February 22–24, 2017
Monterey, CA, USA

I0047543

**Association for
Computing Machinery**

Advancing Computing as a Science & Profession

FPGA'17

Proceedings of the 2017 ACM/SIGDA International Symposium on
Field-Programmable Gate Arrays

Sponsored by:
ACM SIGDA

Supported by:
Altera, DEEPHi, Microsoft Research, Aldec, Algo-Logic, Amazon Web Services, Atomic Rules, Lattice, Micron, Microsemi, Nagase, Xilinx, and Trimberger Family Foundation

Association for Computing Machinery

Advancing Computing as a Science & Profession

The Association for Computing Machinery
2 Penn Plaza, Suite 701
New York, New York 10121-0701

Notice to Past Authors of ACM-Published Articles
ACM intends to create a complete electronic archive of all articles and/or other material previously published by ACM. If you have written a work that has been previously published by ACM in any journal or conference proceedings prior to 1978, or any SIG Newsletter at any time, and you do NOT want this work to appear in the ACM Digital Library, please inform permissions@acm.org, stating the title of the work, the author(s), and where and when published.

ISBN: 978-1-4503-4354-1 (Digital)

ISBN: 978-1-4503-4942-0 (Print)

Additional copies may be ordered prepaid from:

ACM Order Department
PO Box 30777
New York, NY 10087-0777, USA

Phone: 1-800-342-6626 (USA and Canada)
+1-212-626-0500 (Global)
Fax: +1-212-944-1318
E-mail: acmhelp@acm.org
Hours of Operation: 8:30 am – 4:30 pm ET

Printed in the USA

FPGA 2017 Chairs' Welcome

We are delighted to welcome you to the 2017 ACM International Symposium on Field-Programmable Gate Arrays (ACM FPGA 2017). ACM FPGA is the premiere forum for the presentation of new and exciting research on all aspects of FPGA technology, which include:

- Novel FPGA architectures and circuits.
- Advances in CAD tools for FPGAs, in areas such as technology mapping, placement, routing, and others.
- High-level design methodologies that permit FPGA design at higher levels of abstraction.
- Virtualization infrastructure to facilitate and ease the use of FPGAs in the datacenter/cloud context.
- New applications for FPGAs, particularly their use as accelerators for achieving higher computational throughput and energy efficiency.

The conference also provides the opportunity for FPGA researchers and practitioners from around the world to connect with long-time friends, meet new ones, and network with one another in beautiful Monterey, California, famous worldwide for its spectacular coast, Fisherman's Wharf, and Cannery Row.

This year we received 101 submissions, of which 25 were accepted as full research papers (10 pages) to appear in the main conference or the pre-conference special-session on deep learning, and 5 papers were accepted as short research papers (6 pages). All full and short papers appear in these proceedings. In addition, 29 submissions were selected to be presented as posters; abstracts of these appear in these proceedings.

Recent years have seen the deployment of FPGAs in datacenters by Microsoft, Baidu, Amazon, and other companies. This year, the evening panel will consider the topic, "FPGAs in the Cloud", to discuss the opportunities and obstacles for achieving widespread FPGA usage in the cloud.

The symposium kicks off with the co-located Workshop on Overlay Architectures for FPGAs (OLAF). An overlay is an abstraction layer implemented on top of an FPGA whose purpose is to improve ease-of-use and engineering productivity. Following this, we will have a special session on "The Role of FPGAs in Deep Learning", with a tutorial and research paper presentations. The deep learning topic has exploded in importance in the past year with deep neural networks producing state-of-the-art results in image recognition, language translation, game playing, and other tasks. It will be fascinating to see whether, in the years ahead, FPGAs gain a prominent role for realization of accelerators in this burgeoning area.

We would like to thank the members of the Program Committee and secondary reviewers, whose names appear on the following pages, and who devoted considerable time and effort in evaluating the submissions and providing thoughtful feedback to the authors. We would like to thank Prof. George Constantinides from Imperial College London for moderating the panel session, Dr. Andrew Ling from Intel for chairing the pre-conference special session on deep learning, and Profs. Hayden So and John Wawrzynek for organizing the OLAF workshop. Special thanks to Lisa Tolles, Cindy Edwards, Joanne Lateulere and John Lateulere for logistical support, and our sponsors for making FPGA 2017 possible.

Welcome to ACM FPGA 2017!

Jason H. Anderson
Program Chair
University of Toronto, Canada

Jonathan Greene
General Chair
Microsemi, USA

Table of Contents

Session: Interconnect and Routing
Session Chair: Sinan Kaptanoglu *(Microsemi)*

Session: Architecture
Session Chair: Steve Wilton *(University of British Columbia)*

Session: CAD Tools
Session Chair: Lesley Shannon *(Simon Fraser University)*

Session: Panel: FPGAs in the Cloud
Session Chair: George Constantinides *(Imperial College London)*

Session: High-Level Synthesis – Tools and Applications
Session Chair: Stephen Neuendorffer *(Xilinx)*

Session: Graph Processing Applications

Session: Virtualization and Applications

Session: Applications

Poster Session 1

Poster Session 3

FPGA 2017 Organization

FPGA 2017 Sponsor and Corporate Patrons

Sponsors:

siG da (acm)

Gold Corporate Patrons:

ALTERA
now part of Intel

DEEPHi

Microsoft
Research

Silver Corporate Patrons:

ALDEC
THE DESIGN VERIFICATION COMPANY

ALGORITHMS IN LOGIC
ALGO-LOGIC
HTTP://ALGO-LOGIC.COM

amazon web services

Atomic Rules

LATTICE SEMICONDUCTOR

Micron

NAGASE

Microsemi.

XILINX

ALL PROGRAMMABLE™

Logistics Support:

Trimberger Family
Foundation

OLAF'17: Third International Workshop on Overlay Architectures for FPGAs

Hayden Kwok-Hay So
Department of Electrical and Electronic
Engineering
University of Hong Kong
Hong Kong
hso@eee.hku.hk

John Wawrzynek
Department of Electrical Engineering and
Computer Sciences
University of California, Berkeley
Berkeley, CA 94720
johnw@eecs.berkeley.com

ABSTRACT

The Third International Workshop on Overlay Architectures for FPGAs (OLAF) is held in Monterey, California, USA, on Feburary 22, 2017 and co-located with FPGA 2017: The 25th ACM/SIGDA International Symposium on Field Programmable Gate Arrays. The main objective of the workshop is to address how overlay architectures can help address the challenges and opportunites provided by FPGA-based reconfigurable computing. The workshop provides a venue for researchers to present and discuss the latest developments in FPGA overlay architecture and related areas. We have assembled a program of six refereed papers with panel discussions with prominent experts in the field.

CCS Concepts

•**Computer systems organization** → **Reconfigurable computing;** *Parallel architectures; Multiple instruction, multiple data; Single instruction, multiple data; Cellular architectures;* •**Hardware** → **Reconfigurable logic and FPGAs;**

Keywords

FPGA; Overlay architecture

1. BACKGROUND

The OLAF workshop was started in response to the growing interest in utilizing virtual coarse-grain architectures overlaying fine-grained FPGAs. Overlay architectures, such as arrays of soft processor cores, and vector processors, originally emerged from academic research to address the challenges of providing familiar programming models and abstractions to users of FPGAs. In a wide variety of applications, these architectures demonstrated their effectiveness to not only supply users with convenient programming models and tools but also their ability to take advantage of inherent computational efficiency of FPGAs. These systems, such as

those for supporting openCL, are also now finding use in commercial systems. While originally developed to address design productivity, overlay architectures provide other benefits, such as enhanced debugging, design portability, security, domain specific optimizations, hardware platform independance, support for partial reconfiguration, and user independence from vendor specific tools. As the complexity of FPGA platforms continue to grow exponentially, it is anticipated that the use of overlay architectures on FPGAs will increase and become mainstream practice.

2. SCOPE

Prospective authors were invited to submit full papers (up to six pages) describing original results or extended abstracts (not exceeding two pages) describing work-in-progress. Contributions were sought in, but not limited to, the following topics:

- New overlay architectures
- Application of overlay architectures
- Tools for designing and generating overlays
- Debugging
- Tools and practices to improve design productivity and usability of FPGAs
- FPGA Virtualization
- FPGAs in cloud datacenters
- Time-multiplexed architectures
- Rapid compilation
- High-level synthesis
- Cross vendor development frameworks

3. FORMAT

The selected papers were organized into two sessions, each with a series of oral presentation. This year, to promote attendee interaction and group discussion, we follow each set of oral presentation by a panel discussion designed to delve deeper into the topics covered by the oral presentations and to look forward to new opportunites and challenges.

We would like to thank all the authors and attendees for their participation.

FPGA '17 February 22-24, 2017, Monterey, CA, USA

© 2017 Copyright held by the owner/author(s).

ACM ISBN 978-1-4503-4354-1/17/02.

DOI: http://dx.doi.org/10.1145/3020078.3030012

The Role of FPGAs in Deep Learning

Andrew Ling
Intel Corp.
Toronto, ON
andrew.ling@intel.com

Jason Anderson
University of Toronto
Toronto, ON
janders@eecg.toronto.edu

ABSTRACT
Deep learning has garnered significant visibility recently as an Artificial Intelligence (AI) paradigm, with success in wide ranging applications such as image and speech recognition, natural language understanding, self-driving cars, and game playing (e.g., Alpha Go). This special session is devoted to exploring the potential role of FPGAs in this important fast-evolving domain.

CCS Concepts
•Computing methodologies → Machine learning approaches; •Hardware → Hardware accelerators;

Keywords
FPGAs, machine learning, deep learning

1. INTRODUCTION
2012 saw a breakthrough in computer vision, where for the first time, deep convolutional neural networks (CNNs) produced state-of-the-art accuracy in image recognition [2]. Since then, advances in CNNs have continued unabated [3, 4] and they have been applied to a range of areas including speech recognition, game playing, language translation, and other areas. The importance of neural networks, as well as their scope of application looks set to further explode in the years ahead.

Deep neural networks have tens to hundreds of millions of parameters, making their training and application compute intensive. In the machine learning community, these tasks have been primarily accomplished using multi-core processors (CPUs) and graphics processing units (GPUs). With modern CPUs and GPUs, applying an already-trained neural network (inference) to perform a task can be achieved rapidly (though perhaps at modest energy efficiency); however, training typically requires days or even weeks of compute time.

For FPGAs to be able to participate in the deep-learning revolution, they must be able to show a compelling value proposition in end markets, or be competitive against other processors in terms of cost, speed or power. Presently, although FPGAs have shown some market success in deep learning, the deep-learning market is still dominated by multi-core CPUs and GPUs. However, recent work on reduced-precision neural networks (e.g., [1]) bodes well for FPGAs, as unlike GPUs, FPGAs permit datapaths to be precisely tailored to the needed precision. Furthermore, due to the flexibility of FPGAs in terms of logic and IOs, they may have a compelling total-cost-of-ownership (TCO), particularly in the multi-node domain.

2. SESSION OVERVIEW
The special session will commence with a tutorial on deep learning and recent research trends, with the intent of bringing the ACM FPGA community up-to-speed on the area. Following this, a paper by Intel considers the question of whether FPGAs can "beat" GPUs in the neural network context, considering both speed and energy efficiency. The Intel paper looks at full-precision neural networks, as well as reduced precision and examines the conditions necessary for FPGAs to provide a benefit over GPUs. This is followed by four papers describing innovative research on using FPGAs to implement neural-network accelerators. Techniques considered include implementing binarized neural networks on FPGAs, the use of OpenCL high-level synthesis for accelerator design, and performing computations in the frequency domain.

3. REFERENCES
[1] I. Hubara, M. Courbariaux, D. Soudry, R. El-Yaniv, and Y. Bengio. Binarized neural networks. In *Neural Information Processing Systems*, pages 4107–4115, 2016.
[2] A. Krizhevsky, I. Sutskever, and G. E. Hinton. ImageNet classification with deep convolutional neural networks. In *Neural Information Processing Systems*, pages 1106–1114, 2012.
[3] K. Simonyan and A. Zisserman. Very deep convolutional networks for large-scale image recognition. *CoRR*, abs/1409.1556, 2014.
[4] C. Szegedy, W. Liu, Y. Jia, P. Sermanet, S. E. Reed, D. Anguelov, D. Erhan, V. Vanhoucke, and A. Rabinovich. Going deeper with convolutions. In *IEEE Conference on Computer Vision and Pattern Recognition*, pages 1–9, 2015.

FPGA '17 February 22-24, 2017, Monterey, CA, USA
© 2017 Copyright held by the owner/author(s).
ACM ISBN 978-1-4503-4354-1/17/02.
DOI: http://dx.doi.org/10.1145/3020078.3030013

Can FPGAs Beat GPUs in Accelerating Next-Generation Deep Neural Networks?

Eriko Nurvitadhi[1], Ganesh Venkatesh[1], Jaewoong Sim[1], Debbie Marr[1],
Randy Huang[2], Jason Gee Hock Ong[2], Yeong Tat Liew[2],
Krishnan Srivatsan[3], Duncan Moss[3], Suchit Subhaschandra[3], Guy Boudoukh[4]

[1]Accelerator Architecture Lab, [2]Programmable Solutions Group, [3]FPGA Product Team, [4]Computer Vision Group
Intel Corporation

ABSTRACT

Current-generation Deep Neural Networks (DNNs), such as AlexNet and VGG, rely heavily on dense floating-point matrix multiplication (GEMM), which maps well to GPUs (regular parallelism, high TFLOP/s). Because of this, GPUs are widely used for accelerating DNNs. Current FPGAs offer superior energy efficiency (Ops/Watt), but they do not offer the performance of today's GPUs on DNNs. In this paper, we look at upcoming FPGA technology advances, the rapid pace of innovation in DNN algorithms, and consider whether future high-performance FPGAs will outperform GPUs for next-generation DNNs.

The upcoming Intel® 14-nm Stratix™ 10 FPGAs will have thousands of hard floating-point units (DSPs) and on-chip RAMs (M20K memory blocks). They will also have high bandwidth memories (HBMs) and improved frequency (HyperFlex™ core architecture). This combination of features brings FPGA raw floating point performance within striking distance of GPUs. Meanwhile, DNNs are quickly evolving. For example, recent innovations that exploit sparsity (e.g., pruning) and compact data types (e.g., 1-2 bit) result in major leaps in algorithmic efficiency. However, these innovations introduce irregular parallelism on custom data types, which are difficult for GPUs to handle but would be a great fit for FPGA's extreme customizability.

This paper evaluates a selection of emerging DNN algorithms on two generations of Intel FPGAs (Arria™ 10, Stratix™ 10) against the latest highest performance Titan X Pascal GPU. We created a customizable DNN accelerator template for FPGAs and used it in our evaluations. First, we study various GEMM operations for next-generation DNNs. Our results show that Stratix 10 FPGA is 10%, 50%, and 5.4x better in performance (TOP/sec) than Titan X Pascal GPU on GEMM operations for pruned, Int6, and binarized DNNs, respectively. Then, we present a detailed case study on accelerating Ternary ResNet which relies on sparse GEMM on 2-bit weights (i.e., weights constrained to 0,+1,-1) and full-precision neurons. The Ternary ResNet accuracy is within ~1% of the full-precision ResNet which won the 2015 ImageNet competition. On Ternary-ResNet, the Stratix 10 FPGA can deliver 60% better performance over Titan X Pascal GPU, while being 2.3x better in

performance/watt. Our results indicate that FPGAs may become the platform of choice for accelerating next-generation DNNs.

Keywords
Deep Learning, Accelerator, Intel Stratix 10 FPGA, GPU.

1. INTRODUCTION

The exponential growth of digital data such as images, videos, and speech, from myriad sources (e.g., social media, internet-of-things) is driving the need for analytics to extract knowledge from the data. Data analytics often rely on machine learning (ML) algorithms. Among ML algorithms, deep convolutional neural networks (DNNs) offer state-of-the-art accuracies for important image classification tasks, and therefore are becoming widely adopted.

Mainstream current-generation DNNs (e.g., AlexNet, VGG) rely heavily on dense matrix multiplication operations (GEMM) on 32-bit floating-point data (FP32). Such operations are well-suited for GPUs, which are known to do well on regular parallelism and are equipped with many floating-point compute units and high-bandwidth on-chip and off-chip memories. As such, recent GPUs are becoming more widely used for accelerating DNNs, since they can offer high performance (i.e., multi-TFLOP/s) for mainstream DNNs.

While FPGAs have provided superior energy efficiency (Performance/Watt) than GPUs for DNNs, they have not been known for offering top performance. However, FPGA technologies are advancing rapidly. The upcoming Intel Stratix 10 FPGA [17] will offer more than 5000 hardened floating-point units (DSPs), over 28MB of on-chip RAMs (M20Ks), integration with high-bandwidth memories (up to 4x250GB/s/stack or 1TB/s), and improved frequency from the new HyperFlex technology, thereby leading to a peak 9.2 TFLOP/s in FP32 throughput. In comparison, the latest Nvidia Titan X Pascal GPU offers 11 TFLOPs in FP32 throughput. This means that FPGA performance may be just within striking distance.

Moreover, DNN algorithms are evolving rapidly. Recent developments point toward next-generation DNNs that exploit network sparsity [4,5,6] and use extremely compact data types (e.g., 1bit, 2bit) [1,2,3,4,5]. These emerging DNNs offer orders of magnitude algorithmic efficiency improvement over "classic" DNNs that rely on dense GEMM on FP32 data type, but they introduce irregular parallelism and custom data types, which are difficult for GPUs to handle. In contrast, FPGAs are designed for extreme customizability. FPGAs shine on irregular parallelism and custom data types. An inflection point may be near!

FPGA'17, February 22-24, 2017, Monterey, CA, USA.
© 2017 ACM. ISBN 978-1-4503-4354-1/17/02...$15.00.
DOI: http://dx.doi.org/10.1145/3020078.3021740

The key question is: For next-generation DNNs, can FPGAs beat GPUs in performance? This paper is the first to shed light on the answer by offering the following contributions:

- First, we survey key trends in next-generation DNNs that exploit sparsity and compact data types. We cover pruned sparse networks [6], low N-bit networks [6,7], 1-bit binarized networks [1,2,3], and 2-bit sparse ternary networks [4,5].

- Second, we develop a customizable DNN hardware accelerator template for FPGA that can support various next-generation DNNs. The template offers first-class hardware support for exploiting sparse computation and custom data types. It can be customized to produce optimized hardware instances for FPGA for a user-given variant of DNN.

- Third, using the template, we evaluate various key matrix multiplication operations for next-generation DNNs. Our evaluation is done on the current- and next-generation of FPGAs (Arria 10, Stratix 10) and the latest high-performance Titan X Pascal GPU. We show that Stratix 10 FPGA is able to offer 10%, 50%, and 5.4x better in performance (TOP/sec) than Titan X Pascal GPU on GEMM operations for pruned, Int6, and binarized DNNs, respectively. We also show that both Arria 10 and Stratix 10 FPGAs offer compelling energy efficiency (TOP/sec/watt) relative to Titan X GPU.

- Lastly, we conduct a case study on Ternary ResNet [5], where the key operation is multiplication of two sparse matrices. One matrix has FP32 values, and the other has ternary 2-bit values (i.e., weights are constrained to 0,+1,-1). The accuracy of Ternary ResNet [5] is within ~1% of the best reported accuracy of the most recent 2015 ImageNet competition winner (i.e., full-precision ResNet). For Ternary ResNet, the Stratix 10 FPGA can deliver 60% better performance than Titan X Pascal GPU, while being 2.3x better in performance/watt.

The rest of the paper is organized as follows. Section 2 provides background on DNN, FPGA, and GPU trends. Section 3 discusses our customizable DNN hardware accelerator template, which we use to derive FPGA implementation instances to evaluate against the GPU. Section 4 compares various types of GEMMs for next-generation DNNs. Section 5 presents a case study on Ternary ResNet on FPGAs and GPUs. Section 6, 7, and 8 offers discussions, related work, and concluding remarks.

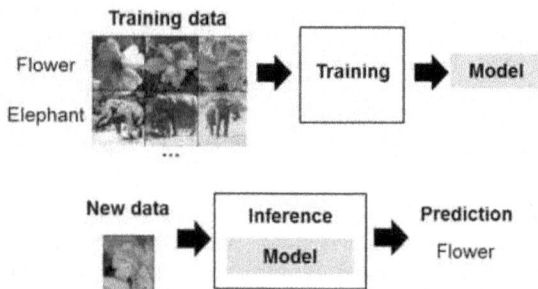

Figure 1. Machine learning for data analytics. The training phase creates a model from known training data. The model is then used during inference to make predictions on new data.

2. BACKGROUND
2.1 Deep Neural Networks Overview

Classification vs. Training. Many data analytics workloads rely on machine learning (ML) algorithms. A typical ML setup for data analytics consists of two phases, as illustrated in Figure 1. First, the training phase iteratively works on a known set of data samples (e.g., various images and its known categories in Figure 1) to create a model with predictive power. Then, the inference phase uses the model to make predictions for newly seen data samples (e.g., predicting a category of a newly seen image, in Figure 1). Section 4 of this paper focuses on key matrix operations used in both inference and training phases, while the case study presented in Section 5 focuses on the inference phase.

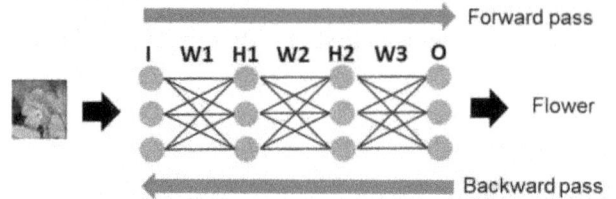

Figure 2. An example neural network with 4 fully connected layers (input I, hidden H1 and H2, output O). Inference does only forward pass. Training iteratively does forward and backward passes to update weights (W1, W2, W3).

Neural Networks Basics. As mentioned earlier, deep convolutional neural network (DNN) is a class of ML algorithms that are widely used because they offer state-of-the-art inference accuracies. Neural networks can be formulated as graphs, where nodes represent neurons and edges represent connections across the neurons. Each neuron and edge is associated with a value. Neuron values are often referred to as activation values, and edge values as network weights. The graph is structured as layers of neurons. Figure 2 illustrates a 4-layer network, with an input layer and an output layer, and two hidden layers between them.

The neural network computation works by going through each layer in the network. For a given layer, each neuron's value is calculated by multiplying and accumulating all the values of the previous layer's neurons with the corresponding edge weights. Thus, the computation heavily relies on multiply-accumulate operations. The DNN computation consists of forward and backward passes, as illustrated in Figure 2. The forward pass takes a sample at the input layer, goes through all hidden layers, and produces a prediction at the output layer. For inference, only the forward pass is needed to obtain a prediction for a given sample. For training, the prediction error from the forward pass is then fed back during the backward pass to update the network weights – this is called the back-propagation algorithm. Training iteratively does forward and backward passes to refine network weights until the desired accuracy is achieved.

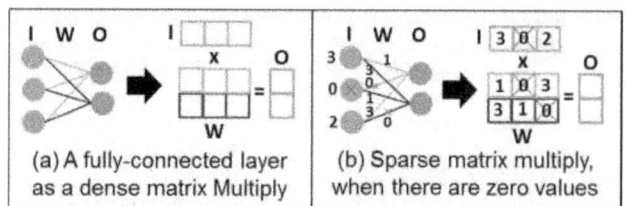

Figure 3. Fully connected layers can be formulated as matrix multiplications. When there are zeros, the computation becomes sparse matrix multiply. Though not illustrated here, convolution layer can also be formulated as matrix multiply.

There are different types of DNN layers. A fully connected (FC) layer connects all the neurons in one layer to all the neurons in the next layer (as in Figure 3). A convolutional layer connects only to groups of neighbor neurons. Activation and normalization layers transform neuron values. And, pooling layers merge a group of neuron values. Modern DNNs typically have multiple sets of each type of layers. Each one has a convolutional layer, followed by some combination of activation (i.e., ReLU) layers, batch normalization layers, and pooling layers (to reduce the size of the computation for the later layer and to avoid overfitting). FC layers were used in earlier networks (e.g., AlexNet, VGG). Recent networks (e.g., ResNet) use only very few or no FC layers. For modern DNNs, most computation is on the convolution layers (e.g., [8] reports ~90% time spent on convolutions)

Network Layers as Matrix Multiply. The fully-connected and convolutional layers can be formulated as matrix multiplication. In practice, such formulation may make it more amenable for high-performance implementations (e.g., by using an optimized math library, such as Intel MKL). Figure 3(a) shows an illustration, where a 3-neuron input layer (I) and a 2-neuron output layer (O) are formulated as dense vectors, and the weights (W) are formulated as a 2x3 dense matrix. The computation multiplies the vector of input neurons with the weight matrix.

2.2 Trends in Deep Neural Networks

Trend 1: Deeper networks lead to more accuracy, but these large models are becoming intractable to process. In recent years, many have shown that deeper neural networks can deliver greatly improved inference accuracies. Table 1 shows the winners of the well-known ILSVRC challenge on ImageNet dataset for the past several years. As shown in the table, the accuracy has increased tremendously since 2012, with a 4.5x reduction in the top-5 error rate (16.4 to 3.5%), but the number of layers has also gone up 19x (8 layers in AlexNet to 152 layers in ResNet). Deeper networks require more computation to perform.

Table 1. Recent DNNs are deeper and more accurate. Furthermore, larger model makes processing intractable, leading to recent focus on more efficient DNN algorithms.

Network	Top-5 Error %	Depth (#layers)	Model Size (MB)
AlexNet (ILSVRC'12)	15.3	8	240
VGG (ILSVRC'14)	7.3	19	500
GoogLeNet (ILSVRC'14)	6.7	22	24
ResNet (ILSVRC'15)	3.57	152	240

Along with deeper networks, early networks were greatly increasing the number of parameters, consequently leading to larger model sizes. In 2012, AlexNet had 60M parameters (240MB, 4B/parameter), while in 2014 VGG had a ~2x larger model. The increase in model size significantly increases the computational requirements, memory bandwidth, and storage needed to move and store the model. Therefore, more recent DNNs necessarily designed the networks to be more efficient. For example, GoogLeNet uses a composition of varying size filters, to allow for deeper network, while having a manageable model size. ResNet utilizes a "shortcut" connection to skip layers, enabling sharing of weights across more layers, resulting in a very deep network with a model size smaller than VGG.

Trend 2: Improving efficiency by using more compact data types. Another avenue for improving DNN efficiency is to use more compact data types. Many researchers have shown (e.g., [6,7,10,11]) that it is possible to represent data in much less than 32-bits, demonstrating the use of 8-4 bits (depending on the

network) leads to only a small reduction in accuracy compared to full precision. Data types which are more compact than 32-bit single precision floating point are becoming the new norm. As an evidence of this, the latest GPUs are providing native support for FP16 and Int8 data types. Moreover, popular DNN frameworks, such as TensorFlow, provide support for such data types as well.

Interestingly, very recently, there are many active research efforts that study *extremely compact data representation*. In particular, research on binarized neural networks (BNNs) [1,2,3] investigates the use of 1-bit data types, by constraining values to +1 or -1. The most efficient variant of BNNs proposes using 1-bit for both neurons as well as weights. The brilliance of doing this is that not only is the storage size and bandwidth demand dramatically lower (32x smaller than FP32), but the computation of 1-bit "multiply-accumulate" can be done without multiplications or additions! The computation boils down to an xnor followed by a bitcounting operation. We provide details on how to do this in Section 3.

BNNs have comparable accuracies to state-of-the-art full precision networks for small datasets (e.g., CIFAR10). However, the BNN accuracy on larger datasets (e.g. ImageNet) has not yet been realized. Nevertheless, BNN research is very active and rapidly advancing. For example, a BNN variant called BinaryNet [2] demonstrated a near state-of-the-art accuracy on CIFAR10 in early 2016, but was not evaluated on ImageNet. In August of 2016, a new work [3] reported evaluations of ImageNet using BinaryNet and proposed a new variant of BNN called XNOR-net. The work shows that BinaryNet achieves only half the accuracy of AlexNet on ImageNet, but XNOR-net gets within 22% of AlexNet accuracy. Given the rapid rate of advances in this research, even better accuracy may be achieved in the near future.

Ternary neural networks (TNNs) [4,5] are another class of network that proposes extremely low bit-width. TNNs constrained weight values to 0, +1, or -1, which can be represented in 2 bits. Recently [5], TNNs have been shown to provide comparable accuracy on ImageNet, within 1% of full-precision ResNet-152, which is the latest ILSVRC winner. However, such TNNs still rely on FP32 neuron values. Thus, the multiply-accumulate computations are done between FP32 neurons and 2-bit weights. While this makes computation more efficient (detailed in Section 3), the efficiency gain is not as great as that of BNNs.

Trend 3: Improving efficiency by taking advantage of sparsity. There are many studies on exploiting sparsity (i.e., the presence of zeros) in DNN neurons and weights. In recent years, most networks use Rectified Linear Unit (ReLU) as the activation function, which zeroes out negative neuron values. It has been reported [8] that ~50% of neuron values in popular networks (e.g., AlexNet, VGG) are zeros. Computation on such zero-valued neurons is unnecessary. As illustrated in Figure 3(b), in the presence of zero values, the computation becomes sparse matrix multiplication, which requires fewer operations than dense matrix.

Furthermore, there are also research efforts to exploit sparsity on the weight values [6]. Such research show that it is possible to make network weights sparse while maintaining accuracy, by zeroing out ("pruning") weights that are deemed to be not important. The recent result in [6] shows that such pruning on AlexNet and VGG-16 results in up to 91% and 96% sparsity for certain layers, without sacrificing accuracy. In our own experiments, based on the approach in [6], we are able to achieve ~85% sparsity for AlexNet convolutional layers, and even more in fully connected layers, for ImageNet dataset, with only ~1%

degradation in accuracy. We were also able to prune GoogleNet with only ~0.2% drop in accuracy, while achieving ~65% sparsity for all convolution layers, except for the first layer.

Another method to sparsify weights is by ternarization. As mentioned earlier, TNNs constrain weights to 0, +1, or -1. Thus, it introduces many zeros to the weights. A Ternarized ResNet that delivers comparable accuracy to full-precision ResNet introduces ~50% sparsity to the weights.

Other Trends. DNN research is rapidly evolving and there are trends not covered in this paper. We offer discussions on these in Section 6. Nevertheless, we believe that sparsity exploitation and the use of extremely compact data types are two major trends likely to become the norm in the next-generation DNNs. Therefore, we focus on these in the remainder of the paper.

2.3 GPU vs. FPGA Trends

GPUs are known to do well on data parallel computation that exhibits regular parallelism and demands high floating point compute throughput. Across generations, GPUs offer increased FLOP/s, by incorporating more floating-point units, on-chip RAMs, and higher memory bandwidth. For example, the latest Titan X Pascal offers peak 11 TFLOP/s of 32-bit floating-point throughput, a noticeable improvement from the previous generation Titan X Maxwell that offered 7 TFLOP/s peak throughput. However, GPUs can face challenges from issues, such as divergence, for computation that exhibits irregular parallelism. Further, GPUs support only a fixed set of native data types. So, other custom-defined data types may not be handled efficiently. These challenges may lead to underutilization of hardware resources and unsatisfactory achieved performance.

Meanwhile, FPGAs have advanced significantly in recent years. There are several FPGA trends to consider. First, there are much more on-chip RAMs on next-generation FPGAs. For example, Stratix 10 [17] offers up to ~28 MBs worth of on-chip RAMs (M20Ks). Second, frequency can improve dramatically, enabled by technologies such as HyperFlex. Third, there are many more hard DSPs available. Fourth, off-chip bandwidth will also increase, with the integration of HBM memory technologies. Fifth, these next-generation FPGAs use more advanced process technology (e.g., Stratix 10 uses 14nm Intel technology). Overall, it is expected that Intel Stratix 10 can offer up to 9.2 TFLOP/s of 32bit floating-point performance. This brings FPGAs closer in raw performance to state-of-the-art GPUs. Unlike GPUs, the FPGA fabric architecture was made with extreme customizability in mind, even down to bit-levels. Hence, FPGAs have the opportunity to do increasingly well on the next-generation DNNs as they become more irregular and use custom data types.

In addition, the software ecosystem for FPGAs is advancing as well. High-level FPGA programming tools (e.g., Altera OpenCL SDK) are now commercially available. They allow programming FPGAs at a higher level of abstraction than RTL (e.g., Verilog). These tools make FPGAs more accessible to developers who are not hardware experts. FPGAs are integrating into mainstream compute systems, e.g., alongside a server CPU in an upcoming Intel Xeon®+FPGA offering [12], inside a network card, or as a "GPU form factor" PCIe card. These trends can speed up FPGA adoption into the mainstream systems. Indeed, there are ongoing efforts from leading technology companies to incorporate FPGAs into datacenters (e.g., [12,13]).

3. CUSTOMIZABLE HARDWARE ARCHITECTURE TEMPLATE FOR DNNS

We have developed customizable hardware architecture "template" for DNNs, which takes into account the emerging DNN trends mentioned in Section 2 (i.e., sparsity, compact data types). The template can be configured to derive hardware instances (i.e., RTL implementation) for a given user-specified DNN variant. Such instances can then be mapped to FPGA (or ASIC). We use this template to facilitate our evaluations of next-generation DNNs on FPGAs and to compare them against GPUs, which we will discuss in the next two sections. Meanwhile, we describe our customizable DNN hardware template in this section.

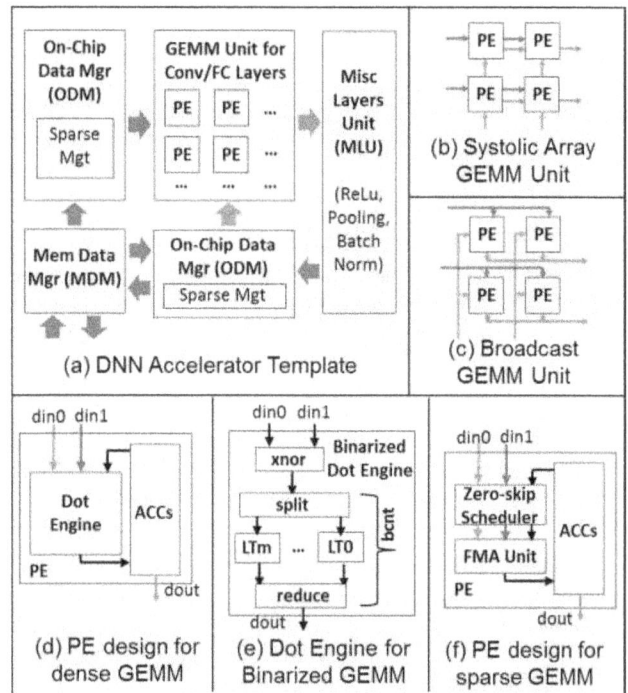

Figure 4. Customizable hardware architecture template for DNNs. (a) shows top-level design. (b) and (c) show variants of GEMM unit supported by our template. (d) and (f) show PE designs for handling dense and sparse data. (e) shows optimization for binarized GEMM, where multiply-accumulate operation is done using xnor and bitcounting.

3.1 Overview

The top-level design of our template is shown in Figure 4(a). The design consists of Memory and On-chip data management units (MDM, ODM), GEMM Unit to compute convolutional and fully connected layers, and Misc Layers Unit (MLU) to compute the other DNN layer types (ReLU, Batch Norm, Pool).

The design works as follows. First, weights and input neurons are loaded into on-chip buffers in ODM from memory. The convolution and fully-connected layers are computed by dynamically flattening the weights and input feature maps (neurons) onto blocked matrix operations, as in [10]. The GEMM Unit performs such matrix operations and outputs the result to MLU, which then performs the ReLu/BatchNorm/Pooling layers, as dictated by the desired DNN configuration. The output goes into the on-chip buffer in ODM, to be read by the next convolution/FC layer. If there is not enough buffer in ODM, the output is spilled out to memory by MDM.

The GEMM Unit consists of multiple processing elements (PEs). The GEMM Unit is customizable to use systolic-based [14] or broadcast-based [15] architecture across PEs, as shown in Figures 4(b) and 4(c). PE is customizable to be able to perform one or more multiply-accumulate operations.

In overall, the template is customizable to use various GEMM and PE architectures (systolic/broadcast; sparse/dense) and data types (1bit/2bit/Nbit/FP), as well as the typical sizing parameters (e.g., number of PEs, GEMM units, buffer sizes, etc.).

3.2 Support for Emerging DNNs

Our architecture template incorporates features to exploit sparsity and to handle compact data types, which are needed by emerging DNNs. We describe these features below.

3.2.1 Support for N-bit data type

FPGAs have been known to be extremely flexible to handle various data types. Many prior DNN works (e.g., [6,7,10,11]) have shown promising results implementing customized N-bit data. Our architecture template can also support customization to N-bit data. PEs can be customized to handle varying width of dot product calculations based on data type width. Accordingly, the data management units (ODM, MDM) can be customized to handle packing/unpacking of the desired N-bit data types.

3.2.2 Support for Sparse Pruned DNNs

There are many existing studies on processing sparse matrices (e.g., in HPC applications). However, such studies typically use matrices that are extremely sparse (i.e., 1% or less non-zeros). We observe that the sparsity in DNNs is not as extreme (i.e., ~5-50% non-zeros). Therefore, instead of utilizing a sparse matrix format (e.g., CSR), we opted to use a dense format, but dynamically checked/tracked zeros and skipped zero computation (i.e., similar to the approach from [8]). Specifically, prior to feeding data to GEMM Unit, on-chip data manager checks for zero values and includes metadata (index or bitvector) to identify the locations of the zeros in the block of data providing to the GEMM unit. Each processing element (PE) inside the GEMM unit will read a set of matrix elements along with the metadata. It will then schedule computation based on information in the metadata. Those zero elements are not scheduled onto the multiply-accumulate compute units inside the PE, therefore reducing number of cycles needed to complete the matrix operations and improving overall performance. The design of the PE to support sparsity is shown in Figure 4(f). In contrast, the PE design for regular dense computation is shown in Figure 4(d).

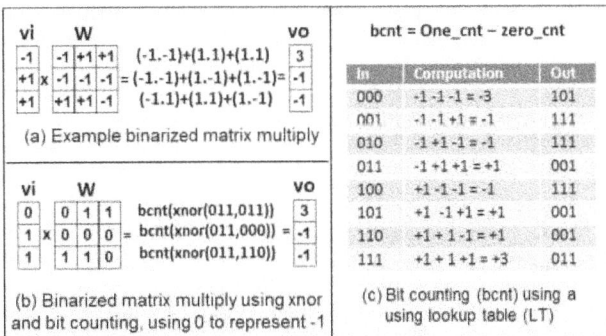

Figure 5. Binarized Matrix Multiplication. By representing -1 as 0, standard multiply and add operations (a) can be replaced by xnor and bit counting operations (b), where bit counting can be done using a lookup table (c).

3.2.3 Support for Binarized DNNs

In binarized DNNs (BNNs), both weight and neuron values are constrained to +1 or -1. Therefore, the key operation in BNNs is 1-bit matrix multiplication. Figure 5(a) shows an example of a 1-bit matrix multiply. To improve computation efficiency -1 can be represented as zeros, and computation can be done using an xnor followed by a bit counting operation (as in Figure 5(b)). The bit counting itself can further be implemented using a lookup table, as shown in Figure 5(c). Our DNN architecture template provides a customization option for a PE that performs N-bit dot products using the aforesaid approach, as depicted in Figure 4(e).

3.2.4 Support for Ternarized DNNs

Lastly, the support for Ternarized DNNs (TNNs) in our architecture is as follows. In TNNs, weights are constrained to 0, +1, or -1, but neurons are still using N-bit precision. In this case, we represent ternary weights using 2 bits, with 1 bit indicating whether the value is 0 and another bit indicating whether the value is +1 or -1 (as in BNNs). The PE uses the 1-bit zero indicator in the same way as the metadata bits used to exploit sparsity in Section 3.2.2. As such, whenever there is an operation against a zero weight, the operation will be skipped and not be scheduled onto the PE's compute unit(s). If the weight is either +1 or -1, instead of performing multiplication against N-bit precision neuron values, we simplify the computation by negating the sign of the neuron value (i.e., a sign bit flip if neuron is floating-point, or negation if it is fixed point). As such, PE for ternary computation does not require a multiplication unit.

4. EVALUATION OF MATRIX MULTIPLY FOR NEXT-GENERATION DNNs

Matrix multiplication is a key operation in DNNs. It is important to have a thorough understanding of the achievable peak performance of this key operation on the platforms studied. For this reason, we evaluate matrix multiplication on a variety of matrix and data types. We selected dense and sparse matrices, 32-bit floating point data types vs. narrow bit-width data types, and even an extremely compact binarized 1-bit data type.

Table 2. FPGAs and GPU under study. Based on [16,17,18]

Type	Arria 10 1150 FPGA	Stratix 10 2800 FPGA	TitanX Pascal GPU
Peak FP32 TFLOPs	1.36	9.2	11
On-chip RAMs	6.6 MB (M20Ks)	28.6 MB (M20Ks)	13.5 MB (RF, SM, L2)
Memory BW	Assume same as Titan X	Assume same as Titan X	480 GB/s

4.1 Methodology

Since we would like to understand the top possible performance achievable by FPGAs and GPUs for the types of matrix multiplications under study, we allow freely choosing matrix sizes that provide the best performance for the target platform. This ended up being in the range of dimensions of 2K-4K. We also chose amenable batch sizes (i.e., number of independent matrix multiplications), since batching is a common practice when running DNNs on GPUs to maximize throughput.

The specific FPGAs and GPU studied are shown in Table 2. We include two generations of FPGAs (Arria 10 and Stratix 10) and compare them with the Titan X Pascal GPU, the latest and highest performance GPU available for purchase at this paper's submission deadline (September of 2016).

To make a fair FPGA comparison to the GPU, we decided to allow the FPGA to have the same memory capacity and bandwidth as the GPU. Although readily-available FPGA cards have less capable memory system than the GPU card, integrated HBM stacks in the upcoming Stratix 10 will allow FPGA packages and cards to have the equivalent memory bandwidth and capacity as the GPU cards. We want to evaluate the potential fundamental advantages of FPGA vs. GPU rather than penalizing our FPGA study with memory limitations that can be addressed with packaging and card-level solutions.

For our FPGA evaluation, we derived RTL instances from our DNN hardware template, with customizations selected to optimize for the matrix operations under study. Then, we use Altera Quartus™ software, EPE tool [19], analytical modeling, and simulations to estimate performance and power. For Stratix 10, which has been announced, but not yet available, we use Quartus Early Beta release. Note that its quality is not necessarily reflective of future more mature releases of Quartus for Stratix 10.

For our GPU evaluation, we conduct real system measurements on the Nvidia Titan X Pascal card. We use nvprof to collect performance and power numbers.

4.2 "Classic" DNNs

Current mainstream (i.e., "classic") DNNs, such as AlexNet, VGG, Googlenet, ResNet, etc., typically rely on dense matrix multiplication on single-precision floating point numbers (FP32).

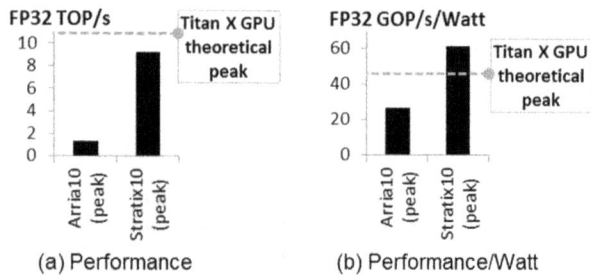

Figure 6. Matrix multiplication results for "Classic" DNNs. It operates on dense matrices with FP32 data type

For GPU, we measured the FP32 dense matrix multiplication performance using the cuBLAS library in the Nvidia CUDA Toolkit 8.0 RC. Most of the instructions in the cuBLAS SGEMM implementation are FMAs, leading to high compute efficiency. The peak theoretical performance of Titan X Pascal is 11 TFLOPs, and we achieved 10.88 TFLOPs with the cuBLAS matrix multiplication library call.

FP32 dense matrix multiplication is a sweet spot for GPUs, not FPGAs, so we did not create an optimized FPGA implementation for this. We present comparison of peak numbers based on the FPGA and GPU datasheets instead (in Figure 6).

As Figure 6(a) shows, Stratix 10 with its far greater number of DSPs will offer much improved FP32 performance compared to the Arria 10, bringing the Stratix 10 within striking distance to Titan X performance. However, the peak FP32 TOP/s still lags behind the GPU. It could be possible for FPGAs to win in performance/Watt. Figure 6(b) shows that the Stratix 10 can be up to ~40% better than Titan X if we assume the FPGA peak TOP/s.

4.3 Sparse (Pruned) DNNs

As described in Section 2, next-generation DNNs are likely to operate on sparse matrices. Pruning [6] is a recent, popular technique to make DNN weights sparse without little or no loss in accuracy. For our study, we replicated the pruning results for AlexNet from [6] using our in-house software reference. We also ran further experiments to fine-tune (e.g., pruning threshold, number of re-training iterations) and optimize our results. We are able to achieve on average ~85% sparsity in the convolution layers of AlexNet with less than a 1% degradation in accuracy (fully connected layers are even more sparse). Hence, our evaluation uses matrices with 85% sparsity (i.e., 15% non-zeros).

4.3.1 Sparse Matrix Multiply on GPU

Evaluating sparse matrix multiply for pruned DNNs can be challenging for GPUs. Modern GPU architectures employ what is known as a single-instruction multiple-thread (SIMT) execution model, in which multiple threads execute the same sequence of instructions, on different data, in a lock step fashion. As such, although a few threads may skip zero computation, the corresponding SIMT lanes simply remain idle while the threads on the other SIMT lanes perform non-zero computation. In addition, checking for zeros in the matrices adds extra instructions to the execution kernel, which reduces compute efficiency.

Another approach is to use sparse linear algebra libraries for zero-skipping. However, existing GPU libraries such as cuSPARSE are targeted for traditional sparse matrix operations that perform on extremely sparse matrices with less than 1% of zeros (e.g., well-known in the High-Performance Computing domain). Also, for sparse matrix multiplication, the input matrices need to be converted to one of the standard sparse matrix formats such as compressed sparse row (CSR) or compressed sparse column (CSC). Since the matrices in DNNs are not extremely sparse (i.e., ~5%-50% sparsity), using these sparse libraries leads to large overhead.

To address this problem, we wrote our own sparse matrix multiply implementation. Our implementation uses dense matrix format, but it checks and skips zeros dynamically in a similar way as our FPGA implementation. Our implementation is a modification on top of an optimized open-source MAGMA [29] dense matrix multiply library. While we would have liked to implement our algorithm on top of cuBLAS, the code for cuBLAS is not open-source. The MAGMA library is one of the most optimized open-source GPU libraries that we could find.

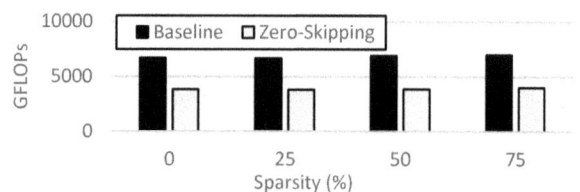

Figure 7. GPU performance on sparse (zero-skipping) GEMM versus dense GEMM for various sparsity levels. Zero-skipping sparse GEMM performs worse than normal dense GEMM.

Figure 7 shows the comparison between the baseline SGEMM (without zero-skipping) and SGEMM with zero-skipping for varying sparsity levels. As explained before, dynamically checking zero values degrades performance as it needs to execute more non-useful instructions, without increasing SIMT utilization. Across the different sparsity percentages, zero-skipping kernel performs worse than without zero-skipping. Hence, for comparison against FPGA, we use GPU performance on dense matrix multiplication. This is because the GPU performance is far better on dense matrix, computing all the multiplications, including the zeros. Specifically, we use the cuBLAS library in the Nvidia CUDA Toolkit 8.0 RC.

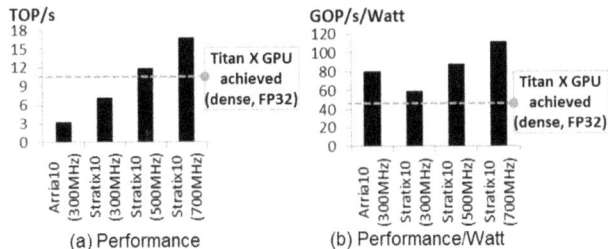

Figure 8. Matrix multiplication results for DNNs with pruning. It operates on sparse matrices with FP32 data type. We use 85% sparsity, based on pruned AlexNet experiments. For GPU, we report achieved performance on FP32 dense matrix multiply, since we found that sparse matrix multiplication lead to GPU performance degradation.

4.3.2 Sparse Matrix Multiply on FPGA

For FPGA, we use the design described in Section 3.2.2. Since on FPGA we can detect and skip zero computation in a fine grained manner, at 85% sparsity we observe ~4x speedups in cycle count, as our GEMM Unit is able to skip many zeros.

For Stratix 10, we made conservative, moderate, and aggressive performance projections. The conservative estimate is based on mapping and scaling up our GEMM implementation for Arria 10 directly to Stratix 10 without doing any optimization for HyperFlex to achieve higher frequency. Hence, the conservative estimate uses 300MHz frequency, matching the Arria 10 design. The moderate and aggressive projections anticipate frequency boosts from HyperFlex to 500MHz and 700MHz, respectively.

4.3.3 FPGA vs. GPU

The performance and performance/watt for FPGAs and GPU under study is shown in Figure 8. As shown in Figure 8(a), even the conservative 300 MHz estimate for Stratix 10 is only ~34% worse in performance than GPU. The moderate estimate using 500 MHz brings Stratix 10 performance to ~10% better than GPU, and the aggressive estimate improves it even further.

In terms of performance/watt, Figure 8(b) shows that FPGAs offer more compelling results than GPU across the board. Arria 10 offers 16% better performance/watt over GPU, with Stratix 10 offering even further improvements.

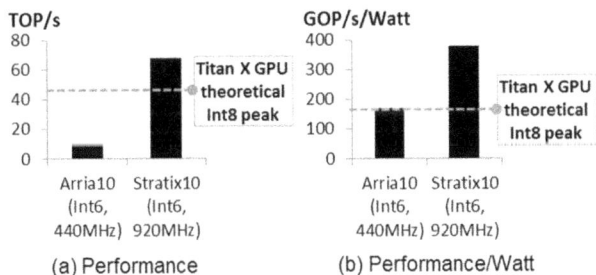

Figure 9. Matrix multiplication results for DNNs with compact data types. It operates on dense matrices. We use 6-bit (Int6) data type for FPGA. For GPU, which does not have native support for Int6, we use theoretical peak Int8 GPU performance for comparison.

4.4 Compact Narrow-Bitwidth DNNs

As described in Section 2, there is significant prior work in quantizing data to reduce computation requirements and bit-widths to values smaller than 32-bit floating point. While 8-bit or larger data types were used in the past DNN proposals, there are trends towards even smaller sub-8-bit data types [6,7]. Here, we evaluate dense matrix multiplication using the Int6 data type.

We use FPGA implementation based on systolic GEMM (shown in Figure 4(b)) that is well optimized for frequency. It can achieve 440MHz for Arria 10 and 920MHz in Stratix 10. For GPU, we use theoretical peak Int8 performance for Titan X, since GPU does not have native support for Int6 computations.

Our evaluation results are shown in Figure 9. As Figure 9(a) shows, Stratix 10 Int6 performance is more than 50% better than the Titan X theoretical peak Int8 performance (Titan X Int6 performance is expected to not be better than Int8). As Figure 9(b) shows, performance/watt of FPGA is either comparable (Arria 10) or more than 2x better (Stratix 10) than Titan X GPU.

4.5 Binarized DNNs

Recent "binarized" DNNs have proposed using extremely compact 1bit data types. As detailed earlier, 1bit matrix multiplications in binarized DNNs can be done more optimally using xnor and bitcounting operations.

For GPU evaluation, we use a binary matrix multiply kernel (xnor_gemm) from BinaryNet [2], which is based on the blocked version of matrix multiply in the CUDA Programming Guide. In the xnor_gemm implementation, instead of performing FMA operations for matrix multiply, each CUDA thread performs xnor and population count operations to compute one element of the resulting matrix. The population count operation is supported in Nvidia GPUs via __popc() (for 32-bit) and __popcll() (for 64-bit) intrinsic functions. When these intrinsics are used in the CUDA kernel, the CUDA compiler maps __popc() to a single instruction and __popcll() to a few instructions.

On Titan X Pascal, 32 32-bit population count operations can be issued every cycle per Streaming Multiprocessor (SM), which leads to 1024 "binary ops" per cycle per SM. As Titan X can issue up to 128 FP32 FMA instructions every cycle per SM, the peak throughput of "binary ops" over FP32 operations is 4x. In our Titan X Pascal, we achieve 45.6 TOPs for binary GEMM performance.

For FPGA, we use systolic array GEMM unit with the PE for binarized DNNs, which we described earlier in Section 3.2.3. Our PE is configured to do 256-wide binary dot product operations. We synthesized our implementation to Arria 10 and Stratix 10. For validation, we also deployed and ran the design on an Arria 10 development system.

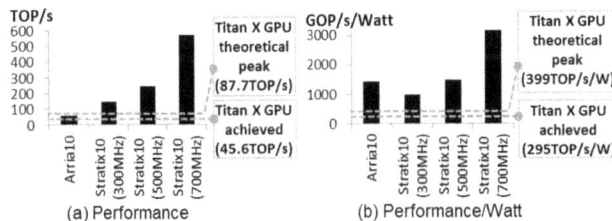

Figure 10. Matrix multiplication results for binarized DNNs. It operates on dense matrices with 1bit data types. Multiply and add operations are replaced with xnor and bitcount.

Our evaluation results are shown in Figure 10. Stratix 10 can deliver 3x (conservative) to 12x (aggressive) better performance than achieved performance on Titan X GPU, and 70% (conservative) and over 6x (aggressive) than theoretical performance of Titan X. Meanwhile, Arria 10 can deliver 25% better performance than achieved Titan X GPU performance. In terms of performance/watt, the Arria 10 and Stratix 10 can deliver 3x to over 10x better energy efficiency relative to Titan X.

5. TERNARY RESNET CASE STUDY

In the previous section, we evaluated key operations in various emerging DNNs. In this section, we zoom in on a specific DNN. In particular, we report a case study on accelerating Ternary version of the state-of-the-art ResNet [5].

5.1 Ternary ResNet Overview

Ternary DNNs (i.e., Ternary Weight Networks) [4,5] have recently proposed constraining neural network weights to +1, 0, or -1, allowing for weights to be represented with just 2 bits, while simultaneously introducing more sparsity to these weights. Neurons are still represented using full precision (FP32). The reported ImageNet accuracy results on Ternary DNNs have been very compelling. The earlier paper [4] in May 2016 reported only 1.8% top-5 accuracy degradation on Ternary ResNet-18 relative to full precision ResNet-18 (i.e., 86.2% Ternary vs. 88% full precision accuracies). The very recent work [5] in September 2016 reports only 0.64% accuracy degradation for ResNet-152 (i.e., 93.2% ternary vs. 93.84% full precision). This work also reports accuracy for ternary ResNet-50, which is within 1% accuracy of full precision ResNet-50. We focus on ResNet-50 here, since its accuracy is close to ResNet-152 (within ~1.2%), but requires much less computation.

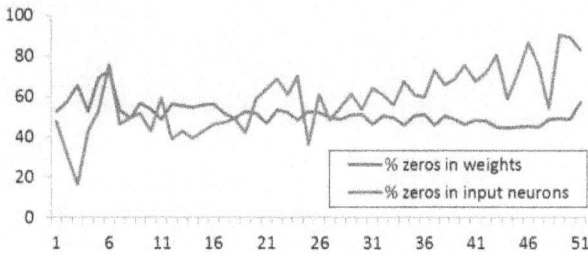

Figure 11. Sparsity of Ternary ResNet-50. The x-axis shows the different layers of ResNet-50. The y-axis shows percentages of zeros for each layer. Sparsity results for the ternary weights and runtime neuron values are provided.

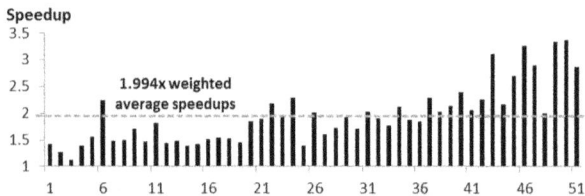

Figure 12. FPGA accelerator speedups from exploiting sparsity for each Ternary ResNet-50 layer. E.g., 1.5 means that enabling sparse support to skip zeros leads to 1.5x faster run (in cycle count) over normal dense processing.

5.2 Software Reference and Sparsity Study

Our software reference is based on the work in [5], which is built on top of the Torch framework for ResNet [20]. We ran our own experiments on ImageNet dataset with Ternary ResNet. Indeed, we were able to obtain accuracies mentioned earlier.

First, to understand the opportunity for sparsity exploitation, we collected average sparsity data for the resulting weights from training with Ternary ResNet-50. Since ResNet uses ReLU as the activation function, we also report runtime sparsity at the input neuron values. Figure 11 shows the results.

As Figure 11 shows, the sparsity varies layer by layer. On a weighted average across the layers, the weights are 51% sparse and the neurons are 60% sparse. This means, that in the upper bound, there can be 70-80% overall sparsity across both the weights and neurons. In an ideal case, if it is possible to avoid the 70-80% unnecessary zero computations with perfect efficiency, the upper bounds for speedups are 3.3x-5x. While this is promising, in practice the actual speedups depend on whether the compute platform can avoid these zero computations efficiently.

5.3 FPGA Evaluation

We used the hardware template detailed in Section 3 and considered several possible instances of RTL implementations for Ternary ResNet-50. In particular, we enabled customizations for ternary DNNs discussed in Section 3.2.4.

First, we customized for 2bit ternary data format, and replaced multiplication with a sign bit manipulation. Thus, our PE only contains a floating-point accumulator. Nevertheless, a single Stratix 10 DSP block contains an FP32 multiplier and an FP32 adder. Even though we are not using the multiplier, we still have to use an entire DSP for our accumulator, so we do not gain any DSP savings in this case. We do obtain ALM and M20K savings from having very compact 2-bit ternary data representation.

Second, we evaluated different configurations for zero skipping support. Generally, there is a tradeoff between the aggressiveness of our sparse data scheduler to skip zero computations and the FPGA resources needed and frequency. A more aggressive sparse scheduler can look further ahead to a larger set of weights and/or neurons, and identify and skip larger portions of zeros dynamically. However, it costs more resources and may impact frequency if it introduces data dependencies.

For this study, we chose a simper design more amenable to frequency optimizations. Specifically, we opted for a less aggressive but simpler sparse scheduler, at the expense of less opportunity to skip zero computations. Furthermore, instead of having the sparse scheduler skip zeros on both neurons and weights, we chose to skip only zero neurons, as they use wider 32-bit data type and sparser than the weights. Zero skipping only on neurons lets us use only one of the "Sparse Mgt" unit outside of the GEMM unit (i.e., inside "ODM" in Figure 4(a)) and to simplify "zero-skip scheduler" inside each PE. Based on ResNet-50 layer dimensions, we customize our DNN accelerator with GEMM units with 4x8 PEs and 8 FMA units/PE.

Figure 12 shows our simulation results. We get only ~2x reduction in cycle count from skipping zeros, even though as stated earlier the upper bounds for exploiting sparsity are 3.3x-5x speedups. More comprehensive design exploration is needed to find an optimal design point. We leave this for a future study.

Because we exploit sparsity less aggressively, we ended up with a simpler more regular design that is amenable to frequency optimizations. The design runs at 450 MHz, even without explicitly optimizing for HyperFlex yet. Due to time constraints, we are not yet able to fully optimize our design. We are also using

Quartus Early Beta release for Stratix 10. Even though this is the latest version available to us at present, it may or may not reflect the synthesis result of more mature future releases of Quartus for Stratix 10. Due to this, we made projections with conservative, moderate, and aggressive optimization targets. Our conservative estimate targets 450MHz, which we currently already achieved without explicit optimizations for HyperFlex. HyperFlex has been reported to enable much higher frequency (e.g., 896MHz in 400G Ethernet CRC assembly [22]), so we use 600MHz and 750MHz as our moderate and aggressive projections.

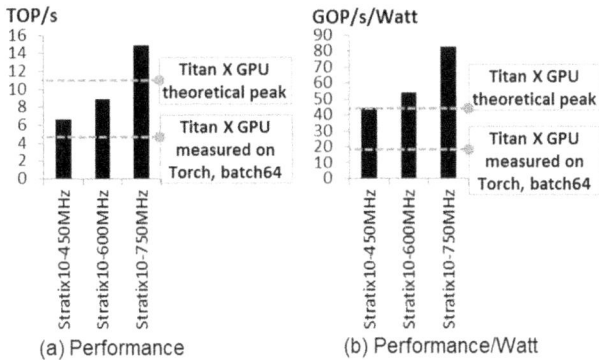

Figure 13. Ternary ResNet-50 results for ImageNet problem size, on Titan X GPU and Stratix 10 FPGA. For Stratix 10, we provide conservative, moderate, and aggressive estimates. For GPU, we provide the best achieved performance on Torch among the various settings we experimented with. Our GPU result is better than existing performance number [20,21].

5.4 GPU Evaluation

We ran Torch for ImageNet and Ternary ResNet-50 on a Titan X Pascal GPU to collect performance numbers. We tried multiple batch sizes, and found that batch of 64 gives the best performance. We used cuDNN 5 with the most aggressive performance setting. cuDNN not only supports highly optimized matrix operations as in cuBLAS, but it also supports many other optimizations, including mathematical transforms such as Winograd [23]. cuDNN chooses the best approach to compute the DNN workload given to it. Since our FPGA does not currently support all the optimizations in cuDNN (including Winograd), we believe that we are allowing the GPU to do the best it can do given its current software ecosystem. This includes using algorithm/mathematical optimizations that our FPGA design does not currently support.

To obtain an aggregated performance number, we collected execution times for many samples. We excluded samples that run much slower than others since they are not compute bound (i.e., they have non trivial data access time). We average 200 compute-bound samples to get our GPU result. Overall, we found that the achieved Ternary ResNet performance is 6.6 TFLOP/s on average, much less than the Titan X theoretical peak of 11 TFLOP/s.

We sanity checked our result against other ResNet GPU performance numbers we could find [20,21]. [21] reported execution time for ResNet-50 using the same Torch framework we use, on a Titan X Pascal. Our achieved performance (TOP/sec) is ~3x better than what was reported there. We notice that [21] used batch 16 and did not use cuDNN, which may explain the performance gap. There is also a ResNet-50 execution time reported in [20], but it was for a Titan X Maxwell. We scaled their

number up to Pascal by accounting for increased performance (i.e., 11 TFLOP/s peak in Titan X Pascal vs 7 TFLOP/s Titan X Maxwell). Our achieved performance is ~50% better than their reported number projected up for Pascal. Hence, we believe that our GPU achieved performance number is quite reasonable.

Finally, we also attempted to take advantage of ternarization in the GPU compute kernel, by avoiding multiplication and instead using a sign bit flip. However, after further study, we believe that the GPU is not able to take advantage of this optimization. This is because instruction throughput of 32-bit bitwise operations (e.g., AND, OR, XOR) is the same as the one of 32-bit floating point operations. For example, Titan X Pascal which supports CUDA Compute Capability 6.1 has the same throughput of 128 operations per cycle per multiprocessor for both operations. Therefore, either a multiply operation or a sign bit flip operation would still require a single instruction in GPU, with the same throughput. Hence, using a sign bit flip instead of a multiply would not improve GPU performance. Therefore, we opted to represent ternary value as float and used cuDNN.

5.5 FPGA vs. GPU Results

The performance and performance/watt of Stratix 10 FPGA and Titan X GPU for ResNet-50 is shown in Figure 13. To calculate throughput (TOP/sec), we divide the total operations in ResNet-50 by the execution time.

Even for the conservative performance estimate, Stratix 10 is already ~60% better than achieved Titan X performance. The moderate and aggressive estimates are even better, delivering 2.1x and 3.5x speedups over Titan X. Interestingly, the Stratix 10 aggressive 750MHz estimate can deliver 35% better performance compared to theoretical peak performance of Titan X. In terms of performance/watt, Stratix 10 delivers much better improvements over Titan X, compared to pure performance, from 2.3x to 4.3x across conservative to aggressive estimates.

We still need to do real measurements on the actual Stratix 10 FPGAs when they become commercially available, to verify the estimates presented here. However, these estimated results are very exciting evidence that next-generation Stratix 10 FPGA can potentially deliver leadership performance over the state-of-the-art high-performance GPU on next-generation DNNs.

6. DISCUSSION: OTHER DNN TRENDS

DNNs are rapidly advancing, and this paper does not cover all the DNN trends. Below are two other emerging DNN trends not studied in this paper, which we expect to be good for FPGAs.

Mathematical Transforms (e.g., Winograd). The first trend is in optimizations using mathematical transforms. In particular, Winograd transformation [23] has been shown to be amenable to small DNN filters (e.g., 3x3) that are common in state-of-the-art DNNs. Fast Fourier Transforms (FFTs) have also been shown to be amenable for larger filters (5x5 and above), which are still used in some DNNs. FPGAs have been known to be an efficient platform for FFTs (e.g., [24]), and one could expect that they would be well-suited for Winograd transformations as well. These transforms are often computable in a streaming data fashion and involve an arbitrary set of mathematical operators. And, there are many possible transformation parameters that lead to different compositions of mathematical operators. Such computation properties (arbitrary composition of operations on streaming data) are likely to be amenable to FPGAs.

Compression. There are various compression techniques that have been proposed for DNNs, such as weight sharing [6], hashing [25], etc. These techniques require find-grained data accesses, with indexing and indirection on lookup tables, which an FPGA fabric is particularly good at.

7. RELATED WORK

To the best of our knowledge, this is the first paper that projects performance of DNNs on Stratix 10, provides comparison against the latest Titan X Pascal GPU, and offers comprehensive coverage for many emerging DNNs (i.e., sparse, binary, ternary).

FPGA Accelerators. There has been a plethora of prior work focusing on FPGA-based deep learning accelerators (e.g., [10,11]). However, these works target older generation FPGAs, with many of them targeting embedded FPGA platforms. In contrast, this paper projects deep learning acceleration on state-of-the-art Stratix 10 FPGA for high-performance applications. Furthermore, prior works do not provide comparison to the latest high-performance Titan X Pascal GPU. And, their accelerators do not cover all of the variety of emerging DNN optimizations that we evaluate here.

ASIC Accelerators. Aside from FPGA acceleration, there have also been many works focusing on ASIC accelerators for deep learning (e.g., [8,9,26]). Most of these studies focus on "classic" DNNs that rely on dense matrix computation. There are more recent ASIC accelerators [8,9] that have been optimized for sparse DNNs and compact data types. Unlike these works, we focus on FPGAs in this paper.

FPGA vs. GPU Studies. Finally, there are existing studies that compare FPGAs against GPUs. The work in [27] compares BLAS matrix operations among CPU, FPGA, and GPUs. The work in [28][30] compare Neural Networks implemented on CPU, FPGA, GPU, and ASIC. However, these studies target older generation FPGAs and GPUs, while we target the latest Stratix 10 FPGA and Titan X Pascal GPU. Moreover, these prior studies do not focus on all emerging DNNs that are studied in this paper.

8. CONCLUSION

Can FPGAs beat GPUs in performance for next-generation DNNs? Our evaluation of a selection of emerging DNN algorithms on two generations of FPGAs (Arria 10 and Stratix 10) and the latest Titan X GPU shows that current trends in DNN algorithms may favor FPGAs, and that FPGAs may even offer superior performance. We created a customizable DNN hardware template for FPGAs and used this to study various GEMM operations for next-generation DNNs on FPGAs and GPUs. Our results show that projected Stratix 10 performance is 10%, 50%, and 5.4x better in performance (TOP/sec) than Titan X Pascal GPU on GEMM operations for pruned, Int6, and binarized DNNs, respectively. We also presented a case study on Ternary ResNet, which relies on sparse GEMM on 2-bit weights, and achieved accuracy within ~1% of the full-precision ResNet. On Ternary-ResNet, the Stratix 10 FPGA is projected to deliver 60% better performance over Titan X Pascal GPU, while being 2.3x better in performance/watt. Our results indicate that FPGAs may become the platform of choice for accelerating DNNs.

9. REFERENCES

[1] M. Courbariaux, Y. Bengio, J-P. David "BinaryConnect: Training Deep Neural Networks with binary weights during propagations," NIPS 2015.

[2] M. Courbariaux, I. Hubara, et al., "Binarized Neural Networks: Training Deep Neural Networks with Weights and Activations Constrained to +1 or -1," arXiv:1602.02830 [cs.LG].

[3] M. Rastegari, V. Ordonez, J. Redmon, A. Farhadi "XNOR-Net: ImageNet Classification Using Binary Convolutional Neural Networks," arXiv:1603.05279 [cs.CV]

[4] F. Li, B. Liu. "Ternary Weight Networks," arXiv:1605.04711 [cs.CV]

[5] G. Venkatesh, E. Nurvitadhi, D. Marr, ".Accelerating Deep Convolutional Networks Using Low-Precision and Sparsity," ICASSP, 2017.

[6] S. Han, H. Mao, W. J. Dally, "Deep Compression: Compressing Deep Neural Networks with Pruning, Trained Quantization, and Huffman Coding," ICLR 2016.

[7] P. Gysel, et al., "Hardware-Oriented Approximation of Convolutional Neural Networks," ICLR Workshop 2016.

[8] J. Albericio, P. Judd, T. Hetherington, et al, "Cnvlutin: Ineffectual-Neuron-Free Deep Convolutional Neural Network Computing," ISCA 2016.

[9] S. Han, X. Liu, et al., "EIE: Efficient Inference Engine on Compressed Deep Neural Network," ISCA 2016.

[10] N. Suda, V. Chandra, et al., "Throughput-Optimized OpenCL-based FPGA Accelerator for Large-Scale Convolutional Neural Networks," ISFPGA 2016.

[11] J. Qiu, et al., "Going Deeper with Embedded FPGA Platform for Convolutional Neural Network," ISFPGA 2016.

[12] P.K. Gupta, "Accelerating Datacenter Workloads," Keynote at FPL 2016. Slides available at www.fpl2016.org.

[13] A. Putnam, A. M. Caulfield, et al., "A Reconfigurable Fabric for Accelerating Large-Scale Datacenter Services," ISCA 2014.

[14] S. Y. Kung, "VLSI Array Processors," Prentice-Hall, Inc. Upper Saddle River, NJ, USA, 1987.

[15] A. Pedram, et al., "A High-Performance, Low-Power Linear Algebra Core," ASAP 2011.

[16] Altera Arria 10 Website. https://www.altera.com/products/fpga/arria-series/arria-10/overview.html

[17] Altera Stratix 10 Website. https://www.altera.com/products/fpga/stratix-series/stratix-10/overview.html

[18] Nvidia Titan X Website. http://www.geforce.com/hardware/10series/titan-x-pascal

[19] Altera's PowerPlay Early Power Estimators (EPE) and Power Analyzer, https://www.altera.com/support/support-resources/operation-and-testing/power/pow-powerplay.html

[20] S. Gross, M. Wilber, "Training and investigating Residual Nets," http://torch.ch/blog/2016/02/04/resnets.html

[21] J. C. Johnson, "cnn-benchmarks", available at https://github.com/jcjohnson/cnn-benchmarks

[22] G. Baeckler, "HyperPipelining of High-Speed Interface Logic," ISFPGA Tutorial, 2016.

[23] A. Lavin, S. Gray, "Fast Algorithms for Convolutional Neural Networks," arXiv:1509.09308 [cs.NE].

[24] P. D'Alberto, P. A. Milder, et al., "Generating FPGA Accelerated DFT Libraries," FCCM 2007.

[25] W. Chen, J. Wilson, et al., "Compressing Neural Networks with the Hashing Trick," ICML 2015.

[26] Y. Chen, T. Luo, S. Liu, et al., "Dadiannao: A machine-learning supercomputer," Int. Symposium on Microarchitecture (MICRO), 2014.

[27] S. Kestur, et al., "BLAS Comparison on FPGA, CPU and GPU," IEEE Annual Sym. on VLSI (ISVLSI), 2010

[28] E. Nurvitadhi, J. Sim, D. Sheffield, et al, "Accelerating Recurrent Neural Networks in Analytics Servers: Comparison of FPGA, CPU, GPU, and ASIC," FPL 2016.

[29] MAGMA: Matrix Algebra on GPU and Multicore Architectures. Website: http://icl.cs.utk.edu/magma/

[30] E. Nurvitadhi, D. Sheffield, J. Sim, et al, "Accelerating Binarized Neural Networks: Comparison of FPGA, CPU, GPU, and ASIC," FPT 2016.

Accelerating Binarized Convolutional Neural Networks with Software-Programmable FPGAs

Ritchie Zhao[1,*], Weinan Song[2], Wentao Zhang[2], Tianwei Xing[3], Jeng-Hau Lin[4],
Mani Srivastava[3], Rajesh Gupta[4], Zhiru Zhang[1,*]

[1]School of Electrical and Computer Engineering, Cornell University, USA
[2]School of Electronics Engineering and Computer Science, Peking University, China
[3]Department of Electrical Engineering, University of California Los Angeles, USA
[4]Department of Computer Science and Engineering, University of California San Diego, USA
*{rz252, zhiruz}@cornell.edu

Abstract

Convolutional neural networks (CNN) are the current state-of-the-art for many computer vision tasks. CNNs outperform older methods in accuracy, but require vast amounts of computation and memory. As a result, existing CNN applications are typically run on clusters of CPUs or GPUs. Research on FPGA acceleration of CNN workloads has achieved reductions in power and energy consumption. However, large GPUs outperform modern FPGAs in throughput, and the existence of compatible deep learning frameworks give GPUs a significant advantage in programmability.

Recent work in machine learning demonstrates the potential of very low precision CNNs — i.e., CNNs with binarized weights and activations. Such binarized neural networks (BNNs) appear well suited for FPGA implementation, as their dominant computations are bitwise logic operations and their memory requirements are greatly reduced. A combination of low-precision networks and high-level design methodology may help address the performance and productivity gap between FPGAs and GPUs. In this paper, we present the design of a BNN accelerator that is synthesized from C++ to FPGA-targeted Verilog. The accelerator outperforms existing FPGA-based CNN accelerators in GOPS as well as energy and resource efficiency.

1. Introduction

Deep convolutional neural networks (CNNs) have become an important class of machine learning algorithms widely used in computer vision and artificial intelligence. While CNNs have been known to researchers for decades, they were popularized after demonstrating high accuracy at the 2012 ImageNet recognition challenge [15]. Subsequently, CNNs have become the state-of-the-art for image classification, detection, and localization tasks. Research in CNNs and other areas of deep learning continues at a rapid pace, with hundreds of new papers published each year introducing new models and techniques. One indicator of this rate of progress is the improvement in the top-5 accuracy of the ImageNet competition winner over the years: 84.7% in 2012 [15] to 96.4% in 2015 [10].

One challenge to the widespread deployment of CNNs is their significant demands for computation and storage capacity. The VGG-19 network, for instance, contains over 140 million floating-point (FP) parameters and performs over 15 billion FP operations to classify one image [22]. Consequently, the training and inference of modern CNNs is almost exclusively done on large clusters of CPUs and GPUs [4]. One additional benefit of such platforms is the availability of compatible deep learning frameworks such as Caffe [12], Theano [24], or TensorFlow [9], which allow users to make use of the latest models or to train a custom network with little engineering effort.

While CPU and GPU clusters are currently the go-to platforms for CNN and many other machine learning applications, a customized hardware solution on FPGA can offer significant improvements in energy efficiency and power dissipation. These factors may be critical in enabling the increased use of CNNs in low-power settings such as unmanned drones or embedded computing. Recent work by Microsoft has even explored cost-effective acceleration of deep learning on FPGAs at datacenter scale [18]. There are also efforts in the academic community on FPGA-based CNN accelerators [27, 19] as well as tools for generating them automatically [23, 26]. Yet, there remains a sizable gap between GPU and FPGA platforms in both CNN performance *and* design effort. The latter is especially distressing given the rate of algorithmic innovation in deep learning — an FPGA-based CNN accelerator (or CNN design compiler) is unlikely to support the most up-to-date models, putting them at a severe competitive disadvantage.

We observe two trends which may help overcome these obstacles. The first is a series of recent papers in the machine learning community regarding very-low-precision CNNs. Networks with binary weights [6], or binary weights *and* activations [7, 21] have in certain cases demonstrated accuracy comparable to full precision nets. Such *binarized neural networks* (BNNs) may be the key to efficient deep learning on FPGA. Binarization reduces storage and memory bandwidth requirements, and replace FP operations with binary operations which can be very efficiently performed on the LUT-based FPGA fabric.

Concerning the cost and effort of FPGA implementation, we see a steady improvement in FPGA design automation tools over the past decade. High-level synthesis (HLS) tools such as Xilinx Vivado HLS [5] and LegUp [1] enable a user to write code in a high-level programming language, then algorithmically compile that code down to a register-transfer level (RTL) design specification. More recent tools such as Intel FPGA SDK for OpenCL [8] and Xilinx SDSoC [13] offer further automation features for generating the hardware-software interface and on-chip memory network. In the context of deep learning, these tools have the potential to critically reduce time-to-market on new accelerator designs and thus reduce the aforementioned innovation gap.

In this paper we present the design of a BNN accelerator for FPGAs. In order to take full advantage of the binarized values and operations, our design differs in multiple aspects from CNN accelerators in literature. Our specific contributions are as follows:

- To our best knowledge, we are the first to study FPGA acceleration for very low precision CNNs. Compared to their full-precision counterparts, such networks are potentially a better fit for the LUT-based fabric and limited on-chip storage in modern FPGAs.

- We employ an HLS design methodology for productive development of our FPGA-based BNN accelerator. Existing HLS work has examined loop ordering, unrolling, and local buffering for CNNs [27]. Our HLS implementation leverages these optimizations, and further propose novel BNN-specific hardware constructs to ensure full throughput and hardware utilization across the different input feature sizes.

- We implement our BNN classifier on a low-cost FPGA development board (ZedBoard) and show promising improvements over CPU and embedded GPU baselines as well as existing FPGA accelerators. Our source code is publicly available on the authors' websites.

The rest of this paper is organized as follows: Section 2 gives a primer on CNNs and BNNs; Section 3 describes our BNN accelerator design; Section 4 provides some details on our HLS code; Section 5 reports our experimental findings, Section 6 reviews previous work on FPGA-based CNN accelerators; and we conclude the paper in Section 7.

2. Preliminaries

In this section we briefly review the basic principles and terminology of CNNs, the differences between a CNN and BNN, and the specific CIFAR-10 BNN model that our accelerator will target.

2.1 Convolutional Neural Network Primer

A CNN is a machine learning classifier that typically takes in a multi-channel image and produces the probabilities of that image belonging to each output class. A typical CNN consists of a pipeline of connected *layers*. Each layer takes as input a set of *feature maps (fmaps)*, performs some computation on them, and produces a new set of fmaps to be fed into the next layer. The input fmaps of the first layer are the channels of the input image. Layers may require configuration values known as *parameters*, which must first be determined by *training* the CNN offline on pre-classified data. Once the parameters are finalized, the CNN can be deployed for *inference* — the classification of new data points. For most practical machine learning applications, the first-class concerns are the accuracy and execution time of online classification. This paper will thus focus on accelerating the inference task without compromising accuracy.

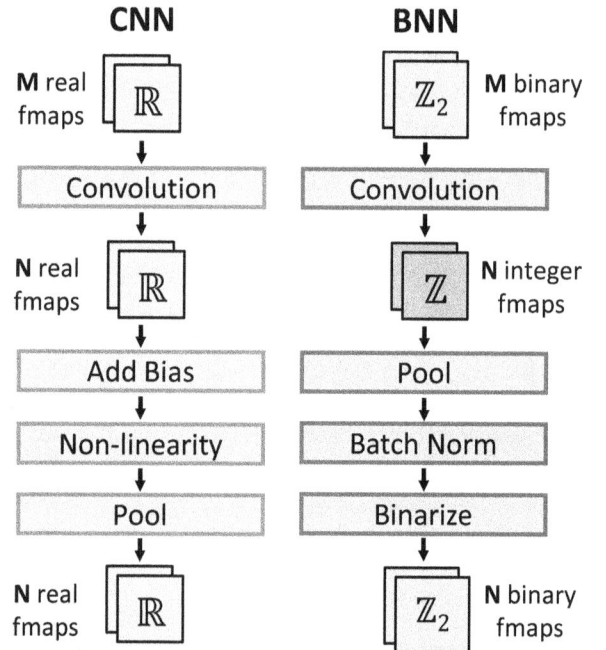

Figure 1: **Comparison of CNNs and BNNs** — Left: the order of operations in a CNN for a conv and pool layer. Right: the (modified) order of operations in the BinaryNet BNN [7]. Pooling is performed early and a batch normalization precedes the binarization to minimize information loss. Biases have been removed from the BNN.

Below we describe three layer types which are found in most CNNs, including our CIFAR-10 BNN model.

Convolutional (conv) layers convolve each input fmap with a $K \times K$ weight filter. The conv results are summed, added with a bias, and passed through a non-linearity function (such as ReLU or sigmoid) to produce a single output fmap. In this paper, we assume conv layers *pad* the input fmaps at the borders to produce output fmaps of the same size. Equation (1) below shows the operation of a conv layer with M input fmaps $\mathbf{x}_1, ..., \mathbf{x}_M$, N output fmaps $\mathbf{y}_1, ..., \mathbf{y}_N$, and non-linearity f.

$$\mathbf{y}_n = f(\sum_{m=1}^{M} \mathbf{x}_m * \mathbf{w}_{n,m} + b_n) \qquad (1)$$

The parameters of this conv layer are $M \times N \times K \times K$ weights and N biases.

Pooling layers maps each input fmap to an output fmap whose every pixel is the max/mean of a $K \times K$ window of input pixels. Unlike conv layers the windows do not overlap, and the output fmaps are K times smaller in each dimension. Pooling layers are inserted throughout a CNN to gradually reduce the size of the intermediate feature maps.

Dense or fully-connected (FC) layers take an input vector of 1×1 feature maps (pixels) and perform a dot product with a weight vector. The result is added to a bias and passed through a non-linearity to produce a single 1×1 output. Equation (2) below shows the operation of a FC layer with M input pixels, N output pixels, and non-linearity f.

$$y_n = f(\sum_{m=1}^{M} x_m w_{n,m} + b_n) \qquad (2)$$

The parameters are $M \times N$ weights and N biases.

2.2 Binarized Neural Networks

A BNN is essentially a CNN whose weights and fmap pixels are binarized to -1 or +1; they can be seen as an extreme example of the quantized, reduced-precision CNN models commonly used for hardware acceleration. In this paper we focus on an architecture developed by Courbariaux et al. in [6] and later refined in [7]. The first paper binarizes only the weights while the follow-up binarizes both weights and fmaps. We focus on the latter version and refer to it as the BinaryNet architecture/model. This architecture achieves near state-of-the-art results on both CIFAR-10 and SVHN datasets at time of publication. Other more recent work on low precision networks promise accuracy close to state of the arts on ImageNet [16, 28].

In the BinaryNet model, the weights and outputs of both conv and FC layers are binarized using the Sign function (i.e., positive weights are set to +1 and negatives to -1). Figure 1 illustrates the flow of data through a conv and pooling layer in both a CNN and a BNN. For the CNN, the order of operations matches Equation (1) and the fmaps are real-valued at all times. In the BNN, the feature maps go from binary to integer (after convolution) until it is binarized

again. Biases have been removed (see Section 3.1). Pooling in the BNN is always performed on the integer data.

The BNN also introduces a new layer type — **Batch normalization** [11] layers reduce the information lost during binarization by linearly shifting and scaling the input distribution to have zero mean and unit variance. This reduces quantization error compared to an arbitrary input distribution. [1] The transformation is given in Equation (3) below,

$$y = \frac{x - \mu}{\sqrt{\sigma^2 + \epsilon}} \gamma + \beta \qquad (3)$$

where x and y are input and output, respectively, μ and σ are statistics collected over the training set, γ and β are trained parameters, and ϵ is to avoid round-off problems. During inference, all parameters are fixed, so we need only be concerned with efficiently applying Equation (3) to each input fmap pixel. Each output fmap require its own set of batch norm parameters.

The primary advantages of BNNs over their higher precision counterparts are twofold:

1. The convolution operation in Equation (1) (which nominally requires a $K \times K$ element multiply-accumulate) can now be implemented as a bitwise XNOR between two $K \times K$ bit vectors and a popcount. This is highly relevant to FPGA design, as these operations can be implemented very efficiently in the logic fabric.

2. Assuming comparable numbers of feature maps and FC layer units, binarizing weights and fmaps greatly reduces their memory size. This is again compelling for FPGAs as existing FPGA accelerators are typically constrained in performance by a combination of on-chip storage space and off-chip memory bandwidth.

2.3 CIFAR-10 BNN Model

The CIFAR-10 dataset [14] contains sixty thousand 32×32 3-channel images consisting of photos taken of real world vehicles and animals. The images come from 10 classes (airplane, truck, cat, etc.) and are divided into a training set of 50000 and a test set of 10000.

The BinaryNet architecture consists of six conv layers followed by three FC layers. All conv layers use 3×3 filters and edge padding, and all conv/FC layers apply batch norm before binarization. There is a 2×2 max pooling layer after the 2nd, 4th, and 6th conv layers. The first conv layer is different from the rest: its input is the image, which is floating-point, not binary; its weights are still binary. The architecture is summarized in Table 1; the size of the fmaps gets smaller deeper into the network, and that the first two dense layers contain most of the weights.

---

[1] Batch normalization can also speed up training and regularize the activations in full-precision CNNs, but this is beyond the scope of this paper.

Layer	Input Fmaps	Output Fmaps	Output Dim	Output Bits	Weight Bits
Conv1	3	128	32	128K	3456
Conv2	128	128	32	128K	144K
Pool	128	128	16	32K	
Conv3	128	256	16	64K	288K
Conv4	256	256	16	64K	576K
Pool	256	256	8	16K	
Conv5	256	512	8	32K	1.1M
Conv6	512	512	8	32K	2.3M
Pool	512	512	4	8192	
FC1	8192	1024	1	1024	8.0M
FC2	1024	1024	1	1024	1.0M
FC3	1024	10	1	10	10K
Total					13.4M
Conv					4.36M
FC					9.01M

Table 1: **Architecture of the BinaryNet CIFAR-10 BNN** — The weight bits exclude batch norm parameters, whose total size after optimization (see Section 3.1) is 0.12M bits, less than 1% of the size of the weights.

Training of the CIFAR-10 BNN model was done using open-source Python code provided by Courbariaux et al. [2], which uses the Theano and Lasagne deep learning frameworks. We reached 11.58% test error out-of-the-box, in line with their results. Their paper also presents more advanced training techniques such as stochastic binarization, which further reduce error rate. We did not use them in this work. Different training schemes do not affect the inference pass or the compatibility of our accelerator.

3. FPGA Accelerator Design

In this section, we first outline how we optimize the BinaryNet model for hardware, then describe the design of our system and the specific compute units.

3.1 Hardware Optimized BNN Model

As with the design of conventional CNN accelerators, a key optimization we made to the BNN model is parameter quantization. While the weights are already binarized, the biases and batch norm parameters are real numbers. During bias quantization, we noticed that nearly every bias was much smaller than 1. Given that the inputs have magnitude 1, we tried setting the biases to zero and observed no effect on accuracy. We then retrained the network with biases removed from the model, and reached a test error of 11.32%. For the rest of the paper we use this as the baseline error rate.

A second optimization involved noting that the batch norm calculation (Equation (3)) is a linear transformation, and can thus be formulated as $y = kx + h$, where:

$$k = \frac{\gamma}{\sqrt{\sigma^2 + \epsilon}} \quad \text{and} \quad h = \beta - \frac{\mu\gamma}{\sqrt{\sigma^2 + \epsilon}} \quad (4)$$

[2] https://github.com/MatthieuCourbariaux/BinaryNet

This reduces the number of operations and cuts the number of stored parameters to two. Furthermore, the BNN always binarizes immediately after batch norm. Thus we do not need the magnitude of y, only the sign, allowing us scale k and h by any multiplicative constant. We exploit this property during quantization by scaling each k and h to be within the representable range of our fixed-point implementation. Empirical testing showed that k and h can be quantized to 16 bits with negligible accuracy loss while being a good fit for power-of-2 word sizes. We also quantized the floating point BNN inputs to 20-bit fixed point. Table 2 summarizes the impact of each algorithmic modification on test error. The HLS accelerator has the same accuracy as the C++ code.

3.2 Retraining for +1 Edge-Padding

One complication in the BinaryNet model is the interaction between binarization and edge padding. The model binarizes each activation to -1 or +1, but each input fmap is edge padded with zeros, meaning that a convolution can see up to 3 values: -1, 0, or +1. Thus the BinaryNet model actually requires some 2-bit operators (though the fmap data can still be stored in binary form). We managed to modify and retrain the BinaryNet model to pad with +1, eliminating the zeros and creating a truly binarized CNN. This +1 padded BNN achieves a test error of 11.82% in Python and 12.27% in C++/FPGA, only slightly worse than the original.

For our FPGA implementation we used the 0 padded BNN as the resource savings of the +1 padded version was not particularly relevant for the target device.

Source	Model	Padding	Test Error
From [7]	-	0	11.40%
Python	Default	0	11.58%
Python	no-bias	0	11.32%
Python	no-bias	+1	11.82%
C++	no-bias, fixed-point	0	11.46%
C++	no-bias, fixed-point	+1	12.27%

Table 2: **Accuracy of the BNN with various changes** — no-bias refers to retraining after removing biases from all layers and fixed-point refers to quantization of the inputs and batch norm parameters.

3.3 System Architecture

Our system architecture, shown in Figure 2(a), consists of three compute units, data and weight buffers, a direct memory access (DMA) system for off-chip memory transfer, and an FSM controller. The three compute units work on different types of layers: the *FP-Conv* unit for the (non-binary) first conv layer, the *Bin-Conv* unit for the five binary conv layers, and the *Bin-FC* unit for the three binary FC layers. Of the three, the Bin-Conv and Bin-FC units must handle different numbers of input and output fmaps, and (in the case of Bin-Conv) different fmap sizes.

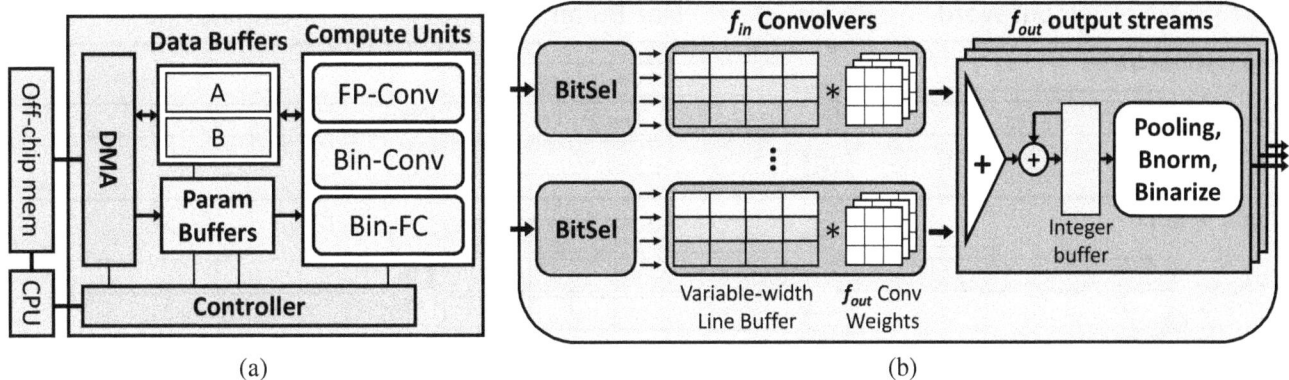

Figure 2: **Architectural diagrams of our BNN accelerator** — (a) system-level block diagram showing the three compute units, buffers, and how the accelerator is connected to the CPU and off-chip memory hierarchy; (b) architecture of the Bin-Conv unit with input and output parallelization factors $f_{in} = 2$ and $f_{out} = 3$. The unit can stream in two words per cycle and produce three output fmaps per invocation.

The storage of intermediate data in our accelerator differs from most existing designs. In full-precision CNN accelerators, the size of a single set of fmaps between two layers typically exceed the size of FPGA on-chip storage. This necessitates the continuous transfer of fmaps to and from off-chip RAM. However, as Table 1 shows, the size of the largest set of fmaps in our BNN is only 128K bits, which easily fits on-chip even in smaller FPGAs. Our design uses two in-out data buffers A and B of equal size. One layer reads from A and write its outputs to B; then (without any off-chip data transfers) the next layer can read from B and write to A. Thus, off-chip memory transfers are only needed for the input image, output prediction, and loading each layer's weights.

Unlike the fmaps, there is only enough memory on-chip to store a portion of a layer's weights. Multiple accelerator invocations may be needed for a layer; in each invocation we load in a new set of weights and produce a new set of fmaps. The next invocation produces the next set of fmaps, and etc, until all output fmaps have been generated and stored in the on-chip data buffer. Invoking the accelerator requires passing it arguments such as pointers to the weights, the layer type and size, the fmap size, and whether pooling should be applied. Inside the accelerator, the controller decodes these inputs and coordinates the other modules.

3.4 Compute Unit Architectures

In our accelerator, each compute unit must store *binarized* data to the on-chip RAMs at the end of its execution. As Figure 1 reveals, the first operation of a conv or FC layer transforms the binary inputs to integers; we make sure each unit will also perform the subsequent batch-norm, pooling, and binarization before writing data out to the buffers. One of our design goals is to limit the amount of integer-valued intermediate data buffered inside each compute unit,

FP-Conv — The fixed-point conv unit utilizes the well-known line buffer architecture for 2D convolutions. Because this unit only targets a single layer, we hardwire it to handle

a 3-channel 32×32 input. While the input pixels are 20-bit fixed-point, the weights are binarized, so we can replace the multiplies in the conv operation with sign inversions. We fully parallelize across the three input channels: each cycle we stream in three input pixels, add them to three line buffers, and compute a $3 \times 3 \times 3$ convolution. The result is put through batch norm and binarization to produce one output bit per cycle. Greater parallelism in this unit is achievable, but the first conv layer takes up a very small portion of the overall runtime, and we focused our efforts elsewhere.

Bin-Conv — The binary conv unit is the most critical component of the accelerator, as it will be responsible for the five binary conv layers which take up the vast majority of the runtime. The unit must maintain high throughput and resource efficiency while handling different input widths *at runtime*; our design targets 8, 16, or 32, and can support larger power-of-two widths with minor changes. To efficiently compute a convolution, multiple rows of input pixels need to be buffered for simultaneous access. However, a standard line buffer (i.e., from video processing applications) is unsuitable for this task due to two reasons:

1. A line buffer must be sized for the largest input fmap; in this case it must have a width of 32. This not only causes buffer under-utilization when the fmap is 16 or 8 wide, it also leads to loss of throughput, as we can only perform as many convolutions per cycle as the input width.

2. A line buffer is designed to shift one pixel per cycle to always store the most recent rows. However, with binarized inputs we have access to not one but many lines of new pixels each cycle (for instance, a 32-bit word can hold 4 lines from an 8×8 fmap). This radically changes how we should update the line buffer.

In full precision CNN accelerators, the size problem can be addressed by tiling, where input fmaps are processed in tiles which are always the same size. This is unsuitable in a BNN since the fmaps are typically very small in terms of number

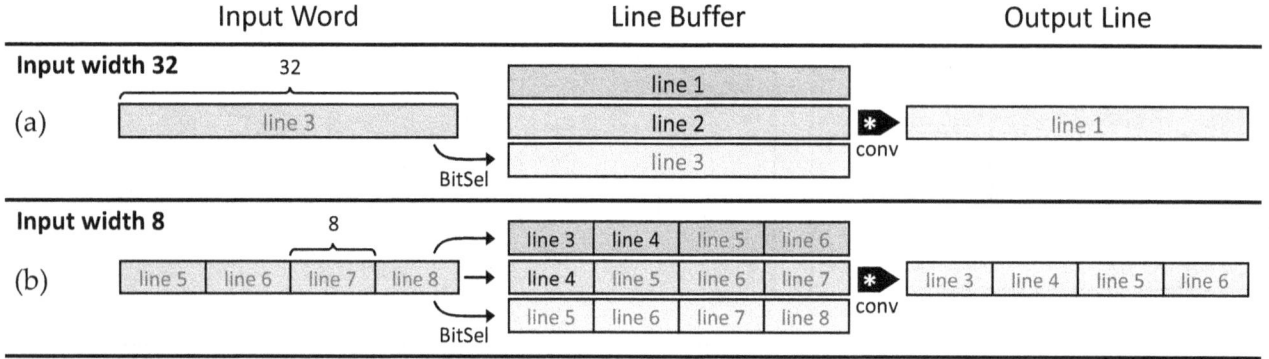

| Input Word | Line Buffer | Output Line |

Figure 3: Example usage of the variable-width line buffer — we show how a 32-bit input word is divided up by BitSel and inserted into the VWLB. The line buffer has height 3 and width 32. Sliding a 3×3 conv filter across the VWLB produces 32 output pixels, ignoring edge effects. (a) for a 32-wide input fmap, each row of the VWLB stores one line and applying the conv filter produces one 32-wide output line; (b) for an 8-wide input fmap, each row of the VWLB stores four lines and applying the conv filter produces four consecutive 8-wide output lines given the mapping of input lines to banks shown.

of bits. One possible solution to the second problem is to reorganize the data so each bit in an input word comes from a different fmap, and assign each bit to a separate line buffer. However, this requires an exorbitant number of line buffers and is not area efficient.

To address the above issues, we introduce two new modules: the *BitSel* module and the *variable-width line buffer* (VWLB). Figure 2(b) shows the basic structure of the Bin-Conv unit, whose execution proceeds in two phases. In the first phase, input fmaps from the on-chip buffers are streamed in on the left side, through the BitSel modules, and into the VWLBs. The Convolver modules compute the partial conv sums and accumulates them in the integer buffers. The BitSel is responsible for reordering the input bits so that the Convolver logic can be agnostic of the fmap width. In Figure 2(b), f_{in} is the input parallelization factor — the Bin-Conv unit accepts f_{in} input words per cycle and the data buffers are partitioned to match this rate. f_{out} is the output parallelization factor — each Convolver applies f_{out} 3 × 3 conv filters per cycle to the data in the VWLB and generates partial sums for f_{out} different fmaps. The first phase ends when all input fmaps in the current layer have been processed. At this point each integer buffer contains a finished conv map. In the second phase we compute max pooling, batch norm, and binarization to produce f_{out} binary output fmaps. Note that max-pooling and binarization are non-linear operations, so we cannot apply them to partially finished conv maps and accumulate afterwards.

Figure 3 explains the operation of the BitSel and VWLB in greater detail. The diagram assumes we have a word size of 32 bits and a 3×3 conv filter, which requires a VWLB with three rows and 32 elements per row. We demonstrate how the VWLB works for input fmap widths 32 and 8 and ignore edge padding for the sake of simplicity.

1. For a 32-wide input, each word contains exactly one line. Each cycle, the VWLB shifts up and the new 32-bit line

is written to the bottom row. We can then slide the 3×3 conv window across the VWLB to generate one 32-bit line of conv outputs.

2. For an 8-wide input, each word contains four lines. We split each VWLB row into four banks, and map each input line to *one or more* VWLB banks. The mapping is done in such a way that sliding the conv window across the VWLB produces four consecutive 8-bit output lines. Each cycle the VWLB shifts both up and to the left.

The BitSel is responsible for slicing the input word and mapping the slices to the row banks. Because the smallest input width is 8, each slice and VWLB bank is sized at 8 bits. For a 32-wide input, BitSel maps four contiguous 8-bit slices to the bottom row. For an 8-wide input, the mapping is more complex, but still highly regular and can be computed in hardware with just adds and shifts. Each pixel in the output lines in Figure 3 is an integer conv sum, and each sum is accumulated at a different location in the integer buffer.

The BitSel and VWLB provides three primary advantages: (1) the VWLB achieves full hardware utilization regardless of input width, (2) a new input word can be buffered every cycle, and (3) the BitSel deals with various input widths by itself, allowing the actual buffer and convolution logic to be fixed. Note that the VWLB used in our design differs from Figure 3 in a few details. First, we have neglected edge padding. The actual VWLB contains two additional elements per bank to hold horizontal pad bits; vertical padding is handled by inserting lines of zeros. Second, because the pad bits are 0 rather than +1 or -1, we must make each element in the VWLB two bits instead of one. The conv operation is performed between the 2-bit data and 1-bit weights, and can be implemented as sign inversion and accumulate.

Bin-FC — The binary FC unit is comparatively simple. Each cycle we read in f_{in} data words and an equal number of weight words. f_{in} here is the input parallelization factor just as in Bin-Conv. Because there is no edge padding in an FC layer the computations can be truly binary. We perform a dot product between the data and weight words by applying a bitwise XOR operation and then summing the resulting bits with a popcount. Similar to the Bin-Conv unit, we accumulate the sum in an integer buffer and apply binarization after all inputs have been processed. Note that the FC layers are typically bound by memory bandwidth of the off-chip connection, rather than the throughput of the accelerator.

Data Buffers — To accommodate multiple reads per cycle, the data buffers are partitioned into f_{in} banks, and feature maps are interleaved across the different banks. Figure 4 shows an example with $f_{in} = 2$ and four words per fmap. The data words are read sequentially by address, so a compute unit always accesses f_{in} consecutive fmaps in parallel.

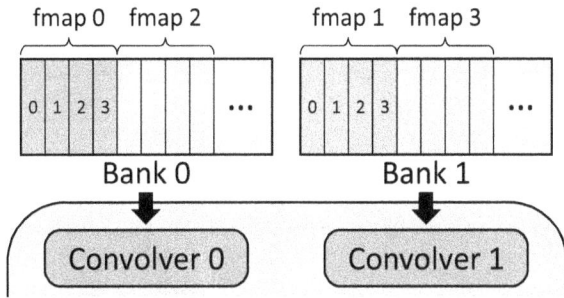

Figure 4: **Example of data buffer banking** — The compute unit and memory system have $f_{in} = 2$. Each fmap contains four words which are laid out sequentially. The fmaps are interleaved across banks, and both Bin-Conv and Bin-FC benefit from this banking.

4. HLS Accelerator Implementation

Figure 5 shows the HLS pseudocode for the front half of the Bin-Con unit, and demonstrates a key difference between BNN and CNN hardware design. For a CNN the code typically loops over an fmap processing one pixel at a time; key design decisions include loop ordering and unroll factors (see [27] for a good example). In our BNN accelerator, the basic atom of processing is not a pixel but a word. The example code is designed to sustain one word per cycle throughput over the entire input feature map set. Each fmap consists of `words_per_fmap` words, a number which differs between layers. As it processes the input set, the code updates the weights on each new fmap and accumulates the conv results in `outbuf`. We call `BitSel` and `conv` inside the loop to instantiate the BitSel units and conv logic as shown in Figure 2(b). To increase the number of input streams we can tile the loop and unroll the inner loop body.

A key design decision here is the input word size, which controls the level of parallelism across the pixels of an fmap. To guarantee correctness, `words_per_fmap` must be an integer greater than zero; this constrains the word size to at most the size of the smallest input fmap ($8 \times 8 = 64$ bits in our case). The word size restriction is not a significant limiting

```
1  VariableLineBuffer linebuf;
2  ConvWeights wts;
3  IntegerBuffer outbuf;
4
5  for (i = 0; i < n_input_words; i++) {
6    #pragma HLS pipeline
7
8    // read input word, update linebuffer
9    WordType word = input_data[i];
10   BitSel(linebuf, word, input_width);
11
12   // update the weights each time we
13   // begin to process a new fmap
14   if (i % words_per_fmap == 0)
15     wts = weights[i / words_per_fmap];
16
17   // perform conv across linebuffer
18   for (c = 0; c < LINE_BUF_COLS; c++) {
19     #pragma HLS unroll
20     outbuf[i % words_per_fmap][c] +=
21       conv(c, linebuf, wts);
22   }
23 }
```

Figure 5: **HLS pseudocode for part of the Bin-Conv unit** — the pseudocode implements a pipeline which reads and performs convolution on one input word each cycle. Many details are left out; the goal is to illustrate how our design can be expressed in high-level code.

factor in our design, as 64 is already a very large parallelization factor (it means we perform 64 convolutions per cycle), and there are other sources of parallelism to exploit in the BNN. We chose a word size of 64 bits for the data buffers and sized each data buffer A and B at 2048 words, which is just enough to store the largest set of fmaps in the BNN.

We also explored different values for f_{in} and f_{out} in Bin-Conv. It was observed that both have roughly similar effects on execution time, but increasing f_{out} has a more severe effect on total area. f_{in} controls the number of BitSels and VWLBs while f_{out} controls the number of pooling/batch norm units and integer buffers. In terms of logic a BitSel and a pooling/batch norm unit is similar, but each VWLB contains 32×3 2-bit registers while each integer buffer contains 32×32 12-bit registers. Thus all else being equal it is better to increase f_{in}. This result shows the importance of minimizing the storage of intermediate values and only committing binarized data to memory.

We use Xilinx SDSoC as the primary design tool for our BNN application. SDSoC takes as input a software program with certain functions marked as "hardware". It invokes Vivado HLS under the hood to synthesize the "hardware" portion into RTL. In addition, it automatically generates the data motion network and DMA necessary for memory transfer between CPU and FPGA based on the specified software-hardware partitioning. We selected a DMA engine built for contiguous memory since it has the highest throughput, and a neural network's data and weights can be laid out contiguously. We used directives to ensure that data is only transferred on the first and last accelerator invocation; weights are transferred on every invocation.

5. Experimental Results

We evaluate our design on a ZedBoard, which uses a low-cost Xilinx Zynq-7000 SoC containing an XC7Z020 FPGA alongside an ARM Cortex-A9 embedded processor. We make use of Xilinx SDSoC 2016.1 as the primary design tool, which leverages Vivado HLS and Vivado to perform the actual HLS compilation and FPGA implementation. We compared our design against two server-class computing platforms: an Intel Xeon E5-2640 multicore processor (**CPU**) and an NVIDIA Tesla K40 GPU (**GPU**). We also compared against an NVIDIA Jetson TK1 embedded GPU board (**mGPU**). As BNNs are a recent development, our baseline applications will not be as well optimized compared to CNN baselines (where implementations can be found in frameworks such as Caffe). The CPU and GPU baselines are adapted from code provided in [7]. The code leverages Theano, and calls OpenBLAS for CPU and CUDA for GPU. However, it does not perform bitwise optimizations since they are not natively supported in Theano, and instead uses floating-point values binarized to -1 and +1. For the baselines we used the BNN model with no biases and k and h, and on the GPU we always used the largest batch size.

Power measurement is obtained via a power monitor. We measured 4.5W idle and 4.7W max power on the Zedboard power supply line when running our BNN. This indicates the dynamic power consumption of the FPGA is very low.

Table 3: **Comparison of different configurations** — Last row shows the resources available on the device; **Runtime** is in milliseconds. * indicates our chosen configuration.

f_{in}	LUT	FF	BRAM	DSP	Runtime
1	25289	28197	86	3	17.5
2	35291	37125	87	3	10.8
4	38906	36771	87	3	7.98
8*	46900	46134	94	3	5.94
Dev.	53200	106400	140	220	-

Table 3 shows the performance and resource utilization of our accelerator using different values of f_{in} for the Bin-Conv and Bin-FC units. All numbers are post place and route. In our experiments f_{out} is set to 1 for reasons outlined in Section 4. Performance scaling is clear, though the scaling is less than unity due to memory transfer and other overheads. We use $f_{in} = 8$ for the rest of the experiments.

We compare the performance of our accelerator to the various baselines in Table 4. As raw throughput depends heavily on device size, we also show the power consumption and the throughput per Watt. The FPGA design obtains 15.1x better performance and 11.6x better throughput per Watt over **mGPU**, which has a similar power envelope. Against the x86 processor, it achieves a 2.5x speedup. While the binary conv layers were faster, the FC layers were slower, which is unsurprising as the FC layers are bound by external memory bandwidth. Versus **GPU**, the FPGA is 8.1x worse in performance. But as expected, it has much lower power consumption and better throughput per Watt.

To show that the FC layers are indeed limited by memory bandwidth, we created a design where the FC computations are removed but the memory transfers are kept. The new execution time of the FC layers is within 5% that of the original, demonstrating that there is not much to gain by further parallelizing them beyond the current design.

Table 4: **Performance comparison** — **Conv1** is the first FP conv layer, **Conv2-5** are the binary conv layers, **FC1-3** are the FC layers. A – indicates a value we could not measure. Numbers with * are sourced from datasheets. The last row shows power efficiency in throughput per Watt.

	Execution time per image (ms)			
	mGPU	CPU	GPU	FPGA
Conv1	–	0.68	0.01	1.13
Conv2-5	–	13.2	0.68	2.68
FC1-3	–	0.92	0.04	2.13
Total	90	14.8	0.73	5.94
Speedup	1.0x	6.1x	123x	15.1x
Power (Watt)	3.6	95*	235*	4.7
imgs/sec/Watt	3.09	0.71	5.83	35.8

Table 5 compares our implementation against state-of-the-art FPGA accelerators found in literature — all numbers are retrieved from the respective papers. Note that two of the comparisons are against larger FPGAs while one is against the same device. Throughput is shown in giga-operations-per-second (GOPS), and we count adds and multiplies following [27]: each binary xor, negation, or addition counts as one operation. Our BNN accelerator beats the best known FPGA accelerators in pure throughput, and is also much more resource and power efficient. BNNs save especially on the number of DSPs since multiplication/division is only needed for batch norm and not for the compute-intensive conv or FC calculations. The metrics of throughput per kLUT and throughput per Watt are especially important — due to the relative novelty of the BNN, we were only able to obtain a suitable network for CIFAR-10 while previous work shows results for larger ImageNet networks. However, our data provides evidence that the BNN is algorithmically better suited for FPGA than CNN, enabling far more efficient usage of resource and power. With a more advanced network and larger device, our design should scale up and achieve similar gains. Very recent work on low-precision

CNNs have also made great strides into achieving near state-of-the-art accuracy on the ImageNet dataset [16, 28].

Table 5: **Comparison of our work against state-of-the-art FPGA accelerators** — GOPS counts multiplies and adds per second. * indicates values approximated from charts.

	[23]	[19]	[25]	Ours
Platform	Stratix-V GSD8	Zynq 7Z045	Zynq 7Z020	Zynq 7Z020
Capacity (kLUTs)	695	218.6	53.2	53.2
Clock(MHz)	120	150	100	143
Power(W)	19.1	9.6	-	4.7
Precision	8-16b	16b	-	1-2b
GOPS (conv)	136.5	187.8	-	318.9
GOPS (all)	117.8	137.0	12.73	207.8
kLUTs	120*	182.6	43.2	46.9
DSPs	760*	780	208	3
GOPS/ kLUT	0.98	0.75	0.29	4.43
GOPS/ Watt	6.17	14.3	7.27	44.2

While it may not be completely fair to compare GOPS between a binarized and conventional network, it is currently the (de facto) standard practice for hardware accelerator studies to compare reduced and full-precision implementations that use different data types.

6. Related Work

Our paper owes much to the groundbreaking work on BNNs in the machine learning community [6, 7]. These papers contain some discussion on the advantages of BNNs over CNN for hardware, but to our best knowledge we are the first to present a working FPGA implementation.

There have been many studies on the design of CNN accelerators for FPGA. Zhang et al. [27] describe how to optimize an HLS design by reordering and tiling loops, inserting the proper pragmas, and organizing external memory transfers. Ensuing publications have mostly eschewed HLS in favor of RTL designs. Qiu et al. [19] propose an architecture that computes conv and FC layers on the same hardware, as well as dynamic fixed-point quantization. Their paper demonstrates an area-efficient accelerator for AlexNet on the Xilinx ZC706 board.

A related line of research focuses on creating CNN design compilers which can generate optimized hardware for a family of models. These works typically use a set of RTL modules combined with a design space exploration tool to find the optimal architectural parameters. Rahman et al. [20] propose a scalable array-based CNN accelerator with heavy input reuse. Motamedi [17] uses a roofline model for performance to guide hardware generation. Wang [26] proposes DeepBurning, which targets a variety of CNN architectures and performs data layout optimization.

OpenCL frameworks for deep learning on FPGA have also been proposed. Suda et al. [23] use parameterized OpenCL alongside analytical models for performance and resource, enabling a genetic algorithm to search for the optimal configuration. Venieris and Bouganis [25] study the use of synchronous dataflow to capture CNN workloads and use graph partitioning to control resource consumption.

There is also a great deal of research work on ASIC CNN co-processors. Among the most well know is the DianNao line of architectures [2]. The Eyeriss paper [3] contains a comprehensive study of popular dataflows for spatial architectures and derive an optimal one.

Our approach differs from existing work in two major ways: (1) we are the first to study BNNs for FPGA acceleration; (2) we make use of a C-based HLS methodology and propose design constructs to maximize throughput on different layers. Existing CNN accelerators on FPGA are not well-equipped to handle BNNs due significant differences in compute and storage requirements, and layer organization. Our final design differs greatly from previous work.

7. Conclusions and Future Work

We are the first to implement an accelerator for binarized neural networks on FPGA. BNNs feature potentially reduced storage requirements and binary arithmetic operations, making them well suited to the FPGA fabric. However, these characteristics also render CNN design constructs such as input tiles and line buffers ineffective. We introduce new design constructs such as a variable-width line buffer to address these challenges, creating an accelerator radically different from existing work. We leverage modern HLS tools to write our design in productive, high-level code, and our accelerator outperforms existing work in raw throughput, throughput per area, and throughput per Watt.

Future BNN work should focus both on algorithmic and architectural improvements. On the algorithmic side we would like to explore techniques to reduce model size. From the architectural side one action item is to implement a low-precision network for ImageNet, which would involve a much larger and more complicated accelerator design.

Acknowledgements

This research was supported in part by DARPA Award HR0011-16-C-0037, a DARPA Young Faculty Award, NSF Awards #1337240, #1453378, #1512937, and a research gift from Xilinx, Inc. The Tesla K40 GPU used for this research was donated by the NVIDIA Corporation.

References

[1] A. Canis, J. Choi, M. Aldham, V. Zhang, A. Kammoona, T. Czajkowski, S. D. Brown, and J. H. Anderson. LegUp: An Open-Source High-Level Synthesis Tool for FPGA-Based Processor/Accelerator Systems. *ACM Trans. on Embedded Computing Systems (TECS)*, 13(2):24, 2013.

[2] T. Chen, Z. Du, N. Sun, J. Wang, C. Wu, Y. Chen, and O. Temam. Diannao: A Small-Footprint High-Throughput Accelerator for Ubiquitous Machine-earning. *Int'l Conf. on Architectural Support for Programming Languages and Operating Systems (ASPLOS)*, Mar 2014.

[3] Y.-H. Chen, T. Krishna, J. Emer, and V. Sze. Eyeriss: An Energy-Efficient Reconfigurable Accelerator for Deep Convolutional Neural Networks. *Int'l Symp. on Computer Architecture (ISCA)*, Jun 2016.

[4] A. Coates, B. Huval, T. Wang, D. J. Wu, A. Y. Ng, and B. Catanzaro. Deep Learning with COTS HPC Systems. *Int'l Conf. on Machine Learning (ICML)*, pages 1337–1345, Jun 2013.

[5] J. Cong, B. Liu, S. Neuendorffer, J. Noguera, K. Vissers, and Z. Zhang. High-Level Synthesis for FPGAs: From Prototyping to Deployment. *IEEE Trans. on Computer-Aided Design of Integrated Circuits and Systems (TCAD)*, Apr 2011.

[6] M. Courbariaux, Y. Bengio, and J.-P. David. BinaryConnect: Training Deep Neural Networks with binary weights during propagations. *Advances in Neural Information Processing Systems (NIPS)*, pages 3123–3131, 2015.

[7] M. Courbariaux, I. Hubara, D. Soudry, R. El-Yaniv, and Y. Bengio. Binarized Neural Networks: Training Deep Neural Networks with Weights and Activations Constrained to +1 or -1. *arXiv e-print*, arXiv:1602.02830, Feb 2016.

[8] T. S. Czajkowski, U. Aydonat, D. Denisenko, J. Freeman, M. Kinsner, D. Neto, J. Wong, P. Yiannacouras, and D. P. Singh. From OpenCL to High-Performance Hardware on FPGAs. *Int'l Conf. on Field Programmable Logic and Applications (FPL)*, pages 531–534, Aug 2012.

[9] M. A. et al. TensorFlow: Large-Scale Machine Learning on Heterogeneous Systems, 2015. Software available from tensorflow.org.

[10] K. He, X. Zhang, S. Ren, and J. Sun. Deep Residual Learning for Image Recognition. *arXiv e-print*, arXiv:1512.0338, Dec 2015.

[11] S. Ioffe and C. Szegedy. Batch Normalization: Accelerating Deep Network Training by Reducing Internal Covariate Shift. *arXiv e-print*, arXiv:1502.03167, Mar 2015.

[12] Y. Jia, E. Shelhamer, J. Donahue, S. Karayev, J. Long, R. Girshick, S. Guadarrama, and T. Darrell. Caffe: Convolutional architecture for fast feature embedding. *arXiv preprint*, arXiv:1408.5093, 2014.

[13] V. Kathail, J. Hwang, W. Sun, Y. Chobe, T. Shui, and J. Carrillo. SDSoC: A Higher-level Programming Environment for Zynq SoC and Ultrascale+ MPSoC. *Int'l Symp. on Field-Programmable Gate Arrays (FPGA)*, pages 4–4, Feb 2016.

[14] A. Krizhevsky and G. Hinton. Learning Multiple Layers of Features from Tiny Images, 2009. Master's Thesis. Department of Coumputer Science, University of Toronto.

[15] A. Krizhevsky, I. Sutskever, and G. E. Hinton. Imagenet Classification with Deep Convolutional Neural Networks. *Advances in Neural Information Processing Systems (NIPS)*, pages 1097–1105, 2012.

[16] F. Li and B. Liu. Ternary Weight Networks. *arXiv e-print*, arXiv:1605.04711, May 2016.

[17] M. Motamedi, P. Gysel, V. Akella, and S. Ghiasi. Design Space Exploration of FPGA-Based Deep Convolutional Neural Networks. *Asia and South Pacific Design Automation Conf. (ASP-DAC)*, pages 575–580, Jan 2016.

[18] K. Ovtcharov, O. Ruwase, J.-Y. Kim, J. Fowers, K. Strauss, and E. Chung. Accelerating Deep Convolutional Neural Networks Using Specialized Hardware. *Microsoft Research*, Feb 2015.

[19] J. Qiu, J. Wang, S. Yao, K. Guo, B. Li, E. Zhou, J. Yu, T. Tang, N. Xu, S. Song, et al. Going Deeper with Embedded FPGA Platform for Convolutional Neural Network. *Int'l Symp. on Field-Programmable Gate Arrays (FPGA)*, pages 26–35, Feb 2016.

[20] A. Rahman, J. Lee, and K. Choi. Efficient FPGA Acceleration of Convolutional Neural Networks using Logical-3D Compute Array. *Design, Automation, and Test in Europe (DATE)*, pages 1393–1398, Apr 2016.

[21] M. Rastegari, V. Ordonez, J. Redmon, and A. Farhadi. XNOR-Net: ImageNet Classification Using Binary Convolutional Neural Networks. *European Conference on Computer Vision (ECCV)*, Oct 2016. arXiv:1603.05279.

[22] K. Simonyan and A. Zisserman. Very Deep Convolutional Networks for Large-Scale Image Recognition. *arXiv e-print*, arXiv:1409.15568, Apr 2015.

[23] N. Suda, V. Chandra, G. Dasika, A. Mohanty, Y. Ma, S. Vrudhula, J.-s. Seo, and Y. Cao. Throughput-Optimal OpenCL-based FPGA Accelerator for Large-Scale Convolutional Neural Networks. *Int'l Symp. on Field-Programmable Gate Arrays (FPGA)*, pages 16–25, Feb 2016.

[24] Theano Development Team. Theano: A Python framework for fast computation of mathematical expressions. *arXiv e-print*, arXiv:1605.02688, May 2016.

[25] S. I. Venieris and C.-S. Bouganis. fpgaConvNet: A Framework for Mapping Convolutional Neural Networks on FPGAs. *IEEE Symp. on Field Programmable Custom Computing Machines (FCCM)*, May 2016.

[26] Y. Wang, J. Xu, Y. Han, H. Li, and X. Li. DeepBurning: Automatic Generation of FPGA-based Learning Accelerators for the Neural Network Family. *Design Automation Conf. (DAC)*, page 110, Jun 2016.

[27] C. Zhang, P. Li, G. Sun, Y. Guan, B. Xiao, and J. Cong. Optimizing FPGA-based Accelerator Design for Deep Convolutional Neural Networks. *Int'l Symp. on Field-Programmable Gate Arrays (FPGA)*, pages 161–170, Feb 2015.

[28] S. Zhou, Y. Wu, Z. Ni, X. Zhou, H. Wen, and Y. Zou. DoReFar-Net: Training Low Bitwidth Convolutional Neural Networks with Low Bitwidth Gradients. *arXiv e-print*, arXiv:1606.06160, Jul 2016.

Improving the Performance of OpenCL-based FPGA Accelerator for Convolutional Neural Network

Jialiang Zhang and Jing Li

Department of Electrical and Computer Engineering
University of Wisconsin-Madison
{jialiang.zhang, jli}@ece.wisc.edu

Abstract

OpenCL FPGA has recently gained great popularity with emerging needs for workload acceleration such as Convolutional Neural Network (CNN), which is the most popular deep learning architecture in the domain of computer vision. While OpenCL enhances the code portability and programmability of FPGA, it comes at the expense of performance. The key challenge is to optimize the OpenCL kernels to efficiently utilize the flexible hardware resources in FPGA. Simply optimizing the OpenCL kernel code through various compiler options turns out insufficient to achieve desirable performance for both compute-intensive and data-intensive workloads such as convolutional neural networks .

In this paper, we first propose an analytical performance model and apply it to perform an in-depth analysis on the resource requirement of CNN classifier kernels and available resources on modern FPGAs. We identify that the key performance bottleneck is the on-chip memory bandwidth. We propose a new kernel design to effectively address such bandwidth limitation and to provide an optimal balance between computation, on-chip, and off-chip memory access. As a case study, we further apply these techniques to design a CNN accelerator based on the VGG model. Finally, we evaluate the performance of our CNN accelerator using an Altera Arria 10 GX1150 board. We achieve 866 Gop/s floating point performance at 370MHz working frequency and 1.79 Top/s 16-bit fixed-point performance at 385MHz. To the best of our knowledge, our implementation achieves the best power efficiency and performance density compared to existing work.

1. INTRODUCTION

Convolutional Neural Networks (CNNs) are widely used in computer vision, speech recognition, natural language processing and text classification. Over the past decade, the accuracy and the performance of CNN has improved significantly, mainly due to the enhanced neural network structures enabled by massive datasets and increased computational resources benefits from the CMOS scaling to train the models in reasonable time.

In recent years, FPGA has become an attractive solution to accelerate CNN classification [1, 2] for its flexibility, short time-to-market, and energy efficiency [3], especially with the recent release of a new-generation high level synthesis (HLS) tool, i.e., OpenCL, which greatly reduces the time and complexity of the programming process. For instance, prior work [4] successfully demonstrated an optimized OpenCL FPGA accelerator for CNN classifiers.

While OpenCL framework provides a high-level programming interface which allows programmers to reuse their code from other platforms, thus significantly enhancing programmability and portability, this comes at the expense of performance. Therefore, it is imperative to optimize the kernel design to maximize hardware resource utilization for better performance.

In this work, to achieve a high performance CNN accelerator, we first propose an analytic model to guide our kernel design to achieve a better mapping from OpenCL kernels to FPGA hardware. We borrow the insights from the roofline model in [1] and further improve it by taking both on-chip and off-chip memory bandwidth into consideration. The core concept of the model is to introduce two key metrics, *machine balance,* and *code balance.* Such balance models quantify the difference between available resources provided by native hardware (FPGA devices) and actual resources demanded by the application (CNN classification kernel). Thus, it can help to pinpoint the performance bottlenecks in the implementation of an OpenCL-based FPGA accelerator for CNNs and provide optimization opportunities.

As a case study, we further apply the model to perform a comprehensive analysis on one of the most popular CNN models: Very Deep Convolutional Networks (VGG) [5], which has also been studied in prior works [2, 4]. From our analysis, a key learning is that the performance of existing OpenCL FPGA CNN accelerators is inherently limited by the "unbalanced" hardware resources. More specifically, the on-chip memory bandwidth cannot match the computational throughput and the off-chip memory bandwidth. Experimental results confirmed that: 1) the computational resources are heavily under-utilized and 2) on-chip and off-chip data accesses are not well balanced. Both observations are due to the inefficient bandwidth utilization of on-chip memory. However, these works either focus on optimizing the computational throughput by increasing parallelism (loop unrolling, vectorization) using the pragma directives provided by the OpenCL SDK without considering memory or optimizing the external memory access through data reuse or advanced memory modules such as Hybrid Memory Cube (HMC) and High Bandwidth Memory (HBM) [6]. Nevertheless, to our best knowledge, there are no efforts to develop a systematic and generic optimization methodology to guide accelerator design accounting for all factors, especially the on-chip memory bandwidth.

Our study further reveals that the inefficiencies of on-chip memory bandwidth are fundamentally due to the current OpenCL kernel design. While designing the kernel, explicit parallel kernel

FPGA '17, February 22-24, 2017, Monterey, CA, USA

© 2017 ACM. ISBN 978-1-4503-4354-1/17/02. . . $15.00

DOI: http://dx.doi.org/10.1145/3020078.3021698

code is translated into a replication of custom compute units. To match the computational throughput and minimize external memory access, on-chip (local) memories will need to be replicated as well. Such a replication scheme quickly drains on-chip memory resources, making the computational-intensive applications become memory-bound. More importantly, from the hardware perspective, the native on-chip memory bandwidth has not been improved much over technology generations (Table 1), making it even more challenging to bridge the gap between computation and memory resources with existing techniques. To address this issue, we propose a novel design for a CNN classification kernel. In particular, the new kernel design is comprised of : **(i)** a two-dimensional interconnection between PEs and the local memory system, as compared with the one-dimensional interconnection in the existing OpenCL kernel design. It enables efficient data sharing without memory replication and thereby increases the effective on-chip memory bandwidth by orders of magnitude. **(ii)** a two-dimensional dispatcher to support the proposed interconnection between PEs and local memory. We also develop a work-item scheduling technique to further optimize memory resource usage. **(iii)** a shared buffer technique, which can be used in conjunction with (i) and (ii) to further reduce the external memory bandwidth requirement. We summarize the key contributions as follows:

- We propose an analytical model to quantitatively characterize the correlation between the performance of CNN classification kernels and available resources on FPGAs.

- We apply the model to perform an in-depth analysis on VGG and identify that the key performance bottleneck is on-chip memory bandwidth.

- We propose a novel kernel design to effectively address the on-chip memory bandwidth limitation and to provide an optimal balance between computation, on-chip and off-chip memory access.

- We conduct experiments to verify the effectiveness of the proposed techniques. To the best of our knowledge, our implementation achieves the **highest performance, energy efficiency and performance density** compared to state-of-the-art OpenCL FPGA CNN implementations.

The rest of the paper is organized as follows. Section 2 presents the background of OpenCL FPGA and the state-of-the-art CNN implementations. In Section 3, we present an analytical performance model and apply it to analyze the performance bottlenecks of implementing a CNN accelerator using OpenCL FPGA. In Section 4, we present a novel kernel and dispatcher design to address the performance bottlenecks. Section 5 presents a detailed case study on CNN using the proposed kernel design with an optimization technique. Section 6 presents the experimental results of our CNN design and validates proposed techniques. Section 7 concludes the paper.

2. BACKGROUND

In this section, we first provide an overview of the OpenCL stack, and then present the background of the convolutional neural network (CNN) and its state-of-art OpenCL FPGA implementations.

2.1 OpenCL Stack on FPGA

In Figure 1, we summarize the OpenCL stack on the FPGA platform, which contains two components: the host API and the

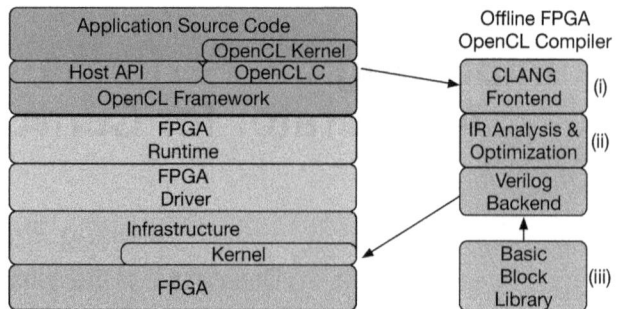

Figure 1: Overview of OpenCL FPGA stack. OpenCL FPGA provides extra flexibility in configuring the hardware architecture in an offline compilation process.

OpenCL device kernel. Under the OpenCL framework, device vendors provide two device specific layers: runtime and driver, to interface with the upper-level programming framework and the underlying hardware.

Unlike GPU and other fixed architectures, at the core, the OpenCL compilation flow for FPGAs offers additional flexibility in customizing hardware tailored for a specific application. In particular, the OpenCL kernels for FPGA must be compiled *offline* [7] into a set of configurable primitive operations provided by the vendor. We note that these primitives used in FPGA's compilation are analogous to processor instructions, e.g., load/store, arithmetic operation and synchronization operation, etc.. Nonetheless, they can be pre-compiled into custom hardware modules in FPGAs and placed in the kernel database of the system as an IP library.

As shown in Figure 1, the offline kernel compiler is based on the LLVM framework and the compilation process is composed of three components: CLANG frontend, LLVM-optimizer and a custom backend which invokes the IP library to generate custom hardware for each basic block and connect them using flexible routing resources on the FPGA. However, such flexibility also creates challenges for performing optimization in significantly enlarged design spaces in the hardware/software domain. If not handled properly, the unoptimized kernel implementation may severely degrade performance.

The OpenCL FPGA framework is depicted in Figure 2. It consists of an infrastructure region, which includes a PCIe DMA engine, an external DRAM controller, and a kernel region. The kernel connects to the SOC Bus (e.g AXI or Avalon) in the infrastructure region to interact with external DRAM and the Host. Based on the current OpenCL FPGA kernel design, *work-items* are execution instances of a kernel and are grouped by *work-groups*. The kernel region has three major components: a dispatcher, a compute subsystem organized hierarchically into compute units (CUs) and processing elements (PEs), and a local memory subsystem. The dispatcher is responsible for scheduling work-groups (work-items) to the CUs (PEs) as well as host/device memory transfers. The CUs execute work-groups in lockstep. All CUs share a global memory and constant memory while each CU has its own local memory. The PE array in each CU can be organized in one, two or three dimensions using the OpenCL attribute *num_compute_units()*. In Figure 2(c), we show a 2×2 PE organization. We note that even though PEs can be arranged in high-dimension, the interconnection between PEs and the local memory system is still one-dimensional.

2.2 FPGA Accelerator for CNN

The Convolutional Neural Network (CNN) is currently the most popular deep learning architecture in the domain of artificial intel-

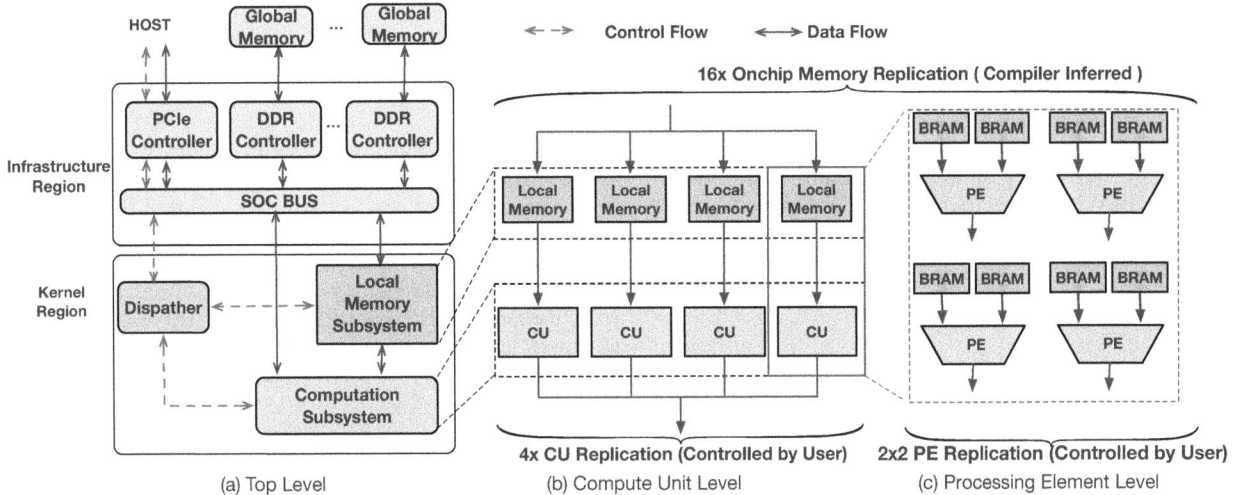

Figure 2: OpenCL FPGA framework:(a) Top level ;(b) Compute unit (CU); (c) Processing element(PE)

ligence (AI) [8] and computer vision (CV) [5, 9, 10]. CNNs are typically organized into alternating convolutional and pooling neural network layers followed by a number of fully-connected layers. The detailed operations of CNNs can be found in prior work [9]. Similar to other supervised learning algorithms, CNNs have a feed-forward path for recognition and a backward path for training. In practice, the training phase is typically conducted offline and the pre-trained model is deployed for online classification.

Most recently, the advances in FPGA hardware and design tools have reignited interests in implementing CNNs on FPGAs. For instance, [1, 2] use high-level synthesis (HLS) tools to develop CNN accelerators on FPGA with soft microprocessors and embedded hard microprocessors, respectively.

There are also efforts to develop FPGA CNN accelerators using OpenCL. For example, [4] attempts to find optimal parallel CU/PE configurations for different workloads to achieve desired computational throughput. However, in order to serve the concurrent memory requests from parallel CUs/PEs and to minimize the penalty of external memory access, the compiler automatically replicates the local memory (BRAM) by the same factor [7]. For instance, in Figure 2, we show the kernel design used by [4], with 4 CUs. Each of the CUs contains a 2×2 PE array, which provides 16x more parallelism in computation but inevitably increases the on-chip memory consumption by a factor of 16 as well. In the following section, we will analyze the impact of the PE/BRAM replication on accelerator performance.

3. DESIGN CHALLENGE OF AN OPENCL BASED FPGA ACCELERATOR FOR CNN APPLICATION

In this section, we present an analytical performance model to characterize the resource requirement of a given kernel and the available hardware resources of FPGA. Based on the model, we will perform an in-depth analysis on the design challenges of implementing a CNN accelerator using OpenCL FPGA.

3.1 Performance Model

The performance of an OpenCL FPGA accelerator design can be determined by a large number of factors. Among them, the most critical one is data access. As explained in section 1, the hardware resources in state-of-the-art FPGAs are inherently unbalanced,i.e.,

computation vs. memory, on-chip memory vs. off-chip memory. However, theoretical peak performance can only be approached by providing a "balanced" data flow. The problem is becoming more pronounced in implementing CNN classifiers which demand high throughput in processing.

To quantitatively evaluate the performance limiting factors in OpenCL FPGA accelerator implementations, we borrow insights from the roofline model in [1] and develop an improved analytical performance model considering both on-chip and off-chip memory bandwidth. The model is based on the following assumptions: (i) The applications of interest are bandwidth bounded, not latency bounded. A large set of streaming applications, including CNNs, fall into this category [11]. (ii) Computation and memory access overlap perfectly. External memory access is coalesced well to achieve the maximum streaming bandwidth. (iii) The performance is determined by the slowest datapath in the memory hierarchy. All faster paths are assumed to be infinitely fast.

The central concept of our model is the introduction of "machine balance" B_m, which is used to quantify the balance between memory bandwidth and computational bandwidth of a system. As shown in Equation(1), it is defined as the ratio of the maximum achievable memory bandwidth bw_{max} to peak arithmetic performance (P_{max}) provided by hardware.

$$B_m = \frac{\text{Memory Bandwidth}}{\text{Peak Performance}} = \frac{bw_{max}}{P_{max}} \qquad (1)$$

To substitute the generic memory bandwidth bw_{max} with on-chip memory bandwidth bw_m^{on} and off-chip memory bandwidth bw_m^{off}, we further introduce two more metrics, B_m^{on} and B_m^{off}, defined as the machine balance for on-chip and off-chip memory respectively. Note that the machine balance B_m is largely determined by hardware and can be used to identify if a specific OpenCL FPGA platform provides adequate resources for an application.

On the other hand, from the application perspective, we introduce "code balance" B_c which reflects the memory bandwidth requirement of a specific OpenCL kernel program. In contrast to machine balance, B_c is inherently determined by the application itself. Similar to machine balance, we further define B_c^{on} and B_c^{off} as the code balance for on-chip memory and off-chip memory respectively. The calculation of B_c^{off} is given by Equation (2).

$$B_c = B_c^{off} = \frac{\text{Data Size}}{\text{Total No. of Operation}}, \qquad (2)$$

Unlike B_c^{off}, the calculation of B_c^{on} can be converted into first calculating B_c^i, the code balance for each arithmetic instruction (Equation (3)) and then taking an averaged value across all the arithmetic instructions in a kernel (Equation (4)). For instance, operations like mul and add, which need two input words to perform one arithmetic operation, have a $B_c^i = 2$. Similarly, operations like MAC, which need two inputs to perform two consecutive multiply and add operations, have a B_c^i of 1.

$$B_c^i = \frac{\text{Instruction Input (\emph{Words})}}{\text{No. of Operations (\emph{Ops})}}, \qquad (3)$$

$$B_c^{on} = \frac{1}{N} \sum_N B_c^i, \qquad (4)$$

In addition to balancing computation to data access, the bandwidth matching between on-chip and off-chip memory is equally important for performance. For that, we further compare B_c^{on} with B_c^{off}. The difference between them indicates the degree of data locality (data reuse among instructions) that a program inherently possesses. The larger the difference, the higher the locality. In principle, one data fetched from external memory and buffered on-chip should be reused at least $\frac{B_c^{on}}{B_c^{off}}$ times to match the on-chip memory bandwidth with the off-chip memory bandwidth for maximum efficiency. We define γ as the data reuse ratio and the memory subsystem should be designed to satisfy $\gamma \leq \frac{B_c^{on}}{B_c^{off}}$ for optimal usage.

With the proposed balance model, we can compare the difference between machine balance and code balance and use $\frac{B_m^{\{on,off\}}}{B_c^{\{on,off\}}}$ to quantitatively characterize the gap between the resource requirement of an OpenCL kernel and the available hardware resources provided by the FPGA. The larger the difference, the wider the gap, and the worse the accelerator performance. As shown in Equation 5, we can use it to identify the performance bottleneck in an accelerator design, i.e., compute-bound or memory-bound. If $\frac{B_m^{\{on,off\}}}{B_c^{\{on,off\}}} < 1$, which indicates the memory bandwidth requirement of a kernel is larger than the available memory bandwidth provided by native hardware, i.e., it becomes *memory-bound*. In that case, the compute units become under-utilized and have to stall to wait for the data, resulting in performance degradation. Otherwise, it is compute-bound. Therefore, the arithmetic performance P can be expressed as

$$P^{\{on,off\}} = \begin{cases} P_{max}, & \frac{B_m^{\{on,off\}}}{B_c^{\{on,off\}}} \geq 1, \quad \text{(comp. bound)}, \\[2ex] \frac{bw_{max}^{\{on,off\}}}{B_c^{\{on,off\}}}, & \frac{B_m^{\{on,off\}}}{B_c^{\{on,off\}}} < 1, \quad \text{(mem. bound)}, \end{cases} \qquad (5)$$

In the case of a memory-bound application, we can further provide more insights as to whether the performance is limited by on-chip memory or off-chip memory in the memory hierarchy using Equation (6).

$$P = \min\left(P^{on}, P^{off}\right) = \min\left(\underbrace{\frac{bw_{max}^{on}}{B_c^{on}}}_{\substack{\text{On-chip}\\\text{Mem BW}\\\text{Bounded}}}, \underbrace{\frac{bw_{max}^{off}}{B_c^{off}}}_{\substack{\text{Off-chip}\\\text{Mem BW}\\\text{Bounded}}}, \underbrace{P_{max}}_{\substack{\text{Comp.}\\\text{Bounded}}}\right), \qquad (6)$$

Thus, the overall performance is determined by the minimum

value between the projected performance bounded by on-chip memory P^{on} and by off-chip memory P^{off}. Ideally, it is desirable to keep $\frac{B_m^{\{on,off\}}}{B_c^{\{on,off\}}}$ equal to 1 to ensure a perfect balance between computation and memory resources to achieve the best utilization and maximum throughput. However, in practice, it is not feasible as it not only varies with hardware platforms but also with workloads. To achieve the peak performance, it is desirable to keep it larger than 1 in order to make good use of FPGA's abundant computational resources for better performance. As the code balance B_c is fixed by the algorithm itself, the most effective way to improve the ratio is to improve B_m^{on} or B_m^{off}. However, as we will discuss in next subsection, the existing OpenCL FPGA implementations for applications like CNN classifiers are inherently bounded by on-chip memory ($\frac{B_m}{B_c} < 1$).

3.2 Performance Analysis

In this subsection, we will apply the balance model to analyze the performance limiting factors when implementing an OpenCL FPGA accelerator for CNN classification. We will compare the machine balance of modern FPGA devices of three technology generations (28nm, 20nm, 16/14nm) with the code balance of a CNN classifier using the VGG19 model [5], which is the winner of Imagenet 2014 competition.

In Table 1, we list the machine balance B_m^{on} and B_m^{off} for on-chip and off-chip memory respectively, in conjunction with other essential hardware resources from the largest commercially available FPGA devices over three technology generations (28nm, 20nm, 16/14nm). We note that to calculate the B_m^{on}, we adopt the memory replication strategy based on the existing kernel design in OpenCL FPGA as described in Section 2. We can see that B_m^{on} is almost constant for different technology nodes, which indicates the computational resources increase proportionally with respect to the on-chip memory bandwidth. In other words, the design space has not changed over generations of FPGA devices from the hardware perspective. However, the B_m^{off} is improved dramatically at the 16/14nm technology node due to the availability of advanced memory modules such as HBM, HMC, and bandwidth engine (BE2) [6].

In Table 2, we also list both on-chip code balance B_c^{on} and off-chip code balance B_c^{off} with workload specific information including data size, number of operations of the convolution (CONV) layer and fully-connect (FC) layer in the VGG model [5], as CONV layers and FC layers constitute the majority of the computation in the VGG model.

To gain more insights on the performance limiting factors for implementing the VGG model, we follow the methodology developed in Section 3.1 and calculate the $\frac{B_m}{B_c}$ for both CONV layers and FC layers considering both on-chip and off-chip memory access. Let us first consider off-chip memory bandwidth. In Figure 3(a), we show that $\frac{B_m^{off}}{B_c^{off}}$ for CONV layers are all greater than 1 except for the 14nm FPGA devices with DDR DRAM, which indicates the off-chip memory bandwidth is *not* the bottleneck. In Figure 3(b), we show that $\frac{B_m^{off}}{B_c^{off}}$ for FC layers is smaller than 1, which indicates its performance is limited by external memory bandwidth. However, as FC layers contribute only a small fraction to the overall computation (1.2 %), its impact on performance can be considered negligible.

Compared to off-chip memory access, we show that the on-chip memory bandwidth indeed becomes the bottleneck. As shown in Figure 3(c), $\frac{B_m^{on}}{B_c^{on}}$ for all layers is less than 1, which indicates that the CNN classifier is bounded by the on-chip memory bandwidth. To make it worse, unlike external memory bandwidth, which can be

Table 1: Comparison of resources and performance of the largest commercial FPGA over generations

	28nm	20nm	16/14nm
Amount of DSP	3600	5520	12288
DSP frequency (MHz)	741	741	891
Arith. Perf. (GFLOP/sec)	5335	8180	21897
Amount of BRAM	1470	2160	3908
Capacity of BRAM(Mb)	52.9	75.9	454.5
bw_{max}^{on} (GWords/s)	3586	7128	15526
bw_{max}^{off} (GWords/s)	70.3	76.8	96^1, 1000^2
B_m^{on}	0.168	0.217	0.177
B_m^{off}	0.0033	0.0026	0.0010^1, 0.014^2

^{1}DDR4 SDRAM
^{2}HBM

Table 2: Problem size and number of operations of CONV and FC layers in VGG model

Layer group	Size of Input Feature (k)	Size of weight (k)	Size of Output Feature (k)	Ops (GOPs)	Percent of Total Operations	B_c^{off}	B_c^{on}
CONV1	336	38	6422	3.8	8%	0.0021	1
CONV2	240	221	3211	5.5	21%	0.0010	1
CONV3	280	2064	3211	12.9	36%	0.00062	1
CONV4	140	8257	1605	12.9	26%	0.00087	1
CONV5	401	9437	401	3.6	8%	0.00277	1
FC1	25	102760	4096	0.0002	0.04 %	0.5	1
FC2	4	16777	4096	0.00003	0.04 %	0.5	1
FC3	4	4096	1000	0.000008	0.04 %	0.5	1

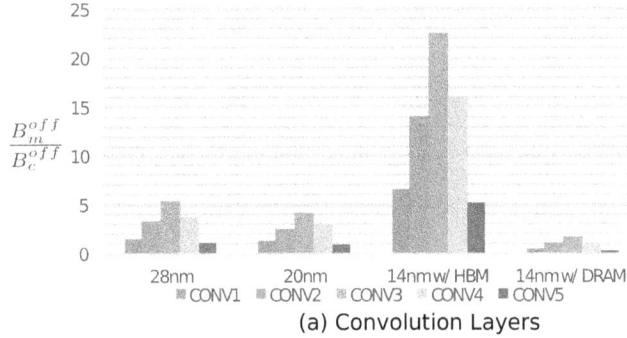

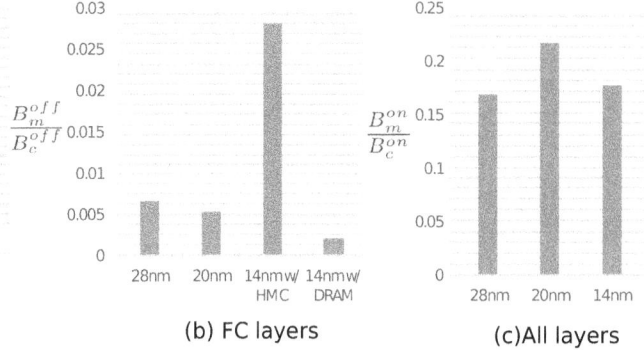

Figure 3: (a) $\frac{B_m^{off}}{B_c^{off}}$ for CONV Layers; (b) $\frac{B_m^{off}}{B_c^{off}}$ for FC layers; (c) $\frac{B_m^{on}}{B_c^{on}}$ for all layers; (d) $\frac{B_c^{on}}{B_m^{off}}$ for all layers

improved by advanced memory modules, from previous machine balance studies, we show that the on-chip memory bandwidth has not changed over generations with respect to computational bandwidth.

As discussed in Section 3.1, another key factor that should be taken into account for performance is the balance between the on-chip memory bandwidth and off-chip memory bandwidth. From Table 2, we see a dramatic difference between B_c^{on} and B_c^{off} for all CONV layers, which indicates high data locality and thus great data reuse potential. We will need to leverage it to make on-chip memory design meet the data reuse ratio requirement defined in Section 3.1 to achieve balanced on-chip to off-chip data access.

To conclude, our analysis shows that the on-chip memory bandwidth is the bottleneck for implementing the OpenCL FPGA accelerator for CNN classification and should be matched with both computational throughput and the off-chip memory bandwidth for higher performance. Hence, to fully exploit the potential of an OpenCL FPGA platform to achieve the optimal CNN implementation, we should: (i) Increase B_m^{on} by improving the on-chip memory bandwidth usage. (ii) Meet the requirement of the data reuse ratio $\gamma \leq \frac{B_c^{on}}{B_c^{off}}$ to match the on-chip memory bandwidth with off-chip memory bandwidth.

4. DESIGN METHODOLOGY

From the analysis in the Section 3.2, we know that matching the code balance B_c and the machine balance B_m is the key towards a high performance OpenCL FPGA accelerator for CNN classification. In this section, we will present a novel kernel design for CNN classification, which can achieve more efficient on-chip memory bandwidth usage by improving B_m^{on} and balance on-chip and off-chip memory access to meet the requirement of data reuse. In the rest of the section, we will present the detailed design methodol-

ogy: 1) introducing a two-dimensional multi-cast interconnection between PEs and local memory; 2) developing a two-dimensional dispatcher to accommodate the change in kernel design.

4.1 CNN Classifier Kernel Design

The interconnection between compute units (CUs) and local memories (BRAMs) defined in the existing OpenCL kernel are shown in Figure 2. As we can see, even though the PEs can be organized as an array with up to three dimensions, the interconnection between local memory and PEs is still in one-dimension, i.e., each PE is connected to a dedicated BRAM port. When replicating PEs to achieve parallelism in performing computation, BRAM will have to be replicated by the same factor. Thus, the B_m^{on} of the kernel design in [4] can be calculated as follows.

$$B_m^{on} = \frac{N_{\text{BRAM}} \cdot f_{\text{DSP}}}{N_{\text{DSP}} \cdot f_{\text{BRAM}}}, \quad (7)$$

where N_{DSP} is the number of DSP slices, N_{BRAM} is the number of BRAM, f_{DSP} is the working frequency of the DSP slices and f_{BRAM} is the working frequency of BRAM as listed in Table 1.

The underlying reason for low B_m^{on} in the existing CNN implementation using OpenCL FPGA can be stated as follows: while fully exploiting data level parallelism by replicating PEs, the unnecessary memory replication quickly used up all on-chip BRAM resources. To improve B_m^{on}, the key is to improve the efficiency of BRAM usage.

On the other hand, when taking a closer look at the data access pattern of matrix multiplication which is the key kernel in CNN, as shown in Equation (8), we can see that each vector from the matrix A needs to be multiplied by n vectors from the matrix B and vice versa. Such data access patterns create opportunities for reusing the data from one on-chip BRAM port by multiple PEs.

$$(AB)_{ij} = \sum_k A_{ik} B_{kj} \qquad \forall i < m, j < n \qquad (8)$$

By leveraging such a data access pattern and the flexible FPGA routing architecture, we propose a novel two-dimensional interconnection between PEs and local memory which effectively supports the sharing of data from the same local memory port of BRAMs by multiple PEs as shown in Figure 4, as compared with the one-dimensional interconnection defined in the existing kernel design (Figure 2). In other words, we use *multicast* connections between PEs and the local memory instead of *unicast* connections. Such interconnection not only improves on-chip memory bandwidth usage without replication but also improves on-chip data reuse to meet the reuse ratio requirement for reducing external memory access.

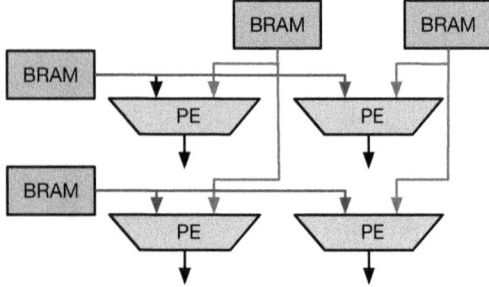

Figure 4: Proposed two-dimensional PE-to-local memory interconnection

We note that in order to support 2-D interconnection between PEs and the local memory system, the dispatcher will need to be modified accordingly. The details of necessary modifications will be explained in Section 4.2. With the proposed 2-D interconnection, the BRAM requirement for N_{DSP} PEs is reduced from $\mathcal{O}(N_{\text{DSP}})$ to $\mathcal{O}(\sqrt{N_{\text{DSP}}})$ and therefore B_m^{on} is improved by $\sqrt{N_{\text{DSP}}}$.

$$B_m^{on\prime} = \sqrt{N_{DSP}} \cdot \frac{N_{BRAM} \cdot BW_{BRAM}}{N_{DSP} \cdot f_{BRAM}} = \sqrt{N_{DSP}} B_m^{on} \qquad (9)$$

We also improve the data reuse by a factor of $\sqrt{N_{DSP}}$ without consuming extra on-chip memory resources, compared to the traditional 1-D PE-to-local memory interconnection. Using the largest FPGA device at the 14/16 nm technology node, we can increase B_m^{on} from 0.177 to 19.62 while improving data reuse by the same factor (110 $\times$).

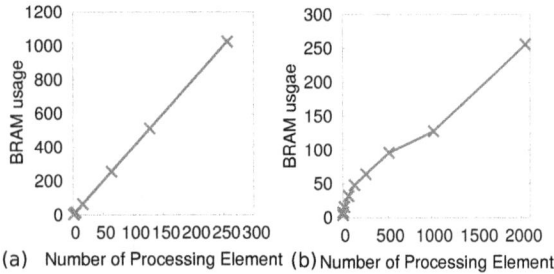

Figure 5: BRAM usage for (a) traditional one-dimensional and (b) proposed two-dimensional interconnection between PEs to local memory when varying the number of PEs using Arria10 AX1150 FPGA

We conduct two preliminary experiments to confirm the effectiveness of the proposed technique. We use the matrix multipli-

cation kernel from the Altera OpenCL library [7] as our baseline. We vary the number of PEs in one CU and obtain the corresponding BRAM usage. In Figure 5(a), we show that the BRAM usage increases linearly when increasing the number of PEs. However, the growth stops at the point of 256 PEs, as if we further increase the number of PEs to 512, the BRAM usage exceeds the limitation of our Altera Arria10 AX1150 FPGA which has 1963 DSP slices and 1500 on-chip BRAMs. We can see that the computational resources are heavily under-utilized when BRAM usage reaches 100% using the traditional 1-D interconnection between PEs and local memory. On the contrary, in Figure 5(b), with the proposed 2-D interconnection, we can make full use of all the 1963 PEs with only 256 on-chip BRAM usage, significantly saving on-chip BRAM bandwidth. We note that the proposed PE-to-memory interconnection can also be applied to accelerate other algorithm kernels, which exhibit similar data access patterns to matrix multiplication.

We have already shown that the proposed matrix multiplication kernel design can significantly improve B_m^{on} and also the on-chip data reuse by a factor of $\sqrt{N_{DSP}}$ by using the 2-D interconnection and the 2-D dispatcher without necessarily increasing the on-chip memory usage. However, it is still not sufficient to meet the data reuse requirement targeting the Altera Arria10 AX1150 FPGA. To address this issue, we add a buffer to further improve the on-chip data reuse and to reduce external memory access. This buffer serves two purposes: **(i)** coalescing memory access from different memory banks in the shared memory system to fully utilize the external memory bandwidth. **(ii)** Leveraging the data locality in the data access stream, such as sliding windows in the convolution layer computation. In the case of CNN, we will present a line buffer design in Section 5. Note that the buffer is not necessarily needed for all FPGA devices as long as the on-chip hardware resources meet the data reuse ratio requirement.

4.2 Two-Dimensional Dispatcher

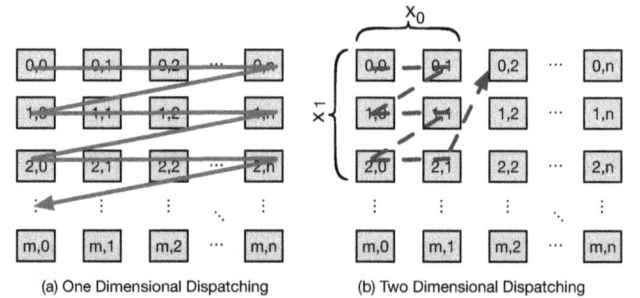

Figure 6: Conceptual diagram illustrating (a) traditional one-dimensional dispatcher and (b) proposed two-dimensional dispatcher ($x_0 = 2, x_1 = 3$)

For the conventional 1-D interconnection between PEs and local memory, the current OpenCL dispatcher always schedules the work-items along the lower dimension as shown in Figure 6(a). However, in order to accommodate our 2-D interconnection with data sharing, we propose to dispatch work-items to compute units in a two dimensional manner. The 2D dispatcher can be implemented by adding a new dispatching policy (x_0, x_1). As shown in Figure 6(b), the 2D dispatcher divides work-items into work groups with a size of x_1 in the x dimension and x_2 in the y dimension, and performs the work-item scheduling and work-group scheduling along the lowest dimension within each division. In section 5.3, we will present the optimal scheduling policy based on the workload and available hardware resources.

5. IMPLEMENTATION OF AN OPENCL FPGA ACCELERATOR FOR CNN

In this section, we will apply the techniques proposed in Section 4 to implement a full-fledged OpenCL FPGA CNN accelerator based on the VGG model [5]. We will first present the overall architecture and implementation of each CNN layer. Then, we discuss the optimization of the scheduling policy to minimize the requirement of the external DRAM bandwidth.

5.1 Overall Architecture

The accelerator kernel has three major components as shown in Figure 2(a). The dispatcher receives pointers of kernel inputs and outputs from the PCI-e controller, and issues read and write commands to the external DRAM controller. The shared buffer uses a 512-bit Avalon memory mapped bus master to receive the data read from external DRAM. Since there is only one external memory channel on our development board, we only need to have a single global read port. The DDR4 channel has a 64-bit double data rate (DDR) bus width and the DRAM controller operates at a quarter clock rate. As we can achieve a kernel frequency larger than the output data rate of DDR memory controller ($2133\,\mathrm{MHz}/8 = 266.5\,\mathrm{MHz}$), we can fully utilize the external DRAM bandwidth.

Given the fixed PE resources (DSP slices) per FPGA device, we can vary the number of CUs and the size of the PE array per CU. As shown in Figure 7(a), in this design, we choose to assign each compute unit (CU) a 16×16 PE array. The reason to choose a dimension of 16 is that each BRAM provides data width of 32 bits and thereby 16 of them can form a 512-bit data bus which equals the bus width of external DRAM and eases the design interface between compute units and the shared buffer. As discussed in Section 4.1, with the 2D interconnection between PEs and local memory, a 16×16 PE array can achieve a B_m^{on} of 2.83 which is larger than B_c^{on} (1) in Table 2.

5.2 Detailed Implementation

A typical CNN classifier has several tens of layers, which run sequentially. Each layer reads the feature map from its previous layer and outputs a series of new feature maps, based on the parameters of the CNN model typically called "weights". Finally, the CNN classifier outputs the probability of each feature. Convolution (CONV) and Fully Connected (FC) layers are the two basic layers that constitute the majority of the computation for all CNN models. In addition, a pooling layer is typically added after convolution layers. In the rest of this section, we will present the implementation of each layer.

5.2.1 Convolution Layer

The convolution operation constitutes over 90% of the total operations in the VGG model. Therefore, to improve the overall performance of a CNN accelerator, the key is to optimize the performance of convolution. The two-dimensional convolution can be described by Equation (10)

$$out(f_o, x, y) = \sum_{f_i=0}^{N_{if}} \sum_{k_x=0}^{K} \sum_{k_y=0}^{K} wt(f_o, f_i, k_x, k_y) \times in(f_i, x + k_x, y + ky). \tag{10}$$

where $out(f_o, x, y)$ and $in(f_i, x + k_x, y + ky)$ are the output and input feature of neurons at the location (x, y) in the feature map

f_o and f_i respectively. $wt(f_o, f_i, k_x, k_y)$ is the weights at the location (k_x, k_y) which get convolved with the input feature map f_i and f_o. We use the similar flatten and rearrangement method as [4] to convert the two-dimensional convolution into matrix multiplication. Figure 7(b) shows the overall data flow of performing a convolution. Weights and input feature maps are stored in DRAM and placed in the order of x,y and f_i.

As shown in Figure 8, we implement a line buffer [12] between local memory and external memory to flatten and rearrange data. The goal is to minimize the random data access penalty from external memory and to improve on-chip data reuse. The line buffer streams data from external memory which has a continuous address and converts it into the data order for 2D convolution. By leveraging the data access pattern of 2D convolution, which is a 2D sliding window and has strong data locality, the line buffer can reduce the bandwidth requirement of external memory substantially.

In addition, to hide the external memory access latency, we fill the line buffer using a ping-pong mechanism to pipeline the data access and computation. More specifically, we choose to fill the 256 memory locations at one time, as 256 is not only half of the Altera M20K memory depth but also the maximum data burst size of the DDR4 interface. Each compute unit, which has 256 floating DSP slices (PEs), calculates 256 vector products in parallel by reusing the data from 16 row memory ports and 16 column memory ports as shown in Figure 7(a).

5.2.2 Fully Connected Layer

Fully connected layers calculate the inner products between input features and weights to get the output features as shown in Equation (11),

$$out(f_o) = \sum_{f_i=0}^{N_{if}} wt(f_o, f_i) \times in(f_i) \tag{11}$$

As the inner product calculation in FC layers is also the key operation in CONV layers, we can reuse the architecture from section 5.2.1 to implement it. However, as the weights do not provide any locality, we can only apply the data sharing technique to the input feature. From the previous study in Section 3.2, we know that the performance of FC layers are bounded by external memory. Fortunately, the FC layers only contribute a small portion of computation, so they will not add too much to the runtime. In this work, we use one column of DSPs (PEs) in Figure 7(a) to implement FC layers to make the computational bandwidth match the maximum streaming bandwidth that the DDR4 memory interface can provide.

5.2.3 Pooling Layer

The pooling layer outputs the average or the maximum value of a local area of the input feature map. Pooling layers can be expressed as Equation (12),

$$out(f_o, x, y) = \max_{0 < (k_x, k_y) < k} in(f_i, x + k_x, y + k_y), \tag{12}$$

where k is the pooling kernel size. We implement a similar line buffer as in Section 5.2.1, which uses the connections between different register stages to accomplish the window selection. In our design, we use a 4-input comparator to get the maximum value of a 2×2 window. It is mainly used to buffer data from the output of compute units and then to feed to the pooling layer after convolution.

5.3 Optimization of Work-item Scheduling

As shown in Section 5.2, we can reduce the external memory access to the desired number under the condition that we have un-

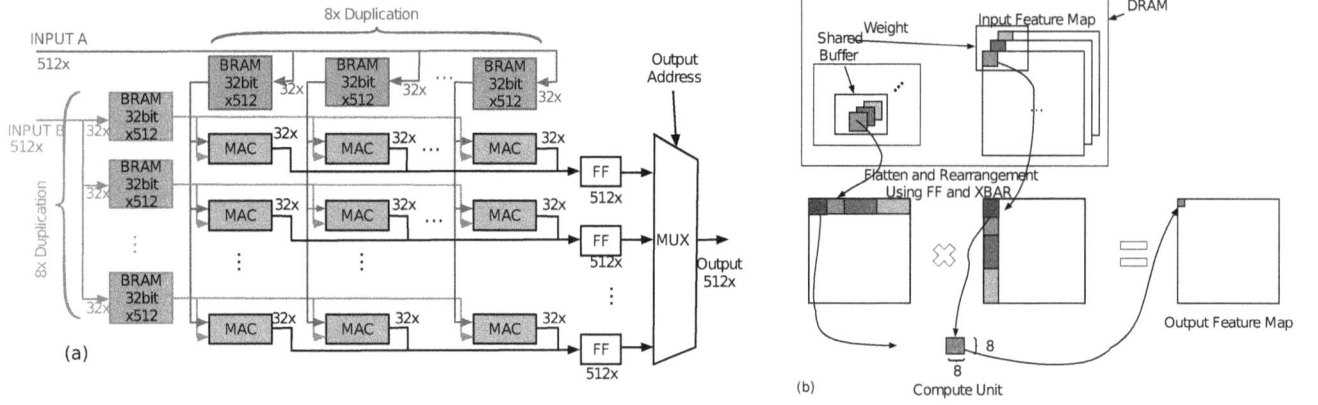

Figure 7: (a) The architecture of proposed CNN accelerator; (b) Convert 3-D convolution into matrix multiplication on proposed architecture

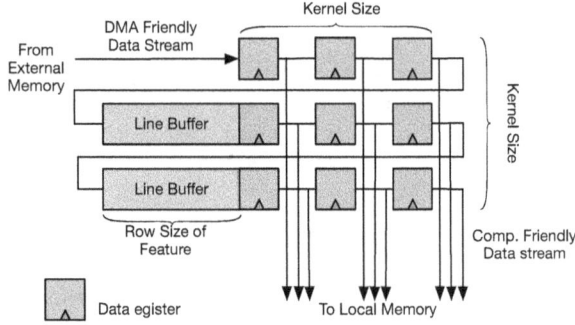

Figure 8: Design of line buffer

Table 3: Work-item scheduling optimization results of convolution layers for the VGG kernel with a 16×16 PE Array and up to 512 M20K BRAMs

Layer	Optimal $<x_1, x_2>$	Req. of DRAM BW with optimal 2-D scheduling	Req. of DRAM BW with 1-D scheduling
CONV1	<6,13>	14.5GB/s	123.9GB/s
CONV2	<6,4>	10.8GB/s	89.8GB/s
CONV3	<5,3>	11.5GB/s	92.6GB/s
CONV4	<7,9>	10.7GB/s	82.1GB/s
CONV5	<4,5>	11.6GB/s	94.6GB/s

limited on-chip memory capacity to hold all input feature maps and weights in BRAM, which in practice, however, is unlikely to be the case. In this section, we present an optimization technique to adaptively change the scheduling policy of the proposed 2-D dispatcher to trade on-chip memory bandwidth with the capacity to satisfy both requirements under device-specific constraints of on-chip memory.

Given the number of input features N_{if}, output features N_{of}, the size of input feature $size_{in}$, output feature $size_{out}$, kernel size $size_k$ and available on-chip memory resources, we minimize the external DRAM bandwidth requirement by solving the following optimization problem:

$$\min_{x_0, x_1, x_2} \quad a\frac{x_0}{x_1} + b\frac{x_0}{x_2} + c\frac{1}{x0}, \tag{13}$$
$$s.t. \quad x_0 x_1 + x_1 x_2 < size_{on-chip},$$

Table 4: FPGA resource utilization

	Available Resources	Proposed	Baseline	Ratio
DSP	1518	1320(86%)	576 (38%)	2.26x
BRAM	2713	1250 (46%)	1648 (60%)	0.75x
Logic	1506k (38%)	437k (43%)	237k (16%)	1.84x
Frequency	-	370 MHz	320 MHz	1.15x

$$a = \frac{N_{of} \cdot size_{if}^2 \cdot}{size_k^2},$$
$$b = N_{of} \cdot size_{if}^2, \tag{14}$$
$$c = N_{if} \cdot size_k^2 \cdot size_{of}^2 \cdot N_{of},$$

where a is the column size of the kernel buffer, b is the row size of the input feature buffer, x_0 is the column size of the kernel buffer and the row size of the input feature buffer, x_1 is the row size in kernel buffer and x_2 is the column size of the input feature buffer. Note that x_1 and x_2 are the scheduling parameters for the 2-D dispatcher. As x_0, x_1 and x_2 are all integer variables and the feasible set is small, we search over all the points in the feasible set to obtain the minimum value. In Table 3, we list the results of optimal scheduling policy of the VGG model and we can observe that the optimal scheduling policy can reduce at least 80% of the external memory bandwidth requirement.

6. EXPERIMENTAL RESULTS

In this section, we first present the modified OpenCL workflow and our evaluation setup. Then, we present the experimental results to validate the effectiveness of the proposed techniques and compare with prior work.

6.1 OpenCL Workflow and Experimental Setup

We use an Arria10 FPGA development board from Altera and list its specifications in Table 4. The board consists of an Altera Arria10 GX1150 FPGA and a 1GB DDR4 SDRAM module with 12GB/s bandwidth. The board also provides an interface to measure the voltage and current of all power rails for power monitoring.

We use Altera OpenCL SDK 16.0.211 as the OpenCL FPGA compiler and use Altera Quartus Pro 16.0.211 as the FPGA implementation tool. We implement the proposed kernel design in

Table 5: Experiment results of CNN accelerator based on VGG

Layer	Number of Operations (GOPs)	Proposed		Baseline		Speedup
		Duration (ms)	Perf. (Gops/s)	Duration (ms)	Perf. (GOP/s)	
CONV1	3.87	3.5	1098.04	21.3	181.6	6.03x
CONV2	5.55	4.4	1232.04	26.8	207.11	5.95x
CONV3	9.25	6.8	1329.57	41.4	223.35	5.94x
CONV4	9.25	7.4	1347.77	45.0	205.25	6.56x
CONV5	2.31	1.8	1223.32	10.9	210.73	5.82x
CONV TOTAL	30.69	23.9	1284.94	145.5	207.7	6.18x
FC6	0.029	4.1	7.25	4.8	6.09	1.19x
FC7	0.034	5.2	6.58	6.2	5.52	1.19x
FC8	0.0082	1.8	4.50	2.1	3.78	1.19x
FC TOTAL	0.073	11.1	6.6	13.2	5.52	1.19x
TOTAL	30.76	35.5	866	158.8	196	4.41x

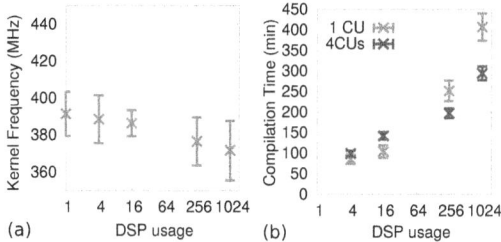

Figure 9: (a)Kernel frequency under different DSP usage; (b) Kernel compilation time under different DSP usages and CU/PE organizations

System Verilog and package it into the OpenCL IP library based on the instructions in [13]. The Verilog kernel has four 512-bit Avalon memory mapped interfaces to communicate with the external DRAM controller and uses a 6-port Avalon streaming interface to receive pointers and other parameters from the host.

The host machine is equipped with an Intel Xeon E5-1630V3 CPU with 64GB DDR4-2133 SDRAM and is running Ubuntu Linux 14.04.3. We follow the methodology in [4] and implemented the baseline design on the same Arria 10 platform. We also use the Caffe [14] convolutional learning framework as our CPU baseline. We extract the input image, pre-trained weights and output features from Caffe. We compare the result of our implementation with result from Caffe to verify the functional correctness.

6.2 Results and Discussion

In this subsection, we first compare the resource utilization with the baseline design, followed by the kernel frequency and compilation time. Then, we show the micro benchmark of our CNN accelerator and compare it with the baseline implementation. Finally, we compare our overall performance with prior work. Note that we implemented both single precision floating point and fixed point versions. Except for the data in Table 6, all the data were obtained from the floating point implementation.

The placement and routing are accomplished by Altera OpenCL SDK, and the resource utilization is reported in Table 4. To achieve a higher working frequency, we use register duplication to limit the maximum fan-out to 100. We found that the paths with the highest fan-out are the control signals, which are generated by the dispatcher and connected to all of the PEs. As the widths of control signals are typically 1 bit, register duplication will not significantly

increase the usage of flip-flop. We can see that our implementation has nearly used all of the computational resources (DSPs) with no more than half of on-chip memory. On the contrary, the DSP utilization of the baseline implementation can only achieve 38% and cannot be further improved as the required BRAM usage will exceed the device capacity.

To ensure that increasing the number of PEs sharing the same BRAM port will not introduce noticeable performance degradation, we report the kernel frequency for various cases. We first fix the number of CUs to be 1 while gradually increasing the number of PEs inside a CU. We then change the synthesis seed to check if the fanout of a single memory port increases and reduce the working frequency of the kernel. We extract the working frequency from the OpenCL implementation report. As shown in Figure 9 (a), the kernel frequency slightly decreases from 390MHz to 380MHz when the number of PEs per memory port increases from 1 to 1024.

To further check if our implementation increases the place-and-route complexity, we also log the Quartus compilation time for various CU/PE organizations under the constraints of keeping the same total computational resources. In particular, we consider 1 and 4 CUs while increasing the number of PEs per CU. As shown in Figure 9 (b), the compilation time for the 1 CU design is larger than the design with 4 CUs as increasing the number of PEs per CU increases the pressure for global routing and thus increases compilation time. This result also indicates that given the same computational resource budget, we should assign a smaller number of PEs to each CU and use a larger number of CUs.

In Table 5, we summarize the execution time and performance of each layer group and compare them with the baseline implementation. We can see the performance of the CONV1 layer is much lower than other convolution layers as the performance is bounded by the external memory bandwidth. This is mainly because the Arria10 FPGA development board only uses 1 out of 4 DRAM channels. From Table 3, we can see the required DRAM bandwidth is 14.5GB/s, which is higher than the achievable bandwidth of single channel DDR4 2133 SDRAM. We can also see the proposed design outperforms the baseline implementation by 6.18x for convolution layers and achieves 4.41x improvement in overall performance. Despite the performance gain from working frequency (1.12x) and DSP utilization (2.15x), as listed in Table 4, the proposed design also benefits from the line buffer, which guarantees the DRAM accesses have continuous addresses to achieve the maximum DRAM bandwidth.

In Table 6, we compare our work with previous work. We show our CNN accelerator achieves a floating point performance of 866

Table 6: Comparison with previous CNN implementations

	ISCA2010 [15]	FCCM16 [16]	FPGA15 [1]	FPGA16 [4]	FPGA16 [2]	Our Impl.	
FPGA	Viretex5 SX240T	Zynq XC7Z020	Virtex7	Strtix V GSD8	Zynq XC7Z045	Arria10 GX1150	
Frequency (MHz)	200 MHz	100 MHz	100MHz	120MHz	150MHz	370MHz	385MHz
CNN size (Gops)	0.52	5.48	1.33	30	30.76	30.76	
Precision	fixed	fixed	float	fixed	fixed	float	fixed
DSP Utilization	-	95/110	1120/1400	727/1963	- /780	1320/1518	2756/3036
BRAM Utilization	-	18/280	1024/2060	1500/2567	972/2180	1250/2713	1450/2713
Performance (Gops/s)	16	12.73	61.6	47.5	136.97	866	1790
Performance Density (ops/DSPslices/cycle)	-	0.6	0.44	0.36	1.17	2.8	3.06
Power Efficiency (Gops/s/W)	-	7.27	3.31	1.84	14.22	20.75	47.78

Gop/s and 1.79 Top/s fixed point performance which significantly outperforms prior work. As different experiments use different FPGA platforms and CNN models, it is challenging to have a fair apple-to-apple comparison. To address it, in the table, we further list the performance density which is defined as the number of arithmetic operations that one DSP slice executes in one cycle to characterize the efficiency of a design, i.e., whether or not it utilizes all available computational resources on a FPGA device. The performance density also eliminates the impact of the clock frequency. As shown in Table 6, our implementation has the highest performance density. In addition, we also achieve the highest power efficiency compared to prior work.

7. CONCLUSION

In this paper, we present a new kernel design methodology to implement a high performance CNN accelerator using OpenCL FPGA. In particular, by quantitatively modeling the performance with respect to resources, we present a comprehensive case study on a popular CNN model. When implementing CNN, we find the on-chip memory bandwidth is 6x smaller than the available computational bandwidth in state-of-the-art FPGA devices and thus severely limits the performance due to heavily underutilized computational resources. To address the problem, we propose a 2-D interconnection between PEs and local memory, which can effectively reduce the on-chip memory bandwidth requirement. Furthermore, we design a 2D dispatcher with an optimized scheduling policy to further minimize the external memory requirements by leveraging the data locality of the CNN. Finally, we present the design details of a convolutional learning classification accelerator using the VGG model. Our implementation on the Altera Arria 10 achieves a 1.79 Top/s throughput under 385MHz working frequency with an energy efficiency of 47.78 Gops/s/W and outperforms prior work.

ACKNOWLEDGEMENTS

We appreciate the insightful comments and feedback from the anonymous reviewers. We thank Intel/Altera for the donation of the development tool and hardware. We especially thank Jeff Nigh for his kind help.

8. REFERENCES

[1] C. Zhang, P. Li, G. Sun, Y. Guan, B. Xiao, and J. Cong, "Optimizing fpga-based accelerator design for deep convolutional neural networks," in *Proceedings of the 2015 ACM/SIGDA International Symposium on Field-Programmable Gate Arrays*, ACM.

[2] J. Qiu, J. Wang, S. Yao, K. Guo, B. Li, E. Zhou, J. Yu, T. Tang, N. Xu, S. Song, *et al.*, "Going deeper with embedded fpga platform for convolutional neural network," in *Proceedings of the 2016 ACM/SIGDA International Symposium on Field-Programmable Gate Arrays*, ACM, 2016.

[3] A. Putnam, A. M. Caulfield, E. S. Chung, D. Chiou, K. Constantinides, J. Demme, H. Esmaeilzadeh, J. Fowers, G. P. Gopal, J. Gray, *et al.*, "A reconfigurable fabric for accelerating large-scale datacenter services," in *2014 ACM/IEEE 41st International Symposium on Computer Architecture (ISCA)*, IEEE, 2014.

[4] N. Suda, V. Chandra, G. Dasika, A. Mohanty, Y. Ma, S. Vrudhula, J.-s. Seo, and Y. Cao, "Throughput-optimized opencl-based fpga accelerator for large-scale convolutional neural networks," in *Proceedings of the 2016 ACM/SIGDA International Symposium on Field-Programmable Gate Arrays*, ACM, 2016.

[5] K. Simonyan and A. Zisserman, "Very deep convolutional networks for large-scale image recognition," *arXiv preprint arXiv:1409.1556*, 2014.

[6] Xilinx, "The rise of serial memory and the future of ddr." http://www.xilinx.com/support/documentation/white_papers/wp456-DDR-serial-mem.pdf, 2015.

[7] T. S. Czajkowski, D. Neto, M. Kinsner, U. Aydonat, J. Wong, D. Denisenko, P. Yiannacouras, J. Freeman, D. P. Singh, and S. D. Brown, "Opencl for fpgas: Prototyping a compiler," in *Proceedings of the International Conference on Engineering of Reconfigurable Systems and Algorithms (ERSA)*, 2012.

[8] Y. LeCun, L. Bottou, Y. Bengio, and P. Haffner, "Gradient-based learning applied to document recognition," *Proceedings of the IEEE*, vol. 86, no. 11, 1998.

[9] A. Krizhevsky, I. Sutskever, and G. E. Hinton, "Imagenet classification with deep convolutional neural networks," in *Advances in neural information processing systems*, 2012.

[10] S. Ren, K. He, R. Girshick, and J. Sun, "Faster r-cnn: Towards real-time object detection with region proposal networks," in *Advances in neural information processing systems*, pp. 91–99, 2015.

[11] G. Hager and G. Wellein, *Introduction to High Performance Computing for Scientists and Engineers*. Boca Raton, FL, USA: CRC Press, Inc., 1st ed., 2010.

[12] B. Bosi, G. Bois, and Y. Savaria, "Reconfigurable pipelined 2-d convolvers for fast digital signal processing," *IEEE Transactions on Very Large Scale Integration (VLSI) Systems*, Sept 1999.

[13] Altera, "Altera sdk for opencl best practices guide," 2016.

[14] Y. Jia, E. Shelhamer, J. Donahue, S. Karayev, J. Long, R. Girshick, S. Guadarrama, and T. Darrell, "Caffe: Convolutional architecture for fast feature embedding," *arXiv preprint arXiv:1408.5093*, 2014.

[15] S. Chakradhar, M. Sankaradas, V. Jakkula, and S. Cadambi, "A dynamically configurable coprocessor for convolutional neural networks," in *ACM SIGARCH Computer Architecture News*, vol. 38, ACM, 2010.

[16] S. I. Venieris and C.-S. Bouganis, "fpgaconvnet: A framework for mapping convolutional neural networks on fpgas,"

Frequency Domain Acceleration of Convolutional Neural Networks on CPU-FPGA Shared Memory System[*]

Chi Zhang, Viktor Prasanna
Ming Hsieh Department of Electrical Engineering
University of Southern California, Los Angeles, USA 90089
{zhan527, prasanna}@usc.edu

ABSTRACT

We present a novel mechanism to accelerate state-of-art Convolutional Neural Networks (CNNs) on CPU-FPGA platform with coherent shared memory. First, we exploit Fast Fourier Transform (FFT) and Overlap-and-Add (OaA) to reduce the computational requirements of the convolutional layer. We map the frequency domain algorithms onto a highly-parallel OaA-based 2D convolver design on the FPGA. Then, we propose a novel data layout in shared memory for efficient data communication between the CPU and the FPGA. To reduce the memory access latency and sustain peak performance of the FPGA, our design employs double buffering. To reduce the inter-layer data remapping latency, we exploit concurrent processing on the CPU and the FPGA. Our approach can be applied to any kernel size less than the chosen FFT size with appropriate zero-padding leading to acceleration of a wide range of CNN models. We exploit the data parallelism of OaA-based 2D convolver and task parallelism to scale the overall system performance.

By using OaA, the number of floating point operations is reduced by 39.14% ∼ 54.10% for the state-of-art CNNs. We implement VGG16, AlexNet and GoogLeNet on Intel QuickAssist QPI FPGA Platform. These designs sustain 123.48 GFLOPs/sec, 83.00 GFLOPs/sec and 96.60 GFLOPs/sec, respectively. Compared with the state-of-the-art AlexNet implementation, our design achieves 1.35x GFLOPs/sec improvement using 3.33x less multipliers and 1.1x less memory. Compared with the state-of-art VGG16 implementation, our design has 0.66x GFLOPs/sec using 3.48x less multipliers without impacting the classification accuracy. For GoogLeNet implementation, our design achieves 5.56x improvement in performance compared with 16 threads running on a 10 Core Intel Xeon Processor at 2.8 GHz.

[*]This work is supported by the US NSF under grants ACI-1339756 and CCF-1320211. This work is also supported in part by Intel Strategic Research Alliance funding. Equipment grant from the Intel Hardware Accelerator Research Program is gratefully acknowledged.

FPGA '17, February 22-24, 2017, Monterey, CA, USA

© 2017 ACM. ISBN 978-1-4503-4354-1/17/02. . . $15.00

DOI: http://dx.doi.org/10.1145/3020078.3021727

Keywords

Convolutional Neural Networks; Discrete Fourier Transform; Overlap-and-Add; CPU; FPGA; Shared Memory; Double Buffering; Concurrent Processing

1. INTRODUCTION

Convolutional Neural Network (CNN)[9, 15, 17, 20] has been widely used in image recognition, video analysis and natural language processing. Its high computational complexity and need for real-time performance in many applications, has lead to several efforts to accelerate CNN. Various accelerators and libraries have been developed on FPGA[4, 13, 16, 21], GPU[14], multi-core processor[23] for both inference and training.

Due to the high computational complexity of the convolutional layer, prior work has addressed parallelism of the computation by unrolling the 2D convolution to matrix multiplication[12] or reducing the number of operations using Fast Fourier Transform[10]. However, parallelization by unrolling encounters a bottleneck due to limited on-chip memory of FPGAs. Even though FFT provides an asymptotically superior approach, the large gap between the input feature map size and kernel size makes it very inefficient. Other attempts include compressing the model using approximation[22] and data quantization techniques[13] while sacrificing some classification accuracy.

Recently, heterogeneous architectures employing FPGA accelerators have become attractive including Xilinx Zynq, Convey-HC2 and Intel QuickAssist QPI FPGA Platform[19, 8, 11]. The shared memory and high speed interconnection in these platforms makes data communication more efficient between the CPU and the FPGA compared with earlier platforms. The flexibility of CPU and massive parallelism of FPGA makes accelerating large scale CNNs promising. Our design effectively uses the CPU-FPGA platform as follows:

- We exploit the massive parallelism of FPGA to accelerate the most computationally intensive and universal operation (2D convolution) and leave the other layer specific work to the general purpose processor. This makes our approach highly flexible and applicable to a wide range of CNN architectures.

- We characterize the parallelism of our FPGA accelerator by data parallelism and task parallelism. Data parallelism is determined by the convolver design while task parallelism is determined by the number of convolvers operating in parallel. We carefully optimize the design to effectively use the available FPGA resources.

We develop a highly-parallelized convolver in frequency domain on FPGA and a software engine on CPU for inter-layer data remapping including ReLU layer. The CPU is also responsible for optional pooling layer, normalization layer and fully-connected layer after the convolutional layers. The main contributions of this paper are:

- We make a quantitative analysis of the required number of floating point operations in convolutional layers by space convolution[1] and by using Fast Fourier Transform (FFT) and Overlap-and-Add (OaA) [18].

- We propose a highly-parallelized OaA-based 2D convolver architecture on FPGA to accelerate the convolutional layers.

- To make a fair comparison among various convolvers, we use a composite performance metric in signal processing called *Delay-Multiplier (DM)* Product. We demonstrate the superiority of OaA-based convolver by showing that there always exists a FFT size such that the *DM* Product of OaA-based convolver is less than that of space convolver for typical kernel sizes.

- We exploit double buffering technique on FPGA to reduce the memory access latency. We make a quantitative analysis of the tradeoff between the on-chip memory consumption and the memory access latency.

- We propose a novel data layout in the shared memory for efficient data communication between CPU and FPGA. We also propose a software engine on CPU to perform data remapping between layers working concurrently with FPGA.

- We evaluate our work by implementing VGG16[15], AlexNet[9] and GoogLeNet[17] on Intel QuickAssist QPI FPGA Platform. Experimental results show that our designs achieve 2.28x $\sim$ 4.5x improvement in resource efficiency and 0.48x $\sim$ 1.90x improvement in power efficiency.

2. BACKGROUND

2.1 CNN in Frequency Domain

Typically, a CNN contains four building blocks, known as convolutional layer, ReLU layer, pooling layer and fully-connected(FC) layer. The overall architecture of a CNN is a connection of several such building blocks to form a very deep classification system.

2.1.1 Convolutional Layer

Throughout this paper, we use the following notations.

- Input feature maps of size $N_{in} \times N_{in} \times D_{in}$

- D_{out} kernels, each of size $F \times F \times D_{in}$

- Output feature maps of size $N_{out} \times N_{out} \times D_{out}$

The convolutional layer serves as a feature extractor. For each $N_{in} \times N_{in}$ input feature map[2], it performs 2D convolution with the shifting $F \times F$ kernel map of the same depth in each kernel with stride S. Then D_{in} output maps are

---

[1]We use space convolution to refer to direct convolution.
[2]We assume that zero-padding before the convolutional layer is included in N_{in}.

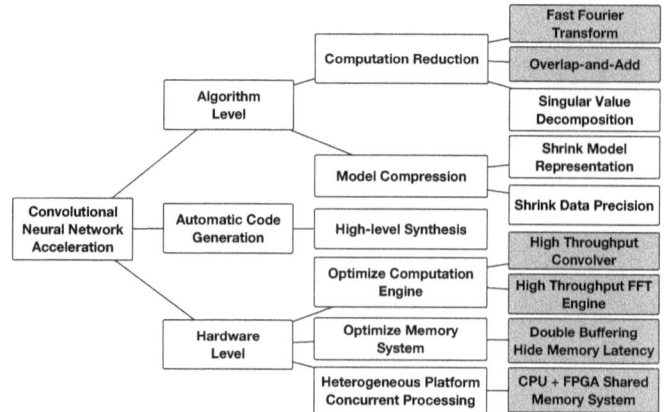

Figure 1: Summary of Various Approaches to Accelerate CNN

summed up to obtain one output feature map. This process is repeated for all D_{out} kernels to obtain the complete $N_{out} \times N_{out} \times D_{out}$ output feature maps. Note that

$$N_{out} = \frac{N_{in} - F}{S} + 1 \qquad (1)$$

2D Convolution and 2D FFT. 2D Convolution can be computed using 2D Fast Fourier Transform (FFT) as follows[18]:

$$y = \text{CONV2}(x, f) = \text{IFFT2}(\text{FFT2}(x).*\text{FFT2}(f)) \qquad (2)$$

where x is a $N_{in} \times N_{in}$ input, f is a $F \times F$ kernel, y is the output of size $N_{out} \times N_{out}$. 2D FFT can be computed as 1D FFT of each row followed by 1D FFT of each column.

Using 2D FFT reduces the computation complexity of a convolutional layer from $\Theta(N_{in}^2 F^2)$ to $\Theta(N_{in}^2 \log N_{in})$. However, it is worth noticing that the overhead of FFT and additional operations due to zero-padding and stride cannot be neglected, especially when dealing with small kernels as in most CNNs. In traditional signal processing, Overlap-and-Add (OaA) [18] is used to efficiently calculate the discrete convolution of a long input signal with a small kernel. By using OaA, we can further reduce the computational complexity of a convolutional layer to $\Theta(N_{in}^2 \log F)$ [6].

2.1.2 Other Layers

Besides convolutional layer, CNN also contains three other layers including ReLU layer, pooling layer and fully-connected layer. It is still challenging to compute these layers in frequency domain due to the non-linearity of ReLU layer. The computation of a fully-connected layer can be viewed as large matrix-vector multiplication, which has been optimized on FPGA in earlier designs[13].

3. RELATED WORK

We summarize various approaches to accelerate CNN and highlight our focus in Figure 1. Currently, there are three main approaches to accelerate CNN including algorithm, automatic code generation and hardware. Using FFT to reduce the convolutional layer computation complexity is studied in [10, 6]. Using singular value decomposition (SVD) to accelerate fully-connected layer on FPGA is studied in [13].

In order to compress the CNN model, a new architecture called SqueezeNet is studied in [7]. Another effort to compress the model is to shrink the data precision from 32-bit

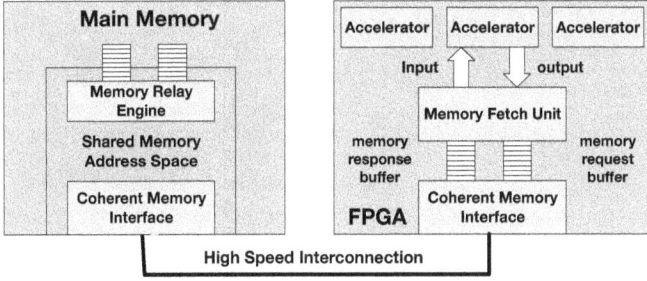

Figure 2: CPU-FPGA Shared Memory Model

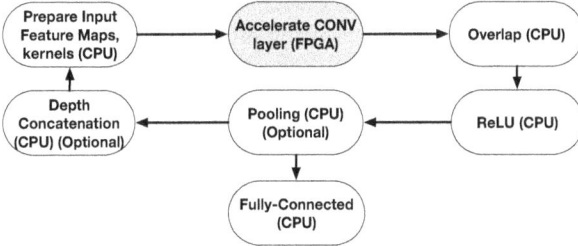

Figure 3: Proposed Mapping

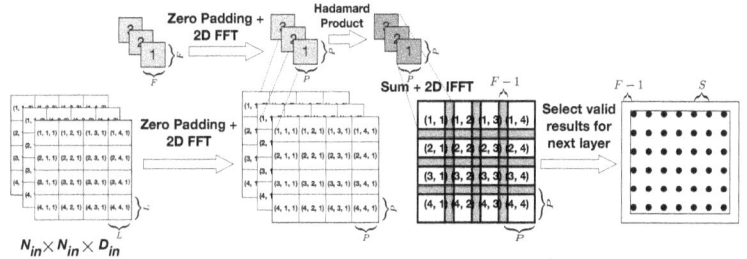

(a) 2D OaA for original input feature maps layout (Only one kernel is shown above)

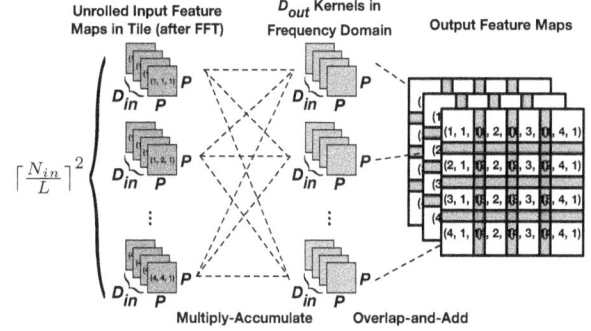

(b) 2D Overlap-and-Add for unrolled input feature maps tiles

Figure 4: Illustration of 2D Overlap-and-Add

floating point to 16 bit or even 8 bit fixed-point while preserving classification accuracy.

Hardware-level optimization is targeted for FPGA implementation. A high throughput convolver and a FFT engine has been studied in [2]. For large-scale CNN acceleration on FPGA, memory system optimization is the key to sustaining peak performance on a FPGA. A general strategy is to balance the computation throughput and memory bandwidth. Data buffering techniques can be used to hide the memory access latency. Concurrent processing on FPGA and CPU can further improve performance.

4. SYSTEM-LEVEL FRAMEWORK

4.1 Shared Memory Model

The shared memory model of CPU-FPGA platform is shown in Figure 2. Similar to the CPU load/store instruction, FPGA can send memory access request to the coherent memory system to perform read/write operations. A memory fetch unit and memory request and response buffer is implemented on FPGA.

The address space of the CPU user program is the entire main memory while the FPGA can only access a portion of it. To transfer data between the shared memory address space and the CPU thread private address space, a memory relay engine is implemented as a thread on the CPU.

In the shared memory model, the FPGA can be viewed as a special thread, which operates on the same set of data with CPU. Using a synchronization mechanism, CPU and FPGA can process different portions of the shared data concurrently.

4.2 Mapping Choices on CPU and FPGA

The CPU-FPGA heterogeneous platform provides a flexible CPU for light-weight operations and a FPGA for high performance parallel computing. Besides, the shared memory model provides an easy and efficient mechanism for FPGA to access data. Thus, various design choices can be made to accelerate CNNs. We identify our design choices in Figure 3.

As mentioned in [21], the convolutional layer occupies more than 90% of the total computation time in a CNN. Also, the convolution operations can be fully pipelined and parallelized on FPGA when transformed into frequency domain. The convolutional layer is mandatory inside all CNNs. By using Overlap-and-Add, we can build a generic convolver on FPGA for any kernel size less than the chosen FFT size.

The overlap varies with respect to the kernel size. The computation time required by performing overlap is much smaller compared with the time to perform 2D convolution. The ReLU layer is a threshold function, which takes very little time to compute on the CPU. The pooling layer takes the maximum value over a certain window, which is also a light-weight computation. The depth concatenation is optional and can be performed while the CPU is rearranging the data output from the FPGA. The shared memory model enables concurrent processing on the CPU and the FPGA, which reduces the overall computation latency further.

5. FREQUENCY DOMAIN 2D CONVOLVER

The 2D convolver is the key computation engine on FPGA to accelerate CNN inference. A "traditional" convolver on reconfigurable architecture is studied in [1]. Note that it cannot be used for different kernel sizes at run time. Also, the data parallelism of the design is too low to support high throughput computations. To address these issues, we propose a high throughput 2D convolver based on FFT and Overlap-and-Add (OaA) [18].

5.1 2D Overlap-and-Add

In traditional signal processing, Overlap-and-Add (OaA) is used to efficiently calculate the discrete convolution of a very long input signal with a small filter. Typical kernel sizes in CNN are $1 \times 1, 3 \times 3, 5 \times 5$ and 7×7, which are much

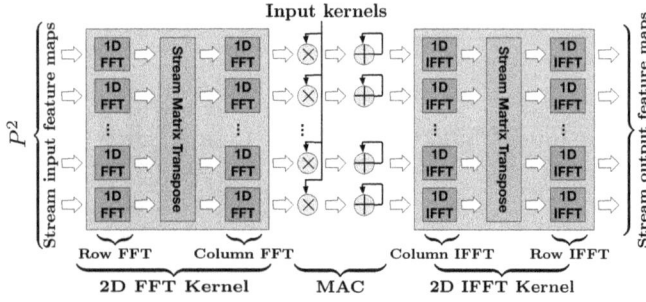

Figure 5: Diagram of OaA-based 2D Convolver

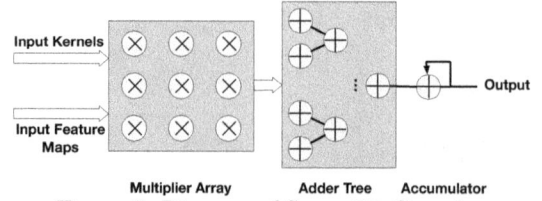

Figure 6: Diagram of Space 2D Convolver

smaller compared with the input feature map size. This makes OaA suitable for this task.

The 2D Overlap-and-Add technique is illustrated in Figure 4a. The input is a $N_{in} \times N_{in} \times D_{in}$ feature map and D_{out} kernels, each size $F \times F \times D_{in}$. The steps of 2D Overlap-and-Add are:

1. Choose the row and column FFT size P, such that $P \geq F$ and P is a power of 2.

2. Pad each $F \times F$ kernel map to $P \times P$ and perform P point 2D FFT to each map inside each kernel. (Note this can be performed in advance and stored in the main memory for inference)

3. Divide the input feature map into $L \times L$ tiles (If N_{in} is not divisible by L, use zero padding), where $L + F - 1 = P$. Then, pad each $L \times L$ tile to $P \times P$ and perform P point 2D FFT to each tile.

4. For each (i, j) pair, perform Hadamard Product of each input feature tile $(i, j, 1), \ldots, (i, j, D_{in})$ with corresponding kernel map $1, 2, \ldots, D_{in}$ of kth kernel. Then sum them up and perform P point 2D inverse FFT (IFFT) to obtain output tile (i, j, k).

5. Each output tile (i, j, k) overlaps with its neighboring tile with a stride of width $F - 1$ as shown in Figure 4a. The green stride is overlapped by 2 tiles and red stride is overlapped by 4 tiles. Add all the overlapped items to produce one output feature map.

6. Note that not all the computed results are used as input feature maps for the next layer. First, crop out the boundary region of width $F - 1$. Then, select the results with a stride of S as shown in Figure 4a.

7. Repeat Step 3 to 6 for all D_{out} kernels and concatenate the results in depth to obtain the complete output feature map.

Note that in Step 4, it is valid to perform the sum first and then perform 2D IFFT due to the linearity of IFFT. This will significantly reduce the amount of computations performed in IFFT.

5.2 OaA-based 2D Convolver

The proposed OaA-based 2D convolver is shown in Figure 5. It contains three stages including 2D FFT Kernel, Multiply-and-Accumulate (MAC) and 2D IFFT Kernel. The data parallelism of this architecture is P^2, where P is the 1D FFT size. The MAC unit must support complex numbers. A canonical complex number multiplier contains 3 floating-point multipliers [5].

To illustrate how the input data is fed into the convolver, we redraw the 2D Overlap-and-Add for the unrolled input feature tiles in Figure 4b. There are in total $\lceil \frac{N_{in}}{L} \rceil^2$ input feature tiles. For each kernel, we perform MAC with all the input tiles and overlap the results to obtain one output feature map. We then repeat the process for all the kernels to obtain the complete output feature maps.

The input of the convolver is one $P \times P$ tile of each input feature map and $P \times P$ map with the same depth of certain kernel. Note that the architecture shown in Figure 5 does not perform final overlapping. The reason is that the overlapped stride width is determined by the kernel size, which can change at run time for different layers. It is inefficient to build a specific hardware module compared with performing overlapping on CPU, given that it is a light-weighted computation.

The main motivation to use OaA to perform 2D convolution is to reduce the number of floating point operations asymptotically as well as increase the data parallelism. The computational complexity of space convolution and OaA convolution is $O(N_{in}^2 F^2)$, $O(N_{in}^2 \log F)$ respectively[3][6]. However, given that the kernel size is often small, the constant factor cannot be ignored and detailed analysis needs to be performed.

5.3 Performance Analysis

We assume the convolvers are all pipelined and no pipeline bubbles are fed into the convolver during any clock cycle. For space convolver, the kernels are in time domain. For OaA-based convolver, the kernels are in frequency domain.

5.3.1 Performance Metric

We consider the *Delay-Multiplier* Product in traditional signal processing as a key performance metric to compare convolver designs employing various algorithms. It is defined as the delay (# of cycles) to process a complete convolutional layer times the number of multipliers used. Since we only compare the performance of the computation engines:

- Power consumption of the convolver is proportional to the number of multipliers.

- Area of the convolver is proportional to the number of multipliers.

Thus, the *Delay-Multiplier* Product is an approximation to *Delay-Power* Product, which is the energy dissipated by the design. Note that the *Delay-Power* Product is also an approximation to the *Area-Delay* Product, which is a key metric to evaluate the efficiency of a hardware design.

---

[3]We consider FFT-based convolution as a special case of OaA-based convolution, where $L = N_{in}$.

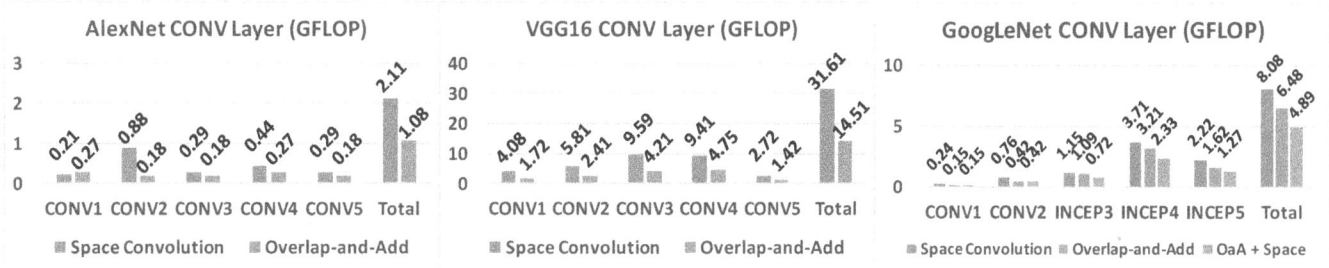

| | (a) AlexNet (2012) | (b) VGG16 (2014) | (c) GoogLeNet (2014) |

Figure 7: Floating Point Operations required in various state-of-art CNNs

Table 1: # of multipliers needed for various 1D FFT kernels

FFT size	4	8	16	32
# of multipliers	0	4	24	88

Table 2: Space-OaA convolver DM ratio with various kernel and FFT sizes, $S = 1$, $N_{in} \gg F$

Kernel size	3	3	3	5	5	7
FFT size	4	8	16	8	16	8
DM ratio	0.75	1.01	0.77	1.25	1.56	0.61
Kernel size	7	7	9	9	11	11
FFT size	16	32	16	32	16	32
DM ratio	2.12	2.31	2.25	3.25	1.89	4.09

5.3.2 Space Convolver

We show the diagram of a space 2D convolver in Figure 6. It consumes $F \times F$ multipliers and can produce 1 valid output every $\frac{1}{D_{in}}$ clock cycle. Thus, the total latency[4] D_{space} is

$$D_{space} = (\frac{N_{in} - F}{S} + 1)^2 \cdot D_{in} \cdot D_{out} \qquad (3)$$

The delay-multiplier product is

$$DM_{space} = (\frac{N_{in} - F}{S} + 1)^2 \cdot D_{in} \cdot D_{out} \cdot F^2 \qquad (4)$$

5.3.3 OaA Convolver

According to Figure 4b, for each input tile and kernel pair, we need D_{in} cycles to process. There are $\lceil \frac{N_{in}}{L} \rceil^2 \cdot D_{out}$ such pairs. Thus,

$$D_{OaA} = \lceil \frac{N_{in}}{L} \rceil^2 \cdot D_{in} \cdot D_{out} \qquad (5)$$

The number of multipliers needed in various FFT sizes is shown in Table 1. In addition, we need P^2 complex multipliers to perform MAC, each containing 3 floating point multipliers [5]. Thus, the delay-multiplier product of OaA convolver is:

$$DM_{OaA} = \lceil \frac{N_{in}}{L} \rceil^2 \cdot D_{in} \cdot D_{out} \cdot (3P^2 + 4P \cdot N_{mult}) \qquad (6)$$

where N_{mult} is the number of multipliers in each 1D FFT kernel.

5.3.4 Performance Comparison

DM Product comparison. To compare OaA convolver with space convolver, we define the space-OaA convolver DM

---

[4]We ignore the latency to fill and drain the pipeline since they are too small compared with the total processing time.

ratio as

$$DM \text{ ratio} = \frac{DM_{space}}{DM_{OaA}} = \frac{(\frac{N_{in} - F}{S} + 1)^2 \cdot F^2}{\lceil \frac{N_{in}}{L} \rceil^2 \cdot (3P^2 + 4P \cdot N_{mult})} \qquad (7)$$

We assume the stride is 1 and $N_{in} \gg F$ as in most convolutional layers. Using $P = L + F - 1$, we can simplify Eq 7 as:

$$DM \text{ ratio} = \frac{(P - F + 1)^2 F^2}{3P^2 + 4P \cdot N_{mult}} \qquad (8)$$

We show the space-OaA convolver DM ratio with typical kernel and FFT sizes in Table 2. As shown in Table 2, for each typical kernel size 3, 5, 7, 9, 11, we can always find a FFT size such that the OaA convolver is superior to space convolver in terms of *Delay-Multiplier* Product as emphasized in bold. In practice, we choose the FFT size to maximize the DM ratio given on-chip resource and memory bandwidth constraints.

Computational Complexity. The total number of floating point operations required by various state-of-the-art CNNs using space convolution and OaA convolution is shown in Figure 7. For AlexNet, VGG16 and GoogLeNet, using OaA convolution can reduce the the total number of floating point operations by 48.82%, 54.10%, 19.79%, respectively, compared with the space convolution. Note that in GoogLeNet Inception Module, more than half of the convolutional layers use 1×1 kernels; in this case using overlap-and-add is not advantageous. If we use space convolution in convolutional layers with 1×1 kernels and use OaA convolution for the rest of the convolutional layers, we can reduce the the total number of floating point operations by 39.43% as shown in Figure 7c grey bars.

Reduced computational complexity can lead to less execution time and higher energy efficiency given the same computational resources (# of multipliers). We define the throughput as the number of outputs produced in each cycle by the convolver. It is determined by the hardware mapping of the algorithm. For OaA-based convolver, the throughput is $O(P^2)$ as shown in Figure 5, whereas the throughput of the adder-tree based space convolver is $O(1)$ as shown in Figure 6.

Flexibility. The OaA convolver can be exploited to accelerate **any kernel size** less than the FFT size P **at run time** if the data in the shared memory is appropriately zero-padded. This can be easily achieved by choosing the corresponding tile size L and performing data rearrangement using the CPU for different convolutional layers.

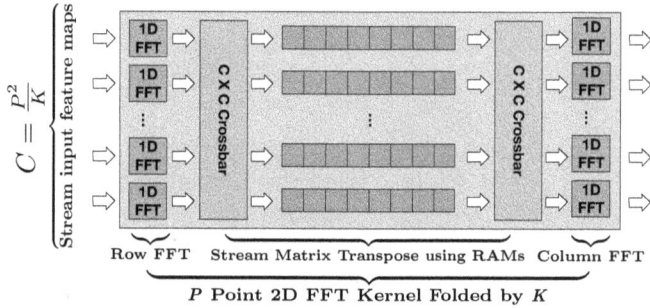

Figure 8: An example of folding 2D FFT Kernel

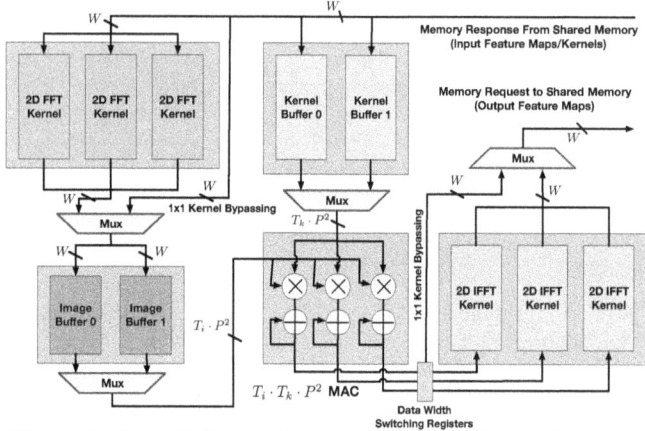

Figure 9: Overall System Design on FPGA, $T_i = 3, T_k = 1$

6. OVERALL SYSTEM DESIGN

In Section 5, we assumed that the convolvers are running at the peak performance with no pipeline stalls. However, this may not be true if the design is bounded by memory bandwidth. This causes the computation engines on the FPGA to be stalled waiting for the input data from the external memory. The data parallelism of the 2D convolver may be larger than the communication channel data width. In this case, we need to fold the 2D FFT Kernel to match the communication channel data width and make the design scalable.

6.1 Folding 2D FFT Kernel

In order to match data parallelism with the communication channel data width W, we can reduce the data parallelism of the 2D FFT kernel. As shown in Figure 8, we fold it by a factor of K, where $1 \leq K \leq P$ and K is a divisor of P such that $W \approx \frac{P^2}{K}$. The data parallelism after folding is $\frac{P^2}{K}$ and the number of 1D FFT kernels required is $\frac{2P}{K}$. In order to support streaming matrix transpose for data arriving in consecutive cycles, we apply the techniques described in [3]. Matrix transpose is a special form of data permutation and by storing the data using intermediate RAMs, we can achieve matrix transpose for data arriving in consecutive cycles. The additional on-chip memory needed for folding 2D FFT kernel is $8P^2$ bytes.

6.2 Overall System Diagram

The overall system is shown in Figure 9. The input data from shared memory can be either input feature maps or kernels. The input feature map data is sent to 2D FFT Ker-

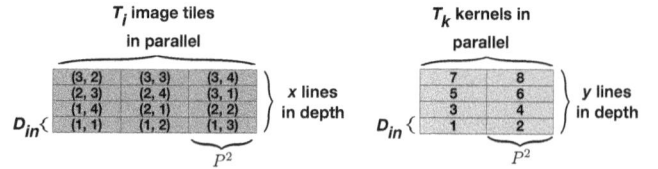

(a) On Chip Memory Layout for Image and Kernel

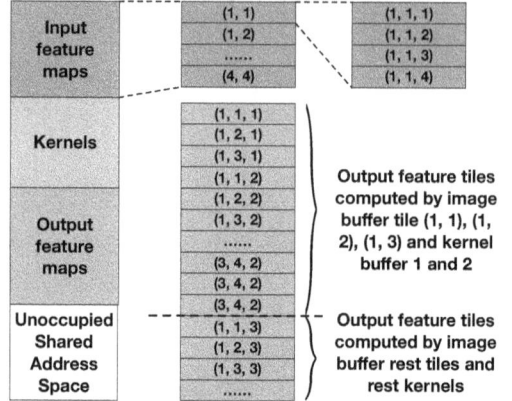

(b) Data Layout in Shared Memory Address Space

Figure 10: Data Layout for Convolutional Layer with 4×4 input feature map and 3×3 kernels, $T_i = 3, T_k = 2, x = 4 \cdot D_{in}, y = 4 \cdot D_{in}$

nel and the frequency domain input feature map is stored in the image buffers. The kernel data is directly stored in the kernel buffers. The MAC array is the main computation engine, which reads data from the image and kernel buffers and performs MAC operations. Each accumulated result is sent to 2D IFFT kernel and the output data is sent to the shared memory. The data width switching registers are needed to match the MAC array output data parallelism with the communication channel data width. Note that the switcher registers will not overflow since the MAC array produces results every D_{in} cycles. Since the focus of this paper is CNN inference, we can assume that all the kernels are in frequency domain. These can be precomputed and stored in the main memory. In this section, we further explore **task parallelism** to scale the system performance. We define,

- T_i: The number of input feature maps processed in parallel in each cycle.

- T_k: The number of kernel maps processed in parallel in each cycle.

Note that we need to perform MAC operations between each input feature map and each kernel map. Thus, the total system task parallelism $T_t = T_i T_k$. Figure 9 illustrates the design for $T_i = 3, T_k = 1$.

As mentioned in Section 5, it is inefficient to perform convolution layer with 1×1 kernel in frequency domain. Thus, a **1-by-1 kernel bypassing** is added to the original data path as shown in Figure 9. In this case, the input feature maps are directly stored and the kernels are in time domain. The 2D IFFT is also bypassed and accumulated results are sent directly to the shared memory. To support 1-by-1 kernel bypassing, we design the MAC array to support both real numbers and complex numbers.

```
read_address_image = 0; read_address_kernel = 0;
for image_start_line = 0 to x − 1 by D_in
  current_image_line = image_start_line;
  for current_kernel_line = 0 to y − 1
    read_address_image = current_image_line;
    read_address_kernel = current_kernel_line;
    if current_image_line == image_start_line + D_in − 1
      current_image_line = image_start_line;
    else
      current_image_line = current_image_line + 1;
    end
  end
end
```

Code 1: Image and Kernel Buffer Read Address Computation

6.3 Optimizing Memory Subsystem

6.3.1 Data Layout

Input feature maps and kernels. We show the shared memory data layout in Figure 10b. The input feature maps and kernel data is stored tile by tile instead of the original 3D array. This enables the FPGA to access data through continuous virtual addresses instead of scattered pointers; this improves the cache performance due to high spatial locality.

On-chip memory. The data layout for on-chip input feature maps and kernels is also tile by tile as shown in Figure 10a. The P^2 data in one input feature map tile or one kernel map is unrolled and stored in parallel as shown in Figure 10a. Let x and y denote the depth of image and kernel buffer, respectively. An example of $x = 4 \cdot D_{in}$, $y = 4 \cdot D_{in}$ is shown in Figure 10a.

Output feature maps. The output feature map layout is determined by the image buffer depth x and the kernel buffer depth y. A pseudo-code to compute the read address of image and kernel buffers is shown in Code 1.

An example of the output feature map data layout in shared memory is shown in Figure 10b, where $x = 4 \cdot D_{in}$, $y = 4 \cdot D_{in}$ and the input feature map size is 4×4 and the kernel size is 3×3.

6.3.2 Double Buffering

To reduce the FPGA-memory traffic and enable full overlap of the memory access and the computation, double buffering technique is exploited as shown in Figure 9. Double buffering is only effective when the computation time is greater than the time to bring the same amount of data to on-chip memory of the FPGA. The data access pattern proposed in Code 1 satisfies this requirement because it takes $O(xy)$ time to perform computations while $O(x + y)$ time to bring the same amount of data to the on-chip memory. However, the on-chip memory will soon become the bottleneck. In this case, we can use only one image buffer and the latency to bring the input feature maps to on-chip memory cannot be fully hidden. The additional delay increased due to using only one image buffer is $4N_{in}^2 D_{in}/B$.

6.3.3 Timing Analysis

A detailed timing diagram of on-chip memory write destination, read source buffer and memory write request is shown in Figure 11. i, k denote the image buffer and the

kernel buffer, respectively. At any time, only one image buffer and kernel buffer is activated to produce buffered data and the other image and kernel buffer is used for buffering data from the shared memory. Suppose the memory read bandwidth is B, the FPGA operating frequency is f. Then according to Code 1, the time to consume one kernel buffer is

$$t_{kernel,consume} = \frac{x}{D_{in}} \cdot y \cdot \frac{1}{f} \qquad (9)$$

Each kernel buffer contains $T_k \cdot P^2 \cdot y$ complex numbers. Thus, the time to fill one kernel buffer is[5]

$$t_{kernel.fill} = \frac{T_k \cdot P^2 \cdot y \cdot 8}{B} \qquad (10)$$

In order to hide the kernel memory access latency, the inequality $t_{kernel,fill} < t_{kernel,consume}$ must be satisfied. Thus,

$$x > \frac{8T_k P^2 D_{in} f}{B} \qquad (11)$$

Another constraint is that we have to fill the vacant image buffer during the time slots between filling kernel buffer and consuming kernel buffer within one image buffer output period as shown in Figure 11. Thus,

$$(x \cdot \frac{y}{D_{in}} \cdot \frac{1}{f} - \frac{T_k \cdot P^2 \cdot y \cdot 8}{B}) \cdot \frac{D_{in} \cdot D_{out}}{y \cdot T_k} > \frac{T_i \cdot P^2 \cdot x \cdot 8}{B} \qquad (12)$$

This leads to,

$$x > \frac{8P^2 D_{in} D_{out} f T_k}{D_{out} B - 8T_i P^2 f T_k} \qquad (13)$$

where $D_{out} B - 8T_i P^2 f T_k > 0$. Thus,

$$x > \max \left(\frac{8T_k P^2 D_{in} f}{B}, \frac{8P^2 D_{in} D_{out} f T_k}{D_{out} B - 8T_i P^2 f T_k} \right) \qquad (14)$$

where $D_{out} B - 8T_i P^2 f T_k > 0$. Note that there is no constraint on the kernel buffer depth y and it can be arbitrarily small as long as it can hold the largest kernel among all the convolutional layers. The total on-chip memory M_{total} needed by the design is

$$M_{total} = (x \cdot P^2 \cdot T_i + y \cdot P^2 \cdot T_k) \cdot 2 \qquad (15)$$

6.3.4 CPU-FPGA Concurrent Processing

As shown in Figure 3, CPU performs overlap, ReLU, pooling and optional depth concatenation, which varies with different convolutional layers. These light-weight tasks are well suited for CPU and can be overlapped with the FPGA.

Synchronization Mechanism. The synchronization between the CPU and the FPGA is through a shared flag as shown in Figure 11. After FPGA completes each output tile of each output feature map, it sets a shared flag in the shared memory. Once the CPU detects the set flag, it performs overlap, ReLU, rearranges the data for the next layer.

6.4 Performance and Resource Estimation

The performance and resource consumption of our design employing double buffering and single image buffer is shown in Table 3, where N_{in} is input feature map size, L is OaA tile size, D_{in} is the number of input feature maps, D_{out} is the number of output feature maps, f is FPGA operating

---
[5]In this paper, we use 32-bit single precision floating-point.

Time

Memory Write Destination	i0	k0	k1	i1	k0	i1	...	i1	k0	i1	k1	i0	k0	i0	...	i0	k0	i0
Read Image Buffer Source	wait	i0										i1						
Read Kernel Buffer Source	wait	k0	k1		...			k1	k0		k1		...					k1
Memory Write Request		Data 0	Flag	Data 1	Flag	Data 2	Flag	Data 3	Flag	Data 4	Flag
CPU		Rearrage 0		Rearrage 1		Rearrage 2		Rearrage 3

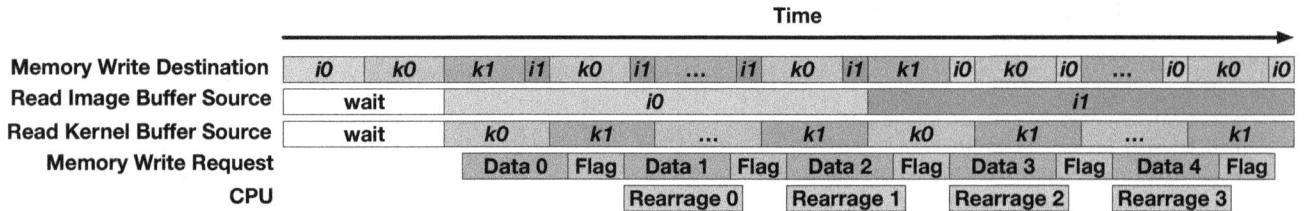

Figure 11: Timing Diagram

Table 3: Theoretical Performance and Resource Consumption

	double buffering	single image buffer
Delay	$\lceil \frac{N_{in}}{L} \rceil^2 D_{in} D_{out}/f$	$\lceil \frac{N_{in}}{L} \rceil^2 D_{in} D_{out}/f$ $+ 4N_{in}^2 D_{in}/B$
Multipliers	$3P^2 + 4PN_{mult}/K$	$3P^2 + 4PN_{mult}/K$
Memory	$P^2(2xT_i + 2yT_k + 8)$	$P^2(xT_i + 2yT_k + 8)$

frequency, B is memory bandwidth, K is 2D FFT folding factor, P is the FFT size, N_{mult} is the number of multipliers in 1D FFT kernel, T_i (T_k) is the image (kernel) task parallelism, x (y) is the image (kernel) buffer depth.

We also give an estimation of the performance and resource consumption by using single image buffer. According to the analysis in Section 6.3.3, the image buffer is often large and the kernel buffer is small. Using single image buffer can make the design practical for FPGAs with limited on-chip memory. The additional delay introduced to bring the input feature maps to FPGA is $4N_{in}D_{in}/B$, which is considerably small compared with the total processing time.

7. EXPERIMENTS AND RESULTS

7.1 Experimental Setup

We conducted our experiments on Intel Heterogeneous Architecture Research Platform (HARP), which is a pre-production of Intel QuickAssist QPI FPGA Platform[8]. It integrates 10 Core Intel Xeon E5-2600 v2 processor and Altera Stratix V FPGA with 6.25 MB BRAM on chip. The CPU and FPGA exchange data through a shared memory; this platform is an example of the model described in Section 4. The high speed interconnection in HARP is Intel QuickPath Interconnection (QPI), which achieves 5.0 GB/s bandwidth according to our own experiments. The QPI data width W is 64 bytes. A direct-mapped coherent cache of 64 KB is implemented on FPGA to reduce the data access latency. Results in this work were generated using preproduction hardware and software from Intel, and may not reflect the performance of production or future systems.

We conducted experiments on AlexNet, GoogLeNet and VGG16 using HARP. We measured the execution time of each group layer inside the three CNNs. We measured the CPU-FPGA sequential execution time; in this case the CPU waits for all the results from the FPGA and then performs overlap and ReLU. We also measured the concurrent execution time; in this case the CPU processes the partial results from the FPGA using the synchronization model discussed in Section 6.3.4.

7.2 Performance Evaluation

We show the overall design parameters in Table 4. Based on the number of DSPs available, the task parallelism is

Table 4: Design Parameters for AlexNet, VGG16 and GoogLeNet

Parameter	Design Value
Task Parallelism $T_t = T_i T_k$	1
# of image buffers	1
Image buffer depth x	8192
# of kernel buffers	2
Kernel buffer depth y	512 (AlexNet, VGG16) 1024 (GoogLeNet)
FFT size	8
2D FFT folding factor K	4

Table 5: Resource used in our design, 4.0 MB BRAM required by VGG16 and AlexNet. 5.0 MB BRAM required by GoogLeNet.

Resource	Registers (K)	Logic (ALM)	32-bit float Multipliers	DSP	BRAM (MB)
Used	266	200522	224	224	4.0/5.0
Available	939	234720	256	256	6.25

set to 1. Based on the available on-chip memory, we use a single image buffer of depth 8192. In AlexNet/VGG16, the maximum kernel depth is 512. In GoogLeNet, the maximum kernel depth is 832. Thus, we choose the kernel depth y to be 512 for AlexNet/VGG16 and 1024 for GoogLeNet. According to DM ratio analysis in Section 5, we choose FFT size to be 8, which is superior to space convolver in terms of $Delay\text{-}Multiplier$ Product for most kernel sizes in CNNs in our experiments based on the available on-chip memory and measured bandwidth. The Intel HARP QPI data width supports 16 32-bit floating point data access in parallel. Thus, we can shrink the 2D FFT data parallelism to 16 and the corresponding folding factor K is 4.

The resource consumption is shown in Table 5 for the design parameters in Table 4. According to Table 5, we conclude that the number of available DSPs is the bottleneck for the chosen design parameters.

Most of the kernel sizes in AlexNet, VGG16 and GoogLeNet convolutional layers is less than the chosen FFT size. Thus, they can be accelerated using the design parameters described in Table 4. Only one exception occurs in CONV1 of AlexNet, whose kernel size is 11 and stride is 4. Accelerating convolutional layers with large stride using frequency domain convolution is not attractive compared with space convolution. Hence, we choose to directly implement it on the CPU.

7.2.1 Tradeoff Analysis

On-chip Memory Consumption vs. Sustained Performance. The peak performance is achieved when there is no pipeline stalls in the computation engines. The sustained performance is determined by the number of the computation engine pipeline stalls and the total computation time. It

Table 6: Execution Time for VGG16 and AlexNet

Layer (Group)	VGG16 Execution Time (ms)					AlexNet Execution Time (ms)			
	FPGA (Theoretical)	FPGA (Actual)	CPU	Sequential	Concurrent	FPGA (Actual)	CPU	Sequential	Concurrent
CONV1	30.96	31.53	7.76	39.29	32.74	-	17.17	17.17	17.17
CONV2	44.36	46.01	4.18	50.19	46.48	7.86	0.09	7.95	7.94
CONV3	81.92	82.27	3.54	85.81	82.75	4.42	0.12	4.54	4.50
CONV4	81.92	82.77	1.37	84.14	82.90	6.64	0.15	6.79	6.71
CONV5	17.69	18.36	0.27	18.63	18.40	4.42	0.11	4.53	4.49
CONV Total	256.85	262.94	17.12	280.06	**263.27**	**23.34**	17.64	40.98	**40.81**

Table 7: Performance Comparison with the State-of-Art CNN Implementations on FPGA

Platform	[21]	[13]	This Work	
	Virtex7 VX485t	Zynq XC7Z045	Intel QuickAssist QPI FPGA	
Clock (MHz)	100	150	200	
Data Precision	32-bit float	16-bit fixed	32-bit float	
Bandwidth (GB/s)	12.8	4.2	5.0	
CNN Model	AlexNet	VGG16-SVD	AlexNet	VGG16
BRAM	4.5 MB	2.13 MB	4.0 MB	4.0 MB
DSP, Multipliers	2240, 747	780, 780	224, 224	224, 224
Throughput (CONV) (GFLOPs/sec)	61.62	187.80	83.00	123.48
Delay (CONV) (ms)	21.61	163.42	CPU:17.17 FPGA:23.64	263.27
Power (FPGA) (W)	18.61	9.63	13.18	13.18
Delay×Multipliers	16142	127467	9141/5295	58972
Resource Efficiency (GFLOPs/sec/Multiplier)	0.082	0.241	0.37	0.55
Power Efficiency (GFLOPs/sec/W)	3.31	19.50	6.30	9.37
Classification Accuracy	Lossless	Lossy	Lossless	
Flexibility	Any CNN	Limited	Any CNN	

Table 8: Resources for implementing multipliers

Multipliers	DSP
16-bit fixed point (Xilinx)	1
32-bit fixed point (Xilinx)	2
32-bit float point (Xilinx)	3
32-bit float point (Altera)	1

is determined by to what extent we can overlap the computation with the memory access latency. We show the impact of on-chip memory on sustained performance versus peak performance ratio in Figure 12.

Energy vs. FFT Size. It is shown in Section 5.3 that larger FFT size reduces the DM Product, which leads to the reduction of energy consumption of the convolvers. However, the energy consumed by on-chip memory to sustain peak performance increases. Thus, in an energy constrained system, we should tradeoff between the on-chip memory energy consumption and the convolver energy consumption.

7.2.2 VGG16 and AlexNet

We show the execution time of various layers in VGG16 and AlexNet in Table 6. Note that the VGG16 execution time of each layer is very close to the predicted value using our analysis. The predicted value is obtained using Table 3. The variation between predicted and actual results is due to the delay to fill and drain the pipelines. The sequential CPU-FPGA total execution time of VGG16 is 280.06 ms while the concurrent total execution time is 263.27 ms. The CPU-FPGA concurrent processing through shared memory reduces the total execution time by 6.0%. However, the advantage of concurrent processing is not noticeable in AlexNet since the execution time on CPU is much smaller than that of FPGA.

Table 9: GoogLeNet Convolutional Layer Performance

GoogLeNet (convolutional layer only) Execution Time (ms)		
Layer	CPU (16 thds)	CPU (1 thd) + FPGA
CONV1	38.53	12.70
CONV2	117.13	17.14
Inception3	91.05	16.16
Inception4	173.21	29.16
Inception5	45.45	8.48
Total	465.37	83.64
Throughput (GFLOPs/sec)	**17.36**	**96.60**

Comparison with State-of-the-Art. We show the comparison of our work with two state-of-art CNN implementations on FPGA in Table 7. Since the number of multipliers consumed is not directly available in [21, 13], we convert the DSP consumption to multipliers consumption using Table 8. Compared with the state-of-the-art AlexNet implementation, our design achieves 1.35x GFLOPs/sec and similar delay with 3.33x less multipliers and 1.1x less memory. Compared with the state-of-the-art VGG16 implementation[13], our design has 0.66x throughput with 3.48x less multipliers without sacrificing the classification accuracy.

Resource and Power Efficiency Comparison. Table 7 shows that our design improves resource efficiency by 4.5x and 2.28x compared with state-of-the-art CNN implementations[21, 13]. Compared with state-of-art AlexNet and VGG16 implementations, our design improves power efficiency by 1.90x and 0.48x. The reasons for having lower power efficiency compared with [13] is: 1) Our design consumes more BRAMs. 2) Our design uses floating-point operations, which limits the system task parallelism and overall performance. 3) Design in [13] is only optimized for VGG16 while our design is applicable to any CNN with maximum kernel size less than the chosen FFT size.

Fully-Connected (FC) Layer. We implemented the FC layer directly on CPU using 16 threads. The FC layer can be viewed as matrix-vector multiplication, which is bounded by memory bandwidth. The execution time for FC1, FC2, FC3 in VGG16 is 115.74 ms (16.10 ms with SVD), 19.30 ms and 4.71 ms, respectively. It outperforms the FC layer implementation on FPGA in [13].

7.2.3 GoogLeNet

We also implemented GoogLeNet on Intel HARP and the results are shown in Table 9. Our experiments show that we improve the performance by 5.56x compared with 16 threads running on 10 Core Intel Xeon CPU at 2.8 GHz. The software was compiled with gcc using optimization level O3 and OpenMP.

Scalability. The major issue to increase the thread-level parallelism to compute the convolutional layer lies in the

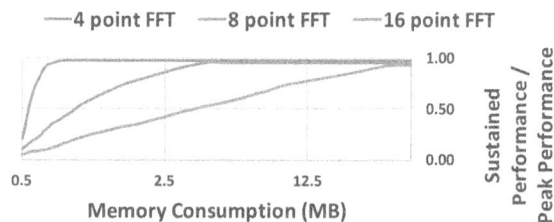

Figure 12: Sustained Performance versus Peak Performance ratio vs. Memory Consumption. The x-axis is in log scale

cost to maintain cache coherency. For FPGA based design, the parallelism can always be increased if the memory bandwidth and the FPGA on-chip resources increase.

8. DISCUSSION

Platform Choice. A CPU-FPGA based design will consume more power than FPGA-only based design. However, the CPU adds more flexibility to the design. Moreover, since most of the computational complexity is in the convolutional layers, the CPU performs simple operations and data rearrangement. Thus the power consumption of the CPU will not increase significantly as the CNN size increases.

Automatic Code Generation. Our framework provides a complete solution to accelerate CNN on FPGA including intra-layer data rearrangement. Widely used CNNs' convolutional layers mainly consist of small kernels. Thus, by zero-padding various kernel sizes to fit a chosen FFT size, and using FPGA to accelerate it by exploiting massive parallelism, we can achieve large performance improvement for various CNN models. We can use our framework to develop an automatic code generation tool so high-level users can specify CNN models and generate the design.

Fixed Point vs. Floating Point. Many previous approaches use fixed point instead of floating point for computations. The advantage is less resource consumption and higher power efficiency. However, it may penalize the classification accuracy.

9. CONCLUSION

In this paper, we first exploited Overlap-and-Add to reduce the computation complexity of the convolutional layers. Then, we proposed a 2D convolver in frequency domain to accelerate convolutional layers on FPGA. To optimize the memory system, we exploited the double buffering technique to overlap the computation with the memory access. Finally, we implemented 3 state-of-art CNN models including AlexNet, VGG16 and GoogLeNet on Intel QuickAssist QPI FPGA Platform. Future work includes employing our design to more CNN models, conducting experiments using fixed point data as well as automatic generation of optimized designs.

10. REFERENCES

[1] B. Bosi, G. Bois, and Y. Savaria. Reconfigurable Pipelined 2D Convolvers for Fast Digital Signal Processing. *IEEE Trans. On Very Large Scale Integration (VLSI) Systems*, 1999.

[2] R. Chen and V. K. Prasanna. Energy Optimizations for FPGA-based 2-D FFT Architecture. In *High Performance Extreme Computing Conference (HPEC), 2014 IEEE*, pages 1–6, Sept 2014.

[3] R. Chen, S. Siriyal, and V. K. Prasanna. Energy and Memory Efficient Mapping of Bitonic Sorting on FPGA. In *Proceedings of the 2015 ACM/SIGDA International Symposium on Field-Programmable Gate Arrays*, FPGA '15, pages 240–249, New York, NY, USA, 2015. ACM.

[4] C. Farabet, Y. Lecun, K. Kavukcuoglu, B. Martini, P. Akselrod, S. Talay, and E. Culurciello. Large-Scale FPGA-Based Convolutional Networks. In R. Bekkerman, M. Bilenko, and J. Langford, editors, *Scaling Up Machine Learning*, pages 399–419. Cambridge University Press, 2011. Cambridge Books.

[5] M. Hemnani, S. Palekar, P. Dixit, and P. Joshi. Hardware optimization of complex multiplication scheme for DSP application. In *Computer, Communication and Control (IC4), 2015 International Conference on*, pages 1–4, Sept 2015.

[6] T. Highlander and A. Rodriguez. Very Efficient Training of Convolutional Neural Networks using Fast Fourier Transform and Overlap-and-Add. *CoRR*, abs/1601.06815, 2016.

[7] F. N. Iandola, M. W. Moskewicz, K. Ashraf, S. Han, W. J. Dally, and K. Keutzer. SqueezeNet: AlexNet-level accuracy with 50x fewer parameters and <0.5MB model size. *CoRR*, abs/1602.07360, 2016.

[8] Intel Inc. Xeon+FPGA Platform for the Data Center. https://www.ece.cmu.edu/ calcm/carl/lib/ exe/fetch.php?media=carl15-gupta.pdf.

[9] A. Krizhevsky, I. Sutskever, and G. E. Hinton. ImageNet Classification with Deep Convolutional Neural Networks. In F. Pereira, C. J. C. Burges, L. Bottou, and K. Q. Weinberger, editors, *Advances in Neural Information Processing Systems 25*, pages 1097–1105. Curran Associates, Inc., 2012.

[10] M. Mathieu, M. Henaff, and Y. LeCun. Fast Training of Convolutional Networks through FFTs. *CoRR*, abs/1312.5851, 2013.

[11] Micron Technology, Inc. The Convey HC-2 Computer. https://www.micron.com/about/about-the-convey-computer-acquisition.

[12] Y. Qiao, J. Shen, T. Xiao, Q. Yang, M. Wen, and C. Zhang. FPGA-accelerated deep convolutional neural networks for high throughput and energy efficiency. *Concurrency and Computation: Practice and Experience*, pages n/a–n/a, 2016. cpe.3850.

[13] J. Qiu, J. Wang, S. Yao, K. Guo, B. Li, E. Zhou, J. Yu, T. Tang, N. Xu, S. Song, Y. Wang, and H. Yang. Going Deeper with Embedded FPGA Platform for Convolutional Neural Network. In *Proceedings of the 2016 ACM/SIGDA International Symposium on Field-Programmable Gate Arrays*, FPGA'16. ACM, 2016.

[14] D. Scherer, H. Schulz, and S. Behnke. *Accelerating Large-Scale Convolutional Neural Networks with Parallel Graphics Multiprocessors*, pages 82–91. Springer Berlin Heidelberg, Berlin, Heidelberg, 2010.

[15] K. Simonyan and A. Zisserman. Very Deep Convolutional Networks for Large-Scale Image Recognition. *CoRR*, abs/1409.1556, 2014.

[16] N. Suda, V. Chandra, G. Dasika, A. Mohanty, Y. Ma, S. Vrudhula, J.-s. Seo, and Y. Cao. Throughput-Optimized OpenCL-based FPGA Accelerator for Large-Scale Convolutional Neural Networks. In *Proceedings of the 2016 ACM/SIGDA International Symposium on Field-Programmable Gate Arrays*, FPGA '16, pages 16–25, New York, NY, USA, 2016.

[17] C. Szegedy, W. Liu, Y. Jia, P. Sermanet, S. E. Reed, D. Anguelov, D. Erhan, V. Vanhoucke, and A. Rabinovich. Going Deeper with Convolutions. *CoRR*, abs/1409.4842, 2014.

[18] Wikipedia. https://en.wikipedia.org/wiki/Multidimensional_discrete_convolution#Overlap_and_Add.

[19] Xilinx Inc. Zynq-7000 All Programmable SoC. http://www.xilinx.com/products/silicon-devices/soc/zynq-7000.html.

[20] M. D. Zeiler and R. Fergus. Visualizing and Understanding Convolutional Networks. *CoRR*, abs/1311.2901, 2013.

[21] C. Zhang, P. Li, G. Sun, Y. Guan, B. Xiao, and J. Cong. Optimizing FPGA-based Accelerator Design for Deep Convolutional Neural Networks. In *Proceedings of the 2015 ACM/SIGDA International Symposium on Field-Programmable Gate Arrays*, FPGA '15, pages 161–170, New York, NY, USA, 2015.

[22] X. Zhang, J. Zou, X. Ming, K. He, and J. Sun. Efficient and Accurate Approximations of Nonlinear Convolutional Networks. *CoRR*, abs/1411.4229, 2014.

[23] A. Zlateski, K. Lee, and H. S. Seung. ZNN - A Fast and Scalable Algorithm for Training 3D Convolutional Networks on Multi-Core and Many-Core Shared Memory Machines. *CoRR*, abs/1510.06706, 2015.

Optimizing Loop Operation and Dataflow in FPGA Acceleration of Deep Convolutional Neural Networks

Yufei Ma, Yu Cao, Sarma Vrudhula[†], Jae-sun Seo

School of Electrical, Computer and Energy Engineering
[†]School of Computing, Informatics, Decision Systems Engineering
Arizona State University, Tempe, USA

{yufeima, yu.cao, vrudhula, jaesun.seo}@asu.edu

ABSTRACT

As convolution layers contribute most operations in convolutional neural network (CNN) algorithms, an effective convolution acceleration scheme significantly affects the efficiency and performance of a hardware CNN accelerator. Convolution in CNNs involves three-dimensional multiply and accumulate (MAC) operations with four levels of loops, which results in a large design space. Prior works either employ limited loop optimization techniques, e.g. loop unrolling, tiling and interchange, or only tune some of the design variables after the accelerator architecture and dataflow are already fixed. Without fully studying the convolution loop optimization before the hardware design phase, the resulting accelerator can hardly exploit the data reuse and manage data movement efficiently. This work overcomes these barriers by quantitatively analyzing and optimizing the design objectives (e.g. required memory access) of the CNN accelerator based on multiple design variables. We systematically explore the trade-offs of hardware cost by searching the design variable configurations, and propose a specific dataflow of hardware CNN acceleration to minimize the memory access and data movement while maximizing the resource utilization to achieve high performance. The proposed CNN acceleration scheme and architecture are demonstrated on a standalone Altera Arria 10 GX 1150 FPGA by implementing end-to-end VGG-16 CNN model and achieved 645.25 GOPS of throughput and 47.97 ms of latency, which is a >3.2× enhancement compared to state-of-the-art FPGA implementations of VGG model.

Keywords

Convolutional neural networks; FPGA; hardware acceleration.

1. INTRODUCTION

FPGA-based CNN accelerators are gaining popularity because of higher energy efficiency than GPUs [8-12], greater flexibility due to reconfigurability and shorter turn-around time than ASICs. They also allow low latency operation by enabling the customization of the acceleration architecture and utilizing of hundreds to thousands of on-chip DSP blocks. The large number of operations (>1G) and kernel weights (>50M) in the state-of-the-art deep CNN algorithms have become a well-known challenge for their implementations on embedded platforms, which are constrained by limited hardware computing resources and costly off-chip communication. In addition, the high variability in the sizes of the different convolution layers may prevent the full utilization of the available computing resources for all the layers. Moreover, the increasing scale and complexity of CNN algorithms to achieve higher accuracy further exacerbate the energy consumption for computation, communication and memory. In fact, the energy cost of the increased data movement and memory accesses due to the large number of operations often exceeds the energy cost of computation [6][15]. Therefore, an energy-efficient accelerator should target fully utilizing computation resources as well as minimizing data movement and memory access.

Since convolution operations often constitute more than 90% of the total CNN operations [2][3][4][6][11], an effective acceleration scheme of convolution requires proper management of the parallel computations and the organization of data storage and access across multiple levels of memories, e.g. off-chip DRAM, on-chip SRAM and local registers. Convolution is comprised of four levels of loops sliding along both kernel and feature maps, resulting in a large design space to explore various choices for implementing parallelism, sequencing of computations, and partitioning the large data set into smaller chunks to fit into on-chip memory. These problems can be handled by the existing loop optimization techniques [7][17], such as loop unrolling, tiling and interchange. Although some CNN accelerators have adopted these techniques [7][9][10][14], the impact of these techniques on design efficiency and performance has not been systematically studied. Instead, most prior works only explore the design space after the hardware architecture or the parallelism scheme has been fixed, and optimize their implementation by only tuning the design variables within their architecture. Without fully studying the loop operations of three-dimensional convolutions, it is difficult to efficiently customize the dataflow and architecture for high-throughput CNN implementations.

In this paper, we provide an in-depth analysis of the three loop optimization techniques for convolution operations and also use corresponding design variables to numerically characterize the acceleration scheme. By this means, the design objectives of CNN accelerators can be quantitatively estimated based on the configurations of the design variables. By searching through the configurations of design variables that minimize the estimated objectives, an efficient dataflow aimed at minimizing the data movements and memory access is determined. Then a corresponding architecture is also designed that fully utilizes the computing resources for high performance, which is uniform and reusable for all the layers. The proposed acceleration scheme and architecture was validated by implementing a large-scale CNN algorithm, VGG-16 [3] for image recognition [1], on the Altera Arria 10 GX 1150 FPGA, and demonstrated throughput of 645.25 GOPS and end-to-end latency of 47.97 ms.

FPGA'17, February 22–24, 2017, Monterey, CA, USA.
© 2017 ACM. ISBN 978-1-4503-4354-1/17/02…$15.00.
DOI: http://dx.doi.org/10.1145/3020078.3021736

for (no = 0; no < Nof; no ++) ──────→ Loop-4
    for (y = 0; y < Noy; y =+ S) ⎫
        for (x = 0; x < Nox; x =+ S) ⎬ ──────→ Loop-3
            for (ni = 0; ni < Nif; ni ++) ──────→ Loop-2
                for (ky = 0; ky < Nky; ky ++) ⎫
                    for (kx = 0; kx < Nkx; kx ++) ⎬ ──────→ Loop-1

$$pixel_L(no; x, y) \mathrel{+}= pixel_{L-1}(ni; x + kx, y + ky) \times weight_{L-1}(ni, no; kx, ky);$$
$$pixel_L(no; x, y) = pixel_L(no; x, y) + bias(no);$$

Figure 1. Four levels of convolution loops, where L denotes the index of convolution layer and S denotes the sliding stride.

The rest of the paper is organized as follows. Section 2 proposes the key design variables that are used to numerically characterize the loop optimization techniques for accelerating the convolution loops. Section 3 describes the quantitatively analysis and estimation of hardware accelerator objectives based on the loop optimizing design variables. Section 4 discusses the acceleration schemes used in recent state-of-the-art CNN accelerators. Section 5 presents the optimization process of minimizing the design objectives and the optimized acceleration scheme with specific design variables. A corresponding dataflow and computing architecture is proposed in Section 6 for accelerating convolution and pooling operations. Section 7 analyzes the experimental results and compares with prior works. Conclusions are presented in Section 8.

2. ACCELERATION OF CONVOLUTION LOOPS

2.1 General CNN Accelerator System

As recent deep CNN algorithms involve a large amount of data and weights, on-chip memory is usually insufficient to store the entire data, requiring external memory with ~GB capacity. Therefore, a typical CNN accelerator consists of three levels of hierarchy: 1) external memory, 2) on-chip buffers, and 3) register files and processing engines (PEs). The basic flow is to fetch data and weights from external memory to on-chip buffer, and then feed them into registers and PEs. After the PE computation completes, results are transferred back to on-chip buffers and to the external memory if necessary, which will be used as the next layer inputs.

2.2 Convolution Loops

Convolution is the main operation in CNN algorithms, which involves three-dimensional multiply and accumulate (MAC) operations of input feature maps and convolution kernel weights. Convolution is comprised of four levels of loops as shown in the pseudo codes in Figure 1 and illustrated in Figure 2. To efficiently map and perform the convolution loops, three loop optimization techniques [7][17], namely, loop unrolling, loop tiling and loop interchange, are employed to customize the computation and communication patterns of the accelerator with three levels of memory hierarchy.

Loop unrolling determines the parallelism scheme of certain convolution loops, and thus the required size of registers and PEs. Loop tiling determines the required capacity of on-chip buffers. It divides the loops into multiple blocks, and the data of the executing block are read from external memory and stored in on-chip buffers. Loop interchange determines the computation order of the four loops and thus affects the dataflow between the adjacent levels of memory hierarchy.

2.3 Loop Optimization and Design Variables

As shown in Figure 2, multiple parameters are used to describe the dimensions of the feature and kernel maps of each convolution layer for a given CNN model. For the given set of parameters, the hardware design variables of loop unrolling and loop tiling will determine the acceleration factor and hardware footprint. All parameters and variables used in this work are listed in Table 1.

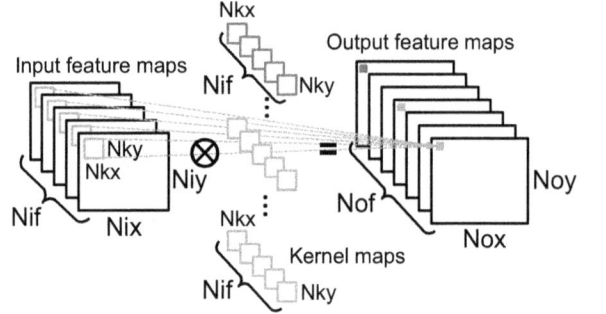

Figure 2. Convolution operation and its parameters.

The width and height of one kernel window is described by (Nkx, Nky). (Nix, Niy) and (Nox, Noy) define the width and height of one input and output feature map, respectively. Nif and Nof denote the number of input and output feature maps, respectively. The loop unrolling design variables are (Pkx, Pky), Pif, (Pox, Poy), and Pof, which denote the number of parallel computations along different feature or kernel map dimensions. The loop tiling design variables are (Tkx, Tky), Tif, (Tox, Toy), and Tof, which represent the portion of data of the four loops stored in local or on-chip buffers. The constraints of these parameters and variables are given by $1 \leq P* \leq T* \leq N*$, where N*, T* and P* denote any parameter or variable that has a prefix of capital N, T and P, respectively. For

Table 1. Convolution Loop Parameters and Design Variables

	Kernel Window (width/height)		Input Feature Map (width/height)		Output Feature Map (width/height)		# of Input Feature Maps	# of Output Feature Maps
Convolution Loops	Loop-1		Loop-3		Loop-3		Loop-2	Loop-4
Convolution Dimensions	Nkx	Nky	Nix	Niy	Nox	Noy	Nif	Nof
Loop Tiling	*Tkx*	*Tky*	*Tix*	*Tiy*	*Tox*	*Toy*	*Tif*	*Tof*
Loop Unrolling	*Pkx*	*Pky*	*Pix*	*Piy*	*Pox*	*Poy*	*Pif*	*Pof*

instance, $1 \leq Pkx \leq Tkx \leq Nkx$. By default, $P*$, $T*$ and $N*$ are applied to all convolution layers.

The relationship of input and output variables can be computed by Equations (1)-(3), where S is the stride of the sliding window and the zero padding size is included in Nix, Niy, Tix and Tiy.

$$Nix = (Nox - 1)S + Nkx$$
$$Niy = (Noy - 1)S + Nky \quad (1)$$

$$Tix = (Tox - 1)S + Nkx$$
$$Tiy = (Toy - 1)S + Nky \quad (2)$$

$$Pix = Pox$$
$$Piy = Poy \quad (3)$$

The parameters or variables ($N*$, $T*$, $P*$) determine the configurations of the three levels of memory hierarchy from external memory to on-chip buffers to registers and PEs.

2.3.1 Loop Unrolling

As illustrated in Figure 3, unrolling different convolution loops directs parallelization of different computations, which affects the optimal PE array architecture with respect to the data reuse opportunities and memory access patterns.

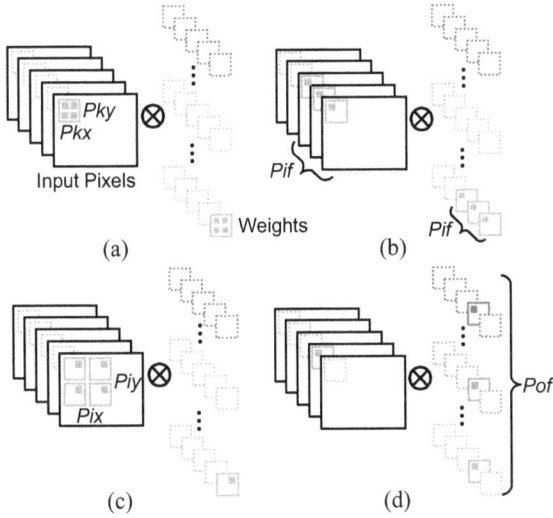

Figure 3. Loop unrolling: (a) unroll Loop-1; (b) unroll Loop-2; (c) unroll Loop-3; (d) unroll Loop-4.

Loop-1 unrolled (Figure 3(a)): in this case, the inner product of $Pkx \times Pky$ pixels and weights from different (x, y) locations in the same feature and kernel map are computed every cycle. This inner product requires an adder tree with fan-in $Pkx \times Pky$ to sum the $Pkx \times Pky$ parallel multiplication results, and an accumulator to add the adder tree output with the previous partial sum.

Loop-2 unrolled (Figure 3(b)): in every cycle, Pif number of pixels/weights from Pif different feature/kernel maps at the same (x, y) location are required to compute the inner product. The inner product operation results in the same computing structure as in unrolling Loop-1 but with a different adder tree fan-in of Pif.

Loop-3 unrolled (Figure 3(c)): in every cycle, $Pix \times Piy$ number of pixels from different (x, y) locations in the same feature map are multiplied with the identical weight, or this weight can be reused by $Pix \times Piy$ times. Since the $Pix \times Piy$ parallel multiplication contributes to independent $Pix \times Piy$ output pixels, $Pix \times Piy$ accumulators are used to serially accumulate the multiplier outputs and no adder tree is needed.

Loop-4 unrolled (Figure 3(d)): in every cycle, one pixel is multiplied with Pof weights at the same (x, y) location but from Pof

different kernel maps, and this pixel is reused by Pof times. The computing structure is identical to the case of unrolling Loop-3 using Pof multipliers and accumulators and no adder tree.

The unrolling variable value of the four convolution loops collectively determines the total number of parallel MAC operations as well as the number of required multipliers (Pm):

$$Pm = Pkx \times Pky \times Pif \times Pix \times Piy \times Pof. \quad (4)$$

2.3.2 Loop Tiling

On-chip memory of FPGAs is not always large enough to store the entire data of deep CNN algorithms altogether. Therefore, it is reasonable to use denser external DRAMs to store the weights and the intermediate pixel results of all layers.

Loop tiling is used to divide the entire data into multiple blocks, which can be fit into the on-chip buffers. With proper assignments of the loop tiling size, the locality of data can be increased to reduce the number of external memory accesses, which incurs long latency and high power consumption. The loop tiling sets the lower bound on the required on-chip buffer size. The required size of input pixel buffer is $Tix \times Tiy \times Tif \times$ (pixel_datawidth). The size of weight buffer is $Tkx \times Tky \times Tif \times Tof \times$ (weight_datawidth). The size of output pixel buffer is $Tox \times Toy \times Tof \times$ (pixel_datawidth).

2.3.3 Loop Interchange

Loop interchange determines the sequential computation order of the four convolution loops. There are two kinds of loop interchange, namely intra-tiling and inter-tiling loop orders. Intra-tiling loop order determines the pattern of data movements from on-chip buffer to register files or PEs. Inter-tiling loop order determines the data movement from external memory to on-chip buffer. The innermost loop is computed first and the outermost loop is computed at the end. Loops that are fully unrolled within the tiling block ($P* = T*$) are set to be the innermost intra-tiling loops by default. Loops with tiling size covering the full loop dimension ($T* = N*$) are the innermost inter-tiling loops by default.

3. ANALYSIS ON DESIGN OBJECTIVES OF CNN ACCELERATOR

In this section, we provide a quantitative analysis of the impact of the loop design variables ($P*$ and $T*$) on the following design objectives that our CNN accelerator aims to minimize:

1) *Computing latency* depends strongly on the loop unrolling factors $P*$, but also be affected by inefficient utilization of PEs and external memory transactions.
2) The requirement of *partial sum storage* is mainly determined by the order of loop computation. The earlier the final pixel output can be obtained, the fewer the number of partial sums that needs to be stored.
3) To reduce *the number of on-chip buffer accesses*, the pixels and weights fetched from the on-chip buffer need to be reused as much as possible, which is largely determined by the loop unrolling strategy.
4) *The number of external memory accesses* primarily relies on the size of on-chip buffers, which is determined by the loop tiling variables $T*$.

3.1 Computing Latency

The number of multiplication operations per layer (Nm) is

$$Nm = Nif \times Nkx \times Nky \times Nof \times Nox \times Noy. \quad (5)$$

Ideally, the number of computing cycles per layer should be Nm/Pm. However, for different loop unrolling and tiling sizes, the multipliers cannot necessarily be fully utilized for every convolution dimension.

The number of actual computing cycles per layer (#_cycles) is

$$\#\_cycles = \#inter\text{-}tiling\_cycles \times \#intra\text{-}tiling\_cycles, \qquad (6)$$

where

$$\#inter\text{-}tiling\_cycles =$$
$$\lceil Nif/Tif \rceil \lceil Nkx/Tkx \rceil \lceil Nky/Tky \rceil \lceil Nof/Tof \rceil \lceil Nox/Tox \rceil \lceil Noy/Toy \rceil, \qquad (7)$$

$$\#intra\text{-}tiling\_cycles =$$
$$\lceil Tif/Pif \rceil \lceil Tkx/Pkx \rceil \lceil Tky/Pky \rceil \lceil Tof/Pof \rceil \lceil Tox/Pox \rceil \lceil Toy/Poy \rceil. \qquad (8)$$

Here we assume that the multipliers receive input data continuously without idle cycles. If the ratio of N* to T* or T* to P* is not an integer, the multipliers or the external memory transactions are not fully utilized. In addition to considering computing latency, memory transfer delay must also be considered for the overall system latency.

3.2 Partial Sum Storage

A partial sum (psum) is the intermediate result of the inner product operation that needs to be accumulated over several cycles to obtain one final output data. Therefore, partial sums need to be stored in memory for the next few cycles and sometimes have to be moved between PEs. An efficient acceleration strategy has to minimize the number of partial sums and process them locally as soon as possible to reduce data movements.

The flow chart to calculate the number of partial sums stored in memory (#psum) is shown in Figure 4. To obtain one final output pixel, we need to finish Loop-1 and Loop-2. Therefore, if both Loop-1 and Loop-2 are fully unrolled, there are no partial sums that need to be stored. If the loop tile size can cover all pixels and weights used in Loop-1 (Tkx = Nkx & Tky = Nky) and Loop-2 (Tif = Nif), then the partial sums can be consumed within this tile as described in Equations (4.2) – (4.5) inside Figure 4. In this case, the number of partial sums, determined by P* or T*, is small and can be stored in local registers (Equation (4.2)) or at most in on-chip buffers (Equation (4.3)). If the loop tile cannot include all data for Loop-1 and Loop-2, partial sums from one tile need to be stored in on-chip or off-chip memory until it is consumed by another tile as in Equations (4.6) – (4.9) inside Figure 4. In this case, the partial sums need to be stored at least in on-chip buffers (Equation (4.6)) or even in external memory (Equation (4.7)). The loop computing order also affects the number of partial sums, and the earlier Loop-1 and Loop-2 are computed, the fewer are the number of partial sums. The requirement to store partial sums in different levels of memory hierarchy significantly worsens data movements and associated energy cost [6], since partial sums involve both read and write memory operations and typically require higher precision than pixels and weights.

3.3 Data Reuse

Reusing pixels and weights reduces the number of read operations of on-chip buffers. There are mainly two types of data reuse: spatial reuse and temporal reuse. *Spatial reuse* means that, after reading data from on-chip buffers, a single pixel or weight is used for multiple parallel multipliers within one clock cycle. On the other hand, *temporal reuse* means that a single pixel or weight is used for multiple consecutive clock cycles.

Having Pm parallel multiplications per cycle requires Pm pixels and Pm weights to be fed into the multipliers. The number of distinct weights required per cycle is:

$$Pwt = Pof \times Pif \times Pkx \times Pky \qquad (9)$$

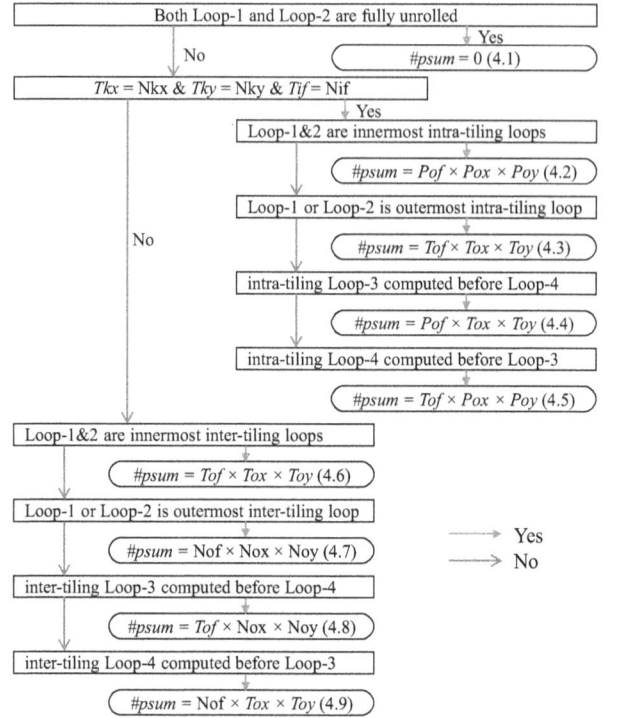

Figure 4. Flow chart that determines the total number of partial sums that needs to be stored in memory.

If Loop-1 is not unrolled (Pkx = 1, Pky = 1), the number of distinct pixels required per cycle (Ppx) is:

$$Ppx = Pif \times Pix \times Piy \qquad (10)$$

Otherwise, Ppx is:

$$Ppx = Pif \times ((Pix\text{-}1)S + Pkx) \times ((Piy\text{-}1)S + Pky) \qquad (11)$$

Note that 'distinct' only means that the pixels/weights are from different feature/kernel map locations and their values may be the same. The number of times a weight is spatially reused in one cycle is:

$$Reuse\_wt = Pm / Pwt = Pix \times Piy \qquad (12)$$

where the spatial reuse of weights is realized by unrolling Loop-3 (Pix > 1 or Piy > 1). The number of times of a pixel is spatially reused in one cycle (Reuse_px) is:

$$Reuse\_px = Pm / Ppx \qquad (13)$$

If Loop-1 is not unrolled, Reuse_px is:

$$Reuse\_px = Pof \qquad (14)$$

otherwise, Reuse_px is:

$$Reuse\_px = \frac{Pof \times Pkx \times Pky \times Pix \times Piy}{((Pix-1)S + Pkx) \times ((Piy-1)S + Pky)} \qquad (15)$$

The spatial reuse of pixels is realized by either unrolling Loop-4 (Pof > 1) or unrolling both Loop-1 and Loop-3 together. Only unrolling Loop-1 (Pix=1, Piy=1) or only unrolling Loop-3 (Pkx=1, Pky=1) hampers reusing pixels, and Reuse_px = Pof.

If Loop-3 is the innermost intra-tiling loop, the weights can be reused for Tox×Toy/(Pox×Poy) consecutive cycles. If Loop-4 is the innermost intra-tiling loop, the pixels can be reused for Tof/Pof consecutive cycles.

3.4 Access of On-chip Buffer

With the data reuse, the number of on-chip buffer accesses can be significantly reduced. Without any data reuse, the total read operations from on-chip buffers for both pixels and weights are Nm, as every multiplication needs one pixel and one weight. With data reuse, the total number of read operations from on-chip buffers for weights becomes:

$$\#read\_wt = \text{Nm} / Reuse\_wt \qquad (16)$$

and the total number of read operations of buffers for pixels is:

$$\#read\_px = \text{Nm} / Reuse\_px \qquad (17)$$

If the final output pixels cannot be obtained within one tile, their partial sums are stored in on-chip buffers. The number of write and read operations to/from on-chip buffers for partial sums per cycle is $2 \times Pof \times Pox \times Poy$, where all partial sums generated by Loop-1 (Pkx, Pky) and Loop-2 (Pif) are already summed together right after multiplications. The total number of write and read operations to/from on-chip buffers for partial sums is:

$$\#wr\_rd\_psum = \#\_cycles \times (2 \times Pof \times Pox \times Poy) \qquad (18)$$

The number of times output pixels are written to on-chip buffers (i.e. $\#write\_px$) is identical to the total number of output pixels in the given CNN model. Finally, the total number of on-chip buffer accesses is:

$$\#buffer\_access = \\ \#read\_px + \#read\_wt + \#wr\_rd\_psum + \#write\_px \qquad (19)$$

3.5 Access of External Memory

In our analysis, both the weights and intermediate results of pixels are assumed to be stored in external memory (DRAM), which is a necessity when mapping large-scale CNNs on moderate FPGAs. The costs of DRAM accesses are higher latency and energy than block memory accesses [6][15][16], and therefore it is important to reduce the number of external memory accesses to improve the overall performance and energy efficiency. The minimum number of DRAM accesses is achieved by having sufficiently large on-chip buffers and proper loop computing orders, such that every pixel and weight needs to be transferred from DRAM only once. Otherwise, the same pixel or weight has to be read multiple times from DRAM to be consumed for multiple tiles.

The flow chart to estimate the number of DRAM accesses is shown in Figure 5, where $\#DRAM\_px$ and $\#DRAM\_wt$ denote the number of DRAM access of one input pixel and one weight, respectively. After fetched out of DRAM, all data should be exhaustedly utilized before being kicked out of the buffer. Therefore, if the tile size or the on-chip buffer can fully cover either all input pixels or all weights of one layer, the minimum DRAM access can be achieved as Equation (5.8) inside Figure 5. By computing Loop 3 first, weights stored in buffer are reused and $\#DRAM\_wt$ is reduced as in Equation (5.1) and (5.5). Similarly, by computing Loop-4 first, pixels can be reused to reduce $\#DRAM\_px$ as in Equation (5.3) and (5.6). However, computing Loop-3 or Loop-4 first may postpone the computation of Loop-1 or Loop-2, which would lead to a large number of partial sums.

The DRAM access of output pixels is not considered in the analysis because it is constant as every output pixel is written to DRAM only once. As Nkx > S, there are overlaps of pixels on the boundary of two tiles, and these pixels may be read twice by the two tiles. Since the number of the additional read is negligible, we do not include them in the analysis.

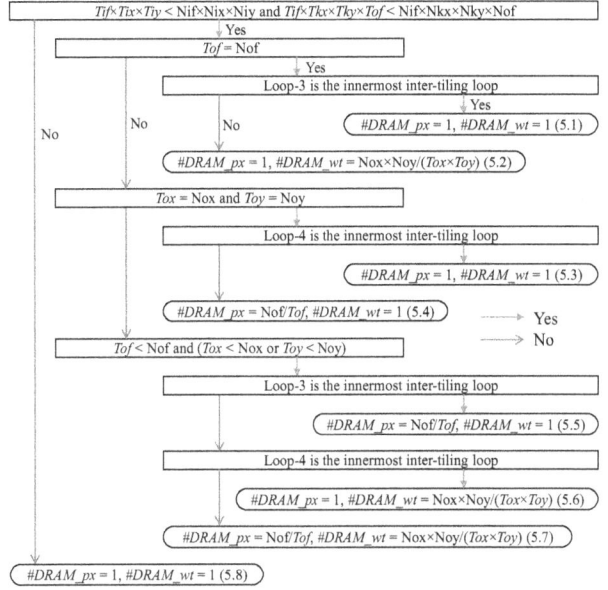

Figure 5. Flow chart that determines the average number of DRAM accesses of a single pixel and a single weight.

4. LOOP OPTIMIZATION IN RELATED WORKS

In this section, the acceleration schemes of the state-of-the-art hardware CNN accelerators are compared. The loop unrolling strategy of current designs can be categorized into the four types:

(A) Unroll Loop-1, Loop-2, Loop-4 [9][10][12][14]
(B) Unroll Loop-2, Loop-4 [7][11]
(C) Unroll Loop-1, Loop-3 [5][6]
(D) Unroll Loop-3, Loop-4 [13]

By unrolling Loop-1, Loop-2 and Loop-4 in type-(A), parallelism is employed in kernel maps, input feature maps and output feature maps. However, kernel window size (Nkx × Nky) is normally very small (≤11×11) so that it cannot provide sufficient parallelism and other loops need to be further unrolled. A more challenging problem is that the size of kernel window may vary considerably across different convolution layers in a given CNN model (e.g., AlexNet [2], ResidualNet [4]), which may cause workload imbalance and inefficient utilization of the PEs. To address this, PEs need to be configured differently for layers with different kernel window sizes [8], which increases the control complexity.

In type-(C), every row in the kernel window is fully unrolled (Pkx = Nkx) and Loop-3 is also partially unrolled [5][6]. By this means, pixels can be reused by the overlapping caused by Loop-1 and Loop-3 as in Equation (15), and weight reuse can also be realized by unrolling Loop-3 as in Equation (12). However, Loop-4 is not unrolled and further pixel reuse cannot be achieved. The issue caused by unrolling Loop-1 also affects type-(C).

In type-(A) and type-(B), Loop-3 is not unrolled, which implies that weights cannot be reused. Type-(B) only unrolls Loop-2 and Loop-4, but Nif × Nof of the first convolution layer is usually small (≤3×96) and cannot provide sufficient parallelism.

In type-(D), both Loop-3 and Loop-4 are unrolled so that both pixels and weights can be reused. In addition, Nox×Noy×Nof (≥ 13×13×64) is very large across all the convolution layers in AlexNet [2] and VGG [3] so that high level of parallelism can be achieved even for largest FPGA available with ~3,600 DSP blocks. By this means, a uniform configuration and structure of PEs can be applied for all the convolution layers. [13] unrolled Loop-3 and Loop-4, however the choice and impact of such parallelism scheme is not quantitatively analyzed.

Loop tiling has been used in prior hardware CNN accelerators to fit the large-scale CNN models into limited on-chip buffers. However, only a few prior works [10][13] have shown their tiling configurations that determine the on-chip buffer size, and the trade-off between the loop tiling size and the number of external memory accesses is not explored. The tiling size in [13] does not cover Loop-1 and Loop-2, e.g., $Tkx = Tky = Tif = 1$, which could significantly increase the number and movements of partial sums.

The impact of loop interchange has not been rigorously studied in prior works, but it can greatly impact the number of partial sums as well as the resulting data movements and memory access.

5. PROPOSED ACCELERATION SCHEME

Based on the design objectives and analysis in Section 3, the optimization process of our acceleration scheme is presented in this section, which includes appropriate selection of the convolution loop design variables.

5.1 Minimizing Computing Latency

We set variables P^* to be the common factors of T^* for all the convolution layers to fully utilize PEs, and T^* to be the common factors of N^* to make full use of external memory transactions. For CNN models with only small common factors, it is recommended to set $\lceil N^*/T^* \rceil - N^*/T^*$ and $\lceil T^*/P^* \rceil - T^*/P^*$ as small as possible to minimize the inefficiency caused by the difference in sizes of CNN models. Based on the number of DSP blocks in our Arria 10 FPGA (= 1,518), we target the number of parallel multiplications Pm to be around 3,000 (one DSP block supports two 18-bit×18-bit multiplications), to fully utilize the available computing resources and minimize the latency.

5.2 Minimizing Partial Sum Storage

To reduce the number and movements of partial sums, both Loop-1 and Loop-2 should be computed as early as possible or unrolled as much as possible. To avoid the drawback of unrolling Loop-1 as discussed in Section 4 and maximize the data reuse as discussed in Section 3.3, we decide to unroll Loop-3 ($Pox>1$ or $Poy>1$) and Loop-4 ($Pof>1$). By this means, we cannot attain zero partial sum storage as Equation (4.1) inside Figure 4.

Constrained by $1 \leq P^* \leq T^* \leq N^*$, the least number of partial sum storage is achieved by Equation (4.2) among Equations (4.2) – (4.9) inside Figure 4. To satisfy the condition for Equation (4.2), we serially compute Loop-1 and Loop-2 first and ensure the required data of Loop-1 and Loop-2 are buffered, i.e., $Tkx = Nkx$, $Tky = Nky$ and $Tif = Nif$. Therefore, we can achieve $Pof \times Pox \times Poy$ number of partial sums, which can be retained in local registers with minimum data movements.

5.3 Minimizing Access of On-chip Buffer

The number of on-chip buffer accesses is minimized by unrolling Loop-3 to reuse weights as shown in Equation (12) and unrolling Loop-4 to reuse pixels as shown in Equation (14). By keeping the data used in Loop-1 in local registers, the sliding window across overlapped pixels can also be reused, similar to Equation (15), which unrolls both Loop-1 and Loop-3. As our partial sums are kept on local registers, they do not add overhead to the buffer access and storage.

5.4 Minimizing Access of External Memory

As we first compute Loop-1 and Loop-2 to reduce partial sums, we cannot achieve the minimum number of DRAM access described in Equation (5.1) and (5.3) inside Figure 5, where neither the pixels nor the weights are fully buffered for one convolution layer. Therefore, we can only attain the minimum DRAM access by assigning sufficient buffer size for either all pixels or all weights of each layer as in Equation (5.8) inside Figure 5.

Then, the design optimization of minimizing the on-chip buffer size while having minimum DRAM access is formulated as below:

$$\text{minimize } bits\_BUF\_px\_wt$$
$$\text{subject to } \#Tile\_px_L = 1 \text{ or } \#Tile\_wt_L = 1 \quad (20)$$
$$\text{with } \forall L \in [1, \#CONVs],$$

where $\#Tile\_px_L$ and $\#Tile\_wt_L$ denote the number of tiling blocks for input pixels and weights of layer L, respectively, and $\#CONVs$ is the number of convolution layers. $bits\_BUF\_px\_wt$ is the sum of pixel buffer size ($bits\_BUF\_px$) and weight buffer size ($bits\_BUF\_wt$), which are given by,

$$bits\_BUF\_px\_wt = bits\_BUF\_px + bits\_BUF\_wt. \quad (21)$$

Both pixel and weight buffers need to be large enough to cover the data in one tiling block for all the convolution layers. This is expressed as

$$bits\_BUF\_px = \text{MAX}(words\_px_L) \times \text{pixel\_datawidth}$$
$$\text{with } L \in [1, \#CONVs] \quad (22)$$

$$bits\_BUF\_wt = \text{MAX}(words\_wt_L) \times \text{weight\_datawidth}$$
$$\text{with } L \in [1, \#CONVs], \quad (23)$$

where $words\_px_L$ and $words\_wt_L$ denote the number of pixels and weights of one tiling block in layer L, respectively. These are expressed in terms of loop tiling variables as follows.

$$words\_px_L = Tix_L \times Tiy_L \times Tif_L + Tox_L \times Toy_L \times Tof_L \quad (24)$$
$$words\_wt_L = Tof_L \times Tif_L \times Tkx_L \times Tky_L \quad (25)$$

where $words\_px_L$ is comprised of both input and output pixels. The number of tiles in Equation (20) is also determined by T^* variables,

$$\#Tile\_px_L = \lceil Nif_L/Tif_L \rceil \times \lceil Nox_L/Tox_L \rceil \times \lceil Noy_L/Toy_L \rceil \quad (26)$$
$$\#Tile\_wt_L =$$
$$\lceil Nkx_L/Tkx_L \rceil \times \lceil Nky_L/Tky_L \rceil \times \lceil Nif_L/Tif_L \rceil \times \lceil Nof_L/Tof_L \rceil \quad (27)$$

By solving Equation (20), we can find an optimal configuration of T^* variables that result in minimum DRAM access and on-chip buffer size. However, since we have already set $Tkx = Nkx$, $Tky = Nky$, $Tif = Nif$ as in Section 5.2, we can only achieve a sub-optimal solution by tuning Tox, Toy and Tof, resulting in larger buffer size requirement. If the available on-chip memory is sufficient, we set $Tox = Nox$ so that an entire row can be stored in the on-chip buffer to benefit the DMA transactions with continuous data.

Finally, we have to solve Equation (20) by searching Toy and Tof, because it has a non-linear objective function and constraints with integer variables. Since Toy and Tof in VGG-16 consist of 2 × #CONVs = 26 variables and some variables can have up to 6 candidate values constrained by $T^*/P^* =$ power of 2 and $T^* \leq N^*$, the total number of Toy and Tof configurations is 7.2×10^{13}, which becomes an enormous solution space. Therefore, we only randomly sample ~3.6×10^9 configurations, which takes the MATLAB scripts to run for ~5 hours on two desktops. The obtained minimum solution for $bits\_BUF\_px\_wt$ results in an on-chip buffer size of 20.8 Mbits with pixel_datawidth = 16 and weight_datawidth = 8. As 20.8 Mbits is already <50% of our FPGA on-chip RAM capacity, we did not continue the optimizing process that may lead to a better solution than 20.8 Mbits.

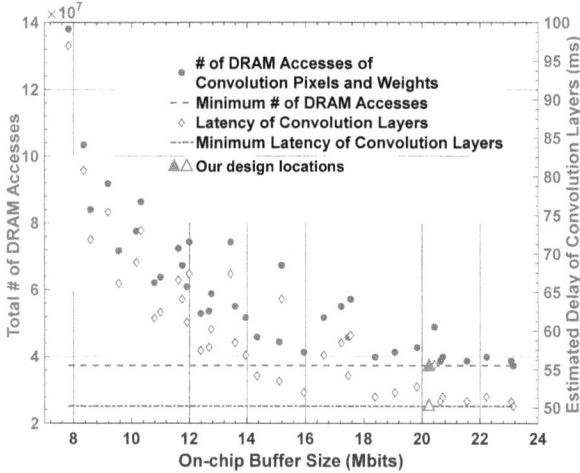

Figure 6. As a function of on-chip buffer size, the total number of DRAM accesses and estimated delay of convolution layers are shown.

If the configurations of Tkx = Nkx, Tky = Nky, Tif = Nif and Tox = Noy are kept, a smaller on-chip buffer can be used but the number of DRAM accesses will increase, as illustrated in Figure 6. The number of DRAM accesses in Figure 6 are obtained by randomly sampling ~5.1×10^9 Toy and Tof configurations using ~9 hours on the same desktops, and only the minimum result is kept for a specific interval of buffer size. The estimated theoretical delay of convolution layers in Figure 6 includes computing latency with 3,136 parallel MAC operations at 150MHz and DRAM transfer delay, which we assumed as 0.46ns per DRAM access. The minimum on-chip buffer requirement is 7.8 Mbits by minimizing Toy and Tof. If 7.8 Mbits still cannot meet the on-chip memory capacity, Equation (20) should be solved without the Tox = Nox constraint, or change the loop tiling strategy.

5.5 Optimized Loop Design Variables

According to the aforementioned optimization process, we propose an acceleration scheme for a high-performance and low-communication CNN accelerator.

5.5.1 Loop Unrolling

For all the convolution layers, we set uniform unrolling factors as Pkx = 1, Pky = 1, Pif = 1, Pox = 14, Poy =14 and Pof = 16, which enables Pm = 3,136 parallel multiplications, based on Section 5.1 5.2 and 5.3. By setting P^* to be constant across all the convolution layers, a uniform structure and mapping of PEs can be realized to reduce the architecture complexity.

5.5.2 Loop Tiling

For loop tiling, we set Tkx = Nkx, Tky = Nky, Tif = Nif as discussed in Section 5.2 so that data used in Loop-1 and Loop-2 are all buffered and Tox = Nox to benefit DMA transaction. Details of Toy and Tof are described in Section 5.4.

5.5.3 Loop Interchange

For loop interchange, we first serially compute Loop-1 and then Loop-2 as described in Section 5.2. Finally, we compute Loop-3 and Loop-4, where the exact computation order of these two loops does not have a pronounced impact on the cost, based on our P^* and T^* choices.

6. PROPOSED CNN ACCELERATOR

A hardware CNN accelerator with a new dataflow and PE architecture is proposed to implement the optimized acceleration scheme in Section 5.5 and minimize latency, on-/off-chip memory access, and data communication.

6.1 Convolution Dataflow

The dataflow of input pixels from on-chip buffers to local register arrays to PEs is shown in Figure 7. Unrolling Loop-3 provides us the opportunity to reuse overlapped input pixels by kernel window sliding. A register array is designed to reuse these data by data movements between registers similar to the dataflow in [6], which is realized by unrolling both Loop-1 and Loop-3.

The numbers in Figure 7 (e.g., 14) denote the (y, x) location of pixels (e.g., (y=1, x=4)) in the input feature map. In this example, Pox = 3, Poy = 3, and the number of input pixel buffer and register arrays equals Poy. Pixels of one tiling block (Tix = 8, Tiy = 6) are first stored in input pixel buffers row-by-row as shown in blue color. At clock cycle 0, pixels at address 0 are loaded into the corresponding registers as shown by blue dashed box to blue solid box with zero padding masked. With Nkx = Nky = 3 in this example, pixels are shifted within register arrays at cycle 1,2,4,5,7,8 as shown by green arrows, where sliding overlapped pixels are reused. At cycle 3 and 6, new pixels are transferred from Input Pixel BUF 1 and BUF 2 to the 3rd register array (R3*), respectively, and old pixels are shifted and reused across register arrays (R3*→R2*, R2*→R1*) as depicted by arrows from dashed yellow box to solid yellow boxes. For simplicity's sake, not every data movement is shown in Figure 7. After Nkx×Nky cycles, we complete one kernel window sliding (Loop-1) and move to the next input feature map with the same dataflow. After Nkx×Nky×Nif cycles, both Loop-1 and Loop-2 are completed and we obtain $Pox×Poy×Pof$ final output pixels. The MAC units can continuously receive and compute input data from buffers without idle cycles. This dataflow is scalable to Nkx and Nky by only changing the control logic for sequential computing. As we judiciously do not unroll Loop-1, our dataflow has no partial sum movements between MAC units, and input pixels are also reused by Pof MAC units as shown in Figure 8 by unrolling Loop-4, both of which are not achieved in [6].

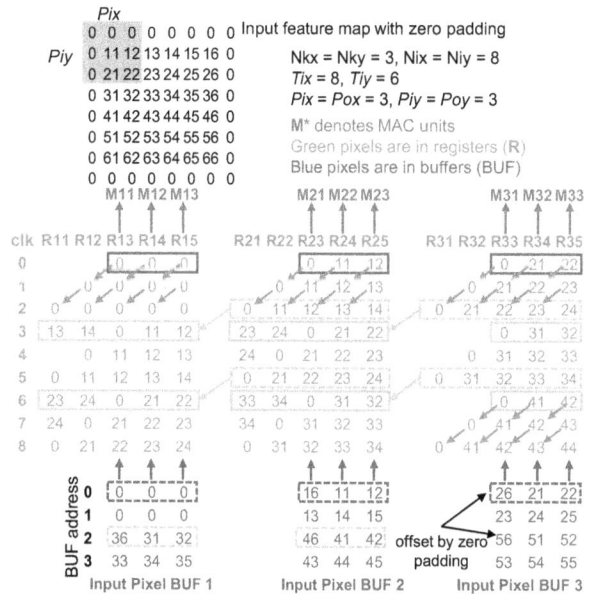

Figure 7. Dataflow of input pixels in convolution layers.

6.2 Convolution PE Architecture

The computing architecture of convolution layers is designed according to the proposed dataflow shown in Figure 8, which is comprised of $Pox \times Poy \times Pof$ PEs and Poy input pixel register arrays. Every PE in our architecture is an independent MAC unit consisting of one multiplier followed by an accumulator. As Loop-1 and Loop-2 are not unrolled, no adder tree is needed to sum the multiplier outputs. The partial sum is consumed inside each MAC unit, such that the data movements of partial sums are minimized. Pixels read from input pixel buffers are shared by Pof MAC units and sliding overlapped pixels can also be reused within the register arrays. Every input pixel buffer is connected with its corresponding register array, except for the first two buffers that are also connected to the Poy-th register array determined by the dataflow. Weights read from weight buffers are shared by $Pox \times Poy$ MAC units. The proposed architecture is implemented with parameterized Verilog codes and is highly scalable to different CNN models in FPGAs or even ASICs by modifying design variables such as Pox, Poy and Pof.

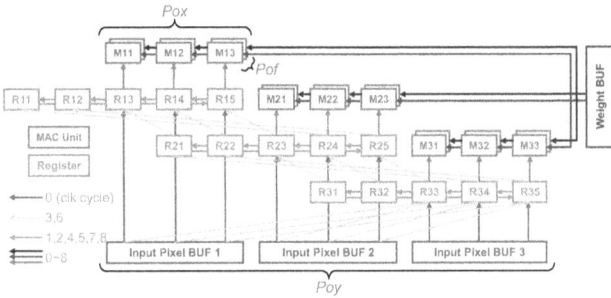

Figure 8. Convolution acceleration architecture.

After the completion of Loop-1 and Loop-2, the partial sums need to be added with biases as in Figure (1) to obtain the final output pixels. Therefore, every $Nkx \times Nky \times Nif$ cycles, MAC units output the partial sums into the adders to add with biases. Since $Nkx \times Nky \times Nif > Poy$ for all the layers, we serialize the $Pox \times Poy \times Pof$ MAC outputs into Poy cycles. Then, we only need $Pox \times Pof$ adders to add the biases in parallel, and the bandwidth of output pixel buffer can also be reduced by a factor of Poy. The bias adder results are truncated to be pixel_datawidth, and the location of the retained bits inside the bias adder results are moved according to the range of the data values in different layers, which allows dynamically adjusting the decimal points to achieve higher effective precision with the same data width. The rectified linear unit (ReLU) activation operation is performed after truncation with a 2-to-1 multiplexer, which uses the sign bit as the select signal and the truncated pixel and zero as the inputs. Finally, the outputs of ReLU are written into Pof output pixel buffers, where one buffer continuously stores $Pox \times Poy$ pixels on the same feature map. These processes after MAC compuations are not included in Figure 8.

6.3 Pooling Dataflow and PE Architecture

Pooling is commonly used to reduce the feature map dimension by replacing pixels within a kernel window (e.g., 2×2, 3×3) by their maximum or average value. Figure 9 shows the dataflow and PE architecture of the pooling layers. The output pixels from previous convolution layers are stored row-by-row in the output pixel buffers. As pooling operation only need pixels, after one tiling of convolution finished, we directly compute pooling with pixels read from output pixel buffers to eliminate the access of external memory. The unrolling factors of all the pooling layers are the same as the convolution layers, except for $Poy = 1$, as the width of output pixel buffer is only Pox. By this means, we can enable $Pox \times Pof$ parallel pooling operations, which is large enough considering much less operations in pooling layers compared to convolution layers. Four register arrays are used to reshape the pooling input pixels and hide the buffer read latency. At clock cycle 0 and 1, pixels at address 0 and 1 are loaded to the left and right part of both

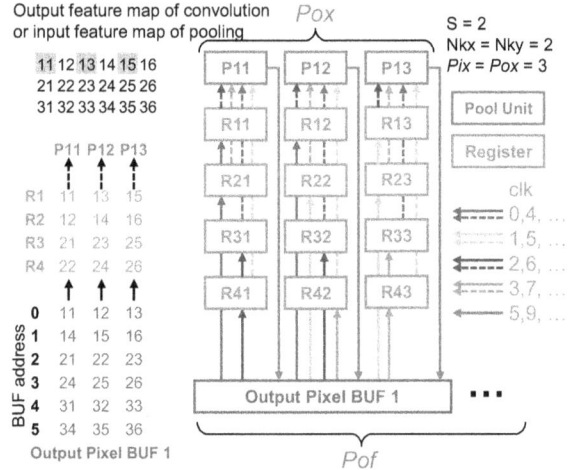

Figure 9. Pooling acceleration dataflow and architecture.

Table 2. Comparison with Previous CNN FPGA Implementations

	[13] AlexNet	[12] AlexNet	[11] AlexNet	[10] VGG	[9] VGG	[8] VGG	This work: VGG
FPGA	Virtex-7 VC 707	Virtex-7 VC709	Stratix-V GXA7	Zynq XC7Z045	Stratix-V GSD8	Virtex-7 VX690t	**Arria-10 GX 1150**
Frequency (MHz)	160	156	100	150	120	150	**150**
# Operations (GOP)	1.33	1.46	1.46	30.76	30.95	30.95	**30.95**
Number of Weights	2.33 M	60.95 M	60.95 M	50.18 M	138.3 M	138.3 M	**138.3 M**
Precision (all fixed)	32 bit	16 bit	8-16 bit	16 bit	8-16 bit	16 bit	**8-16 bit**
DSP Utilization	2,688 (96%)	2,144 (60%)	256 (100%)	780 (89%)	1,963[d]	3,600[d]	**1,518 (100%)**
Logic Utilization[a]	45K (9.2%)	274K (63%)	121K (52%)	183K (84%)	262K[d]	693K[d]	**161K (38%)**
On-chip RAM[b]	543 (53%)	956[b] (65%)	1,552 (61%)	486 (87%)	2,567[d]	1,470[d]	**1,900 (70%)**
Latency/Image (ms)	-	8×2.56[c]	12.75	224.6	262.9	151.8	**47.97**
Throughput (GOPS)	147.82	565.94	114.5	136.97	117.8	203.9	**645.25**

[a.] Xilinx FPGAs in LUTs and Altera FPGAs in ALMs
[b.] Xilinx FPGAs in BRAMs (36 Kb) and Altera FPGAs in M20K RAMs (20 Kb)
[c.] The reported delay of one pipeline stage is 2.56 ms and the number of pipeline stages equals 8.
[d.] The resource utilization is not reported in the original papers. The total available resources of the used FPGAs are listed.

the 1st (R1*) and 2nd (R2*) register arrays, respectively. The operations for 3rd (R3*) and 4th (R4*) register arrays are similar. Aided by this dual buffer technique, pixels can be continuously fed into PEs without idle cycles. The PEs for max-pooling are made of comparators. The outputs of pooling are written back to the output pixel buffers and then transferred to the external memory.

6.4 Fully-connected Layers

The inner-product layer or fully-connected (FC) layer is a special form of the convolution layer with $Nkx = Nky = Nox = Noy = 1$, or there are no Loop-1 and Loop-3. Therefore, we only unroll Loop-4 and reuse the same PE array used in convolution layers for all the fully-connected layers. Contrary to convolution layers, FC layers normally have large amount of weights but small amount of operations, which makes the throughput of FC layers primarily bounded by the off-chip communication speed. Due to this, dual FC weight buffers are used to overlap the inner-product computation with off-chip communication. FC layer output pixels are directly stored in on-chip buffers as their size is small (<20 KB).

7. EXPERIMENTAL RESULTS

7.1 System Setup

The proposed hardware CNN accelerator is demonstrated by implementing VGG-16 CNN model [3], which has 13 convolution layers, 5 pooling layers, 3 FC layers and 138.3 million parameters. We used a Nallatech 385A board that includes two banks of 4GB DDR3L SDRAM and an Altera Arria 10 GX 1150 FPGA, which consists of 1,150K logic elements, 1,518 DSP blocks and 2,713 M20K memory blocks.

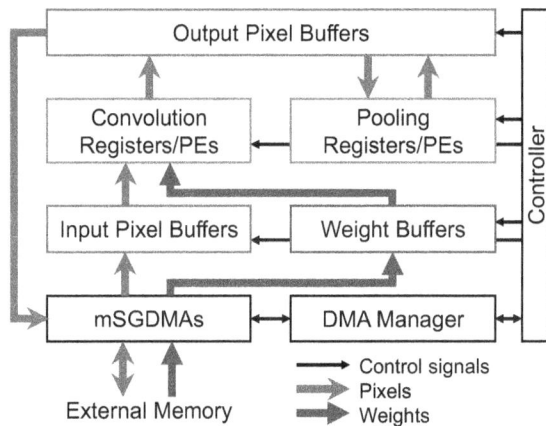

Figure 10. Top-level CNN acceleration system.

The overall CNN acceleration system on the FPGA chip shown in Figure 10 is coded in parametrized Verilog scripts and compiled by Quartus Prime synthesis tool. With two SDRAM banks, both kernel and feature maps are separated into these two banks to enable full off-chip communication. Two Modular Scatter-Gather DMA (mSGDMA) engines provided by Altera are used to simultaneously read and write from/to these two SDRAM banks. After the input images and weights are loaded into SDRAMs, the CNN acceleration process starts. When the computation of one tiling loop completes, the output pixels are transferred to SDRAM, and then the weights and pixels for the next tiling loop are loaded from SDRAM to on-chip buffers. The controller governs the iterations of the four convolution loops and the layer-by-layer sequential computation. The buffer read and write addresses are also generated by the controller.

The fixed point data representation is used with 16-bit pixels, 8-bit weights, and 30-bit partial sums. The decimal points can be dynamically adjusted according to the ranges of pixel values in different layers to fully utilize the existing data width [10][11]. By this means, the top-1 and top-5 ImageNet classification accuracy degradation is within 2% compared with software full precision implementation [8][9][10].

7.2 Analysis of Experimental Results

The performance and specifications of the CNN accelerator is summarized and compared with other CNN FPGA implementations in Table 2. In Arria 10 FPGA, one DSP block can support two 18-bit×18-bit multiplications and our Arria 10 FPGA has 1,518 DSP blocks, which can support 3,036 multiplications in parallel. Our unrolling strategy needs $Pm = Pox×Poy×Pof = 3,136$ multiplications, and the remaining 100 multipliers are implemented by logic elements. The breakdown of the processing time per image of VGG-16 model is shown in Figure 11. The computation time of convolution layers dominates the total latency by 70.0%. DMA_conv, which consumes 10.1% of the overall latency, includes the SDRAM transaction delay of convolution weights and input/output pixels. The FC computing time is hidden by FC weights transfer delay through DMA, shown as DMA_FC.

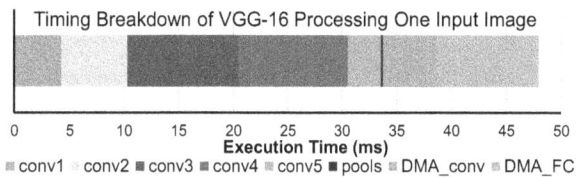

Timing Breakdown of VGG-16 Processing One Input Image

Execution Time (ms)

■ conv1 ■ conv2 ■ conv3 ■ conv4 ■ conv5 ■ pools ■ DMA_conv ■ DMA_FC

Figure 11. Latency breakdown of VGG-16 acceleration.

The breakdown of our on-chip RAM (total of 1,900 M20K blocks) utilization is: convolution pixel/weight buffers (70.1%), FC buffers (11.9%), FIFOs for clock crossing (3.1%) and DMA (11.7%). The actual M20K bits (27.2 Mbits) used for convolution buffers is larger than the optimized results of 20.8 Mbits, because the required memory depth value is not a power of 2.

The power of 385A FPGA card can only be supplied through a PCIe slot, which makes it difficult to directly measure the power consumption. Instead, we use Altera PowerPlay Power Analyzer to simulate our power consumption. The total thermal power is 21.2 W consisting of sources from DSP (3.6%), M20K (15.0%), logic cells (16%), clock (12.9%), transceiver (15.7%), I/O (13.2%) and static consumption (23.5%).

7.3 Comparison with Prior Works

The reported results from recent CNN FPGA accelerators are listed in Table 2. [13] only implements convolution layers in AlexNet and uses the similar strategy as us to unroll Loop-3 and Loop-4, which can also achieve high DSP utilization. However, their 32-bit data width forces the multipliers to use much more DSP blocks than our design. In addition, their tiling strategy is only along Loop-3 and Loop-4, which significantly postpones the acquisition of the final pixels resulting in more memory accesses and data movements of partial sums.

In [8][12], the layer-by-layer computation is pipelined using different part of one or multiple FPGAs resources. Pipelining of each layer may increase hardware utilization thus achieve high throughput by preventing computing engines from being idle caused by the imbalance of different layers. However, with the highly increasing number of convolution layers [4], it becomes very difficult to map different layers onto different resources and balance the computation among all the pipeline stages. In addition, pipelining can increase the throughput but not necessarily the latency. On the contrary, our uniform architecture can also be fully utilized by all the convolution layers and is highly scalable to be applied to other CNNs with more layers, e.g. the ResidualNet [4].

Batch computing with multiple input images is applied in [6][8][12]. The biggest advantage of this technique is to share the weights transferred from off-chip DRAM among multiple images and thus increase the throughput at the cost of increased latency per image and external memory storage of multiple images. As the DRAM transaction delay of kernel weights accounts for a signification portion (~22%) in our system latency as shown in Figure 11, batch computing could also benefit our throughput considerably by effectively hiding the DMA weight transfer delay. Benefit from batch computing and using 2,144 DSP blocks, which enables high parallelism degree, [12] also achieves high throughput of 565.94 GOPS for AlexNet.

With the optimized CNN acceleration scheme and low-communication dataflow, the proposed CNN accelerator uses uniform unrolling factors for all the convolution layers and fully utilizes all the DSP resources to achieve 3.2–5.6× throughput improvement than [8][9][10][11][13] and 3.2–5.5× less latency than prior VGG implementations [8][9][10].

8. CONCLUSION

In this paper, we present an in-depth analysis of convolution loop acceleration strategy by numerically characterizing the loop optimization techniques. The relationship between accelerator objectives and design variables are quantitatively investigated, and we provide design guidelines for an efficient acceleration strategy. A corresponding new dataflow and architecture is proposed to minimize data communication and enhance throughput. Our CNN accelerator demonstrated VGG-16 CNN model on Arria 10 FPGA, achieving 645.25 GOPS of throughput and 47.97 ms of latency per image, which outperforms all prior VGG FPGA implementations by >3.2×.

9. ACKNOWLEDGMENT

This work was supported in part by the NSF I/UCRC Center for Embedded Systems through National Science Foundation grant 1361926 and 1535669, and Samsung Advanced Institute of Technology.

10. REFERENCES

[1] O. Russakovsky, et al. ImageNet large-scale visual recognition challenge. In *Int. J. Computer Vision*, 2015.

[2] A. Krizhevsky, et al. ImageNet classification with deep convolutional neural networks. In *Neural Information Processing Systems (NIPS)*, 1097-1105, 2012.

[3] K. Simonyan, et al. Very Deep Convolutional Networks for Large-Scale Image Recognition. In *Int. Conf. Learning Representations (ICLR)*, 2015.

[4] K. He, et al. Deep residual learning for image recognition. In *IEEE Conf. on Computer Vision and Pattern Recognition (CVPR)*, 2016.

[5] Y.-H. Chen, et al. Eyeriss: An Energy-Efficient Reconfigurable Accelerator for Deep Convolutional Neural Networks. In *IEEE Int. Solid-State Circuits Conf. (ISSCC)*, 2016.

[6] Y.-H. Chen, et al. Eyeriss: A Spatial Architecture for Energy-Efficient Dataflow for Convolutional Neural Networks", In *ACM/IEEE Int. Symp. Computer Architecture (ISCA)*, 2016.

[7] C. Zhang, et al. Optimizing FPGA-based accelerator design for deep convolutional neural networks. In *ACM Int. Symp. on Field-Programmable Gate Arrays (FPGA)*, 2015.

[8] C. Zhang, et al. Energy-Efficient CNN Implementation on a Deeply Pipelined FPGA Cluster. In *ACM Int. Symp. on Low Power Electronics and Design (ISLPED)*, 326-331, 2016.

[9] N. Suda, et al. Throughput-optimized OpenCL-based FPGA accelerator for large-scale convolutional neural networks. In *Int. Symp. on Field-Programmable Gate Arrays (FPGA)*, 16-25, 2016.

[10] J. Qiu, et al. Going deeper with embedded FPGA platform for convolutional neural network. In *ACM Int. Symp. on Field-Programmable Gate Arrays (FPGA)*, 26-35, 2016.

[11] Y. Ma, et al. Scalable and Modularized RTL Compilation of Convolutional Neural Networks onto FPGA, In *Int. Conf. Field-Programmable Logic and Applications (FPL)*, 2016.

[12] H. Li, et al. A High Performance FPGA-based Accelerator for Large-Scale Convolutional Neural Networks, In *Int. Conf. Field-Programmable Logic and Applications (FPL)*, 2016.

[13] A. Rahman, et al. Efficient FPGA acceleration of Convolutional Neural Networks using logical-3D compute array. In *Design, Auto. & Test in Europe Conf. (DATE)*, 2016.

[14] M. Motamedi, et al. Design space exploration of FPGA-based Deep Convolutional Neural Networks. In *Asia and South Pacific Design Auto. Conf. (ASP-DAC)*, 2016.

[15] S. Han, et al. Deep Compression: Compressing Deep Neural Networks with Pruning, Trained Quantization and Huffman Coding. In *Int. Conf. Learning Representations (ICLR)*, 2016.

[16] S. Han, et al. EIE: Efficient Inference Engine on Compressed Deep Neural Network. In *ACM/IEEE Int. Symp. Computer Architecture (ISCA)*, 2016.

[17] D. Bacon, et al. Compiler transformations for high-performance computing. In *ACM Computing Surveys (CSUR)*, Volume 26 Issue 4, Pages 345-420, 1994.

An OpenCL™ Deep Learning Accelerator on Arria 10

Utku Aydonat, Shane O'Connell, Davor Capalija, Andrew C. Ling, Gordon R. Chiu

Intel Corporation
Toronto, Canada
utku.aydonat|shane.oconnell|davor.capalija|andrew.ling|gordon.chiu@intel.com

ABSTRACT

Convolutional neural nets (CNNs) have become a practical means to perform vision tasks, particularly in the area of image classification. FPGAs are well known to be able to perform convolutions efficiently, however, most recent efforts to run CNNs on FPGAs have shown limited advantages over other devices such as GPUs. Previous approaches on FPGAs have often been memory bound due to the limited external memory bandwidth on the FPGA device. We show a novel architecture written in OpenCL™, which we refer to as a Deep Learning Accelerator (DLA), that maximizes data reuse and minimizes external memory bandwidth. Furthermore, we show how we can use the Winograd transform to significantly boost the performance of the FPGA. As a result, when running our DLA on Intel's Arria 10 device we can achieve a performance of 1020img/s, or 23img/s/W when running the AlexNet CNN benchmark. This comes to 1382 GFLOPs and is 10x faster with 8.4x more GFLOPS and 5.8x better efficiency than the state-of-the-art on FPGAs. Additionally, 23 img/s/W is competitive against the *best publicly known* implementation of AlexNet on nVidia's TitanX GPU.

Keywords

Deep Neural Network, Convolution Neural Network

1. INTRODUCTION

Convolutional neural nets (CNNs) have become widely adopted in various computer vision applications including driver assist and image classification. More recently, FPGAs have shown promise in efficiently implementing CNNs [21, 16, 13, 20, 11, 2, 12, 14, 4]. Unfortunately, the vast majority of FPGA implementations of CNNs have only implemented the convolutional layers limiting the benefit of the approach since other layers may quickly become the bottleneck of the neural net [20]. There has been work in implementing all the layers on the FPGA [20, 16, 13], however, when compared to some of the best results publicly known for GPUs [3, 9], FPGA performance have fallen short significantly.

FPGA '17, February 22-24, 2017, Monterey, CA, USA

© 2017 ACM. ISBN 978-1-4503-4354-1/17/02. . . $15.00

DOI: http://dx.doi.org/10.1145/3020078.3021738

One of the reasons that FPGAs have not been able to achieve good performance against GPUs is due to their limited external memory bandwidth. CNNs are often solved using matrix-multiplication based approaches, which require large amounts of data to be moved between the compute units and external memory [16]. Additionally, previous FPGA architectures for CNNs have not been able to take advantage of the peak operations of the device leading to low performance [21, 16, 13, 20].

To address the problems above, we introduce a novel architecture described in OpenCL and provide the following contributions:

- A methodology to minimize bandwidth of convolutional and fully-connected layers by caching all intermediate feature-maps on-chip in *stream-buffers*. In conjunction with batching images during fully-connected layers, which is similar to what is used in [20], we are able to reduce the external bandwidth requirements by an order-of-magnitude for both the convolutional and fully-connected layers.

- A design space exploration methodology that leverages analytical models for resource usage and throughput and is able to find the optimal architecture configuration, for a specific FPGA device and CNN, to get maximum throughput.

- An approach that leverages the Winograd transformation to reduce the multiply-accumulate operations of the convolutions [18].

Due to the contributions above we are able to implement all layers of AlexNet [7] on Intel's Arria 10 FPGA and achieve over 10x better throughput and 8.4x more GFLOPS than the state-of-the-art FPGA implementation of AlexNet [20]. Furthermore, we show that, to the best of our knowledge, this is the first FPGA implementation whose performance per watt is competitive against the same generation *highly-optimized* TitanX GPU results [3, 9, 10].

The rest of the paper is organized as follows. Section 2 has background on CNNs and related work. Section 3 describes the DLA architecture. Section 4 describes our analytical model for design space exploration. Finally, Sections 5 and 6 describe our results.

2. BACKGROUND

Deep neural networks are machine learning algorithms that are inspired by the structure and function of the human brain. They consist of several interconnected artificial neurons that are modeled after the neurons of the human nervous system. An artificial neuron accepts numerical input from other neurons, and produces an output. For DNNs, the output is computed as a dot-product of its inputs and its unique set of learnable weights. Subsequently, a non-linear *activation function* (e.g. tanh, ReLU, sigmoid) is applied to the dot-product result. This output is then used as input by other neurons. Neural networks have been used to solve many complex problems to which robust solutions cannot be designed by hand such as image recognition, handwritten text, gesture, and speech recognition; game-playing and decision making (e.g. AlphaGo); face identification; and object detection.

2.1 Convolutional Neural Networks

Convolutional neural networks (CNNs) are neural networks that excel in classifying images and videos. They have garnered a considerable amount of attention in recent years due their ability to achieve state-of-the-art results in image recognition and object detection. CNNs are neural nets that consist primarily of *convolution* layers in which each neuron is connected only to a small, nearby region of neurons in the previous layer. This local connectivity is intentionally designed into the network topology with the goal of exploiting the local correlation in the input data. This connectivity restriction, together with the additional property that groups of neurons within one convolution layer also share learnable weights, allows the outputs of neurons in the layer to be computed using 3-dimensional convolution.

Although a CNN can be described from a neuronal perspective, it is more instructive, for the discussion that follows, to view it as a directed graph of *computational layers*. Each node represents a layer that accepts one or more *n*-dimensional arrays as input, performs some computation, and produces one or more *n*-dimensional arrays as output. The edges of the graph represent the producer-consumer relationships between the layers of the network. The data arrays that layers within the network consume and produce are often referred to as *feature maps*.

In AlexNet, a convolution layer accepts a 3-dimensional array with depth C, height H, and width W as input, and produces a 3-dimensional array with depth K, height P, and width Q. The output feature map is computed by convolving the input feature map with K *filters*, and applying an activation function element-wise to the result. Each filter is also a 3-dimensional array with depth C, height R, and width S which consists of learnable weights. The convolution of the input feature map with one filter produces one 2-dimensional array referred to as a *channel* or *plane* of the output feature map. The entire output feature map is obtained by concatenating depth-wise the K channels produced by convolving each of the K filters with the input feature map. An illustration of the images is shown in Figure 3.

2.2 AlexNet

AlexNet [7] consists of the following layers:

- **Convolution** - The previous section describes the functionality of convolution layers. In AlexNet, all convolution layers use the ReLU or ramp function $f(x) = \max(0, x)$ as their activation function. In addition, each convolution layer also has K scalar bias terms that are added to corresponding output feature map channels before applying the ReLU function.
- **Cross-channel local response normalization** - A nor-

malization layer scales each element in its input feature map by a factor that is a function of the elements at the same location in adjacent channels as the element being normalized. The dimensions of the output and input feature maps are identical.

- **Max pooling** - A max pooling layer strides a two-dimensional window across each channel of the input feature map and propagates the element of maximum value in the window through to the output feature map. Compared to the input feature map, the output feature map has the same depth, smaller height, and smaller width.
- **Fully-connected(dense)** - A fully connected layer is a convolution layer in which $H = R$ and $C = W = S = 1$ (which in turn implies that $P = Q = 1$). That is, the height and width of each filter is equal to the height and width of the input feature map. Described from a neuronal perspective, a fully-connected layer is one in which each neuron is connected to every neuron in the previous layer (hence the name fully-connected). Since the input feature map and each filter have the same dimensions, no striding occurs when computing the output feature map. As a result, it is more convenient to think of the output as a matrix-vector product $\mathbf{v_o} = \mathbf{W}\mathbf{v_l}$ where $\mathbf{v_i}$ is a flattened version of the input feature map containing $n_i = C \times H \times W$ elements, $\mathbf{W}$ is a $n_o = K$ by n_i matrix in which row k is a flattened version of the kth filter, and $\mathbf{v_o}$ is the output feature map. It is possible to process a batch of b different input feature maps from b different images at once by replacing $\mathbf{v_i}$ with an n_i by b matrix $\mathbf{V_i}$ in which column k is the flattened input feature map corresponding to the kth image in the batch. The aforementioned equation then becomes $\mathbf{V_o} = \mathbf{W}\mathbf{V_i}$, where $\mathbf{V_o}$ is an n_o by b matrix in which column k is the flattened output feature map corresponding to the kth image in the batch. This method of processing multiple images at once in a fully-connected layer will feature prominently in the upcoming discussion.
- **Softmax** - A softmax layer normalizes the values in the input feature map by applying the softmax function to it. Consequently, the sum of the elements in the output feature map is unity.

At a high level, AlexNet consists of five convolution layers, followed by three fully-connected layers, and a softmax layer. There is a normalization layer after the each of the first two convolution layers. Finally, there is a max-pooling layer after the two aforementioned normalization layers, and between the last convolution layer and the first fully-connected layer. The final softmax layer outputs a 1000-element vector containing probabilities that the input image belongs to each of the 1000 possible classes in the ImageNet Large Scale Visual Recognition Competition (ILSVRC [15]). More details regarding the structure and function of AlexNet can be found in [7].

2.3 Related Work

FPGAs have been shown to be a practical means to solve CNNs [21, 16, 13, 20, 11, 2, 12, 14, 4]. In [16], the authors use a matrix-multiply approach to solve both convolutional and fully-connected layers which is similar to GPU and CPU approaches that convert 3D convolutions into 2D matrix-multiplications. Written in OpenCL, they are able to run all layers on the FPGA but unfortunately end up being severely external memory bound such that the average GOPs they achieve is relatively low. To solve the memory bottleneck, in [13] the authors introduce a singular value decomposition approach to significantly reduce the data required, and hence memory bandwidth, of the fully connected layers. They empirically show that this has approximately

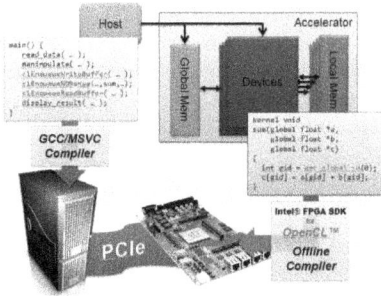

Figure 1: Intel FPGA SDK for OpenCL Host-Device Setup and Flow.

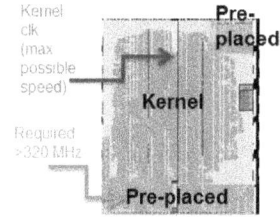

Figure 2: OpenCL FPGA Platform on an Intel's Device.

1% impact on the overall accuracy of the neural network when applied to image classification.

Conversely, the work in [21, 20] use a roofline model that allows users to maximize compute resources on the FPGA given the memory bandwidth constraints. In [20], the authors describe Caffeine which is a runtime reconfigurable CNN FPGA accelerator. In Caffeine, the throughput is improved significantly over previous approaches by creating a model to realistically reflect DDR transfers and also provide a *convolutional MM representation* where they are able to maximize data reuse of weight filters by batching input feature maps of the fully-connected layers. They show that they are able to improve the performance of CNN on FPGAs by 3x, and they are 1.5x more energy efficient than the K40 GPU. Unfortunately, when compared to nVidia's last generation TitanX GPU [3, 9] the power efficiency of the FPGA is still 5.8x worse. Additionally, the authors of [20] show that the GOPs of each layer is relatively low where they are only able to achieve 14.7% of the GOPs of the KU060 device when running at 200MHz.

Our approach differs from the previous work as we significantly reduce memory bandwidth without loss of accuracy by caching all feature-maps on-chip. Additionally, we show that our architecture is *compute-bound*, such that we can efficiently use all the DSP resources, and ensure that they are occupied (i.e. doing useful work) the majority of the time and leverage Winograd transforms to reduce the number of required operations. Finally, we show how we use a design space exploration methodology to find the optimal configuration of our architecture for a specific FPGA device and CNN. All of these factors lead to a performance efficiency that is competitive against nVidia's TitanX GPU.

2.4 Intel FPGA SDK for OpenCL

The Intel FPGA SDK for OpenCL allows users to program FPGAs with OpenCL. OpenCL is an open parallel programming language that is vendor agnostic and is supported by many vendors [6].

Currently, OpenCL uses a master-slave model where a master host device is used to control all memory transfers and execution of the kernels. A user is required to write a host program, which calls a predefined OpenCL API to control the accelerator device. On the device side, the user writes OpenCL kernel functions that are compiled to the accelerator. This model is illustrated in Figure 1.

One of the key challenges for using FPGAs is that they have traditionally required a hardware design methodology.

Because of the reconfigurable nature of FPGAs, timing-sensitive components such as DDR memory controllers must be timing closed to ensure they work correctly. The Intel FPGA SDK for OpenCL avoids these problems by providing a pre-generated platform for the OpenCL programmer. An illustration of the platform on the FPGA device is shown in Figure 2. As illustrated, the platform has pre-placed components whose resources are reserved for the platform, and cannot be used for the algorithmic portion of the OpenCL kernel code.

Our DLA is written with OpenCL, where OpenCL kernels are used to define the DLA architecture, and the host runtime is used to coordinate the data transfers of the images with the kernel execution in an efficient manner.

3. DLA ARCHITECTURE

Our Deep Learning Accelerator (DLA) implements *all layers* of AlexNet on the FPGA and is defined using the Intel FPGA SDK for OpenCL.

3.1 Design Goals

Our DLA is targeted for high-performance. In most CNN topologies, the total amount of floating-point computation is dominated by the convolution layers. For instance, in AlexNet, convolutions are 92% of the total floating point operations. Hence, the DLA hardware is optimized to maximize the throughput of the convolution layers by exploiting parallelism in computations. Each convolution layer consists of multiple nested loops that iterate over the dimensions of input features, filters, and output features. As shown in [21], it is possible to choose different combinations of these loops to vectorize in order to speedup the convolution operations. On the FPGA, vectorizing a loop means spatially distributing the computations of that loop across multiple DSP blocks that exist on the device. For maximum performance, our DLA vectorizes the loops that provide sufficient parallelism such that as many DSPs as possible are used every cycle for useful computations. Additionally, the DLA architecture ensures that the processing elements (PEs) are able to solve both the convolutional and fully-connected layers without sacrificing performance.

Our DLA is also aimed to be flexible and achieve good performance with other CNN topologies, besides AlexNet. Hence, convolution loops are chosen for vectorization such that enough parallelism exists not just in AlexNet but in a wide range of CNN topologies. Consequently, adapting our DLA for a different CNN topology will not require vectorizing different loops, but will just require changing the vectorization factors according to the dimensions of that topology. This is similar to what is claimed in [20] and is not discussed in detail in this work.

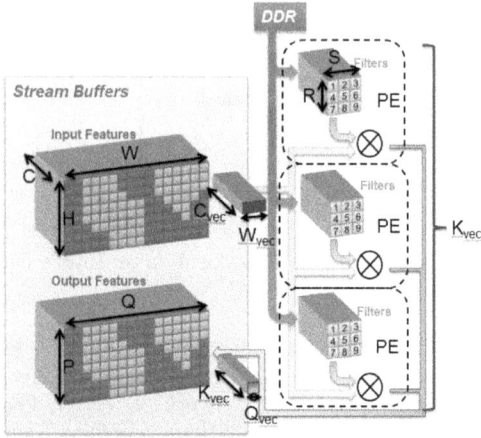

Figure 3: The overview of Convolution Execution.

3.2 Convolution Layers

To improve throughput, parallelism is extracted from four dimensions of a convolution layer: output feature columns (Q), output feature maps (K), input feature maps (C), and input feature columns (W). The vectorization factors for each of these dimensions are respectively referred to as Q_{vec}, K_{vec}, C_{vec}, and W_{vec}. Each cycle, Q_{vec} horizontal output features in K_{vec} output feature maps are computed by convolving an input feature region W_{vec} wide and C_{vec} deep. This is illustrated in Figure 3, for $C_{vec} > 1$, $K_{vec} = 3$, $W_{vec} = 2$, and $Q_{vec} = 1$. The relationship between W_{vec} and Q_{vec} depends on the number of filter and feature pixels that are multiplied per output result. For example, in equation 1, for each output, a vector of three feature and filter pixels are used. In this case $W_{vec} = S_{vec} + Q_{vec} - 1$, where S_{vec} is the size of the filter vector (e.g. $S_{vec} = 3$ in equation 1). If a larger W_{vec} is desired, a larger S_{vec} is required for each output computation.

Vectorizing the W and Q dimensions is also useful for the arithmetic optimizations which will be discussed in section 3.3. Because convolution layers usually process large number of input and output feature maps, enough parallelism can be extracted in these dimensions to use all the DSPs by breaking up the convolution operations into individual dot-products that are processed by PEs.

The PEs act as dot-product solvers for the features and filter weights. Each PE receives the same input features, illustrated as a $1 \times W_{vec} \times C_{vec}$ stick in Figure 3, and convolves them with the filter weights, of size $1 \times S_{vec} \times C_{vec}$, to produce a vector of Q_{vec} output features for one output feature map. Hence, at any given time K_{vec} PEs will be computing K_{vec} different output feature-maps. In other words, K output feature maps are computed in K/K_{vec} tiles. Convolution layers are mapped onto the architecture in Figure 3 in a time-multiplexed fashion, i.e. layers are executed one at a time in succession. This is possible because the sizes of C_{vec}, K_{vec}, Q_{vec} and W_{vec} can be independent of the image size, filter size, and number of input maps and output maps, thus solving different convolution layers simply requires different sequences of $1 \times W_{vec} \times C_{vec}$ sticks of input feature maps and filter data to be read and sent to the PEs.

Our DLA takes advantage of the mega-bytes of on-chip storage available on the FPGA device by storing the fea-

tures and the filter weights in on-chip RAMs. The features are stored in a double buffer and data is broadcast to PEs in a daisy-chain fashion every cycle. The daisy-chain structure is formed by the PEs where each PE receives a stick of input feature data for processing, and also passes the data to an adjacent PE (PE daisy-chain arrangement illustrated in Figure 7). This is much more efficient for placing the DLA on the FPGA since the FPGA is a 2D grid of logic. The outputs of the PEs are stored back into the double buffer. The filters are stored in caches inside the PEs. The purpose of the on-chip storage is to avoid unnecessary external memory accesses because the amount of features and filter weights loaded every cycle depends on the vectorization parameters and can easily exceed the available external memory bandwidth. On-chip storage allow the re-use of data by taking advantage of the temporal data locality. More specifically, double buffers allow the re-use of the input feature maps because same input features are convolved with different filters to compute different output feature maps. In addition, filter caches allow the re-use of the filter weights because same filter weights are convolved with different input features to compute each output feature map.

3.3 Arithmetic Optimizations

In addition to providing parallelization, vectorizing on W and Q allows multiple multiply-accumulate operations to be simplified through Winograd transformations as described here [18]. Lavin et al. [8] showed that Winograd's minimal filter algorithms [18] can be used to derive algorithms for CNNs. These algorithms can be applied when the convolution stride is 1 and can reduce the arithmetic complexity, resulting in faster execution. It has also been shown that the reduction in arithmetic complexity can exceed what can be achieved with other FFT-based methods for small filters. The AlexNet topology uses small 3×3 filters in most of its convolution layers, hence, can take advantage of the Winograd transformations. Furthermore, because the current trend is towards deeper CNN topologies with small filters (e.g. GoogLeNet [17]) other CNN topologies can also take advantage of the Winograd transformations.

$$
\begin{aligned}
o_0 &= (f_0, f_1, f_2) \cdot (i_0, i_1, i_2) \\
o_1 &= (f_0, f_1, f_2) \cdot (i_1, i_2, i_3) \\
o_2 &= (f_0, f_1, f_2) \cdot (i_2, i_3, i_4) \\
o_3 &= (f_0, f_1, f_2) \cdot (i_3, i_4, i_5)
\end{aligned}
\tag{1}
$$

In our DLA, each PE generates four horizontal output pixels in parallel (i.e. $Q_{vec} = 4$) where each output is formed by doing a dot-product between three filters and three inputs as shown in equation 1. In standard convolutions, this requires 12 multiplications and additions every cycle which is shown in equation 1 where o_i is an output pixel, f_i is a filter weight, and i_i is an input pixel. With the Winograd minimal filtering algorithms, we perform the four dot-products in equation 1 with only six multiplications and additions using techniques described in [18], and denoted as $F(4, 3)$. All Winograd arithmetic transformations are done on-chip and the flow is illustrated in Figure 4 which shows how we transform three filter coefficients and six feature inputs into six Winograd filters and six Winograd input features (i.e. $W_{vec} = 6$). The six values are multiplied together to form six Winograd outputs, which then are transformed back to four output features.

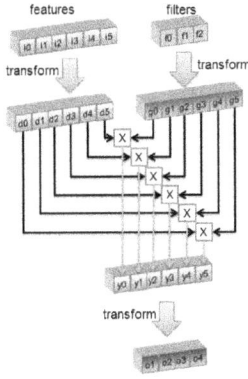

Figure 4: Winograd Flow

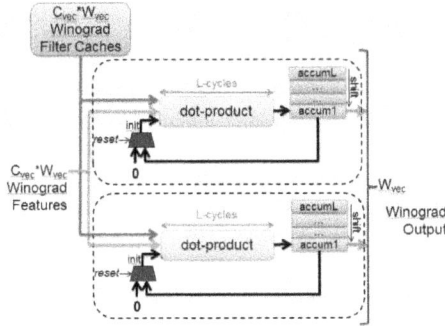

Figure 5: The overview of a PE.

3.4 PEs

Figure 5 shows an overview of a single PE hardware. It consists of dot-product units, accumulators, and caches.

Each dot-product unit multiplies and accumulates the Winograd transformed input features and the filter weights. The vector size of the dot-product unit is determined by the C_{vec} parameter as shown in Figure 5. Each PE contains W_{vec} of such dot-product units. Hence, a sub-region of size $1 \times W_{vec} \times C_{vec}$ is convolved every cycle. Once the total input feature region is convolved, Q_{vec} output features are completed.

Each dot-product unit takes as input $C_{vec} \times W_{vec}$ features, $C_{vec} \times W_{vec}$ transformed filter weights, and an *init* bus as shown in Figure 5. To support Winograd, we take $C_{vec} \times S_{vec}$ filters and convert them to $C_{vec} \times W_{vec}$ transformed filter weights. The *init* bus is set to zero when *reset* is set, which represents the start of a new output feature computation. If *reset* is not set, then *init* is set to the current accumulator value so that the accumulator is incremented by the dot-product result. If the *done* signal is set, the dot-product result is sent out. This happens when the very last dot-product is completed for an output feature. Otherwise, the result of the dot-product continues to be stored in the accumulator.

The accumulators are implemented as shift-registers. At any given cycle, each shift-register location contains the partial sum that belongs to a specific output feature. The size of this shift-register depends on the latency L of the dot-product unit. That is, the same shift-register value that is used as the *init* value in the dot-product will be updated

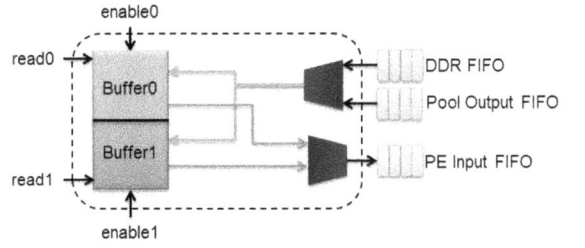

(a) A single stream buffer.

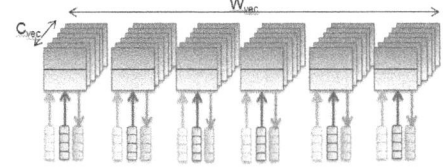

(b) The array of stream buffers.

Figure 6: Stream buffer hardware.

with the result of the dot-product, L cycles later. Hence, at any given cycle, each PE keeps L different partial sums that belong to L different output features for each dot-product unit. Because each dot-product unit is fully-pipelined, L different output computations are *interleaved*. That is, for L consecutive cycles, input features and filter weights for different output features will be fed into a dot-product unit in a sequence. In our implementation, we interleave both in the W (L_w) and H (L_h) direction.

Filter weights are stored in PE caches implemented in on-chip RAMs. Every cycle, $W_{vec} \times C_{vec}$ transformed filter weights are loaded from these caches and fed onto the dot-product units. Hence, $W_{vec} \times C_{vec}$ caches, or memory banks, are used in order to get the necessary on-chip memory read bandwidth. A single filter weight can be loaded from each cache every cycle.

Filter weights are stored in the caches before the corresponding convolution layer starts. To avoid idle computation cycles, the DLA uses double-buffering and overlaps convolutions with the PE cache updates. While filter weights are loaded from the caches for a particular convolution layer, filter weights for the next convolution layer are also prefetched onto the caches.

Every cycle, the W_{vec} outputs of each PE are sent to the ReLU unit for the Winograd output transform as explained in Section 3.3.

3.5 Stream Buffers

Stream buffers shown in Figure 6 are implemented in on-chip RAMs in order to store the feature data and to stream it to PEs. Each stream buffer is double-buffered similar to filter caches. Before the first convolution layer starts, the images are loaded from the DDR and stored in buffers. During the convolution layer execution, while feature data for a convolution layer is being streamed into the PEs, the outputs of convolutions are simultaneously stored into the buffers. There are a total of $W_{vec} \times C_{vec}$ stream buffers. The width of feature maps is divided into W_{vec} buffers, and the depth is divided into C_{vec} buffers. Hence, a total of $W_{vec} \times C_{vec}$ stream buffers provide sufficient on-chip bandwidth for streaming an input feature region of size $1 \times W_{vec} \times C_{vec}$ to

PEs every cycle. The output features, on the other hand, are generated in a different layout. More specifically, each PE generates Q_{vec} features in a cycle, hence, a total region of $1 \times Q_{vec} \times K_{vec}$ is generated in a cycle. A crossbar network is generated in order to store this region in $1 \times W_{vec} \times C_{vec}$ buffers.

3.6 Shared Exponent FP16

Using half-precision (FP16) instead of single-precision (FP32) floating point operations can significantly reduce the resource requirement of each PE. However, although FP32 is natively supported on Arria 10's DSP blocks, FP16 is not, which leads to additional logic use. To reduce this overhead, we use a shared exponent technique which allows us to perform the multiplications in fixed-point, which significantly reduces the overhead required to perform the FP16 dot-products. This technique works by leveraging the fact that Arria 10 DSP blocks can be fractured into two 18×18 integer multipliers [1] such that before sending the feature and filter data into each PE, we transform all the values into 18-bit numbers, using the maximum exponent found in the group. Since the exponent matches for all the numbers, they can be treated as fixed-point numbers and can be sent directly to the 18×18 integer multipliers. After the dot-product is performed, the number is shifted back to 10-bits, and the exponent and sign bit is added back to the top 6 bits, reforming the 16-bit floating point value, which is stored back into the stream buffer. Note that the shared exponent transform is performed on the data prior to entering the PEs and thus only need to be applied once and can be shared across all PEs.

3.7 Fully Connected Layers

The DLA executes the fully-connected layers on the same PEs described in section 3.4. This approach makes the most efficient use of the dot-product units since these units are kept busy during the convolution and the fully-connected layers.

Due to the different characteristics of computations in fully-connected and convolutional layers, PEs need to be configured differently. Specifically, the ratio of the total filter weights used in computations to the total amount of the computation is significantly higher in fully-connected layers than in convolution layers. In other words, there is significantly less re-use of the fully-connected layer filter weights during the classification of a single image. Hence, storing these filters in PE caches does not give any benefits. Moreover, loading these filters from DDR uses significantly more bandwidth, which may become a performance bottleneck.

In order to alleviate the above issues, the DLA processes fully-connected layers in image batches. After all convolution layers are completed layer by layer for a single image, the last layer will dump the image back out to external memory to batch up the images. Once a large enough batch of images are available, the batch of images is processed together during each of the fully-connected layers. This allows sharing the fully-connected filter weights between the classification of different images, and hence, reducing the external memory bandwidth usage. In other words, filters are shared and same filter weights are multiplied with different image features to produce the output features of different images. This is in contrast to the convolution layers where features are shared and same features are multiplied with different fil-

ter weights to produce different output feature maps. Hence, during the fully-connected layers, filter weights are streamed into the PEs and PE caches store the features for different images that are pre-loaded before computation starts. The caches are sized to accommodate not only the convolution filters but also the batches of images that need to be processed in parallel during fully-connected layers.

The fully-connected layers are executed with the following configuration (summarized in Table 1).

1. No Winograd transformations are applied because features and filters are convolved to generate only a single output.

2. Before starting the compute, features are pre-loaded into the PE caches. For instance, if the image batch size is S_{batch}, each PE will store N different image features, where N is equal to S_{batch}/K_{vec}.

3. During fully-connected layer computation, the W_{vec}/N dot-product units in each PE are used to process one image.

4. Each cycle, F unique filter weights are loaded from the DDR and streamed into the PEs, where F is equal to $(W_{vec}/N) \times C_{vec}$. Each PE receives the same filter weights and multiplies them with different image features.

5. Similar to the convolution configuration, L different output computations are interleaved.

6. W_{vec}/N partial sums in each PE are summed to produce N outputs from each PE.

Configuration	Convolution	Fully-Connected
Winograd Transformation	Yes	No
Batch Size	1	S_{batch}
Streamed Data	Features	Filters
Cached Data	Filters	Features
Dot-Products per Image	W_{vec}	W_{vec}/N

Table 1: Configuration of PEs during convolution and fully-connected layers.

3.8 Overall Architecture

CNN algorithms often include other layers in addition to convolution and fully-connected layers. For instance, AlexNet contains normalization, max-pooling, and ReLU layers. Hence, our DLA contains additional hardware to support these different types of layers to enable the entire topology to be executed on the FPGA.

Figure 7 shows the DLA hardware support for all the AlexNet layers. The PEs, as discussed earlier, perform the dot-products for convolution and fully-connected layers. The StreamBuffer unit manages the stream buffers, applies the Winograd transformations to features, and streams the transformed features to the first PE. The StreamBuffer unit also fetches the filter data from DDR and sends it to the PEs. The features are forwarded through all the PEs via the daisy-chained input connections between them. The outputs of the PEs are sent to the ReLU unit again via daisy-chained output connections. ReLU unit applies the Winograd output transformations and non-linearity functions. The throughput of ReLU unit and all the subsequent units are higher than the total throughput of the PEs in order to avoid stalls. The outputs of the ReLU unit are sent to the normalization unit, which applies the normalization formula across the feature maps. Because PEs compute feature maps in tiles, normalizing a tile requires buffering of convolution outputs from the previous tile. The outputs of the normalization unit are

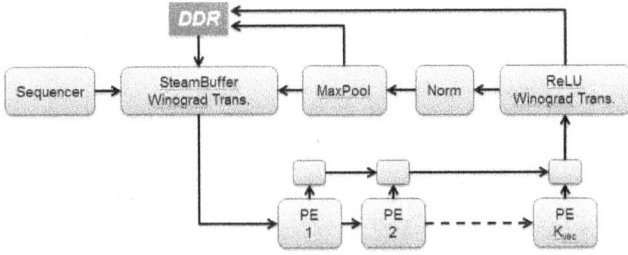

Figure 7: Overall DLA Architecture.

sent to the pooling unit which computes the maximum value in a window. Because each feature map is pooled independently, no data buffering is necessary between the feature map tiles. If more convolution layers are to follow, the output of the pooling unit is stored back onto the stream buffer for further processing. Following the last convolution layer, the outputs of the pooling unit are stored to external memory. At the start of the fully-connected layers, these features are read back from external memory and loaded onto the PE caches as described earlier. Also, the ReLU output is sent directly to DDR, without applying Norm or Pool.

The DLA includes several control signals, such as stream buffer read/write addresses, PE cache read/write addresses, PE done/reset signals, normalization/pooling bypass signals, etc. These signals are generated by the sequencer unit which is configured according to the topology of the CNN algorithm being executed. The sizes of input/output images, intermediate features, filters, normalization/pooling windows, convolution strides, etc. are used in calculating the exact cycles certain actions are taken at or the addresses that are accessed. Hence, executing a different CNN algorithm on the same hardware requires just changing the sequencer configuration.

In AlexNet, the normalization and pooling operations are not always performed after every convolution layer. Hence, these units can be by-passed depending on the topology that is being executed. This makes extending this architecture to support software configurability relatively straightforward because the sequence of layers bypassed can be changed after the FPGA is programmed and is similar to the work in [20].

All the units described above are written as OpenCL kernels. Each kernel executes independently and concurrently. The connections between the kernels are implemented as FIFOs using the Intel channel API.

4. DESIGN SPACE EXPLORATION AND ANALYTICAL MODELS

One of the benefits of our architecture is that the resource usage of the PE array, stream buffers, and filter caches can be analytically modeled using the C_{vec}, K_{vec}, W_{vec}, and Q_{vec} parameters.

For 16-bit floating point precision, equation 2 models the DSP usage for all the PE elements, which assumes that each DSP block can perform two 16-bit floating point multiplies and two 16-bit floating point adds and no Winograd. If Winograd is applied, we divide equation 2 by 2 and add on a constant factor of 200. The constant factor is an over estimate, and accounts for the on-chip Winograd transforms as shown in Figure 4 and the value chosen is applicable

to the $F(4,3)$ Winograd transforms we use. The stream buffers and filter caches M20K usage can be modeled using equation 3 and 4 respectively, which assumes a given M20K can store 1024 16-bit floating point values by forming a 2 word wide by 512 deep memory [1]. Equation 3 models the number of M20Ks required to store the largest input and output feature map for any given layer (represented by the $MAX(Depth_{in} + Depth_{out})$). C is the number of input feature maps for a given layer, H and W are the feature map height and width. Equation 4 models the number of M20Ks required to store all filter weights for a single output feature map. This is scaled up by the number of PEs (i.e. K_{vec}) since each PE processes one output feature map at any given time. Note that for the filter caches the depth is not considered since the filters don't require the entire M20K depth (i.e. there are less than 512 words needed).

$$N_{dsps} = (W_{vec} - Q_{vec} + 1) \times Q_{vec} \times K_{vec} \times C_{vec} \times 0.5 \quad (2)$$

$$N_{banks} = W_{vec} \times C_{vec}$$
$$Depth = C \times W \times H / N_{banks}$$
$$N_{M20K} = CEIL(\frac{MAX(Depth_{in} + Depth_{out})}{512 \times 2}) \times N_{banks}$$
$$\quad (3)$$

$$N_{banks} = W_{vec} \times C_{vec}$$
$$N_{M20K} = N_{banks} \times K_{vec}/2 \quad (4)$$

Expected throughput is modeled using the vector dimensions (C_{vec}, K_{vec}, W_{vec}, and Q_{vec}), feature map sizes, output map sizes, filter sizes, and DDR bandwidth utilization. For a single convolutional layer, the number of cycles to process an image is shown in equation 5. Here, C is the number of input feature maps, K is the number of output feature maps, Q is the width of the output feature map, P is the height of the output feature map. DSP_{eff} represents the efficiency of the DSPs and models any quantization issues due to Q_{vec} and interleaving width-wise (L_w) and height-wise (L_h) as described in section 3.4, where we ignore quantization effects on C and K for simplicity (e.g. if C_{vec} does not divide C evenly). For example, if the output image is 20 wide, and $Q_{vec} = 3$ with no interleaving (i.e. $L_h = L_w = 1$), on the 7th cycle, only the first two values of Q_{vec} will have useful output, the last value will be dropped. In this case, the $DSP_{eff} = 20/(CEIL(6.67) \times 3) = 95\%$. N_{cycles} are the number of cycles required to generate all output feature-maps for the layer, assuming there are no memory bandwidth constraints. $BYTE_{req}$ are the total bytes of prefetched filter weights required to be loaded from DDR during the convolution layer where R_{next} and S_{next} are the filter dimensions of the next convolution layer, and C_{next} is the number of feature map layers in the next convolutional layer, and $BYTE_{ddr}$ are the total number of bytes that can be transferred during the convolutional layer assuming that there is one DDR memory interface that is 64 bytes wide. N_{real} is the estimated number of cycles required taking into account any DDR bandwidth limitations of the device.

$$DSP_{eff} = Q/(CEIL(Q/(Q_{vec} \times L_w)) \times Q_{vec} \times L_w) \times$$
$$P/(CEIL(P/(L_h)) \times L_h)$$
$$N_{flops} = 2 \times K \times C \times Q \times P \times DSP_{eff}$$
$$N_{cycles} = N_{flops}/(N_{dsps} \times 2)$$
$$BYTE_{req} = K_{next} \times R_{next} \times S_{next} \times C_{next} \times 2$$
$$BYTE_{ddr} = 64 \times N_{cycles}$$
$$N_{real} = N_{cycles} \times BYTE_{req}/BYTE_{ddr}$$
$$(5)$$

For fully-connected layers, the number of cycles is shown in equation 7 which calculates the cycles required for an entire batch of images. Here, K and C are the number of input and output feature maps for the fully-connected layer and S_{batch} is the batch size used. For fully-connected layers, $BYTE_{req}$ are the total bytes of the filter weights that need to be loaded. Also, we ignore any quantization effects for fully-connected layers, since empirically we show that DSP efficiency is close to 100% (shown later in Table 2).

$$S_{batch} = K_{vec} \times 2$$
$$N_{flops} = 2 \times K \times C \times S_{batch}$$
$$N_{cycles} = N_{flops}/(N_{dsps} \times 2)$$
$$BYTE_{req} = C \times K \times 2$$
$$BYTE_{ddr} = 64 \times N_{cycles}$$
$$N_{real} = N_{cycles} \times BYTE_{req}/BYTE_{ddr}$$
$$(6)$$

To get the final throughput in terms of images per second, we divide the clock frequency of the design by the total cycles for all layers to process. For fully-connected layers, we have to normalize to one image so we divide by the batch size, S_{batch}. We ignore the execution time of other layers, such as Norm and ReLU, since these are executed concurrently with the convolutional or fully-connected layers, and have a negligible execution overhead.

$$T_{all} = f_{max}/(\Sigma_{conv}(N_{real}) + \Sigma_{fc}(N_{real}/S_{batch})) \quad (7)$$

Using both the resource usage estimates and throughput models, we can find the optimal C_{vec} and K_{vec} value for a given FPGA device, assuming all other values are set by the user (e.g. f_{max}, W_{vec}, etc). A curve of this is shown in the results section in Figure 8.

5. EXPERIMENTAL EVALUATION

We evaluate our DLA by implementing the AlexNet topology on Intel's Arria 10 dev kit which contains a A10-1150 device (20nm). We use a batch size of 1 for convolution layers, and 96 for the fully connected layers as described in Section 3.7. We use only one bank of DDR4x64 at 1200MHz with a total bandwidth of 17GB/s to reduce the power required for the FPGA. We compare against the work in [16] and [20]. Additionally, we compare against the *best known* results for nVidia's TitanX GPU (28nm) taken from [3]. Note that nVidia used 28nm for its last generation GPU and skipped the 20nm node, which is why TitanX is used in this comparison. When measuring throughput, we measure the total system throughput, which includes all the data transfers of the images to the FPGA using the ILSVRC data set [15], which would be incurred in a real application, which is not done in [20] nor [3]. In order to hide the latency of

Layer	Eff. GFLOPS	Act. GFLOPS	Eff.
Conv1	2,308	1,154	82.9%
Conv2	1,740	870	62.5%
Conv3	1,960	980	72.4%
Conv4	1,960	980	72.4%
Conv5	1,743	871	62.6%
Fc6	1,389	1,389	99.8%
Fc7	1,386	1,386	99.6%
Fc8	1,378	1,378	99.0%

Table 2: The average GFLOPS achieved of convolutional and fully-connected layers and DSP efficiency when using an 8×48 configuration. Shows both effective GFLOPS (Eff. GFLOPS) due to Winograd and actual GFLOPS (Act. GFLOPS).

the transfers, we pipeline the execution of the DLA with the image data transfers from host to FPGA DDR memory. Also note that the data precision vary from fixed and floating point in the studies in [16, 20, 3] and our work. Previous work [16, 5] have shown the limited impact of 16-bit fixed point when compared to 16-bit floating point and is not described here.

6. RESULTS

To illustrate the efficiency of our architecture, we show the GFLOPS of the DLA for each fully-connected and convolutional layer in Table 2 as well as the DSP efficiency. Here, we define DSP efficiency as the percentage of time the DSP is occupied and doing useful computation.

It is clear that for most layers, DSP efficiency and GFLOPS are relatively high, which is required to be competitive against the GPU. The DSP efficiency differs between layers because vectorization factors (W_{vec}, Q_{vec}, K_{vec}, C_{vec}, S_{vec}) lead to different quantization inefficiencies for different feature, filter and output dimensions as described in equation 5. For instance, Conv2 has the lowest efficiency because it uses 5×5 filter weights which are sub-optimally vectorized with 1×3 tile sizes used. Moreover, FC layers have close to ideal efficiency because the dimensions of their input features, filter weights, and output features are large with respect to the vectorization factors, i.e. how many features and filters are loaded and how many output features are computed every cycle as discussed in Section 3.7.

We should note that for Conv1, we achieve a high efficiency even though the number of input feature maps for the first layer is three, which is not wide enough to fill up the vector 8 dot-product units in each PE (i.e. 3 is less than $C_{vec} = 8$). In order to get around this limitation, we fold the three input feature maps to create 48 sub-feature maps, such that we can saturate the dot-product width.

Figure 8 plots the achievable throughput for various C_{vec} and K_{vec} values, using the Arria 10 1150 device. Here, we assume f_{max} is 300MHz, $Q_{vec} = 4$, and $W_{vec} = 6$, and we only explore positions where K_{vec} are even multiples of C_{vec} (areas which are not even multiples are 0 in Figure 8), which leads to a more efficient memory structure for the stream buffers and filter cache. Note that the highlighted red circle is one of the peak throughput numbers with $C_{vec} = 8$ and $K_{vec} = 48$. This is our final configuration which achieves a throughput of 1020 img/s.

To validate our analytical models presented in Section 4,

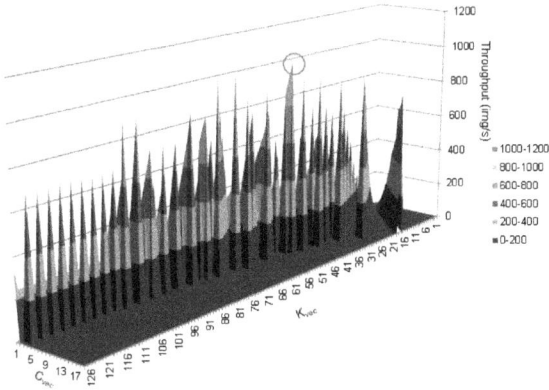

Figure 8: Plot of expected throughput for various C_{vec} and K_{vec} values.

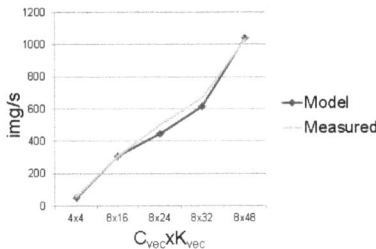

Figure 9: A comparison of empirical data against analytical model for A10-1150 device.

we plot predicted img/s given by our models and the measured performance, as shown in Figure 9. Note that in Figure 9 we scale down the model img/s predictions provided by equations 5 and 7 by 16% to account for any inefficiencies in the pipelined data transfers and the overhead of data movement between the host processor and FPGA, which is included in the measured throughput values. 16% is used because this was measured as the average difference between the system-level throughput and the FPGA device throughput. As shown in the graph, our model throughput predictions match very closely to the actual measurements.

6.1 Resource Usage

To show the impact of the shared exponent floating point optimization described in Section 3.6, we show the resource usage of a single PE using true half-precision dot-products (Half-type) vs shared exponent dot-products in Table 3. The shared exponent significantly reduces resource usage since we can leverage the DSP fully, whereas when using the half-type, a lot of logic must be used to normalize and compute the 16-bit floating point multiplications and perform the dot-product. Also, it should be noted that no impact to accuracy was seen to the top-1 and top-5 error rate (56% and 79% respectively) between our shared exponent implementation and 32-bit floating point.

Table 4 shows the final resource usage of an 8×48 ($C_{vec} \times K_{vec}$) configuration running on the Arria 10 1150 device running at 303MHz.

6.2 FPGA Comparisons to the state-of-the-art

Table 5 and Table 6 shows our comparisons against prior

FP16 config	ALMs	Reg
Half-type	10.7K	26K
Shared Exponent	3.3K	10.6K

Table 3: Resource usage of PE without shared exponent optimizations (Half-type) and with shared exponent optimizations.

ALMs	Reg	M20K	DSPs	Freq.
246K (58%)	681K	2487 (92%)	1476 (97%)	303 MHz

Table 4: Resource usage and clock frequency on the Arria 10 1150 device, for an 8×48 configuration running at 303MHz.

work on FPGAs and GPUs respectively. As Table 5 shows, we achieve 8.4x more GFLOPS when compared to the latest Ultrascale (KU 20nm [19]) result, which uses a batch size 32 for the fully-connected layers, and 19x more GFLOPS than the latest Stratix V result, both running AlexNet. It is important to note that in [20] the authors are only able to use 50% of DSP resources and claim that this is due to a limitation in SDAccel when using partial reconfiguration. However, even if they were able to use 100% of DSPs, the 8.4x gap would still not be closed since they are only able to achieve a 14.7% efficiency of their DSPs, which assumes a 1.1 TOPS for the KU060 device at 200MHz used in [20].

We should note that in [20] and [16], they show better GOPS numbers for VGG of 266 GOPS and 118 GOPS respectively. Since our architecture is also applicable to VGG, which is based on convolutional and fully-connected layers as well, our performance will not be impacted negatively with the VGG topology. In fact, since VGG is more regular, DSP efficiency is improved on previous work [20] and we believe that this should also benefit the DLA architecture.

Finally, in Table 6 we show a comparison of our work against the best known nVidia results for the TitanX and M4 running AlexNet with image sizes of 224×224 and batch size 128 (note that the M4 white paper doesn't specify batch size) . The TitanX card has a peak 6.1 TFLOPS, compared to the 1150 Arria 10 device which has 1.3 TFLOPS and as Table 6 shows, the TitanX is able to beat our work in terms of raw performance. However, when normalized against power consumption, we are competitive with both nVidia devices [3, 10]. Also note that the img/s/W numbers shown in Table 6 are 5.8x better than the img/s/W for AlexNet presented in [20].

6.2.1 Discussion on performance comparisons

There are several simplifications the authors do in [3] which can significantly boost the performance of the TitanX result shown in Table 6 including the *removal* of communication overhead and the use of random data instead of the ILSVRC database set. As such, we suspect that the raw performance numbers are overly optimistic and, unlike our

Stratix V (28nm)[16]	KU060 (20nm) [20]	DLA (20nm)
72.4 GOPS	165 GOPS	1382 GFLOPS

Table 5: A comparison of our DLA against [20, 16] for AlexNet. For the DLA, effective flops shown due to Winograd.

	img/s	Watts (W brd)	Peak Ops	img/s/W
DLA (20nm)	1020	45	1.3TFLOPS	23
KU060 (20nm)	104	25	3.6TOPS	4
TitanX (28nm)	5120	227	6.1TFLOPS	23
M4 (28nm)	1150	58	2.2TFLOPS	20

Table 6: A comparison of the DLA at 303MHz against [20] and [3, 10]. KU060 peak operations are integer, the rest are 32-bit floating pt.

throughput measurements, do not reflect the actual throughput of a production system. Additionally, the KU060 104 img/s is estimated using Figure 10d in [20], which assumes no execution overhead for data transfers and ignores the execution time of the non-linear layers (i.e. Pool, Norm, ReLU), which again is overly optimistic. Due to these simplifications, we suspect that the relative system performance benefit of our DLA is much larger than what is reported in Table 6.

7. CONCLUSIONS

We describe a novel architecture written in OpenCL, DLA, targeted for computing CNNs on FPGAs. We demonstrate an approach that reduces the required memory bandwidth by an order-of-magnitude through the use of an on-chip stream buffer that efficiently stores input and output feature maps. Additionally, we demonstrate a vectorization approach that achieves over 60% DSP efficiency and uses the Winograd transform to significantly reduce the DSPs required to perform the convolution layers. Because of these improvements, we are able to achieve an overall system-level performance that is 10x faster than the state-of-the-art on FPGAs when running AlexNet and is competitive in energy efficiency with the best known results on nVidia's TitanX GPU at 23 img/s/W.

Future work includes mapping other CNNs such as GoogLeNet and VGG to our architecture, and exploring how run-time reconfigurability may impact performance of our architecture.

8. ACKNOWLEDGEMENTS

We would like to thank Stephen Weston for his insightful comments and Kevin Jin for the experimental data.

9. REFERENCES

[1] Altera. *Arria 10 Device Overview*. White Paper A10-OVERVIEW. Altera Corporation, Jan. 2015.

[2] S. Cadambi, A. Majumdar, M. Becchi, S. Chakradhar, and H. P. Graf. A programmable parallel accelerator for learning and classification. In *Proceedings of the 19th International Conference on Parallel Architectures and Compilation Techniques*, PACT '10, pages 273–284, New York, NY, USA, 2010. ACM.

[3] S. Chintala. convnet-benchmarks, 2016.

[4] C. Farabet, C. Poulet, J. Y. Han, and Y. LeCun. Cnp: An fpga-based processor for convolutional networks. In *2009 International Conference on Field Programmable Logic and Applications*, pages 32–37, Aug 2009.

[5] S. Gupta, A. Agrawal, K. Gopalakrishnan, and P. Narayanan. Deep learning with limited numerical precision. In D. Blei and F. Bach, editors, *Proceedings of the 32nd International Conference on Machine Learning (ICML-15)*, pages 1737–1746. JMLR Workshop and Conference Proceedings, 2015.

[6] Khronos. The open standard for parallel programming of heterogeneous systems, 2015.

[7] A. Krizhevsky, I. Sutskever, and G. E. Hinton. Imagenet classification with deep convolutional neural networks. In *Advances in Neural Information Processing Systems*, NIPS '12, pages 1097–1105, 2012.

[8] A. Lavin. Fast algorithms for convolutional neural networks. *CoRR*, abs/1509.09308, 2015.

[9] nVidia. GPU-Based Deep Learning Inference: A Performance and Power Analysis, November 2015.

[10] NVIDIA. Nvidia(r) tesla(r) m4 gpu accelerator, Apr. 2016.

[11] K. Ovtcharov, O. Ruwase, J.-Y. Kim, J. Fowers, K. Strauss, and E. Chung. Accelerating deep convolutional neural networks using specialized hardware, February 2015.

[12] M. Peemen, A. A. A. Setio, B. Mesman, and H. Corporaal. Memory-centric accelerator design for convolutional neural networks. In *2013 IEEE 31st International Conference on Computer Design (ICCD)*, pages 13–19, Oct 2013.

[13] J. Qiu, J. Wang, S. Yao, K. Guo, B. Li, E. Zhou, J. Yu, T. Tang, N. Xu, S. Song, Y. Wang, and H. Yang. Going deeper with embedded fpga platform for convolutional neural network. In *Proceedings of the 2016 ACM/SIGDA International Symposium on Field-Programmable Gate Arrays*, FPGA '16, pages 26–35, New York, NY, USA, 2016. ACM.

[14] M. Sankaradas, V. Jakkula, S. Cadambi, S. Chakradhar, I. Durdanovic, E. Cosatto, and H. P. Graf. A massively parallel coprocessor for convolutional neural networks. In *Proceedings of the 2009 20th IEEE International Conference on Application-specific Systems, Architectures and Processors*, ASAP '09, pages 53–60, Washington, DC, USA, 2009. IEEE Computer Society.

[15] Stanford Vision Lab. Imagenet large scale visual recognition challenge (ilsvrc), 2015.

[16] N. Suda, V. Chandra, G. Dasika, A. Mohanty, Y. Ma, S. Vrudhula, J.-s. Seo, and Y. Cao. Throughput-optimized opencl-based fpga accelerator for large-scale convolutional neural networks. In *Proceedings of the 2016 ACM/SIGDA International Symposium on Field-Programmable Gate Arrays*, FPGA '16, pages 16–25, New York, NY, USA, 2016. ACM.

[17] C. Szegedy, W. Liu, Y. Jia, P. Sermanet, S. E. Reed, D. Anguelov, D. Erhan, V. Vanhoucke, and A. Rabinovich. Going deeper with convolutions. *CoRR*, abs/1409.4842, 2014.

[18] S. Winograd. *Arithmetic Complexity of Computations*, volume 33. Siam, 1980.

[19] Xilinx. *UltraScale Architecture and Product Overview*. Preliminary Product Specification. Xilinx Corporation, June 2016.

[20] C. Zhang, Z. Fang, P. Zhou, and J. Cong. Caffeine: Towards uniformed representation and acceleration for deep convolutional neural networks. In *Proceedings of the 2016 International Conference On Computer Aided Design*, ICCAD '16, New York, NY, USA, 2016. ACM.

[21] C. Zhang, P. Li, G. Sun, Y. Guan, B. Xiao, and J. Cong. Optimizing fpga-based accelerator design for deep convolutional neural networks. In *Proceedings of the 2015 ACM/SIGDA International Symposium on Field-Programmable Gate Arrays*, FPGA '15, pages 161–170, New York, NY, USA, 2015. ACM.

FINN: A Framework for Fast, Scalable Binarized Neural Network Inference

Yaman Umuroglu*†, Nicholas J. Fraser*‡, Giulio Gambardella*, Michaela Blott*,
Philip Leong‡, Magnus Jahre† and Kees Vissers*
*Xilinx Research Labs; †Norwegian University of Science and Technology; ‡University of Sydney
yamanu@idi.ntnu.no

ABSTRACT

Research has shown that convolutional neural networks contain significant redundancy, and high classification accuracy can be obtained even when weights and activations are reduced from floating point to binary values. In this paper, we present FINN, a framework for building fast and flexible FPGA accelerators using a flexible heterogeneous streaming architecture. By utilizing a novel set of optimizations that enable efficient mapping of binarized neural networks to hardware, we implement fully connected, convolutional and pooling layers, with per-layer compute resources being tailored to user-provided throughput requirements. On a ZC706 embedded FPGA platform drawing less than 25 W total system power, we demonstrate up to 12.3 million image classifications per second with 0.31 µs latency on the MNIST dataset with 95.8% accuracy, and 21906 image classifications per second with 283 µs latency on the CIFAR-10 and SVHN datasets with respectively 80.1% and 94.9% accuracy. To the best of our knowledge, ours are the fastest classification rates reported to date on these benchmarks.

1. INTRODUCTION

Convolutional Neural Networks (CNNs) have dramatically improved in recent years, their performance now exceeding that of other visual recognition algorithms [14], and even surpassing human accuracy on certain problems [24, 29]. They are likely to play an important role in enabling ubiquitous machine vision and intelligence on all kinds of devices, but a significant computational challenge remains. Modern CNNs may contain millions of floating-point parameters and require billions of floating-point operations to recognize a single image. Furthermore, these requirements tend to increase as researchers explore deeper networks. For instance, AlexNet [14] (the winning entry for ImageNet Large Scale Visual Recognition Competition (ILSVRC) [23] in 2012) required 244 MB of parameters and 1.4 billion floating point operations (GFLOP) per image, while VGG-16 [25] from ILSVRC 2014 required 552 MB of parameters and 30.8 GFLOP per image.

While the vast majority of CNNs implementations use floating point parameters, a growing body of research demonstrates this approach incorporates significant redundancy. Recently, it has been shown [5, 27, 22, 12, 32] that neural networks can classify accurately using one- or two-bit quantization for weights and activations. Such a combination of low-precision arithmetic and small memory footprint presents a unique opportunity for fast and energy-efficient image classification using Field Programmable Gate Arrays (FPGAs). FPGAs have *much* higher theoretical peak performance for binary operations compared to floating point, while the small memory footprint *removes* the off-chip memory bottleneck by keeping parameters on-chip, even for large networks. Binarized Neural Networks (BNNs), proposed by Courbariaux et al. [5], are particularly appealing since they can be implemented almost entirely with binary operations, with the potential to attain performance in the teraoperations per second (TOPS) range on FPGAs.

In this work, we propose FINN, a framework for building scalable and fast BNN inference accelerators on FPGAs. FINN-generated accelerators can perform millions of classifications per second with sub-microsecond latency, thereby making them ideal for supporting real-time embedded applications such as augmented reality, autonomous driving and robotics. Compute resources can be scaled to meet a given classification rate requirement. We demonstrate FINN's capabilities with a series of prototypes for classifying the MNIST, SVHN and CIFAR-10 benchmark datasets. Our classification rate results surpass the best previously published results by over 48× for MNIST, 2.2× for CIFAR-10 and 8× for SVHN. To the best of our knowledge, this is the fastest reported neural network inference implementation on these datasets. The novel contributions are:

- Quantification of peak performance for BNNs on FPGAs using a roofline model.
- A set of novel optimizations for mapping BNNs onto FPGA more efficiently.
- A BNN architecture and accelerator construction tool, permitting customization of throughput.
- A range of prototypes that demonstrate the potential of BNNs on off-the-shelf FPGA platforms.

The rest of this paper is organized as follows: Section 2 provides background on CNNs, BNNs, and their hardware implementations. Section 3 discusses BNNs accuracy and peak performance on FPGAs. Section 4 describes FINN's architecture and optimizations. Section 5 presents the experimental evaluation, and Section 6 concludes the paper.

2. BACKGROUND

This work is focused on *supervised* learning, in which the goal is to find a function, $g(\mathbf{x}_i)$, which approximates a mapping $\mathbf{x}_i \to y_i \ \forall \ i$, where $\{\mathbf{x}_i, y_i\}$ is an input/output pair known as a training example. Furthermore, only the *inference* problem is studied, the parameters, w, being assumed to have been learned offline.

2.1 Convolutional Neural Networks

A *multilayer perceptron* is a type of Artificial Neural Network (ANN) which has its neurons arranged in multiple layers, with neurons taking the output of all neurons of the previous layer as inputs. Mathematically, the output, $a_{l,n}$, for the nth neuron in the lth layer of a fully connected network is calculated as follows:

$$a_{l,n} = f_{act}(\sum_{s=0}^{S_l} w_{l,n,s} a_{l-1,s} + b_{l,n}) \ , \qquad (1)$$

where $w_{l,n,s}$ is weight of the sth synapse connected to the input of the nth neuron in the lth layer, $b_{l,n}$ is a bias term, f_{act} is the activation function, and S_l is the number of synapses connected to each neuron in the lth layer. Popular activation functions include: the hyperbolic tangent function, $f_{act}(a) = tanh(a)$; and the rectified linear unit (ReLU), $f_{act}(a) = max(0, a)$.

CNNs [15] are a variant of multilayer perceptrons, in which a layer only receives inputs from a small *receptive field* of the previous layer. This approach greatly reduces the number of parameters involved and allows local features (e.g., edges, corners) to be found [15]. A basic 2D convolutional layer in a neural network is similar to a fully connected layer except that: a) each neuron receives an image as inputs and produces an image as its output (instead of a scalar); b) each synapse learns a small array of weights which is the size of the convolutional window; and c) each pixel in the output image is created by the sum of the convolutions between all synapse weights and the corresponding images. The output of the lth convolutional layer, which takes as input S_l images of dimension $R_l \times C_l$, the pixel, $p_{l,n,r,c}$, at location (r, c) of the nth output image is calculated as follows:

$$p_{l,n,r,c} = f_{act}(\sum_{s=0}^{S_l} \sum_{j=0}^{J_l} \sum_{k=0}^{K_l} w_{l,n,s,j,k} p_{l-1,n,r+j,c+k}) \ , \qquad (2)$$

where $J_l \times K_l$ are the dimensions of the convolution window. As discussed in Section 4, a 2D convolutional layer can be reduced to a matrix multiply followed by an elementwise activation function. CNN topologies are composed from a few common primitives: convolutional layers, *pooling* layers and fully connected layers.

Pooling layers can be considered as simple downsamplers of 2D images. A basic max pooling layer divides an image into small sub-tiles of a given window size and then replaces each sub-tile with its largest element. An average pooling layer is similar but uses the average function instead of max.

2.2 Binary Neural Networks

Although floating point numbers are a natural choice for handling the small updates that occur during neural network training, the resulting parameters can contain a lot of redundant information [8]. One of several possible dimensions possessing redundancy is precision [27]. An extreme case

are BNNs in which some or all the arithmetic involved in computing the outputs are constrained to single-bit values. We consider three aspects of binarization for neural network layers: binary input activations, binary synapse weights and binary output activations. If all three components are binary, we refer to this as *full binarization*, and the cases with one or two components as *partial binarization*.

Kim and Smaragdis [12] consider full binarization with a predetermined portion of the synapses having zero weight, and all other synapses with a weight of one. They report 98.7% accuracy with fully-connected networks on the MNIST dataset, and observe that only XNOR and bitcount operations are necessary for computing with such neural networks. XNOR-Net by Rastegari et al. [22] applies convolutional BNNs on the ImageNet dataset with topologies inspired by AlexNet, ResNet and GoogLeNet, reporting top-1 accuracies of up to 51.2% for full binarization and 65.5% for partial binarization. DoReFa-Net by Zhou et al. [32] explores reduced precision during the forward pass as well as the backward pass, and note that this opens interesting possibilities for training neural networks on FPGAs. Their results includes configurations with partial and full binarization on the SVHN and ImageNet datasets, including best-case ImageNet top-1 accuracies of 43% for full and 53% for partial binarization.

Finally, the work by Courbariaux et al. [5] describes how to train fully-connected and convolutional networks with full binarization and batch normalization layers, reporting competitive accuracy on the MNIST, SVHN and CIFAR-10 datasets. Training for this work was performed using their open source implementation. We use the acronym CNN to refer to conventional or non-binarized neural networks for brevity throughout the rest of this paper.

2.3 Neural Networks in Hardware

A great deal of prior work on mapping neural networks to hardware exist both for FPGAs and as ASICs. We refer the reader to the work by Misra and Saha [16] for a comprehensive survey. We cover a recent and representative set of works here, roughly dividing them into four categories based on their basic architecture: 1) a single processing engine [20, 31, 4, 2], usually in the form of a systolic array, which processes each layer sequentially; 2) a streaming architecture [28, 1], consisting of one processing engine per network layer; 3) a vector processor [7] with instructions specific to accelerating the primitives operations of convolutions; and 4) a neurosynaptic processor [6], which implements many digital neurons and their interconnecting weights.

Systolic arrays: Zhang et al. [31] describes a single processing engine style architecture, using theoretical roofline models tool to design accelerators optimized for the execution of each layer. Ovtcharov et al. [20] implement a similar style architecture, but achieved a $3\times$ speedup over Zhang et al. [31]. Eyeriss by Chen et al. [4] use 16-bit fixed point rather than floating point, and combine several different data reuse strategies. Each 2D convolution is mapped to 1D convolutions across multiple processing engines, allowing for completely regular access patterns for each processing element. The authors report that their data reuse provides $2.5\times$ better energy efficiency over other methods. YodaNN by Andri et al. [2] have a similar design as Zhang et al. [31] but explore binary weights for fixed sized windows.

Streaming architectures: Venieris and Bouganis [28] proposed a synchronous dataflow (SDF) model for mapping

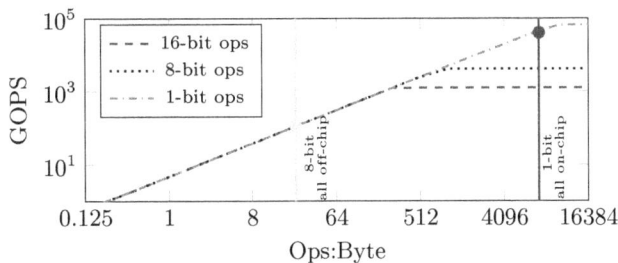

Figure 1: Roofline model for a ZU19EG.

CNNs to FPGAs, which is a similar approach to ours. The main difference is that our design is optimized for BNNs while their design targets conventional CNNs. Their designs achieve up to 1.62× the performance density of hand tuned designs. Alemdar et al. [1] implement fully-connected ternary-weight neural networks with streaming and report up to 255K frames per second on the MNIST dataset, but concentrate on the training aspect for those networks.

Vector processors: Farabet et al. [7] describe a programmable ConvNet Processor (CNP), which is a RISC vector processor with specific macro-instructions for CNNs including 2D convolutions, 2D spatial pooling, dot product and an element-wise non-linear mapping function. The authors also created a tool to compile a high level network description into host code which is used to call the CNP.

Neurosynaptic processors: TrueNorth [6] is a low power, parallel ASIC with 4096 neurosynaptic cores, each implementing 256 binary inputs, 256 neurons and a 256×256 array of synapses. An internal spiking router can connect any input on any core to any neuron on any core, allowing many network topologies to be implemented on fixed hardware.

The authors are not aware of any publication that demonstrates end-to-end mapping of BNNs onto FPGAs. In comparison to prior art, the binary network inference engine can significantly increase classification rates, while reducing power consumption and minimizing latency. This currently comes at the cost of a small drop in accuracy for larger networks, however we believe a) there are use cases that do not require the highest level of accuracy, or can be solved with smaller networks (such as classification of playing cards or handwritten digits [15]) and b) that accuracy can be improved by increasing network sizes [27], an ongoing topic in machine learning research.

3. BNN PERFORMANCE AND ACCURACY

3.1 Estimating Performance Using Rooflines

To estimate and compare BNN performance with fixed-point CNN, we use a *roofline model* [30] which considers memory bandwidth, peak computational performance and arithmetic intensity (the number of mathematical operations performed for each byte of off-chip memory read or written). The intersection of the roofline curve with a vertical line for a particular arithmetic intensity, gives the theoretical peak performance point, which is either *compute-bound* or *memory-bound*. In particular, we consider the binarized [32, 22] and 8-bit fixed-point [26] implementations of the popular AlexNet [14], both of which require 1.4 billion operations (GOPS) to classify one image.

Using the methodology described in [17], we develop a

roofline model for a Xilinx Zynq UltraScale+ ZU19EG FPGA[1]. The resulting roofline model is depicted in Figure 1. We first observe that the FPGA's compute-bound performance is 66 TOPS for binary operations, which is about 16× higher compared to 8-bit and 53× higher compared to 16-bit fixed point operations. However, reaching the compute-bound peak is only possible if the application is not memory-bound. The compact model size of BNNs provides another key benefit. Since the binarized AlexNet requires only 7.4 MB of parameters (compared with 50 MB for 8-bits), the entire neural network model can be kept in on-chip memory. The arithmetic intensities for the binarized and 8-bit fixed point AlexNet variants are shown with vertical lines. Thus, the BNN is almost able to reach the computational peak, while the peak performance of the fixed-point CNN is bound by the memory bandwidth. Based on these observations, with a design that reaches 75% of the peak, we estimate a throughput of $0.75 \cdot \frac{66 \text{ TOPS}}{1.4 \text{ GOPS}} \approx 35000$ images per second.

Using the same model, it should be possible to extend the comparison to CPUs and GPUs, but little data is available on peak binary synaptic operation performance since BNNs are relatively new. For instance, [5] mentions 6 cycles per 32 synapses (64 binary operations) on recent NVIDIA GPUs, which would yield a computational peak of about 26 TOPS on a Tesla K40 with 2880 cores running at 875 MHz, and 16666 images per second for binarized AlexNet.

3.2 Accuracy–Computation Tradeoffs

A tradeoff between network size, precision and accuracy exists [27] so if one would like to achieve a certain classification accuracy for a particular problem, which approach leads to the most efficient solution? 1) A regular ANN with floating point precision? 2) A larger network, but a BNN? To gain more insight into this issue, we conducted a set of experiments on the MNIST dataset that compare accuracy of floating point and binary precision for the same topology. The binary networks are obtained via replacing regular layers by their binary equivalents, as described by Courbariaux et al. [5]. We also binarize the input images for the BNN as our experiments show that input binarization works well for MNIST. Since the space of possible network topologies that can be trained is infinite, we adopted the approach in [27] to simplify the problem. We fix the network topology to a 3 hidden layer, fully connected network while scaling the number of neurons in each layer, and plot the resulting accuracy in Table 1 along with the number of parameters and operations per frame. A few trends are apparent for this problem and network configuration space: 1) similar to what was found in by Sung et al. [27], as the network size increases, the difference in accuracy between low precision networks and floating point networks decreases; and 2) in order to achieve the same level of accuracy as floating point networks, BNNs require 2–11× more parameters and operations. Note that we show the accuracy for networks trained using 32-bit floating point numbers, but it is likely that this could be reduced to 8-bit fixed point without a significant change in accuracy [10]. Our BNN performance estimates from Section 3.1 suggest a 16× speedup for BNN over 8-bit fixed point, which is greater than the 2–11× increase in parameter and operation size. Thus, we expect that BNNs with compara-

---

[1]We assume 4.8 GB/s off-chip memory bandwidth, 350 MHz clock and the following operation cost function: 2.5 LUTs for 1-bit, 40 LUTs for 8-bit, 8 LUTs and 0.5 DSPs for 16-bit.

Table 1: Accuracy results - BNN vs floating point NN.

Neurons/layer	Binary Err. (%)	Float Err. (%)	# Params	Ops/frame
128	6.58	2.70	134,794	268,800
256	4.17	1.78	335,114	668,672
512	2.31	1.25	932,362	1,861,632
1024	1.60	1.13	2,913,290	5,820,416
2048	1.32	0.97	10,020,874	20,029,440
4096	1.17	0.91	36,818,954	73,613,312

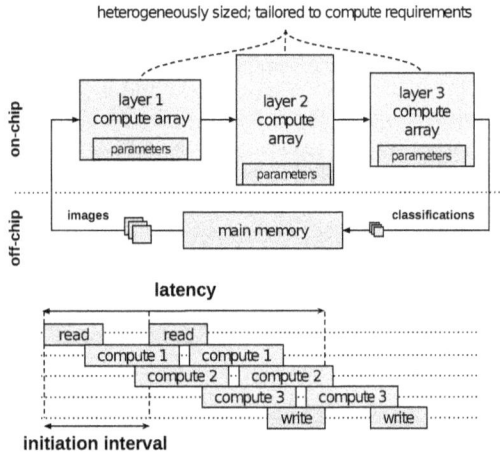

Figure 2: Heterogeneous streaming architecture and schedule.

ble accuracy will be faster than fixed-point networks, even though they may require more parameters and operations.

4. BNNs ON RECONFIGURABLE LOGIC

4.1 Architecture

We adopted a *heterogeneous streaming* architecture as shown in Figure 2 for this work. We build a custom architecture for a given topology rather than scheduling a operations on top of a fixed architecture. Separate compute engines are dedicated to each layer, which communicate via on-chip data streams. Each engine starts to compute as soon as the previous engine starts to produce output. Additionally, owing to the compact model size of BNNs, all neural network parameters are kept in on-chip memory. This avoids most accesses to off-chip memory, minimizes the *latency* (the time to finish classifying one image) by overlapping computation and communication, and minimizes the *initiation interval*: a new image can enter the accelerator as soon as the first compute array is finished with the previous image. The separate mapping of layers to compute arrays also enables heterogeneity. By tailoring compute arrays separately for each layer's requirements, we can avoid the "one-size-fits-all" inefficiencies and reap more of the benefits of reconfigurable computing. This requires a different bitfile when the neural network topology is changed but we consider this an acceptable cost for the performance gains obtained.

A BNN accelerator may have various constraints imposed upon it depending on the use case. User-imposed constraints include the choice of FPGA and platform, desired classification throughput in frames per second (FPS) and clock frequency. Simultaneously, the BNN topology constrains how the compute resources must be allocated to obtain an efficient heterogeneous streaming architecture. FINN offers parameterizable building blocks and a way of controlling the classification throughput, as described in Sections 4.3

and 4.4. To achieve portability, we chose a commercial high level synthesis tool, Vivado High-Level Synthesis (HLS), for the implementation. The tool enables faster development cycles via high-level abstractions, and provides automated pipelining to meet the clock frequency target.

4.2 BNN-specific Operator Optimizations

BNNs have several properties that enable a more efficient mapping to FPGAs without affecting the network accuracy, which we describe in the following subsections. We assume that the methodology described in [5] is used for training all BNNs in this paper, where all BNN layers have the following properties (unless otherwise stated):

- Using 1-bit values for all input activations, weights and output activations (full binarization), where an unset bit represents -1 and a set bit represents +1.

- Batch normalization prior to the activation function.

- Using the following activation function:
  $\text{Sign}(x) = \{+1 \text{ if } x \geq 0, -1 \text{ if } x < 0\}$

4.2.1 Popcount for Accumulation

The regular and value-constrained nature of BNN computations enable computing binary dot products with fewer hardware resources. Let Y be the number of input synapses (or *fan-in*) for a given neuron, with the number of +1-valued synapse inputs denoted as Y_1 and -1-valued synapses as Y_0. As there are only two possible values (-1 and +1) for any synapse input, $Y = Y_0 + Y_1$. Therefore, by counting the number of synapses for only one value, it is possible to infer the summed response for the entire neuron.

The practical consequence for hardware is that the summation of a binary dot product can be implemented by a *popcount* operation that counts the number of set bits instead of accumulation with signed arithmetic. Our experiments with Vivado HLS indicate that popcount-accumulate requires approximately half the number of LUT and FF resources to implement compared to signed-accumulate. For instance, with a target $F_{\text{clk}} = 200$ MHz, a 128-bit popcount-accumulate requires 376 LUTs and 29 FFs, while a 128-bit bipolar-accumulate requires 759 LUTs and 84 FFs.

4.2.2 Batchnorm-activation as Threshold

All BNN layers use batch normalization [11] on convolutional or fully connected layer outputs, then apply the sign function to determine the output activation. We show how the same output can be computed via thresholding.

Let a_k be the dot product (pre-activation) output of neuron k, and $\Theta_k = (\gamma_k, \mu_k, i_k, B_k)$ be the batch normalization parameters learned during training for this neuron. The output a_k^b is computed as $a_k^b = \text{Sign}(\text{BatchNorm}(a_k, \Theta_k))$, with $\text{BatchNorm}(a_k, \Theta_k) = \gamma_k \cdot (a_k - \mu_k) \cdot i_k + B_k$. Figure 3 shows the dot product input vs output activation for three example neurons. Depending on parameter values, the plot may be shifted towards the left or right, or be flipped horizontally, but a threshold τ_k for a change in the output activation is always present. Solving $\text{BatchNorm}(\tau_k, \Theta_k) = 0$ we can deduce that $\tau_k = \mu_k - (B_k/(\gamma_k \cdot i_k))$.

To make the thresholds compatible with the positive-only operations in Section 4.2.1), the computed threshold is averaged with the neuron fan-in S to obtain $\tau_k^+ = (\tau_k + S)/2$. Observing how neuron C activates with an opposite sign threshold to neurons A and B in Figure 3, all neurons can be

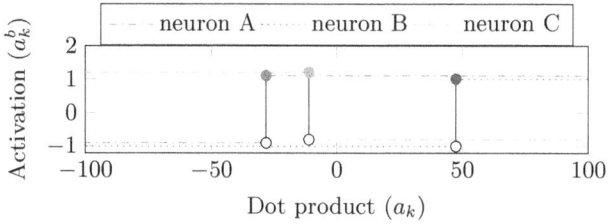

Figure 3: Three examples of binary neuron activations with batch normalization. A slight vertical offset is added for clarity.

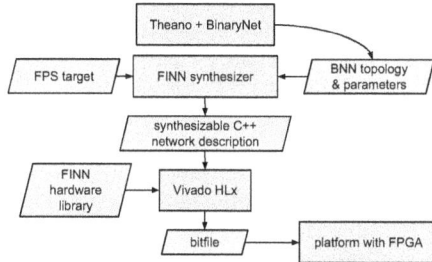

Figure 4: Generating an FPGA accelerator from a trained BNN.

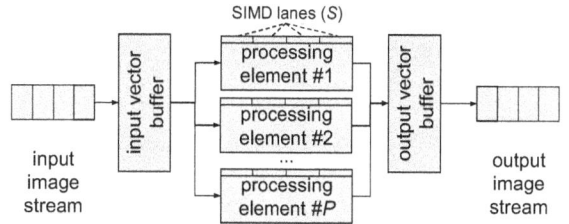

Figure 5: Overview of the MVTU.

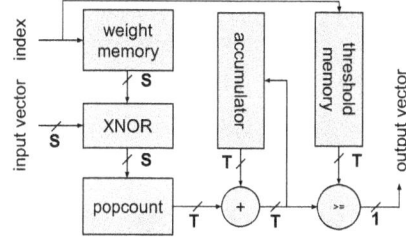

Figure 6: MVTU PE datapath. **Bold** indicates bitwidth.

made to activate using a greater-than threshold by flipping the signs of a neuron's weights if $\gamma_k \cdot i_k < 0$.

Using these techniques, we can compute the output activation using an unsigned comparison and avoid computing the batch normalized value altogether during inference. τ_k^+ itself is fixed for a trained network and can be computed from the batchnorm parameters at compile time. Synthesis reports from Vivado HLS for 16-bit dot product output values indicate that regular batchnorm-and-sign activation requires 2 DSPs, 55 FFs and 40 LUTs, whereas the threshold activation we describe here only requires 6 LUTs.

4.2.3 Boolean OR for Max-pooling

The networks described in [5] perform pooling prior to activations, i.e. pooling is performed on non-binarized numbers, which are then batch normalized and fed into the activation function. We show that the same layer outputs can be derived by max pooling *after* the activations without having to re-train the network. Let $a_1, a_2, \ldots a_Y$ be the positive dot product outputs that will be processed by max-pooling. In accordance with Section 4.2.2, the output would be computed as $a^b = (\text{Max}(a_1, a_2, \ldots a_Y) > \tau^+)$. Due to the distributivity of Max, the output will be *true* if *any* of $a_1, a_2, \ldots a_S$ are greater than τ^+. Therefore, the same result can be computed as $a^b = (a_1 > \tau^+) \vee (a_2 > \tau^+) \ldots \vee (a_Y > \tau^+)$. As the threshold comparisons are already computed for the activations, max-pooling can be effectively implemented with the Boolean OR-operator. We note that similar principles apply for min-pooling (as Boolean AND) and average-pooling (as Boolean majority function) as well.

4.3 FINN Design Flow and Hardware Library

Figure 4 illustrates the design flow for converting a trained BNN into an FPGA accelerator. The user supplies a FPS target alongside a Theano-trained BNN to the FINN synthesizer. The synthesizer first determines the folding parameters (Section 4.4) to meet the FPS target and applies the optimizations from Section 4.2, then produces a synthesizable C++ description of a heterogeneous streaming architecture. The architecture is composed of building blocks from the FINN hardware library described in the following subsections.

4.3.1 The Matrix–Vector–Threshold Unit

The Matrix–Vector–Threshold Unit (MVTU) forms the computational core for our accelerator designs. The vast majority of compute operations in a BNN can be expressed as matrix–vector operations followed by thresholding. For instance, the pre-activation output $\mathbf{a_N}$ of the fully connected neural network layer at index N is given by matrix-vector product $\mathbf{a_N} = \mathbf{A} \cdot \mathbf{a_{N-1}^b}$ where $\mathbf{A}$ is the synaptic weight matrix and $\mathbf{a_{N-1}^b}$ are the activations from the previous layer. The post-activation output can then be computed by $\mathbf{a_N^b} = \mathbf{a^N} > \tau_{\mathbf{N}}^+$, where the thresholds $\tau_{\mathbf{N}}^+$ are determined as described in Section 4.2.2. Convolutions can also be implemented as matrix–vector products, as will be described in Section 4.3.2. As such, the MVTU implements fully-connected layers as a standalone component, and is also used as part of the convolutional layers.

The overall organization of the MVTU is shown in Figure 5. Internally, the MVTU consists of an input and output buffer, and an array of Processing Elements (PEs) each with a number of SIMD lanes. The number of PEs (P) and SIMD lanes (S) are configurable to control the throughput as discussed in Section 4.4.1. The synapse weight matrix to be used is kept in On-Chip Memory (OCM) distributed between PEs, and the input images stream through the MVTU as each one is multiplied with the matrix. Each PE receives exactly the same control signals and input vector data, but multiply-accumulates the input with a different part of the matrix. In terms of the taxonomy described in [4], this architecture is both *weight stationary* (since each weight remains local to the PE) and *output stationary* (since each popcount computation remains local to the PE).

Figure 6 shows the datapath of an MVTU PE. It computes the dot product between the input vector and a row of the synaptic weight matrix and compares the result to a threshold, producing a single-bit output. The dot product computation itself consists of an XNOR of the vectors, after which the number of set bits in the result is counted (see Section 4.2.1) and added to the accumulator register. Once the entire dot product is accumulated, it is thresholded. The accumulator, adder and threshold memory bitwidth can be scaled down to $T = 1 + \log_2(Y)$ for additional resource savings.

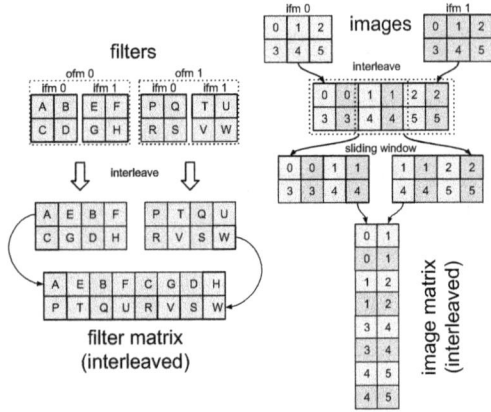

(a) Lowering with interleaved channels.

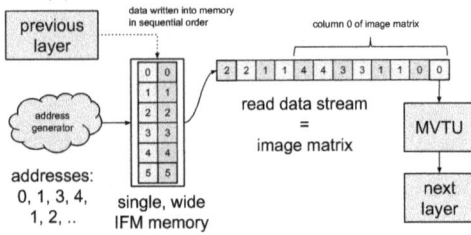

(b) SWU operation.

Figure 7: Convolution using interleaved channels.

Finally, it is worth pointing out that the MVTU architectural template can also support partial binarization for non-binarized outputs and inputs. Removing the thresolding stage provides non-binarized outputs, while using regular multiply-add instead of XNOR-popcount can handle non-binarized inputs These features are used in the first and last layers of networks that process non-binary input images or do not output a one-hot classification vector.

4.3.2   Convolution: The Sliding Window Unit

Convolutions can be *lowered* to matrix-matrix multiplications [3], which is the approach followed in this work. The weights from the convolution filters are packed into a *filter matrix*, while a sliding window is moved across input images to form an *image matrix*. These matrices are then multiplied to generate the output images.

The convolutional layer consists of a Sliding Window Unit (SWU), which generates the image matrix from incoming feature maps, and a MVTU that actually computes the matrix–matrix product using a different column vector from the image matrix each time. In order to better cater for the SIMD parallelism of the MVTU and minimize buffering requirements, we *interleave* the feature maps such that each pixel contains all the Input Feature Map (IFM) channel data for that position, as illustrated in Figure 7a. Since the dot product to compute a Output Feature Map (OFM) pixel includes all IFMs pixels at a certain sliding window location, those IFM pixels can be processed in any order owing to the commutative property of addition. Note that interleaving the filter matrix has no additional cost since it is done offline, and interleaving the input image can be done on-the-fly in the FPGA. Storing the pixels in this fashion allows us to implement the SWU with a single wide OCM instead of multiple narrow OCMs, and also enables the output of the MVTU to be directly fed to the next layer without any

transposition. As illustrated in Figure 7b, the incoming IFM data is simply stored at sequential addresses in a buffer, then the memory locations corresponding to each sliding window are read out to produce the image matrix.

Although not required by any of the networks described in this work, the SWU also pads the images if necessary. One interesting observation is that with the bipolar number representation used in this work, there is no number corresponding to zero. Therefore, in order to maintain a true binary datapath for activations, images must be padded with our representation or either a 1 or a -1. Future work will look into what impact this has on the accuracy of trained networks, but early experiments suggest that there is very little difference in accuracy, with respect to [5].

4.3.3   The Pooling Unit

The Pooling Unit (PU) implements max-pooling as described in Section 4.2.3. To implement $k \times k$ max-pooling on a $D_H \times D_W$ binary image of C channels, the PU contains $C \cdot k$ line buffers of D_W bits each. As with the rest of our component library, the PU operates in a streaming fashion. The input image is gradually streamed into the line buffers. When at least k rows of the image have arrived, each k consecutive bits of the line buffer are OR'ed together to produce horizontal subsampling for each channel. These are then OR'ed together with the other line buffers to produce vertical subsampling, the results are streamed out, and the oldest line buffers are refilled with the next row of pixels.

4.4   Folding

In terms of the MVTU description given in Section 4.3.1, each PE corresponds to a *hardware neuron*, while each SIMD lane acts as a *hardware synapse*. If we were to dimension each MVTU in a network with a number of hardware neurons and synapses equal to the number of neurons and synapses in a BNN layer, this would result in a fully parallel neural network that could classify images at the clock rate. However, the amount of hardware resources on an FPGA is limited, and it is necessary to time-multiplex (or *fold*) the BNN onto fewer hardware synapses and neurons. We now describe how the folding is performed subject to user constraints.

The work by Venieris et al. [28] describes a method for folding neural networks expressed as streaming dataflow graphs, with focus on formalizing the folding and design space exploration. In this work, we consider a simpler variant that only controls the folding of matrix–vector products to achieve a given FPS requirement set by the user, and focus on *how* the folding is implemented in terms of the workload mapping. As almost all computations in BNNs are expressed as matrix–vector multiplications, implementing folding for matrix–vector multiplication already enables a great degree of control over the system throughput. Folding directly affects the resource and power consumption of the final system as well, which we explore in Section 5.

4.4.1   Folding Matrix–Vector Products

Folding matrix–vector products is achieved by controlling two parameters of the MVTU: P the number of PEs, and S the number of SIMD lanes per PE. These determine how the matrix is partitioned between the PEs. A P-high, S-wide tile of the matrix is processed at a time, with each row in the tile mapped to a different PE, and each column to a different SIMD lane. For a $X \times Y$ matrix, we refer to $F^n = X/P$

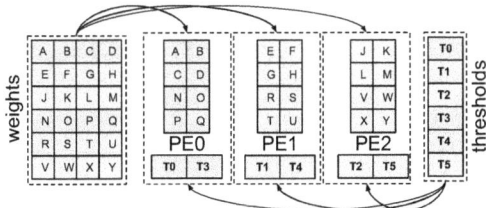

Figure 8: Neuron and synapse folding for MVTU.

as the *neuron fold* and $F^s = Y/S$ as the *synapse fold*. The *total fold* F is then obtained as $F = F^n \cdot F^s$, which is also the number of cycles required to complete one matrix–vector multiply. Note that F^n and F^s should be integers to avoid padding the weight matrix. As an example, Figure 8 shows how a 6×4 weight matrix is partitioned between three PEs with two SIMD lanes each. Here, each matrix-vector multiply will take $F^n \cdot F^s = (6/3) \cdot (4/2) = 4$ cycles.

The same principle applies for convolutional layers, but these always have an inherent amount of folding due to our current matrix–matrix product as multiple matrix–vector products implementation. For convolutional layers, the total fold is $F = F^m \cdot F^n \cdot F^s$, where F^m is a network-dependent constant due to multiple matrix-vector products, and is equal to the number of output pixels from the convolution.

4.4.2 Determining F^n and F^s

Avoiding the "one-size-fits-all" inefficiencies requires tailoring each MVTU's compute resources to layer requirements. The guiding principle here is *rate-balancing* the heterogeneous streaming architecture: the slowest layer (with $II_{\max}$) will determine the overall throughput, so each layer should use a roughly equal number of cycles to process one image. As this is a streaming system, the classification throughput FPS will be approximately $\frac{F_{\text{clk}}}{II_{\max}}$, where F_{clk} is the clock frequency. For a fully-connected layer, the total fold F is equal to the initiation interval (II). Therefore, balancing a fully-connected BNN can be achieved by using F^n and F^s such that $F^n \cdot F^s = \frac{F_{\text{clk}}}{\text{FPS}}$ for each layer. Depending on the BNN and the FPS requirements, the number of memory channels or sliding window generation may constitute bottlenecks. For such cases, we match the throughput of all other layers to the bottleneck in order not to waste resources.

5. EVALUATION

5.1 Experimental Setup

To evaluate FINN, we created a number of prototypes that accelerate BNNs inference on the MNIST [15] (28×28 handwritten digits), CIFAR-10 [13] (32×32 color images in 10 categories) and cropped SVHN [18] (32×32 images of Street View House Numbers) datasets. Each prototype combines a BNN topology with a different use case scenario. We consider three different BNN topologies for classifying the datasets as follows:

- **SFC** and **LFC** are three-layer fully connected network topologies for classifying the MNIST dataset, with different numbers of neurons to demonstrate accuracy-computation tradeoffs (Section 3.2). SFC contains 256 neurons per layer and achieves 95.83% accuracy, while LFC has 1024 neurons per layer and achieves 98.4%

accuracy. These networks accept 28x28 binary images and output a 10-bit one-hot vector indicating the digit.

- **CNV** is a convolutional network topology inspired by BinaryNet [5] and VGG-16 [25]. It contains a succession of (3x3 convolution, 3x3 convolution, 2x2 maxpool) layers repeated three times with 64-128-256 channels, followed by two fully connected layers of 512 neurons each. We use this topology for classifying both the CIFAR-10 (with 80.1% accuracy) and SVHN (with 94.9% accuracy) datasets, with different weights and thresholds. Note that the inputs to the first layer and the outputs from the last layer are not binarized; CNV accepts 32x32 images with 24 bits/pixel, and returns a 10-element vector of 16-bit values as the result.

To further demonstrate the flexibility of the framework, we consider two usage scenarios for each BNN topology to guide the choice of parametrization:

- **max** is the maximum performance scenario where it is desirable to reach the peak FPS permitted by the platform, topology and FINN's architecture.

- **fix** represents a scenario with a fixed FPS requirement, which is often determined by an I/O device for real life applications. For instance, consider a 640×480 video stream at 30 FPS, which is to be chopped up into 32×32 tiles for neural network inference. Handling this task with real-time performance would require a BNN inference rate of 9000 FPS, which we set as the requirement for this usage scenario.

We use shortened names to refer to the prototypes, e.g. CNV-fix refers to the prototype that implements the **CNV** topology for the **fix** usage scenario. For each prototype, the folding factors (Section 4.4) were determined to meet the requirements of its usage scenario, and the FINN design flow (Section 4.3) was followed to generate the hardware accelerator. Vivado HLS and Vivado version 2016.3 were used for the bitfile synthesis. A target clock frequency of 200 MHz was used for both Vivado HLS and Vivado, and to run the resulting accelerator unless otherwise stated. The salient properties of the topologies and folding factors for the prototypes are summarized in Table 2.

All prototypes have been implemented on the Xilinx Zynq-7000 All Programmable SoC ZC706 Evaluation Kit running Ubuntu 15.04. The board contains a Zynq Z7045 SoC with dual ARM Cortex-A9 cores and FPGA fabric with 218600 LUTs and 545 BRAMs. The host code runs on the Cortex-A9 cores of the Zynq. It initializes 10000 images with test data in the Zynq's shared DRAM, launches and times the accelerator execution to measure classification throughput, then measures accuracy by comparing against the correct classifications. Two power measurements P_{chip} and P_{wall} are provided for each experiment; P_{chip} using the PMBus interface to monitor the FPGA power supply rails, and P_{wall} using a wall power meter for the total board power consumption. The measurements are averaged over a period of 10 seconds while the accelerator is running.

5.2 Results

Table 3 provides an overview of the experimental results, in terms of classification throughput, latency to classify one image, FPGA resource usage and power. The **max** scenario

Table 2: Summary of workloads.

Topology	Params (Mbits)	Ops (M)	Off-chip I/O (B)	Op.Int. (Ops/B)
SFC	0.3	0.6	112	5970
LFC	2.9	5.8	112	51968
CNV	1.5	112.5	3092	36400

Prototype	Per-Layer Total Fold (F)
SFC-max	13, 16, 16, 16
SFC-fix	12544, 16384, 16384, 2560
LFC-max	104, 128, 128, 128
LFC-fix	13312, 16384, 16384, 10240
CNV-max	8100, 7056, 5184, 7200, 5184, 4608, 8192, 8192, 1280
CNV-fix	16200, 14112, 10368, 14400, 10368, 9216, 16384, 16384, 1280

Table 3: Summary of results from FINN 200 MHz prototypes.

Name	Thr.put (FPS)	Latency (µs)	LUT	BRAM	P_{chip} (W)	P_{wall} (W)
SFC-max	12361 k	0.31	91131	4.5	7.3	21.2
LFC-max	1561 k	2.44	82988	396	8.8	22.6
CNV-max	21.9 k	283	46253	186	3.6	11.7
SFC-fix	12.2 k	240	5155	16	0.4	8.1
LFC-fix	12.2 k	282	5636	114.5	0.8	7.9
CNV-fix	11.6 k	550	29274	152.5	2.3	10

results are perhaps the best summary of the potential of BNNs on FPGAs, with SFC-max achieving 12.3 million classifications per second at 0.31 µs latency while drawing less than 22 W total power. All **fix** results meet and exceed the 9000 FPS requirement by 30% due to folding factors being integers, though lower throughput and power could have been achieved by using a slower clock. We focus on particular aspects of the results in the following subsections.

5.2.1 Maximum Throughput and Bottlenecks

To assess the quality of results for the **max** scenarios, we compare the achieved performance (XNOR–popcount operations per second) with the peak throughput in TOPS indicated by the roofline model. Figure 9 presents a roofline model (Section 3.1) for the ZC706, assuming 90% LUT utilization, 200 MHz clock frequency and 1.6 GB/s of DRAM bandwidth. The vertical lines show the arithmetic intensities for the topologies, and the actual operations per second values from corresponding prototypes with **max** usage scenarios are indicated as points on those lines. All **max** prototypes achieve performance in the TOPS range, but are bottlenecked due to different factors. CNV-max achieves 2.5 TOPS and is *architecture-bound*. The current SWU design does not scale as well as the MVTU and constitutes a bottleneck, which will be addressed in future work. Despite its higher complexity, observe that CNV-max actually requires ~2× fewer LUTs

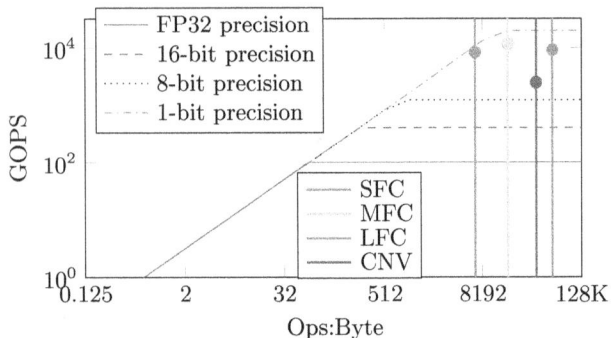

Figure 9: ZC706 roofline with topologies and **max**-datapoints.

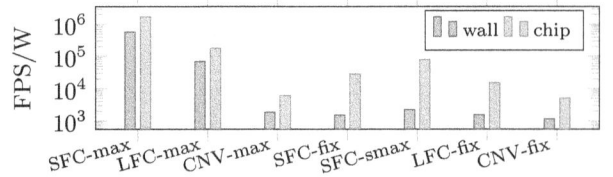

Figure 10: Prototype energy efficiency.

than SFC-max since the folding parameters for CNV-max are chosen in accordance with the maximum performance dictated by the bottleneck. SFC-max achieves 8.2 TOPS and is *memory-bound*. Observe that the SFC arithmetic intensity line intersects the memory-bound (sloped) part of the roofline, thus the performance cannot be scaled up without adding more DRAM memory bandwidth. LFC-max achieves 9.1 TOPS, which is 46% of the roofline, and is *resource-bound*. As folding factors are integers, the smallest increment is 2× which roughly doubles the resource cost. The FPGA has enough LUTs but not enough BRAMs to accommodate doubled resource cost, thus leaving ~30% of BRAMs unused. A 3x512-neuron fully connected topology, labeled MFC in Figure 9, was able to achieve 11.6 TOPS and 6238 kFPS with 95% of the device BRAMs.

5.2.2 Energy Efficiency

It is desirable to minimize the energy spent per image classification, which corresponds to maximizing FPS per Watt when many images are to be classified. To help evaluate the energy efficiency, Figure 10 plots the achieved FPS per Watt for the prototypes for both the wall power and FPGA power readings. In general, we see that the higher FPS prototypes have better energy efficiency, with SFC-max offering 583066 FPS per W of total power and outperforming all other prototypes by at least an order of magnitude. It is also worth noting that the board's idle power consumption is about 7 W, which forms a lower bound on all wall power measurements, and could be improved by e.g. using LPDDR memory.

To maximize energy efficiency with a fixed target FPS, is it better to use a highly parallel design at low clock frequency, or a less parallel design at high clock frequency? We ran an additional experiment to investigate this question by slowing down the SFC-max prototype to meet the **fix** FPS requirement of 9000 FPS. By clocking it at 250 kHz, we obtained a classification throughput of 15731 FPS with 0.2 W of FPGA power. The result is labeled SFC-smax in Figure 10, and is over 2× more energy efficient than SFC-fix. This suggests that a high degree of parallelism benefits energy efficiency as long as the FPGA resources are available.

5.2.3 Resource Efficiency

We consider two aspects of resource efficiency for FINN: how efficiently the compute units are used during runtime (*runtime efficiency*), and how efficiently FPGA resources are turned into compute units (*mapping efficiency*).

To assess runtime efficiency, we divide the FPS-based (actual) operations per cycle ($\frac{FPS \cdot Ops}{F_{clk}}$) by the (peak) number of synaptic operations per cycle from the design ($\sum 2 \cdot P \cdot S$). The prototypes exhibit good runtime efficiency, with ~70% for **CNV**, ~80% for **SFC** and ~90% for **LFC**. The efficiency can be increased further by fine-tuning the folding factors between different layers.

Evaluating the mapping efficiency directly on the proto-

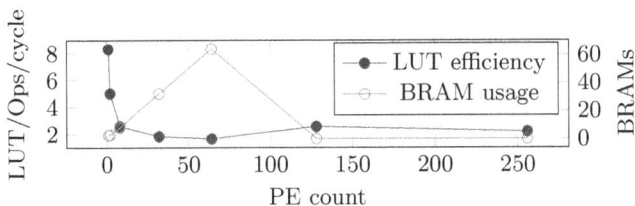

Figure 11: Mapping resource efficiency.

types loses some insight, since **CNV** uses LUTs on SWU and PU, while fully-connected topologies do not. Instead, for a single 256×256 fully-connected layer, we fix $S = 64$ and vary P, and plot the LUTs per synaptic operation in Figure 11, which should be minimized to maximize efficiency. The LUTs per operation decreases with higher P since the fixed-size control logic is amortized between more PEs and reaches a minimum of 1.83 for $P = 64$, but increases again for $P > 64$. To understand why, we also plot the number of BRAMs used in the same figure. Although all designs have the same number of BNN parameters, the number of BRAMs increases with P since each PE needs its own weight and threshold memories. This also means a significant part of the BRAM storage capacity is unused for $1 < P \leq 64$, since the same amount of network parameters is divided between a greater number of memories. This is also visible for SFC-fix and SFC-max, which use the same network parameters, but have almost $10\times$ difference in the number of BRAMs used (15.5 vs 130.5) since SFC-max has more compute elements working in parallel. Here, with $P > 64$, so little of each BRAM is used that Vivado HLS implements the weight and threshold memories using LUTs, which causes the LUTs per operation to increase. Thus, the depth and number of BRAMs, and the LUT-to-BRAM ratio of the FPGA plays a key role in determining how well the resources will be utilized by a BNN. For instance, on another FPGA with the same amount of LUTs but twice the number of half-depth BRAMs, LFC-max could achieve $2\times$ throughput.

5.3 Comparison to prior work

From an application perspective, we suggest that the current best way to compare different platforms is to simply compare their accuracy, FPS and power consumption when working on the same benchmark datasets (MNIST, CIFAR-10 and SVHN). This comparison is provided in Table 4, and is divided into three sections: our results, prior work on low-precision (< 4 bits) networks, and prior work with higher-precision (> 4 bits) networks.

When it comes to pure image throughput, our designs outperform all others. For the MNIST dataset, we achieve an FPS which is over $48/6\times$ over the nearest highest throughput design [1] for our SFC-max/LFC-max designs respectively. While our SFC-max design has lower accuracy than the networks implemented by Alemdar et al. [1] our LFC-max design outperforms their nearest accuracy design by over $6/1.9\times$ for throughput and FPS/W respectively. For other datasets, our CNV-*max* design outperforms TrueNorth [6] for FPS by over $17/8\times$ for CIFAR-10 / SVHN datasets respectively, while achieving $9.44\times$ higher throughput than the design by Ovtcharov et al. [20], and $2.2\times$ over the fastest results reported by Hegde et al. [9]. Our prototypes have classification accuracy within 3% of the other low-precision

works, and could have been improved by using larger BNNs.

A recent work by Nurvitadhi et al. [19] compares binary matrix-vector operation performance and efficiency on FPGA, ASIC, GPU and CPU. Their results indicate that CPU and GPUs are severely underutilized for binary synaptic operations, and that FPGAs are only ~8× less energy efficient than ASICs in this case. As they do not provide results on end-to-end network implementations, we do not include them in Table 4. Our 11.6 TOPS MFC prototype (Section 5.2.1) is 20% faster than the 9.6 TOPS reported in their work.

6. CONCLUSION

This work demonstrates the performance and energy efficiency potential of recently proposed BNNs for image classification. They are particularly well-suited for FPGA implementations as parameters can be fit entirely in OCM and arithmetic is simplified, enabling high computational performance. The novel parameterizable dataflow architecture and optimizations presented enable unprecedented classification rates, minimal power consumption and latency, while offering the flexibility of C++ design entry and the scalability required for accelerating larger and more complex networks. We hence believe that this technology is eminently suitable for embedded applications requiring real-time response, including surveillance, robotics and augmented reality. Future work will focus on providing support for non-binary low precision, implementing larger networks like AlexNet, higher performance convolutions, and a more thorough design space exploration. Finally, FINN assumes that all BNN parameters can fit into the available OCM of a single FPGA. Supporting external memory, multi-FPGAs implementations and reconfiguration [28] could improve the utility of our approach.

Acknowledgments

The authors would like to thank the NTNU HPC lab and colleagues at Xilinx Research Labs for their support. This work was supported under the Australian Research Councils Linkage Projects funding scheme (project number LP130101034).

7. REFERENCES

[1] H. Alemdar, N. Caldwell, V. Leroy, A. Prost-Boucle, and F. Pétrot. Ternary Neural Networks for Resource-Efficient AI Applications. *CoRR*, abs/1609.00222, 2016.

[2] R. Andri, L. Cavigelli, D. Rossi, and L. Benini. YodaNN: An ultra-low power convolutional neural network accelerator based on binary weights. *CoRR*, abs/1606.05487, 2016.

[3] K. Chellapilla, S. Puri, and P. Simard. High performance convolutional neural networks for document processing. In *Proc. ICFHR*. Suvisoft, 2006.

[4] Y.-H. Chen, J. Emer, and V. Sze. Eyeriss: A spatial architecture for energy-efficient dataflow for convolutional neural networks. In *Proc. ACM/IEEE ISCA*. IEEE, 2016.

[5] M. Courbariaux, I. Hubara, D. Soudry, R. El-Yaniv, and Y. Bengio. Binarized Neural Networks: Training Deep Neural Networks with Weights and Activations Constrained to +1 or -1. *CoRR*, abs/1602.02830, 2016.

[6] S. K. Esser, P. A. Merolla, J. V. Arthur, A. S. Cassidy, R. Appuswamy, A. Andreopoulos, D. J. Berg, J. L.

Table 4: Comparison to prior work. Metrics not reported by prior work are indicated by dashes (-), and our estimates by ~ .

Name	Dataset	Platform	Precision	Err. (%)	kFPS	P_{chip} (W)	P_{wall} (W)	kFPS/P_{chip}	kFPS/P_{wall}	GOPS
SFC-max	MNIST	ZC706	1	4.17	12,361	7.3	21.2	1693.29	583.07	8,265.45
LFC-max	MNIST	ZC706	1	1.60	1,561	8.8	22.6	177.39	69.07	9,085.67
MFC-max	MNIST	ZC706	1	2.31	6,238	11.3	28.5	552	218.8	11,612.86
CNV-max	CIFAR-10	ZC706	1	19.90	21.9	3.6	11.7	6.08	1.87	2,465.5
CNV-max	SVHN	ZC706	1	5.10	21.9	3.6	11.7	6.08	1.87	2,465.5
Alemdar et al. [1]	MNIST	Kintex-7 160T	2	2.24	255.10	0.32	-	806.45	-	~96.68
Alemdar et al. [1]	MNIST	Kintex-7 160T	2	1.71	255.10	1.84	-	138.50	-	~448.47
Alemdar et al. [1]	MNIST	Kintex-7 160T	2	1.67	255.10	2.76	-	92.59	-	~864.03
Park and Sung [21]	MNIST	ZC706	3	-	70	4.98	-	14.06	-	~210
TrueNorth [6]	CIFAR-10	TrueNorth	1	16.59	1.249	0.2044	-	6.11	-	-
TrueNorth [6]	SVHN	TrueNorth	1	3.34	2.526	0.2565	-	9.85	-	-
CaffePresso [9]	MNIST	Keystone-II	16	-	5	-	14	-	0.357	44.82
CaffePresso [9]	CIFAR-10	Keystone-II	16	-	10	-	14	-	0.714	146.14
CaffePresso [9]	MNIST	Parallella	32	-	0.64	-	5	-	0.129	5.78
CaffePresso [9]	CIFAR-10	Parallella	32	-	0.1	-	5	-	0.019	1.40
Ovtcharov et al. [20]	CIFAR-10	Stratix V D5	32	~11-26	2.32	-	25	-	0.093	-

McKinstry, T. Melano, D. R. Barch, et al. Convolutional Networks for Fast, Energy-Efficient Neuromorphic Computing. *CoRR*, abs/1603.08270, 2016.

[7] C. Farabet, C. Poulet, J. Y. Han, and Y. LeCun. CNP: An FPGA-based processor for convolutional networks. In *Proc. IEEE FPL*, pages 32–37. IEEE, 2009.

[8] S. Han, H. Mao, and W. J. Dally. Deep Compression: Compressing Deep Neural Network with Pruning, Trained Quantization and Huffman coding. *CoRR*, abs/1510.00149, 2015.

[9] G. Hegde, Siddhartha, N. Ramasamy, and N. Kapre. CaffePresso: An Optimized Library for Deep Learning on Embedded Accelerator-based platforms. In *Proc. CASES*, 2016.

[10] F. N. Iandola, M. W. Moskewicz, K. Ashraf, S. Han, W. J. Dally, and K. Keutzer. SqueezeNet: AlexNet-level accuracy with 50x fewer parameters and< 1MB model size. *CoRR*, abs/1602.07630, 2016.

[11] S. Ioffe and C. Szegedy. Batch normalization: Accelerating deep network training by reducing internal covariate shift. In *Proc. ICML*, pages 448–456, 2015.

[12] M. Kim and P. Smaragdis. Bitwise neural networks. *CoRR*, abs/1601.06071, 2016.

[13] A. Krizhevsky and G. Hinton. Learning multiple layers of features from tiny images. *Technical Report*, 2009.

[14] A. Krizhevsky, I. Sutskever, and G. E. Hinton. Imagenet classification with deep convolutional neural networks. In *Proc. NIPS*, pages 1097–1105, 2012.

[15] Y. LeCun, L. Bottou, Y. Bengio, and P. Haffner. Gradient-based learning applied to document recognition. *Proc. of the IEEE*, 86(11):2278–2324, 1998.

[16] J. Misra and I. Saha. Artificial neural networks in hardware: A survey of two decades of progress. *Neurocomputing*, 74(1–3):239–255, 2010.

[17] S. Muralidharan, K. O'Brien, and C. Lalanne. A Semi-Automated Tool Flow for Roofline Anaylsis of OpenCL Kernels on Accelerators. *Proc. Workshop on H2RC*, 2015.

[18] Y. Netzer, T. Wang, A. Coates, A. Bissacco, B. Wu, and A. Y. Ng. Reading digits in natural images with unsupervised feature learning. *NIPS Workshop on Deep Learning and Unsupervised Feature Learning*, 2011.

[19] E. Nurvitadhi, D. Sheffield, J. Sim, A. Mishra, G. Venkatesh, and D. Marr. Accelerating Binarized Neural Networks: Comparison of FPGA, CPU, GPU, and ASIC. In *Proc. ICFPT*, 2016.

[20] K. Ovtcharov, O. Ruwase, J.-Y. Kim, J. Fowers, K. Strauss, and E. Chung. Accelerating deep convolutional neural networks using specialized hardware, February 2015.

[21] J. Park and W. Sung. FPGA based implementation of deep neural networks using on-chip memory only. In *Proc. IEEE ICASSP*, pages 1011–1015. IEEE, 2016.

[22] M. Rastegari, V. Ordonez, J. Redmon, and A. Farhadi. XNOR-Net: ImageNet Classification Using Binary Convolutional Neural Networks. In *ECCV*, 2016.

[23] O. Russakovsky, J. Deng, H. Su, J. Krause, S. Satheesh, S. Ma, Z. Huang, A. Karpathy, A. Khosla, M. Bernstein, A. C. Berg, and L. Fei-Fei. ImageNet Large Scale Visual Recognition Challenge. *IJCV*, 115(3):211–252, 2015.

[24] J. Schmidhuber. Deep learning in neural networks: An overview. *Neural Networks*, 61:85–117, 2015.

[25] K. Simonyan and A. Zisserman. Very deep convolutional networks for large-scale image recognition. *CoRR*, abs/1409.1556, 2014.

[26] N. Suda, V. Chandra, G. Dasika, A. Mohanty, Y. Ma, S. B. K. Vrudhula, J. Seo, and Y. Cao. Throughput-Optimized OpenCL-based FPGA Accelerator for Large-Scale Convolutional Neural Networks. In *Proc. ACM/SIGDA ISFPGA*, pages 16–25, 2016.

[27] W. Sung, S. Shin, and K. Hwang. Resiliency of deep neural networks under quantization. *CoRR*, abs/1511.06488, 2015.

[28] S. I. Venieris and C.-S. Bouganis. fpgaConvNet: A Framework for Mapping Convolutional Neural Networks on FPGAs. In *Proc. IEEE FCCM*, pages 40–47. IEEE, 2016.

[29] T. Weyand, I. Kostrikov, and J. Philbin. Planet - photo geolocation with convolutional neural networks. *CoRR*, abs/1602.05314, 2016.

[30] S. Williams, A. Waterman, and D. A. Patterson. Roofline: an insightful visual performance model for multicore architectures. *Commun. ACM*, 52(4):65–76, 2009.

[31] C. Zhang, P. Li, G. Sun, Y. Guan, B. Xiao, and J. Cong. Optimizing FPGA-based accelerator design for deep convolutional neural networks. In *Proc. ACM/SIGDA ISFPGA*, pages 161–170. ACM, 2015.

[32] S. Zhou, Z. Ni, X. Zhou, H. Wen, Y. Wu, and Y. Zou. DoReFa-Net: Training low bitwidth convolutional neural networks with low bitwidth gradients. *CoRR*, abs/1606.06160, 2016.

ESE: Efficient Speech Recognition Engine with Sparse LSTM on FPGA

Song Han[1,2], Junlong Kang[2], Huizi Mao[1,2], Yiming Hu[2,3], Xin Li[2], Yubin Li[2], Dongliang Xie[2]
Hong Luo[2], Song Yao[2], Yu Wang[2,3], Huazhong Yang[3] and William J. Dally[1,4]
[1] Stanford University, [2] DeePhi Tech, [3] Tsinghua University, [4] NVIDIA
[1] {songhan,dally}@stanford.edu, [2] song.yao@deephi.tech, [3] yu-wang@mail.tsinghua.edu.cn

ABSTRACT

Long Short-Term Memory (LSTM) is widely used in speech recognition. In order to achieve higher prediction accuracy, machine learning scientists have built increasingly larger models. Such large model is both computation intensive and memory intensive. Deploying such bulky model results in high power consumption and leads to a high total cost of ownership (TCO) of a data center.

To speedup the prediction and make it energy efficient, we first propose a *load-balance-aware pruning* method that can compress the LSTM model size by 20× (10× from pruning and 2× from quantization) with negligible loss of the prediction accuracy. The pruned model is friendly for parallel processing. Next, we propose a scheduler that encodes and partitions the compressed model to multiple PEs for parallelism and schedule the complicated LSTM data flow. Finally, we design the hardware architecture, named Efficient Speech Recognition Engine (ESE) that works directly on the sparse LSTM model.

Implemented on Xilinx XCKU060 FPGA running at 200MHz, ESE has a performance of 282 GOPS working directly on the sparse LSTM network, corresponding to 2.52 TOPS on the dense one, and processes a full LSTM for speech recognition with a power dissipation of 41 Watts. Evaluated on the LSTM for speech recognition benchmark, ESE is 43× and 3× faster than Core i7 5930k CPU and Pascal Titan X GPU implementations. It achieves 40× and 11.5× higher energy efficiency compared with the CPU and GPU respectively.

Keywords

Deep Learning; Speech Recognition; Model Compression; Hardware Acceleration; Software-Hardware Co-Design; FPGA

1. INTRODUCTION

Deep neural network is becoming the state-of-the-art method for speech recognition [6, 13]. Long Short-Term Memory (LSTM) and Gated Recurrent Unit (GRU) are two popular types of recurrent neural networks (RNNs) used for speech

FPGA '17, February 22 - 24, 2017, Monterey, CA, USA

© 2017 Copyright held by the owner/author(s). Publication rights licensed to ACM.
ISBN 978-1-4503-4354-1/17/02... $15.00

DOI: http://dx.doi.org/10.1145/3020078.3021745

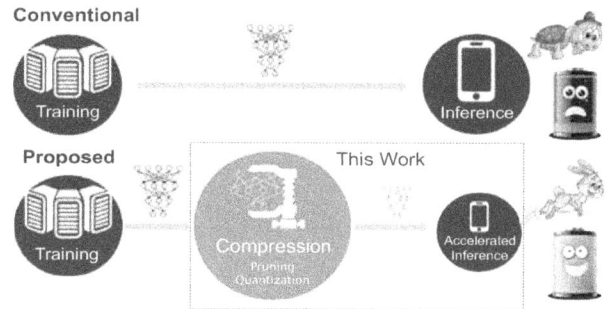

Figure 1: Proposed efficient DNN deployment flow: model compression+accelerated inference.

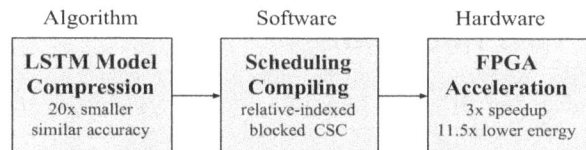

Figure 2: ESE optimizes LSTM computation across algorithm, software and hardware stack.

recognition. In this work, we evaluated the most complex one: LSTM [14]. A similar methodology could be easily applied to other types of recurrent neural network.

Despite the high prediction accuracy, LSTM is hard to deploy because of its high computation complexity and high memory footprint, leading to high power consumption. Memory reference consumes more than two orders of magnitude higher energy than ALU operations, thus our focus narrows down to optimizing the memory footprint.

To reduce memory footprint, we design a novel method to optimize across the algorithm, software and hardware stack: we first optimize the algorithm by compressing the LSTM model to 5% of it's original size (10% density and 2× narrower weights) while retaining similar accuracy, then we develop a software mapping strategy to represent the compressed model in a hardware-friendly way, finally we design specialized hardware to work directly on the compressed LSTM model.

The proposed flow for efficient deep learning inference is illustrated in Fig. 1. It shows a new paradigm for efficient deep learning inference, from Training=>Inference, to Training=>Compression=>Accelerated Inference, which has advantage of inference speed and energy efficiency compared with conventional method. Using LSTM as a case study for the propose paradigm, the design flow is illustrated in Fig. 2.

The main contributions of this work are:

1. We present an effective model compression algorithm for LSTM, which is composed of pruning and quantization. We highlight our load balance-aware pruning and automatic flow for dynamic-precision data quantization.

2. The recurrent nature of RNN and LSTM produces complicated data dependency, which is more challenging than feedforward neural nets. We design a scheduler that can efficiently schedule the complex LSTM operations with memory reference overlapped with computation.

3. The irregular computation pattern after compression posed a challenge on hardware. We design a hardware architecture that can work directly on the sparse model. ESE achieves high efficiency by load balancing and partitioning both the computation and storage. ESE also supports processing multiple speech data concurrently.

4. We present an in-depth study of the LSTM and speech recognition system and did optimization across the algorithm, software, hardware boundary. We jointly analyze the trade-off between prediction accuracy and prediction latency.

2. BACKGROUND

Speech recognition is the process of converting speech signals to a sequence of words. As shown in Fig. 3, the speech recognition system contains the front-end and back-end, where front-end unit is used for extracting features from speech signals, and back-end processes the features and output the text. The back-end includes acoustic model (AM), language model (LM), and decoder. Here, Long Short-Term Memory (LSTM) recurrent neural network is used in the acoustic model.

The feature vectors extracted from front-end unit are processed by acoustic model, then the decoder uses both acoustic and language models to generate the sequence of words by maximum a posteriori probability (MAP) estimation, which can be described as

$$\hat{\mathbf{W}} = \arg\max_{\mathbf{W}} P(\mathbf{W}|\mathbf{X}) = \arg\max_{\mathbf{W}} \frac{P(\mathbf{X}|\mathbf{W})P(\mathbf{W})}{P(\mathbf{X})}$$

where for the given feature vector $\mathbf{X} = X_1 X_2 \ldots X_n$, speech recognition is to find word sequence $\hat{\mathbf{W}} = W_1 W_2 \ldots W_m$ with maximum posterior probability $P(\mathbf{W}|\mathbf{X})$. Because $\mathbf{X}$ is fixed, the above equation can be rewritten as

$$\hat{\mathbf{W}} = \arg\max_{\mathbf{W}} P(\mathbf{X}|\mathbf{W})P(\mathbf{W})$$

where $P(\mathbf{X}|\mathbf{W})$ and $P(\mathbf{W})$ are the probabilities computed by acoustic and language models respectively in Fig. 3 [20].

In modern speech recognition system, LSTM architecture is often used in large-scale acoustic modeling and for computing acoustic output probabilities. In the speech recognition pipeline, LSTM is the most computation and memory intensive part. Thus we focus on accelerating the LSTM.

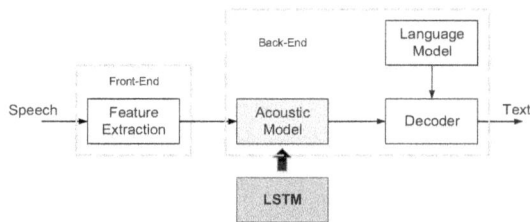

Figure 3: Speech recognition engine: LSTM is used in acoustic model. LSTM takes more than 90% time in the whole computation pipeline.

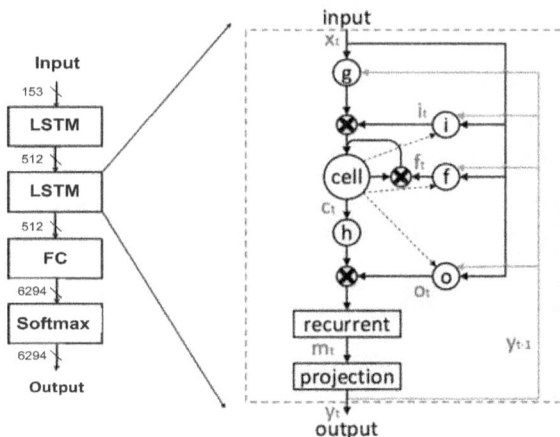

Figure 4: Data flow of the LSTM model.

The LSTM architecture is shown in Fig. 4, which is the same as the standard LSTM implementation [19]. LSTM is one type of RNN, where the input at time T depends on the output at $T - 1$. Compared to the traditional RNN, LSTM contains special memory blocks in the recurrent hidden layer. The memory cells with self-connections in memory blocks can store the temporal state of the network. The memory blocks also contain special multiplicative units called gates: input gate, output gate and forget gate. As in Fig. 4, the input gate i controls the flow of input activations into the memory cell. The output gate o controls the output flow into the rest of the network. The forget gate f scales the internal state of the cell before adding it as input to the cell, which can adaptively forget the cell's memory.

An LSTM network accepts an input sequence $x = (x_1; \ldots; x_T)$, and computes an output sequence $y = (y_1; \ldots; y_T)$ by using the following equations iteratively from $t = 1$ to T:

$$i_t = \sigma(W_{ix}x_t + W_{ir}y_{t-1} + W_{ic}c_{t-1} + b_i) \quad (1)$$

$$f_t = \sigma(W_{fx}x_t + W_{fr}y_{t-1} + W_{fc}c_{t-1} + b_f) \quad (2)$$

$$g_t = \sigma(W_{cx}x_t + W_{cr}y_{t-1} + b_c) \quad (3)$$

$$c_t = f_t \odot c_{t-1} + g_t \odot i_t \quad (4)$$

$$o_t = \sigma(W_{ox}x_t + W_{or}y_{t-1} + W_{oc}c_t + b_o) \quad (5)$$

$$m_t = o_t \odot h(c_t) \quad (6)$$

$$y_t = W_{ym}m_t \quad (7)$$

Here the big O dot operator means element-wise multiplication, the W terms denote weight matrices (e.g. W_{ix} is the matrix of weights from the input to the input gate), and W_{ic}, W_{fc}, W_{oc} are diagonal weight matrices for peephole connections. The b terms denote bias vectors, while σ is the logistic sigmoid function. The symbols i, f, o, c and m are respectively the input gate, forget gate, output gate, cell activation vectors and cell output activation vectors, and all of which are the same size. The symbols g and h are the cell input and cell output activation functions.

3. MODEL COMPRESSION

It has been widely observed that deep neural networks usually have a lot of redundancy [11, 12]. Getting rid of the redundancy won't hurt prediction accuracy. From the hardware perspective, model compression is critical for saving the computation as well as memory footprint, which means lower latency and better energy efficiency. We'll discuss two steps of model compression that consist of pruning and quantization in the next three subsections.

3.1 Pruning

In the pruning phase we first train the model to learn which weights are necessary, then prune away weights that are not contributing to the prediction accuracy; finally, we retrain the model given the sparsity constraint. The process is the same as [12]. In step two, the saliency of the weight is determined by the weight's absolute value: if the weight's absolute value is smaller than a threshold, then we prune it away. The pruning threshold is empirical: pruning too much will hurt the accuracy while pruning at the right level won't.

Our pruning experiments are performed on the Kaldi speech recognition toolkit [17]. The trade-off curve of the percentage of parameters pruned away and phone error rate (PER) is shown in Fig.6. The LSTM is evaluated on the TIMIT dataset [8]. Not until we prune away more than 93% parameters did the PER begins to increase dramatically. We further experiment on a proprietary dataset which is much larger: it has 1000 hours of training speech data, 100 hours of validation speech data, and 10 hours of test speech data, we find that we can prune away 90% of the parameters without hurting word error rate (WER), which aligns with our result on TIMIT dataset. In our later discussions, we use 10% density (90% sparsity).

3.2 Load Balance-Aware Pruning

On top of the basic deep compression method, we highlight our practical design consideration for hardware efficiency. To execute sparse matrix multiplication in parallel, we propose the load balance-aware pruning method, which is very critical for better load balancing and higher utilization on the hardware.

Pruning could lead to a potential problem of unbalanced non-zero weights distribution. The workload imbalance over PEs may cause a gap between the real performance and peak performance. This problem is further addressed in Section 4.

Load-balance-aware pruning is designed to solve this problem and obtain hardware-friendly sparse network, which produces the same sparsity ratio among all the submatrices. During pruning, we make efforts to avoid the scenario when the density of one submatrix is 5% while the other is 15%. Although the overall density is about 10%, the submatrix with a density of 5% has to wait for the other one with more computation, which leads to idle cycles. Load-balance-aware pruning assigns the same sparsity quota to submatrices, thus ensures an even distribution of non-zero weights.

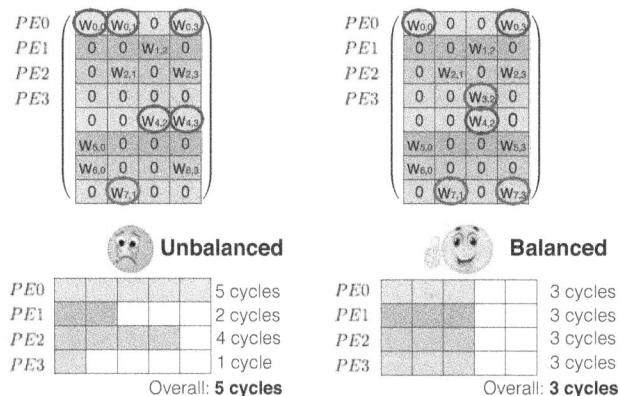

Figure 5: Load Balance Aware Pruning and its Benefit for Parallel Processing

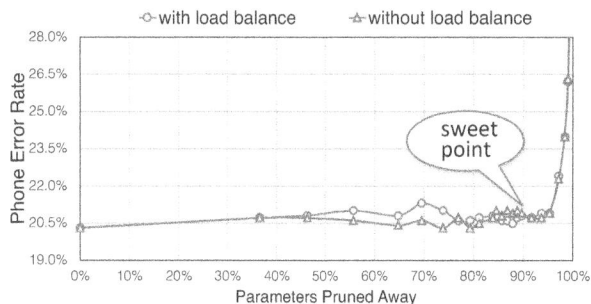

Figure 6: Accuracy curve of load-balance-aware pruning and original pruning.

As illustrated in Fig. 5, the matrix is divided into four colors, and each color belongs to a PE for parallel processing. With conventional pruning, PE_0 might have five non-zero weights while PE_3 may have only one. The total processing time is restricted to the longest one, which is five cycles. With load-balance-aware pruning, all PEs have three non-zero weights; thus only three cycles are necessary to carry out the operation. Both cases have the same non-zero weights in total, but load-balance-aware pruning needs fewer cycles. The difference of prediction accuracy with / without load-balance-aware pruning is very small, as shown in Fig. 6. There is some noise around 70% sparsity, so we put more experiments around 90% sparsity, which is the sweet point. We find the performance is very similar.

To show that load-balance-aware pruning still obtains comparable prediction accuracy, we compare it with original pruning on the TIMIT dataset. As demonstrated in Fig.6, the accuracy margin between two methods is within the variance of pruning process itself.

3.3 Weight and Activation Quantization

We further compressed the model by quantizing 32bit floating point weights into 12bit integer. We used linear quantization strategy on both the weights and activations.

In the weight quantization phase, the dynamic ranges of weights for all matrices in each LSTM layer are analyzed first, then the length of the fractional part is initialized to avoid data overflow.

The activation quantization phase aims to figure out the

Table 1: Weight Quantization under different Bits.

Weight Matrices[1]		Min	Max	Integer	Decimals		
					16bit	12bit	8bit
LSTM1	W_gifo_x[2]	-4.9285	5.7196	4	8	4	0
	W_gifo_r[2]	-0.6909	0.7140	1	11	7	3
	bias	-3.0143	2.1120	3	13	9	5
	W_ic	-0.6884	0.9584	1	15	11	7
	W_fc	-0.6597	0.7204	1	15	11	7
	W_oc	-1.5550	1.3325	2	14	10	6
	W_ym	-0.9373	0.8676	1	11	7	3
LSTM2	W_gifo_x	-1.0541	1.0413	2	10	6	2
	W_gifo_r	-0.6313	0.6400	1	11	7	3
	bias	-1.5833	1.8009	2	14	10	6
	W_ic	-0.9428	0.5158	1	15	11	7
	W_fc	-0.5762	0.6202	1	15	11	7
	W_oc	-1.0619	1.4650	2	14	10	6
	W_ym	-1.0947	1.0170	2	10	6	2

[1] Only weights in LSTM layers are qunantized.
[2] In Kaldi, Wcx, Wix, Wfx, Wox are saved together as W_gifo_x, and so does W_gifo_r mean.

Table 2: Activation Function Lookup Table.

Activation	Min	Max	sampling range	sampling points
Sigmoid Input	-51.32	59.16	-64-64	2048
Tanh Input	-104.7	107.4	-128-128	2048

Table 3: Other Activation Quantization.

Activation	Min	Max	Width	Decimals
LSTM Input	-7.611	8.166	16	11
Intermediate Results	-107.8	109.4	16	8

Table 4: PER Before and After Compression.

Quantization Scheme	Phone Error Rate %
32bit floating original network	20.4%
32bit floating pruned network	20.7%
16bit fixed pruned network	20.7%
12bit fixed pruned network	**20.7%**
8bit fixed pruned network	84.5%

optimal solution to the activation functions and the intermediate results. We build lookup tables and use linear interpolation for the activation functions, such as sigmoid and tanh, and analyze the dynamic range of their inputs to decide the sampling strategies. We also investigated how many bits are enough for the intermediate results of the matrices operations.

We explore different data quantization strategies of weights with real network trained under TIMIT corpus. The sparsity of LSTM layers after pruning and fine-tune procedure is about 88.8% (i.e. a density of 11.2%). Performing the weight and activation quantization, we can achieve 12bit quantization without any accuracy loss. The data quantization strategies are shown in Table.1,2 and Table.3. For the lookup tables of activation functions sigmoid and tanh, the sampling ranges are [-64, 64], [-128, 128] respectively, the sampling points are both 2048, and the outputs are 16bit with 15bit decimals. All the results are obtained under Kaldi framework.

For TIMIT, as shown in Table.4, the PER is 20.4% for the original network, and change to 20.7% after pruning and fine-tune procedure when 32-bit floating-point numbers are used. The PER remains as 20.7% without any accuracy loss under 16/12-bit quantization, and deteriorated to 84.5% while 8-bit quantization is employed.

4. ENCODING AND COMPILING

The LSTM computation includes sparse matrices multiplication, element-wise multiplication, and memory reference.

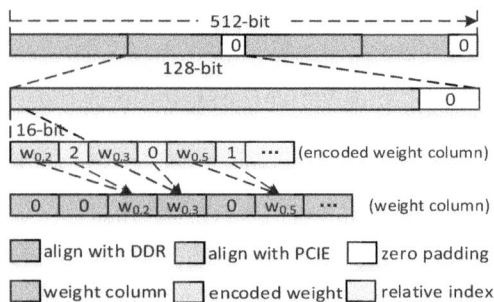

Figure 7: Encoding in CSC format and data align using zero-padding.

We design a data flow scheduler to make full use of the hardware accelerator.

Data is divided into n blocks by row where n is the number of PEs in one channels of our hardware accelerator. The first n rows are put in n different PEs. The $n+1$ row are put in the first PE again. This ensures that the first part of the matrix will be read in the first reading cycle and can be used in the next step computation immediately.

Because of the sparsity of pruned matrices. We only store the nonzero number in weight matrices to save redundant memory. We use relative row index and column pointer to help store the sparse matrix. The relative row index for each weight shows the relative position from the last nonzero weight. The column pointer indicates where the new column begins in the matrix. The accelerator will read the weight according to the column pointer.

Considering the byte-aligned bit width limitation of DDR, we use 16bit data to store the weight. The quantized weight and relative row index are put together(i.e. 12bit for quantized weight and 4bit for relative row index).

Fig.7 shows an example for the compressed sparse column (CSC) storage format and zero-padding method. We locate one column in weight matrix through a pointer, and calculate the absolute address of weights by accumulating relative indexes. In Fig.8, we demonstrate the computation pattern using a simple example. Given an input vector that has 6 elements $\{a_0, a_1, a_2, a_3, a_4, a_5\}$, and a weight matrix contains 8×6 elements. There are 2 PEs to calculate $a_3 \times w[3]$, where a_3 is the fourth element in the input vector and $w[3]$ represents the fourth column in the weight matrix.

5. HARDWARE IMPLEMENTATION

In this section, we first present challenges in hardware design and then propose the Efficient Speech Recognition Engine (ESE) accelerator system and detail how ESE accelerates the sparse LSTM.

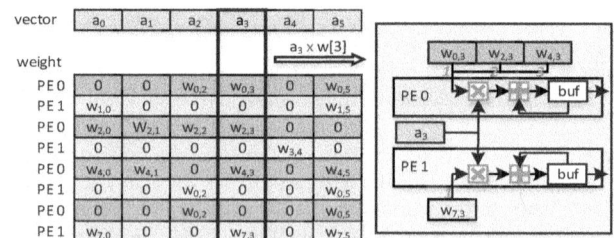

Figure 8: The computation pattern: non-zero weights in a column are assigned to 2 PEs, and every PE multiply-add their weights with the same element from the shared vector.

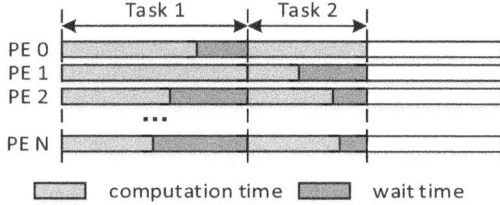

Figure 9: Imbalanced workload results in more waiting time.

5.1 Motivation

Although pruning and quantization can reduce memory footprint, some new challenges are introduced. General purpose processors cannot implement these challenges efficiently.

First, irregular computation is introduced by compression. After pruning, dense computation becomes sparse computation; After quantization, the weight and index are not byte-aligned. Instead, they must be grouped to be byte-aligned: we group the 4-bit pointer, and 12-bit weight into 2 bytes.

Second, load imbalance introduced by sparsity will reduce the hardware efficiency. In the sparse LSTM, a single element in the voice vector will be consumed by multiple PEs. As a result, operations of all PEs have to be synchronized. It will create a long waiting period if some PEs have fewer non-zero weights, as shown in Fig.9.

Moreover, general-purpose processors cannot fully exploit the parallelism in the compressed LSTM network. In the custom design, however, we have the freedom to take advantage of the parallelism both inter sparse SpMV operation and intra SpMV operation.

Many challenges exist in the specialized hardware accelerator design on FPGA. First, customized decoding circuits are needed to recover the original weight matrix. The index is relative, so accumulation is needed to recover the absolute index. We use only 4-bits to represent relative offset. If a real offset is more than 16, the largest offset that 4 bits can represent, a padding zero is introduced.

Second, data representation should be carefully designed. The data width of PCIE interface, external DDR3 memory interface, and data itself are not aligned. Moreover, the dynamic-precision quantization makes hardware computation on different data more complex and irregular. Bit shifts are necessary for different layers.

Third, a carefully designed scheduler/controller is needed. The LSTM network involves a complicated data flow and many different types of weights. Computations in the LSTM network have dependency with each other. Some computation can be executed concurrently, while other computation has to be executed sequentially. Moreover, the hardware design should support input vector sharing in the multi-channel system, which aims to perform multiple LSTM networks with different voice vectors concurrently. Therefore, a carefully designed scheduler is necessary for a highly pipelined design, which can overlap the data communication and computation.

5.2 System Overview

Fig.10 (a) shows the overview architecture of ESE system. It is a CPU+FPGA heterogeneous architecture to accelerate LSTM. The whole system can be divided into three parts: the hardware accelerator on a FPGA chip, the software program on CPU, and the external memory on the FPGA board.

Software part consists of a CPU and host memory. It

Table 5: Two types of LSTM operations: matrix-vector multiplication and element-wise multiplication.

Target	SpMV Group	ElemMul Group
i_t	$W_{ix}x_t, W_{ir}y_{t-1}$	$W_{ic}c_{t-1}$
f_t	$W_{fx}x_t, W_{fr}y_{t-1}$	$W_{fc}c_{t-1}$
c_t	$W_{cx}x_t, W_{cr}y_{t-1}$	f_tc_{t-1}, i_tg_t
o_t	$W_{ox}x_t, W_{or}y_{t-1}$	$W_{oc}c_t$
m_t	N/A	o_th_t
y_t	$W_{ym}m_t$	N/A

communicates with FPGA via the PCI-Express bus. In the initialization procedure, it sends parameters and data structure information of the LSTM model to FPGA. It can transmit voice vectors and receive corresponding results if the hardware accelerator on FPGA is ready.

The external memory together with the FPGA chip on one development board stores all the parameters and voice vectors. The on-chip BRAM is limited while the amount of data in the LSTM model is large. The accelerator accesses the DRAM through memory controller (MEM Controller), which is built using the memory interface generator (MIG) IP.

On the FPGA chip, we put the ESE Accelerator, ESE Controller, PCIE Controller, MEM Controller, and On-chip Buffers. The ESE Accelerator consists of Processing Elements (PEs) which take charge of the majority of computation tasks in the LSTM model. PE is the basic computation unit for a slice of voice vectors with partial weight matrix. Each ESE channel implements the LSTM network for one voice vector sequence independently. On-chip buffers, including input buffer and output buffer, prepare data to be consumed by PEs and store the generated results. ESE Controller determines the behavior of other circuits on FPGA chip. It schedules PCIE/MEM Controller for data-fetch and the LSTM computation pipeline flow of ESE Accelerator. The accelerator reads parameters and voice vectors from and writes computation results to the DRAM memory. When MEM Controller is in the idle state, the accelerator can read results currently stored in the memory and feed them to the software part.

5.3 ESE Controller (Scheduler)

The most expensive operations are sparse matrix vector multiplication (SpMV) and element-wise multiplication (ElemMul). We partition most operations, involved in the LSTM network described by equations (1) to (6), into the such two categories, as shown in Table 5.

LSTM is a complicated dataflow. We want to meet the data dependency and ensure more parallelism at the same time. Fig.11 shows the state machine in the ESE scheduler. It overlaps computation and memory reference. From state INITIAL to STATE_6, ESE accelerator completes the computation of a LSTM. The first three lines operations are fetching weights, pointers, and vectors/diagonal matrix/bias respectively to prepare for the next computation. Operations in the fourth line are matrix-vector multiplications, and that in the fifth line are element-wise multiplications (indigo blocks) or accumulations (orange blocks). Operations in the horizontal direction have to be executed sequentially, while those in the vertical direction can be executed concurrently. For example, we can calculate $W_{fr}y_{t-1}$ and i_t con-

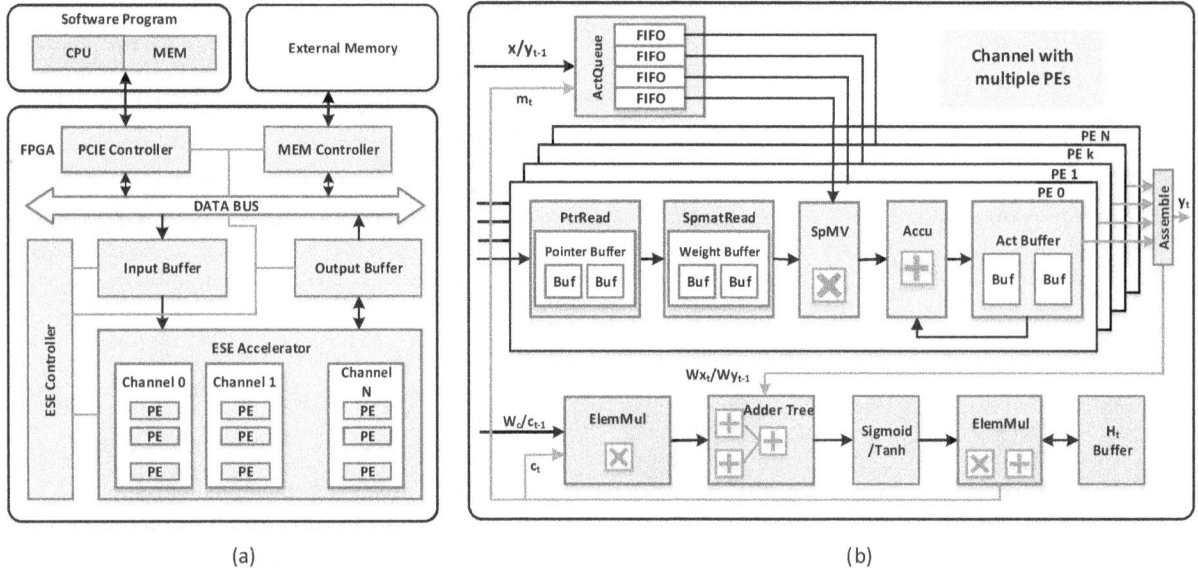

Figure 10: The Efficient Speech Recognition Engine (ESE) accelerator system: (a) the overall ESE system architecture; (b) one channel with multiple processing elements (PEs).

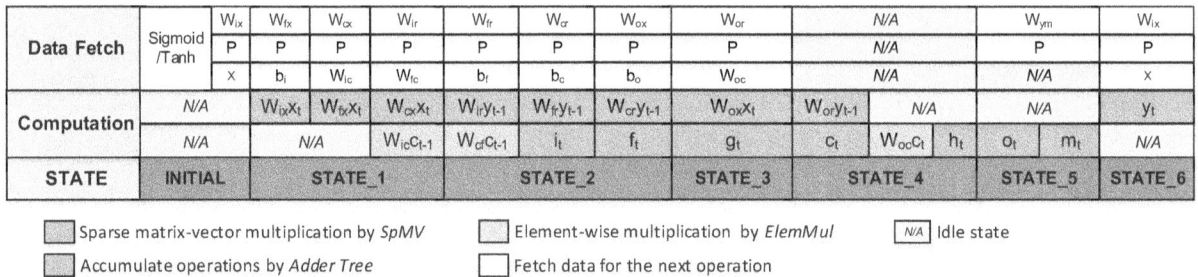

		W_{ix}	W_{fx}	W_{cx}	W_{ir}	W_{fr}	W_{cr}	W_{ox}	W_{or}	N/A	W_{ym}	W_{ix}
Data Fetch	Sigmoid /Tanh	P	P	P	P	P	P	P	P	N/A	P	P
		x	b_i	W_{ic}	W_{fc}	b_f	b_c	b_o	W_{oc}	N/A	N/A	x
Computation	N/A	$W_{ix}x_t$	$W_{fx}x_t$	$W_{cx}x_t$	$W_{ir}y_{t-1}$	$W_{fr}y_{t-1}$	$W_{cr}y_{t-1}$	$W_{ox}x_t$	$W_{or}y_{t-1}$	N/A	N/A	y_t
	N/A	N/A	$W_{ic}c_{t-1}$	$W_{cf}c_{t-1}$	i_t	f_t	g_t	c_t	$W_{oc}c_t$	h_t	o_t	m_t / N/A
STATE	INITIAL	STATE_1		STATE_2			STATE_3	STATE_4		STATE_5	STATE_6	

- (shaded) Sparse matrix-vector multiplication by *SpMV*
- (shaded) Accumulate operations by *Adder Tree*
- (shaded) Element-wise multiplication by *ElemMul*
- (white) Fetch data for the next operation
- N/A Idle state

Figure 11: The state flow of ESE accelerator system: operations in the horizontal direction and vertical direction are executed sequentially and concurrently respectively.

currently, because the two operations are not dependent on each other in the LSTM network, and they can be executed by two independent computation units. $W_{ir}y_{t-1}/W_{ic}c_{t-1}$ and i_t have to be executed sequentially, because i_t is dependent on the former operations in LSTM network.

$W_{ix}x_t$ and $W_{fx}x_t$ are not dependent on each other in the LSTM network, but they cannot be calculated concurrently because they have resource conflict. Weights are stored in one external memory because even after compression the real world network cannot fit in the limited block RAM (4.25MB). Other parameters and input vector are stored in the other piece of DDR3 memory. Pointers are required for the same computations as weights, because we use pointers to look up weights in the compressed LSTM network. But pointers have small quantity and are accessed every time. Note that x, bias b, and diagonal matrix W_c are not accessed at the same time, and all these parameters have a relatively small quantity. Therefore, pointers, vectors, diagonal matrix and bias can be stored in the same external memory and can be prepared well during weight fetching period.

The latency of the element-wise operations and non-linear functions is not on the critical path. These operations are executed in parallel with the matrix-vector multiplication and weights-fetching.

5.4 ESE Channel Architecture

Fig.10 (b) shows the architecture of one ESE channel with multiple PEs. It is composed of Activation Queue (ActQueue), Sparse Matix-vector Multiplier (SpMV), Accumulator, Element-wise Multiplier (ElemMul), Adder Tree, Sigmoid/Tanh Units, and local buffers.

Activation Vector Queue (ActQueue). ActQueue consists of several FIFOs. Each FIFO stores some elements of the input voice vector a_j for each PE. ActQueue is shared by all the PEs in one channel, while each FIFO is owned by each PE independently.

ActQueue is used for decoupling the imbalanced workload among different PEs. Load imbalance arises when the number of multiply accumulation operations performed by every PE is different, due to the imbalanced sparsity. Those PEs with fewer computation tasks have to wait until the PE with the most computation tasks finishes. Thus if we have a FIFO, the fast PE can fetch a new element from the FIFO and won't need to be blocked by slow PEs. The data width of FIFO is 16-bit, and the depth is adjusted from 1 to 16 to investigate its effects on the latency, and the results are discussed in experiment section. These FIFOs are built on the distributed RAM on chip.

Sparse Matrix Read (SpmatRead). Pointer Read Unit (PtrRead) and Sparse Matrix Read (SpmatRead) manage the encoded weight matrix storage and output. The start and end pointers p_j and p_{j+1} for column j determine the start location and length of elements in one encoded weight column that should be fetched for each element of a voice vector. SpmatRead uses pointers p_j and p_{j+1} to look up the non-zero elements in weight column j. Both PtrRead and SpmatRead consist of ping-pong buffers. Each buffer can store 512 16-bit values and is implemented with block rams. Each 16-bit data in SpmatRead buffers consists of a 4-bit index and a 12-bit weight.

Sparse Matrix-vector Multiplication (SpMV). Each element in the voice vector is multiplied by its corresponding weight column. Multiplication results in the same row of all new vectors are summed to generate an element in the result vector, which is a local reduce. In ESE, $SpMV$ multiplies an element from the input activation by a column of weight, and the current partial result is written into the partial result buffer $ActBuffer$. Accumulator $Accu$ sums the new output of $SpMV$ and previous data stored in Act Buffer. Multiplier instantiated in the design can perform $16bitx12bit$ functions.

Element-wise Multiplication (ElemMul). $ElemMul$ in Fig.10 (b) generates one vector by consuming two vectors. Each element in the output vector is the element-wise multiplication of two input vectors. There are 16 multipliers instantiated for element-wise multiplications per channel.

Adder Tree. $AdderTree$ performs summation by consuming the intermediate data produced by other units or bias data from input buffer.

Sigmoid/Tanh. They are the non-linear modules applied as activation functions to some intermediate summation results.

Here we explain how ESE computes i_t. In the initial state, PE receives weight W_{ix}, pointers P and voice vector x. Then SpMV calculates $W_{ix}X_t$ in the first phase of STATE_1. $W_{ir}y_{t-1}$ and $W_{ic}c_{t-1}$ are generated by SpMV and ElemMul respectively in the first phase of STATE_2. In the second phase of STATE_2, Adder Tree accumulates these output and bias data from the input buffer and then the following non-linear activation function unit Sigmoid/Tanh produces intermediate data i_t. PE will fetch required parameters in the previous phase to overlap with the computation. The other LSTM network operations are similar. In Fig.11, either SpMV or ElemMul is in the idle state at some phases. This is because both matrix-vector multiplication and element-wise multiplication consume weight data, while PE cannot pre-fetch enough weight data for both computations in the period of one phase.

5.5 Memory System

In the hardware design, on-chip buffers are built upon a basic idea of double-buffering, in which double buffers are operated in a ping-pong manner to overlap data transfer with computation. We use two pieces of 4GB DDR3 DRAMs as the off-chip memory, named DDR_1 and DDR_2 in Fig.12. We design a memory controller (MEM Controller). Fig.12 shows the MEM Controller architecture. On the one hand, it receives instructions from ESE Controller and schedules the data flow among ESE accelerator, PCIE interface, and DDR3 interface. On the other hand, it rearranges received data into structures required by the destination interface. We take the data flow of result y as an example. Data y at the output port of PE is 16-bit wide, while the PCIE interface is 128-bit wide. In order to increase

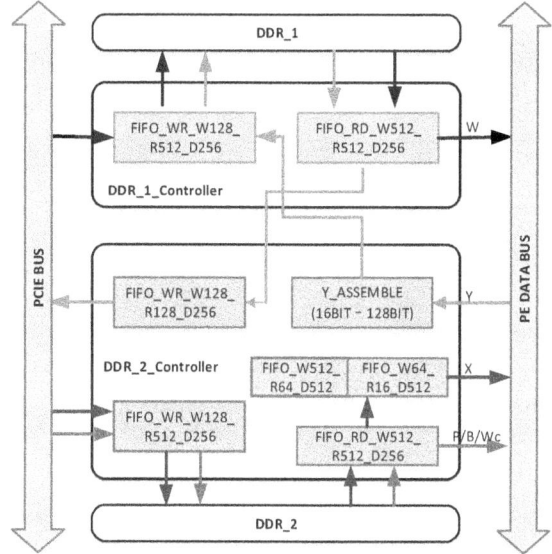

Figure 12: Memory management unit.

the data transmission speed, we assemble eight 16-bit data into one 128-bit value by Y_ASSEMBLE unit. Then it will be stored in DDR_1 temporarily and fed back to the software via PCIE interface when both PCIE and DDR_1 are in idle state. The behavior described above is shown as the green arrow line in Fig.12. Similarly, vector x is split into 32 16-bit values from a 512-bit value through asynchronous FIFOs. Moreover, asynchronous FIFOs, FIFO_WR_XX and FIFO_RD_XX, also play an important role of asynchronous clock domains isolation.

6. EXPERIMENTAL RESULTS

In this section, the performance of the hardware system is evaluated. First, we introduce the environment setup of our experiments. Then, hardware resource utilization and comprehensive experimental results are provided.

6.1 Experimental Setup

The proposed ESE hardware system is built on XCKU060 FPGA running at 200 MHz. Two external 4GB DDR3 DRAMs are used. Our host program is responsible for sending parameters and vectors into the programmable logic part, and collecting corresponding results.

We use TIMIT dataset to evaluate the performance of model compression. TIMIT is an acoustic-phonetic continuous speech corpus. It contains broadband recordings of 630 speakers of eight major dialects of American English, each reading ten phonetically rich sentences. We also use a proprietary, much larger speech recognition dataset which contains 1000 hours of training data, 100 hours of validation data and 10 hours of test data.

Our baseline software program runs on i7-5930k CPU and Pascal Titan X GPU. We use MKL BLAS / cuBLAS on CPU / GPU for dense matrix operation implementations, and MKL SPARSE / cuSPARSE on CPU / GPU for sparse matrix implementations.

6.2 Resource Utilization

Table 6 shows the resource utilization for our ESE design configured with 32 channels and each channel has 32 PEs on XCKU060 FPGA. The ESE accelerator design almost fully utilizes the FPGA's hardware resource.

Table 6: ESE Resource Utilization.

	LUT	LUTRAM[1]	FF	BRAM[1]	DSP
Avail.	331,680	146,880	663,360	1,080	2,760
Used	293,920	69,939	453,068	947	1,504
Utili.	88.6%	47.6%	68.3%	87.7%	54.5%

[1] LUTRAM is 64b each, BRAM is 36Kb each.

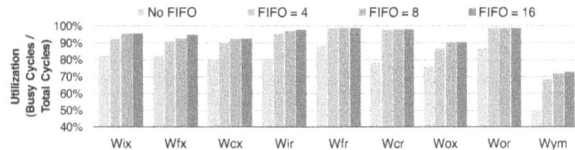

Figure 13: FIFO improves load balancing and decreases latency. The ALU utilization is more than 90% when FIFO depth is 8 for load balancing.

We configure each channel with 32 PEs, which is determined by balancing computation and data transfer. It is required that the speed of data transfer is no less than that of computation in order not to starve the DSP. As a result, we get equation 8. The expression to the left of the equal sign means that the amount of computations is divided by the computation speed. Multiplied by 2 in the numerator part means each data need multiplication and accumulation operations, and that in the denominator part indicates twice multiply-accumulate operations for 2 bytes (16-bit). ESE implements the multiply-accumulate operation in a pipeline manner. The expression to the right represents the cycles that ESE fetch the required amount of data from external memory. In our hardware implementation, both the frequencies of PE and memory interface controller are 200MHz. The width of external DRAM is 512-bit. Therefore, the proper number of PEs per channel is 32.

$$\frac{data\_size \times compress\_ratio \times 2}{PE\_num \times 2 \times freq\_PE}$$
$$\geq \frac{data\_size \times compress\_ratio \times 16bit}{ddr\_width \times freq\_ddr} \qquad (8)$$

FIFO Depth. ESE uses FIFO to decouple the PEs and solves load imbalance problem. Load imbalance here means the number of non-zero weight assigned to every PE is different. The FIFO for each PE reduces the waiting time for PEs with fewer computations. We adjust the cache depth to investigate its effect. The FIFO width is 16-bit, and its depth is set 1, 4, 8, 16 respectively. In Fig.13, when there's FIFO depth is one (no FIFO), the utilization, which is defined as busy cycle divided by total cycles, is low (80%) due to load imbalance. When the FIFO depth is 4, the utilization is above 90%. When FIFO depth is increased to 8 and 16, the utilization increased but has a marginal gain. Thus we chose the FIFO depth to be 8. Note that even when the FIFO depth is 8, the last matrix (Wym) still has low utilization. This is because that matrix has very few rows and each PE has few elements, and thus the FIFO cannot fully solve this problem for this matrix.

6.3 Accuracy, Speed, and Energy Efficiency

We evaluate the trade-off between accuracy and speedup of ESE in Fig.15. The speedup increases as more parameters get pruned away. The sparse model which is pruned to 10% achieved 6.2× speedup over the dense baseline model.

Table 7: Power consumption of different platforms.

Platform	CPU Dense	CPU Sparse	GPU Dense	GPU Sparse	ESE
Power	111W	38W	202W	136W	**41W**

Figure 14: Measured at the socket, the total power consumption of the machine with FPGA fully loaded is 132W. Without FPGA the idle machine consumes 91W. Subtracting the two, ESE consumes 41W.

Comparing the red and green line, we find that load-balance-aware pruning improves the speedup from 5.5× to 6.2×.

We measured power consumption of CPU, GPU and ESE. CPU power is measured by the pcm-power utility. GPU power is measured with nvidia-smi utility. We measure the power consumption of ESE by taking difference with / without the FPGA board installed. ESE takes 41 watts; CPU takes 111 watts(38 watts when using MKLSparse), GPU takes 202 watts (136 watts when using cuSparse).

The performance comparison of LSTM on ESE, CPU, and GPU is shown in Table 8. The CPU implementation used MKL BLAS and MKL SPBLAS for dense/sparse implementation, and the GPU implementation used cuBlas and cuSparse. We optimized the CPU/GPU speed by combining the four matrices of i, f, o, c gates that have no dependency into one large matrix. Both mklSparse and cuSparse implementation observed significant lower utilization of peak CPU/GPU performance for the interested matrix size (relatively small) and sparsity (around 10% non-zeros). We implement the whole LSTM on ESE. The model is pruned to 10% non-zeros. There are 11.2% non-zeros taking padding zeros into account. On ESE, the total throughput is 282 GOPS with the sparse LSTM, which corresponds to 2.52 TOPS on the dense LSTM. Processing the LSTM with 1024 hidden elements, ESE takes 82.7 us, CPU takes 6017.3/3569.9 us (dense/sparse), and GPU takes 240.2/287.4 us (dense/sparse). With batch=32, CPU sparse is faster than dense because CPU is good at serial processing, while GPU sparse is slower than dense because GPU is throughput oriented. With no batching, we observed both CPU and GPU are faster for the sparse LSTM because the saving of memory bandwidth is more salient.

Performance wise, ESE is 43× faster than CPU 3× faster than GPU. Considering both performance and power consumption, ESE is 197.0×/40.0× (dense/sparse) more energy efficient than CPU, and 14.3×/11.5× (dense/sparse) more energy efficient than GPU. Sparse LSTM makes both CPU and GPU more energy efficient as well, which shows the advantage of our pruning technique.

Plat.			ESE on FPGA (ours)							CPU		GPU	
Matrix	Matrix Size	Sparsity (%)[1]	Compres. Matrix (Bytes)[2]	Theoreti. Comput. Time (µs)	Real Comput. Time (µs)	Total Operat. (GOP)	Real Perform. (GOP/s)	Equ. Operat. (GOP)	Equ. Perform. (GOP/s)	Real Comput. Time (µs)		Real Comput. Time (µs)	
										Dense	Sparse	Dense	Sparse
W_{ix}	1024×153	11.7	36608	2.9	**5.36**	0.0012	218.6	0.010	1870.7	1518.4[3]	670.4	34.2	58.0
W_{fx}	1024×153	11.7	36544	2.9	**5.36**	0.0012	218.2	0.010	1870.7				
W_{cx}	1024×153	11.8	37120	2.9	**5.36**	0.0012	221.6	0.010	1870.7				
W_{ox}	1024×153	11.5	35968	2.8	**5.36**	0.0012	214.7	0.010	1870.7				
W_{ir}	1024×512	11.3	118720	9.3	**10.31**	0.0038	368.5	0.034	3254.6	3225.0[4]	2288.0	81.3	166.0
W_{fr}	1024×512	11.5	120832	9.4	**10.01**	0.0039	386.3	0.034	3352.1				
W_{cr}	1024×512	11.2	117760	9.2	**9.89**	0.0038	381.2	0.034	3394.5				
W_{or}	1024×512	11.5	120256	9.4	**10.04**	0.0038	383.5	0.034	3343.7				
W_{ym}	512×1024	10.0	104832	8.2	**15.66**	0.0034	214.2	0.034	2142.7	1273.9	611.5	124.8	63.4
Total	3248128	11.2	728640	57.0	**82.7**	0.0233	282.2	0.208	2515.7	6017.3	3569.9	240.3	287.4

[1] Pruned with 10% sparsity, but padding zeros incurred about 1% more non-zero weights.

[2] Sparse matrix index is included, and weight takes 12 bits, index takes 4 bits => 2 Bytes per weight in total.

[3] Concatenating W_{ix}, W_{fx}, W_{cx} and W_{ox} into one large matrix $W_{\mathrm{ifoc\_x}}$, whose size is 4096×153.

[4] Concatenating W_{ir}, W_{fr}, W_{cr} and W_{or} as one large matrix $W_{\mathrm{ifoc\_r}}$, whose size is 4096×512. These matrices don't have dependency and combining matrices can achieve 2× speedup on GPU due to better utilization.

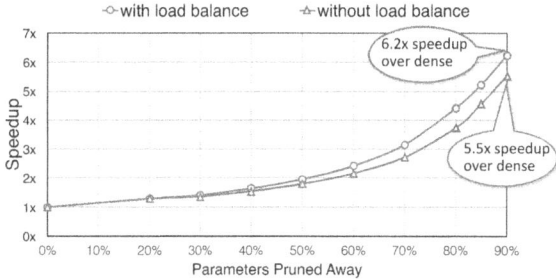

Figure 15: Computation latency decreases as the sparsity increases. Running the sparse model is 4.2× faster over the dense model, both run on ESE. Load balance aware pruning helps speedup.

7. RELATED WORK

Deep Compression Deep Compression [11] is a method that can compress convolutional neural network models by 35x-59x without hurting the accuracy. It comprises of pruning, weight sharing and Huffman coding. However, the compression rate is targeting CNN and image recognition. In this work we target LSTM and speech recognition. The method also differs from the previously proposed 'Deep Compression' in that we catered specially for FPGA design. During pruning, we enforce each row have the same amount of weight to enforce hardware load balancing. During quantization, we use linear quantization instead of non-linear quantization, which made it possible to directly use the integer ALU. We also eliminate the Huffman Coding step which introduced extra decoding overhead but marginal gain.

CNN Accelerators Many custom accelerators have been proposed for CNNs. DianNao [2] implements an array of multiply-add units to map large DNN onto its core architecture. Due to limited SRAM resource, the off-chip DRAM traffic dominates the energy consumption. DaDianNao [3] and ShiDianNao [5] eliminate the DRAM access by having all weights on-chip (eDRAM or SRAM). However, these DianNao-series architectures are CNN proposed to accelerate CNN, and the weights are uncompressed and stored in the dense format. In this work, we target LSTM neural network and speech recognition, and data compression is also supported in our ESE architecture. Our work in this paper is also distinguished itself with Angel-Eye architecture, which also has the compression, compilation and acceleration, but it is for CNN and image recognition tasks [9, 18].

EIE Accelerator The EIE architecture proposed by Han et al. [10] can performs inference on compressed network model and accelerates the resulting sparse matrix-vector multiplication with weight sharing. With only 600mW power consumption, EIE can achieve 102 GOPS processing power on a compressed network corresponding to 3 TOPS/s on an uncompressed network, which is 24000× and 3400× more energy efficient than a CPU and GPU respectively. But EIE is also not designed for LSTM and speech recognition, ESE in this paper is targeted for LSTM and ESE has many considerations for FPGA while EIE is for ASIC, which leads different design optimization. Besides, EIE use codebook-based quantization, but ESE use direct quantization.

Sparse Matrix-Vector Multiplication Accelerators To pursue a better computational efficiency on machine learning and deep learning, several recent works focus on using FPGA as an accelerator for Sparse Matrix-Vector Multiplication (SpMV). Zhuo et al. [21] proposed an FPGA-based design on Virtex-II Pro for SpMV. Their design outperforms general-purpose processors, but the performance is limited by memory bandwidth. Fowers et al. [7] proposed a novel sparse matrix encoding and an FPGA-optimized architecture for SPMV. With lower bandwidth, it achieves 2.6× and 2.3× higher power efficiency over CPU and GPU respectively while having lower performance due to lower memory bandwidth. Dorrance et al. [4] proposed a scalable SMVM kernel on Virtex-5 FPGA. It outperforms CPU and GPU counterparts with >300× computational efficiency and has 38-50× improvement in energy efficiency. For compressed deep networks, previously proposed SpMV accelerators can only exploit the static weight sparsity. In this paper, we use the relative indexed compressed sparse column (CSC) format for data storing, and we develop a scheduler which can map a complicate LSTM network on ESE accelerator.

GRU on FPGA Nurvitadhi et al presented a hardware accelerator for Gated Recurrent Network (GRU) on Stratix V and Arria 10 FPGAs [16]. This work shows that FPGA can provide superior performance/Watt over CPU and GPU. In our work, we present a FPGA accelerator for LSTM network. It also demonstrates a higher efficiency FPGA comparing with CPU and GPU. Different from theirs, our ESE is especially designed for sparse LSTM model. It can achieve more benefits but also introduces a more difficult hardware design.

LSTM on FPGA In order to explore the parallelism for RNN/LSTM, Chang presented a hardware implementation of LSTM network on Zynq 7020 FPGA from Xilinx with

2 layers and 128 hidden units in hardware [1]. The implementation is 21 times faster than the ARM Cortex-A9 CPU embedded on the Zynq 7020 FPGA. Lee accelerated RNNs using massively parallel processing elements (PEs) for low latency and high throughput on FPGA [15]. These implementations did not support sparse LSTM network, while our ESE can achieve more speed up by supporting sparse LSTM.

8. CONCLUSION

In this paper, we present Efficient Speech Recognition Engine (ESE) that works directly on compressed sparse LSTM model. ESE is optimized across the algorithm-software-hardware boundary: we first propose a method to compress the LSTM model by 20× without sacrificing the prediction accuracy, which greatly saves the memory bandwidth of FPGA implementation. Then we design a scheduler that can map the complex LSTM operations on FPGA and achieve parallelism. Finally we propose a hardware architecture that efficiently deals with the irregularity caused by compression. Working directly on the compressed model enables ESE to achieve 282 GOPS (equivalent to 2.52 TOPS for dense LSTM) on Xilinx XCKU060 FPGA board. ESE outperforms Core i7 CPU and Pascal Titan X GPU by factors of 43× and 3× on speed, and it is 40× and 11.5× more energy efficient than the CPU and GPU respectively.

9. ACKNOWLEDGMENT

This work was supported by National Natural Science Foundation of China (No.61373026, 61622403, 61261160501).

We would like to thank Wei Chen, Zhongliang Liu, Guanzhe Huang, Yong Liu, Yanfeng Wang, Xiaochuan Wang and other researchers from Sogou for their suggestions and providing real-world speech data for model compression performance test.

10. REFERENCES

[1] A. X. M. Chang, B. Martini, and E. Culurciello. Recurrent neural networks hardware implementation on FPGA. *CoRR*, abs/1511.05552, 2015.

[2] T. Chen, Z. Du, N. Sun, J. Wang, C. Wu, Y. Chen, and O. Temam. Diannao: a small-footprint high-throughput accelerator for ubiquitous machine-learning. In *ASPLOS*, 2014.

[3] Y. Chen, T. Luo, S. Liu, S. Zhang, L. He, J. Wang, L. Li, T. Chen, Z. Xu, N. Sun, and O. Temam. Dadiannao: A machine-learning supercomputer. In *MICRO*, December 2014.

[4] R. Dorrance, F. Ren, et al. A scalable sparse matrix-vector multiplication kernel for energy-efficient sparse-blas on FPGAs. In *FPGA*, 2014.

[5] Z. Du, R. Fasthuber, T. Chen, P. Ienne, L. Li, T. Luo, X. Feng, Y. Chen, and O. Temam. Shidiannao: shifting vision processing closer to the sensor. In *ISCA*, pages 92–104. ACM, 2015.

[6] D. A. et al. Deep speech 2: End-to-end speech recognition in english and mandarin. *arXiv, preprint arXiv:1512.02595*, 2015.

[7] J. Fowers, K. Ovtcharov, K. Strauss, et al. A high memory bandwidth fpga accelerator for sparse matrixvector multiplication. In *FCCM*, 2014.

[8] J. S. Garofolo, L. F. Lamel, W. M. Fisher, J. G. Fiscus, and D. S. Pallett. Darpa timit acoustic-phonetic continous speech corpus cd-rom. nist speech disc 1-1.1. *NASA STI/Recon technical report n*, 93, 1993.

[9] K. Guo, L. Sui, et al. Angel-eye: A complete design flow for mapping cnn onto customized hardware. In *ISVLSI*, 2016.

[10] S. Han, X. Liu, H. Mao, J. Pu, A. Pedram, M. A. Horowitz, and W. J. Dally. Eie: efficient inference engine on compressed deep neural network. *arXiv preprint arXiv:1602.01528*, 2016.

[11] S. Han, H. Mao, and W. J. Dally. Deep Compression: Compressing deep neural networks with pruning, trained quantization and huffman coding. *ICLR*, 2016.

[12] S. Han, J. Pool, J. Tran, and W. J. Dally. Learning both weights and connections for efficient neural networks. In *Proceedings of Advances in Neural Information Processing Systems*, 2015.

[13] A. Hannun, C. Case, J. Casper, B. Catanzaro, G. Diamos, E. Elsen, R. Prenger, S. Satheesh, S. Sengupta, A. Coates, and A. Ng. Deep speech: Scaling up end-to-end speech recognition. *arXiv, preprint arXiv:1412.5567*, 2014.

[14] S. Hochreiter and J. Schmidhuber. Long short-term memory. *Neural computation*, 1997.

[15] M. Lee, K. Hwang, J. Park, S. Choi, S. Shin, and W. Sung. Fpga-based low-power speech recognition with recurrent neural networks. *arXiv preprint arXiv:1610.00552*, 2016.

[16] E. Nurvitadhi, J. Sim, D. Sheffield, A. Mishra, S. Krishnan, and D. Marr. Accelerating recurrent neural networks in analytics servers: Comparison of fpga, cpu, gpu, and asic. In *Field Programmable Logic and Applications (FPL), 2016 26th International Conference on*, pages 1–4. EPFL, 2016.

[17] D. Povey, A. Ghoshal, G. Boulianne, L. Burget, O. Glembek, N. Goel, M. Hannemann, P. Motlicek, Y. Qian, P. Schwarz, et al. The Kaldi speech recognition toolkit. In *IEEE 2011 workshop on automatic speech recognition and understanding*, 2011.

[18] J. Qiu, J. Wang, et al. Going deeper with embedded FPGA platform for convolutional neural network. In *FPGA*, 2016.

[19] H. Sak et al. Long short-term memory recurrent neural network architectures for large scale acoustic modeling. In *INTERSPEECH*, pages 338–342, 2014.

[20] L. D. Xuedong Huang. *An Overview of Modern Speech Recognition*, pages 339–366. Chapman & Hall/CRC, January 2010.

[21] L. Zhuo and V. K. Prasanna. Sparse matrix-vector multiplication on fpgas. In *FPGA*, 2005.

Quality-Time Tradeoffs in Component-Specific Mapping:

How to Train Your
Dynamically Reconfigurable Array of Gates with Outrageous Network-delays

Hans Giesen
giesen@seas.upenn.edu

Raphael Rubin
rafi@seas.upenn.edu

Benjamin Gojman
bgojman@acm.org

André DeHon
andre@acm.org

Department of Electrical and Systems Engineering
University of Pennsylvania, 200 S. 33rd St., Philadelphia, PA 19104

ABSTRACT

How should we perform component-specific adaptation for FPGAs? Prior work has demonstrated that the negative effects of variation can be largely mitigated using complete knowledge of device characteristics and full per-FPGA CAD flow. However, the cost of per-FPGA characterization and mapping could be prohibitively expensive. We explore lightweight options for per-FPGA mapping that avoid the need for *a priori* device characterization and perform less expensive per FPGA customization work. We characterize the tradeoff between Quality-of-Results (energy, delay) and per-device mapping costs for 7 design points ranging from complete mapping based on knowledge to no per-device mapping. We show that it is possible to get 48–77% of the component-specific mapping delay benefit or 57% of the energy benefit with a mapping that takes less than 20 seconds per FPGA. An incremental solution can start execution after a 21 ms bitstream load and converge to 77% delay benefit after 18 seconds of runtime.

Keywords

FPGA; Variation; Component-Specific Mapping

1. INTRODUCTION

Process variation is large in today's CMOS technology and continues to grow as feature sizes scale down. At minimum feature size, this results in nominally identical devices that have a large range of threshold voltages and hence operating delays. As a result, we are forced to use large, non-minimum feature sizes, at the expense of higher capacitance, and to use high operating voltages that lead to greater dynamic and leakage energy to accommodate the worst-case fabricated devices on today's multi-billion transistor integrated circuits. Consequently, we pay a large energy penalty for variation that threatens to increase the energy used per LUT evaluation as we scale to smaller feature sizes and undermine the traditional benefits of feature-size scaling.

FPGAs, unlike ASICs, can mitigate the impact of variation by assigning functions to resources **after** fabrication, when process variation has already occurred. Resources that use transistors at the extreme tails of the device characteristic distribution can be avoided. Slow resources can be assigned off the critical path. This allows resources to use smaller transistors and operate at lower voltages. Full mapping benefits can reduce energy by 2-3× and allow the continued reduction of energy at smaller feature sizes [26].

Full component-specific mapping requires both an extensive per-chip resource characterization phase [14] and per-chip mapping phase [26] in contrast to the conventional one-mapping-fits-all (OMFA) model that performs mapping only once to be used across any number of specific FPGA components. When full characterization may take days and mapping times run into hours, this cost can be prohibitive.

Lightweight repair schemes that precompute alternate resources and select among them [19, 16, 28] provide more practical schemes for pure defect tolerance. By performing a single precomputation of alternative resources, this reduces the per-FPGA mapping time down to seconds. This basic idea can be applied to variation: *identify the slow paths that limit operation and replace them with faster, precomputed alternatives.* In this paper, we identify and explore a range of algorithms for timing repair exploiting these precomputed alternatives and characterize their costs and benefits.

We first review variation and component-specific mapping (Sec. 2) and precomputed alternatives (Sec. 3). We tune the routing architecture (Sec. 4) to the variation mitigation problem, and then describe the mapping algorithms (Sec. 5). Sec. 6 describes our methodology, Sec. 7 present our experimental results, and Sec. 8 discusses their implications.

Our novel contributions include:
- Show how to adapt lightweight, load-time route alternative selection to address variation.
- Show how to adapt incremental, in-system repair to address variation.
- Characterize time (runtime, measure) and quality (delay, energy) achievable across 7 design points between OMFA and full CAD, perfect-knowledge mapping.

FPGA '17, February 22 - 24, 2017, Monterey, CA, USA

© 2017 Copyright held by the owner/author(s). Publication rights licensed to ACM.
ISBN 978-1-4503-4354-1/17/02. . . $15.00

DOI: http://dx.doi.org/10.1145/3020078.3026124

2. BACKGROUND

2.1 Process Variation

Even identically drawn transistors in a modern VLSI technology will differ from each other [4, 30]. Nominal critical dimensions now measure in single or double-digit nanometers, meaning the presence or absence of individual atoms has a significant impact on performance. Phase-shift masking, etching, and lensing effects result in approximate feature definition [3]. Differences in local oxide thickness [2], random dopant fluctuation [1], and stochastic dopant placement provide a strong random component to the composition of each transistor. As a result, key characteristics, such as the threshold voltage (V_{th}), vary widely from chip-to-chip and from device-to-device within a single chip.

These effects directly impact the delay of each resource in the FPGA [32]. In modern, short-channel, velocity-saturated transistors operating above threshold, delay scales linearly in $V_{dd} - V_{th}$, such that devices slow down as V_{th} increases. On a 65 nm FPGA, Gojman measures a spread of over 100 ps for nominally identical paths within a LAB [14] and nominally identical interconnect segments [13], and these spreads increase as features sizes shrink.

Variation also limits our ability to scale down operating voltage, resulting in higher dynamic energy [7]. Since delay above threshold is proportional to $V_{dd} - V_{th}$, we are forced to increase V_{dd} to offset high V_{th} values, increasing the dynamic operating energy that scales as $C(V_{dd})^2$. Design functionality depends on all used devices being able to switch, and design delay is determined by the slowest of numerous parallel paths. With random V_{th} variation, this means we sample the V_{th}-distribution millions-to-billions of times on today's FPGAs, and the worst device among those sampled will be the limiting V_{th} for operation.

One way to combat variation is to increase device size, which increases energy through increased switching capacitance. For random dopant variation, variance scales roughly as $\frac{1}{\sqrt{L \cdot W}}$, where L and W are the length and width of the transistor [18]. By scaling up device widths, we reduce the relative effects of variation. However, this also directly increases the device capacitance and indirectly increases the wire capacitance by making the chip larger and hence wires longer. This reverse scaling of device size increases the C in the dynamic operating energy $C(V_{dd})^2$.

2.2 Component-Specific Mapping

The idea of component-specific mapping for defects has a history that predates FPGAs. We have long accepted that hard disks will not be manufactured perfectly and use defect maps to avoid the small fraction of sectors that cannot reliably store data. The TERAMAC computer provided the first large-scale use of defect identification and component-specific mapping for FPGA-like architectures [9]. This required a complete run of the placement and routing tools that were aware of the defects in the machine. Wong and Gojman extended the characterization of resources from defects to variation, showing how a modern FPGA with adjustable clocks can self-characterize the delay of individual resources [33, 14]. Using a Configured Test Circuit (CTC) on the FPGA fabric, they measure the delay of specific resource sets. Mehta extended the component-specific mapping concept to variation mitigation, building upon the data that Wong and Gojman showed how to extract [26].

The TERAMAC and Mehta model accepts that we must first measure devices and bring that information into the routing and perhaps placement phase. This means we must measure and store gigabytes of information for each chip, and we must run the CAD tools uniquely for each chip—a contrast from the component-independent model where we only need to generate a single mapping that can be reused across any number of chips.

To avoid the cost of full chip mapping, we can design the architecture or architectural mapping to allow small edits to the bitstream to exchange bad resources for good ones. Lach first showed how to strategically reserve spare LUTs and precompute alternate mappings that allow any defective LUT to be replaced locally [19]. Rubin showed how to reserve spare wiring tracks and precompute alternate routes to locally avoid interconnect defects [28]. These solutions accept a loss of efficiency from the full mapping approach in order to avoid the cost of computing a completely unique mapping for each chip. They also invest additional up-front costs to precompute alternatives to defects in order to minimize the per-chip mapping costs.

2.3 Temperature, Activity, and Aging

Beyond manufacturing variation, environmental and usage effects can also impact the delay of individual resources, and aging can change their delay over time [31]. Component-specific mapping allows us to reduce the manufacturing margins, but may still need margins for these other environment and usage effects. To the extent environment effects impact the die uniformly, such as ambient temperature, dynamic voltage scaling [8] used on top of component-specific mapping can reduce the level of margining. Local variation in chip activity [36] can cause resource delays to diverge from the delays captured by isolated CTC tests [22]. The online-monitoring techniques we adapt from COSMIC TRIP [12] (Sec. 5.5) capture these effects, while the algorithms that use CTC testing will not. Periodic re-characterization of the delays can reduce the necessary aging margins, which becomes more viable with the lightweight load-time techniques we describe here or can be eliminated with COSMIC TRIP.

3. CHOOSE-YOUR-OWN-ADVENTURE

All of our lightweight algorithms build on Choose-Your-own-Adventure (CYA) precomputed alternatives [28]. The CYA bitstream is organized by 2-point nets and contains multiple alternative paths for each 2-point net route. A 2-point net links a single source to a single destination; a full net with fanout to multiple destinations is represented by a collection of 2-point nets. At load time, the bitstream loader configures each 2-point net, then performs a simple test to validate that the configured route successfully transmits the intended signal. If it works, the loader keeps the path and proceeds to load the next 2-point net. If it fails, it tries one of the alternatives for the 2-point net stored in the bitstream. The loader does not require significant state or decision making; it simply loads bit patterns and branches on success failure indications from tests. The original CYA formulation suggested it could be an extension of the existing FSM that controlled bitstream loading. We expect the supervisory processors on the Stratix-10 [17] could be programmed to perform CYA bitstream loading.

The standard CYA approach to bitstream construction is to split the FPGA routing resources into two sets—a *base set* for normal routing and a *reserved* set to use for repairs. A normal Pathfinder [25] route is used within the base set to produce a base route. Every net in the application netlist has a route within the base resources, and the base resources for a net are reserved exclusively for that net. Alternate routes for each 2-point net are then identified from reserved resources and the unused base resources. These alternatives are allocated non-exclusively. Since most 2-point nets will use their base route, the alternatives will only be lightly used. Identifying multiple alternative routes for each 2-point net deals both with the cases where other nets do use resources that conflict with some alternative routes and the cases where the alternatives themselves are unusable.

The key goal of Rubin's CYA alternative generation was to maximize diversity in order to minimize the chance that the alternative set would be unable to provide a defect-free path [28]. For timing-repair, we also care about the delay of the routes. Consequently, we tuned the cost function to prioritize alternative path generation by path delay with care to avoid duplicate paths.

4. ARCHITECTURE

As noted, CYA bitstream generation splits the channels in the architecture into two domains: base tracks and reserved spare tracks that are only available to alternative routes. Channels are interconnected via a modified Wilton S-box [24]. Fig. 1a represents a traditional Wilton S-box in a segment length 1 architecture. Tracks and connections entirely in the base domain are shown in black. Blue identifies the spare domain. A significant fraction of the connections is depicted in red, indicating cross-domain connections. These pose two problems: First, the spare tracks are reserved during base routing, so tracks that attempt to cross the boundary become dead-ends. Second, although base tracks are not reserved during alternative generation, they are often occupied, meaning these cross-domain connections also result in blocked paths for the alternatives. Fig. 2 illustrates how these dead-ends (red connections) increase the delay from a CLB to different channels. We eliminated the dead-ends by modifying the Wilton S-box such that base tracks never cross over to reserved tracks and vice versa. The modified S-box (Fig. 1b) can be regarded as two separate Wilton S-boxes, one of which switches among the base tracks, and the other among reserved tracks.

We also split the C-boxes so that extra CLB pins are connected only to spare tracks, and base CLB pins to base tracks. This saves area by omitting switches that would almost never be used. A drawback is that base tracks cannot be utilized by alternatives, even in situations where not all base tracks are occupied. The population of switches connecting spare tracks to extra CLB pins is controlled by $F_{C_{in,extra}}$ and $F_{C_{out,extra}}$. Their counterparts $F_{C_{in}}$ and $F_{C_{out}}$ are limited to the base tracks and regular CLB pins.

When Rubin used CYA for defect-tolerance, he only addressed the presence of spare paths. Considering delay and energy, a good alternative should also maintain or reduce delay. Even before considering variation, delay depends on the number of segments that a path traverses, the segment lengths, the fan-in of S-box multiplexers and CLB input pins. Sparse C-box population results in segments that are not connected to all CLB outputs and inputs, and segment staggering means that not all tracks can get from the source to destination using the same number of segments in a path.

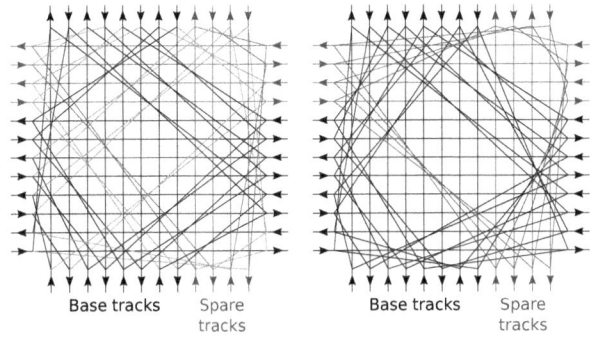

(a) Original Wilton S-Box   (b) Modified Wilton S-Box
Blue links show Reserved Tracks; Red links show switch connections that become unusable when we partition Base and Reserved Tracks.

Figure 1: S-Box Optimized for Reserved Tracks

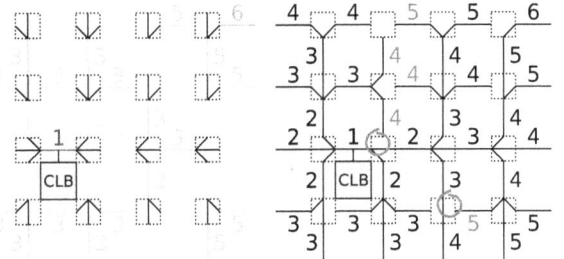

(a) No dead-ends   (b) With dead-ends
Red numbers in the (b) figure highlight delays that are larger than in the (a) figure due to the dead-end connections highlighted with red circles.

Figure 2: Effect of Dead-Ends in S-Box on Delay

To guarantee that the architecture will have good timing alternatives for every 2-point net, we derived a formula relating the number of distinct good timing alternatives, N_{alts}, of a 2-point net to the spare architectural resources:

$$N_{alts} = \left\lfloor \frac{O_s}{4} \right\rfloor \lfloor Tracks/output \rfloor \lfloor Inputs/track \rfloor \quad (1)$$

Here, $\frac{O_s}{4}$ is the number of extra CLB output pins per CLB side. These pins are only available for alternative routes. The formula guarantees that there will at least N_{alts} connections from every CLB to a spare track that connects to the destination at the optimal stagger offset. The formula considers alternatives different as long as at least one section of the path (CLB pin or track) differs. The number of spare tracks connected to an output is

$$Tracks/output = \min\left(Round\left(F_{C_{out,extra}} \frac{W_s}{2} \right), \left\lfloor \frac{W_s}{2L_{seg}} \right\rfloor \right),$$

where $\frac{W_s}{2}$ is the number of spare tracks in one direction. The min operator limits $Tracks/output$ to the number of output multiplexers in a channel. The inputs per track is

$$Inputs/track = \frac{\left\lfloor \frac{I_s}{4} \right\rfloor Tracks/input}{\frac{W_s}{2}} \quad (2)$$

with I_s as number of extra CLB input pins. Switches connecting to these pins are equally distributed among the tracks, so we computed $Inputs/track$ by dividing the number of

Table 1: Fast Alternatives Architectures Parameters

Guaranteed fast alternatives	1	2
Regular input pins	27	27
Regular output pins	8	8
$F_{C_{in}}$	0.15	0.15
$F_{C_{out}}$	0.2	0.3
Segment length	4	4
Extra input pins (I_s)	16	16
Extra output pins (O_s)	4	8
$F_{C_{in,extra}}$	0.25	0.25
$F_{C_{out,extra}}$	0.1	0.1
Spare tracks (W_s)	16	16
Overhead Area Sparing (% base)	20.8	21.7

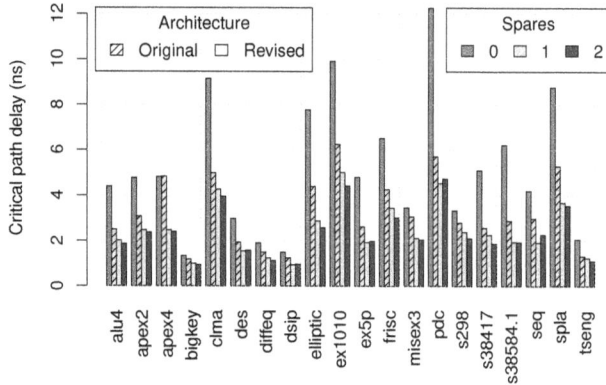

Figure 3: Architecture and Spare Provisioning Impact for Full-Path Pathfinder Selection at $V_{dd} = 0.60$V, 64 Alternatives

switches by the number of tracks in one direction. The number of tracks per input is provided by

$$Tracks/input = Round\left(F_{C_{in,extra}}\frac{W_s}{2}\right). \quad (3)$$

To guarantee that alternatives can use segments with the same length, we modified the S-box connectivity at the edge of the FPGA, and we restricted the number of reserved tracks to multiples of $2L_{seg}$. We also ensure that the fan-in of multiplexers in the reserved domain is never higher than the fan-in in the base domain. Tab. 1 summarizes the architecture parameters selected for our experiments.

Fig. 3 shows the impact of the switchbox rewiring and spare allocation on the Pathfinder Selection algorithm. For the same resources (1 guaranteed fast alternative), the split-domain Wilton increases the potential gains from repair by 45% and reduces minimum channel width 10%. Using one guaranteed alternative saves 50% (geomean) delay, and a second provides marginal additional benefit.

5. MAPPING ALGORITHMS

In this section, we describe the algorithms that we characterize. Tab. 2 summarizes the key characteristics of the algorithms to highlight their differences.

5.1 OMFA

As a baseline, One-Mapping-Fits-All (OMFA) is the standard component-independent mapping. Working on nomi-

nal delay estimates for routing resources, VPR-Pathfinder routing [25, 23] is performed once, and the same mapping of nets to resources is used for all chips. The only time required to map a design with OMFA is the load time, which is configuration bandwidth dominated.

$$T_{omfa} = N_{bits} \times T_{bit} \quad (4)$$

We use N_{bits} estimates from [28], using VPR to supply detail switch counts, and take $T_{bit} = 1$b/ns after the Virtex-5 [34].

5.2 Full Knowledge

For the highest-quality mapping, we perform a normal VPR-Pathfinder-style placement and routing based on a routing graph where the delay over every link in the network is set to match the specific FPGA component. We assume CTC-style measurement of basic resources to obtain the link delays. Resources are decomposed into Discrete Units of Knowledge or DUKs from [14]. Pathfinder routing [25] is already designed to find shortest paths in this routing graph with irregular, heterogeneous delays, and techniques from [26] allow us to represent per-switch delays in VPR [23].

Full Knowledge routing requires a processor capable of running a full Pathfinder router to produce the component-specific bitstream. In typical operation, we imagine this would be performed once, before the FPGA platform is deployed. The bitstream would then be stored in configuration ROM or flash memory on the FPGA platform.

To estimate Full Knowledge mapping time, we include both the time to run VPR routing on the component delays, T_{vpr}, and the time to measure all the paths, $N_{dukpaths}$, necessary to compute all DUKs in the FPGA.

$$T_{full} = T_{vpr} + T_{dmeas} \times N_{dukpaths} \quad (5)$$

We estimate the number of DUKs and paths based on [13]:

$$N_{dukpaths} = 2 \cdot N_{segments} \cdot (2L_{seg} + 1) + \quad (6)$$
$$\left(1 + N_{ch} \cdot F_{cout} \cdot L_{seg} \cdot F_{cin} \cdot \frac{N_{ins}}{2}\right)5K \cdot N_{luts} \cdot N_{outs}$$

We estimate T_{dmeas} as 2 seconds, based on observations that 4 DUKs can be measured on average per configuration in less than 8 seconds. We expect these numbers are conservative and could be significantly reduced with appropriate tuning. From prior work (e.g., [12]), we know algorithm runtime and testing are the dominant time components. We keep the models simple for illustration, omitting lower-order contributors such as load and reconfiguration time for algorithms with large testing and algorithm time.

5.3 CYA Defect-Only

CYA performs greedy, load-time selection among the alternatives. We adapt CYA for timing optimization by testing each 2-point net alternative, not just for functionality, but also for operation at a specified delay. We use a CTC measurement technique like the one from Wong or Gojman [33, 14] to test if a path will run at a specified delay. Load-time selection simply tests for a performance threshold and takes the first alternative that meets the specified performance; it does not characterize the performance of alternatives or try to select the highest-performance alternative.

The simplest load-time selection is a defect-only case where the timing test is set to some large threshold value (e.g., 10 ns). Defect-only CYA tests at this large threshold value

Table 2: Key Algorithm Characteristics

Algorithm	When	Measure		Base Rsrv	Alter- nates	Greedy?	Delay Type	State Bytes
		How	What					
Full Knowledge	Mfg.	CTC	All DUKs	N	N/A	No	Static	100M
Pathfinder Repair	Load	CTC	Paths + Repair DUKs	Y	Route	No	Static	10M
Pathfinder Selection	Load	Binary CTC	Paths + Repair Paths	Y	Precomp.	No	Static	10M
Incr. CYA	Operation	DDFFL	Delay at LUT (MD)	Y	Precomp.	By Slack	Observ.	1M
CYA Slack-Budget	Load	Binary CTC	Paths	Y	Precomp.	By Net	Static	10
CYA Defect-Only	Load	Binary CTC	Paths	Y	Precomp.	By Net	Static	10
OMFA	Never	N/A	N/A	N	N/A	N/A	Static	10

to filter out resources that are slow enough to be considered defective. Tab. 2 marks algorithms that only use CTC measurements to decide whether a path meets a threshold as "Binary CTC" to distinguish them from cases where the algorithm uses a series of CTC measurements to estimate the delay of a path or resource.

The Defect-Only CYA load time is dominated by testing alternatives for the threshold cutoff, T_{thresh}:

$$T_{defect-CYA} = N_{atry} \times N_{tmeas} \times T_{thresh} \qquad (7)$$

N_{atry} is the total number of alternatives tried during the load. Threshold measurement count, N_{tmeas}, is set to 1000.

5.4 CYA Slack-Budget

A more sophisticated option tests each path against a required time (RT). We could set the required time to the nominal delay for the path for each 2-point net. However, we can achieve the nominal delay for the circuit even when off-critical path 2-point net links do not make their nominal delay. That is, there is slack on these paths, and we can allow 2-point nets to use some of that slack. As a result, we budget the slack along the 2-point nets in a path from inputs to outputs. For this work, we use a very simple slack-budgeting scheme where each 2-point net in a path gets its delay-proportional share of the total path slack ($Slack(2pt_i) = Slack(Path(i)) \times \frac{Delay(2pt_i)}{Delay(CriticalPath)-Slack(Path(i))}$). Each 2-point net may be part of multiple paths that have differing initial slack, which results in unclaimed path slack after this formula is applied. Therefore, we distribute slack by repeatedly applying this formula until all the residual slacks are negligible or entirely distributed. More sophisticated slack-budgeting schemes are known in the literature (e.g., [11]), but we leave those for future work. Finally, we scale the delay budgets to match the timing target for each load, resulting in a required time:
$RT_i = \frac{DelayTarget}{Delay(CriticalPath)} \times (Delay(2pt_i) + Slack(2pt_i))$.
Slack-Budget CYA performs a binary search to determine the minimum $DelayTarget$ achievable.

Slack-Budget CYA loading is the same as Defect-Only CYA, except that it uses the per-net timing target delay, T_{targ}, determined from slack budgeting. For simplicity in estimation, we conservatively use the target circuit delay:

$$T_{sbudget-CYA} = N_{atry} \times N_{cmeas} \times DelayTarget \qquad (8)$$

N_{atry} includes all alternatives tried across all delay targets in the binary search.

5.5 Incremental CYA

The CYA Slack-Budget greedy selection of the first "good-enough" alternative may not allocate fast resources where they are most needed. In the Incremental CYA algorithm, we postpone delay measurement and circuit customization to runtime, where they are performed in parallel with the main circuit operation. This effectively reduces the initial preparation time to the time needed for the defect CYA algorithm. Furthermore, testing is performed in the final environment with the full circuit configured, meaning temperature and activity effects are included in the characterization. During operation the algorithm performs measurements to locate the slowest resource and replaces the slowest path with an unused and non-conflicting CYA alternative path. As customization takes place incrementally, a circuit can already take advantage of delay improvements before the algorithm completes. Since repairs are made in order of need, the slowest paths get the first chance to select from available alternatives, providing a form of *list scheduling* [15]. Computations that can tolerate variable delay, such as best-effort and streaming dataflow computation, can start performing useful work immediately during this initial tuning phase. Tasks with real-time requirements may not meet their full-speed operation goals until a number of repairs have occurred. As we show in Sec. 7, timing repair can typically be achieved in tens of seconds.

Our algorithm is an adaptation of COSMIC TRIP [12], which was originally devised to deal with circuit slowdown caused by aging. As in COSMIC TRIP, we assume an FPGA equipped with Difference Detectors with First-Fail Latches (DDFFL) [20] connected to every LUT output to establish whether signals attain their final value at a time instant that precedes the end of the clock period by a configurable amount of time. The time between the start of the clock period and the latest arrival time for errorless operation is called the maximum delay MD_i of a LUT i. From the MD_i estimates, the algorithm computes the relative lateness, RL_i of every LUT. RL_i indicates the additional time that a LUT needs to produce an output value compared to its predecessors and its nominal delay. The LUT with the relative lateness that most exceeds its slack is selected for repair.

In COSMIC TRIP, the slack, $Slack_i$, was derived from the MD_i estimates before the circuit was affected by aging. When incremental repair is applied to reduce a timing margin, there is no equivalent to delays before aging to use as basis of the slack computation. Therefore, the search algorithm must be revised to accommodate variation. We constrain the slowest-LUT search to the critical path because any delay improvement in the remaining circuitry will not affect the minimum clock period of the circuit as a whole. We identify the critical-path LUTs by determining the LUTs that minimize the slack computed from the current timing errors. Every repair potentially affects the trajectory of the critical path, so we incrementally recompute the slack during every search, increasing the per-repair costs over COSMIC TRIP. When a LUT has been repaired, we must update the MD_i's and $Slack_i$'s in the network. However, only the MD_i intervals of the repaired LUT and its recursive fanout cone need to be reset and remeasured. We can reuse the MD_i's outside of the cone, reducing the time to updated the MD_i estimates compared to the initial estimation.

The incremental repair algorithm has much higher complexity than the CYA loader and requires megabytes of memory. We imagine it running on an attached processor such as the embedded ARM core on modern Zynq and Arria SoCs.

For Incremental CYA, we first run defect-only CYA, and then perform incremental repair attempts during operation.

$$T_{incr-CYA} = T_{defect-CYA} + T_{incr} \qquad (9)$$

The incremental repairs require both algorithm time to compute the next measurement or repair attempt and operational cycles during which the DDFFL collects samples.

$$T_{incr} = T_{incr-select} + N_{tot-eval-cyc} \times T_{cycle} \qquad (10)$$

However, the circuit may be performing useful work during the algorithm time and the computation, just not at the final rate of operation. An alternate indication of the cost of the algorithm is the lost time compared to running at the final operating speed.

$$T'_{incr} = \left(\frac{T_{incr-select}}{T_{cycle}} + N_{tot-eval-cyc} \right) \\ \times (T_{cycle} - T_{final-cycle}) \qquad (11)$$

5.5.1 Observed and Worst-Case Delays

Conventional vendor CAD maps designs for worst-case delays with large margins. Component-specific mapping can map to the specific delays of a particular chip. However, the worst-case delays calculated with static timing analysis may still be larger than the delay paths typically seen in the chip. This may be in part due to false paths in the netlist graph that are not sensitizible [10, Ch. 8] or due to real paths that are, nonetheless, activated very rarely [27]. VPR timing estimates do not eliminate false paths, and even the best false-path estimates are necessarily conservative.

One fundamental difference of Incremental CYA is that it actively optimizes *observed* delays rather than worst-case delays. A path that is never sensitized does not contribute to the delay (MD) and lateness (RL) calculations. This can allow Incremental CYA to operate faster than a static timing analysis might predict. It also means that Incremental CYA will not repair a path before it is sensitized; consequently, it will never spend resources repairing a false path.

5.6 Pathfinder Repair

To make loading simple and fast, CYA makes several simplifications relative to a Full Knowledge route. Most notably, it splits base and reserved tracks, it uses a limited number of full LUT-to-LUT paths, and it performs alternative selection in a greedy fashion rather than using Pathfinder-style negotiated congestion. To characterize the effects of these limitations, we create two intermediates points between Full Knowledge routing and CYA. These algorithms can be viewed as limit studies providing insight into how much quality we are compromising by each of the individual simplifications.

In Pathfinder Repair, we look specifically at the impact of the base and reserved track split where we only reroute nets that fail to meet their timing, and we reroute these using only the routing resources available to CYA—the reserved tracks. The entire design is routed using the base resources with their nominal delay, just as for a CYA design. However, rather than pre-computing alternatives, the algorithm performs full-knowledge characterization of the reserved resources, and full Pathfinder negotiated-congestion routing for the two-point nets whose base routes do not meet the timing target. We implement this modification inside VPR by identifying only the failed two-point nets as the logical graph to route and marking only the reserved resources as available for routing. As a result, the Pathfinder Repair route has the highest quality possible for a design with the base/reserved track split. It sacrifices quality by not ripping up good routes in the base to reuse their resources, but, as a result, it saves time by only performing component-specific routing on nets that fail to meet timing in the base route.

Pathfinder Repair will require a processor and memory with the full capabilities to represent the detail FPGA routing graph for the reserved tracks and run full VPR-style routing. It must also be able to perform DUK measurements and DUK computations for the reserved track resources.

Pathfinder Repair requires DUK measurement time, repair time, $T_{vpr-repair}$, and time to measure each 2-point net to see if it meets its required timing target:

$$T_{path-repair} = T_{vpr-repair} + T_{dmeas} \times N_{dukpaths} \\ + N_{2pt} \times N_{cmeas} \times T_{cycle} \qquad (12)$$

$N_{dukpaths}$ here uses Eq. 6 with $N_{ch} = W_s$, since Pathfinder Repair only needs to characterize the reserved resources. Since repair time only needs to route the failing nets on the smaller set of reserved tracks, routing time is lower than Full Knowledge routing ($T_{vpr-repair} < T_{vpr}$). We set N_{cmeas} to 2^{15} to match the Full Knowledge measurements.

5.7 Pathfinder Selection

Pathfinder Selection is designed as a mid-point between Pathfinder Repair and CYA to characterize the impact of using a limited set of LUT-to-LUT paths rather than performing full-knowledge route selection. That is, a key simplification in CYA is that it keeps only a small number of LUT-to-LUT path alternatives rather than performing a search on the route resource graph to explore available paths. This is what allows the CYA loader to be simple and avoid representing the route graph. CYA also allocates these LUT-to-LUT paths in a greedy manner; this also simplifies state and decision making. Pathfinder Selection keeps the limited LUT-to-LUT paths used by CYA, but performs Pathfinder-style negotiated congestion among the nets that fail to meet timing in the base route and their alternative paths in order to perform the repair. Compared to Pathfinder Repair, this characterizes the impact of only using a limited number of LUT-to-LUT paths. Compared to CYA, this characterizes the impact of greedy route selection. Pathfinder Selection is implemented in a modified VPR Pathfinder router where we restrict path expansion for a net to the set of precomputed alternatives that meet its slack budget target. As with CYA and Pathfinder Repair, we limit the set of 2-point nets to route to the set that fails to meet timing in the base route.

Pathfinder Selection has the same processor and memory needs as Pathfinder Repair since it must represent the individual routing resources to detect conflicts. Pathfinder Selection does not need to measure or compute DUKs since it operates entirely on LUT-to-LUT paths.

Pathfinder Selection replaces the runtime of full VPR with the runtime of Pathfinder negotiation on precomputed alternatives paths, $T_{vpr-select}$, and DUK characterization with 2-point alternative target delay filtering.

$$T_{path-select} = T_{vpr-select} + N_{2pt} \times N_{cmeas} \times T_{targ} \\ + N_{2pt} \times N_{alt} \times N_{cmeas} \times T_{targ} \quad (13)$$

6. METHODOLOGY

We compare the various algorithms on the Toronto 20 benchmark [5] set. We use VPR 5.0.2 [23] for placement and extend it with timing-target routing [29]. Our target architecture is an Island-style architecture [6] with 6-input LUTs ($K = 6$) and 8 base LUTs per cluster ($N = 8$) and a segment length of 4 using the split Wilton switchbox (Sec. 4), making it similar to the Stratix-IV [21]. Routes are performed with a base track allocation set at the minimum number of routing channels for the design. We add sparing to guarantee at least one alternative as fast as the base routes (i.e., 16 spare inputs, 4 spare outputs, $W_s = 16$ reserved tracks, with $F_{C_{out,extra}} = 0.20$ and $F_{C_{in,extra}} = 0.15$) as described in Sec. 4. Except for the OMFA and Full Knowledge mapping, all cases use separated base and reserved tracks. Full knowledge mapping performs its single route on the full set of base and reserved resources.

We use a 22-nm CMOS process modeled by the Predictive Technology Model (PTM) [35] with a typical operating $V_{dd} = 0.8$V and Gaussian distributed threshold voltage with $\mu_{V_{th}} = 400$mV, $\sigma_{V_{th}} = 36$mV. We construct an FPGA "chip" by independently sampling each transistor's threshold voltage from this distribution and use the same set of 20 "chips" across all 7 algorithms. For most results, rather than presenting the characteristics of individuals, we present the 95% yield point—the delay or energy achieved by the second slowest or second highest energy chip in the batch of 20.

For Full Knowledge mapping and repair, routing starts with a complete delay map for the resources in the network. For load-time CYA, we simulate the CYA loader algorithm. For iterative repair CYA, we simulate both the DDFFL data collection and the repair algorithm.

The algorithm time for mapping can be directly converted to energy assuming constant operating power for the mapping processor during the computation.

$$E_{alg} = T_{alg} \times P_{proc} \quad (14)$$

We run our algorithms on a laptop-class Intel Core i7-5600U processor at 2.6 GHz, monitor power consumption with PowerTop, and estimate $P_{proc} \approx 0.19$ W. To run the full set of experiments, we also run jobs on a cluster of 2.7 GHz Intel Xeon processors and scale the runtime to match the laptop-class processor used for timing and power estimates.

7. EXPERIMENTS

Fig. 4 shows an illustrative Incremental CYA repair sequence using the **des** benchmark. We use boxplots to characterize the distribution of the 20 chips, the thick line marks the median and the box captures the two quartiles on either side of the median, with the circles denoting the outliers. Before repair, the design has a large range of potential delays,

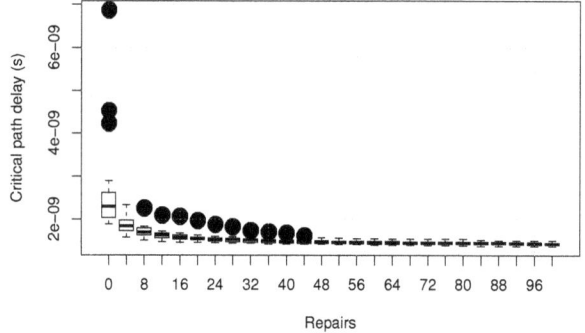

For each repair point, a boxplot characterizes the delay achieved for the set of 20 "chips" used in the experiment. Circles represent the outlier data points.

Figure 4: Incremental CYA Delay vs. Repairs for des for One Fast Alternative Sparing at $V_{dd} = 0.60$V, 64 Alternatives

spread over 5 ns, depending on how the randomly sampled slow resources happen to align with the critical path. If we had to guarantee 95% yield, we would be forced to treat this design as operating at 4.5 ns. However, after the first few repairs, the median drops below 2 ns and the worst-case chip is under 2.3 ns. As repairs continue, the distribution tightens. By 100 repairs, the delay is 1.4 ns, and the entire spread in the distribution is less than 0.13 ns. These 100 repairs occur over a period of one second.

Fig. 5 shows how Incremental CYA makes use of alternatives. We see the largest gains come from having one fast alternative, with some additional gains going to 4 alternatives. Only a couple of designs show additional improvement with 16 alternatives, and the 64 alternatives provides no significant gains. The guarantee of only one or a few fast alternatives coupled with the cost function prioritization that makes sure the most promising alternatives are selected first, and hence kept in the smaller alternative sets, means that the algorithm can generally satisfy the design without going very deep into the alternative set.

Fig. 6 shows how the algorithms compare. Two designs (clma, ex1010) do not achieve 95% yield at 0.6V for OMFA. Slack-budget CYA is always able to improve over OMFA, with the improvement often being substantial. For a few designs, the worst-case, Incremental CYA shows little or no improvement over the defect-CYA that is run as a prefix to the incremental improvement. Nonetheless, the observed delay for Incremental CYA always achieves delays below Slack-budget CYA, showing that the incremental repair is effective in practice. Pathfinder Selection is only slightly better than Slack-budget CYA, suggesting that the greedy path selection in CYA has a modest effect on solution quality. Pathfinder Selection can be worse than observed delays for Incremental CYA since it is optimizing for static timing analysis. Full Knowledge achieves the lowest delays, as expected, but clearly shows that the slack-budget and Incremental CYA are closer to it than to the OMFA delays. Pathfinder Repair is only moderately worse than Full Knowledge, suggesting that algorithms do not sacrifice much quality for the simplification of only repairing slow paths. The larger gap between Pathfinder Selection and Pathfinder Repair, more

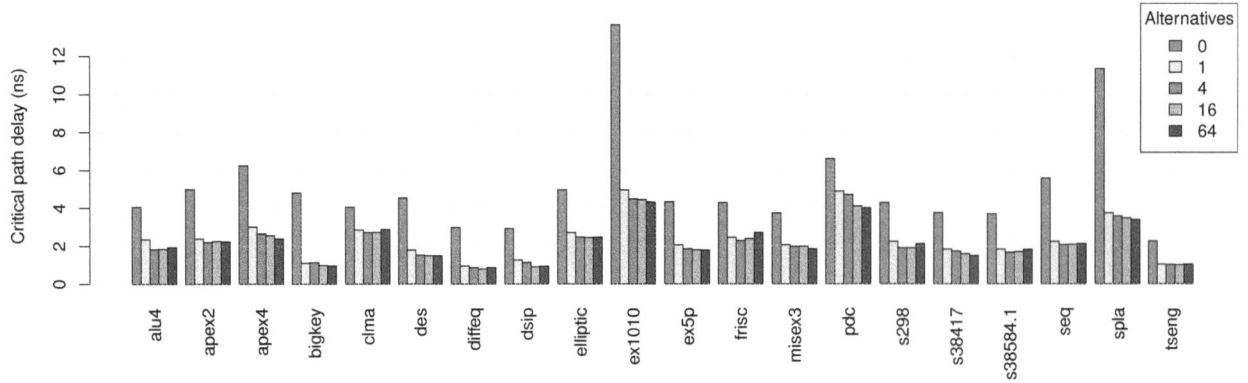

Figure 5: Delay vs. Alternatives for Incremental CYA with One Fast Alternative Sparing at $V_{dd} = 0.60$V

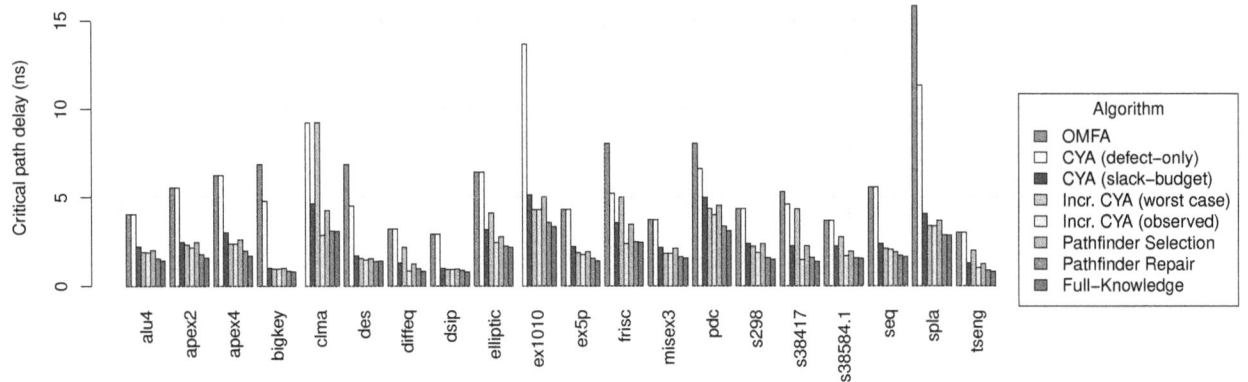

Figure 6: Delay for All Algorithms for One Fast Alternative Sparing at $V_{dd} = 0.60$V and 64 Alternatives

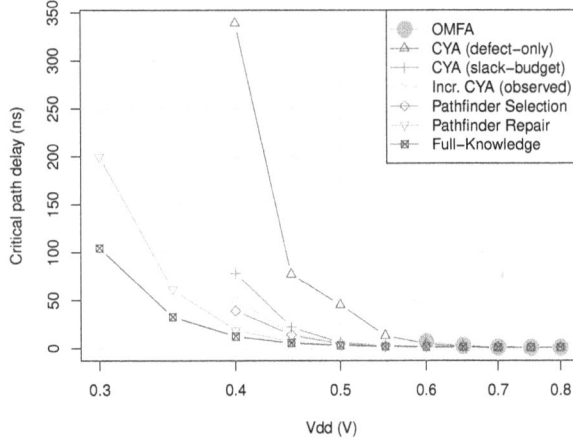

Figure 7: Delay vs. Voltage for des with One Fast Alternative Sparing, 64 Alternatives

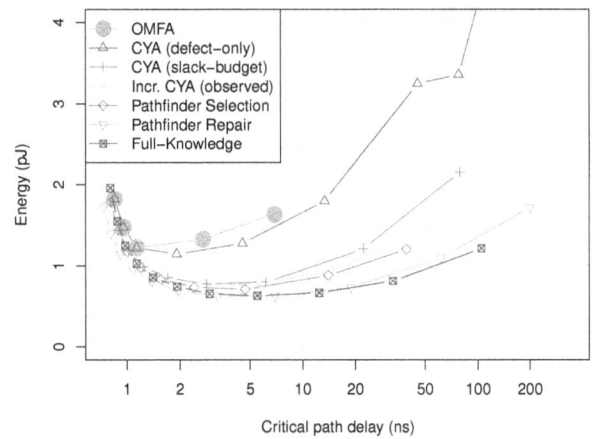

Figure 8: Energy vs. Delay for des with One Fast Alternative Sparing, 64 Alternatives

evident in Fig. 9 and 10, shows that the limited set of full-path alternatives does have a quality impact. This suggests that additional tuning to generate a better or larger set of alternatives might be able to improve CYA quality.

As we lower the voltage, the delay increases and variation has a larger impact on chip delay. Fig. 7 shows how the algorithms stack up on delay for specific voltages. OMFA cannot guarantee 95% operational yield below 0.60 V, while Full Knowledge and Pathfinder Repair can scale down to 0.30 V. Various CYA alternatives and Pathfinder Selection can scale to 0.40 V. At 0.80 V the delay improvement among algorithms is small and undifferentiated. As voltage drops, we see larger separation among the algorithms.

Up to the point where leakage dominates, the lower voltage of operation turns into reduced energy (see Fig. 8). Component-specific repair allows the design to operate to and past the minimum energy point. The ability to reduce the delay at lower voltages, reduces the leakage penalty, allowing the component-specific repairs to shift the energy minimum down to lower energy points at greater delays.

In Figs. 9 and 10, we plot the quality resulting from the algorithms against the time required for mapping and loading. Raw bitstream loads can occur in hundredths of a second, while Full Knowledge mappings take 10^7–10^8 seconds. Defect-only, Slack-budget, and Incremental CYA map in 1–10 seconds. Incremental CYA delay results are within

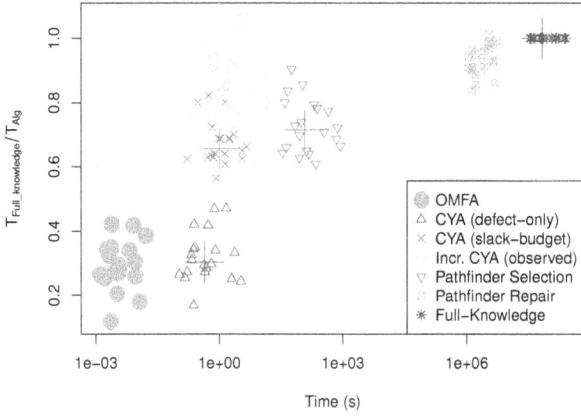

Figure 9: Delay vs. Mapping Time with One Fast Alternative Sparing at $V_{dd} = 0.60$V, 64 Alternatives

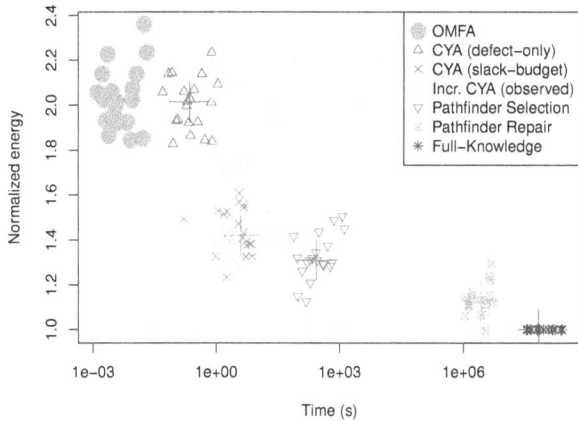

Figure 10: Energy vs. Mapping Time with One Fast Alternative Sparing, 64 Alternatives

$\frac{0.16}{1.0-0.29} \approx 23\%$, and energy results within $\frac{0.44}{2.02-1} \approx 43\%$ of the Full Knowledge mapping.

Tab. 3 summarizes how the algorithms fare when we use them to minimize energy while achieving a delay only 20% larger than the nominal delay. Knowledge mapping schemes spend their dominant time characterizing the chip. Tab. 3 separates measurement time from mapping time, so we can also reason about their delay to get the design running on the FPGA assuming we already have a delay map. Furthermore, we expect the characterization times can be reduced by tuning, including simply running fewer measurement samples, perhaps at the expense of less accurate characterization. From the breakdowns in the table, we can see that the mapping time alone can cost two orders of magnitude more time than the CYA algorithms.

8. DISCUSSION

Slack-budget CYA gets half-way to the delay benefits of full-knowledge mapping, with under ten seconds of measurement and mapping time. At the expense of more sophisticated on-chip measurement and algorithms, Incremental CYA maps just as fast and closes over half of the remaining gap. These show that it is possible to achieve much of the potential benefits of component-specific with lightweight schemes that run quickly.

Table 3: Quality vs. Mapping Costs with One Fast Alternative Sparing Targeting $1.2 \cdot Delay_{nominal}$

Algorithm	T_{FK}/T_{alg}	E/E_{FK}	T_{meas} (s)	T_{alg} (s)	E_{cust} (J)
OMFA	0.98	1.4	0.0	0.0045	0.00086
CYA (def. only)	0.98	1.4	0.021	0.0	0.021
CYA (Sl. budg.)	1.02	1.3	0.063	0.0	0.057
Incr. CYA	1.01	1.1	0.050	0.84	0.18
Pathfinder Sel.	1.02	1.3	14	13	15
Pathfinder Rep.	1.03	1.0	$1.4 \cdot 10^6$	125	$4.6 \cdot 10^5$
Full Knowledge	1.00	1.0	$3.4 \cdot 10^7$	396	$1.6 \cdot 10^7$
geomean aggregates					

Note that the Incremental CYA achieves break-even energy within 20 minutes of operation. As we see in Tab. 3, customization for Incremental CYA costs around 0.18 J and typically reduces it by $0.3E_{FK}$. Assuming that a clock cycle using the Full Knowledge algorithm costs around 1.1 pJ, the savings would be around 0.33 pJ, meaning the cost of customization is repaid after 5.5×10^{11} operations, or, assuming a 2 ns typical cycle time, around 1090 seconds (18 minutes).

Only Incremental CYA fully deals with in-system timing variation and aging. As such, the gap between Incremental CYA and a margined Full Knowledge is likely to be smaller in practice than illustrated here. Alternately, using Incrementally CYA on top of a Full Knowledge routed base route could achieve the high quality of Full Knowledge without needing additional margins.

9. CONCLUSION

Component-specific mitigation of delay variation can be quite tractable. While Full Knowledge characterization and mapping can take megaseconds (days), Slack-budget CYA typically achieves over 50% of the potential delay recovery and over 50% of the potential energy recovery, with under twenty seconds of load-time mapping. Incremental CYA requires similar tuning time and achieves comparable energy recovery (57% average) while achieving over 70% (77% average) of the delay recovery. With these lightweight schemes, energy break-even occurs in hours.

Acknowledgements

H. Giesen was supported by the Leggett Family Fellowship. This research was funded in part by DARPA/CMO contract HR0011-13-C-0005. Any opinions, findings, and conclusions or recommendations expressed in this material are those of the authors and do not reflect the official policy or position of the Department of Defense or the U.S. Government.

10. REFERENCES

[1] A. Asenov. Random dopant induced threshold voltage lowering and fluctuations in sub-0.1 μm MOSFET's: A 3-D "atomistic" simulation study. *IEEE Trans. Electron Devices*, 45(12):2505–2513, December 1998.

[2] A. Asenov. Intrinsic threshold voltage fluctuations in decanano MOSFETs due to local oxide thickness variation. *IEEE Trans. Electron Devices*, 49(1):112–119, January 2002.

[3] A. Asenov, S. Kaya, and A. R. Brown. Intrinsic parameter fluctuations in decananometer MOSFETs

introduced by gate line edge roughness. *IEEE Trans. Electron Devices*, 50(5):1254–1260, May 2003.

[4] K. Bernstein, D. J. Frank, A. E. Gattiker, W. Haensch, B. L. Ji, S. R. Nassif, E. J. Nowak, D. J. Pearson, and N. J. Rohrer. High-performance CMOS variability in the 65-nm regime and beyond. *IBM J. Res. and Dev.*, 50(4/5):433–449, July/September 2006.

[5] V. Betz and J. Rose. FPGA Place-and-Route Challenge. <http://www.eecg.toronto.edu/~vaughn/challenge/challenge.html>, 1999.

[6] V. Betz, J. Rose, and A. Marquardt. *Architecture and CAD for Deep-Submicron FPGAs*. Kluwer Academic Publishers, Norwell, Massachusetts, 02061 USA, 1999.

[7] D. Bol, R. Ambroise, D. Flandre, and J.-D. Legat. Interests and limitations of technology scaling for subthreshold logic. *IEEE Trans. VLSI Syst.*, 17(10):1508–1519, 2009.

[8] C. T. Chow, L. S. M. Tsui, P. H. W. Leong, W. Luk, and S. J. E. Wilton. Dynamic voltage scaling for commercial FPGAs. In *ICFPT*, pages 173–180, 2005.

[9] W. B. Culbertson, R. Amerson, R. Carter, P. Kuekes, and G. Snider. Defect tolerance on the TERAMAC custom computer. In *FCCM*, pages 116–123, April 1997.

[10] S. Devadas, A. Ghosh, and K. Keutzer. *Logic Synthesis*. McGraw-Hill, New York, 1994.

[11] S. Ghiasi, E. Bozorgzadeh, S. Choudhuri, and M. Sarrafzadeh. A unified theory of timing budget management. In *ICCAD*, pages 653–659, 2004.

[12] H. Giesen, B. Gojman, R. Rubin, and A. DeHon. Continuous online self-monitoring introspection circuitry for timing repair by incremental partial-reconfiguration (COSMIC TRIP). In *FCCM*, pages 111–118, 2016.

[13] B. Gojman and A. DeHon. GROK-INT: Generating real on-chip knowledge for interconnect delays using timing extraction. In *FCCM*, pages 88–95, 2014.

[14] B. Gojman, S. Nalmela, N. Mehta, N. Howarth, and A. DeHon. GROK-LAB: Generating real on-chip knowledge for intra-cluster delays using timing extraction. *ACM Tr. Reconfig. Tech. and Sys.*, 7(4):5:1–5:23, Dec. 2014.

[15] R. Graham. Bounds on multiprocessor timing anomalies. *SIAM J. Appl. Math*, 7:416–429, 1969.

[16] C. He, M. F. Jacome, and G. de Veciana. A reconfiguration-based defect-tolerant design paradigm for nanotechnologies. *IEEE Design and Test of Computers*, 22(4):316–326, July-August 2005.

[17] D. L. How and S. Atsatt. Sectors: Divide conquer and softwarization in the design and validation of the Stratix 10 FPGA. In *FCCM*, pages 119–126, May 2016.

[18] K. J. Kuhn. Reducing variation in advanced logic technologies: Approaches to process and design for manufacturability of nanoscale cmos. In *IEDM*, pages 471–474, 2007.

[19] J. Lach, W. H. Mangione-Smith, and M. Potkonjak. Low overhead fault-tolerant FPGA systems. *IEEE Trans. VLSI Syst.*, 6(2):212–221, June 1998.

[20] J. M. Levine, E. Stott, G. A. Constantinides, and P. Y. Cheung. Online measurement of timing in circuits: for health monitoring and dynamic voltage & frequency scaling. In *FCCM*, pages 109–116, 2012.

[21] D. Lewis, E. Ahmed, D. Cashman, T. Vanderhoek, C. Lane, A. Lee, and P. Pan. Architectural enhancements in Stratix-III and Stratix-IV. In *FPGA*, pages 33–42, 2009.

[22] T. A. Linscott, B. Gojman, R. Rubin, and A. DeHon. Pitfalls and tradeoffs in simultaneous, on-chip FPGA delay measurement. In *FPGA*, pages 100–104, February 2016.

[23] J. Luu, I. Kuon, P. Jamieson, T. Campbell, A. Ye, W. M. Fang, and J. Rose. VPR 5.0: FPGA CAD and architecture exploration tools with single-driver routing, heterogeneity and process scaling. In *FPGA*, pages 133–142, 2009.

[24] M. I. Masud and S. Wilton. A new switch block for segmented FPGAs. In *FPL*, pages 274–281, 1999.

[25] L. McMurchie and C. Ebeling. PathFinder: A Negotiation-Based Performance-Driven Router for FPGAs. In *FPGA*, pages 111–117, 1995.

[26] N. Mehta, R. Rubin, and A. DeHon. Limit Study of Energy & Delay Benefits of Component-Specific Routing. In *FPGA*, pages 97–106, 2012.

[27] K. Minkovich and J. Cong. Mapping for better than worst-case delays in LUT-based FPGA designs. In *FPGA*, pages 56–64, 2008.

[28] R. Rubin and A. DeHon. Choose-Your-Own-Adventure Routing: Lightweight Load-Time Defect Avoidance. *ACM Tr. Reconfig. Tech. and Sys.*, 4(4), December 2011.

[29] R. Rubin and A. DeHon. Timing-Driven Pathfinder Pathology and Remediation: Quantifying and Reducing Delay Noise in VPR-Pathfinder. In *FPGA*, pages 173–176, 2011.

[30] P. Sedcole and P. Y. K. Cheung. Parametric yield modeling and simulations of FPGA circuits considering within-die delay variations. *ACM Tr. Reconfig. Tech. and Sys.*, 1(2), June 2008.

[31] E. A. Stott, J. S. J. Wong, P. Sedcole, and P. Y. K. Cheung. Degradation in FPGAs: measurement and modelling. In *FPGA*, page 229, 2010.

[32] T. Tuan, A. Lesea, C. Kingsley, and S. Trimberger. Analysis of within-die process variation in 65nm FPGAs. In *ISQED*, pages 1–5, March 2011.

[33] J. S. Wong, P. Sedcole, and P. Y. K. Cheung. Self-measurement of combinatorial circuit delays in FPGAs. *ACM Tr. Reconfig. Tech. and Sys.*, 2(2):1–22, June 2009.

[34] Xilinx, Inc., 2100 Logic Drive, San Jose, CA 95124. *Virtex-5 FPGA Configuration User Guide*, September 2008. UG191 <http://www.xilinx.com/bvdocs/userguides/ug191.pdf>.

[35] W. Zhao and Y. Cao. New generation of predictive technology model for sub-45 nm early design exploration. *IEEE Trans. Electron Dev.*, 53(11):2816–2823, 2006.

[36] K. M. Zick and J. P. Hayes. On-line sensing for healthier FPGA systems. In *FPGA*, pages 239–248, 2010.

Synchronization Constraints for Interconnect Synthesis

Alex Rodionov and Jonathan Rose
The Edward S. Rogers Sr. Department of Electrical and Computer Engineering
University of Toronto
Toronto, Ontario, Canada
{arod, Jonathan.Rose}@ece.utoronto.ca

ABSTRACT

Interconnect synthesis tools ease the burden on the designer by automatically generating and optimizing communication hardware. In this paper we propose a novel capability for FPGA interconnect synthesis tools that further simplifies the designer's effort: automatic cycle-level synchronization of data delivery. This capability enables the creation of interconnect with significantly reduced hardware cost, provided that communicating modules have fixed latency and do not apply upstream backpressure. To do so, the designer specifies constraints on the lengths, in clock cycles, of multi-hop logical communication paths. The tool then uses an integer programming-based method to insert balancing registers into optimal locations, satisfying the designer's constraints while minimizing register usage. On an example convolutional neural network application, the new approach uses 43% less area than a FIFO-based synchronization scheme.

Keywords

Convolutional Neural Networks; FPGA Interconnect Synthesis

1. INTRODUCTION

Interconnect synthesis and system integration tools, such as Altera Qsys[2], Xilinx IPI[21], and LatticeMico[16], provide a higher-level design entry method than manually writing HDL: they automate the creation of the hardware that connects functional modules together. Similarly, Network-on-Chip (NoC) architectures like CONNECT[18], Split+Merge[12], and Hoplite[13] provide ready-made interconnect solutions for FPGA designs. These tools and architectures simplify the creation of large, complex hardware systems.

A consequence of designing at this level of abstraction is that the implementation of the interconnect is hidden from the designer behind a standardized signaling protocol like Avalon[2] or AXI[4]. As a result, a functional module *can not* assume, in general, that the interconnect will provide a

FPGA '17, February 22 - 24, 2017, Monterey, CA, USA

© 2017 Copyright held by the owner/author(s). Publication rights licensed to ACM.
ISBN 978-1-4503-4354-1/17/02... $15.00

DOI: http://dx.doi.org/10.1145/3020078.3021729

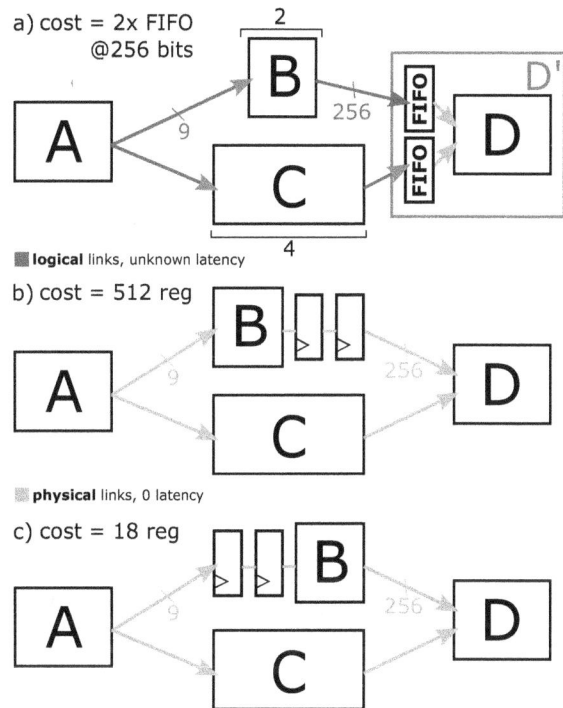

Figure 1: Three solutions for ensuring that inputs at module D arrive at the same time: a) Using an automated system-building tool and modifying module D (as D') by adding FIFOs at its inputs, or building the interconnect manually and adding two pipeline stages b) after or c) before module B.

specific end-to-end latency, or that the latency will even be constant during system operation.

This presents a challenge when functional modules require synchronized data arrival from two or more sources. To guarantee synchronization even in the face of unknown interconnect latency, FIFOs or similar constructs can be inserted just before the functional module inputs, and dequeued when the module sees fit.

The alternative would be to manually create the interconnect with explicit, fixed, known latencies, such that the data arrives at each functional module input at the correct clock cycle by design. While this removes the area penalty incurred by FIFOs, it requires significantly more effort for the designer. They must either create the interconnect in HDL, giving up the productivity advantage of automated tooling, or (if their tools allow) manually specify the locations of registers in the interconnect. Not only must they add the correct *number* of registers, but they could potentially select among many equally-valid *locations* to insert them, with some yielding higher area usage than others.

Figure 1 illustrates a motivating example, containing four functional modules, of such a synchronization problem. Here, modules B and C are internally fully pipelined with fixed input-to-output latencies of 2 and 4 clock cycles, respectively. Each takes a 9-bit input and produces a 256-bit output, as a block RAM might commonly do, for example. Module D requires matching inputs to arrive during the same clock cycle.

If a tool is used to build this system, the four modules would be connected with abstract logical links that are synthesized to an implementation with an unknown latency. The designer may employ the solution shown in Figure 1(a), where module D is wrapped inside a new module D' that adds two 256 bit wide FIFOs to synchronize the data arrival at the inputs.

However, if the designer had full control over the design of the interconnect, they may opt instead to use balancing registers to add the correct, fixed amount of extra latency to synchronize data arrival, and avoid the unnecessary hardware complexity of FIFOs. Two equally-valid solutions are shown in Figures 1(b) and 1(c), with the latter having the lower area usage of 18 (versus 512) registers. The choice of (c) over (b) may be trivial to see in this example, but a larger more complex system would present the designer with less-obvious choices.

In this paper, we propose augmenting an interconnect synthesis tool with the ability to automatically create area-optimal, fixed-latency interconnect in response to the synchronization needs of the designer's application, effectively enabling solutions such as Figure 1(c) to be generated automatically.

This is accomplished by accepting, from the designer, a set of *synchronization constraints*, which take the form of equations or inequalities that relate the end-to-end latencies of one or more logical links and a constant. The tool then satisfies these constraints during interconnect creation by inserting the correct number of balancing registers, favouring solutions that use the minimal amount of total registers.

The problem of synchronizing pipelined systems with delay buffers is itself not novel, as will be discussed in Section 2. However, existing system-building tools for FPGAs lack this capability; adding it would allow their use in constructing new classes of applications, such as systolic arrays[15], beyond the traditional use cases of "processor plus memory-mapped IP cores" or streaming dataflow pipelines.

To this end, we will demonstrate the creation of an FPGA-based implementation of a convolutional neural network (CNN) accelerator using our new synchronization constraint enabled system building methodology. Its area and performance will be compared against a similar system built using a FIFO-based synchronization approach resembling Figure 1(a).

We will present a review of previous work on the synchronization problem in Section 2 and our own interconnect synthesis-specific formulation in Section 3, where we augment our own open-source GENIE interconnect synthesis tool[19, 20] with the ability to apply synchronization con-

straints. This is followed, in Section 4, by the description of the CNN accelerator example design. Section 5 evaluates and compares its clock frequency and area against other design approaches. Finally, we conclude in Section 6.

2. PREVIOUS WORK

The optimization problem of inserting the minimal amount of delay elements to satisfy the synchronization of fixed-latency pipelined computation blocks is a form of *buffer minimization problem* and has been well-studied[11]. The integer programming based approach that we will use to solve it in Section 3.4 is a basic approach that has had refinements made by others to improve its asymptotic runtime complexity through decomposition approaches[7] or graph-theoretic reformulations[5].

The buffer minimization problem has also found use in High-Level Synthesis (HLS) tools[9, 6]. There, hardware modules representing operations in a control/data flow graph are scheduled to begin at a certain clock cycle in order to satisfy dependencies, which naturally leads to the same problem of determining the optimal locations for delay element insertion.

Our contribution is to apply this existing buffer minimization problem in the context of FPGA interconnect synthesis tools, thereby exposing synchronization directly to the end user. Existing tools[2, 21, 16] do not have this capability; individual components can stall upstream communication via backpressure, but this complicates the interconnect implementation. Alternatively, the designer could buffer incoming signals manually, as part of their functional modules.

FPGA-based network on chip architectures[18, 12, 13] are not complete system-building tools like the software provided by the FPGA vendors. Furthermore, contention in packet-switched networks makes packet latency variable, preventing global synchronization of transmissions from taking place. Our approach could theoretically be applied to circuit-switched networks[10], however.

Previously, we introduced our own system-building and interconnect synthesis software, GENIE[19, 20], which is based on Split and Merge[12] routing primitives. Although it is capable of creating backpressure-free interconnect, it currently suffers from the same lack of global synchronization capability as the existing vendor-provided tools. In this paper, we augment it with synchronization constraints. This will extend the automation afforded by interconnect synthesis software to the creation of tightly-scheduled pipelined systems, such as systolic arrays, in addition to (and co-existing with) traditional memory-mapped and streaming components.

3. PROBLEM DEFINITION

In this section, we begin with a review of the traditional system representation seen by interconnect synthesis tools, and proceed to augment this with our formalization of synchronization constraints. An integer programming based method will be provided to solve the constraints and generate the necessary interconnect. Two additional post-processing optimizations will be described that further reduce interconnect area usage.

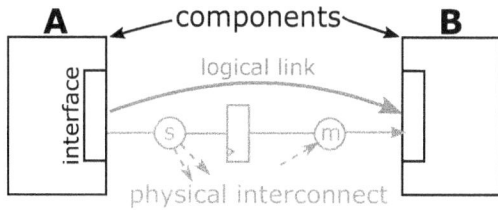

Figure 2: Elements of GENIE's representation of a system, with example generated interconnect.

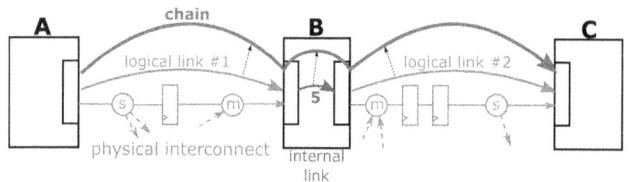

Figure 3: A chain spanning three components A, B, and C, with its constituent two logical links and one internal link within B that has a latency of 5 clock cycles. Each logical link will be realized into example interconnect

3.1 System Representation

First, we review the terminology used to represent a system as seen by a generic interconnect synthesis tool. Although we are extending GENIE in this paper, the concepts presented here should be applicable and relevant to other tools as well.

The designer creates a system containing instances of *components* that represent functional modules. The individual input/output ports of each component are grouped into higher-level connection points called *interfaces* which adhere to some protocol and have well-defined roles for each constituent signal. The designer defines *logical links* between the interfaces of instantiated components to specify that they should communicate. The tool then accepts this system representation as input, and realizes it by instantiating the components and connecting them with physical interconnect according to the logical links.

The structure and details of the generated hardware will differ depending on the tool and interconnect architecture, but in general will include functions for distribution, arbitration, buffering, and conversion. For example, a network-on-chip architecture will instantiate routers that perform most of those functions, joined by wires. The GENIE tool we are extending uses Split nodes for distribution, Merge nodes for arbitration, and FIFOs or registers for buffering depending on whether backpressure is required. The exact arrangement of the primitives used by GENIE to realize the logical specification is defined by an optionally-customizable *topology*. More details can be found in previous work[20].

Figure 2 illustrates an example of the basic elements in a system representation: two component instances A and B are connected with a logical link, which is turned into physical hardware consisting of a split node, a register, and a merge node, which connect to other components in the system that are not shown. This is the baseline which we seek to extend next.

3.2 Internal Links and Chains

In the existing representation, logical links originate and terminate at the interfaces of components. In order to capture the type of global synchronization requirements depicted in the opening example shown in Figure 1, we must first extend the basic system representation of the previous section with the ability to specify communication *through* components.

Internal links serve this purpose – they define a communication path from one of a component's receiving interfaces to one of its transmitting ones. Each internal link has an associated fixed latency, in clock cycles, and is explicitly specified by the designer as part of a component's definition. It is also possible for an interface to participate in multiple internal links within a component, each with a different latency.

We can now define a higher-level type of construct called a *chain*, which captures a transmission beginning at one component, through zero or more intermediate components, and terminating at an ultimate destination. A chain defines a contiguous set of one or more logical links and internal links. Figure 3 illustrates an example of a chain spanning three components - A, B, and C. The intermediate component B has an internal latency of 5 clock cycles.

3.3 Synchronization Constraints

Recall that the goal of this work is to automatically generate interconnect that obeys user-specified synchronization constraints. Now, with the ability to capture multi-component transmissions using chains, we are ready to introduce the formulation of the constraints proper. Given a set of $N \geq 1$ chains $h_1, h_2, \ldots, h_N$, a synchronization constraint takes the form:

$$h_1 \pm h_2 \pm \cdots \pm h_N \ \mathbf{op} \ K \qquad (1)$$

where **op** is a comparison operator (one of $<, \leq, =, \geq, >$), and K is an integer. Each term h_i represents the end-to-end latency, in clock cycles, of that chain. This general form allows the designer to specify arbitrary latency relationships between chains, or to bound the latency of an individual chain. A chain (and its constituent logical links) can participate in multiple constraints.

Figure 4 restates the example system in Figure 1 as an input to GENIE using chains, logical links, and synchronization constraints. The explicitly-specified physical interconnect in the original example has been replaced with logical links between components A, B, C, and D, whose interfaces have been named 'in' and 'out'. The latencies of B and C are captured with internal links. The requirement for D's inputs to arrive simultaneously has been captured as a synchronization constraint between two chains $h_0 = \{A.out \rightarrow B.in, B.out \rightarrow D.in\}$ and $h_1 = \{A.out \rightarrow C.in, C.out \rightarrow D.in\}$, with the constraint being that $h_0 = h_1$.

3.4 Optimization Problem Formulation

The synchronization constraints are used as an input to the tool. The goal is to use them to guide the generation of interconnect. However, in general, there may be *many* legal solutions, differing in the number of total inserted registers; ideally, we would like to find the solution that yields the fewest. This is the well-known buffer minimization problem[11], and this section formalizes a version of it using the system representation terminology introduced previously.

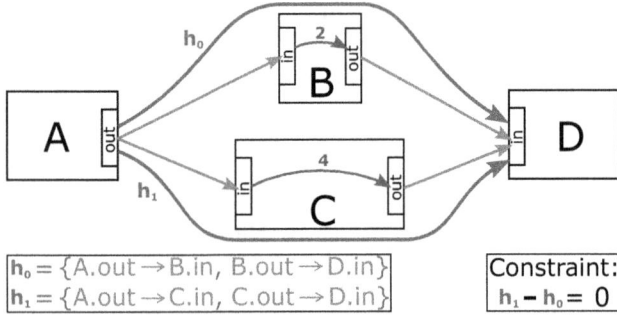

$h_0 = \{A.out \rightarrow B.in, B.out \rightarrow D.in\}$
$h_1 = \{A.out \rightarrow C.in, C.out \rightarrow D.in\}$

Constraint:
$h_1 - h_0 = 0$

Figure 4: The example in Figure 1 restated using a synchronization constraint on an interconnect synthesis problem. The two chains from A to D are constrained by the user to have equal latency.

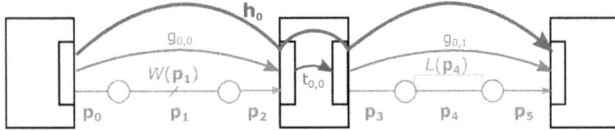

Figure 5: A single chain consisting of one internal link and two logical links, which are synthesized into interconnect containing a total of four primitives and six physical links p_0 through p_5. $W(p_1)$ is the width in bits of link p_1 and $L(p_4)$ is the necessary extra latency, in cycles, of p_4.

Let **C** be the set of all user-provided constraints, each taking the form of Equation 1. For a constraint $c \in \mathbf{C}$, let $\mathbf{H}_c$ represent the set of chains that appear on the left hand side. A chain $h \in \mathbf{H}_c$ has an associated set of logical links, $\mathbf{G}_h$, which is a subset of all logical links **G**. Chains also traverse internal links, that are represented by the set **T**.

The tool realizes logical links into physical interconnect consisting of hardware primitives connected by *physical links*, which directly represent RTL nets. **P** is the set of all physical links. By splicing registers into physical links, cycles of delay can be added in appropriate places to satisfy the overall set of synchronization constraints. If we define $L(p)$ as the number of registers to insert into physical link p, then the goal of the overall optimization problem is to solve $L(p)$ for all $p \in \mathbf{P}$.

We also wish to satisfy the constraints using the minimum total amount of registers. If $W(p)$ represents each physical link's width in bits, then this objective can be codified as the minimization of the following cost function:

$$\# \text{ of registers} = \sum_{p \in \mathbf{P}} W(p)L(p) \qquad (2)$$

Figure 5 illustrates the relationship between an example chain h_0 and its constituent logical, internal, and physical links, as well as the properties W and L of physical links. The latency L of a physical link is a numerical annotation that is only later realized as extra registers.

To solve the set of constraints **C**, each constraint $c \in \mathbf{C}$ is first converted from the form of Equation 1, as provided by the user, into that of Equation 3 by expanding each chain term h_i into its constituent physical links p_i and internal links t_i:

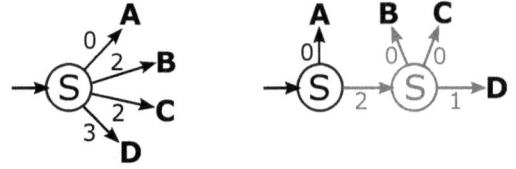

Figure 6: Left: a Split node feeding four physical links with differing latencies. Right: applying systolic retiming, the number of required register stages is reduced from **7** down to **3**.

$$h_1 \pm h_2 \pm \cdots \pm h_N \ \mathbf{op} \ K_c \qquad (1)$$

$$L(p_0) \pm \cdots \pm L(p_N) \ \mathbf{op} \ K_c \pm L(t_0) \pm \dots \pm L(t_M) \qquad (3)$$

The left-hand side consists of unknowns (the latency of physical links to solve for), and the right-hand side of constants (the user's constraint constant K_c together with the fixed latencies of internal links denoted by $L(t_i)$). Interconnect primitives in GENIE have zero latency, but for general applicability, the latencies of interconnect primitives should also be included on the right-hand side.

The resulting system of inequalities is in a canonical form suitable for solving using integer programming: the (nonnegative, integer) unknown variables $L(p)$ are on the left-hand side, and constants are on the right-hand side. A solution to the IP problem yields the values of $L(p)$ for all for all p, subject to the optimization criterion of minimizing the cost function of Equation 2, which is linear with respect to the unknown variables $L(p)$.

Note that additional techniques[7, 5] can be used to improve the asymptotic performance of solving this optimization problem.

3.5 Systolic Retiming Transform

The solution to the optimization problem can lead to scenarios like the left side of Figure 6. Here a Split node (used for distributing signals to different destinations) fans out to four physical links that were assigned three distinct latency values. Realizing this assignment requires 7 register stages - the sum of the 2, 2, and 3 register stages for destinations B, C, and D. However, if we allow for the freedom to change the topology of interconnect primitives *after* initial latency assignment, a less-costly solution can be found, as shown in the right side of the figure where an extra Split node is used to reduce the cost to three register stages. We call this optimization the *systolic retiming transform*.

It is performed after the initial $L(p)$ values have been assigned by the solution of the optimization problem. The overall process is:

1. Sort the Split node's fanout physical links into bins by their latency assignments $L(p)$.

2. Remove the initial Split node.

3. Create a Split node for each bin from step 1.

4. Connect each Split node from step 3 to the original destinations in the respective latency bins, but reset the latency on these new physical links to 0.

5. Connect the Split nodes together with physical links whose latencies are the differences between successive bins.

6. The last Split node can be removed and its sole fanout reassigned to the second-last Split node.

After performing the systolic retiming transform, the updated latency values $L(p)$ on each physical link are used to insert the corresponding number of register stages.

3.6 Long Register Chain Optimization

Current FPGAs can repurpose logic blocks to be used as distributed RAM resources. Although they are not as wide or deep as larger, traditional block RAMs, they still offer more bits of storage per logic block than registers do.

After satisfying the design's synchronization constraints and performing the systolic retiming transform, we perform one final post-processing optimization: long chains of balancing registers are replaced with a single distributed RAM based implementation to reduce area usage. Unlike a FIFO, this memory-based delay element is functionally equivalent to a chain of registers (for example, it preserves non-valid bubble cycles rather than compacting them).

Chains of registers are replaced with memory-based delay elements when the estimated cost is lower. This depends on the length of the chain, the data width, and FPGA-specific architecture parameters such as the maximum depth and width of distributed RAM elements.

As an aside, the introduction of registers embedded directly in the routing fabric of the latest FPGAs[3] will change the cost/benefit analysis of performing this optimization. It may be preferable to leave chains of registers untouched when targeting such architectures.

3.7 Limitations and Scope

Backpressure-free synchronization with balancing registers requires that components have internal links with fixed, static latencies. This will exclude any part of the system that communicates with off-chip peripherals that have non-deterministic latency, such as DRAM controllers. A less-obvious limitation of the presented approach is that it excludes communication patterns in which $N > 1$ sources wish to communicate with 1 sink and the N transmissions are not guaranteed to be mutually-exclusive in time. This scenario implies one or more of the sources would have to be stalled to avoid data loss, implying the need for backpressure and thus non-fixed latency due to the resulting stalls.

A real system may contain a mixture of both types of communication: latency-insensitive with backpressure, and backpressure-free. These regions may even interact with one another. For example: an off-chip memory controller feeding returned read data into an adjoining network of fixed-latency processing modules. It's not possible to determine when valid read data will be returned from memory, but our synchronization constraints could still be applied to the latter region to correctly distribute that data *relative to* its entry into the region.

4. DESIGN EXAMPLE

In this section, we describe a concrete example application for which synchronization constraints can be used effectively: a Convolutional Neural Network (CNN) accelerator targeted

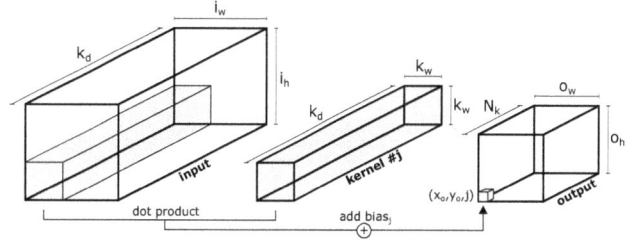

Figure 7: Visualization of the dot product between a kernel and a kernel-sized subvolume of the input. This produces a single output voxel.

towards image classification workloads. There exist many FPGA implementations of CNNs (for example, [23]), and so our goal is not to improve on the state of the art of CNN architecture. Rather, we wish to illustrate the power of synchronization constraints in aiding the creation of a functionally correct, high-performance implementation using an interconnect-centric design flow. We will begin with an overview of the CNN context and then provide a description of the overall design, followed by the implementation details and results in the next section.

4.1 CNN Background

CNNs are a machine learning technique[17] and have been effectively used in applications ranging from image classification [14] and speech recognition[1], to playing the game of Go[22]. CNNs operate in two modes: training and inference. Training 'teaches' the network to classify inputs, and involves feedback. Inference is a feed-forward process that uses the trained neural network to classify inputs. As we have chosen the problem of image classification, training can be performed offline, so we focus only on building hardware to perform inference.

Each input image is split into color channels and stacked together to form a 3-dimensional volume. This image undergoes a chain of different computation stages, each producing an intermediate volume that represents higher-order features of the original image. The final output is a low-dimensional array that directly represents the probabilities of different image categories. The most time-consuming[8] processing stages are the *convolutional layers* from which CNNs derive their name. Our accelerator only implements these.

A convolutional layer convolves its input image with N_k different kernels to produce the output. Each kernel contains weights from off-line training that are constant during inference. The image, kernels, and output can be visualized as 3-dimensional volumes, and the convolution process as a repeated dot product of volumes: Each voxel of the output volume is produced by calculating the dot product of a kernel volume, of width/height k_w and depth k_d, with an equally-sized sub-volume of the image, and then adding a kernel-specific bias constant. This dot product operation, restated as Equation 4, is also visualized in Figure 7.

$$out(x_o, y_o, j) =$$

$$\sum_{x=0}^{k_w-1} \sum_{y=0}^{k_w-1} \sum_{z=0}^{k_d-1} kern_j(x, y, z) \cdot inp(x + x_0, y + y_0, z) \quad (4)$$

$$+ \ bias_j$$

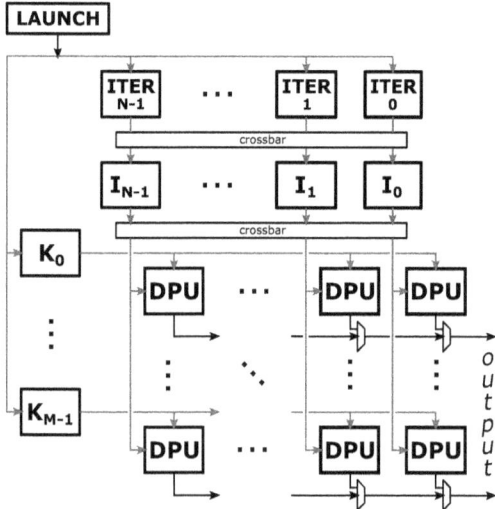

Figure 8: Block diagram of the dot product array. It contains $N \times M$ Dot Product Units, fed by N on-chip image buffers and M kernel buffers.

To generate the entire output volume (and complete the convolution), multiple such dot products must be performed. Each time, a different kernel and/or a different image sub-volume is chosen. The former corresponds to the z coordinate of the output voxel, and the latter to the x and y coordinates of the output. Additionally, When the sub-volume is swept across the input image in the x and y dimensions, the amount it moves within the input is called the *stride*. Equation 4 assumes a stride of 1 for simplicity.

Note that in the overall convolution, many dot product operations share either the same kernel or the same region of the input volume. This is exploited to achieve high parallelism in our hardware implementation, which is described next

4.2 Hardware Design

Our CNN design is able to process a single convolutional stage at a time, with size parameters that are configurable at runtime. The input image volume and kernels are initially stored in off-chip memory and are streamed into on-chip buffers, and the output volume is written back into off-chip memory as well. Voxels are represented using 16-bit fixed-point integers.

We accelerate the convolution by performing many of its constituent dot product operations in parallel. This is implemented with an array of $N \times M$ *dot product units* (DPUs), as shown in Figure 8. Each DPU consumes 16 input voxels and 16 matching kernel voxels per clock cycle, using hardened FPGA DSP blocks to do voxel-wise multiplication and accumulation. The image and kernel data are supplied by N on-chip image and M kernel buffers, each providing 256 bits of data per cycle. They are labeled I_0 through I_{N-1} and K_0 through K_{M-1} respectively, in Figure 8.

Since many DP operations share either kernel or image data, the buffer outputs can be broadcast to many DPUs simultaneously, efficiently utilizing on-chip read bandwidth. Each kernel buffer is broadcast to a row of DPUs, and each image buffer can broadcast to one of the N columns (targeting a different column every clock cycle).

The blocks marked $ITER$ in Figure 8 sequentially generate addresses to read the image buffers, and each $ITER$ unit reads a different image buffer every clock cycle. The kernel buffers also have address-generating logic, but it is built-in, feeding only its associated buffer with a straightforward access pattern, and is thus omitted from the figure for simplicity.

Once all image and kernel buffers have been filled, control logic issues a $LAUNCH$ signal that begins address generation by the $ITER$ units and the kernel buffers' built-in equivalents. The addresses are used to read the respective kernel and image buffers, feeding DPUs with data, which eventually produce a result.

This process is repeated many times, as neither the entire image (nor all the kernels) will necessarily fit into the available on-chip buffers. The synchronization of the delivery of kernel and image data streams to DPUs is the problem which we aim to help solve using the synchronization constraints described in this paper.

5. IMPLEMENTATION AND RESULTS

In this section, we seek to measure the difference in quality of results (area, clock frequency) when building the CNN accelerator system using an interconnect synthesis flow augmented with synchronization constraints. To this end, we build three different versions of the system using GENIE:

1. A basic, unpipelined implementation with no significant synchronization requirements and low performance.

2. A pipelined implementation, which introduces synchronization requirements that are addressed by the manual addition of FIFOs to the functional modules.

3. The same pipelined implementation as Version 2, but with the synchronization requirements solved using the flow described in Section 3.

The first naïve unpipelined version is easy enough to make functionally correct with minimal manual effort, but suffers from low performance as a result.

The second version improves on this by inserting pipeline registers to increase clock frequency, at the cost of complicating the problem of achieving functional correctness, which is solved with the insertion of FIFOs and adds a small amount of extra effort for the designer. This implementation represents a realistic higher-performance solution that a designer may choose, if they do not have access to the synchronization constraint flow presented in this paper.

The third version keeps the performance-increasing pipeline registers from the second version, but uses the synchronization constraint flow to allow GENIE to automatically insert balancing registers, rather than relying on manually-inserted FIFOs. We will demonstrate that this version maintains high performance and uses significantly less area than the FIFO-based design.

5.1 Methodology

All three versions are generated with GENIE. In each, we also vary the number of DPUs in the accelerator by changing the number of columns (N) of the DPU array. This increases the size of the accelerator, adding computational power, while also increasing the distances that signals need to travel.

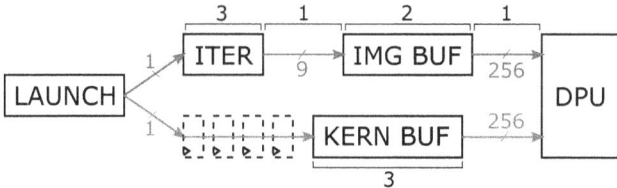

Figure 9: The paths taken by image data (top), and kernel data (bottom) to reach the inputs of a single DPU. Also shown are bit widths of each logical link, and the fixed latencies of design modules and interconnect. Four extra registers are required on the kernel path to achieve balance.

The design was synthesized with Altera Quartus Prime Pro 16.0 and targets an Arria 10 `10AX115S2F45I2SGES` device. We measure clock frequency, register usage, and the number of Adaptive Logic Modules (ALMs). ALMs represent post-packing logic, register, and distributed RAM usage, and thus the overall consumed area (not including DSP blocks).

5.2 Version 1: Unpipelined Implementation

The first version achieves correct operation without optimization of the clock frequency. It represents a realistic first design iteration. The key simplification made in this initial version is that kernel and image data are broadcast combinationally to all DPUs simultaneously, rather than distributed in a systolic pipelined fashion.

For correct operation, kernel and image data must arrive simultaneously at each DPU. In this version, this synchronization is achieved by manual insertion of registers to balance arrival times. The location, and number, of such registers are determined by inspection of the signal paths and existing fixed latencies.

Figure 9 shows the paths taken by the image and kernel data through the computation array toward a single DPU, as well as the fixed latencies of the intervening blocks and generated interconnect. From inspection, it is trivial to balance the two paths by manually inserting four registers between the *LAUNCH* signal generator and a kernel buffer.

Canonically, this register insertion is performed for all kernel buffers individually. Fortunately, since this version of the array broadcasts *LAUNCH* to all kernel buffers simultaneously, a single instance of the four registers can be used, and the output broadcast to *all* of the kernel buffers. In the two other versions of the array, synchronization will be more complicated once this broadcast is removed.

Table 1: Area and Frequency for Unpipelined Array

N	DSP	ALM	REG	F_{max} (MHz)
4	512	14421	40335	333
6	768	21290	56603	265
8	1024	28977	72819	230
11	1408	48349	97250	169

Table 1 shows the speed and area results for various parameterizations of the Version 1 CNN hardware: changing N increases the number of DPUs, and by extension, DSP block usage, ranging from a third of the 1520 available DSPs at $N = 4$, to 93% of the DSPs at $N = 11$. Since the circuit broadcasts data combinationally to all DPUs, it is no

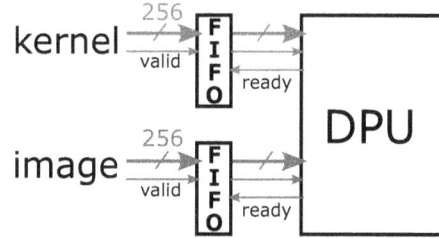

Figure 10: FIFOs are inserted at each DPU to synchronize kernel and image data arrival times. A DPU asserts the *ready* signals to simultaneously dequeue both FIFOs.

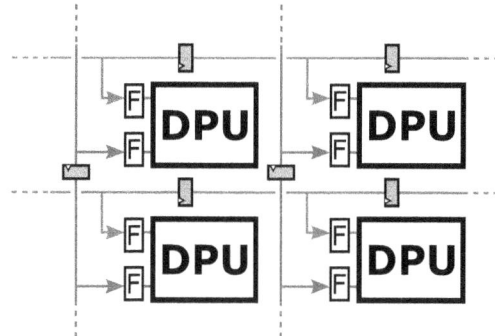

Figure 11: A section of the modified Version 2 DPU array, showing the locations of manually-added pipeline registers as well as the pairs of FIFOs added in front of each DPU.

surprise that the observed clock frequency drops (from 333 to 169 MHz) as the number of DPUs increases – the signals must travel longer distances to reach their destinations. Examination of the most-critical paths from timing analysis confirms this intuition.

5.3 Version 2: FIFO-based Implementation

To achieve higher clock frequencies, we can break up the broadcast of the image and kernel data with pipeline registers. However, this affects the kernel and image data arrival times at each DPU and complicates their synchronization. One solution is to place FIFOs in front of every DPU, as shown in Figure 10.

This requires a manual change to the DPU module, but can be performed once and then replicated aross the entire array. As long as the FIFOs are deep enough to cover the worst case arrival disparity, the designer can independently vary the amount of delivery pipeline stages without concern about functional correctness. Figure 11 illustrates a portion of the array after the insertion of FIFOs and pipeline registers.

Table 2 gives the area and frequency measurements for the Version 2 FIFO-based implementation. The Δ column compares the results with the Version 1 unpipelined system described previously. The clock frequency improves by up to 40% but the average ALM and register usage is increased by 167% and 84% respectively. ALM usage is affected by the FIFOs, as they are configured to use distributed RAM rather than more expensive block RAM.

While using FIFOs to maintain synchronization is simple for the designer to implement, it is not an elegant solution for

101

Table 2: Area and Frequency of Pipelined+FIFO Implementation

N	DSP	ALM	Δ	REG	Δ	F$_{max}$ (MHz)	Δ
4	512	39329	2.73x	40335	1.74x	378	1.13x
6	768	59160	2.78x	103645	1.83x	343	1.30x
8	1024	79976	2.76x	136955	1.88x	321	1.40x
11	1408	117982	2.44x	187181	1.92x	236	1.40x

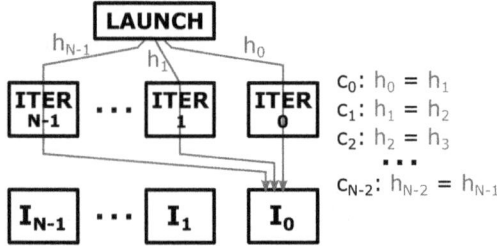

Figure 12: $N-1$ synchronization constraints, c_0 through c_{N-2}, that force all the possible N chains feeding image buffer I_0's address input to have equal latency, avoiding collision of read addresses as they arrive at the buffer.

a system which originally had no backpressure and completely deterministic data arrival times. Ideally, we would like to insert the correct amount of registers in the correct locations automatically, using registers to balance delays instead of FIFOs. This is done in Version 3 below, using synchronization constraints.

5.4 Version 3: Synchronization Constraint Implementation

In this version, we begin with the kernel and image buffer broadcasts manually pipelined in the same systolic fashion as in Figure 11, but *without* the FIFOs for synchronization. Instead, to achieve correct data delivery in the presence of the pipeline registers, we define several sets of synchronization constraints, which GENIE will use to automatically insert the necessary registers to balance delays.

The $ITER$ units have been carefully designed such that, as long as they receive the $LAUNCH$ signal simultaneously, all N of them will *never* send a transmission to the same destination image buffer during the same clock cycle. This temporal mutual-exclusivity of transmissions is critical to avoiding the need for backpressure within the design, and must be preserved all the way from the output of the $ITER$ units to the inputs of the image buffers. Therefore, the first set of constraints ensure exactly this scenario, by demanding that all possible $LAUNCH$ to image buffer chains are of the same length. Figure 12 illustrates these constraints for the first image buffer, I_0. Similar sets of constraints are needed for the remaining image buffers, I_1 through I_{N-1}.

The next set of constraints is intended to fulfill the role previously performed by the FIFOs: to ensure that kernel and image data arrive synchronized at each DPU. This requires the chain supplying the kernel data to a DPU to have the same latency as all chains (from all image buffers) supplying the image data.

Figure 13 illustrates these constraints. Note that we choose a single arbitrary $ITER$ unit for the N image data chains,

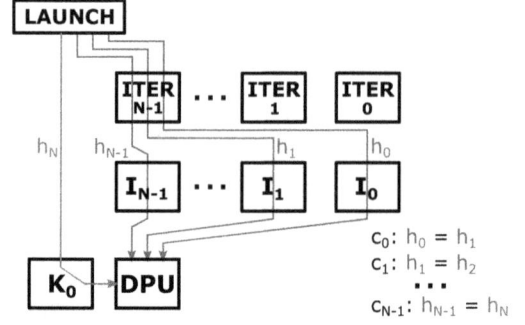

Figure 13: N synchronization constraints, c_0 through c_{N-1}, that force kernel and image data to arrive simultaneously at a DPU.

rather than the quadratic-in-N-sized exhaustive set that traverses through all possible $ITER$s. We are allowed to perform this simplification due to the first set of constraints of Figure 12, which forced all $ITER$-to-image-buffer chains to be equal.

Figure 14 shows the hardware that results from applying this total set of synchronization constraints. As before, four registers have been added to delay the $LAUNCH$ signal before it reaches the first kernel buffer. These four registers were inserted manually in the original unpipelined implementation, but now they are inferred automatically from the constraints.

In addition to these registers, more have been automatically added to balance data arrival. Proceeding down the column of kernel buffers, each buffer receives its 1-bit $LAUNCH$ signal one cycle after the previous – the optimizer naturally favoured delaying the signal here, at the input of the kernel buffers, rather than at the more expensive 256-bit outputs.

Our constraints forbid the optimizer from employing a similar elegant solution for delaying the 1-bit $LAUNCH$ signal to the $ITER$s for image data. This is because each $ITER$ ultimately feeds all DPU columns, and thus can't be individually delayed at the source. The best legal solution was instead to add an increasing number of expensive 256-bit registers at the top of every DPU column to delay the image data.

Table 3: Area and Frequency for Synchronization Constraint-based Array

N	DSP	ALM	REG	F$_{max}$ (MHz)
4	512	21835	68673	376
6	768	32867	101206	343
8	1024	45024	133617	330
11	1408	69218	182658	248

The clock frequency and area usage of the Version 3 hardware are given in Table 3. As with the other two versions, area usage increases and clock frequency decreases with increasing array size.

Figure 15 compares these results to that of the other two versions. Clock frequency remains within 5% of Version 2, which is expected since it uses the same arrangement of pipeline registers. However, this same level of performance is achieved using 43-45% fewer ALMs than Version 2 (Figure 15b). Given that the total number of registers remains

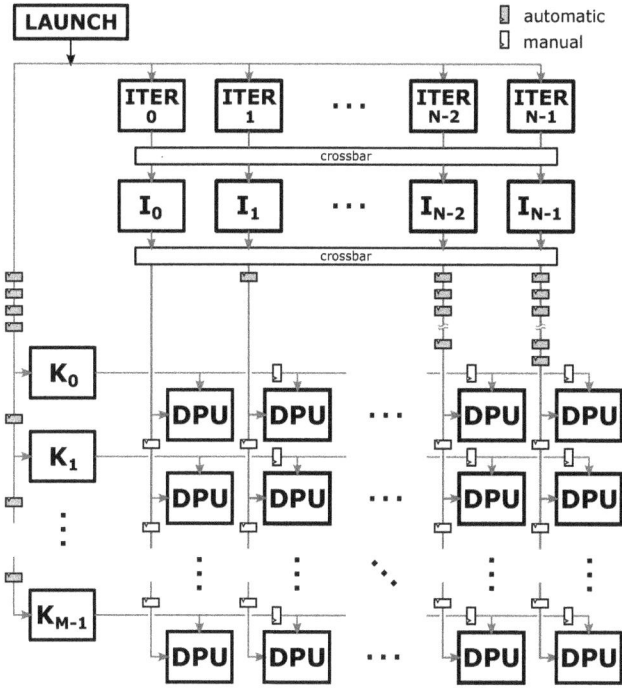

Figure 14: Version 3 DPU array resulting from the application of the synchronization constraints. Automatically-inserted balancing registers are distinguished from the manually-inserted broadcast distribution registers.

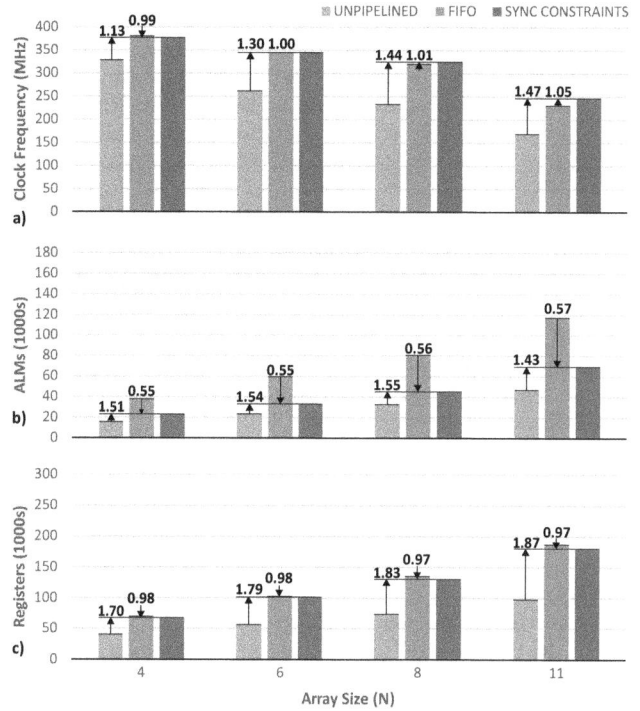

Figure 15: Absolute and relative a) clock frequency, b) ALM usage, and c) register usage of the three array implementations, with varying array size from $N = 4$ to $N = 11$. The relative values compare the synchronization constraint implementation versus the unpipelined and FIFO implementations.

roughly the same (Figure 15c), this observed difference in ALM usage can be attributed to Version 2's per-DPU FIFOs.

Compared to Version 1, Version 3 uses 43% more area (ALMs) to achieve a 47% increase in clock frequency at the largest array size of $N = 11$. Using synchronization constraints, this result was achieved automatically by GENIE and provided an easy way to achieve a correct pipelined implementation of the neural network array without the need to modify any of the functional blocks of the system.

6. CONCLUSION

We have created a means for an interconnect synthesis tool to satisfy data synchronization requirements by automatically inserting the correct number of balancing registers into area-optimal locations within the interconnect. The requirements are represented as inquality-based constraints provided by the designer. For portions of a system that lack backpressure, this automates and therefore simplifies the creation of globally, rather than locally, synchronized interconnect for correct circuit operation.

To illustrate the utility and potential gains of this approach, we applied it to the design of an FPGA-based convolutional neural network accelerator. Here, synchronization constraints were used to help solve a realistic design problem: maintaining correct data synchronization in spite of the insertion of performance-enhancing pipeline registers. The backpressure-free interconnect generated with our approach used less area than a more traditional FIFO-based method of synchronization, which would be a more representative implementation given existing interconnect synthesis tools

and their communication protocols. The end result is that system building tools can more efficiently build interconnect for a new class of applications that contain fixed-latency pipelined modules.

Although the general form of our constraints allow a designer to use them to explicitly add performance-enhancing pipeline registers to a design, rather than manually add them as we have done in our example, this still requires manual intervention by the designer to know *which* paths are critical. In the future, we envision synchronization constraints propagating to the place-and-route stage of synthesis, where back-end tools are already capable of inserting pipeline registers embedded into the FPGA interconnect[3]. With the presence of synchronization constraints, such late-stage physical modifications could be performed on the design while ensuring that the resulting circuit will continue to operate correctly.

7. REFERENCES

[1] O. Abdel-Hamid, A.-R. Mohamed, H. Jiang, L. Deng, G. Penn, and D. Yu. Convolutional Neural Networks for Speech Recognition. *IEEE/ACM Trans. Audio, Speech and Lang. Proc.*, 22(10):1533–1545, Oct. 2014.

[2] Altera. QSys - Altera's System Integration Tool. http://www.altera.com/products/software/quartus-ii/subscription-edition/qsys/qts-qsys.html.

[3] Altera. Stratix 10 FPGA and SOC. https://www.altera.com/products/fpga/stratix-series/stratix-10/overview.html, 2016.

[4] ARM Ltd. AMBA Open Specifications. http://www.arm.com/products/system-ip/amba/amba-open-specifications.php.

[5] E. Boros, P. L. Hammer, and R. Shamir. A Polynomial Algorithm for Balancing Acyclic Data Flow Graphs. *IEEE Trans. Comput.*, 41(11):1380–1385, Nov. 1992.

[6] A. Canis, S. D. Brown, and J. H. Anderson. Modulo SDC scheduling with recurrence minimization in high-level synthesis. In *Field Programmable Logic and Applications (FPL), 2014 24th International Conference on*, pages 1–8, Sept 2014.

[7] P. R. Chang and C. S. G. Lee. A Decomposition Approach for Balancing Large-Scale Acyclic Data Flow Graphs. *IEEE Trans. Comput.*, 39(1):34–46, Jan. 1990.

[8] J. Cong and B. Xiao. *Artificial Neural Networks and Machine Learning – ICANN 2014: 24th International Conference on Artificial Neural Networks, Hamburg, Germany, September 15-19, 2014. Proceedings*, chapter Minimizing Computation in Convolutional Neural Networks, pages 281–290. Springer International Publishing, Cham, 2014.

[9] J. Cong and Z. Zhang. An Efficient and Versatile Scheduling Algorithm Based on SDC Formulation. In *Proceedings of the 43rd Annual Design Automation Conference*, DAC '06, pages 433–438, New York, NY, USA, 2006. ACM.

[10] C. Hilton and B. Nelson. PNoC: a flexible circuit-switched NoC for FPGA-based systems. *IEE Proceedings - Computers and Digital Techniques*, 153(3):181–188, May 2006.

[11] X. Hu, S. C. Bass, and R. G. Harber. Minimizing the Number of Delay Buffers in the Synchronization of Pipelined Systems. *Trans. Comp.-Aided Des. Integ. Cir. Sys.*, 13(12):1441–1449, Nov. 2006.

[12] Y. Huan and A. DeHon. FPGA Optimized Packet-Switched NoC using Split and Merge Primitives. In *Field-Programmable Technology (FPT), 2012 International Conference on*, pages 47–52, Dec 2012.

[13] N. Kapre and J. Gray. Hoplite: Building austere overlay NoCs for FPGAs. In *Field Programmable Logic and Applications (FPL), 2015 25th International Conference on*, pages 1–8, Sept 2015.

[14] A. Krizhevsky, I. Sutskever, and G. E. Hinton. Imagenet classification with deep convolutional neural networks. In *Advances in Neural Information Processing Systems*, page 2012.

[15] H. T. Kung. Why systolic architectures? *IEEE Computer Magazine*, 15(1):37–46, Jan 1982.

[16] Lattice Semiconductor. LatticeMico System Development Tools. http://www.latticesemi.com/en/Products/DesignSoftwareAndIP/EmbeddedDesignSoftware/LatticeMicoSystem.aspx.

[17] Y. Lecun, Y. Bengio, and G. Hinton. Deep learning. *Nature*, 521(7553):436–444, 5 2015.

[18] M. K. Papamichael and J. C. Hoe. CONNECT: Re-examining Conventional Wisdom for Designing Nocs in the Context of FPGAs. In *Proceedings of the ACM/SIGDA International Symposium on Field Programmable Gate Arrays*, FPGA '12, pages 37–46, New York, NY, USA, 2012. ACM.

[19] A. Rodionov, D. Biancolin, and J. Rose. Fine-Grained Interconnect Synthesis. In *Proceedings of the 2015 ACM/SIGDA International Symposium on Field-Programmable Gate Arrays*, FPGA '15, pages 46–55, New York, NY, USA, 2015. ACM.

[20] A. Rodionov and J. Rose. Automatic FPGA system and interconnect construction with multicast and customizable topology. In *Field Programmable Technology (FPT), 2015 International Conference on*, pages 72–79, Dec 2015.

[21] Xilinx Corporation. Accelerating Integration. http://www.xilinx.com/products/design-tools/vivado/integration/.

[22] M. Zastrow. Machine outsmarts man in battle of the decade. *New Scientist*, 229(3065):21 –, 2016.

[23] C. Zhang, P. Li, G. Sun, Y. Guan, B. Xiao, and J. Cong. Optimizing FPGA-based Accelerator Design for Deep Convolutional Neural Networks. In *Proceedings of the 2015 ACM/SIGDA International Symposium on Field-Programmable Gate Arrays*, FPGA '15, pages 161–170, New York, NY, USA, 2015. ACM.

Corolla: GPU-Accelerated FPGA Routing Based on Subgraph Dynamic Expansion

Minghua Shen* and Guojie Luo*⁑

Center for Energy-efficient Computing and Applications, School of EECS, Peking University, China*
Collaborative Innovation Center of High Performance Computing, NUDT, China⁑
{msung, gluo}@pku.edu.cn

ABSTRACT

FPGAs are increasingly popular as application-specific accelerators because they lead to a good balance between flexibility and energy efficiency, compared to CPUs and ASICs. However, the long routing time imposes a barrier on FPGA computing, which significantly hinders the design productivity. Existing attempts of parallelizing the FPGA routing either do not fully exploit the parallelism or suffer from an excessive quality loss. Massive parallelism using GPUs has the potential to solve this issue but faces non-trivial challenges.

To cope with these challenges, this work presents Corolla, a GPU-accelerated FPGA routing method. Corolla enables applying the GPU-friendly shortest path algorithm in FPGA routing, leveraging the idea of problem size reduction by limiting the search in routing subgraphs. We maintain the convergence after problem size reduction using the dynamic expansion of the routing resource subgraphs. In addition, Corolla explores the fine-grained single-net parallelism and proposes a hybrid approach to combine the static and dynamic parallelism on GPU. To explore the coarse-grained multi-net parallelism, Corolla proposes an effective method to parallelize mutli-net routing while preserving the equivalent routing results as the original single-net routing. Experimental results show that Corolla achieves an average of 18.72× speedup on GPU with a tolerable loss in the routing quality and sustains a scalable speedup on large-scale routing graphs. To our knowledge, this is the first work to demonstrate the effectiveness of GPU-accelerated FPGA routing.

1. INTRODUCTION

With the slowdown of Moore's Law, the computing landscape is becoming increasingly parallel and heterogeneous, consisting of a larger number of cores and customized accelerators. FPGAs shows particularly promising as an acceleration technology with its reconfigurability and customizability, owing to that they can provide performance and en-

ergy improvements in a broad range of applications [1, 2, 3]. For example, Microsoft's large-scale FPGA-based cluster has been used thus far to accelerate Bing web search engine and deep neural network processing [4, 5]. Compared with other competitive accelerators like GPUs, FPGAs usually offer much better energy efficiency and can still deliver high performance for datacenter computing infrastructures. However, the increasingly lengthy compilation time associated with FPGA computer-aided design (CAD) algorithms has been a severe limitation to broader adoption of this technology [6].

Routing is one of the most complex and time-consuming steps in the FPGA CAD flow [6]. Since routing quality directly affects the maximum clock frequency and other design metrics such as routability and power, it also becomes a critical step in the design cycle. The PathFinder routing algorithm [8] is in dominant use in the FPGA community due to its superior performance and quality of results. This algorithm enables the nets to negotiate with each other to find a feasible routing. However, this process is often lengthy in runtime, and a promising direction to overcome the runtime challenge is through parallelization [9]. Several recent works on parallelizing the FPGA routing have been reported [10, 11, 12, 13, 14, 15]. However, there is a lack of literature on the GPU acceleration of FPGA routing. In this paper, we explore how to use GPU efficiently for a fast FPGA routing algorithm.

The Graphics Processing Unit (GPU) provides a massively parallel computing platform to cope with the tedious and time-consuming problems [16]. GPU acceleration techniques show excellent performance in applications with the data parallel paradigm. Several algorithms in the area of FPGA CAD have been successful accelerated using GPUs [17, 18, 19, 22]. However, the PathFinder algorithm for FPGA routing is sequential in nature. Dependencies exist in the routing process of different nets, as well as the routing of a single net. Such dependencies violate the requirement of independence in the data parallel paradigm. Accordingly, the existing routing algorithms must be thoroughly revised to take full advantage of GPU acceleration techniques.

The kernel of FPGA routing is, in fact, a single source shortest path (SSSP) solver. Several GPU-based approaches have been proposed to accelerate the SSSP solver [20, 21], but the available speedup is insignificant due to the synchronization cost and the irregularity of memory accesses [22]. Also, the GPU-accelerated path-finding solvers for video games [23] and the global routing problem for ASICs [24] assume the routing structures as rectilinear grids. There-

FPGA '17, February 22-24, 2017, Monterey, CA, USA
© 2017 ACM. ISBN 978-1-4503-4354-1/17/02...$15.00
DOI: http://dx.doi.org/10.1145/3020078.3021732

fore, these parallelization techniques cannot be directly applied to FPGA routing, whose complex routing resources form a general graph. Among the GPU-based SSSP solvers for general graphs, the Bellman-Ford algorithm provides the greatest speedup so far [25, 26], although its worst-case time complexity is inferior to the Dijkstra's algorithm. Moreover, the serial Bellman-Ford algorithm excels when running on a small graph [27].

In this paper, we leverage multiple techniques to enable the usage of the GPU-friendly Bellman-Ford algorithm to increase the speedup and restrict its weakness. Specifically, we observe that the bounding box of the final routing tree of most nets is only slightly larger than the bounding box of the pins. Thus, we can use the Bellman-Ford algorithm in a subgraph defined by a limited-size bounding box to replace the Dijkstra or A* algorithm in FPGA routing. We make use of such observation and idea in our GPU-accelerated routing method, named Corolla. Corolla applies the dynamic expansion strategy of the routing resource subgraph to control the problem size so that it can adopt the GPU-based Bellman-Ford algorithm to achieve a high speedup to route a single net. Moreover, we explore the fine-grained node and edge parallelism in the routing of a single net, and we discuss the possibility to leverage coarse-grained net parallelism to route multiple nets concurrently.

In summary, Corolla presents a novel GPU acceleration technique for FPGA routing. The main contributions of this work are described as follows:

- The GPU-friendly Bellman-Ford algorithm becomes practical for FPGA routing, attributed to our problem size reduction technique by exploiting the coverage estimation and dynamic expansion on routing resource subgraphs.

- We further improve the speedup by considering the single-net and multi-net parallelism. On the single-net parallelization, we propose a hybrid approach that combines the advantages of both the static and dynamic parallelism in the SSSP solver for FPGA routing. On the multi-net parallelization, we present a deterministic net-parallel technique that guarantees equivalent routing results as the original ordered net-by-net routing.

- The proposed method provides an average of 18.72× speedup on GPU. We also analyze it scalability using large-scale routing graphs. To our knowledge, this is the first work on utilizing GPU to efficiently accelerate FPGA routing.

Relying on GPU acceleration, Corolla achieves significantly greater speedups than the publicly available VPR [38] router and the state-of-the-art VPR-based parallel routers. We believe it will have many useful applications and implications for fast physical designs due to the fundamental importance of routing.

2. BACKGROUND

In this section, we review the routing problem and then discuss the negotiation-based PathFinder algorithm.

2.1 FPGA Routing Problem

The routing resources of an FPGA can be modeled as a directed graph $G(V, E)$, the *routing resource graph*, where

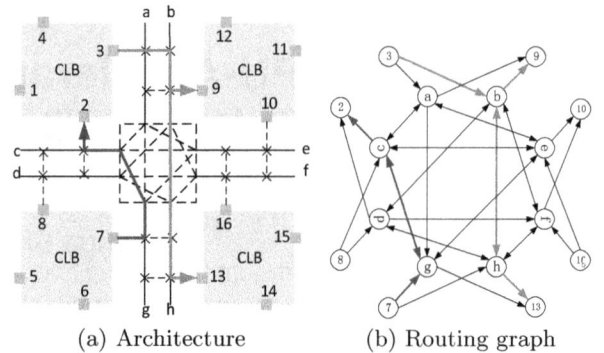

(a) Architecture (b) Routing graph

Figure 1: FPGA routing resource graph.

each vertex v_i represents an electrical pin or a wire segment, and each edge e_{ij} corresponds to a programmable connection between an electrical pin and a wire segment, or a programmable routing switch between two wire segments. Fig. 1(a) shows an example of a partial routing architecture, and the corresponded routing resource graph is shown in Fig. 1(b) with a channel width of two.

The routing problem is to find disjoint paths in $G(V, E)$ to connect the pins of the source and the sinks for each net, as shown in Fig. 1(b). A net N_i has one source node s_i and a few sinks t_{ij} that are logically connected to the source. Both the source and sinks are vertices in V, and thus, the net N_i is a subset of V. The routing of net N_i is to find a subtree in graph G that includes all vertices in N_i, and this subtree is called the routing tree RT_i of net N_i. The source s_i is the root node of RT_i, and the sinks t_{ij} are the terminal nodes. The routing trees for different nets are disjoint in G, to prevent short circuits.

In this paper, we focus on accelerating the engine of the negotiation-based router. The same data structures and algorithms can be applied to a router with various objectives, such as timing.

2.2 PathFinder Algorithm

A summary is described below on the negotiation-based PathFinder algorithm [8]. PathFinder routes one net at a time in each iteration, where congestions are temporally allowed in the intermediate routing solutions. The nets must negotiate with each other to decide who will make a detour around the congested resource nodes in subsequent iterations, until all the congestions are resolved to obtain a complete legal routing solution.

Each iteration rips up an existing routing tree and reroutes it by invoking the maze expansion [7], which computes a path from the source to each sink in the routing resource graph. It is also the most computationally expensive task in FPGA routing. All of the unvisited vertices are first stored in a priority queue based on their cost, and the vertex v_{min} with the minimum cost is extracted during maze expansion. If v_{min} is a sink, a routing path will be constructed by invoking a backtrace procedure. Otherwise, each neighbor v of v_{min}, which has not been previously visited, is inserted into the priority queue and the maze expansion continues until a legal routing tree is found.

Prior work has shown that the maze expansion accounts for about 68% of total runtime [12, 13]. Our effort is to completely revamp and accelerate it using GPU acceleration techniques.

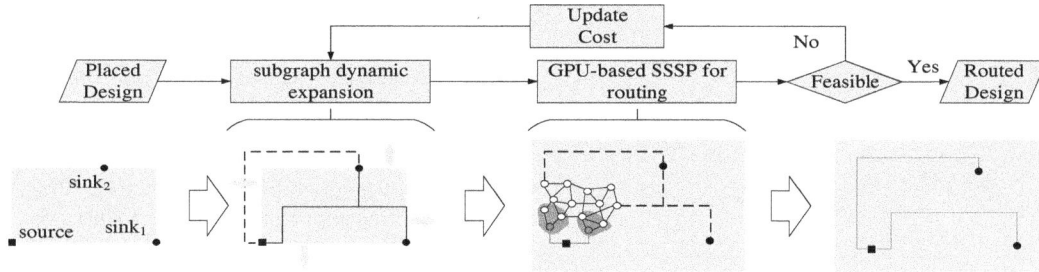

Figure 2: The algorithmic flow of Corolla.

3. OVERVIEW

In this section, we give an overview of Corolla, our GPU-accelerated routing method for FPGAs.

3.1 Motivation

FPGA routing, a tedious and time-consuming process, is sequential in nature. In the coarse grain, the "present costs" in the PathFinder routing algorithm are sequentially updated net after net within an iteration. While in the fine grain, the priority queue in the maze expansion routing of a single net limits the practical concurrency. Such data sharing in the coarse grain and the fine grain violates the requirement of data independence of the GPU-friendly data-parallel paradigm. Thus, the existing routing algorithms are not designed for GPU acceleration and must be revisited.

In this paper, we explore the capability of GPU acceleration for FPGA routing. The computational kernel in FPGA routing is the single-source shortest path (SSSP) solver. Firstly, we present the subgraph dynamic expansion method to enable the use of a GPU-friendly SSSP algorithm for FPGA routing in Section 4. Secondly, we explore different GPU-based parallelizations and propose an efficient hybrid solution, followed by multi-net parallelization in Section 5.

3.2 Algorithmic Flow

The algorithmic flow of Corolla is shown in Fig. 2. In the overall flow, we preserve the negotiation-based framework that iteratively reduces the routing congestion by ripping up and rerouting the nets. In subgraph dynamic expansion, the routing subgraph of each net is extracted according to the *initial coverage* strategy at the first iteration, and its size may be expanded according to the *dynamic expansion* strategy. In the GPU-based SSSP for routing, we propose multiple techniques to improve parallelism and speedup. We explore the node and edge parallelism and a hybrid approach to accelerate the single-net routing on GPU. We also leverage the net parallelism to accelerate the multi-net routing. The kernel of Corolla is the GPU-friendly SSSP algorithm to route every net inside its routing subgraph.

Corolla guarantees deterministic results, although it produces different results from the original PathFinder algorithm. Assume there is a sequential version of Corolla that applies the same subgraph dynamic expansion strategy, it is obvious that the single-net parallelization is sequential equivalent, and we will propose a multi-net parallelization that is also sequential equivalent.

4. SUBGRAPH DYNAMIC EXPANSION

The computational kernel in FPGA routing is a solver

for the single-source shortest path (SSSP) problem, usually using Dijkstra's algorithm or A* search[1]. The fundamental data structure in both algorithms is a priority queue, which causes contentions and bottlenecks in a GPU implementation. Therefore, most existing literature and publicly-available solvers for the GPU-accelerated SSSP algorithm are based on the Bellman-Ford algorithm for a greater parallelism and speedup, although the worst-case sequential time complexity of the Bellman-Ford algorithm is higher than the Dijkstra's algorithm.

To take full advantage of the existing GPU-based SSSP solvers for FPGA routing, our basic idea is to alleviate its time complexity by reducing the problem size. In general, there are at least two approaches to doing so:

1) One is to perform global routing in a coarsened routing graph.

2) The other is to restrict the search space for the SSSP algorithm.

The global routing approach is useful for ASIC routing, but it is less effective for FPGA routing [28]. It may be possible to obtain a pseudo-rectilinear structure from the FPGA routing graph by clustering the routing segment nodes inside the same channel. Taking Fig. 1 as an example, one may cluster the nodes a and b, c and d, e and f, g and h, respectively, so that the clustered nodes form a rectilinear structure for global routing. However, this conversion is not accurate to model the congestion, because it cannot distinguish the congestion cost of the segment nodes in the same channel. According to our analysis of the final routing results of the PathFinder algorithm across multiple benchmarks, we observe that the routing cost of some segment nodes in the same channel differ significantly. The maximum difference (e.g., 24) of the routing cost for the nodes in the same channel usually greater than the mean (e.g., 9) plus one standard deviation (e.g., 10) among the nodes with non-zero costs. Therefore, the global routing approach is not the best choice to reduce the problem size, and we resort to the other approach by restricting the search space.

To ensure the correctness and convergence of the FPGA routing algorithm, we propose the method of *subgraph dynamic expansion* to limit the search space. It contains three essential steps to mitigate the disadvantages of the Bellman-Ford algorithm.

- **Step 1:** subgraph extraction, which is implemented

---

[1]Dijkstra's algorithm and A* search have similar data structures and algorithmic flow. Thus, we only mention Dijkstra's algorithm to compare with the GPU-friendly Bellman-Ford algorithm in the rest of this paper for conciseness.

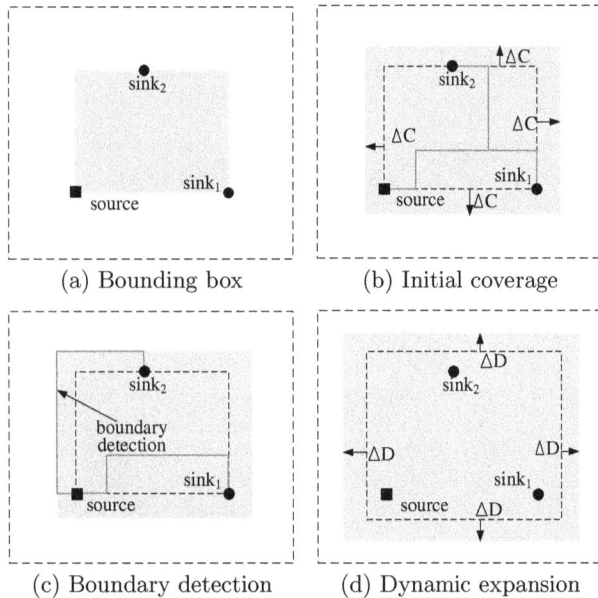

(a) Bounding box   (b) Initial coverage

(c) Boundary detection   (d) Dynamic expansion

Figure 3: The three steps of subgraph dynamic expansion in Corolla: (a) obtain the net bounding box before routing, (b) estimate the initial coverage that provides most nets a sufficiently large subgraph to route, and (c) perform boundary detection to trigger the (d) dynamic expansion to guarantee that the routing subgraph is eventually large enough.

efficiently based on a labeling system that relates the coordinates to the routing resource nodes.

- **Step 2:** initial coverage, which is preprocessed by analyzing the routing results of existing circuits. Our estimation of the initial routing subgraphs provides sufficient routing nodes (e.g., for 98.5% nets in existing circuits), so that each net only needs to explore its routing tree in a small subgraph instead of the overall routing graph.

- **Step 3:** dynamic expansion, which is complementary to initial coverage using a detection strategy to adaptively expand the routing subgraph in a next iteration until a feasible solution is found.

Notice that the key idea of subgraph dynamic expansion is to estimate and find a large-enough routing subgraph for every net to obtain its feasible route. In the initial coverage, we first determine the initial routing subgraphs to cover a significant portion of nets, and then we perform dynamic expansion in case that a few nets need a larger subgraph to find their legal routing trees. This method effectively bounds the number of nodes during the routing exploration, and thus alleviates the complexity overhead of the Bellman-Ford algorithm compared to the Dijkstra's algorithm.

The usage of subgraph dynamic expansion in Corolla is illustrated in Fig. 3. For example in Fig. 3(a), a straightforward estimation of the routing subgraph is the one within the bounding box of *source*, *sink1* and *sink2*. Using the bounding box to estimate the initial subgraph does not provide enough routing resources in many cases, and thus, Corolla determines a good-enough subgraph at the initial coverage stage, as shown in Fig. 3(b). The static estimation is un-

likely 100% accurate, and a detour path outside the initial coverage may be necessary for a legal routing solution. So we apply an adaptive strategy to expand the subgraph, whenever a detour path touching the boundary of the current routing subgraph is detected, as illustrated in Fig. 3(c). Finally, Corolla can find a routing solution inside the estimated and expanded subgraph as shown in Fig. 3(d). Evaluations show that this approach effectively reduces the problem size without affecting the quality of the routing solution.

4.1 Subgraph Extraction

As discussed earlier, due to the limitations of the global routing approach for FPGAs, we resort to the method of restricting the search space (i.e., the routing subgraph) for the GPU-based SSSP solvers. The ideal restricted search space with the minimum number of routing resource nodes should let an SSSP algorithm generate the same or similar result as in the original search space. However, this very ideal case is non-trivial to obtain. In addition, extracting an irregular subgraph requires some timing-consuming graph traversals that affect the efficiency. Thus, we relax the ideal routing resource subgraph to be a net-specific box, which contains sufficient routing resource nodes for the given net. In the following, we present the details how to extract a routing resource subgraph inside a box.

We make the following assumptions for the proposed subgraph extraction. The routing graph consists of pin nodes and segment nodes. A pin node corresponding to a pin of a logic block is assigned with the placement coordinates of this logic block. For every segment node, there exists an edge connecting to a pin node, and this segment node shares the same coordinates with its neighboring pin node. Since some segment nodes are neighbors of two or more pin nodes with different coordinates, these segment nodes have multiple coordinates.

The subgraph corresponding to a box in the FPGA routing region includes all the pin nodes and segment nodes with coordinates inside this box, as well as the routing edges between these nodes. Given any box in the FPGA routing graph, we can efficiently extract the subgraph in the box defined above. In the next two subsections, we will discuss how to determine the size of such box for any given net and guarantee the convergence of the routing algorithm.

4.2 Initial Coverage

The routing subgraph defined in the previous subsection reduces the problem size. The next question is how to find the dimension of the box for the subgraph extraction, given any net to be routed.

As discussed earlier, to ensure the correctness and convergence of the routing algorithm, the box should contain sufficient routing resources for a given net, and its size is expected to be as small as possible. A simple choice is the minimum bounding box of the pins in a given net, which is available before routing. But this simple choice rarely provides enough routing resources. Another choice is the minimum bounding box of the final routing tree, which is of course only available after the routing finishes. This choice provides sufficient routing resources but is impractical and not implementable. To get a good-enough initial subgraph before routing, we propose the *initial coverage* in Corolla to estimate the initial boxes to cover a significant portion of nets with enough routing resources. The idea of this esti-

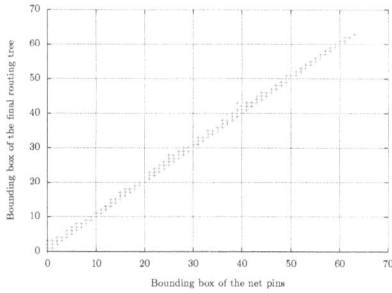

Figure 4: The bounding box of the final routing tree is only slightly larger than the bounding box of the net pins for Δ_C.

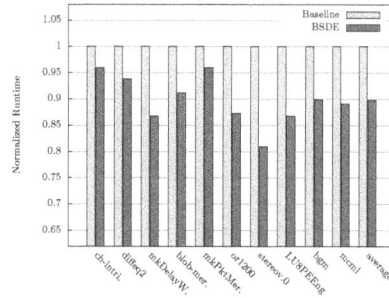

Figure 5: Comparisons of the sequential routing runtime between the baseline and BSDE.

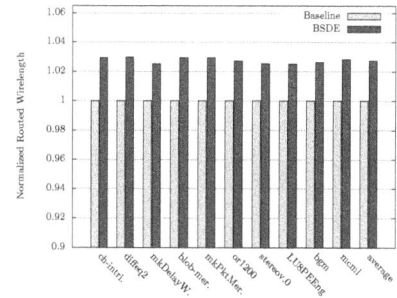

Figure 6: Comparisons of the wirelength degradation between the baseline and BSDE.

Table 1: An example of the initial expansion factor of 0.021 for a 98.5% coverage

Bench.	Δ_C	array	$\dfrac{\Delta_C}{\sqrt{\text{array}}}$	coverage
diffeq2	1	34 × 34	0.029	100%
mkDelayW.	1	48 × 48	0.021	99.8%
blob_mer.	1	51 × 51	0.020	100%
mkPKtMer.	1	58 × 58	0.017	100%
or1200	1	65 × 65	0.015	100%
LU8PEEng	1	53 × 53	0.019	99.3%
bgm	2	73 × 73	0.027	99.5%
mcml	2	101 × 101	0.020	98.7%
average	-	-	0.021	-

mation is based on the statistical data from existing routed circuits.

An important observation is that for most nets, the size of the bounding box of the net pins is only slightly greater than the bounding box of the final routing tree, as illustrated in Fig. 4. Based on this empirical relation based on existing routed circuits, Corolla statistically estimates the size of the boxes for the routing subgraphs during the initial coverage. The box of a given net in the initial coverage is expanded from the four sides of the bounding boxes of net pins by a distance of Δ_C, as illustrated in Fig. 3(b). The estimation of Δ_C relates to the FPGA size, as well as a user-defined percentage of coverage.

Here we describe an example flow to estimate Δ_C given a few circuits with known routing solutions. The distance Δ_C is the difference in the left, right, top and bottom boundary coordinates between the bounding box of the net pins and the bounding box of its final routing tree, which can be collected from these existing circuits. If the user-defined percentage of coverage is 98.5%, we find the smallest coverage that is not less than 98.5% of the nets in every given circuit. We observe that by dividing this value of Δ_C by the FPGA array size, we obtain a similar ratio, 0.021 on average, among many circuits. We call this ratio the *initial expansion factor*. Examples of this initial expansion factor are shown in Table 1.

Therefore, given a new circuit, we can multiply the FPGA array size by the initial expansion factor and round it up to the next integer to obtain Δ_C for the initial coverage. By applying this rule, we can estimate how much we should expand the bounding box to be the initial coverage when constructing of the initial routing resource subgraphs.

4.3 Dynamic Expansion

Though the initial coverage provides enough routing re-

sources for most nets, there are still some outliers. A simple fix is to expand the subgraphs continuously to ensure sufficient routing resources eventually. However, such strategy will increase the routing time due to some unnecessarily large subgraphs. In Corolla, we use the *dynamic expansion* strategy, which contains a detection method to expand a subgraph only when necessary.

The dynamic expansion is based on a boundary detection strategy, which is used to decide whether Corolla continues to expand the size for the routing subgraph of a net. A net is likely to use more routing resources when its routing tree occupies a node on the boundary of the current routing subgraph. Once detected, Corolla expands the box of its routing subgraph on the four sides by a distance of Δ_D[2] in the next iteration. With this boundary detection strategy in dynamic expansion, Corolla can converge using a similar number of iterations as the original PathFinder algorithm.

The subgraph dynamic expansion consists of subgraph extraction, initial coverage, and dynamic expansion. Its purpose is to reduce the problem size to remedy the worst-case time complexity of the Bellman-Ford algorithm, which is GPU-friendly and has efficient GPU-based implementations. Before discussing the GPU acceleration in the next section, here we evaluate the impact of subgraph dynamic expansion on the routing quality and the runtime, as well as the impact of replacing the Dijkstra's algorithm by the Bellman-Ford algorithm. Two approaches are evaluated and compared, including: the original PathFinder algorithm (baseline), and the modified PathFinder algorithm using the Bellman-Ford algorithm with subgraph dynamic expansion (BSDE).

Fig. 5 show the normalized runtime of these two approaches. Though the worst-case time complexity of the Bellman-Ford algorithm is greater than the Dijkstra's algorithm, the runtime of BSDE is obviously better than the baseline with a negligible impact on the routed wirelength. Fig. 6 reports the normalized routed wirelength of the two approaches, where the routed wirelength is increased by about 2.7% on average, and detailed explanation will be presented in Section 6.

Fig. 5 and Fig. 6 illustrate the effectiveness of the Bellman-Ford algorithm combined with subgraph dynamic expansion for FPGA routing. This computational kernel is GPU-friendly and is, therefore, a good candidate for the GPU-accelerated FPGA routing.

---

[2]This parameter is empirically set to one, which is sufficient to find a legal routing solution according to our experiments.

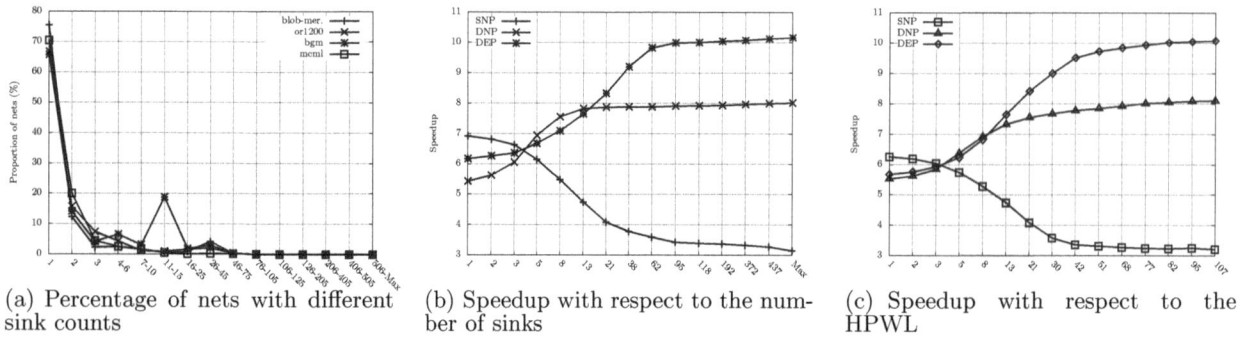

(a) Percentage of nets with different sink counts

(b) Speedup with respect to the number of sinks

(c) Speedup with respect to the HPWL

Figure 7: Hybrid approach by combining SNP, DNP, and DEP.

5. GPU-ACCELERATED ROUTING

In this section, we present the details of acceleration techniques in Corolla.

5.1 Dynamic Parallelism

Dynamic parallelism is an important and useful technique to dynamically exploit the parallelism in irregular computations such as graph algorithms. Moctar and Brisk [13] demonstrate the effectiveness of the dynamic parallelism with multi-threading by using the operator formulation [30] for FPGA routing.

The general idea of the operator formulation to implement dynamic parallelism is to apply a *compute* operator iteratively on a subset of nodes in a graph. At each iteration, the active nodes perform useful computations, and the rest inactive nodes are idle. A *check* operator determines whether a node is active or inactive. The compute operator often accesses neighboring nodes and can activate inactive nodes for further processing. Execution completes when all nodes are inactive and will not be activated again.

For example, in the Bellman-Ford algorithm, a compute operator updates the known shortest path of a node, and a check operator checks whether an upstream of a given node has an updated known shortest path. The operator formulation is a framework that automatically parallelizes a program where the compute and check operators are defined.

In Corolla, we explore the dynamic parallelism of routing resource nodes and edges to accelerate GPU-based FPGA routing.

5.2 Parallelization Exploration

Considering the specific structure of routing resource graphs, the previous experiences of parallelization strategies for general graphs cannot be directly applied to routing resource graphs. Thus, it is necessary to explore and examine the effectiveness of three different kinds of parallelism in the GPU-based Bellman-Ford algorithm for FPGA routing in Corolla:

1. Static node parallelism (SNP), where every node, no matter active or not, is assigned to a thread to process in parallel.

2. Dynamic node parallelism (DNP), where only the active nodes, i.e., the nodes whose known shortest distances to the source node have recently been changed, are assigned to threads to process in parallel.

3. Dynamic edge parallelism (DEP), which is similar to

DNP but considers assigning active edges to threads instead of active nodes.

In SNP, every thread first checks whether its responsible node is active. If active, it then applies the compute operator to update the known shortest path of the active node in each superstep. Every kernel execution on the GPU forms a superstep, and the kernel is invoked again in the next superstep when active nodes exist. All nodes, including active and inactive, are statically assigned to the threads through a block decomposition during the parallelization in every superstep.

In DNP, a centralized worklist with atomic memory operation (AMO) is used to manage the dynamic parallelism. First, an initialization step pre-checks all the nodes and populates the active nodes into the worklist for parallel processing. For example, to route a net, the worklist is initialized with the source node. Second, every thread pulls an active node from the worklist using AMO and then applies the compute operator to the corresponding active node. The newly activated nodes are pushed onto the worklist with AMOs such that only active nodes will be visited in the next iteration. This process is repeated until the worklist becomes empty. Compared with SNP, DNP exposes more parallelism and improves the efficiency by mapping threads to useful computation work. However, the DNP also present its weakness with high memory contention when accessing a shared worklist.

A better implementation can be obtained by exploring the DEP using Merrill's method [31]. Besides focusing on the edges instead of nodes, DEP use a prefix scan to allocate a chunk of memory for each thread to maintain the active nodes so that it relieves the contention of atomic accesses by avoiding AMO. These chunks of memory are assigned to the CUDA blocks, which work in parallel to check the edges in their assigned chunks, using various heuristics to trade-off time and space for a high throughput.

5.3 Hybrid Approach

Either static or dynamic parallelism has its merits and demerits. Although slower than DNP and DEP for large graphs, the static SNP method achieves greater speedup for the low-fanout nets than the dynamic DNP and DEP methods. Our explanation is that the routing subgraph of a low-fanout net only has a small number of routing nodes, so the static assignment of GPU threads to these nodes is efficiently executed on the hardware. In Corolla, we present a hybrid approach to exploit the merits of both the static and dynamic parallelisms.

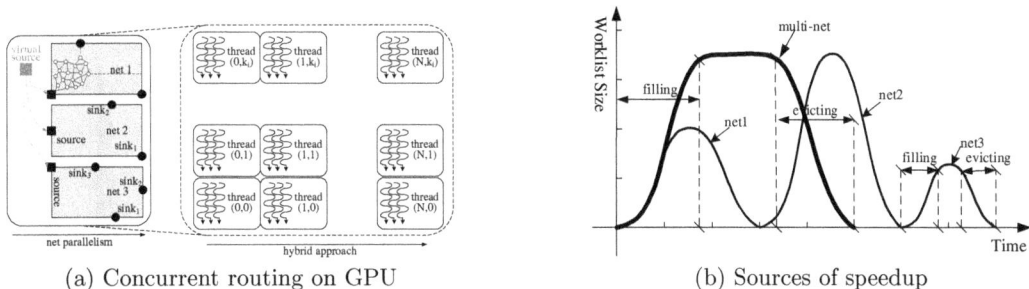

(a) Concurrent routing on GPU

(b) Sources of speedup

Figure 8: Multi-net parallelization using our hybrid approach.

To seek higher speedup for FPGA routing, we analyze how different attributes of a net affect the runtime of different methods. Fig. 7(a) shows the percentage of the nets with a different number of sinks on four representative circuits. The number of low-fanout nets is significantly higher than the high-fanout nets. Thus, there is an opportunity to improve the speedup using a net-specific parallelization strategy. Fig. 7(b) shows the speedup using the SNP, DNP, and DEP methods of the nets with a different number of sinks in the *or1200* circuit. For this specific circuit, we observe that the static SNP method is better than the dynamic methods for the nets with fewer than three sinks, and the dynamic DEP method is superior to the others for the nets with more than thirteen sinks. Moreover, we explore the speedups from the SNP, DNP and DEP methods with respect to the HPWL of the nets and observe similar results, as shown in Fig. 7(c). We also observe similar patterns for other circuits by conducting the same set of experiments.

These results reveal the opportunity to combine different methods to improve the speedup. We propose an efficient hybrid approach that uses SNP for the nets with less than or equal to three sinks and uses DEP for the remaining nets. Though there is a possible gain using the DNP method for the nets with a moderate amount of sinks, these nets only contribute to a small percentage of runtime, and we simply apply DEP instead. We will present experimental evaluations in Section 6.2, which will show that our hybrid approach is as efficient as an "optimal" combination of SNP, DNP, and DEP.

5.4 Multi-Net Parallelization

In the previous subsections, we explore the fine-grained node and edge parallelism using the SNP, DNP, DEP, and the hybrid approaches. In this subsection, we will explore the coarse-grained net parallelism to achieve a further speedup on GPU. Specifically, during the multi-net parallelization, we maintain equivalent routing results as the single-net parallelization.

According to previous works [33], the routing sequence of the nets affects the routing quality. To explore the net parallelism while maintaining deterministic results, we impose a restriction that the routing results are equivalent to the single-net routing according to the original net ordering. The parallelization is done in a greedy fashion: we collect as many as nets as possible according to their original order, and make sure that their concurrent routing will not affect their routing results compared to the single-net routing. By using the routing subgraphs of the nets, this collection

Table 2: Benchmark summary

Bench.	Arch.	Dim.	Nets	CLBs
ch-intri.	k4_N4_90nm	20x20	788	497
sha	k4_N4_90nm	29x29	1946	866
boundtop	k4_N4_90nm	19x19	2380	724
diffeq2	k4_N4_90nm	34x34	3710	1296
diffeq1	k4_N4_90nm	35x35	3953	1450
mkDelayW.	k4_N4_90nm	48x48	5224	1554
blob_mer.	k4_N4_90nm	51x51	6606	2702
mkSMAdap.	k4_N4_90nm	53x53	7154	3126
mkPKtMer.	k4_N4_90nm	58x58	7474	3767
or1200	k4_N4_90nm	65x65	8078	3648
stereov.0	k6_N10_40nm	39x39	9312	1492
stereov.1	k6_N10_40nm	39x39	13553	1401
LU8PEEng	k6_N10_40nm	53x53	16278	2373
bgm	k6_N10_40nm	73x73	27853	4225
stereov.2	k6_N10_40nm	86x86	36479	2802
mcml	k6_N10_40nm	101x101	81282	7934

process can efficiently and precisely check the dependency among the nets in each iteration.

The subgraph extraction approach mentioned in Section 4.1 provides a good indicator for this dependency detection. The collection of the subset of concurrent nets starts with the current net to be routed. Then we gradually add the next a few nets according to the original order to this subset, until the routing subgraph of a next net has overlaps with one of the nets in this subset. It is evident that this subset can be routed in parallel without affecting the routing results. Hence, our multi-net parallelization guarantees deterministic solutions.

Fig. 8(a) demonstrates the concurrent routing of multiple independent nets on GPU. To unify the single-net and multi-net routing, a virtual source node is introduced to directly connect to the actual source nodes of the independent nets. Thus, the independent nets can be combined into a single pseudo net, which can be routed on GPU leveraging the single-net acceleration techniques as discussed previously.

Fig. 8(b) explains the sources of speedup when routing multiple nets in parallel. The vertical axis reveals how the size of the worklist, which is the number of edges processed concurrently in the GPU-based SSSP algorithm, varies with respect to the execution time. The speedup comes from the reduction of the filling time of the worklist at the beginning and the evicting time near the end. So that when we route multiple nets as a single pseudo net, some overheads in these two phrases are eliminated to improve the speedup.

6. EXPERIMENTAL EVALUATIONS

In this section, we present and analyze the acceleration results of Corolla. our GPU-accelerated FPGA routing method based on subgraph dynamic expansion.

111

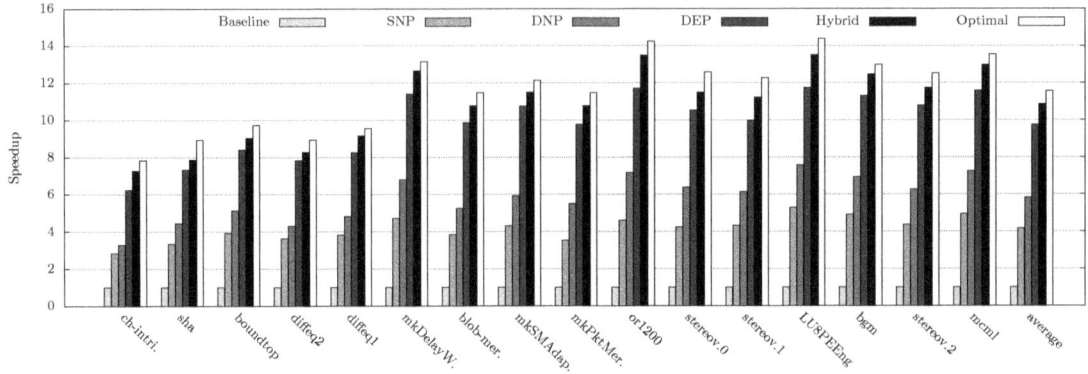

Figure 9: Single-net acceleration on GPU using SNP, DNP, DEP, and Hybrid approach.

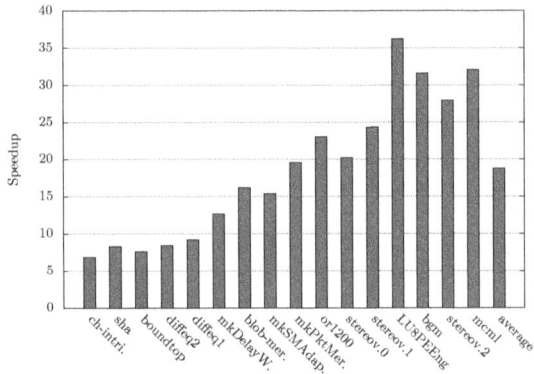

Figure 10: Multi-net acceleration on GPU using the hybrid approach.

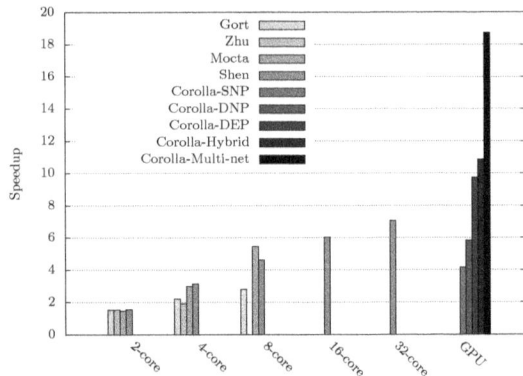

Figure 11: Speedup of SNP, DNP, DEP, Hybrid, and Multi-net routing compared to existing works.

6.1 Experimental Setup

All experiments are performed on a Linux server with a 6-core Intel Xeon E5-2620 CPU at 2.2GHz and 32 GB shared memory, equipped with a Tesla K40c GPU having 2880 cores in 15 streaming multiprocessors and 12 GB video memory. The baseline for comparison is the original VPR 7.0 router [38], which is a sequential program implemented in C. Some of the GPU implementations of the SSSP algorithm are adapted from the source code in the LonestarGPU collection [29].

All experiments are run with sixteen representative circuits from the VTR benchmarks [38] commonly used in

FPGA CAD research. Table 2 summarizes the characteristics of these benchmarks, including the array size of the routing region generated, the number of nets, and the number of configuration logic blocks (CLBs) used. We use ABC [39] for logic synthesis and technology mapping, T-VPack for packing, and VPR placer [38] for placement, respectively. Across all runs, each benchmark is routed using a channel width of $1.3\times$ the minimum channel width needed by VPR, following the same configurations as in the previous works [12, 13, 14].

6.2 Speedup Analysis

Fig. 9 shows the speedups using four different parallelization techniques in Corolla. The speedups of each benchmark are shown in a cluster of bars. The leftmost bar is the baseline, and the next four bars show the speedups of SNP, DNP, DEP, and the hybrid approach in Corolla. To illustrate the effectiveness of our hybrid approach, we include the speedups of an optimal hybrid approach in the last bar. The average speedups over all benchmarks are shown in the last cluster. On average, we achieve a speedup of $4.15\times$, $5.82\times$, $9.75\times$, and $10.86\times$ with the SNP, DNP, DEP, and Hybrid, respectively. The runtime of the optimal hybrid approach is estimated by summing up the fastest possible runtime of each net using either SNP, DNP, or DEP, assuming there is an oracle to predict the optimal selection. The $10.86\times$ speedup of our hybrid approach in Corolla is only slightly less than the speedup of the optimal hybrid approach, $11.57\times$ on average.

We can observe in Fig. 9 that the hybrid approach in Corolla achieves more speedup than the parallel methods of SNP, DNP, and DEP. The reason is that our hybrid approach invokes SNP to route a significant number of low-fanout nets, and routes the timing-consuming multi-sink nets using DEP. Moreover, the hybrid approach is compatible with the coarse-grained parallel methods [12, 14] to achieve a further speedup.

Fig. 10 presents the results of the acceleration of multi-net routing on GPU using the hybrid approach. It can be seen that this approach produces an average speedup of $18.72\times$ using a single GPU. This is a $3.43\times$ improvement over the recent fine-grained parallel router [13], and a $2.67\times$ enhancement over the recent coarse-grained parallel router [14]. We do obtain notable speedups for the four largest benchmarks on the right in the figure, owing to that more independent nets can be combined into a single pseudo net and result in more acceleration on GPU. Moreover, this approach is promising to be extended with the multi-GPU parallelization to improve the speedup greatly [31].

Finally, we list the speedups of previous coarse-grained and fine-grained parallel FPGA routers, compared to the sequential VPR router in Fig. 11. By taking advantage of GPU acceleration, Corolla achieves significant speedups. It is the first work to accelerate FPGA routing using GPU. It is also the first work to achieve near $20\times$ speedup for the FPGA routing problem.

6.3 Quality Analysis

In Fig. 12, we compare the routing quality of the multi-net parallelization in Corolla with the sequential VPR regarding the routed wirelength. The degradation mainly comes from the multi-sink nets. The original VPR router performs the Dijkstra's algorithm many times to obtain a final routing tree. And Corolla directly combines the shortest paths from the single source to the multiple sinks in a single round of the Bellman-Ford algorithm into a full routing tree.

Corolla only introduces a 2.73% degradation in wirelength on average, compared to the original VPR router. This impact is negligible for the scenarios such as the synthesis of reconfigurable FPGA accelerators in datacenters and fast design iterations in early design stages. In the former case, the delay degradation is insignificant compared to the orders of magnitude speedups introduced by FPGA acceleration. And in the latter case, the design quality is not as important as the design productivity.

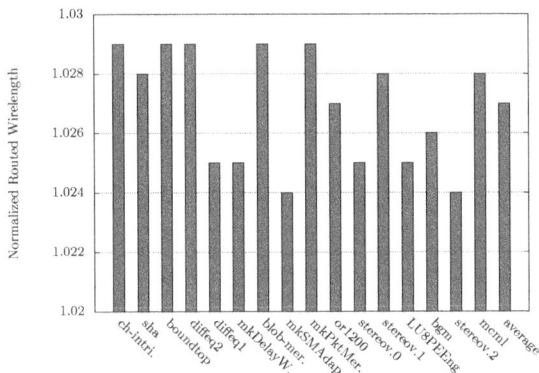

Figure 12: Impacts on the routed wirelength using the multi-net parallelization in Corolla.

6.4 Scalability Analysis

With the FPGA integration density scales, the routing resource graph will continue to grow every generation. Thus, a scalable routing algorithm becomes essential to provide similar speedup when the size of routing graph grows. Here, we evaluate the multi-net parallelization in Corolla on large scale routing graphs.

We construct synthetic designs on large-scale routing graphs based on given benchmarks. The locations of the sources and sinks of the nets in a benchmark are linearly stretched when we extend the FPGA array size from 100×100 to 1000×1000. The routing resource graph for the 1000×1000 array size is at the same scale as the largest benchmark in Titan [6].

Fig. 13 gives the speedups obtained on three representative benchmarks over the sequential VPR router. Corolla achieves the best speedup for the FPGA array size around 500×500. While the speedup decreases slowly when the

FPGA array size grows, Corolla still scales well. The scalability of Corolla is attributed to two reasons: 1) The subgraph dynamic expansion strategy effectively reduces the problem size. 2) The GPU-based SSSP is a variant of the Bellman-Ford algorithm, which makes use of the worklist that behaves similarly to a queue. Actually, in many practical cases, the Bellman-Ford algorithm converges faster than the worst-case analysis [35, 36], and there exist examples [37] that the queue-based Bellman-Ford algorithm spends less computation than the Dijkstra's algorithm. Here, Corolla provides another example that the variant of queue-based Bellman-Ford algorithm is practical for FPGA routing. We observe the same trends for other benchmarks and therefore, these results indicate that Corolla is promising to maintain a similar speedup for large-scale routing graphs.

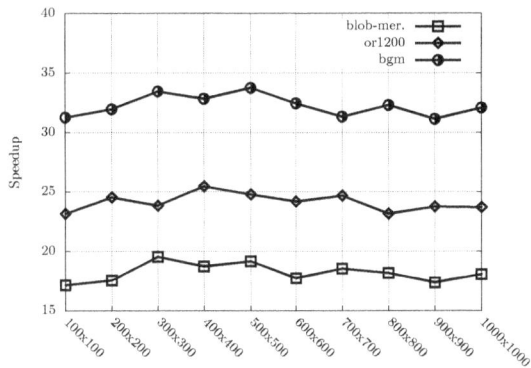

Figure 13: Scalability Analysis with different FPGA array sizes.

7. RELATED WORK

Most of the previous works on parallelizing FPGA routing are motivated by the acceleration of the overall synthesis time. The first parallel PathFinder algorithm is proposed by Chan and Schlag [10]. By modeling the routing problem into a graph or hypergraph matching problem, they analyze how and when the history and present congestion cost of the PathFinder routing algorithm should be synchronized across the processors to ensure convergence while improving parallelism [32]. Although their method is highly sensitive to the order of the nets to be routed, it is still an open problem to determine the best net ordering [33]. Quite noticeable is that a speedup of $2.5\times$ is attainable using three processors on a distributed cluster.

The fine-grained parallelization avoids the influences of net ordering in the PathFinder routing algorithm. Dehon et al. [34] propose the design of a hardware accelerator for FPGA routing. Their simulations predict a speedup of up to three orders of magnitude over PathFinder with 5%-25% loss in solution quality. Zhu et al. [11] partition the high-fanout nets into several low-fanout subnets to be routed in parallel. They achieve a speedup of $1.9\times$ on a quad-core processor platform with 2.3% loss in solution quality. And then Moctar and Brisk [13] explore the dynamic parallelism using the Galois API. They achieve a good speedup of $5.4\times$ using eight threads. Recently, Hoo et al. [15] propose a fully parallel router based on Lagrangian relaxation to decompose the original routing problem into independent subproblems. This approach produces an average speedup of $7\times$ using eight threads, compared to its sequential version.

While the coarse-grained parallelism is sensitive to the net ordering, Gort and Anderson [12] propose a deterministic parallel PathFinder routing algorithm. They partition the nets into subsets, and these subsets are routed in parallel with an efficient synchronization scheme to guarantee the deterministic results. Although they did not emphasize the scalability, it is the first deterministic parallel routing algorithm and achieves a 2.8× speedup using eight cores. Another deterministic parallel router is proposed by Shen and Luo [14], using a partitioning-based parallel routing method. They leverage a dynamic programming algorithm to determine the optimal recursive partitioning strategy. Although it degrades the quality of routed wirelength, the parallel router exploits more parallelism and scales to a 32-core cluster with an average speedup of 7×.

8. CONCLUSIONS

In this paper, we present Corolla, which leverages the GPU techniques to accelerate FPGA routing. In Corolla, we first use the approach of subgraph dynamic expansion to obtain convergent routing results with a reduced problem size. This approach enables the efficient application of the GPU-friendly Bellman-Ford algorithm to replace the Dijkstra's algorithm in PathFinder. We then perform systematic experiments and comparisons among different GPU accelerations of the Bellman-Ford algorithm, including the SNP, the DNP, and the DEP approaches. We point out that we can combine the static SNP and dynamic DEP methods for a greater speedup and exploit the multi-net parallelism, where we achieve an average of 18.72× speedup on GPU.

9. ACKNOWLEDGMENTS

The authors would like to thank the anonymous reviewers for their constructive comments. This work is partly supported by National Natural Science Foundation of China (NSFC) Grant 61520106004.

10. REFERENCES

[1] K. Atasu et al. *Accelerating text analytics queries on reconfigurable platforms*. In Workshop. CARL, 2015.

[2] P. Gupta. *Xeon+fpga platform for the data center*. In Workshop. CARL, 2015.

[3] T. Brewer. *Convey Acceleration of the Memcached and Imagemagick Applications*. In Workshop. CARL, 2015.

[4] A. Putnam et al. *A reconfigurable fabric for accelerating large-scale datacenter services*. In Proc. ISCA, 2014.

[5] K. Ovtcharov et al. *Accelerating deep convolutional neural networks using specialized hardware*. In White paper, 2015.

[6] K. E. Murray and V. Betz. *Titan: Enabling large and complex benchmarks in academic CAD*. In Proc. Field Programmable Logic and Appl., 2013.

[7] C. Lee. *An algorithm for path connections and its applications*. In Proc. IRE Trans. on Electronic Computers, 1961.

[8] L. McMurchie and C. Ebeling. *Pathfinder: A negotiation-based performance-driven router for FPGAs*. In Proc. Field Programmable Gate Arrays, 1995.

[9] B. Catanzaro, K. Keutzer, and B. Su. *Parallelizaing CAD: A timely research agenda for EDA*. In Proc. ACM Design Automation Conference 2008.

[10] P. Chan and M. Schlag, *Acceleration of an FPGA router*. In Proc. Field-Programmable Custom Computing Machines, 1997.

[11] C. Zhu, J. Wang, and J. Lai. *A novel net-partition-based multithreaded FPGA routing method*. In Proc. Field Programmable Logic and Appl., 2013.

[12] M. Gort and J. Anderson. *Deterministic multi-core parallel routing for FPGAs*. In Proc. Field Programmable Logic and Appl., 2010.

[13] Y. Moctar and P. Brisk. *Parallel FPGA routing based on the operator formulation*. In Proc. Design Automation Conf., June 2014.

[14] M. Shen and G. Luo. *Accelerate FPGA routing with parallel recursive partitioning*. In Proc. Int. Conf. on Computer Aided Design, 2015

[15] C. Hoo, A. Kumar, and Y. Ha. *ParaLaR: A parallel FPGA router based on lagrangian relaxation*. In Proc. Field Programmable Logic and Appl., 2015

[16] J. Croix and S. Khatri. *Introduction to GPU programming for EDA*. In Proc. Int. Conf. on Computer Aided Design, 2009.

[17] N. Kapre and D. Ye. *GPU-accelerated high-level synthesis for bitwidth optimization of FPGA datapaths*. In Proc. Field Programmable Gate Arrays, February 21-23, 2016.

[18] D. Chen and D. Singh. *Parallelizing FPGA technology mapping using Graphics Processing Units*. In Proc. Field Programmable Logic and Appl., 2010.

[19] C. Fobel and D. Stacey. *GPU-accelerated wire-length estimation for FPGA placement*. In Proc. Application Accelerators in High-Performance Computing. 2011.

[20] P. Harish and P. Narayanan. *Accelerating large graph algorithms on the GPU using CUDA*. In Proc. High Performance Computing, pp. 197â€“208, 2007.

[21] U. Meyer and P. Sanders. *Delta-stepping: A parallel single source shortest path algorithm*. In Proc. Annual European Symposium on Algorithms, pp. 393â€“404, 1998.

[22] Y. Deng and S. Mu. *Electronic design automation with graphic processors: a survey*. In Proc. Foundations and Trends in Electronic Design Automation, 2013.

[23] A. Bleiweiss. *GPU accelerated pathfinding*. In Proc. Symposium on Graphics Hardware, pp. 65-74, 2008.

[24] Y. Han, K. Chakraborty, and S. Roy. *A global router on GPU architecture*. In Proc. IEEE International Conference on Computer Design, 2013.

[25] F. Busato and N. Bombieri. *An Efficient Implementation of the Bellman-Ford Algorithm for Kepler GPU Architectures*. In Proc. IEEE Transactions on Parallel and Distributed Systems, 2016.

[26] A. Davidson, S. Baxter, M. Garland, and J. Owens. *Work-efficient parallel GPU methods for single-source shortest paths*. In Proc. IEEE 28th International Parallel and Distributed Processing Symposium, 2014.

[27] A. DeHon et al. *GraphStep: A system architecture for sparse-graph algorithm*. In Proc. Field-Programmable Custom Computing Machines, 2006.

[28] V. Betz, J. Rose, and A. Marquardt. *Architecture and CAD for Deep-Submicron FPGAs*. In Proc. Springer, ISBN 0-7923-8460-1, February 1999.

[29] M. Burtscher, R. Nasre, and K. Pingali. *A quantitative study of irregular programs on GPUs*. In Proc. Int. Sym. on Workload Characterization, 2012.

[30] K. Pingali et al. *The tao of parallelism in algorithms*. In Proc. Programming Language Design and Implementation, 2011.

[31] D. Merrill, M. Garland, and A. Grimshaw. *Scalable GPU graph traversal*. In Proc. Principles and Practice of Parallel Programming, 2012.

[32] P. Chan, M. Schlag, C. Ebeling, and L. McMurchie. *Distributed-memory parallel routing for field-programmable gate arrays*. In Proc. IEEE TCAD, 19(8):850â€“862, 2000.

[33] R. Rubin and A. Dehon. *Timing-driven pathfinder pathology and remediation:quantifying and reducing delays noise in VPR-pathfinder*. In Proc. Field Programmable Gate Arrays, 2011.

[34] A. Dehon, R. Huang, and J. Wawrzynek. *Hardware-assisted fast routing*. In Proc. Field-Programmable Custom Computing Machines, 2002.

[35] S. Zhou, C. Chelmis, and V. Prasanna. *Accelerating large-scale single-source shortest path on FPGA*. In Proc. Parallel and Distributed Processing Symposium Workshop, 2015.

[36] A. Dandalis, A. Mei, and V. Prasanna. *Domain specific mapping for solving graph problems on reconfigurable devices*. In Proc. Parallel and Distributed Processing, 1999.

[37] R. Sedgewick and K. Wayne. *Algorithms* In Proc, Addison-Wesley, 4th edition, ISBN: 032157351X, 2011.

[38] J. Rose et al. *VPR 7.0: Next generation architecture and CAD system for FPGAs*. In Proc. ACM Trans. on RETS, 2014.

[39] Berkeley Logic Synthesis and Verification Group. ABC: A system for sequential synthesis and verification. http://www.eecs.berkeley.edu/alanmi/abc/.

Don't Forget the Memory: Automatic Block RAM Modelling, Optimization, and Architecture Exploration

Sadegh Yazdanshenas, Kosuke Tatsumura*, and Vaughn Betz
Department of Electrical and Computer Engineering, University of Toronto, Canada
*Advanced LSI Technology Laboratory, Corporate R&D Center, Toshiba Corporation, Japan
sadegh.yazdanshenas@mail.utoronto.ca, kosuke.tatsumura@toshiba.co.jp,
vaughn@ece.utoronto.ca

ABSTRACT

While academic FPGA architecture exploration tools have become sufficiently advanced to enable a wide variety of explorations and optimizations on soft fabric and routing, support for Block RAM (BRAM) has been very limited. In this paper, we present enhancements to the COFFE transistor sizing tool to facilitate automatic generation and optimization of BRAM for both SRAM and Magnetic Tunnelling Junction technologies. These new capabilities enable investigation of area, delay, and energy trends for various sizes of BRAM or different BRAM technologies. We also validate these trends against available commercial FPGA BRAM data. Furthermore, we demonstrate that BRAMs generated by COFFE can be used to carry out system-level architecture explorations using an area-oriented RAM-mapping flow and the Verilog-To-Routing flow.

Keywords

On-chip Memory; FPGA BRAM; Automatic Transistor Sizing; SRAM; Magnetic Tunnelling Junction

1. INTRODUCTION

FPGAs have undergone a constant evolution since their advent to address dynamic designer requirements and to take advantage of fast-evolving silicon technologies. Throughout this evolution, the capacity and complexity of FPGA on-chip memories have been increasing and different sizes of memories have been used as shown in Table 1 for Altera Stratix FPGAs. The changes in BRAM architecture have mainly been driven by new and generally increasing application demands for memory. Currently, BRAMs constitute roughly a quarter of FPGA fabric area [20] and power [17]. Still, the limiting resource in many applications is the on-chip memory. For instance, [13] presents an FPGA-accelerated implementation of Microsoft Bing's ranking engine where up to 90% of *Block RAMs* (BRAMs) are utilized in the "Scr2" ranking stage with a logic utilization of only 48%. We speculate that increasing memory demand from emerging applications will result in further changes in

FPGA '17, February 22-24, 2017, Monterey, CA, USA
© 2017 ACM. ISBN 978-1-4503-4354-1/17/02...$15.00
DOI: http://dx.doi.org/10.1145/3020078.3021731

FPGA BRAM architecture and possibly in the introduction of more BRAM-rich FPGAs such as Xilinx Ultra Scale+ [4] which has added a larger 288Kb BRAM to increase memory capacity.

Rapid increase in demand for on-chip memory in many FPGA applications, various degrees of freedom in BRAM design such as size, organization (width, depth, banking), and connectivity to routing along with the advent of promising emerging memory technologies such as *Magnetic Tunneling Junction* (MTJ) [18, 21] and *Phase Change Memory* (PCM) [14] create ample opportunities for exploration of FPGA BRAM architectures. However, designing BRAMs is much more challenging than ordinary digital design due to the analog nature of some BRAM components, the importance of variability, and the custom layout style used for efficient RAMs. Hence, extensive BRAM architecture explorations such as those carried out for Stratix V [8] are limited to industry. Currently, academic studies regarding BRAM such as [5] circumvent the lack of BRAM models by using CACTI [11] or interpolating between published industrial data [6]. However, while CACTI is widely used in the processor architecture community, it does not model essential FPGA-specific BRAM components such as width-configurability and connectivity to programmable routing and therefore provides simulation results that may be far from commercial FPGA product BRAMs.

To facilitate BRAM modelling and architecture research in FPGAs, this paper makes the following contributions:

- Extends the COFFE transistor sizing tool [1] [2] to automatically generate functional BRAM models that can be used by architecture and circuit researchers.

- Demonstrates how COFFE can now be used to evaluate BRAMs using emerging memory technologies such as MTJ.

- Shows how these generated BRAM models can be used in architecture-level exploration of FPGAs using a RAM mapper or VTR [10].

2. ARCHITECTURE EXPLORATION CAD

Verilog-To-Routing (VTR) is an open-source academic CAD flow commonly used by FPGA researchers to assess any arbitrary FPGA architecture. VTR takes in a verilog description of a set of circuits and a description of a hypothetical FPGA and performs all the required CAD steps to synthesize, place, and route the circuit on the target FPGA.

---

[1] The latest implementation of COFFE can be downloaded from: http://www.eecg.toronto.edu/~vaughn/software.html

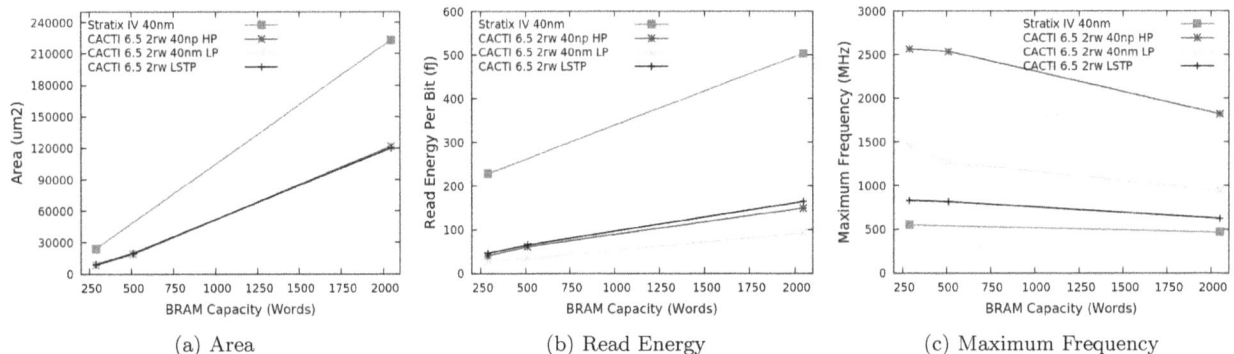

Figure 1: Comparing CACTI at 40nm with Stratix IV 40nm

Table 1: Evolution of On-Chip Memory in Memory-rich Altera Stratix FPGAs

Device and Year	Capacity (Mb)	Memory Types and Capacity Distribution	Noteable Changes
Stratix EP1S80 2002	7	M512: 6% M4K: 23% M576K: 71%	-
Stratix II EP2S180 2004	9	M512: 6% M4K: 38% M576K: 56%	Considerable increase in frequency
Stratix III EP3SE260 2006	16	MLAB: 10% M9K: 48% M144K: 42%	Introduction of MLAB & Change in sizes of all memories
Stratix IV EP4S100G5 2008	27	MLAB: 24% M9K: 42% M144K: 34%	Double MLAB capacity
Stratix V EB 2010	62	MLAB: 18% M20K: 82%	Uses only one type of block RAM
Stratix 10 10SX280 2013	243	MLAB: 6% M20K: 94%	-

Upon completion of the flow, the relative area, speed, and power can be used to rank different architectures, allowing researchers to evaluate various architectural ideas. The most time-consuming part of this process is creating the hypothetical FPGA description. Manual circuit design of an FPGA fabric to obtain reasonably accurate area and delay models can take months. In order to overcome this limitation, several tools have been created that allow automatic generation of hypothetical FPGA architectures by modelling the FPGA soft-fabric [2, 22]. However, so far the BRAMs used in architecture descriptions in the VTR flow are modelled by scaling commercial FPGA BRAMs to the desired technology and size. This limitation prevents researchers from investigating the expediency of novel circuit designs, emerging memory technologies, and alternative organizations.

To the best of our knowledge, CACTI is the only tool that researchers can currently use to model the physical characteristics of an arbitrary memory block [11]. However, CACTI has several shortcomings for FPGAs. Firstly, it models memory blocks with fixed I/O width and therefore does not include the circuitry required for width-configurability which all FPGAs require. Secondly, it doesn't include models for the routing fabric which constitute a considerable part of the BRAM tile. As a result, the simulation results produced by CACTI do not match commercial FPGA BRAM data. Figure 1 provides a quantitative comparison of Stratix IV with CACTI at the same (40nm) technology node. As can be seen, CACTI provides a memory block which takes much less silicon area, consumes

significantly less energy, and operates at a much higher frequency. Such differences could be due to CACTI not modelling the previously described FPGA-specific BRAM components or assuming more aggressive memory optimizations compared with those common in FPGAs. Regardless of the cause, we believe that FPGA academic researchers need open-source BRAM models to evaluate technology, circuit, and architecture modifications more accurately.

There are several existing FPGA transistor sizing tools that we considered for augmentation with BRAM models. We chose not to base our implementation on tools that use linear models of transistors [7, 15] as we wish to model advanced process nodes with high accuracy. In addition, using linear models will limit our implementation to SRAM-based BRAMs while our goal is to be able to model BRAMs that use emerging non-volatile memory technologies such as MTJ which don't have accurate linear models. On the other hand, COFFE [2] uses HSPICE simulations and iterative optimization to obtain a transistor sizing solution in any technology node in a matter of hours. Hence, we have decided to add our BRAM models to COFFE to generate a complete FPGA architecture that includes soft logic, routing, and BRAM.

It is worth mentioning that FPRESSO [22] is a faster, yet less accurate alternative to COFFE for logic blocks. It uses COFFE to generate FPGA-specific components and feeds them into the standard cell design flow. The standard cell flow is not a viable option for BRAM simulations due to the analog nature of some of BRAM components such as sense amplifiers.

3. COFFE ENHANCEMENTS

Figure 2 depicts the major steps of the COFFE transistor sizing tool. COFFE starts by creating a parameterized set of spice netlists representing the key building blocks of the target FPGA. To create these netlists, it requires a process model and specifications of the target architecture. COFFE uses 22nm PTM transistors [1] in its example designs and we have decided to do the same for BRAM. However, for BRAM design, we need more than one transistor model to allow the BRAM core to use low-power (higher V_{TH}, lower leakage) transistors while the rest of the FPGA utilizes high-performance transistors. In addition, MTJ-based BRAMs allow a reduction in the threshold voltage of the low-power transistors as the MTJ itself helps reduce leakage current. To this end, we changed the process models to include up to three different types of transistors: high-performance (logic), low-power (SRAM-based BRAM), and low-power with reduced V_{TH} (MTJ-based BRAM). COFFE uses two different metal models for intra-block and inter-

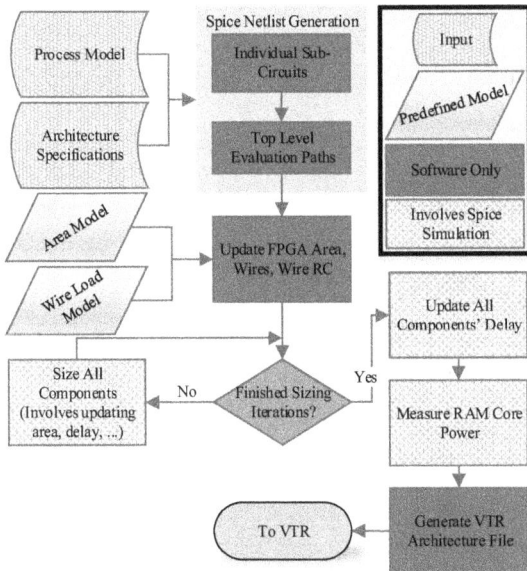

Figure 2: Major Steps in COFFE's algorithm

Table 2: COFFE's required inputs for modeling a BRAM

Parameter	Default: 16K SRAM-based BRAM	Description and range
enable_bram_module	1	Should COFFE simulate a BRAM? { 0	1 }
vdd_low_power	0.95	Memory block operating voltage
number_of_banks	2	Number of memory banks in BRAM { 1	2 }
row_decoder_bits	6	Number of address bits decoded by the row decoder
col_decoder_bits	2	Number of address bits decoded by the column decoder
conf_decoder_bits	5	Number of address bits decoded by the configurable decoder
read_to_write_ratio	1.0	BRAM expected read to write ratio. Used for energy measurement.
memory_technology	SRAM	Used memory technology { SRAM	MTJ }
sense_dv	0.03	Voltage difference required for sense amplifier operation (v)
worst_read_current	15e-7	Worst-case SRAM cell read current (A)
MTJ_Rlow_nominal	2500	Nominal MTJ resistance in low-resistance state (Ω)
MTJ_Rhigh_nominal	6250	Nominal MTJ resistance in high-resistance state (Ω)
MTJ_Rlow_worstcase	3060	Worst case MTJ resistance in low-resistance state (Ω)
MTJ_Rhigh_worstcase	4840	Worst case MTJ resistance in high-resistance state (Ω)

block routing. While we kept this convention, our BRAM-enhanced implementation uses an additional two metal models with user-specified R and C. The first one is used in modelling the wires inside the memory cell array (wordline and bitline). In our example SRAM-based BRAMs, we used a 90nm metal pitch as used by industrial 20nm SRAM cell designs [12]. The second one allows designers to construct MTJ wordline using gate line [19]. In our example MTJ-based BRAMs, we used a 22nm wide gate line for this wire model. We also extended the set of inputs to be able to describe any BRAM module as detailed in subsection 3.1.

As shown in Figure 2, generating the parameterized spice netlist has two separate steps: generating individual subcircuits and generating top-level (along with context) evaluation paths. The required subcircuits and overall BRAM architectures supported by COFFE are presented in subsection 3.2. However, mere generation of subcircuits is insufficient for evaluation and optimizations of circuits. COFFE performs all optimizations and measurements using top-level evaluation paths which include the wave-shaping circuitry, the target circuit, and the load. Unlike logic blocks, some BRAM top-level paths require specification of initial conditions to model the outcome of the previous stage in BRAM operation (e.g. reading can start after precharging the bitlines). Section 3.3 provides examples of how these paths should be generated to evaluate a BRAM module.

After creating of the parameterized spice netlists, COFFE's area and wire load models [2] are used to update FPGA area, wirelength and wire resistance and capacitances. This step is also repeatedly called in the succeeding stage: transistor sizing. Transistor sizing takes almost all of COFFE's runtime. It evaluates parameterized top-level modules and determines the best transistor sizing for each module. COFFE iteratively sizes each subcircuit until the cost-function no longer improves or a specified maximum number of iterations is reached.

Finally, COFFE carries out one final update on all component delays and generates the hypothetical FPGA architecture as a VTR input file. We have added an additional step after the final timing update to measure RAM core power which is detailed in subsection 3.6.

3.1 Extended Set of Inputs

Table 2 lists input parameters that BRAM-enhanced COFFE requires to model BRAMs. It is worth mentioning that among these parameters, those that specify how address bits should be decoded imply how memory cells should be organized into the physical array. In addition, the number of the configurable decoder bits also implies the maximum width of the BRAM block and therefore changes the number of input and output ports. When modelling a SRAM-based BRAM, the user should specify the voltage difference required at the inputs of the sense amplifier for its operation. The user should also supply COFFE with the weakest SRAM cell read current to allow COFFE to model the worst-case memory cell as discussed in subsection 3.4. Both of these parameters can be changed to capture the effect of transistor variability on BRAM. In order to model a MTJ-based BRAM, the user should supply low-state and high-state resistances for both nominal cells and worst-case cells.

3.2 Block RAM Circuit Topologies

3.2.1 The Big Picture

BRAMs and typical RAMs have two major differences. First, BRAMs are width-configurable: they are capable of trading maximum width for additional depth. Hence, they require two local crossbars and an additional decoding stage. Second, a considerable portion of BRAM area comes from its routing. This includes input connection blocks, local crossbars, and output switch boxes. For SRAM, we support both 1-bank and 2-bank architectures. Figure 3a shows the 1-bank SRAM-based architecture. Connection blocks and switch boxes are not shown in this figure but they are con-

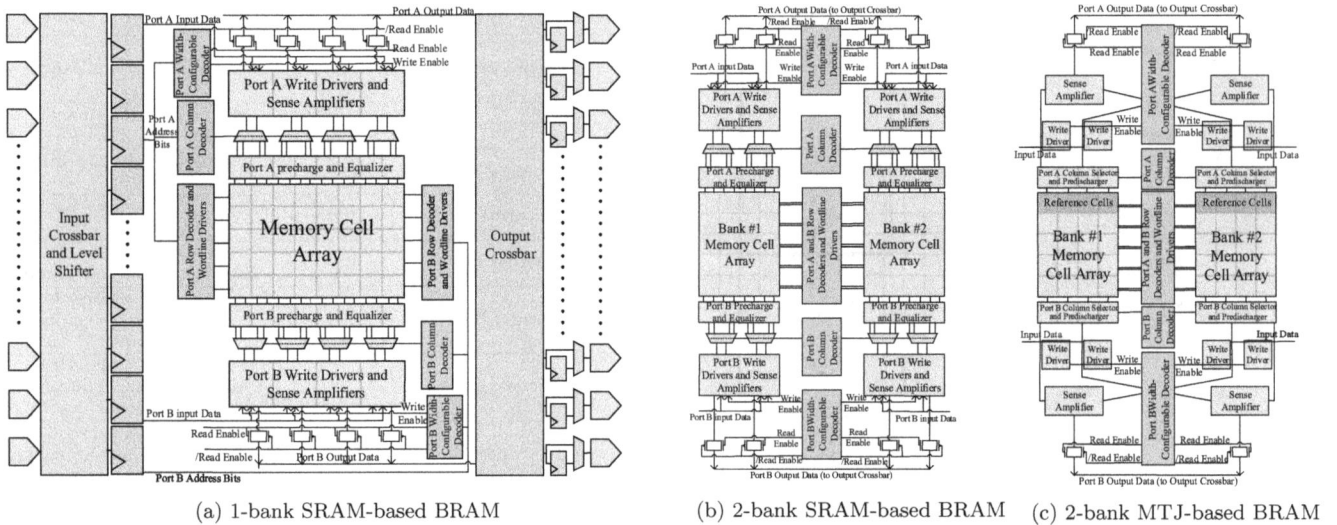

(a) 1-bank SRAM-based BRAM   (b) 2-bank SRAM-based BRAM   (c) 2-bank MTJ-based BRAM

Figure 3: Three supported BRAM architectures

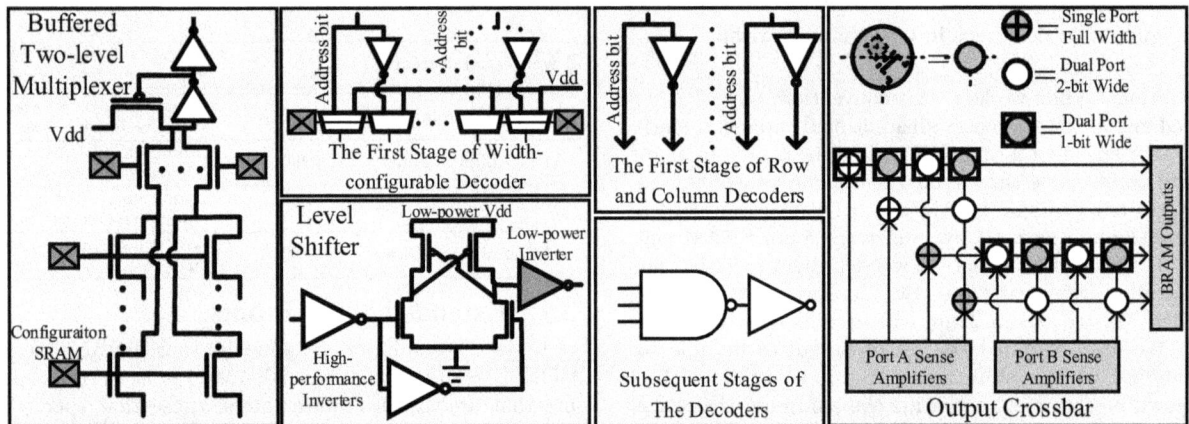

Figure 4: Peripheral circuits common to both SRAM-based and MTJ-based BRAMs

nected to input and output ports respectively. Inputs go through a local crossbar to allow data input duplication for low-width modes. Before connecting to flip flops, signals go through a level shifter to allow the RAM core to operate at a higher voltage with low power transistors. After connecting to the flip flops, signals connect to decoders and write drivers. The flip flops could be further pushed down inside the decoders to improve RAM frequency at the cost of an increase in BRAM setup time and area, but our implementation currently does not support this trade-off.

Figure 3b shows the internals of our 2-bank SRAM-based BRAM architecture. The main difference is in memory cell organization and the fact that one of the address bits will be used for bank selection. Our MTJ-based architecture must be 2-bank as is depicted in Figure 3c. Please note that since the MTJ-based BRAM sense amplifiers require one bitline input from each bank, there are half as many sense amplifiers as there would be in an SRAM-based BRAM. In addition, there is an extra row of reference cells which are used during the read operation.

3.2.2 Peripheral Circuits

Peripheral subcircuits common to both SRAM-based and MTJ-based BRAMs are depicted in Figure 4. COFFE automatically sizes all of the transistors in these subcircuits except for the level shifter for which we use a presized solu-

tion. The two-level multiplexer is used in the input crossbar, input connection blocks, and switch boxes. However, each of these components requires a multiplexer with a different size depending on architectural parameters. In addition, these components have different context (input and load circuits) and require separate simulations. Hence, different multiplexers are created for each component and sized in different contexts.

The row and column decoders have an initial stage of inverters followed by several stages of nand and inverter gates. Depending on the required size of these decoders, COFFE automatically generates each stage in the appropriate context using nand gates with two or three inputs. The main difference between the width-configurable decoder and other decoders is in the first stage. This stage has an additional set of multiplexers choosing between Vdd or an input address bit; programming the SRAM cells appropriately allows the FPGA designs to use different widths of operation. Subsequent stages are created similar to other decoders.

The output crossbar uses pass transistors along with configuration SRAM cells to enable width-configurability. Figure 4 depicts an example of an output crossbar with a maximum width of 4 bits. It also marks switches that are activated in different modes of operation. This crossbar receives 4 inputs from each port and provides 4 outputs. During single-port operation, port A will be the only operational

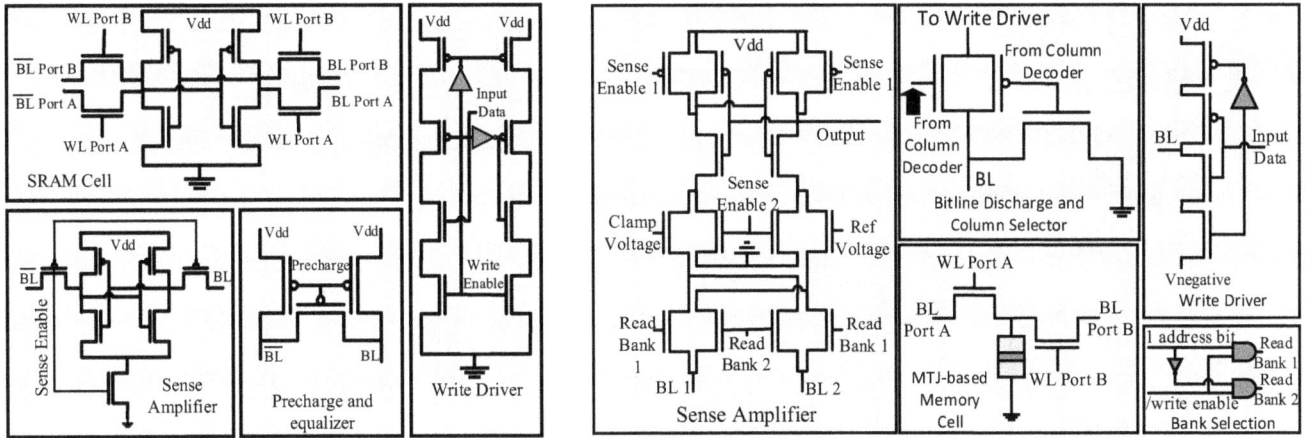

(a) SRAM-specific subcircuits (b) MTJ-specific subcircuits

Figure 5: BRAM core subcircuits for each of the supported technologies

port. As can be seen, this crossbar allows Port A to work in 4-bit, 2-bit, and 1-bit wide modes. During true dual-port (2 r/w ports) operation, half of the maximum width is allowed and each port can operate in 1-bit or 2-bit wide modes. Allowing only half the actual maximum width in the true dual-port mode reduces the number of input and output ports to the programmable routing by nearly 50% and all commercial FPGA BRAMs follow this practice. Hence, we have adopted it as well. COFFE can now automatically generate and size the required crossbar for any given maximum width of operation.

3.2.3 Technology-specific Subcircuits

In addition to peripheral subcircuits, COFFE generates some technology-specific subcircuits which include the memory cell, sense amplifier, write driver, precharge and equalizer (SRAM only), and bitline discharge and column selector (MTJ only) which are depicted in Figure 5. Among these components, the last two are automatically sized by COFFE while the rest should be precisely sized by the designer. We also provide a set of presized components in a 22nm process for both technologies, as detailed in [16].

In order to model a SRAM/MTJ cell other than the one provided in our implementation of COFFE, the user should change the SRAM/MTJ cell description and provide its dimensions for proper wire-length calculations. The user should also provide their own sense amplifier and write driver. Every other component in BRAM is generated and sized by COFFE. Once the user supplies the mentioned components, delay, area, energy calculations for the whole BRAM will be performed by COFFE.

If the user wishes to use COFFE to model another memory technology such as Resistive RAM or PCM, they should also provide the top-level evaluation paths that can be used for evaluation and/or sizing of individual components. Examples of such top-level evaluation paths can be found in the next section.

3.3 Example Top-level Paths

As mentioned before, COFFE obtains a component delay by running spice simulations on top-level paths. In the original COFFE, each top-level path consists of a wave-shaping circuit, a target circuit, and a loading circuit. The input pulse is applied to the wave-shaping circuit and the trigger point for delay measurement is set at the input of the target

circuit. The target point is defined at the output of the target circuit and just before the loading circuit. This allows COFFE to measure the delay of all components in context without simulating the entire circuit. We adapted the same strategy for wordline drivers, output crossbar, and input crossbar in the BRAM. As an example, the wordline driver in context is shown in Figure 6b. However, this strategy couldn't be applied for paths with multiple fan-in or paths that are dependent on a previous state. An example of the former is the decoder as shown in Figure 6a. The last stage of the decoder may have two predecoder components with different sizes and therefore may require simulation in two separate contexts. We altered the spice generation parsing scheme in COFFE to automatically simulate both paths and extract worst rise and fall time delays and average power.

Two examples of top-level paths that include transistor sizing but are sensitive to initial conditions are shown in Figure 7. In this case, bitlines are assigned an initial condition which resembles the previous state of BRAM. Afterwards, the precharge (or predischarge for MTJ) signal is activated until the bitline connecting to the farthest memory cell reaches a target value.

3.4 Modelling The Worst-Case Cell

The impact of on-die variation on BRAM design is much larger than it is on logic and routing; neglecting on-die variation would result in an unrealistically fast and energy-efficient BRAM that is unlikely to function. For example, when reading from an SRAM cell, it should be able to lower the voltage in the bitline by a predefined value. Since the bitline capacitance is very large, the duration of this operation varies greatly among different SRAM cells due to on-die variation and the dense design of memory cells. Hence, in order to guarantee functionality, we use worst-case memory cells in our delay measurements. Modelling MTJ worst-case cells is fairly straightforward. Spice simulation simply uses the worst-case resistance for the target cell when generating top-level paths that measure read/write delays. However, providing a circuit for the worst-case SRAM cell may be too challenging for circuit designers. Instead, they can carry out Monte Carlo simulation on their SRAM cell to measure the effect of V_{TH} variations on read current [3]. COFFE uses this worst-case read current in measuring the sense amplifier delay in two steps as depicted in Figure 8. In the first step, bitlines are initially precharged and a current source

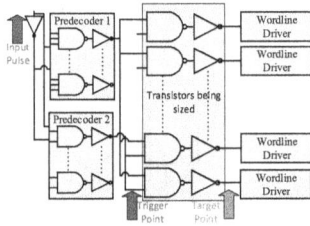 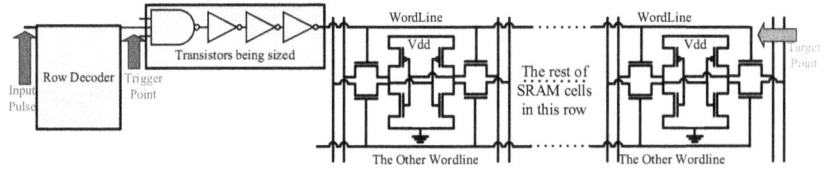

(a) A sample decoder path top-level path (b) Wordline driver top-level path

Figure 6: A sample decoder stage and wordline driver top-level paths

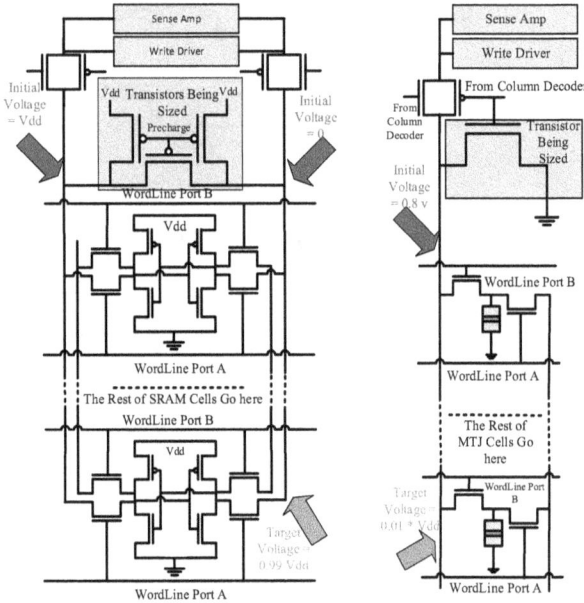 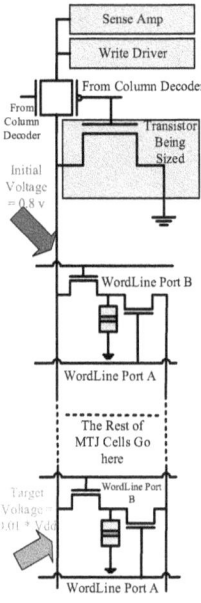 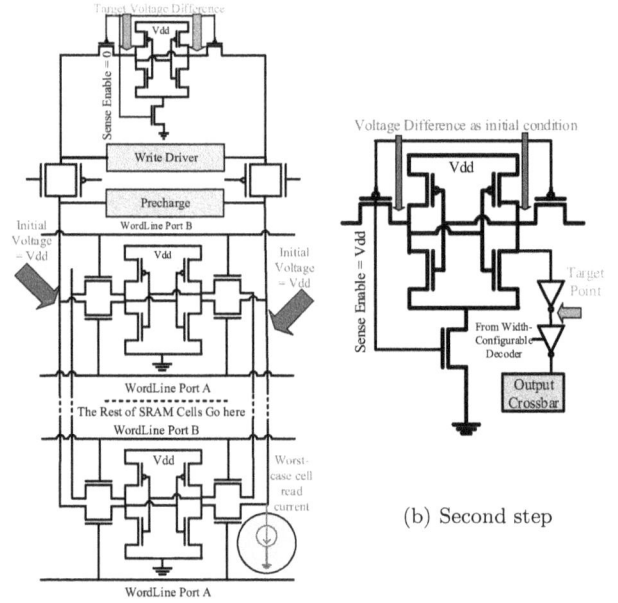 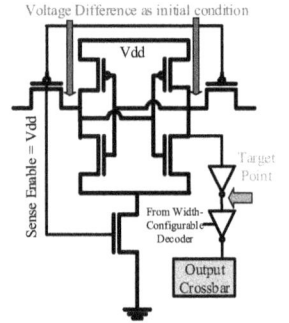

(a) Precharge and equalizer sizing in SRAM-based BRAM

(b) Predischarge in MTJ-based BRAM

Figure 7: Sizing SRAM-based (MTJ-based) Precharge (Predischarge) top-level paths.

(a) First step

(b) Second step

Figure 8: The Top-level paths used to measure sense amplifier delay using worst-case SRAM cell.

connected to the most distant SRAM cell from the sense amplifier, resembling the worst-case SRAM cell, slowly discharges one of the bitlines. The target is to measure how long it takes for the specified voltage difference to be created inside the sense amplifier. In the second stage, the sense amplifier is disconnected from the bitlines and its internal delay is measured. During this stage the sense amplifier amplifies the small voltage difference into one that can cause a trigger in its output inverter.

3.5 Cost-function Optimization

COFFE performs each transistor sizing iteration with the aim of improving the following cost function:

$$Cost = area^a \times delay^d$$

Where area is the area of logic tile and delay is the representative critical path of the logic tile. In order to include BRAM cost in the above equation, we were faced with two options: either to dedicate a portion of area and delay to the BRAM tile or to optimize two separate cost functions. The former resulted in a correlation between logic tile and BRAM size which would make architecture explorations unnecessarily difficult. Hence, we decided to optimize two separate cost functions, one for the BRAM tile and one for the logic tile. We were also faced with the choice of delay for this separate cost function. We tried using RAM frequency as

delay cost but that would result in poor transistor sizing solutions. This is due to the fact that several components are working in parallel in the BRAM; for example, the row decoder and precharge circuits. As COFFE sizes components one by one, it sizes the slower component so that it matches the other component's delay. Any future sizing iterations are futile since they will not result in an improvement in frequency by changing only one module at a time but will result in an increase in area. Therefore, we decided to use the sum of the delay of the BRAM components as the delay criterion in cost function.

3.6 BRAM Core Power

While peripheral circuits' power consumption can be measured along with timing in one spice simulation, measuring RAM core power needs the precise timing of control signals. Hence, after obtaining a final transistor sizing solution, the waveforms shown in Figure 9 are applied to the BRAM to carry out the whole read and write operations and measure power. Figures 9b and 9c show the control signals that are applied during an SRAM-based BRAM write operation. When the BRAM is operating with a width less than the maximum, write is disabled for columns other than those designated for writing by the address bits. We call the operation in such columns *write prevention*. Write prevention is unique to BRAMs since unlike typical memories their operating width can be reduced and traded for addi-

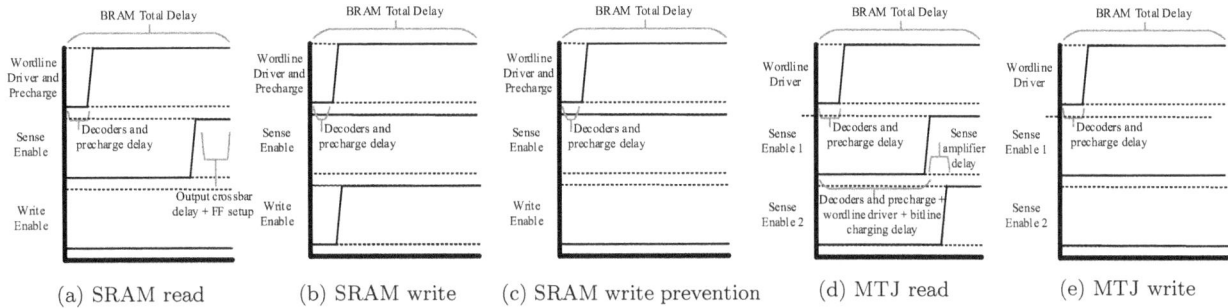

| (a) SRAM read | (b) SRAM write | (c) SRAM write prevention | (d) MTJ read | (e) MTJ write |

Figure 9: Input waves used to measure power components in RAM core

tional depth. In case of MTJs, write prevention results in a near-zero power consumption and hence is not measured.

Another important aspect of BRAM core power measurements is that we need to use nominal cells in this step. While using the worst-case SRAM cell in delay measurements is essential in guaranteeing BRAM functionality, its use for power measurement will underestimate power. The worst-case cell can pull down the bitline just enough to allow the sense amplifier to operate. However, stronger cells will bring bitline down even further causing more power to be consumed in the subsequent precharging stage.

4. BLOCK RAM SIMULATION RESULTS

4.1 Simulation Setup

In this section, we obtain the area, delay, and energy consumption for different BRAM sizes in both SRAM and MTJ technologies. To this end, we run our BRAM-enhanced COFFE to generate and simulate various memory sizes ranging from 8Kb to 256Kb. The inputs that we provide to BRAM-enhanced COFFE for SRAM-based BRAMs are identical to those mentioned in Table 2 for 16K SRAM-based BRAM except that we change decoder sizes to generate different BRAMs. For MTJ-based BRAMs, we use the same decoder configurations and only change memory technology to MTJ. The resistive states of MTJ cells are given to BRAM-enhanced COFFE as shown in Table 2.

4.2 Simulation Results

BRAM area, normalized against the logic block area for a Stratix IV-like 6-LUT logic block is shown in Figure 10a. Since exact area of FPGA BRAMs or logic blocks are not publicly available at 22nm, normalization allows us to verify the results against Stratix IV using the values provided in [20]. As pointed out by this figure, COFFE generates block RAMs that closely follow Stratix IV in terms of the BRAM/logic block area ratio giving us confidence that our RAM designs are indeed representative of those in commercial FPGAs. This figure also shows that MTJ-based BRAMs are more area-efficient when larger BRAMs are used: 8Kb and 256Kb SRAM-based BRAMs are respectively 1.59x and 3.08x larger than their MTJ counterparts. Figure 10b and Figure 10c show the breakdown of area in SRAM-based and MTJ-based BRAMs respectively. Since SRAM cells are larger than MTJ memory cells, SRAM-based BRAM area is usually dominated by memory cells itself while in MTJ-based BRAMs the contribution of other components such as routing become more pronounced. For instance, in 8Kb MTJ-based BRAM, memory cells take only 17% of total area while BRAM routing takes 46% of BRAM area.

The maximum operating frequencies of the generated BRAM modules are depicted in Figure 11a. For the sake of comparison, we have also included Xilinx Ultrascale+ and Altera Arria 10 BRAMs. Our SRAM-based implementation is slightly faster than Arria 10 and Ultrascale+ small memories. We believe this is due to the fact that commercial FPGA CAD tools are more conservative in their timing estimations due to additional guardbands for effects such as device aging. Our model is slower in very large BRAMs compared with Ultrascale+. This is both due to a technology node difference (COFFE 22nm PTM versus Xilinx 16nm FinFETs) and the fact that our implementation is limited to two banks. Using a more aggressive banking, this gap could be reduced at the expense of area. However, our models still provide reasonable trends of SRAM operating frequency. This figure also demonstrates that the gap between SRAM-based and MTJ-based BRAM operating frequencies gets smaller with increasing BRAM size. This is due to the fact that MTJ-based BRAM operating frequency is dominated by cell switching (write) time which is constant regardless of BRAM size as shown in Figure 11c.

The breakdown of SRAM-based BRAM delay components is shown in Figure 11b. The changes in the contributions of different components reflect the changes in the physical structure of the BRAMs. For example, the wordline driver contribution increases from 8k to 16k showing that the number of columns were doubled. From 16k to 32k, the contribution of RAM core delay increases, due to an increased number of rows in memory array. From 32k to 64k, the RAM core contribution decreases while both output crossbar and wordline driver contributions increase due to an increase in the number of columns and input/output width.

Since the energy-efficiency of a BRAM depends on the width of read/write operations, we have included energy consumption per operation per bit for maximum width and 1-bit wide configurations in Figure 12. As depicted in Figure 12a, energy consumption always increases with BRAM capacity regardless of technology. The rate at which this increase occurs, however, is much faster for SRAM-based BRAMs. Hence, MTJ will be more energy-efficient for larger BRAMs and less energy efficient for smaller BRAMs. The exact point at which this transition occurs depends on the width of memory operation. For full-width operation, MTJ-based BRAMs are more energy efficient for BRAMs larger than 64kb while for 1-bit wide operation mode, MTJ-based BRAMs are more energy efficient for all BRAM sizes.

The breakdown of energy consumption for SRAM-based BRAM is shown in Figure 12b. There is no radical change in the breakdown across different BRAM sizes. Write energy is slightly more than read energy for full-width operation but it gets less and less for narrower modes of operation. However, in modes of operation other than full-width, columns that

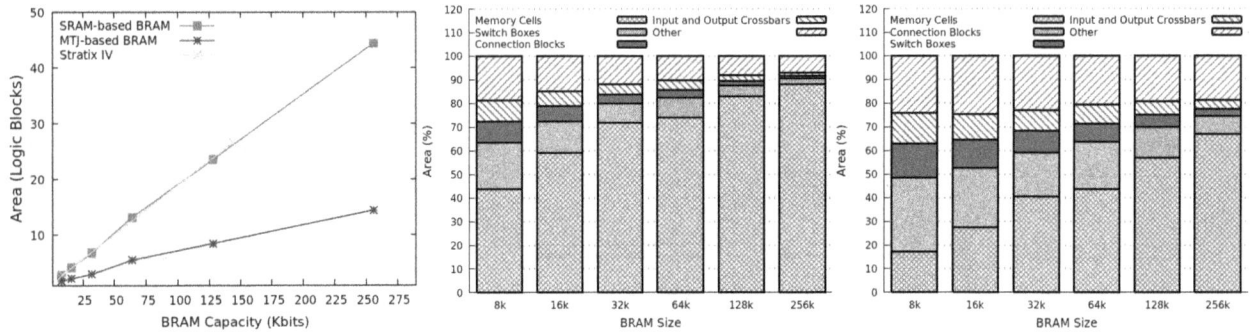

(a) Area as a function of BRAM capacity (b) Area breakdown of SRAM-based BRAM (c) Area breakdown of MTJ-based BRAM

Figure 10: BRAM area trends as generated by COFFE

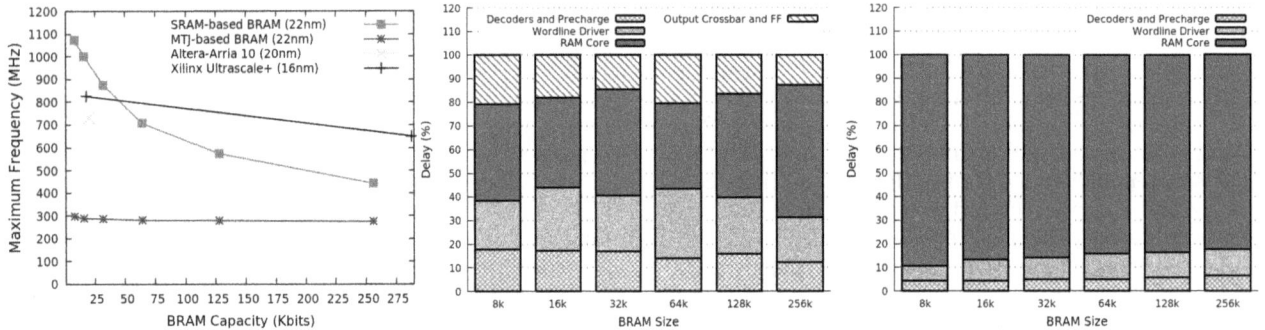

(a) Operating frequency (b) Delay breakdown of SRAM-based BRAM (c) Delay breakdown of MTJ-based BRAM

Figure 11: BRAM delay trends as generated by COFFE

Table 3: The effect of neglecting worst-case SRAM cell modelling on different BRAM parameters

BRAM Capacity (Kbits)	Change in area	Change in delay	Change in energy per bit
8	0.2%	-21.0%	-8.9%
16	0.1%	-19.3%	-6.0%
32	0.2%	-26.9%	-15.0%
64	0.1%	-21.6%	-8.9%
128	0.1%	-30.0%	-19.5%
256	0.3%	-42.0%	-28.7%

don't undergo a write operation undergo a write prevention operation which still consumes energy. On the other hand, MTJ-based BRAMs have very different read and write energy consumptions and see drastic changes in energy breakdown from full-width to 1-bit wide as shown in Figure 12c.

4.3 Importance of Worst-Case SRAM Cell

As previously described, we model the worst-case on-die variation of an SRAM cell. Table 3 shows the impact on area, delay, and energy consumption of using nominal SRAM cells instead of the worst-case cells. As can be seen, the capability to model worst-case SRAM cells is crucial in accurate BRAM modelling; while using nominal cells causes up to 42% and 28.7% underestimation of delay and energy respectively.

5. ARCHITECTURE EXPLORATION

In this section, we carry out FPGA BRAM architecture exploration using BRAM models generated by COFFE. To this end, we first introduce and utilize an area-oriented RAM mapping flow and investigate different BRAMs using a commercial benchmark suite. Afterwards, we use VTR to observe how delay, area, and routability respond to a change in BRAM technology.

5.1 Area-oriented RAM-mapping Flow

We developed an area-oriented RAM-mapping tool that takes a circuit with a list of logical RAMs (design-requested RAMs) along with a target FPGA architecture and maps logical RAMs to physical RAM available in that architecture. We fixed the LUTRAMs in the target architecture to be half of the available logic blocks to simplify our exploration. This value is in line with recent Stratix and Virtex FPGAs. We ran the tool with a benchmark suite that includes 69 industrial circuits[2] used to develop the Stratix-V memory architecture [9]. In order to obtain the trend of RAM-efficiency for a change in the memory-richness of benchmarks, we sorted these 69 circuits in terms of RAM bits to logic block ratio and gradually excluded the lower percentile of circuits from our experiments. We decided to break this exclusion into five steps: all circuits, top 80% (lower 20% excluded), etc. Such exclusion allows us to model the effect of increase in memory demand in more recent applications. For each set of circuits, we performed an exhaustive search to find the best logic block to BRAM count ratio provided by the architecture for each BRAM size.

Figure 13 plots the geometric average chip area required over each benchmark set for various architectures with only one type of BRAM. We normalize this area against the area of the best solution at each x-axis point (circuit set) to make the relative efficiency of each architecture clear. As Figure 13a shows, the best single size of SRAM-based memory for all 5 sets of circuits is 16Kb which is in agreement with BRAM choice in Altera Stratix-V. When we optimize for the entire benchmark suite, the best architecture contains

---

[2]We have partial data from these circuits: Logical RAMs and total logic demand. While this data is enough for RAM-mapping experiments it is insufficient for VTR explorations.

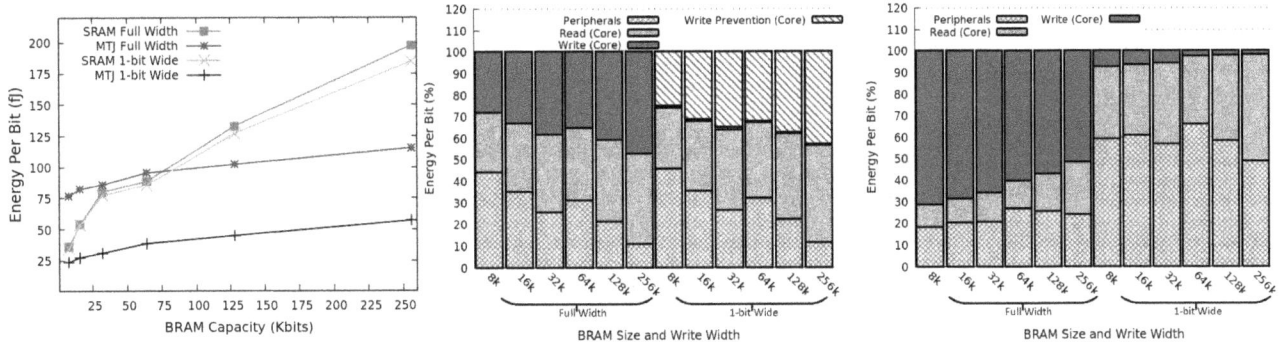

(a) Energy per bit per operation   (b) Energy breakdown of SRAM-based BRAM (c) Energy breakdown of MTJ-based BRAM

Figure 12: BRAM energy trends as generated by COFFE for read/write ratio = 1.0.

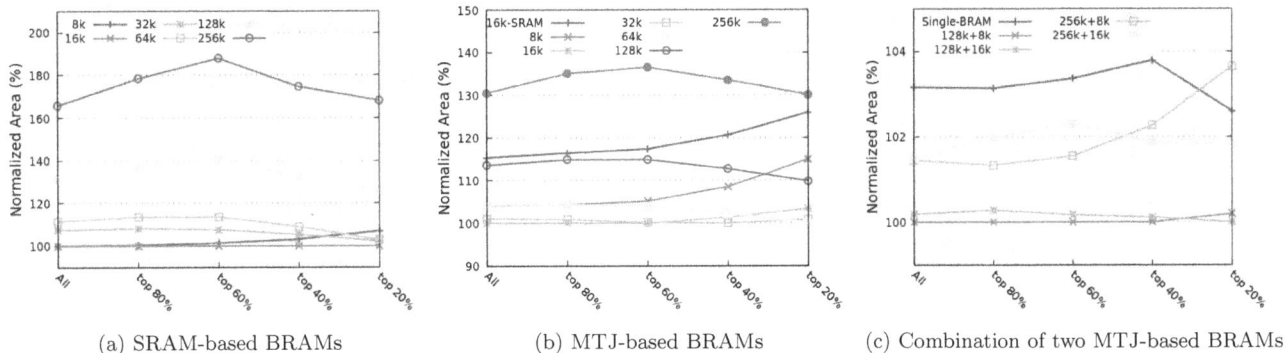

(a) SRAM-based BRAMs   (b) MTJ-based BRAMs   (c) Combination of two MTJ-based BRAMs

Figure 13: Area-optimized RAM-mapping results for various BRAM architectures

11 logic blocks per 16Kb BRAM, whereas if we optimize for the 20% most memory rich designs the best architecture has a 16Kb BRAM for every 7 logic blocks. As circuits become more memory-rich, larger BRAMs are more viable and the 8Kb BRAM size performs even more poorly. The same experiments for MTJ-based BRAMs are shown in 13b. Unlike SRAM-based BRAMs, the best MTJ-based BRAM size changes with the memory richness of circuits and ranges from 16Kb to 64Kb. It is worth mentioning that the gap between the efficient MTJ-based architectures and the 16k-SRAM based solution gets larger (from 15% to 26% required chip area) as memory richness of circuits increases. Another interesting observation is that 128K and 256K MTJ-based BRAMs are never the best solution. However, these two sizes are those with better area, energy, and delay compared to their SRAM-based counterparts. In order to utilize these larger BRAMs, a mix of two types of BRAM are required. Figure 13c shows how the best two-BRAM architecture compare the best single MTJ-BRAM architectures. Using a mixture of two BRAMs can only improve area by about 3% as compared to the single-BRAM solution. The best two-BRAM architectures always use a 128Kb BRAM together with either an 8Kb or a 16Kb BRAM. The architecture should contain more small BRAMs than large; for example for the 20% most memory-rich circuits, the best architecture has one 16Kb BRAM for every 12 logic blocks and one 128Kb BRAM for every 107 logic blocks.

5.2 VTR Flow

While the RAM-mapping flow lets use explore a wide variety of BRAM types using a large number of benchmarks in terms of area, it does not provide any information on delay. In addition, RAM-mapping doesn't enable us to see how the FPGA routing is affected by a change in mem-

ory area. Hence, we used the architecture file generated by COFFE to carry out system-level simulations using VTR. These experiments were carried out using VTR trunk version c5dad5 which provides more realistic connectivity between tall blocks such as BRAM and the routing. Prior to this version of VTR, BRAMs and other tall blocks didn't connect to the routing fabric through the wires that pass over them and only connected to wires at their periphery and hence underutilized the routing fabric. We used 32Kb (VTR's default) SRAM and MTJ-based memories due to space limitations. Both memories start at the second column and are repeated every 8 columns. We decided that the height of these blocks should be equal to their area ratio compared with logic blocks (7 for SRAM, 3 for MTJ) which in case of MTJ-based BRAMs results in an FPGA with more memory using the same die area. Logic blocks and routing are generated using the input parameters shown in Table 4.

Table 5 shows the results of the MTJ-based BRAM architecture normalized to those of the SRAM-based BRAM architecture. Along with each circuit we have shown the ratio of RAM slices to LUTs as a metric of memory-richness. As can be seen, used block area (sum of soft-fabric, DSP, and BRAMs) is reduced in all cases by an average of 18.5%. This is an expected behaviour and matches our simulation results from the previous section since MTJ-based BRAMs are more dense. Routing area varies across different circuits but on average there is a decrease of 10.6%. This decrease, which is more significant in memory-rich circuits, is due to the fact that the reduction in height of BRAMs results in more BRAMs per column and hence enhances routability. Overall, area is decreased by 14.9%. On the other hand, logic delay increases due to the slower speed of MTJ-based BRAMs by an average of 25.1%. However, the increase in total delay is only 1.5% due to a decrease in routing de-

123

Table 4: COFFE input parameters

Architecture Parameter	Value	Process Parameter	Value
N	10	vdd	0.8
K	6	vsram	1
W	320	vsram_n	0
L	4	gate_length	22
I	40	min_tran_width	45
Fs	3	min_width_tran_area	33864
Fcin	0.2	trans_diffusion_length	52
Fcout	0.025		
Or	2		
Ofb	1		
Fclocal	0.5		

Table 5: Change in simulation results after switching BRAM technology to MTJ

Circuit	RAM to LUT Ratio	Block Area	Routing Area	Total Area	Block Delay	Routing Delay	Total Delay	Area-delay Product
mcml	0.3%	-10.5%	0.3%	-4.5%	4.7%	-18.7%	-5.6%	-9.8%
LU32PEEng	6.9%	-13.8%	9.1%	-1.7%	8.7%	-6.0%	0.4%	-1.4%
LU8PEEng	6.2%	-12.7%	4.3%	-4.5%	-4.2%	8.7%	2.7%	-1.9%
ch_intrinstics	1.9%	-14.7%	-1.9%	-9.9%	-1.2%	5.6%	2.9%	-7.3%
mkDelayWorker32B	23.9%	-31.8%	-47.3%	-40.7%	60.2%	-39.9%	2.9%	-39.0%
mkPktMerge	197.8%	-56.9%	-47.8%	-52.8%	140.8%	-33.6%	11.7%	-47.2%
mkSMAdapter4B	7.7%	-15.7%	-0.4%	-9.4%	92.1%	-31.8%	8.3%	-1.9%
or1200	2.1%	-4.8%	3.5%	-0.5%	0.8%	-6.7%	-2.4%	-2.9%
raygentop	1%	-2.6%	2.1%	-0.8%	8.7%	-16.7%	-4.2%	-5.0%
boundtop	1%	-2.6%	0.7%	-1.1%	7.6%	-5.3%	-0.3%	-1.5%
Geometric Mean	4.2%	-18.5%	-10.6%	-14.9%	25.1%	-16.0%	1.5%	-13.6%

lay as a result of enhanced routability. Overall, we can observe 13.6% improvement in area-delay by switching to MTJ-based BRAMs.

6. CONCLUSION

We presented the first automatic FPGA BRAM generator which is capable of modelling and optimizing BRAMs using both SRAM and MTJ technologies. In addition, it can model worst-case cells to capture the effect of on-die variation on BRAMs. We demonstrated that the BRAM-enhanced COFFE results are consistent with published commercial FPGA BRAM data and that it enables investigation of area, delay, and energy trends for different sizes of BRAM and across technologies. We leveraged the BRAM models in carrying out two sets of system-level FPGA BRAM architecture explorations through RAM-mapping and VTR flows. These explorations resulted in interesting conclusions for the best BRAM size depending on the technology and the memory-richness of applications. Furthermore, VTR explorations revealed that in case of memory-rich circuits, using a dense BRAM results in improvements not only in block area, but also in routing area and area-delay.

7. ACKOWLEDGEMENT

We would like to thank David Lewis for invaluable discussions, and the Connaught Scholarship, Toshiba, Intel, and NSERC for funding support.

8. REFERENCES

[1] Predictive technology model. http://ptm.asu.edu/.

[2] C. Chiasson and V. Betz. COFFE: Fully-automated transistor sizing for FPGAs. In FPT, pages 34–41, 2013.

[3] E. Grossar, M. Stucchi, K. Maex, and W. Dehaene. Read stability and write-ability analysis of SRAM cells for nanometer technologies. IEEE Journal of Solid-State Circuits, 41(11):2577–2588, 2006.

[4] Xilinx Inc. Ultrascale architecture and product overview. 2016.

[5] E. Kadric, D. Lakata, and A. DeHon. Impact of memory architecture on FPGA energy consumption. In FPGA, pages 146–155, 2015.

[6] E. Kadric, K. Mahajan, and A. DeHon. Kung fu data energy-minimizing communication energy in FPGA computations. In FCCM, pages 214–221, 2014.

[7] I. Kuon and J. Rose. Exploring area and delay tradeoffs in FPGAs with architecture and automated transistor design. IEEE TVLSI, 19(1):71–84, 2011.

[8] D. Lewis, D. Cashman, M. Chan, J. Chromczak, G. Lai, A. Lee, T. Vanderhoek, and H. Yu.

[9] D. Lewis (Intel). private communication.

[10] J. Luu, et al. VTR 7.0: Next generation architecture and CAD system for FPGAs. TRETS, 7(2):6, 2014.

[11] N. Muralimanohar, R. Balasubramonian, and N. P. Jouppi. CACTI 6.0: A tool to model large caches. HP Laboratories, pages 22–31, 2009.

[12] G. Nallapati, et al. Cost and power/performance optimized 20nm SoC technology for advanced mobile devices. In VLSI Technology, pages 1–2, 2014.

[13] A. Putnam, et al. A reconfigurable fabric for accelerating large-scale datacenter services. In ISCA, pages 13–24, 2014.

[14] M. K. Qureshi, V. Srinivasan, and J. A. Rivers. Scalable high performance main memory system using phase-change memory technology. In ISCA, pages 24–33, 2009.

[15] A. M. Smith, G. A. Constantinides, and P. Y. Cheung. FPGA architecture optimization using geometric programming. IEEE TCAD, 29(8):1163–1176, 2010.

[16] K. Tatsumura, S. Yazdanshenas, and V. Betz. High density, low energy, magnetic tunnel junction based block RAMs for memory-rich FPGAs. In FPT. pages 4–11, 2016.

[17] R. Tessier, V. Betz, D. Neto, A. Egier, and T. Gopalsamy. Power-efficient RAM mapping algorithms for FPGA embedded memory blocks. IEEE TCAD, 26(2):278–290, 2007.

[18] L. Thomas, et al. Perpendicular spin transfer torque magnetic random access memories with high spin torque efficiency and thermal stability for embedded applications. Journal of Applied Physics, 115(17):172615, 2014.

[19] K. Tsuchida, et al. A 64mb MRAM with clamped-reference and adequate-reference schemes. ISSCC, 2010.

[20] H. Wong, V. Betz, and J. Rose. Comparing FPGA vs. custom CMOS and the impact on processor microarchitecture. In FPGA, pages 5–14, 2011.

[21] S. Yuasa, T. Nagahama, A. Fukushima, Y. Suzuki, and K. Ando. Giant room-temperature magnetoresistance in single-crystal fe/mgo/fe magnetic tunnel junctions. Nature materials, 3(12):868–871, 2004.

[22] G. Zgheib, M. Lortkipanidze, M. Owaida, D. Novo, and P. Ienne. FPRESSO: Enabling express transistor-level exploration of FPGA architectures. In FPGA, pages 80–89, 2016.

Architectural enhancements in Stratix V. In FPGA, pages 147–156, 2013.

Automatic Construction of Program-Optimized FPGA Memory Networks

Hsin-Jung Yang
Massachusetts Institute of
Technology, CSAIL
hjyang@csail.mit.edu

Kermin Fleming
Intel Corporation
SSG Group
kermin.fleming@intel.com

Felix Winterstein
Imperial College London
CAS Group
f.winterstein12@imperial.ac.uk

Annie I. Chen
Massachusetts Institute of
Technology, EECS
anniecia@mit.edu

Michael Adler
Intel Corporation
SSG Group
michael.adler@intel.com

Joel Emer
Massachusetts Institute of
Technology, CSAIL
emer@csail.mit.edu

ABSTRACT

Memory systems play a key role in the performance of FPGA applications. As FPGA deployments move towards design entry points that are more serial, memory latency has become a serious design consideration. For these applications, memory network optimization is essential in improving performance. In this paper, we examine the automatic, program-optimized construction of low-latency memory networks. We design a feedback-driven network compiler, which constructs an optimized memory network based on the target program's memory access behavior measured via a newly designed network profiler. In our test applications, the compiler-optimized networks provide a 45% performance gain on average over baseline memory networks by minimizing the impact of network latency on program performance.

1. INTRODUCTION

FPGA-based accelerators have great potential to achieve better performance and energy-efficiency compared to general-purpose solutions because the FPGA permits the tailoring of hardware to a particular application. However, as FPGAs and FPGA-based systems have grown, traditional approaches such as low-level hardware development and system-level hand-tuning have strained in the face of design complexity. To address FPGA programmability challenges, recent work has focused on raising the level of design abstraction by providing high-level programming models [1][2][3][4] as well as offering optimized and reusable service implementations [5][6][7]. However, high-level abstractions and productivity sometimes come at the expense of intelligent control and performance, resulting in a performance gap between a generated system and a manually optimized design. To construct high-performance designs while maintaining high productivity, it is essential to have a compiler that automatically optimizes the abstract service implementations in an application-specific manner on behalf of programmers.

In this work, we focus on FPGA memory systems, the performance of which is critical to the overall program performance for a broad class of applications. Unlike general purpose processors, where the memory system is fixed at design time, FPGAs offer the opportunity to intelligently customize the complete memory system; for example, the number, properties, and topology of cache hierarchies can be selected based on the behavior of a particular program. Furthermore, a specific optimization on FPGA does not need to provide a large average benefit (as is required in processors) because the optimization can be applied only when it can benefit the target application, avoiding unnecessary overhead.

Previous work on multi-level FPGA memory hierarchies has generally focused on the microarchitecture and optimization of on-chip caches to achieve higher cache bandwidth and hit rate [8][9][10]. However, with the rise of serial design entry points for FPGAs, such as C-based kernels compiled through high-level synthesis (HLS), memory latency has become a first-class design consideration. Though parallel, HLS programs are sometimes less parallel than conventional designs written at register transfer level (RTL), making them more sensitive to latency in the memory subsystem. In this work, we focus on the construction of low-latency memory networks. We aim to improve program performance by customizing networks connecting different levels of caches in the memory hierarchy for each target application. Memory network customization is especially valuable when the memory clients of the target program have asymmetric memory access behavior. For example, a memory client that is more latency-sensitive, possibly due to lower data locality or lower request-level parallelism, should be granted a faster network path. Constructing a program-optimized cache network requires the evaluation of cost-performance tradeoffs on a per-application basis. Since the design space of network topologies is quite large, manual exploration is unattractive, and an automated solution is desirable.

In order to automate the design space exploration, we first propose a new communication abstraction for centralized services to separate the functionality of the service network from physical topologies, allowing compilers to optimize the memory network under the proposed abstraction without changing other components in the memory system. To construct a program-optimized network implementation, we need a systematic way of evaluating the performance impact of different network configurations and characterizing the memory access behavior of the program. We therefore introduce a dynamically-configurable network profiler, which can be used to emulate different network topologies for the target application without reconstructing the hardware. In the network profiler, program instrumentation logic is inserted at each memory client in order to measure the client's latency and bandwidth demands.

FPGA '17, February 22-24, 2017, Monterey, CA, USA

© 2017 ACM. ISBN 978-1-4503-4354-1/17/02... $15.00

DOI: http://dx.doi.org/10.1145/3020078.3021748

```
interface MEM_IFC#(type t_ADDR, type t_DATA);
    method void readRequest(t_ADDR addr);
    method t_DATA readResponse();
    method void write(t_ADDR addr, t_DATA data);
endinterface
```

Figure 1: LEAP memory interface

Armed with an abstraction and a means of program introspection, the final step is to develop algorithms for selecting an optimal network topology. We present an integer linear programming (ILP) formulation to determine an optimized tree-based network that minimizes the network latency impact on program performance. We also propose an efficient approximation algorithm that solves this optimization problem in polynomial time using dynamic programming (DP). To implement the optimized physical network, we extend the LEAP Memory Compiler (LMC) proposed in [11]. The compiler takes the profiling results obtained from the network profiler and uses the above optimization techniques to automatically construct an optimized network for the target application.

To test the scalability and robustness of our algorithms, we also consider an emerging class of FPGA workloads: multi-program applications, which we view as representative of future FPGA deployments, especially in the data center context. To support the needs of such deployments and to help amortize large FPGAs, FPGA virtualization has been proposed [12], allowing several user programs to be simultaneously mapped to the same FPGA. On a virtualized FPGA platform, it is common to have a large number of memory clients sharing memory system resources. In order to balance the performance across competing applications, we introduce some quality-of-service controls into the compiler-generated memory network to control fairness among multiple programs.

We evaluate the performance of our automatically-generated cache networks on both single-program and multi-program applications. The single-program applications we target contain HLS-compiled computational kernels that are sensitive to memory latency. For these applications, on average, the program-optimized tree networks achieve a 45% performance gain over the baseline memory networks and a 17% performance gain over the partitioned ring-based networks constructed by the original LMC. For multi-program applications, the tree network with bandwidth control also achieves better fairness by preventing throughput-oriented applications from saturating the memory system bandwidth.

2. BACKGROUND

Our exploration of program-optimized memory network construction builds upon prior work in the automatic synthesis of FPGA memory subsystems: LEAP memories [13][14] and the LEAP Memory Compiler (LMC) [11].

LEAP private memories [13] provide FPGA programs a general, in-fabric memory abstraction with a simple read-request, read-response, write interface as shown in Figure 1. Programmers can instantiate as many memories as needed to store arbitrary data types, and each instantiated memory represents a logically private address space. LEAP memories also support arbitrary address space sizes, which may be larger than the total capacity of FPGA physical memories. To provide the illusion of large address spaces, LEAP exploits the host virtual memory as a backing store and uses FPGA physical memories, including both on-chip and on-board memories, as caches to maintain high performance. LEAP coherent memories [14] extend the private memory abstraction to maintain coherency and consistency of accesses to a shared memory space. A program may declare multiple, independent coherent address spaces.

Similar to the load-store interface of memory systems on general-purpose machines, the abstract interfaces of LEAP memories do not

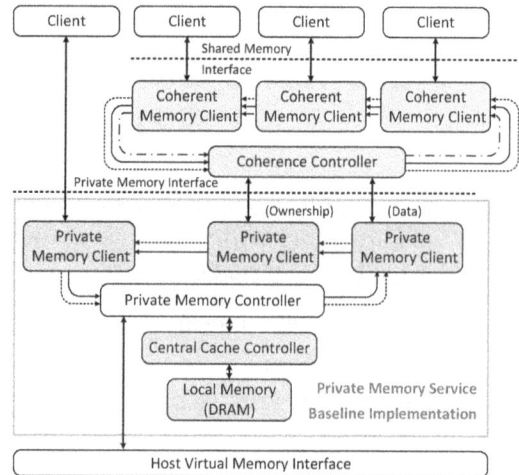

Figure 2: An example of LEAP memory hierarchy

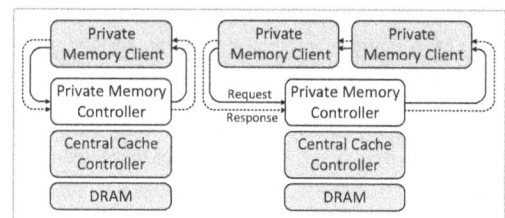

Figure 3: A partitioned ring-based memory network created by LMC

imply any implementation details of the underlying memory system, such as how many levels of cache are in the memory hierarchy or the topology of cache networks. This ambiguity provides compilers significant freedom to construct memory hierarchies based on properties of the target application and the target platform.

Figure 2 shows an example of a typical LEAP memory hierarchy which integrates one private memory and three coherent memories instantiated in the user program. LEAP coherent memories are built on top of the private memory hierarchy: the coherence controller of each shared memory space uses two private memories as data and coherence ownership stores. In each memory client, a local cache can be optionally constructed using on-chip SRAMs. As a baseline, all private memory clients are connected to a single, centralized controller hierarchy, which manages accesses to a central cache implemented with aggregated FPGA board-level memories. Within the central cache, each private and shared memory space is uniquely tagged, enforcing a physical separation.

The LEAP compilation flow is shown in Figure 4. The compiler gathers various LEAP memories instantiated in the user program and assembles them into a memory hierarchy, as in Figure 2. To efficiently utilize the bandwidth of multiple board-level memories on modern FPGAs, instead of building a single large central cache, LMC [11] treats each board-level memory resource as an independent cache managed by a separate controller hierarchy and assigns memory clients to the controller hierarchies in an application-specific fashion. Specifically, LMC measures the traffic sent from each memory client via program instrumentation and uses the measurement as feedback to construct a partitioned memory network, which balances the traffic across controllers. Figure 3 shows an example of the partitioned memory network constructed by LMC.

In both the baseline (Figure 2) and LMC-optimized memory hierarchies (Figure 3), various memory components are connected via LEAP rings [7]. LEAP originally opted for ring-based topologies

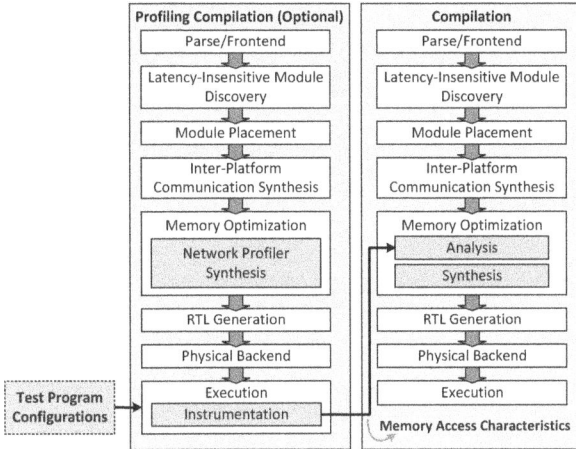

Figure 4: The LEAP compilation flow [15][11], with our augmentations highlighted in blue. We extend the memory optimization phase introduced in LMC to construct more complicated cache networks.

because they are lightweight, largely symmetric, reasonably fair, and easy to assemble. However, as FPGAs and FPGA applications have scaled with Moore's law, the main flaw of ring-based memory networks has been increasingly exposed: latency.

In this work, we seek to alleviate the latency issue present in scaled out FPGA memory systems through the construction of program-optimized tree-based networks. Unlike ring-based networks, tree-based networks can be asymmetric: the compiler can choose both the radix of each interior node and the depth of a given memory client within the network. We extend LMC with algorithms that can synthesize tree-based networks tailored to the latency and bandwidth requirements of a program's memory clients, as measured by program instrumentation. Since the design space is large, we also introduce a network profiler to help explore our algorithmic choices.

3. RELATED WORK

Memory is fundamental to the performance of almost all computational systems. As such, memory systems have long been a focus of intense academic and industrial study. In general-purpose systems, memory architecture is usually determined through human implementation effort due to the high production volume of these systems and their symmetry. However, in lower volume architectures, like embedded SoCs, which have asymmetric use cases, design automation is often employed to optimize the memory system topology.

In the embedded domain, multiple accelerator devices are used to meet performance and energy targets. Multiple automated methods [16][17][18] for building memory networks incorporating such accelerators have been developed. These works propose the generation of custom memory topologies, generally consisting of a combination of shared buses and crossbars of various types based on communication patterns among the accelerators. As with our work, mixed-integer linear formulations have been used to optimize these topologies, given some performance characteristics and goals of the accelerators in the target system. Other works have considered the implementation of SoC-style memory networks in the context of FPGAs [19][20], in which optimization techniques are used to build custom crossbar and bus cascades. None of these works consider the construction of performance-optimized memory topologies for FPGA-based compute accelerators, in particular the case in which a single application may have many simultaneously active memory interfaces that must be balanced to achieve high performance.

A second major difference between our work and prior network synthesis studies lies in the choice of network topologies. Prior works focus almost exclusively on constructing SoC-style networks, which are intended to support memory accesses by a single accelerator and memory-mapped communications between accelerators ganged together to perform some task. This requirement results in very general communication topologies: shared buses and crossbars. We remark that, in FPGA-based compute accelerators, the tasks of communication and memory are usually separated. Communications are typically implemented directly and within the accelerator, while memory systems are confined to state storage. Leveraging this observation, we satisfy the memory needs of accelerators using simpler memory networks than contemplated in prior work, in turn improving key metrics such as area, frequency, and energy.

As FPGAs have grown in their capability as accelerators, several FPGA-specific memory system architectures have been proposed. In this paper, we adopt the LEAP memory and compiler as a base, but we believe most other architectures are sufficiently abstract to be compatible with our approach. CoRAM [6] advocates memory interaction using control threads programmed with a C-like language. CoRAM does not define the memory subsystem backing its programmer interface, and therefore could make use of our optimized memory networks. More traditional FPGA-based processor infrastructures [21][22][23], could also benefit from our work in low-latency memory networks as processors, and especially soft processors, are typically sensitive to memory access latencies. However, the processor memory behavior, as noted above, is typically symmetric when viewed across many workloads. Thus, this class of FPGA programs might not benefit from our optimizations.

Beyond these architectural efforts, researchers have also explored cache microarchitectures and multiple-level memory hierarchies on FPGAs [13][8][24][25]. These works generally assume a fixed, program-invariant memory topology, while our work focuses on optimizing the memory topology on a per-application basis.

4. MOTIVATING EXAMPLE

The advantage of customized memory networks is most salient for applications with a large number of asymmetric memory clients. One example is a high-performance hardware implementation of a *filtering algorithm* [26] for K-means clustering, a widely used machine learning technique for unsupervised partitioning of a data set. K-means clustering partitions a data set into K clusters such that each point belongs to the cluster with the nearest mean. The filtering algorithm prunes the search space of the nearest centers by organizing the data points in a binary search tree (a 'kd-tree' [26]) and finding nearest centers using a tree traversal.

In each iteration, the filtering algorithm traverses the tree starting from the root. Each tree node represents a subset of input data points and the algorithm propagates several candidates for the closest center to each subset down the tree. Our implementation uses three data structures: (i) A kd-tree that is built up from the data points and implemented as a pointer-linked binary tree. (ii) A stack that manages the tree traversal and is implemented as a pointer-linked list, whose head is modified by 'push' and 'pop' operations. (iii) Multiple sets of candidates for the closest center to a data subset. These candidate sets are of variable size and are created and disposed at runtime. The accesses to these data structures are essentially pointer chasing, which makes the execution time of the algorithm very sensitive to the memory access latency.

We parallelize the implementation by splitting the tree and the stack into $P = 8$ partitions and each partition maintains its own center sets. The computational kernels are implemented through high-level synthesis and connected to the LEAP memory system.

```
interface SERVICE_CLIENT_IFC#(type t_REQ, type t_RESP);
    method void sendRequest(t_REQ req);
    method t_RESP receiveResponse();
    method Bool requestNotFull();
    method Bool responseNotEmpty();
endinterface

interface SERVICE_SERVER_IFC#(type t_REQ, type t_RESP,
                              type t_ID);
    method void sendResponse(t_ID client, t_RESP resp);
    method t_REQ receiveRequest();
    method Bool responseNotFull();
    method Bool requestNotEmpty();
endinterface
```

Figure 5: The abstract interfaces of service connections

We instantiate a LEAP private memory for each partition and data structure type, resulting in 24 LEAP memories to store the three different types of data structures. In the baseline LEAP memory hierarchy, all 24 memory clients are connected on a single ring, introducing long network latency. Even if we apply client partitioning mechanisms introduced in LMC on an FPGA with multiple on-board memories, the network latency impact is still significant. To improve performance we need to build a cache network with better scalability.

In addition, we observe that memory clients in the filtering algorithm have different behavior and some are more sensitive to latency than others. For example, stack accesses have very high data locality and all hit in a small first-level cache. Since none of stack access requests reaches the memory network, performance for stack accesses is insensitive to network latency and topology. On the other hand, the LEAP memories storing tree nodes send many read requests to the memory network, because the tree node structures are large, have low data locality, and do not fit in first-level caches. As a result, these memory clients are sensitive to the network latency increase. Increasing network latency for these clients has a significant impact on program performance. To achieve high performance, a program-optimized cache network should provide shorter network latency to the memory clients storing tree nodes by placing these clients closer to the memory controller. In Section 8, we will show that our optimized cache network provides a 44% performance gain over the baseline LEAP memory hierarchy and a 18% performance gain over the partitioned network generated by LMC.

5. COMMUNICATION ABSTRACTION

To automate the construction of program-optimized cache networks, we first introduce a new communication abstraction enabling a clean separation between the functionality of the cache network and physical topologies. This abstraction, which we call a service connection, is designed for centralized services in which a controller takes requests from multiple clients and replies, if necessary.

The service connection abstraction provides clients and servers with request-response-based interfaces as shown in Figure 5. The abstract interfaces allow compilers to construct various network topologies underneath. Figure 6 shows an example of a connected service with three clients and a server, which are instantiated by specifying a service name ("MEM" for example). Semantically, each client is connected to a server with a matched service name via two in-order channels: one for requests, and the other for responses. At compile time, the compiler gathers clients and servers with the same service name, assigns each client with a unique ID, and then constructs an optimized physical network. Requests sent from each client are tagged with the client's ID. The server receives requests from clients, processes the requests, and then sends responses back to the requester by specifying the requester's ID.

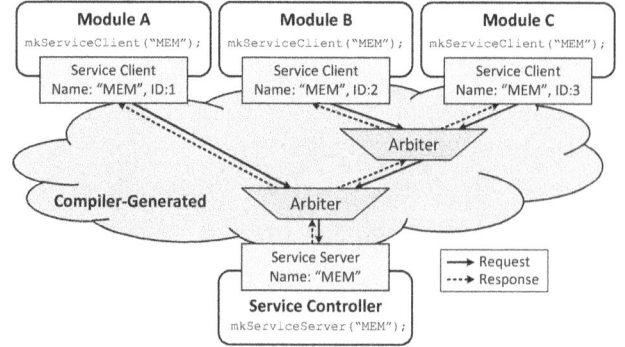

Figure 6: Communication abstraction for centralized services

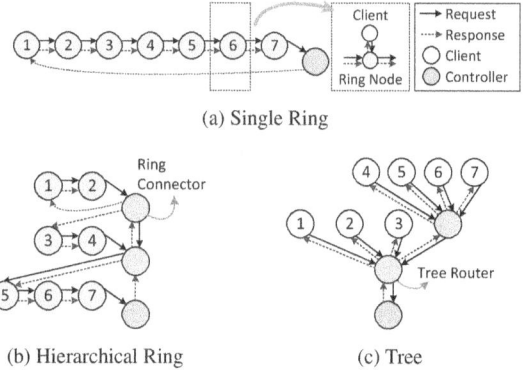

(a) Single Ring

(b) Hierarchical Ring   (c) Tree

Figure 7: Examples of compiler-generated network topologies

This network construction strategy can also be applied to services with multiple servers. For example, the LEAP private memory service may have multiple private memory controllers to manage accesses to multiple on-board memories [11]. In this case, the compiler constructs a separate network for each server and each memory client can be connected to one or multiple servers.

6. NETWORK TOPOLOGIES

With the service connection abstraction, which merely defines the endpoint interfaces, the compiler is free to construct any network topology that connects service clients to their servers. To explore the design tradeoffs, we design the compiler to construct three different types of network topologies: a single-ring, a hierarchical-ring, and a tree network, as shown in Figure 7. Figure 7a is an example of a single-ring network, which works the same as the original LEAP rings. Physically, this network consists of two linear networks: one delivers requests from clients to the controller, and the other delivers responses from the controller to clients. Ring nodes check the requester ID of every incoming response packet and then decide whether to forward the packet to the local client or on the ring. Figure 7b shows an example of a hierarchical-ring network, which consists of multiple levels of rings and ring connectors. Similar to a ring node, a ring connector decides which ring to forward responses by checking the requester ID tagged with the response. The ID of each client is carefully assigned by the compiler in a sequential order, which makes response forwarding much easier at ring connectors. In both single-ring and hierarchical-ring networks, request and response packets are routed in a way so that clients on the same ring observe the same round-trip delay.

Figure 7c is a tree network. Each client is a leaf node and the controller connects to the tree root. The root node and the interior nodes of the tree are tree routers. A tree router forwards requests from its

Algorithm 1 Arbiter with Bandwidth Control

```
 1: procedure REQUESTSCHEDULING(childList, bandwidthList)
 2:    histList ← 0              ▷ Initialize each child's history bits to be zero
 3:    while True do
 4:        activeChildren ← ∅              ▷ Children with requests ready
 5:        hungryChildren ← ∅  ▷ Children with unmet bandwidth targets
 6:        priorityChildren ← ∅        ▷ Children without bandwidth limits
 7:        for i = 1, 2, . . . , LENGTH(childList) do
 8:            c ← childList[i]
 9:            if c has requests ready to send then
10:                activeChildren ← activeChildren ∪ {c}
11:            ▷ hist: number of requests forwarded in the past period
12:            hist ← GETNUMOFONES(histList[i])
13:            if hist < bandwidthList[i].value then
14:                hungryChildren ← hungryChildren ∪ {c}
15:            if bandwidthList[i].limit ≠ True then
16:                priorityChildren ← priorityChildren ∪ {c}
17:        if activeChildren ∩ hungryChildren ≠ ∅ then
18:            candidates ← activeChildren ∩ hungryChildren
19:        else if activeChildren ∩ priorityChildren ≠ ∅ then
20:            candidates ← activeChildren ∩ priorityChildren
21:        ▷ Select the winner from candidates using round-robin
22:        winner ← ROUNDROBIN(candidates)
23:        Forward a request from winner to the output port
24:        for i = 1, 2, . . . , LENGTH(childList) do ▷ Update history bits
25:            if childList[i] is winner then
26:                histList[i] ← histList[i] ≪ 1 + 1
27:            else
28:                histList[i] ← histList[i] ≪ 1
29: end procedure
```

children to its parent node using an arbiter, which is a K-to-1 MUX with bandwidth control, where K is the number of children. Algorithm 1 describes how the arbiter schedules requests from multiple children to the parent node given the bandwidth allocation information of each child. The bandwidth allocation information contains the bandwidth target, which is the number of requests that need to be served within a fixed period of time, and the bandwidth upper limit, which indicates whether the arbiter is allowed to forward requests from the child after its bandwidth target is met. The arbiter first forwards requests from hungry children whose bandwidth targets have not been met yet. If there are no hungry children, the arbiter then forwards requests from children which do not have bandwidth upper limits. If there are multiple candidates, a round-robin algorithm is used to select a winner. The tree router is also responsible for forwarding responses from the parent node to its children based on the requester ID tagged with the response.

The three kinds of network topologies shown in Figure 7 implement different cost-performance tradeoffs. The single-ring network has low design complexity but introduces long network latency when there is a large number of clients. Compared to the single-ring, the hierarchical-ring network has better network scalability with slightly more area overhead introduced by ring connectors. The tree network has the lowest network latency among the three networks but a tree router is much more complicated than a ring connector, especially when the tree router has a large number of children.

Constructing an optimized memory network usually involves the exploration of cost-performance tradeoffs, which may vary from application to application. For example, a program with high data locality may only require a simple cache network, since most memory requests are served in first-level caches, while a program with lower data locality and more memory clients may prefer a tree-based cache network, which has better scalability. In addition, even if a topology has been selected, placing memory clients in the network may still be challenging when the memory clients of the target program

have different latency and bandwidth demands due to asymmetric memory access behavior. A deeply-pipelined client may be able to tolerate longer network latency but have larger bandwidth demands, while a latency-oriented client may be more sensitive to network latency but have smaller bandwidth demands. Therefore, it is essential to develop mechanisms to automate the design space exploration.

7. COMPILER OPTIMIZATION

To automate the construction of memory networks optimized for a particular application, we extend LMC with more detailed program introspection and optimization algorithms for selecting an optimal cache network. Figure 4 shows the extended LEAP compilation flow, which optionally includes profiling compilation to explore the network design tradeoffs on a per-application basis. During profiling compilation, a network profiler is constructed with program instrumentation hardware. The target program is then run with several test configurations to obtain the runtime information of memory access behavior for each memory client. Finally, the target program is recompiled and an optimized memory network is constructed based on the program instrumentation results. Section 7.1 describes the proposed network profiler and how we characterize the memory access behavior for each memory client. Section 7.2 introduces the algorithms by which the compiler synthesizes an optimized network.

7.1 Program Introspection

The goal of a profiling compilation is to understand the memory access behavior of each memory client and to examine the network design tradeoffs for the target application. To evaluate the performance impact of various network configurations, we could build the system several times, each with a different network implementation. However, this approach is very time consuming since each compilation requires full FPGA synthesis, placement, and routing. To facilitate the design space exploration, we design a dynamically-configurable, application-specific network profiler to emulate different network configurations in a single compilation. This network profiler needs not offer optimal performance. It is a measurement tool and can be used to characterize the latency and bandwidth requirements of each memory client in the target application.

Figure 8 shows an example of the application-specific network profiler, which is automatically constructed during profiling compilation. Program instrumentation logic is inserted at each memory client to monitor various runtime memory access properties, including the total number of requests sent from the client, the average request rate, and the average request queueing delay. The request and response ports of each memory client are connected with FIFOs that can be dynamically configured to delay requests/responses for a certain number of cycles. These *latency FIFOs* can be used to measure each client's network latency sensitivity as well as to emulate different network topologies. To configure the delay of the latency FIFOs at runtime, we utilize the LEAP dynamic parameter service, which allows parameter values to be overwritten at runtime through command-line switches.

In the network profiler, each on-board memory is managed by a separate controller hierarchy, and each memory client is connected to all controllers via memory interleaver logic. A memory interleaver partitions a single private memory's address space into multiple interleaved regions [11]. The size of each interleaved region is also dynamically configurable. Each memory client can be assigned to one of the controllers or to multiple controllers with variable-sized interleaved regions at runtime, enabling the performance evaluation of different partitioning algorithms.

The network profiler represents an ideal network with single-cycle latency by directly connecting each memory client to each

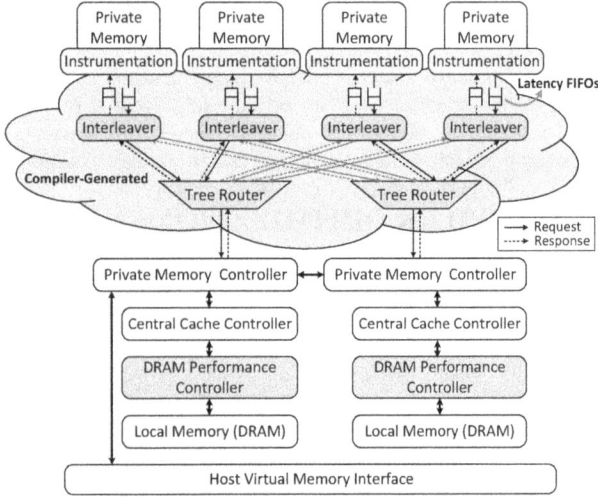

Figure 8: An application-specific network profiler with instrumentation logic and latency FIFOs inserted at each memory client to characterize the client's bandwidth and latency properties.

controller through N-to-1 tree routers, where N is the number of memory clients in the system. For each tree router in the profiler, the assigned bandwidth allocation information, which contains the bandwidth target and the bandwidth upper limit for each client as described in Section 6, is also dynamically configurable, enabling the evaluation of different bandwidth allocation strategies.

The latency FIFOs, the tree routers, and the memory interleavers in the network profiler are all dynamically configurable, enabling the profiler to emulate the performance of different network topologies, such as a singe ring, hierarchical rings, and tree-based networks. For example, to emulate a tree-based network, the delay of latency FIFOs for each client is configured based on the distance between the client and the controller in the target tree network.

This network profiler is a measurement tool that characterizes the network requirements for a particular application and therefore does not need to hit the application's target frequency. Instead, the profiler is usually constructed at a much lower frequency, making the construction of large single-cycle tree routers feasible. In theory, if the network delay and bandwidth allocation for each client are correctly modeled and if the frequency of the profiler is properly scaled down from the application's target frequency, the profiler can achieve very high accuracy. This means the runtime cycle count obtained from the profiling system can be very close to that from the final system with actual network implementation running at target frequency. However, we find that it is difficult to slow down the DRAM operating frequency in the profiling system, resulting in inaccurate performance emulation. To resolve this issue, for each DRAM bank we insert a DRAM performance controller that matches the DRAM latency and throughput to the profiled network.

7.2 Optimized Tree Networks

Armed with the knowledge of program behavior obtained from the network profiler, we can proceed to build a program-optimized cache network. Unless the target program is insensitive to network latency or requires very high operating frequency, the compiler prefers a low-latency tree-based network. The compiler constructs optimized cache networks through three stages: client partitioning, tree topology selection with client placement, and bandwidth allocation.

The compiler first determines the partitioning of the memory clients by passing the profiling results to the partitioning algorithm developed in LMC, which balances the total traffic across controller networks. After partitioning, the next step is to determine the best tree topology of each controller network.

The goal is to construct a tree network that minimizes the network latency impact on program performance. In a tree network, each client is viewed as a tree leaf node, and the controller is the tree root. Ideally, the best solution is to construct a depth-one tree, where the root directly connects to all leaf nodes. However, the complexity of the tree router may result in frequency degradation when there is a large number of leaves. Therefore, to maintain the target frequency, the number of children per tree node is constrained to be no greater than K. To construct an optimal tree network, we need to model the importance of each client, i.e., the impact of placing each leaf node on the overall program performance. This importance factor, which we refer to as latency sensitivity, may be affected by various memory access characteristics of the target client, such as the hit rate of the first-level cache, the memory request rate, or the depth of the computational pipelines. Instead of building a complicated performance model, we define a weight function w_{nd} to be the performance impact introduced by the nth leaf node if placed at tree depth d. This weight function is measured using the network profiler with the following expression:

$$w_{nd} = \frac{\text{runtime(tree with leaf } n \text{ at depth } d \text{ and rest at depth 1)}}{\text{runtime(depth-one tree)}}$$

With this weight function, the original performance maximization problem can be modeled as an optimization problem in which the total tree weight is minimized. Given a leaf node, its weight values are non-decreasing as the tree depth increases. This sets an upper bound for the maximum tree depth given K and the number of leaf nodes. To facilitate problem formulation without the loss of generality, we assume all non-leaf nodes must have exactly K children based on the following two observations: (i) A tree with maximum tree depth D is never optimal if any of the non-leaf nodes at depth $d < (D-1)$ has fewer than K children, because the total tree weight can be decreased by moving a leaf at larger depth to be the child of that node. (ii) We can add dummy leaf nodes with zero weight values so that the non-leaf nodes at depth $D-1$ also have K children, and the dummy leaves would be placed at depth D.

Suppose we are given the number of leaf nodes N, the maximum number of children per node K, the maximum tree depth D, and the weight w_{nd} of placing the nth leaf node at depth d for each $n = 1, \ldots, N, d = 1, \ldots, D$. We can formulate the topology synthesis problem as an integer linear programming (ILP) problem with the following decision variables for each $n = 1, \ldots, N, d = 1, \ldots, D$:

$$\lambda_{nd} \in \{0, 1\} \quad : \quad \text{whether the } n\text{th leaf is at depth } d$$
$$x_d \in \mathbb{Z}_{\geq 0} \quad : \quad \text{number of leaf nodes at depth } d$$
$$y_d \in \mathbb{Z}_{\geq 0} \quad : \quad \text{number of non-leaf nodes at depth } d$$

where $\mathbb{Z}_{\geq 0}$ is the set of nonnegative integers. The problem can be stated formally as:

$$\text{minimize} \quad \sum_{n=1}^{N} \sum_{d=1}^{D} w_{nd} \cdot \lambda_{nd}$$

$$\text{subject to:} \quad \sum_{d=1}^{D} \lambda_{nd} = 1 \quad (n = 1, 2, \ldots, N)$$

$$x_d = \sum_{n=1}^{N} \lambda_{nd} \quad (d = 1, 2, \ldots, D)$$

$$y_0 = 1, \quad y_d + x_d = K \cdot y_{d-1} \quad (d = 1, \ldots, D)$$

$$\lambda_{nd} \in \{0, 1\} \quad (n = 1, \ldots, N; d = 1, \ldots, D)$$

$$x_d \in \mathbb{Z}_{\geq 0}, \quad y_d \in \mathbb{Z}_{\geq 0} \quad (d = 1, \ldots, D)$$

Algorithm 2 Construct a Minimum Weight Tree using DP

1: **procedure** TREECONSTRUCTION($N, D, K, \{a_n\}$)
2:     Sort $\{a_n\}$ so that $a_1 \leq a_2 \leq \cdots \leq a_N$
3:     $V \leftarrow \inf$ $\triangleright$ $V[d][b][m]$: costs
4:     **for** $d = D, D-1, \ldots, 1$ **do** $\triangleright$ Base case: $d = D$
5:         **for** $b = K, 2K, \ldots, \min(\lceil \frac{N}{K} \rceil, (K-1)^d) \cdot K$ **do**
6:             **for** $m = 1, 2, \ldots, N$ **do**
7:                 **if** $b \geq m$ **then** $\triangleright$ Place all m leaves at depth d
8:                     $V[d][b][m] \leftarrow d \cdot \sum_{n=1}^{m} a_n$
9:                 **else if** $d \neq D$ **then**
10:                     $V[d][b][m] \leftarrow$ FINDMIN($V, K, \{a_n\}, d, b, m$)
11: **end procedure**
12: **function** FINDMIN($V, K, \{a_n\}, d, b, m$)
13:     **return** $\min_{x=0,1,..,b\text{-}1} (d \cdot \sum_{n=m\text{-}x+1}^{m} a_n + V[d+1][(b\text{-}x)\cdot K][m\text{-}x])$
14: **end function**

For each leaf node n, if its weight values can be approximated as an affine function of depth d: $w_{nd} = a_n \cdot d + c_n, a_n \geq 0$, the tree topology synthesis problem can be solved using dynamic programming (DP), reducing the problem complexity to polynomial time. We first sort and re-index the leaf nodes so that $a_1 \leq a_2 \leq \cdots \leq a_N$. Under this assumption, there exists an optimal tree in which the depth of node n is nondecreasing in n. Indeed, it is straightforward to verify that if there exists a pair of nodes whose depths are out of order, switching the positions of these nodes would result in a tree with a smaller total weight. This optimality condition allows us to decompose the problem into subproblems at each depth d. Let $V(d, b, m)$ denote the total weight of nodes at depth d or greater in the optimal tree that has m leaf nodes at depth d or greater, and b nodes (including leaf and non-leaf nodes) at depth d. The subproblems can be solved recursively as described in Algorithm 2, and the optimal number of leaf nodes at each depth can be found easily by backtracking the optimal solutions of each subproblem.

After the compiler constructs the optimal tree topology, which minimizes the network latency impact on performance, the final step is to determine the bandwidth allocation for each tree router. The compiler sets each leaf node's bandwidth target based on the client's request rate, which is measured by the program instrumentation logic, and the maximum request rate allowed by the central cache controller and the on-board DRAM. The bandwidth target for a non-root tree router is the sum of the targets of its children. When running multi-program applications, the bandwidth upper limits are set for leaves with large bandwidth demands, in order to control the fairness and prevent throughput-oriented applications from saturating the DRAM bandwidth and slowing latency-oriented applications.

8. EVALUATION

To evaluate the performance of our automatically-generated cache networks, we target a set of single-program and multi-program applications, on the Xilinx VC709 platform, which has two board-level 4GB DDR3 memories. We utilize Vivado HLS to transform HLS benchmarks into RTL implementations and employ Xilinx Vivado 2015.1 for all synthesis and physical implementation work. Also, we use the Gurobi optimizer [27] to solve the ILP problems. All resource utilization and clock rate results in this section are post-place-and-route results.

We examine the following single-program applications, which have a large number of asymmetric memory clients:

Filter: An HLS kernel that implements a filtering algorithm as described in Section 4. The implementation has 8 partitions ($P = 8$) to process independent subtrees and each partition uses 3 LEAP private memories to store different data structures.

Reflect-Tree: An HLS kernel that traverses a binary tree, heap-allocated data structure and swaps the left and right child pointers at each node, producing a mirrored tree in the memory. Similar to *filter*, the tree traversal is managed with a stack, which is implemented with a pointer-linked list. Each list node contains a pointer to a subtree. The head of the list is modified by push and pop operations, which ensures that the tree is traversed in a pre-order fashion. The program visits every node of the tree. Because of its pointer-chasing nature, the execution time of the benchmark is very sensitive to memory access latency. The implementation we target is split into 8 partitions and has 16 LEAP private memories in total.

We also set up the following multi-program applications to evaluate our bandwidth-controllable tree networks:

Cryptosorter-Filter: A multi-program application in which 4 *cryptosorters* [28] are constructed and scheduled to run with 8-partition *filter* ($P = 8$) at the same time. Each *cryptosorter* engine sorts an encrypted memory array, which is stored in a single LEAP private memory, using highly parallel merge-sort engines. It loads a large number of partially ordered lists then merges them using a high-radix sort tree. *Cryptosorter* is throughput-oriented and can consume almost as much bandwidth as the memory system provides. This multi-program application has 28 LEAP private memories: 4 from *cryptosorters* and 24 from *filter*.

Heat-Filter: A multi-program application that includes *heat* and *filter*. *Heat* is a two-dimensional stencil code modeling heat transfer across a surface. *Heat* can be split into multiple worker engines, each of which accesses a LEAP coherent memory. *Heat* is largely throughput-oriented. Workers traverse the shared two-dimensional space in fixed rectangular patterns. In this multi-program application, we construct *filter* with 4 partitions ($P = 4$), and the *heat* implementation has 8 worker engines. The shared memory space for *heat* is interleaved using techniques provided in [11] and is managed by dual coherence controllers. Each controller uses two private memories. This multi-program application has 16 LEAP private memories: 4 from *heat* and 12 from *filter*.

To show the performance benefit of program-optimized cache networks, we compare the performance of the compiler-generated networks with two previous solutions: (i) A baseline LEAP memory hierarchy with a single controller hierarchy to manage accesses to dual DRAMs. All memory clients are connected with a single ring. We refer to this implementation as *baseline*. (ii) A partitioned ring network constructed using LMC. This implementation has two controller hierarchies, and each controller connects to its clients via a single ring. We refer to it as the *single-ring* network configuration in this section. All of our implementations with compiler-generated networks have dual controller hierarchies and the memory clients are partitioned into two groups using the same partitioning mechanism as in the *single-ring* configuration.

8.1 Resource Utilization

Table 1 shows the resource utilization and maximum achievable frequency for different network primitives, including a ring node, which can also be used as a ring connector in hierarchical-ring networks, and K-to-1 bandwidth-controllable tree routers with varying K. As the number of input channels increases, the tree router complexity increases, resulting in larger frequency degradation. In order to maintain the operating frequency of the target application, the compiler needs to set an upper bound of K, limiting the maximum number of children for each interior node in the tree network.

To study the cost-performance tradeoffs of different network topologies, we extract the source code of the compiler-generated network from the target program and build the physical network alone with a standard FPGA tool flow. Table 2 shows the resource

Table 1: Resource utilization for various network primitives

Primitive		Slice LUTS	Slice Registers	f_{max} (MHz)
Ring Node/Connector		626	680	400
Tree Router	$K = 3$	437	577	179
	$K = 5$	826	811	143
	$K = 8$	1337	951	132
	$K = 16$	4501	2840	91
	$K = 32$	19390	11866	71

Table 2: Resource utilization for the cache network in *filter*

Configuration	Slice LUTS	Slice Registers	f_{max} (MHz)
Single Ring	17321	22968	400
Hierarchical Ring	18187	24811	400
Tree ($K = 3$, ILP)	9992	12914	179
Tree ($K = 6$, ILP)	7990	10760	139

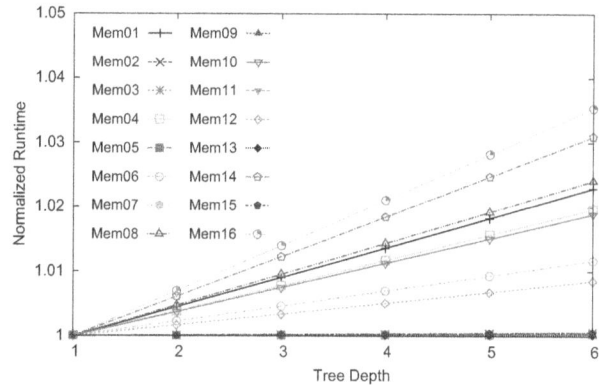

Figure 9: Latency sensitivity of memory clients in *filter*

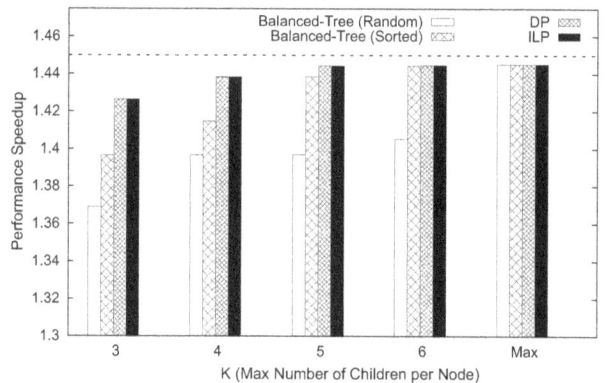

Figure 10: Simulated performance of *filter* with various tree construction algorithms. Performance speedup is calculated by comparing the runtime cycles measured from the network profiler to the runtime of the actual baseline implementation.

utilization and frequency comparison of different network configurations for the cache network in *filter*. Given a fixed number of clients, compared to tree-based networks, ring-based networks can achieve much higher frequency but are less area efficient due to multiple message buffers in each ring node. If programs require high operating frequencies, hierarchical-ring networks, which trade area for maintaining high frequency and improving network scalability, are preferred; otherwise, the compiler would construct tree-based networks, which have lower latency and introduce less area overhead. Since the applications we study all run at a frequency below 130 MHz, as we will show in Section 8.2, tree-based networks with a smaller K are able to maintain the target frequency and provide better performance compared to ring-based networks.

8.2 Single-Program Applications

To construct a tree-based network that minimizes the network latency impact on program performance given an upper bound of K, the compiler first measures the latency sensitivity of each memory client using the network profiler. Figure 9 shows the latency sensitivity measurement of memory clients in *filter*. The data points are client weight values w_{nd} used in the ILP solution as described in Section 7.2. For each memory client in *filter*, its weight values form a straight line and therefore can be approximated as an affine function of tree depth, allowing the compiler to solve the tree construction problem using DP. The slope of each line represents the latency sensitivity, which is a_n in the DP solution described in Section 7.2. The memory clients that store stack data structures are not shown in Figure 9 because they have 100% hit rate in the first-level caches and therefore have zero latency sensitivity. The memory clients storing tree nodes have larger latency sensitivity due to a large number of nonparallel read misses, while the memory clients storing sets of center candidates have higher data locality and thus have latency sensitivity close to zero.

To show the effectiveness of our tree construction algorithms, we first compare the ILP and DP solutions with two other approaches in which a balanced tree with a minimum number of interior nodes is constructed. In a balanced tree, the sum of each leaf's depth is minimized, forming an optimal solution if clients have identical weights. *Balanced-tree (random)* first constructs a balanced tree and then randomly assigns clients to leaves. This approach is also used by our compiler when the profiling compilation is disabled and latency sensitivity of each client is unknown. *Balanced-tree (sorted)* is a greedy approach: it first determines a balanced tree topology and sorts the clients based on their latency sensitivity; then, it assigns latency-sensitive clients to leaves with a smaller tree depth.

Figure 10 shows the simulated performance of *filter* built with the four tree construction algorithms at a varying tree radix K. Since the

weight functions of *filter* clients are very close to affine functions, the tree constructed using DP is identical to that using ILP. As shown in Figure 10, these two solutions achieve good performance even when K is small. When K is larger than 4, the performance of the tree network constructed by DP and ILP is very close to the ideal network (where $K = $ Max). The performance of *balanced-tree (sorted)* increases fast as K increases and reaches a nearly optimal value when $K = 6$, while the performance of *balanced-tree (random)* only slightly increases as K increases from 3 to 6.

We verify the simulated network performance by comparing it to the actual, physical implementation. Since the compiler-generated network module (with K less than 8 for tree-based networks) is not a frequency-limiting module for our test applications, we run all actual, physical implementations at the same frequency to make runtime cycles comparable. Figure 11 shows both the simulated performance and the actual performance of various network configurations for single-program applications. For each network topology, the network profiler is shown to have high accuracy: the performance difference is 1.1%, on average.

In addition, compared to other network topologies, our compiler-optimized tree networks achieve the best performance. For *filter*, the optimized tree network provides a 44% performance gain over the *baseline* and a 18% performance gain over the *single-ring* configuration. For *reflect-tree*, the tree network provides 47% speedup over the *baseline* and 16% speedup over the *single-ring* configuration. We also include a hierarchical-ring configuration, in which the compiler constructs a three-level hierarchical ring based on the latency sensitivity of each client. The hierarchical-ring solution achieves a

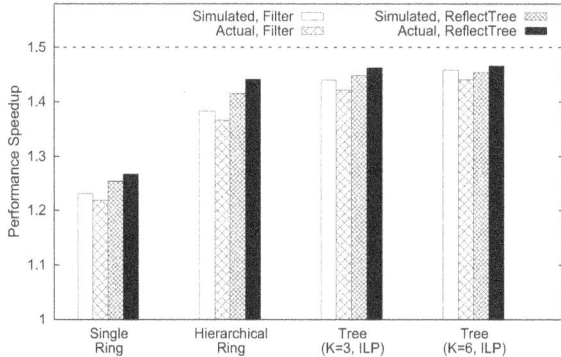

Figure 11: Performance comparison of various network configurations for single-program applications. Performance speedup is calculated by comparing the runtime cycles measured from the profiler and from the actual, physical implementations to the runtime of the actual baseline implementation.

12% performance gain over the *single-ring* configuration for *filter* and a 14% gain for *reflect-tree*, representing an effective approach to reduce the network latency impact at lower complexity.

8.3 Multi-Program Applications

We evaluate the performance of our compiler-optimized cache networks for multi-program applications by comparing the performance slowdown caused by resource sharing. We define the performance ratio r for each program as follows:

$$r = \frac{\text{Performance}_{MP}}{\text{Performance}_{SP}}$$

where Performance_{MP} is the program performance when executing with other programs and Performance_{SP} is the performance measured when executing alone. We also adopt the following fairness metric proposed in [29]:

$$\text{Fairness} = \frac{n}{\sum_{i=1}^{n} \frac{1}{r_i}}$$

where n is the number of programs and r_i is the performance ratio of the ith program. This fairness metric, which ranges from zero to one, is the harmonic mean of performance ratios.

Figure 12 shows the performance comparison of various network configurations when *filer* and *cryptosorter* are scheduled to run simultaneously. To make a fair comparison, we control the number of iterations *filter* executes so that *filter* and *cryptosorter* start and finish at the same time. The performance of *filter* is defined as the number of iterations executed in a fixed period of time. As shown in Figure 12a, *filter* performance slows down a little for *baseline* and *single ring* configurations when *cryptosorter* is constructed on FPGA due to the increased network latency introduced by 4 additional clients. When *filter* is executing with *cryptosorter*, if without bandwidth control, the performance slowdown is over 50% because *cryptosorter* saturates the memory bandwidth, while our bandwidth-controllable tree network reduces the performance slowdown to 5% by limiting the bandwidth consumption of *cryptosorter* clients.

As shown in Figure 12b, when *filter* is constructed, the *cryptosorter* performance slowdown caused by 24 additional clients is larger for the *baseline* and *single-ring* configurations, while the performance of tree-based networks is much less sensitive to the increase of memory clients. When executing with *filter*, if without limitation on bandwidth consumption, *cryptosorter* performance does not slow down because *filter* only consumes little memory

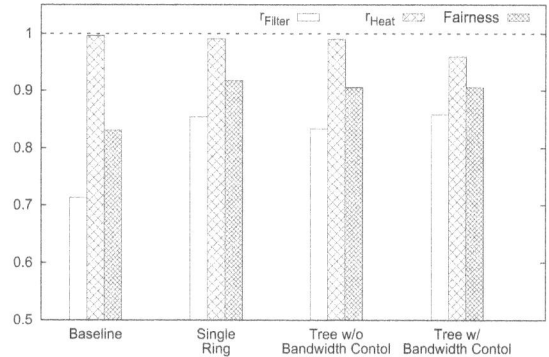

Figure 13: Performance comparison for the *heat-filter* application.

bandwidth. Adding bandwidth limitation to *cryptosorter* clients degrades the *cryptosorter* performance by 13% but achieves much better fairness as shown in Figure 12c.

We also evaluate the performance ratios and fairness for *heat-filter* with different network configurations, as shown in Figure 13. Similar to *cryptosorter*, if without bandwidth limitation, *heat* does not slow down when executing with *filter*, which only has little bandwidth consumption. With partitioned networks, which provide larger memory bandwidth to the clients, the performance slowdown of *filter* is less than 15% when executing with *heat*, even without bandwidth control. The bandwidth consumption of *heat* is smaller than that of *cryptosorter* because of the higher data locality in coherent caches, resulting in a smaller memory bandwidth pressure. Therefore, all partitioned networks can achieve good fairness (above 0.9) when simultaneously executing *heat* and *filter*. Adding bandwidth limitation to *heat* clients in the tree network degrades *heat* performance by 4% and improves *filter* performance by 2%, achieving similar fairness as the tree network without bandwidth control.

9. CONCLUSION

We have presented a feedback-driven compiler that automatically constructs memory networks optimized for the target application. In order to facilitate the design space exploration, we propose a dynamically-configurable network profiler that can be used to characterize the latency and bandwidth requirements of each memory client as well as to evaluate the performance impact introduced by different network topologies. Based on the profiling measurements, the compiler constructs an optimized cache network that minimizes the network latency impact on program performance. Experimental results show that our compiler-optimized network significantly improves the performance of applications that have a large number memory clients with asymmetric memory behavior: it provides a 45% performance gain over the baseline memory network and a 17% gain over the partitioned, ring-based network constructed by LMC, on average. In addition to single-program applications, we also examine a new set of workloads: multi-program applications, which we view as representative of future FPGA deployments. When multiple user programs are executing simultaneously, our compiler-generated network is shown to achieve good cross-application fairness through application-specific bandwidth control.

In this paper, we have demonstrated that applications with asymmetric memory clients can benefit from program-optimized memory networks. As modern FPGA platforms have begun to include asymmetric on-board memory controllers [30][12], one direction for future work is to explore resource-aware memory network optimizations for asymmetric memory controllers with different latency and bandwidth characteristics.

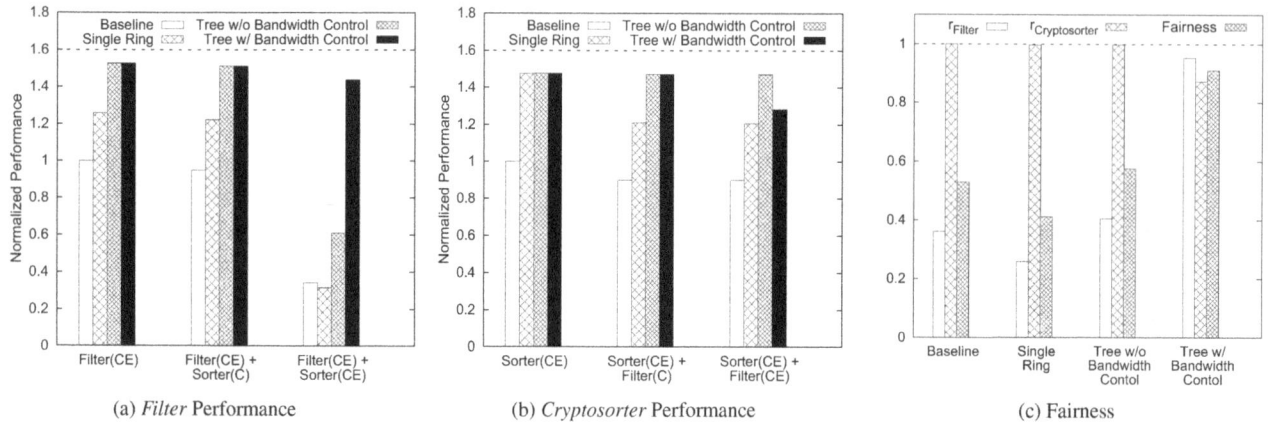

(a) *Filter* Performance   (b) *Cryptosorter* Performance   (c) Fairness

Figure 12: Performance comparison of various network configurations for the *cryptosorter-filter* application. (a) and (b) show the performance of *filter* and *cryptosorter* under different program configuration settings, where C indicates the program hardware is constructed on FPGA and E indicates the program is executed. For each program, the performance is normalized to the performance of the implementation where the program is constructed alone with the baseline memory network.

10. REFERENCES

[1] J. Villarreal, A. Park, W. Najjar, and R. Halstead. Designing modular hardware accelerators in C with ROCCC 2.0. In *FCCM*, 2010.

[2] J. Cong, B. Liu, S. Neuendorffer, et al. High-level synthesis for FPGAs: From prototyping to deployment. *TCAD*, 30(4):473–491, 2011.

[3] A. Canis, J. Choi, M. Aldham, et al. LegUp: An open-source high-level synthesis tool for FPGA-based processor/accelerator systems. *TECS*, 13(2):24, 2013.

[4] Vivado high-level synthesis. http://www.xilinx.com/products/ design-tools/vivado/integration/esl-design.html.

[5] R. Kirchgessner, G. Stitt, A. George, and H. Lam. VirtualRC: a virtual FPGA platform for applications and tools portability. In *FPGA*, 2012.

[6] E. S. Chung, J. C. Hoe, and K. Mai. CoRAM: An in-fabric memory abstraction for FPGA-based computing. In *FPGA*, 2011.

[7] K. Fleming, H.-J. Yang, M. Adler, and J. Emer. The LEAP FPGA operating system. In *FPL*, 2014.

[8] J. Choi, K. Nam, A. Canis, et al. Impact of cache architecture and interface on performance and area of FPGA-based processor/parallel-accelerator systems. In *FCCM*, 2012.

[9] H.-J. Yang, K. Fleming, M. Adler, F. Winterstein, and J. Emer. Scavenger: Automating the construction of application-optimized memory hierarchies. In *FPL*, 2015.

[10] F. Winterstein, K. Fleming, H.-J. Yang, J. Wickerson, and G. Constantinides. Custom-sized caches in application-specific memory hierarchies. In *FPT*, 2015.

[11] H.-J. Yang, K. Fleming, M. Adler, F. Winterstein, and J. Emer. LMC: Automatic resource-aware program-optimized memory partitioning. In *FPGA*, 2016.

[12] Accelerating datacenter workloads. http://fpl2016.org/slides/Gupta%20--%20Accelerating% 20Datacenter%20Workloads.pdf.

[13] M. Adler, K. Fleming, A. Parashar, M. Pellauer, and J. Emer. LEAP Scratchpads: Automatic memory and cache management for reconfigurable logic. In *FPGA*, 2011.

[14] H.-J. Yang, K. Fleming, M. Adler, and J. Emer. LEAP shared memories: Automating the construction of FPGA coherent memories. In *FCCM*, 2014.

[15] K. E. Fleming. *Scalable Reconfigurable Computation Leveraging Latency Insensitive Channels*. PhD thesis, MIT, Cambridge, MA, 2012.

[16] M. Jun, S. Yoo, and E.-Y. Chung. Mixed integer linear programming-based optimal topology synthesis of cascaded crossbar switches. In *ASP-DAC*, 2008.

[17] M. Jun, S. Yoo, and E.-Y. Chung. Topology synthesis of cascaded crossbar switches. *TCAD*, 28(6):926–930, 2009.

[18] A. Cilardo and E. Fusella. Design automation for application-specific on-chip interconnects: A survey. *Integration, the VLSI Journal*, 52:102–121, 2016.

[19] A. Cilardo, E. Fusella, L. Gallo, and A. Mazzeo. Automated synthesis of FPGA-based heterogeneous interconnect topologies. In *FPL*, 2013.

[20] Y.-T. Chen and J. Cong. Interconnect synthesis of heterogeneous accelerators in a shared memory architecture. In *ISLPED*, 2015.

[21] E. Matthews, L. Shannon, and A. Fedorova. Polyblaze: From one to many bringing the Microblaze into the multicore era with Linux SMP support. In *FPL*, 2012.

[22] H. Lange, T. Wink, and A. Koch. MARC II: A parametrized speculative multi-ported memory subsystem for reconfigurable computers. In *DATE*, 2011.

[23] V. Mirian and P. Chow. FCache: A system for cache coherent processing on FPGAs. In *FPGA*, 2012.

[24] D. Göhringer, L. Meder, M. Hübner, and J. Becker. Adaptive multi-client network-on-chip memory. In *RECONFIG*, 2011.

[25] E. Matthews, N. C. Doyle, and L. Shannon. Design space exploration of L1 data caches for FPGA-based multiprocessor systems. In *FPGA*, 2015.

[26] T. Kanungo, D. M. Mount, N. S. Netanyahu, et al. An efficient k-means clustering algorithm: Analysis and implementation. *TPAMI*, 24(7):881–892, 2002.

[27] Gurobi optimization. http://www.gurobi.com.

[28] K. Fleming, M. King, M. C. Ng, A. Khan, and M. Vijayaraghavan. High-throughput pipelined mergesort. In *MEMOCODE*, 2008.

[29] H. Vandierendonck and A. Seznec. Fairness metrics for multi-threaded processors. *CAL*, 10(1):4–7, 2011.

[30] Nallatech 510t FPGA accelerator. http://www.nallatech.com/ nallatech-510t-fpga-datacenter-acceleration/.

NAND-NOR: A Compact, Fast, and Delay Balanced FPGA Logic Element

Zhihong Huang[†] Xing Wei[†] Grace Zgheib[‡] Wei Li[†] Yu Lin[†]
Zhenghong Jiang[†] Kaihui Tu[†] Paolo Ienne[‡] Haigang Yang[†]

[†]Chinese Academy of Sciences
Institute of Electronics, Beijing, China
{huangzhihong, liw, linyu, kelv, yanghg}@mail.ie.ac.cn

[‡]Ecole Polytechnique Fédérale de Lausanne (EPFL)
School of Computer and Communication Sciences, 1015 Lausanne, Switzerland
{grace.zgheib, paolo.ienne}@epfl.ch

ABSTRACT

The And-Inverter Cone has been introduced as an alternative logic element to the look-up table in FPGAs, since it improves their performance and resource utilization. However, further analysis of the AIC design showed that it suffers from the delay discrepancy problem. Furthermore, the existing AIC cluster design is not properly optimized and has some unnecessary logic that impedes its performance. Thus, we propose in this work a more efficient logic element called NAND-NOR and a delay-balanced dual-phased multiplexers for the input crossbar. Our simulations show that the NAND-NOR brings substantial reduction in delay discrepancy with a 14% to 46% delay improvement when compared to AICs. And, along with the other modifications, it reduces the total cluster area by about 27%, when compared to the reference AIC cluster. Testing the new architecture on a large set of benchmarks shows an improvement of the delay-area product by about 44% and 21% for the MCNC and VTR benchmarks, respectively, when compared to LUT-based cluster. This improvement reaches 31% and 19%, respectively, when compared to the AIC-based architecture.

1. INTRODUCTION

Since their first introduction in 1984, *Field-Programmable Gate Arrays (FPGAs)* have increasingly become the main computing power in various fields due to their flexibility and programmability. Having a short time-to-market, reconfigurable capabilities and fast programmability makes the FPGA a reliable computing device in modern digital systems [4, 11].

Most current commercial FPGAs are *SRAM-based (Static Random Access Memory)* FPGAs and have an island-style architecture. In both commercial FPGAs as well as academic research, the FPGA architecture relies mainly on the *Look-up Tables (LUTs)* as the main logic elements in the clusters [2]. A K-input LUT can implement any combinational logic function with K inputs. However, the flexibility of the LUTs comes at the expense of circuit area and delay. Undeniably, the improvement of both the area efficiency and the performance of reconfigurable logic architectures has always been one of the main targets of academic and industrial research [1, 6].

Inspired by modern synthesis tools [3], a new logic element was recently proposed as an alternative logic element for FPGAs [12]. Having a conic structure and composed of multi-level configurable AND and inverter gates, this element is called *And-Inverter Cone (AIC)*. When compared with LUTs, AICs have many advantages: (1) the AIC has a high number of inputs and outputs, which allows it to implement larger, multi-output functions; (2) the AIC structure is similar to the regular expression of Boolean algebra, which allows it to satisfy the logic synthesis requirements and abide by its optimizations for an improved performance; (3) the AIC's area and delay increase linearly and logarithmically with the number of inputs, as opposed to the exponential and linear increase of the LUTs, respectively; (4) intermediate results can be directly reused through the intermediate outputs (known as side outputs) of the AIC, reducing the logic duplication and improving the overall circuit area.

Taking all these advantages into consideration, the AIC is presented as a promising alternative to LUTs in FPGAs. Zgheib et al. [15] presented several AIC cluster architectures, compared them with a state-of-the-art LUT-based FPGA architecture, and concluded that both the AIC and LUT-based architectures have their respective advantages and disadvantages, depending on the application. A new depth-constrained technology-mapping tool was also proposed [7] to optimize the circuits for AICs and improve their results, especially in terms of used area. However, a potential issue in the AIC design has been ignored in the existing research, so far: the input-to-output delay of the AIC can vary a lot, depending on the cone configuration. This variation can have a major impact and is of high importance, since, given

FPGA '17, February 22-24, 2017, Monterey, CA, USA

© 2017 ACM. ISBN 978-1-4503-4354-1/17/02...$15.00

DOI: http://dx.doi.org/10.1145/3020078.3021750

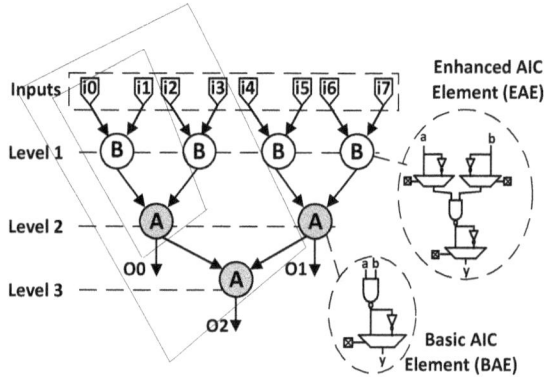

Figure 1: A 3-level AIC (AIC3) with its two types of nodes: Enhanced AIC Element (EAE) and Basic AIC Element (BAE).

its multi-level conic structure, any delay variation that exists in a single AIC node propagates from one level to the other and gets accumulated in the process before reaching the final output. The delay glitch caused by this discrepancy in the cone affects the stability of the overall function and may induce additional dynamic power consumption.

In this paper, we aim at solving the AIC's delay discrepancy problem and propose a more efficient logic element with balanced delays, called NAND-NOR. We also present an improved cluster architecture that reduces the area overhead added with the introduction of AICs into the logic clusters.

The paper starts by presenting the original AIC structure and the delay discrepancy problem, in Section 2. Then, Section 3 proposes the NAND-NOR logic element and analyzes it characteristics. We then introduce a DDM input crossbar and optimized NAND-NOR-based cluster architecture in Section 4. We compare the new architecture, with all its new features, against an LUT-based architecture [15], similar to Stratix-IV, and AIC-based architecture [15] in Section 5. Finally, we summarize our results and conclude in Section 6.

2. LIMITATIONS IN THE AIC DESIGN

The And-Inverter Cone is a multi-level binary tree of cells where each cell is composed of an AND gate with programmable inversions [15], as shown in Figure 1. The AIC has two types of nodes: the *Enhanced AIC Element (EAE)* and the *Basic AIC Element (BAE)*, where the EAE is basically a BAE with programmable input inversions [13].

Figure 2 shows the transistor implementation of the BAE which can be configured as either an AND or NAND gate by selecting either the inverted or non-inverted output, respectively. Despite their many advantages, AICs still have limitations, some of which are already know [15]. However, in this section, we highlight the delay discrepancy problem as well as the inefficiency in the AIC-based cluster design.

2.1 Delay discrepancy problem

Analysis of the AIC shows that the propagation delay of a single node varies with the configuration of the AIC. If the output inversion is needed, then the signal has an additional transistor to go through, increasing the input-to-output delay. This difference in delay can accumulate with every node, as the signal traverses the different AIC levels. To better evaluate the delay difference, we implement the

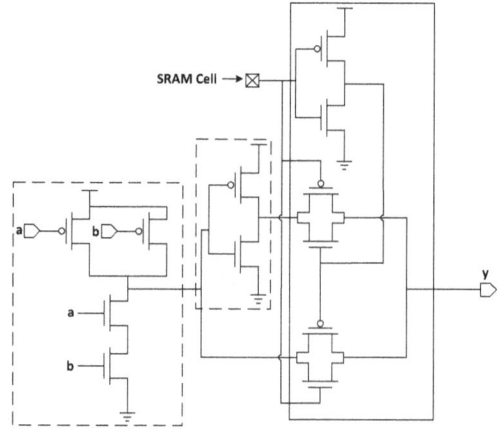

Figure 2: The transistor-level implementation of a BAE.

Table 1: Delay of the AIC, with up to 6 levels, for both the best and worst-case scenarios (ps).

AIC level	Delay of IO path with no inversions	Delay of IO path with all inversions	Average delay	ΔT	σ
AIC6	389.6	577.6	483.6	188	94
AIC5	341.6	504.8	423.2	163.2	81.6
AIC4	274.4	410.4	342.4	136	68
AIC3	215.2	323.2	269.2	108	54
AIC2	148.32	228.8	188.56	80.48	40.24
AIC1	90.64	143.92	117.28	53.28	26.64

AIC cluster with a 40nm standard CMOS technology using the Cadence Virtuoso platform in custom design flow. The delay is measured using Spectre simulator, in typical technology corner. To be able to compare our results with the latest work on AICs [15], we kept the same design environment and simulation parameters. Table 1 shows the simulated delay of up to a 6-level AIC, in the two extreme cases: (1) when no programmable inversion is used in any of the levels and (2) when all the programmable inversions are used in every level, between the input and output. It also shows the difference in delay (ΔT) between the worst and best-case scenarios, as well as the standard deviation.

The results show that, as the number of levels increases, the delay difference between the two extreme cases increases. This is due to the accumulation effect mentioned earlier, which makes the delay discrepancy a critical problem for AICs. For the 6-level AIC, the delay difference can reach 188ps, which means that the delay of the AIC increases by about 50% when all the inversions as added, as opposed to the case when none of the inversions is used. This delay difference is further aggravated in the case of cascaded multi-level AICs.

In combinational circuits, having different arrival times of input signals that must transit simultaneously can result in signal competition and cause signal spikes known as glitches. Such glitches can affect the stability of the circuit or even cause errors. In general, any discrepancy caused by the routing paths can be handled by router's timing analysis. However, since the existing CAD tools do not take into consideration the delay discrepancy due to the logic cell configuration, this problem must be handled separately,

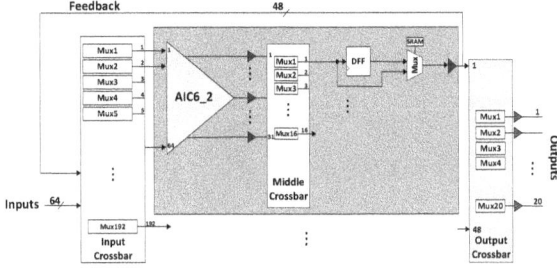

Figure 3: The AIC cluster architecture adopted in the latest AIC paper [15].

otherwise, it will affect the reliability of the AIC-based FP-GAs.

2.2 Inefficiency in existing AIC cluster design

The reference AIC cluster architecture [15] is shown in Figure 3. Although the multiple AIC outputs are highly advantageous in reducing the circuit area, managing all these outputs at the cluster level requires some dedicated hardware. For instance, the middle crossbar is a set of 2-level multiplexers, dedicated solely to reducing the number of AIC outputs; it has a substantial contribution to the delay and area of the cluster.

An analysis of this AIC cluster design shows that the crossbars contribute to about 79% of the total cluster area, and about 43% to 70% of the delay, depending on the selected path. This shows that the crossbars have a major effect on the performance of the AIC-based cluster. Thus, any reduction in the size or number of the crossbar multiplexers used can result in a substantial area reduction and efficiency improvement.

3. NAND-NOR CONE

To overcome the limitations of the AICs discussed in Section 2, especially the delay discrepancy problem, we propose a new cone-based logic element called NAND-NOR.

3.1 NAND-NOR Cone Structure

The NAND-NOR is a new logic element with a conic structure, similar to the AIC, but with nodes that can operate either as a NAND or NOR function, as shown in Figure 4. The NAND-NOR has as well an enhanced type of nodes, used at the first level of the cone, to which programmable input inversions are added. According to De Morgan's theorem [8, 5], any logic function expressed as a combination of AND and NAND operations, which is the representation used by AICs, can be transformed into a function of NAND and NOR operations.

Having programmable inversions at the inputs of the Enhanced NAND-NOR Element adds to its flexibility and allows it to implement eight basic functions: AB, $\bar{A}B$, $A\bar{B}$, $\bar{A}\bar{B}$, $A + B$, $\bar{A} + B$, $\bar{A} + \bar{B}$ and $A + \bar{B}$. Thus, despite the difference in design and configuration, the NAND-NOR and AIC can be logically equivalent and the NAND-NOR can replace the AIC without major CAD tool modifications.

3.2 NAND-NOR Design and Optimization

The transistor-level implementation of the NAND-NOR is shown in Figure 5. As mentioned earlier, and shown in Figures 5b and 5c, the NAND-NOR can be configured either as a NAND gate or a NOR gate, respectively. Compared

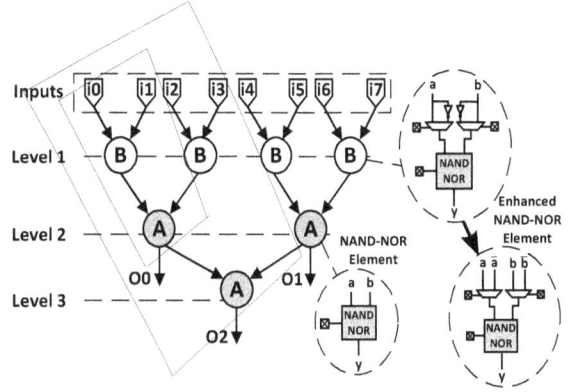

Figure 4: A 3-level NAND-NOR with its different nodes.

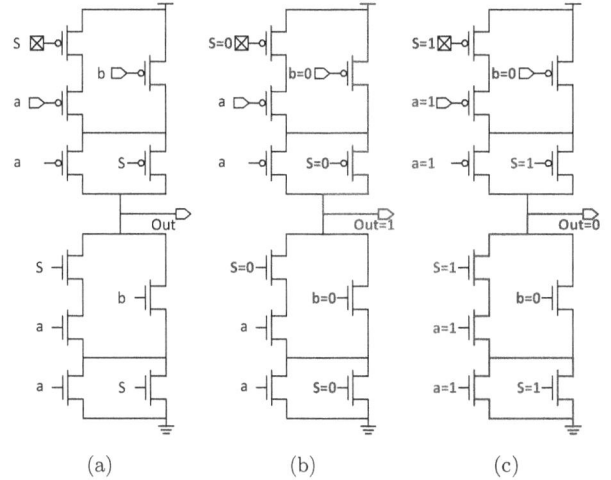

Figure 5: The transistor-level implementation of the NAND-NOR with two configurations: (b) as a NAND gate with input b equals to zero, and (c) as a NOR gate with input a equals to one and b equals to zero.

with the BAE, the NAND-NOR implementation has a simpler structure. The critical path traversed by the signal is reduced from 4 transistors to 2, while the total number of transistors is also reduced from 12 to 10.

We design the NAND-NOR cone circuit using the same technology node and simulate it using the same steps explained in Section 2. Our simulations show that some delay discrepancy exists also between the different NAND-NOR configurations. However this discrepancy can be minimized or even eliminated, theoretically, by optimizing the different transistor sizes. Table 2 shows the post-layout delay results for every level of a 6-level NAND-NOR while temporarily ignoring the input inversions. In this table, the nor_a column shows the delay when the path goes through the a input of the NOR gate of every NAND-NOR level. The same logic applies for the remaining columns. ΔT is the maximum delay difference among the different paths and configurations, with respect to the average delay.

When compared with the AIC [15], the NAND-NOR offers between 14% and 46% improvement in average delay, with 43% to 59% reduction in delay discrepancy, and 64% to 71% improvement in delay's standard deviation, for the different levels. When considering a 6-level cone, the NAND-NOR offers also about 23% area reduction.

Table 2: Delay of the different configurations of a 6-level NAND-NOR (ps).

NAND-NOR Level	nor_a	nor_b	nand_a	nand_b	Average Delay	Average Delay Improvement	ΔT	ΔT Improvement	σ	σ Improvement
6	433.6	423.2	372.8	466.4	424	14.06%	51.2	45.53%	33.59	64.27%
5	375.2	372	321.6	404	368.2	14.94%	46.6	42.89%	29.65	63.66%
4	300.8	298.4	259.2	324.8	295.8	15.75%	36.6	46.18%	23.52	65.42%
3	225.6	224.8	196.8	246.4	223.4	20.50%	26.6	50.74%	17.63	67.35%
2	151.36	151.84	135.04	168	151.56	24.41%	16.52	58.95%	11.65	71.04%
1	67.92	84	76.64	92.24	80.2	46.23%	12.28	53.90%	8.98	66.27%

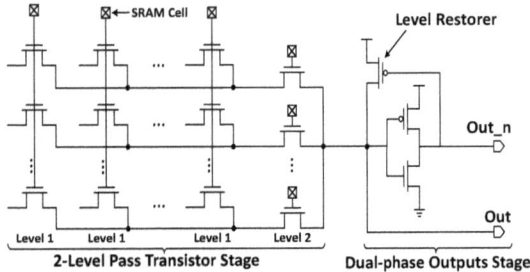

Figure 6: Delay-balanced Dual-phased Multiplexer (DDM).

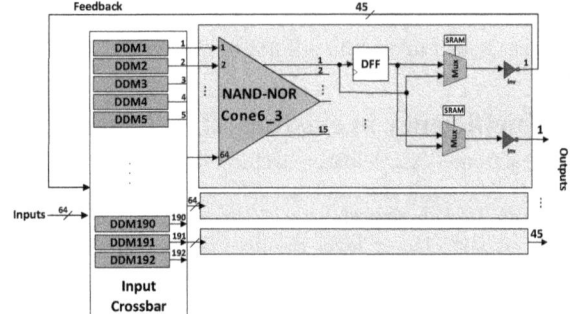

Figure 7: Optimized NAND-NOR cone cluster.

4. DDM CROSSBAR AND CLUSTER OPTIMIZATION

In this section, we try to introduce additional design improvements by balancing the delays of the input signals of the cone through an enhanced input crossbar design. We also try to optimize the overall cluster and improve its inefficiencies through some architectural modifications.

4.1 DDM input crossbar

While testing the NAND-NOR, we noticed that the programmable input inversions for the first level nodes introduce additional delay variations into the design. These cone inputs are delivered using an input crossbar, composed of 192 multiplexers, as shown in Figure 3. Each multiplexer connects only to a single input of the cone, which will then be either inverted or not, depending on the configuration. By that, the load of such multiplexers remains within an acceptable range. Taking all these characteristics into consideration, we suggest using a Delay-balanced Dual-phased Multiplexer (DDM) to deliver the cone inputs.

Figure 6 details the transistor level design of a DDM multiplexer. The 2-level pass-transistor stage is similar to the one used in the Stratix series products [9]. Having the dual-phase outputs stage, we optimize the transistor sizing of the circuit and get both the output and its negation with relatively similar delays.

Having the input crossbar designed as a DDM, the programmable input inversions of the first level nodes of the NAND-NOR cone can be removed, as shown in Figure 4. This results in about 28% area reduction for a 6-level cone, when comparing with the area of the AIC [15]. On top of that, the delay of the crossbar itself is also improved by about 56% due to (i) the removal of the second inverter of the output buffer and (ii) additional transistor optimizations.

4.2 Optimized Logic Cluster

We also try to improve the AIC cluster architecture of Figure 3 by removing the output crossbar and connecting the outputs directly to the connection boxes as the cluster outputs. By doing so, we can reduce the area and delay overhead by limiting the routing flexibility of the outputs.

We also notice that the outputs of the AIC's second level require about half of the cluster resources used to manage the AIC outputs, while being used only to map relatively simple functions. With the help of the new depth-constrained technology-mapping tool [7], we were able to restrict the NAND-NOR's output level to at least the third level, as shown in Figure 7. In this case, the 6-level cone, labeled *cone6_3*, has its outputs generated from level 3 to level 6. This reduces the total number of outputs (of the three cones) from 93 to 45, allowing us to remove the middle crossbar of the cluster.

In addition to that, the existing cluster design uses a single 2-to-1 multiplexer to select between the combinational and sequential versions of each output, for both the feedback and direct output signals. However, such a design can be rather inefficient since, whenever an application requires the same signal in both its combinational and sequential versions, the function generating the output is usually duplicated. To avoid such situations, we add a second multiplexer, as shown in Figure 7, to split between the signal used for feedback and the one used for direct output, allowing for better flexibility.

All the modifications to the cluster, resulting in an optimized NAND-NOR-based architecture, are depicted in Figure 7. The new cluster includes a half populated DDM input crossbar and three NAND-NOR Cone6_3, with outputs starting at the third level.

Figure 8 shows the delay and area comparison between the existing AIC-based cluster architecture [15], a NAND-NOR-based cluster but with a regular input crossbar (labeled *NAND-NOR only*), and the cluster design of Figure 7 with both the NAND-NOR and a DDM input crossbar. The results show that our optimized logic cluster is the most optimal in terms of both delay and area, among the three designs. When compared with the existing AIC cluster [15], our optimized NAND-NOR cluster results in a 27% area re-

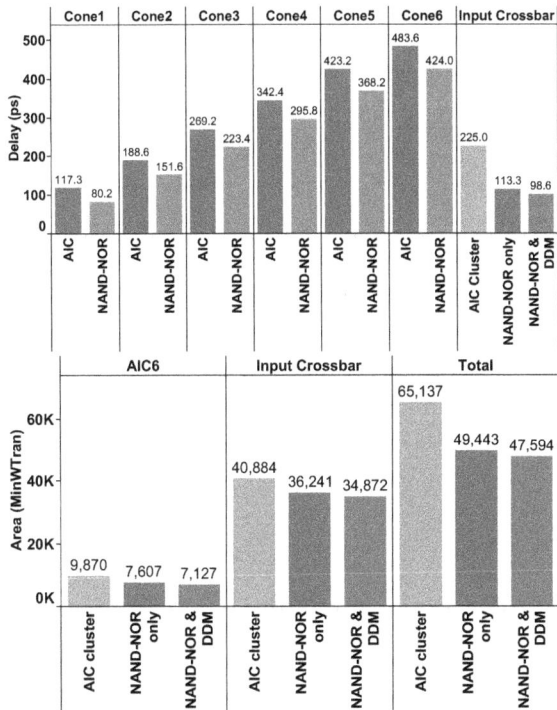

Figure 8: Area and delay comparison of cluster architectures. Note: AIC cluster refers to the reference AIC architecture [15] shown in Figure 3.

duction. Although the delay improvements vary depending on the selected cone configuration, we show that, on average, the NAND-NOR and DDM crossbar are the most delay efficient.

5. EXPERIMENTS AND RESULTS

Now that the cluster is designed and optimized, we test it on a set of benchmarks and compare it to the state-of-the-art architectures.

5.1 Experimental Setup

To test the efficiency of our NAND-NOR cluster, we run the experiments using the VTR flow [10]. However, we replace the default technology mapper, ABC, with the depth-constrained AIC mapper [7]. In fact, since the architectures of the NAND-NOR and AIC are similar and their functionalities can be logically equivalent, we were able to directly use the same netlist generated by the AIC technology mapper [7] and just change the configuration of the cones to support the NAND-NOR. In both cases, the mapper uses the side outputs of the cones.

The overall CAD flow used in the experimental setup is detailed in Figure 9. The area and delay parameters derived in the simulations of Section 4.2 are added to the architecture file, so that they can be used in the packing and routing steps. The other architectural parameters are set to be identical to the reference architecture [15] for a better comparison; more specifically, we use unidirectional wires, a segment length of 4, Wilton switch boxes, and a variable channel width. We also define F_s, Fc_{in} and Fc_{out} to be 3, 0.15, and 0.1 respectively. We select the big 20 MCNC

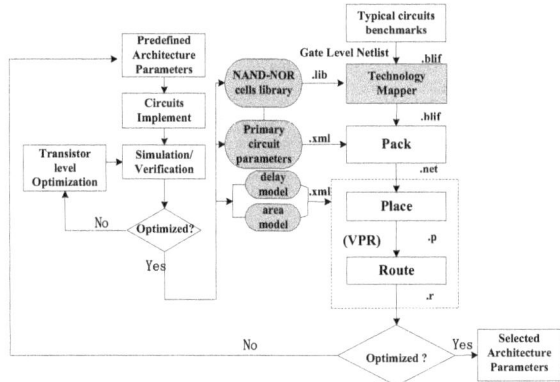

Figure 9: Experimental CAD flow.

benchmarks and the VTR benchmarks [14] that finish within a reasonable time, to test the architecture.

5.2 Results

The selected benchmarks were tested on both the reference AIC architecture and the NAND-NOR architecture. Table 3 shows the delay and area improvement for the MCNC and VTR benchmarks when tested on the NAND-NOR-based FPGA with DDM input crossbar, compared with the LUT-based Stratix IV-like architecture [15] and the reference AIC-based architecture [15]. It also lists the number of clusters needed to implement the circuits with each architecture.

Although, generally, the NAND-NOR architecture does not reduce the number of used clusters, the cluster itself is smaller, as shown in Section 4, which results in an average total area reduction. When compared to the LUT-based FPGA, the delay-area product of the NAND-NOR-based architecture shows 44% and 21% improvement, for the MCNC and VTR benchmarks, respectively. And when compared to the AIC-based architecture, the delay-area product is improved by 31% and 19%, for the MCNC and VTR benchmarks, respectively.

The NAND-NOR architecture can bring worse results in one of these two cases: (i) the delay is compromised for the sake of area improvement (or vice versa) which is mainly decided by the packing and routing algorithms like, for example, for the *steriovision3* benchmark; and (ii) both the delay and area are worse than the LUT-based architecture, which happens in the case of *steriovision1*, a known case for which the technology mapper performs poorly [7].

6. CONCLUSIONS

Several AIC-based FPGA architectures have been previously explored; however, none of these explorations considered the delay discrepancy problem which is particularly important in conic structures like the AIC, due to the multi-level accumulation effect.

An improved and delay balanced logic cone was introduced along with an optimized FPGA cluster architecture, with a DDM input crossbar. With these modifications, we were able to significantly reduce the delay discrepancy, improve the system stability, and provide significant area and delay reduction.

When compared to the AIC structure, the optimized NAND-NOR cone provides about 14% to 46% delay improvement, depending on the number of levels, while the

Table 3: Area, delay and number of clusters for the NAND-NOR architecture vs. the Stratix IV and the AIC architectures.

MCNC Benchmark	Delay Reduction (%)		Area Reduction (%)		Number of Clusters			VTR Benchmark	Delay Reduction (%)		Area Reduction (%)		Number of Clusters		
	w.r.t. LUT	w.r.t. AIC	w.r.t. LUT	w.r.t. AIC	LUT	AIC	NAND-NOR		w.r.t. LUT	w.r.t. AIC	w.r.t. LUT	w.r.t. AIC	LUT	AIC	NAND-NOR
s298	23.45	7.57	50.85	28.27	52	43	49	stereovision0	-40.41	6.45	17.98	17.84	1041	1417	1554
pdc	30.19	19.94	30.17	27.82	193	151	153	ch_intrinsics	28.84	4.36	40.98	13.84	16	13	13
diffeq	29	5.45	18.42	4.72	58	40	48	diffeq1	0.01	5.53	10.45	4.88	37	55	67
alu4	32.79	5.62	24.65	-0.14	62	44	51	mkSMAdapter4B	22.48	11.56	24.57	13.65	114	91	111
misex3	31.94	17.7	34.71	13.47	56	48	47	boundtop	10.89	14.18	32.3	23.39	172	170	182
apex2	22.31	14.74	53.49	32.9	80	76	74	or1200	0.9	4.06	-16.15	18.56	205	198	243
seq	32.81	19.02	42.37	21.69	76	62	61	stereovision1	-48.47	3.67	-19.82	3.5	986	1495	1693
s38417	-23.39	9.45	39.09	36	222	278	315	mkDelayWorker32B	44.84	-0.94	43.49	15.04	55	39	39
bigkey	10.4	4.57	44.77	23.37	80	66	75	raygentop	-0.36	9.83	21.17	20.3	158	194	215
s385841	12.93	-2.64	26.55	16.94	198	152	200	stereovision3	-6.18	-24.91	39.8	15.06	15	12	18
apex4	18.51	16.92	37.45	14.52	57	56	55	diffeq2	-2.36	7.1	1.36	9.52	25	55	64
tseng	3.45	-8.8	8.16	23.94	50	41	55	mkPktMerge	41.39	2.66	2.58	5.41	11	11	11
ex1010	3.06	20.17	44.14	23.25	212	236	235	sha	-37.7	10.61	21.11	26.09	157	232	261
elliptic	26.45	5.93	27.96	19.12	140	93	112	blob_merge	-29.91	2.85	4.28	18.72	387	481	586
dsip	18.69	10.97	48.65	22.69	83	66	76	Geomean	3.13	4.44	18.21	14.96	96	108	123
clma	-1.42	26.71	30.18	24.2	285	381	345								
spla	-8.41	2.1	27.6	20.26	141	155	175								
des	-13.67	26.09	24.33	-12.16	69	119	111								
frisc	27.15	4.91	24.28	23.89	115	106	130								
ex5p	-32.9	38.03	33.83	30.98	47	102	73								
Geomean	14.07	12.92	34.56	20.5	98	92	98								

NAND-NOR cluster offers about 27% area reduction. The new architecture was tested on the MCNC and VTR benchmarks and showed a delay-area product improvement of 44% and 21%, respectively, when compared with the state-of-the-art LUT-based architecture, and 31% and 19% when compared with the reference AIC-based architecture.

7. REFERENCES

[1] E. Ahmed and J. Rose. The effect of LUT and cluster size on deep-submicron FPGA performance and density. *IEEE Transactions on Very Large Scale Integration Systems*, 12(3):288–298, 2004.

[2] V. Betz, J. Rose, and A. Marquardt. *Architecture and CAD for deep-submicron FPGAs*. Kluwer Academic, Boston, Mass., 1999.

[3] R. K. Brayton and A. Mishchenko. ABC: An academic industrial-strength verification tool. In *Proceedings of the International Conference on Computer Aided Verification*, volume 6174 of *Lecture Notes in Computer Science*, pages 24–40. Springer, July 2010.

[4] D. Chinnery and K. Keutzer. *Closing the Gap Between ASIC & Custom: Tools and Techniques for High-Performance ASIC Design*. Springer US, New York, NY., 2002.

[5] P. Hurley. *A Concise Introduction to Logic*. Wadsworth, 2011.

[6] M. Hutton, J. Schleicher, D. Lewis, B. Pedersen, R. Yuan, S. Kaptanoglu, G. Baeckler, B. Ratchev, K. Padalia, and M. Bourgeault. Improving FPGA performance and area using an adaptive logic module. In *Proceedings Field-Programmable Logic and Applications*, pages 135–144. Springer, 2004.

[7] Z. Jiang, G. Zgheib, C. Yu Lin, D. Novo, L. Yang, Z. Huang, H. Yang, and P. Ienne. A technology mapper for depth-constrained FPGA logic cells. In *Proceedings of the 25th International Conference on Field-Programmable Logic and Applications*, pages 1–8, London, Sept. 2015.

[8] K. Levitz and H. Levitz. *Logic and Boolean algebra*. Barron's Educational Series, 1979.

[9] D. Lewis et al. The Stratix II logic and routing architecture. In *Proceedings of the 13th ACM/SIGDA International Symposium on Field Programmable Gate Arrays*, pages 14–20, Monterey, Calif., Feb. 2005.

[10] J. Luu, J. Goeders, M. Wainberg, A. Somerville, T. Yu, K. Nasartschuk, M. Nasr, S. Wang, T. Liu, N. Ahmed, K. B. Kent, J. Anderson, J. Rose, and V. Betz. VTR 7.0: Next generation architecture and CAD system for FPGAs. *ACM Transactions on Reconfigurable Technology and Systems (TRETS)*, 7(2):6:1–6:30, June 2014.

[11] F. Mayer-Lindenberg. Design and application of a scalable embedded systems? Architecture with an FPGA based operating infrastucture. In *9th EUROMICRO Conference on Digital System Design: Architectures, Methods and Tools.*, pages 189–196, 2006.

[12] H. Parandeh-Afshar, H. Benbihi, D. Novo, and P. Ienne. Rethinking FPGAs: Elude the flexibility excess of LUTs with And-Inverter Cones. In *Proceedings of the 20th ACM/SIGDA International Symposium on Field Programmable Gate Arrays*, pages 119–28, Monterey, Calif., Feb. 2012.

[13] H. Parandeh-Afshar, G. Zgheib, D. Novo, M. Purnaprajna, and P. Ienne. Shadow And-Inverter Cones. In *Proceedings of the 23rd International Conference on Field-Programmable Logic and Applications*, pages 1–4, Porto, Portugal, Sept. 2013.

[14] J. Rose, J. Luu, C. W. Yu, O. Densmore, J. Goeders, A. Somerville, K. B. Kent, P. Jamieson, and J. Anderson. The VTR project: architecture and CAD for FPGAs from Verilog to routing. In *Proceedings of the 20th ACM/SIGDA International Symposium on Field Programmable Gate Arrays*, pages 77–86, 2012.

[15] G. Zgheib, L. Yang, Z. Huang, D. Novo Bruna, H. Parandeh-Afshar, H. Yang, and P. Ienne. Revisiting And-Inverter Cones. In *Proceedings of the 22nd ACM/SIGDA International Symposium on Field Programmable Gate Arrays*, pages 45–54, Monterey, Calif., Feb. 2014.

120-core microAptiv MIPS Overlay
for the Terasic DE5-NET FPGA board

Chethan Kumar H B
chethank001@e.ntu.edu.sg
School of Computer Science and Engineering
Nanyang Technological University
Singapore

Prashant Ravi
prashant014@e.ntu.edu.sg
School of Computer Science and Engineering
Nanyang Technological University
Singapore

Gourav Modi
gourav001@e.ntu.edu.sg
School of Computer Science and Engineering
Nanyang Technological University
Singapore

Nachiket Kapre
nachiket@uwaterloo.ca
Electrical and Computer Engineering
University of Waterloo
Waterloo, Canada.

ABSTRACT

We design a 120-core 94 MHz MIPS processor FPGA overlay interconnected with a lightweight message-passing fabric that fits on a Stratix V GX FPGA (5SGXEA7N2F45C2). We use silicon-tested RTL source code for the microAptiv MIPS processor made available under the Imagination Technologies Academic Program. We augment the processor with suitable custom instruction extensions for moving data between the cores via explicit message passing. We support these instructions with a communication scratchpad that is optimized for high throughput injection of network traffic. We also demonstrate an end-to-end proof-of-concept flow that compiles C code with suitable MIPS UDI-supported (user-defined instructions) message passing workloads and stress-test with synthetic workloads.

1. INTRODUCTION

Modern FPGAs now contain millions of LUTs, hundreds of DSP blocks and on-chip RAMs, supported by a rich, configurable, spatial interconnect fabric. However, making effective use of this raw capacity continues to be a challenge to RTL designers. Recent interest in processor-centric overlays such as the GRVI-Phalanx [1] show us how to tile hundreds of lightweight CPU cores into an FPGA with an emphasis of FPGA-centric logic mapping and optimization. Such processor arrays can be programmed in a higher-level programming environment such a C/C++ or OpenCL instead of low-level RTL. We can then focus optimization effort towards customizability and efficiency of the overlay processors. While RISC-V [2] is an interesting and useful open

FPGA '17, February 22 - 24, 2017, Monterey, CA, USA

© 2017 Copyright held by the owner/author(s). Publication rights licensed to ACM.
ISBN 978-1-4503-4354-1/17/02. . . $15.00

DOI: http://dx.doi.org/10.1145/3020078.3021751

platform for collaborative design of processor hardware, the software ecosystem is still not mature. Existing frameworks, compilers, and development environments are substantially more mature for established ISAs such as MIPS, and ARM. For this work, we choose to use the more familiar MIPS ISA [3] with its broader adoption in the embedded markets and well-developed software ecosystem. The MIPS RTL core is made available by Imagination Technologies [4, 5] and is a microAptiv embedded implementation suitable for academic research. While other MIPS-based or MIPS-like FPGA soft processors have been demonstrated [6, 7], we use the newer MIPS3 ISA-capable release from Imagination. It is an alternative effort that complements the RISC-V projects, and we want to provide more options and variations in ISA styles for FPGA overlay research. Starting from an embedded MIPS RTL, and optimizing it for an FPGA implementation, we can make the core more attractive for FPGA overlay designers.

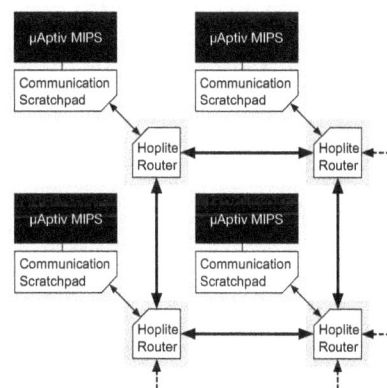

Figure 1: Multi-core μaptiv MIPS arrays interconnected with a Hoplite NoC. RTL modified to support message-passing instructions that do not use cache coherency. Each processor core has separate memory space (scratchpad) dedicated for inter-core communication. Physical implementation merges this with the Register File for efficient use of M20Ks.

In this paper, we make the following contributions to improve the MIPS design for FPGA compatibility:

- **FPGA-centric optimization**: While the original release from Imagination Technologies is silicon tested, it is meant for ASIC substrates without optimizations for FPGA features. We reduce FPGA logic utilization of the processor core to make it suitable for FPGA tiling as well as help improve clock frequency. We quantify the extent of these improvements by measuring resource utilization and frequency of the original MIPS RTL and our optimized solution.

- **Message-Passing support**: Modern FPGAs are wire-rich substrates and communication-centric design is important to expose FPGA capacity to developers. We augment the core with custom instructions and a communication scratchpad to support message-passing functionality. We interface the core with the lightweight Hoplite [8] NoC router. We demonstrate and programming flow to using these instructions in a high-level language such as C. We also simulate RTL for the complete system under various synthetically-generated instruction sequences to stress-test the communication mechanisms.

2. MESSAGE-PASSING MIPS DESIGN

2.1 FPGA-centric optimization

The original MIPS RTL released by Imagination Technologies is a silicon-tested design that has not been optimized for an FPGA implementation. Hence, we first understand the architecture details of the MIPS processor design and identify opportunities for a better matching to the FPGA fabric. The original μaptiv MIPSfpga [5] core occupies 8 K ALMs per core on a DE5-NET board along with 17 M20K RAM blocks while operating at 80 MHz clock frequency. This large footprint makes the core too large for tiling on top of an FPGA device. For instance, we can only fit $\approx$30 cores on the DE5-NET board.

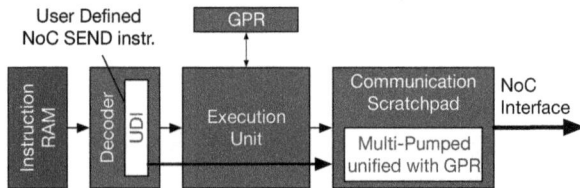

Figure 2: Modifications to MIPS processor pipeline. The instruction and data cache hierarchies have been removed and replaced with Instruction and Data scratchpads. Multiplication unit has been modified to use the Altera DSP block. NoC-specific modifications made to the decoder, along with the addition of a communication-scratchpad.

We make significant structural changes to the RTL to enable lighter weight implementation. The MIPS microarchitecture (with modifications) is shown in Figure 2. The key building blocks of the processor are the ALU (Execution Unit), the Instruction RAM and decoder, along with the general-purpose Register File (GPR). The baseline design uses a cache hierarchy which is not directly suitable for an FPGA overlay. The register file and arithmetic blocks

are not optimized in any way to use the M20Ks or the hard DSP blocks available on the FPGA chip.

- First, we dismantle the complex memory hierarchy that connects the 256 KB RAM through the AHB (AMBA High-Performance Bus) interface into caches inside the core with a flat organization. We directly load the program code into an on-chip Instruction RAM that replaces the expensive cache controllers with single-cycle implementations to drive instructions directly into the decoder. We also replace the data cache with a scratchpad that provide direct physical address space for data storage.

- The instruction cache interface that is included in the MIPSfpga release does not support instruction prefetching which results in very poor IPC rates. In fact, we observed rates as low as 0.25 due to a single allowable fetch every four cycles. The use of single-cycle RAMs to store small MIPS program code inside the core, and modifications to the instruction issue logic eliminate this bottleneck as well.

- Next, we remove unnecessary and unused portions of the RTL including the JTAG interfaces, co-processor connectors, and other peripheral logic that is not directly relevant for correct operation.

- Furthermore, we provide Quartus compiler options to encourage use of DSP units for mapping ALU operations to further reduce area utilization per core.

Next, we show a visual breakdown of resource usage of the unoptimized MIPS processor in Figure 3. From this perspective, it is clear that the cache managers and TLB units occupy bulk of the resource of the core. A leaner core with a flat Instruction+Data RAM would greatly simplify design logic. We can use multi-ported M20K RAM units to implement the register file for tighter implementation. Additionally, we can remap the multiplication logic to use DSP units on the FPGA.

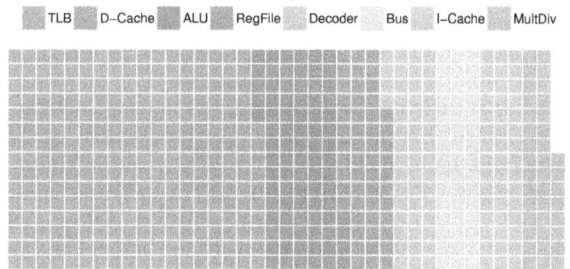

Figure 3: Breakdown of resource usage for the unoptimized MIPS microAptiv core.

We reduce resource usage in the different components of the MIPS organization while retaining functional correctness. We highlight the specific savings per block below:

1. **Execution Datapath (EDP)**: The EDP block consists of the Execution Unit, the Instruction Decoder and the System Co-Processor interface units. The Multiply-Divide Unit (MDU) is connected to the EDP for supporting larger and complicated multiplication and division operations. In adapting this block, we

first redesign the MDU unit, to map to hard DSP blocks on the FPGA to implement signed and unsigned multiplication and fused multiplication-addition operations. The original Verilog used Booth-encoded multiplication directly implemented using logic equations that map to FPGA LUTs. We also removed hardware support for division. A critical modification to the EDP is the adaptation of instruction address generation and interface to the instruction cache. We replace the cache with a simple RAM to hold program code and modify the instruction decode pathway to support this new RAM-based configuration.

2. **Memory Management Unit (MMU) and Translation Lookaside Buffer (TLB)**: The MMU block converts virtual address generated from load and store instructions into physical addresses that map to the global memory space of the system. There are Instruction and Data Caches connected to the MMU. In our simplified MIPS organization, we completely remove the MMU and rely solely on direct physical addressing. This simplification accounts for bulk of the resource utilization reductions as complicated TLB (translation lookaside buffer) and associated circuitry is eliminated. This does mean that we cannot run a full-blown OS or arbitrary code on this MIPS processor. Instead, we have to write C code carefully tailored to this system that is more amenable to coarse-grained parallelization. This simplification also removes the cache controllers, but to retain functional correctness in the instruction decoder, we have to keep certain signal generation logic intact.

3. **Bus Interface Unit (BIU)**: The external peripherals and memory components are connected to the MIPS core through the AHB bus interface. Again, while we can ideally remove this component when tiling the MIPS cores across the FPGA fabric, we had to retain some small portions of this component to ensure the design still operated correctly.

4. **Register File (RF)**: The original register file was implemented directly in FFs to support multi-ported operation. To reduce this cost, we replaced the design with a functionally identical and cycle-compatible multi-pumped [9] M20K-based block with two read ports and one write port. This also resized the RF to hold 512 32b registers.

2.2 Message-Passing Support

Once we have pruned the design, we now integrate communication oriented modifications into the design taking care not to inflate the design size too much. As shown in Figure 2, we modify the µaptiv MIPS RTL to support message-passing instructions. To do this, we have to modify the decoder to interpret the instructions correctly which is achieved through a minor modification of the decoder RTL. We also provide a separate communication-specific address space in the form of scratchpad RAMs. These allow a clean separation between the local address space of the running code, and the address space reserved for global visibility through inter-processor communication. This acts as an extension of the register file dedicated to message passing state and is physically mapped to the same M20K as the Register File. As communication operations do not interfere with

register operations, the number of M20K ports is sufficient to accommodate communication operations along with register operations.

Similar to external memory operations, all interaction with a shared medium such as a NoC may take a variable number of cycles that change with the load on the medium. For instance, when the NoC is congested, a processor may be unable to inject a message into the NoC right away and has to stall. Our decoder RTL has been suitably modified to detect network readiness to determine whether the NoC instruction can execute right away or whether the processor needs to be stalled. A simple implementation is a blocking call that will stall the processor. We support a FIFO-based implementation that queues multiple NoC operations (up to a limit) before the processor must be stalled. At the receiving end of the message, the dedicated multi-pumped M20K port into the communication scratchpad ensure stall-free message receipt.

We use a simple push-based message-passing mechanism that allows communicating processors to perform **write** operations to remote scratchpads. The address space of the communication scratchpads is globally visible, and uniquely addressable from all MIPS cores. We do not yet support request-reply style traffic (*i.e.* remote **read** operations) but expect to do so in the near future through parallel physical request network. Without request-reply style traffic, our NoC does not allow application level deadlock. When we eventually support requests on a separate physical track, the absence of cycles on the same channel will continue to ensure deadlock-free operation. Despite this constraint, the protocol is sufficiently rich to allow us to express bulk synchronous and token dataflow workloads. We use the MIPS **UDI** (User-Defined Instruction) extension to configure the send operation. This allows us to fully customize the interpretation of the certain instruction bits to our application requirements. In our case, we customize the instruction to support NoC operation. The exact interpretation and encoding of 32 bit UDI instruction is shown here.

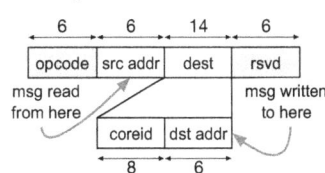

The instruction uses immediate data to encode the source and destination operands of the message to be transmitted over the NoC. Given the 20b field of user-customizable bits in the instruction encoding, we currently support 256 cores (8b address) and 64 scratchpad locations per core (2×6b address).

2.3 Software Support for Message-Passing

We use a ASM intrinsics for supplying message passing instructions directly from the user program in C. Unlike [1], we are capable of executing code produced by the `mips-gcc` toolchain[1]. We use the MIPS *User-Defined Instruction* (UDI) feature to build a simple wrapper for supplying a message-passing workload directly to the C compiler. In Listing 1, we show a sample series of UDI instructions in a C program directly supplying immediate data for the custom **SEND** instruction. The first argument specifies the choice of UDI command (in this case just **SEND**), and the second argument provides the 20b of message passing state including

---

[1]subject to instruction and code size limits

143

the different fields shown in the instruction breakdown earlier (source address, destination MIPS core index, destination address). Note that the UDI start/end instructions are a marker to configure the M20K ports for NoC access, and should be used once for a batch of NoC packets instead of each individual instruction. In addition, we support a global synchronization function that allows all processors to synchronize before safely accessing received data in their communication scratchpads. The reserved bits can be used to either support more than 256 processors, or encode additional priority information to help improve end-to-end packet latencies from important data.

We expect this software API to be useful for bulk synchronous applications that naturally support push-style message passing. Operations or traversals on irregular datastructures such as graphs would be much faster through direct point-to-point messages. It is also possible to build a streaming API using the non-blocking formulation. By adjusting the FIFO depths to application needs, high throughputs can be supported. Token dataflow problems naturally support a message-propagation down a dataflow graph. These are also naturally expressed as send operations.

```
#include <stdio.h>
#include "udi.h"

int main()  {
  mips_udi_i_nv(0x09,0x00000); // UDI Start
  mips_udi_i_nv(0x08,0xFFFFF); // SEND message
  mips_udi_i_nv(0x0A,0x00000); // UDI END
  return 0;
}
```

```
mips-mti-elf-gcc -march=m14kc -c mips.c -o mips.o
```

Listing 1: Code sketch showing example of inline UDI SEND instruction. Also showing a one-line gcc compile command to target the µaptiv MIPS processor.

We show a concrete application example of using our UDI SEND instruction in Listing 2. This is a code sketch for parallel sparse matrix-vector multiply computation operating on integer data. The same code template runs on all cores but on different portions of the matrix. In our implementation, we parallelize the computation by partitioning the matrix across the MIPS cores, assigning a subset of rows to each core. We store the sparse matrix A in a compressed sparse row (CSR) format. The structures a_index and col_index are used to locate non-zero entries in the matrix A with the actual values stored as an array a_nz. The algorithm is iterative, and requires calculation of $b = A \cdot x$ multiple times. The result vector b is processed to build the vector x for the next iteration. Within each core, we loop over the rows m, and process each non-zero entry in A to accumulate the row dot-product result in $b[m]$. Once we compute b, we distribute the results to other cores that will need this in the next iteration using the fanout addressing structure s_index and invcol_index. We use our UDI SEND primitive for quick direct message transfer for b vector values. On a conventional CPU architecture, this would require relying on cache coherency to enforce ordering. On GPUs, we would need to synchronize data through the off-chip DRAM instead. Unlike both these solution, our approach provides an explicit way to perform data transfer over on-chip NoCs.

```
#include <stdio.h>
#include "udi.h"

int main()  {
  // Define SpMV structures
  int *a_index, *col_index,
  int *s_index, *invcol_index;
  int *a_nz, *b, *x;
  int M, m, src, dest, pkt;
  // Loop over non-zeros, to compute Ax=b
  for(m=0; m<M; m++) {
    b[m]=0;
    int edges = a_index[m+1]-a_index[m];
    for(n=0; n<edges; n++) {
      b[m] += a_nz[a_index[m]+n]
        *x[col_index[a_index[m]+n]];
    }
  }
  // Send vector values to cores that need it
  mips_udi_i_nv(0x09,0x00000); // UDI Start
  for(int m=0; m<M; m++) {
    src = &b[m];
    int edges = s_index[m+1]-s_index[m];
    pkt = src<<14;
    for(int n=0; n<edges; n++) {
      // construct packet
      dest = &x[invcol_index[s_index[m]+n]];
      pkt |= dest<<5;
      // send packet
      mips_udi_i_nv(0x08,pkt);
    }
  }
  mips_udi_i_nv(0x0A,0x00000); // UDI End
}
```

Listing 2: Sparse Matrix-Vector Multiplication code sketch with UDI SEND instructions for b vector movement.

3. RESULTS

We map the MIPS processor overlay on the DE5-NET FPGA board. We are able to fit a 120-core implementation after applying optimizations described in Section 2.1. We floorplan the design as shown in Figure 4 to constrain the processors into small wide rectangular regions of the chip. We organize them into two columns to mimic the physical structure of the two DSP columns available on the chip. This columnar structure is highlighted in Figure 5. The DSP block alignment on this chip restricts us into having a X×2 design which can be modified for other chips as per their physical geometry. The careful layout allows the design to run close to the critical path the MIPS execution paths (94 MHz) rather than the inter-MIPS links (200 MHz+). A closer inspection of the timing report shows long combinational paths in the MIPS decoders. While this is relatively easy to pipeline, this has downstream impact on the timings of register accesses, and other dependent operations. We have chosen not to overhaul the delicate silicon-verified pipelines for this work, but seek to identify ways to simplify this critical path as part of future work. Our 120-core implementation is close to exhausting the ALMs on the chip.

In Table 1, we quantify the FPGA logic utilization breakdown of the various constituent blocks of the microAptiv core and show the effect of our optimizations aimed at reducing implementation costs and make it more amenable to lightweight FPGA implementation. A large portion of the savings come from eliminating the Caches (1.7 K ALMs) and

Table 1: FPGA Resource Utilization before and after optimization using Quartus 16.0 Prime Standard Edition on Stratix V FPGA (5SGXEA7N2F45C2) on the Terasic DE5-Net FPGA card.

Module	Before				After			
	ALMs	FFs	DSPs	M20Ks	ALMs	FFs	DSPs	M20Ks
MMU mmu	1771	2499	0	0	0	0	0	0
Execution Datapath m14k_edp	1211	347	0	0	932	345	0	0
Co-Processor m14k_cpz	963	1112	0	0	1406	781	0	0
Decoder m14k_mpc	602	464	0	0	462	325	0	0
Multiply-Divide Unit m14k_mdunit	310	214	0	0	101	71	4	0
I\$ + Ctrl. m14k_icc	428	402	0	4	70	93	0	0
D\$ + Ctrl. m14k_dcc	970	784	0	13	30	36	0	0
Reg. File m14k_rf_reg	602	1138	0	0	56	105	0	1
Bus I/F Unit m14k_biu	614	716	0	0	21	45	0	0
UDI m14k_udi	0	0	0	0	104	141	0	1
Total m14k_top	8144[1]	8430	0	17	2436	2093	2	3[2]

[1]extra ALMs due to other blocks not reported here such as m14k_siu, m14k_ahb. [2]extra M20K due to m14k_ahb block with Instruction RAM.

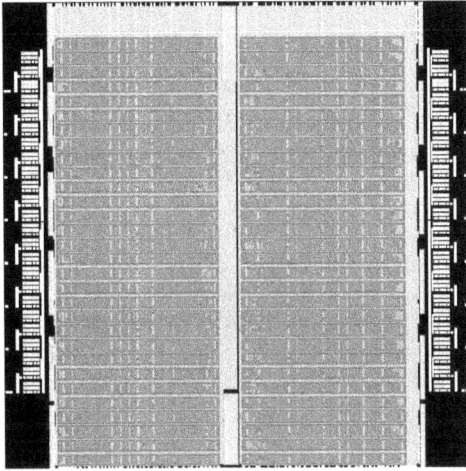

Figure 4: Logilock floorplanning constraints for 64-core design on DE5-NET FPGA board.

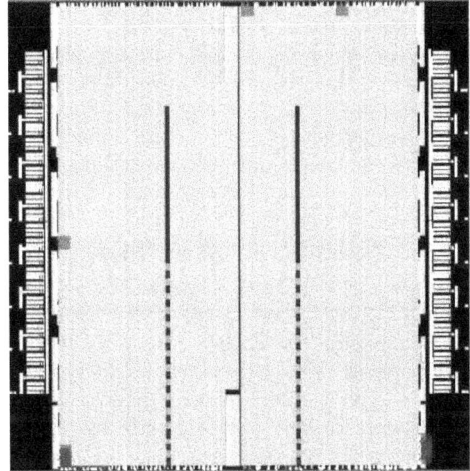

Figure 5: Logilock floorplanning constraints for 64-core design on DE5-NET FPGA board (DSP block columns highlighted in orange and blue).

Caches (1.3 K ALMs). We also efficiently pack the multi-ported Register File to multi-pumped M20K block thereby saving ≈500 ALMs. The newly added NoC interface and instructions consume 300–400 extra ALMs. Overall, we still save 3.3× the resource requirements of the original unoptimized MIPS design.

To verify correctness of the NoC instructions and connectivity, we perform Modelsim simulations of the 120-core MIPS overlay with assembly-level MIPS code generated for various traffic patterns. This also helps us contrast the out-of-the-box performance of the MIPS RTL implementations from Imagination Technologies against our FPGA-optimized configuration. In particular, our modifications to the memory hierarchy and instruction issue logic are crucial to deliver high NoC packet rates. As indicated earlier, the raw MIPS RTL only supports injection rates below 25% due to limits of the instruction issue logic. We modify this logic and streamline the design of the NoC instruction decoding to permit 100% injection rates if so desired (limited by NoC congestion). We simulated the MIPS processor under synthetically-generated traffic patterns and observed similar NoC bandwidth and latency trends as the original Hoplite [8] design.

4. RELATED WORK

In this section we review a prior work on soft processor overlays for communicating applications:

Heracles [10] is an integer-based MIPS-III soft processor array mapped to a Virtex-5 LX330T FPGA board. The multiple cores can communicate with a NoC but retains caches (unlike our design), resulting in an implementation that requires 5.5K LUTs, 2.6K FFs, 75 BlockRAMs and runs at 155 MHz. Furthermore, their virtual-channel based router alone takes 2K LUTs, 2.8K FFs, and runs at 71 MHz. They can fit a 4×4 system on the LX330T board, while our design can scale to 120 cores on the newer, larger DE5-NET board.

The recent GRVI-Phalanx [1] offers a different approach based on RISC-V instead of MIPS instruction sets. The design is extremely lightweight and uses a clustered approach for tight integration of multiple ALUs per Hoplite NoC router. This concentration of ALUs per NoC router is restrictive to applications that demand non-local, intense communication between the parallel elements. Our approach provides a NoC router per MIPS core targeting more irregular problems than the GRVI-Phalanx design. Regardless, the GRVI-Phalanx architecture is a great example of exploiting FPGA features to the fullest extent possible for accelerator integration.

The Adapteva Epiphany [11] ASIC is a 16-core floating-point RISC processor with local scratchpads (no caches) that is supported by NoCs for inter-processor and off-chip communication. The Epiphany processors uses a bespoke RISC instruction set that is incompatible with any standard (industrial or open-source). Our MIPS overlay is a configurable FPGA design that runs an industry-standard MIPS instructions set. We do not currently support floating-point but that can be added easily if required. Furthermore, we are able to use a single NoC for all communication needs by supporting a SEND-only message-passing paradigm. Despite the differences, the programming models of our overlay is very similar to the flat addressing mode of communicating memory elements on the Epiphany chip.

Our prior work [12, 13, 14] describes various approaches for developing overlay FPGA designs supported by NoCs for accelerating the SPICE circuit simulator. In these studies we develop customized VLIW, Dataflow, and Streaming overlays for various phases of SPICE but rely on fast integration with a communicating NoC in all cases. In this paper, we modify a general-purpose MIPS core instead of custom datapaths to support fast communication. This is a harder challenge as the instruction pipelines and memory interfaces are dictated by the MIPS compute organization and offers a constrained space of modification opportunities.

5. CONCLUSIONS AND FUTURE WORK

We implement a 94 MHz 120-core MIPS overlay to the large Stratix V GX FPGA device (5SGXEA7N2F45C2) supported by a lightweight message-passing NoC. We augment the MIPS processor with UDI-based modifications to the decoder and a separate communication scratchpad. This modified hardware can be programmed directly in C using a message-passing API layer with MIPS UDI instrinsics. We use the MIPSfpga RTL released under the Imagination Technologies Academic Program as a starting point for our work. One of our key contributions is the FPGA-specific optimization that significantly prunes the implementation cost by 3–4× by dismantling the complex cache-based memory hierarchy and using the M20K RAM blocks and DSPs wherever possible. We improve permissible injection rates from 25% to 100% through suitable adaptation of the instruction issue logic.

As part of future work we will continue to prune logic utilization of the microAptiv core by customizing a MCU (microcontroller) version of the design. This is less capable and lower performance core, but may provide a better MIPS/LUT efficiency that the GRVI-Phalanx [1] design is able to achieve. The Verilog RTL released by Imagination Technologies is not particularly easy to modify from due to complex ASIC-specific optimizations. Thus, we were sometimes forced to retain certain signals and small code blocks that were vital for correct operation but unnecessary from the system-level perspective. There are still sufficient opportunities for pruning resource costs with a deeper study of the micro-architecture. We aim to boost operating frequencies which are currently bottlenecked in the execution pipeline through appropriate retiming of the design while being careful to retain functional correctness. We also wish to further streamline the NoC interface through clustering and hierarchy to minimize resource overheads. We also want to

support request-reply style NoC traffic to enable pull-style message passing in addition to current SEND instruction support. This is possible by instantiating a physically distinct request network that naturally helps avoid deadlock by isolating requests from replies on separate physical networks.

6. REFERENCES

[1] J. Gray, "GRVI phalanx: A massively parallel RISC-V FPGA accelerator accelerator," *CoRR*, vol. abs/1606.01037, 2016. [Online]. Available: http://arxiv.org/abs/1606.01037

[2] K. Asanović and D. A. Patterson, "Instruction Sets Should Be Free: The Case For RISC-V," 2014.

[3] J. Hennessy, N. Jouppi, S. Przybylski, C. Rowen, T. Gross, F. Baskett, and J. Gill, "MIPS: A Microprocessor Architecture," *SIGMICRO Newsl.*, vol. 13, no. 4, pp. 17–22, Oct. 1982. [Online]. Available: http://dl.acm.org/citation.cfm?id=1014194.800930

[4] S. L. Harris, R. Owen, E. Sedano, and D. C. Martinez, "Mipsfpga: Hands-on learning on a commercial soft-core," in *2016 11th European Workshop on Microelectronics Education*, May 2016, pp. 1–5.

[5] R. Owen, "Mipsfpga university program," https://community.imgtec.com/university/.

[6] H. Nakatsuka, Y. Tanaka, T. V. Chu, S. Takamaeda-Yamazaki, and K. Kise, "Ultrasmall: The smallest mips soft processor," in *2014 24th International Conference on Field Programmable Logic and Applications (FPL)*, Sept 2014, pp. 1–4.

[7] S. Moore and G. Chadwick, "The TIGER-MIPS processor," 2011.

[8] N. Kapre and J. Gray, "Hoplite: Building austere overlay nocs for FPGAs," in *Field Programmable Logic and Applications (FPL), 2015 25th International Conference on*, Sept 2015, pp. 1–8.

[9] C. E. LaForest and J. G. Steffan, "Efficient Multi-ported Memories for FPGAs," in *Proceedings of the 18th Annual ACM/SIGDA International Symposium on Field Programmable Gate Arrays*, ser. FPGA '10. New York, NY, USA: ACM, 2010, pp. 41–50. [Online]. Available: http://doi.acm.org/10.1145/1723112.1723122

[10] M. A. Kinsy, M. Pellauer, and S. Devadas, "Heracles: Fully synthesizable parameterized mips-based multicore system," in *2011 21st International Conference on Field Programmable Logic and Applications*, Sept 2011, pp. 356–362.

[11] L. Gwennap, "Adapteva: More flops, less watts," *Microprocessor Report*, vol. 6, no. 13, pp. 11–02, 2011.

[12] N. Kapre and A. DeHon, "Accelerating SPICE Model-Evaluation using FPGAs," in *2009 17th IEEE Symposium on Field Programmable Custom Computing Machines*, April 2009, pp. 37–44.

[13] ——, "Parallelizing sparse Matrix Solve for SPICE circuit simulation using FPGAs," in *2009 International Conference on Field-Programmable Technology*, Dec 2009, pp. 190–198.

[14] ——, "VLIW-SCORE: Beyond C for sequential control of SPICE FPGA acceleration," in *2011 International Conference on Field-Programmable Technology*, Dec 2011, pp. 1–9.

A Parallelized Iterative Improvement Approach to Area Optimization for LUT-Based Technology Mapping

Gai Liu and Zhiru Zhang
School of Electrical and Computer Engineering, Cornell University, Ithaca, NY
{gl387, zhiruz}@cornell.edu

Abstract

Modern FPGA synthesis tools typically apply a predetermined sequence of logic optimizations on the input logic network before carrying out technology mapping. While the "known recipes" of logic transformations often lead to improved mapping results, there remains a nontrivial gap between the quality metrics driving the pre-mapping logic optimizations and those targeted by the actual technology mapping. Needless to mention, such miscorrelations would eventually result in suboptimal quality of results.

In this paper we propose PIMap, which couples logic transformations and technology mapping under an iterative improvement framework to minimize the circuit area for LUT-based FPGAs. In each iteration, PIMap randomly proposes a transformation on the given logic network from an ensemble of candidate optimizations; it then invokes technology mapping and makes use of the mapping result to determine the likelihood of accepting the proposed transformation. To mitigate the runtime overhead, we further introduce parallelization techniques to decompose a large design into multiple smaller sub-netlists that can be optimized simultaneously. Experimental results show that our approach achieves promising area improvement over a set of commonly used benchmarks. Notably, PIMap reduces the LUT usage by up to 14% and 7% on average over the best-known records for the EPFL arithmetic benchmark suite.

1. Introduction

Modern FPGA designs rely on sophisticated CAD algorithms and tools to achieve high-quality solutions [4]. A very important step in this toolflow is called technology mapping, which transforms a gate-level Boolean logic network[1] into a functionally equivalent netlist composed of look-up tables (LUTs). Minimizing the depth and the total LUT count of

the mapped netlist are two of the typical optimization goals for an FPGA-targeted technology mapper.

A key challenge to technology mapping is that the quality of the mapping solution depends heavily on the structure of the input logic network. It is well known that the problem of restructuring the network for depth- or area-optimal technology mapping is NP-hard [5]. Modern FPGA synthesis tools usually apply a series of structural optimizations to transform the input logic network to be more amicable for technology mapping and other downstream optimizations [8, 11]. Examples of the commonly used logic optimizations include balancing the levels of different paths in a logic network (i.e., balancing), and replacing a sub-network with a smaller one that realizes the same function (i.e., rewriting). In practice, such logic optimizations are usually interleaved with each other and repeatedly applied to better optimize the logic network. While such transformations can effectively reduce the complexity of the logic network in terms of the gate count and/or the number of logic levels, we argue that there still exists considerable room in improving the FPGA mapping quality based on two important observations:

- The mainstream FPGA synthesis frameworks use a fixed predetermined sequence of pre-mapping logic transformations that may not always generate high-quality logic structures. For example, the popular academic tool ABC provides synthesis scripts with more than 20 different optimization sequences [3]. Since the efficacy of these sequences varies across different designs, it is very challenging for a user to quickly identify the best sequence to employ given a new design.
- Miscorrelations exist between the quality metrics driving the pre-mapping logic optimizations and those targeted by the actual technology mapping. Specifically, minimizing the gate count or the number of logic levels may not necessarily translate to reduced LUT count or depth in the final mapped netlist, thereby creating a gap between the optimality at the logic stage and the technology mapping stage.

We use Figure 1 to concretely illustrate the drawbacks of existing techniques. Consider the problem of using 3-input LUTs to map the logic network shown in Figure 1(a), which has four inputs (a-d) and four outputs (o_1-o_4). The original circuit can be implemented using four 3-input LUTs high-

---

[1] In the rest of paper, we use the term *logic network* to denote a pre-mapping gate-level Boolean logic network.

FPGA '17, February 22-24, 2017, Monterey, CA, USA
© 2017 ACM. ISBN 978-1-4503-4354-1/17/02...$15.00
DOI: http://dx.doi.org/10.1145/3020078.3021735

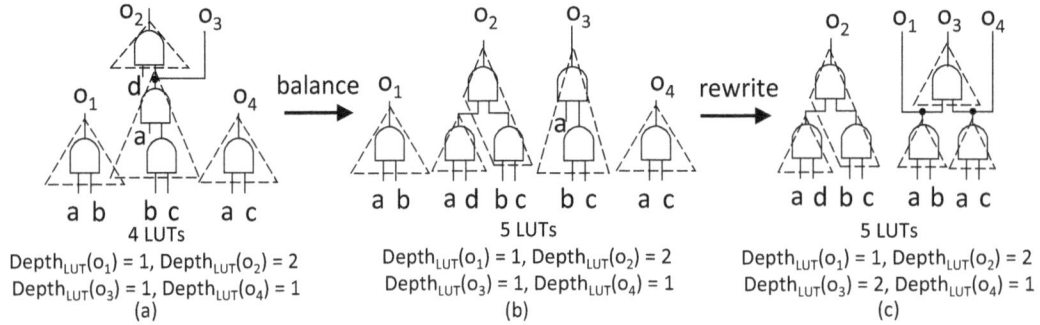

Figure 1. Logic optimizations and mapping on a simple example assuming 3-input LUTs — (a) The original circuit. (b) The circuit after applying `balance`. (c) The circuit after applying `rewrite` to the circuit from (b). Mapping results are indicated with dashed regions.

lighted in Figure 1(a). Suppose we apply two transformations step by step to the network. The first step performs balancing which manages to decrease the depth of the logic network by one as shown in Figure 1(b). The second step uses rewriting to reduce the gate count by one while maintaining the same depth as illustrated in Figure 1(c). While these transformations can successfully simplify the original network, the eventual mapping results are unfortunately worsened in terms of both LUT count and depth if we compare the mapped netlists shown in Figure 1(a) and Figure 1(c). Specifically, the netlist after balancing and rewriting requires one more LUT to map, and the depth of output o_3 also increases by one in the mapped netlist.

Clearly, reducing the depth and area of logic network does not necessarily translate to performance improvements or area savings after mapping. To address this challenge, we propose PIMap — a parallelized iterative improvement approach to area-driven LUT mapping. Unlike existing methods that decouple the logic transformations from technology mapping, PIMap makes use of the actual mapping results to guide a series of randomly proposed structural optimizations. Proposing logic transformations in a probabilistic way allows PIMap to explore a larger design space that cannot be uncovered by fixed optimization sequences. According to our experimental results, PIMap consistently outperforms the state-of-the-art LUT mapping solutions for unconstrained area optimization as well as delay-constrained area minimization.

Since iterative improvement usually comes with nontrivial runtime overhead, we further propose techniques to decompose a large netlist into multiple smaller sub-netlists, and optimize these sub-netlists in parallel across multiple machines. This parallelization framework enables PIMap to handle large circuits with more than 40 thousand LUTs, with a synthesis time in the range of tens to hundreds of seconds. In addition, PIMap also allows the users to easily explore the trade-offs between the design quality and the synthesis effort in runtime.

Our primary technical contributions are as follows:

- We provide a quantitative study on the (mis)correlation between the gate count reduction in the pre-mapping

logic network and the LUT count savings after technology mapping.
- We propose a stochastic iterative improvement algorithm and associated parallelization techniques to enable efficient mapping-in-the-loop area optimization for LUT-based FPGAs.
- We demonstrate promising improvements in area reduction for a set of common benchmarks, including breaking many best-known records for the EPFL arithmetic benchmark suite.

The rest of the paper is organized as follows: Section 2 provides an overview of technology mapping and common logic transformations; Section 3 studies the correlation between the gate count in the logic network and the LUT count after mapping; Section 4 describes the key techniques in PIMap; Section 5 presents the experimental results; Section 6 reviews the related work, followed by conclusions in Section 7.

2. Preliminaries

In this section, we discuss the basics of technology mapping and common logic transformations used in PIMap.

2.1 Overview of Technology Mapping

Generally speaking, technology mappers are divided into structural mappers and functional mappers [12]. Structural mappers consider the input logic network as fixed, and attempt to cover the circuit with K-input LUTs. Functional mappers are allowed to modify the structure of the logic network before mapping to LUTs. In this work we focus on functional mappers for generating higher-quality mapping solutions.

Before covering the logic network with LUTs, functional mappers usually apply a sequence of logic transformations to the network, which we call *moves*. The goal of these moves is to prepare the network for technology mapping so that the subsequent LUT covering step can generate high-quality results in terms of LUT depth or LUT count. We defer the discussion on the details of logic transformation to Section 2.2, and first describe the mechanism of covering a logic network with LUTs.

148

During the LUT covering step in technology mapping, we view the logic network as a directed acyclic graph, where the nodes represent logic gates and the edges capture the connections between the gates. We define a cone C_v at node v as the sub-netlist of v and some of its predecessors so that any path from a node in C_v to v is entirely contained in C_v. A cone is said to be K-feasible if there are no more than K nodes outside C_v that have edges pointing to the nodes in C_v. A cut of C_v is defined to be the set of input nodes of C_v.

In LUT-based FPGAs, we can implement any K-feasible cones using a K-input LUT. Consequently, the mapping problem reduces to the problem of optimally covering the input graph with K-feasible cones [13]. A LUT covering framework generally consists of cut enumeration, cut ranking, cut selection, and final mapping generation. Cut enumeration explores all K-feasible cuts at each node, while cut ranking evaluates the quality of the cuts based on the optimization objective. Cut selection determines the optimal cut for each node based on the ranking information to generate the final covering solution.

2.2 Common Logic Transformations

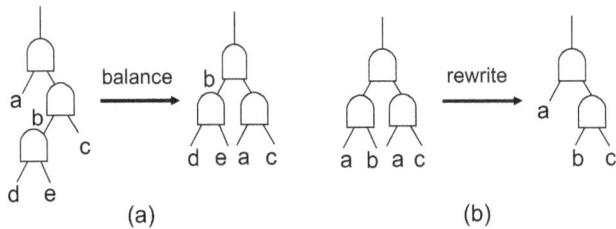

Figure 2. Illustration of two common logic transformations — (a) `balance`: balance the depth of the netlist using associative transform $a(bc) = (ab)c = (ac)b$. (b) `rewrite`: replace a sub-netlist with an equivalent but smaller one.

A logic transformation (or a move) applies optimization on the logic network in order to reduce the size or the number of levels of the network. Figure 2 shows two common logic transformations. The balancing transformation [10] tries to balance the depth of different paths in the netlist using associative transformations in the form as $a(bc) = (ab)c = (ac)b$. An associative transform at a given node is accepted if it reduces the depth of the corresponding node. In Figure 2(a), the balancing move swaps the left child of the output node with the branch that generates node b. As a result, the network is more balanced and the level of the output node is reduced by one.

A rewriting transformation [11] visits each node in the network in a topological order, and enumerates all K-feasible cuts of the subject node. The Boolean function of each cut is then computed and matched against all the equivalence classes of K-variable functions. After trying all the available circuit representations for the given node, the rewriting move picks the one with the largest improvement. Figure 2(b) provides an example of the rewriting transform, where a 3-input function is rewritten to a smaller structure

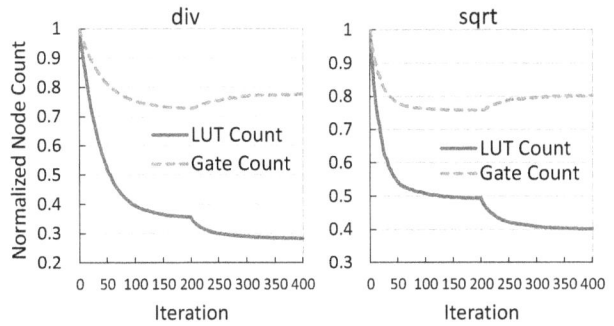

Figure 3. Correlation between gate count in the logic network and post-mapping LUT count — For the first 200 iterations, we perturb the logic network with the objective of reducing gate count. After 200 iterations, we change the objective to reducing LUT count.

shown on the right side. Refactoring is a variation of the rewriting move [10]. It uses a heuristic algorithm to compute a large cut for each node, and then tries to replace the cut with a factored form of the cut function. The transform is accepted if the replacement does not increase the size of the network.

3. Quantitative Study of Correlation between LUT Count and Gate Count

In this section we study the impact of commonly used logic transformations on the gate count in the logic network as well as the corresponding LUT count after technology mapping. Our experimental methodology is to iteratively perturb a given logic network (or a sub-network) to generate a sequence of equivalent design points with varying sizes in terms of gate count and LUT count. More specifically, we use two different strategies to perturb the logic network. The *gate-centric perturbation* enumerates a set of logic transformations to the input network, then greedily accepts the resulting logic networks that reduce the gate count. This way we iteratively generate a sequence of design points with decreasing number of gates, at the same time, the LUT count of each design point is also recorded. With the second strategy called LUT-centric perturbation, we also iteratively apply a set of candidate transformations to the logic network and measure the LUT count after each transformation. However, we only accept the transformations that reduce the LUT count of the resulting mapped netlist. We record both gate count and LUT count upon the acceptance of each transformation.

Here we evaluate two representative designs from the EPFL arithmetic benchmark suite [1], and use and-inverter graph (AIG) as the gate-level representation of the logic network. We use the aforementioned method to apply three transformations in the ABC logic synthesis framework [3] (balance, refactor, rewrite) to generate 400 intermediate design points for each benchmark. Notably, we employ the gate-centric perturbation for the first 200 iterations, and switch to LUT-centric perturbation mode afterwards. Figure 3 shows the normalized LUT count and gate count during the 400 iterations of perturbations. During the initial phase of gate-centric perturbation, the decrease of LUT count coincides with the gate count reduction. Eventually, both descending curves level off, which seems to suggest that little room is left for improving area. Interestingly, when switching to LUT-centric perturbation after 200 iterations, we observe further reduction in LUT count with an increasing gate count. While we are only presenting two benchmarks here due to space limitation, we observe from our experiments very similar trends (to Figure 3) across a broad range of designs, which motivates us to propose PIMap that will be detailed in the next section.

4. PIMap Techniques

PIMap decomposes a large circuit netlist into smaller sub-netlists, and uses an iterative routine to minimize the area of these sub-netlists in parallel. The area minimization routine integrates commonly used logic transformations and technology mappers to progressively improve the design quality. In this section, we describe the PIMap techniques in detail and mainly focus on the unconstrained area optimization. We also show that PIMap can easily be extended to handle depth-constrained area minimization.

4.1 Iterative Area Minimization

The very core of PIMap is an iterative area minimization framework that repeats three major steps: (1) proposing logic transformation moves, (2) evaluating the quality of the move through technology mapping, and (3) determining whether to accept the proposed move. Figure 4 sketches the high-level design flow of this iterative procedure.

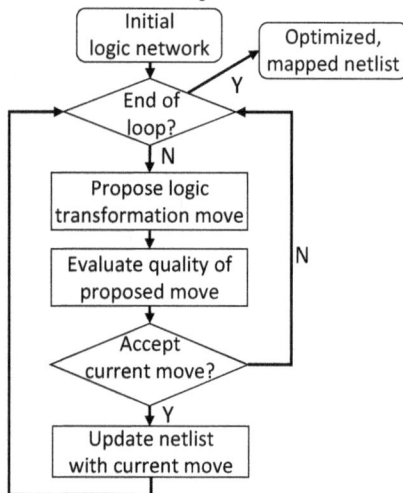

Figure 4. High-level flow chart of the iterative area minimization routine.

Proposing a Transformation Move PIMap makes use of a collection of logic transformation moves, denoted as set T. Each move in T is capable of optimizing a given logic

network for a certain target, such as reducing the number of nodes in the circuit and balancing the node levels of different paths. We further associate T with a discrete probability distribution named P, where the probability of selecting the ith at any iteration is denoted as p_i. At the beginning of each iteration, PIMap randomly chooses one logic transformation from T based on P. The transformed network is then evaluated by invoking an existing area-minimizing technology mapping algorithm.

Evaluating a Move In this step, the transformed netlist is first mapped to K-input LUTs using an existing area-oriented technology mapper. With unconstrained area optimization, we directly tie the quality metric Q of a proposed move to the number of LUTs in the mapped circuit netlist (denoted as N_{LUT}). We note that Q can be extended to include other user-specified factors such as the number of gates in the pre-mapping logic network.

Accepting a Move After obtaining the quality metric of the currently proposed move Q_{curr} and that of the previous iteration, denoted as Q_{prev}, we use the Markov Chain Monte Carlo (MCMC) method to probabilistically determine whether to accept the proposed move [6]. In particular, we employ the Metropolis-Hastings algorithm [7] for calculating the acceptance probability.

This process is detailed in Algorithm 1, which dictates that if the quality of the current move is better than the previous one, we accept the current move unconditionally. Otherwise, we accept the move with a small probability that decreases exponentially as Q_{curr} increases. Probabilistically accepting a move with inferior quality helps PIMap avoid quickly getting stuck in local minima during the search process.[2] Once a move is accepted, we update Q_{prev} to be Q_{curr}, save the updated network, and continue with a new proposal. On the other hand, if the current move is rejected, we do not update Q_{prev} and directly proceed to the next iteration. During the search procedure, we also keep track of the best mapping result and the corresponding circuit netlist. We return the best result at the end of the iterative area minimization routine.

In contrast to the previous methods that apply a fixed sequence of logic transformations, our randomized approach can effectively explore and search a large design space. Moreover, this search is guided by the actual mapping results instead of logic-level design metrics. This combination of a large number (tens or hundreds of iterations) of randomly proposed moves and the mapping-guided search is the key to achieving the superior mapping quality with PIMap.

---

[2] It is worth noting that MCMC and simulated annealing are closely related [9]. Compared to MCMC sampling, simulated annealing has one additional temperature term that decreases over time to control the likelihood of accepting an inferior move. In our experiments, we observe that the temperature term has almost no impact on the convergence rate, thus we decide to directly use the Metropolis-Hastings algorithm to compute the acceptance probability.

Algorithm 1 Calculating acceptance probability
***

if $Q_{curr} < Q_{prev}$ **then**
    ⌊ Accept the current move
else
    // $rand()$: random number between 0 and 1
    if $rand() < e^{-\gamma(Q_{curr}/Q_{prev})}$ **then**
        ⌊ Accept the current move
    else
        ⌊ Reject the current move

4.2 Netlist Extraction and Parallel Optimization

To enable parallel optimization of multiple sub-netlists, PIMap automatically extracts a user-configurable number of non-overlapping sub-netlists from a mapped netlist, and optimize them in parallel through multithreading.

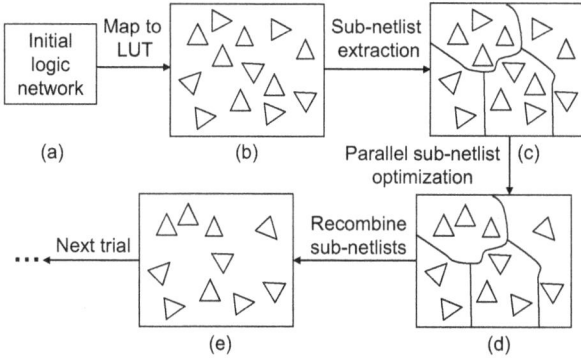

Figure 5. Illustration of netlist decomposition and parallel optimization — (a) Original logic network. (b) Netlist after LUT mapping, where each triangle represents a LUT, the connections between LUTs are omitted. (c) The four sub-netlists after sub-netlist extraction. (d) The four sub-netlists after optimization. (e) The netlist after recombining the four optimized sub-netlists.

Figure 5 conceptually illustrates the netlist extraction and parallel optimization steps. Given an input logic network, we first map it into a circuit netlist composed of LUTs shown as the triangles in Figure 5. We then partition the netlist into multiple sub-netlists, and apply the area minimization technique in Section 4.1 to optimize the sub-netlists in parallel. After optimizing the sub-netlists, we recombine them into a single netlist, and start the next trial of the sub-netlist extraction and optimization. We discuss these two steps in detail below.

Partitioning Mapped Netlists Algorithm 2 describes the steps required to partition a mapped netlist to enable effective parallelization. More specifically, the inputs to our partitioning algorithm include (1) a netlist that has already been mapped to LUTs, (2) a parallelization factor n, and (3) a size constraint M for each sub-netlist, the goal is to extract n non-overlapping sub-netlists with each of which containing no more than M LUTs. It is worth noting that partitioning the mapped netlist allows us to easily merge the opti-

mized sub-netlists to regenerate the complete LUT netlist. More importantly, any improvement to a sub-netlist will directly contribute to the overall LUT savings in the recombined netlist.

Algorithm 2 Extracting sub-netlists
***

Input: A mapped netlist G_0, a parallelization factor n, and a sub-netlist size constraint M.
Output: n sub-netlists $\{G_1, G_2, ..., G_n\}$, each of which contains M LUTs.
// G_{res} is the residual graph of G_0
Initialize $G_{res} = G_0$, and $G_1 = G_2 = ... = G_n = \varnothing$
// extract the ith sub-netlist
for i *from* 1 *to* n **do**
    Randomly pick a node j in G_{res}
    Start from j, visit G_{res} in breadth-first order:
    for *each node* k *during traversal* **do**
        Add node k to G_i
        Remove node k from G_{res}
        if *size of* G_i *reaches* M **then**
            ⌊ break
    // Determine primary inputs (PI) and
          primary outputs (PO) of G_i
    for *each node* k *in* G_i **do**
        for *each fan-in* l *of* k **do**
            if l *is not assigned inside* G_i **then**
                ⌊ Add l to the PI set of G_i
        if (k *is a PO of* G_{res}) *or* (k *is used in* G_{res}) **then**
            ⌊ Add k to the PO set of G_i

return $\{G_1, G_2, ..., G_n\}$

When generating a sub-netlist, our algorithm first randomly picks a *seed*, and expands the sub-netlist using breadth-first search (BFS) from the seed until the number of LUTs in the sub-netlist reaches M. When constructing the sub-netlists, we also maintain a residual graph that contains the nodes not yet added to any sub-netlists. The residual graph is initialized to be the same as the original netlist, and will gradually decrease in size as more sub-netlists are extracted. After generating the first sub-netlist, the algorithm will pick another random seed, and extract the next sub-netlist from the residual graph until all the n sub-netlists have been generated. In case BFS cannot find a cluster of size M, the algorithm extracts another cluster and append it to the sub-netlist until the sub-netlist reaches a size of M LUTs. After the partitioning step, our algorithm assigns the primary inputs (PI) and primary outputs (PO) of each sub-netlist by identifying the nodes that have external fan-ins as well as those that fanout to external nodes.

Optimizing Sub-Netlists After obtaining the sub-netlists from the previous step, PIMap distributes them to available computing resources for independent optimization. We create one thread for each sub-netlist, and assign threads to machines to balance the load. Optionally, PIMap allows the user to use multiple threads to optimize different copies of the same sub-netlist in parallel to increase the likelihood of generating a high-quality solution. After all threads finish execution, a master thread collects the optimized sub-netlists, and combine them to reform the entire design. This combining process involves concatenating all the sub-netlists into a single netlist, and remove the PIs and POs of each individual sub-netlists. Since all sub-netlists are of equal or very similar size, the runtime of different threads are similar to each other. Consequently, the workloads of different threads are highly balanced.

4.3 Overall Flow

We summarize the overall flow of PIMap using the techniques in Sections 4.1 and 4.2. Figure 6 shows the overall flow of PIMap.

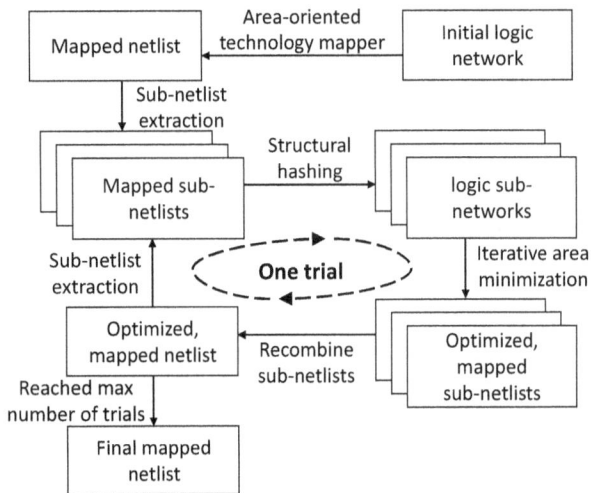

Figure 6. Overall synthesis flow of PIMap.

PIMap takes the initial logic network as the input, and first uses an area-oriented technology mapper to transform the logic network into a mapped netlist. PIMap then uses the sub-netlist extraction technique detailed in Section 4.2 to extract a number of sub-netlists. Since the iterative area minimization requires a gate-level logic network, we apply a netlist decomposition technique, such as structural hashing, to convert the mapped sub-netlist back to the corresponding logic sub-networks. These logic sub-networks are subsequently optimized using the iterative area minimization technique detailed in Section 4.1, which generates the optimized version of the mapped sub-netlists. PIMap then recombines these optimized netlists into a single netlist that is equivalent to the original design.

We define a trial as the four steps including sub-netlist extraction, converting a mapped netlist back to logic network, iterative area minimization, and sub-netlists recombination. At each trial, PIMap repartitions the mapped netlist into a different set of sub-netlists using the technique in Section 4.2 with randomly-selected seed node for each partition. In the rare case where the repartitioned sub-netlists are identical to

the ones from the previous trial, we discard the current partition and repartition the netlist again. This repartition scheme is more effective than a static pre-partitioning, as it allows global cross-boundary optimization that uncovers more area saving opportunities.

In PIMap, the overall optimization flow contains a user-specified number of trials, and the overall flow terminates when it reaches the maximum number of trials or the runtime limit. A highly-optimized and mapped netlist is generated as the final result.

4.4 Extension to Depth-Constrained Area Minimization

PIMap can be extended to support depth-constrained area minimization with only a few modifications to the optimization flow. In depth-constrained area minimization, we assume that the input logic networks are already optimized for depth, and PIMap will try to reduce the area of such networks given that the depth does not increase. To handle depth-constrained area minimization, we modify the PIMap flow in the following aspects:

- We replace the area-oriented technology mapper with a depth-oriented technology mapper so that the depth constraint is likely to be met.

- During each trial, after recombining the optimized sub-netlists, we add a global depth-optimization step that re-maps the logic network using the depth-oriented technology mapper.

- After the global depth-optimization step, we reject the result of the current trial if the design exceeds the depth constraint or the area of the design increases compared to the previous trial. If a current trial is rejected, we reuse the netlist from the previous trial.

The above extensions ensure that the depth constraint is satisfied throughout the optimization flow, while the PIMap techniques are able to minimize the design area under the depth constraint.

5. Experimental Results

We implement the PIMap techniques in C, including the iterative search procedure, the netlist decomposition algorithm, and the routine to manage the parallel optimization across different machines. We integrate the logic optimization moves and the technology mapper in ABC [3] as a static library into PIMap. Throughout the experiment, we use ABC's native AIG as the gate-level representation. In our experiment, we use PIMap to refine designs that are already optimized by existing technology mappers (e.g., optimization scripts from ABC, or the best known results from the EPFL benchmark suite [1]). PIMap can also handle unoptimized designs, and generate final designs without any quality loss, but at the cost of slightly longer runtime.

Table 1. Area reduction using PIMap on the 10 largest MCNC combinational benchmarks — Base = the baseline designs synthesized using ABC's compress2rs script followed by an area-oriented technology mapper (command if -a -K 6); n Trials = result after n number of trials using PIMap; Size = size of the design in terms of number of 6-input LUTs; Dpt = depth of the design defined as the highest LUT level; Time = runtime in seconds; Improv = improvement in size between PIMap and the baseline designs.

Designs	Base Size	Base Dpt	5 Trials Size	Dpt	Time	Improv	10 Trials Size	Dpt	Time	Improv	40 Trials Size	Dpt	Time	Improv
alu4	455	9	425	13	22.3	6.6%	405	15	42.9	11.0%	393	13	168.8	13.6%
apex2	526	12	493	15	22.2	6.3%	488	15	43.1	7.2%	439	17	177.4	16.5%
apex4	568	9	555	13	18.1	2.3%	541	13	38.3	4.8%	526	13	162.4	7.4%
des	631	9	544	8	31.9	13.8%	509	8	62.2	19.3%	477	8	253.0	24.4%
ex1010	606	9	589	11	18.8	2.8%	584	13	39.4	3.6%	556	15	158.5	8.3%
ex5p	332	10	324	11	16.3	2.4%	319	12	34.0	3.9%	304	12	136.9	8.4%
misex3	382	9	352	9	18.6	7.9%	333	10	36.3	12.8%	298	9	153.0	22.0%
pdc	1251	14	1219	19	31.8	2.6%	1200	22	66.6	4.1%	1150	19	266.5	8.1%
seq	627	10	606	12	22.1	3.3%	596	11	43.2	4.9%	567	12	177.0	9.6%
spla	1251	14	1222	18	32.5	2.3%	1191	18	63.8	4.8%	1133	25	250.8	9.4%
geomean						4.8%				7.4%				12.4%

Table 2. Area reduction using PIMap on the EPFL arithmetic benchmarks — Base = the best known results on EPFL benchmarks [1]; n Trials = result after n number of trials using PIMap; Size = size of the design in terms of number of 6-input LUTs; Dpt = depth of the design defined as the highest LUT level; Time = runtime in seconds; Improv = improvement in size between PIMap and the baseline designs.

Designs	Base Size	Base Dpt	5 Trials Size	Dpt	Time	Improv	10 Trials Size	Dpt	Time	Improv	40 Trials Size	Dpt	Time	Improv
adder	201	73	196	68	19.2	2.5%	196	68	37.7	2.5%	194	66	150.5	3.5%
shifter	512	4	512	4	21.1	0.0%	512	4	41.1	0.0%	512	4	164.5	0.0%
divisor	3813	1542	3636	1490	53.1	4.6%	3527	1431	104.3	7.5%	3331	1277	418.1	12.6%
hyp	44635	4194	44095	4341	195.5	1.2%	43677	4431	394.9	2.1%	42164	4542	1604.3	5.5%
log2	7344	142	7036	133	60.9	4.2%	6904	129	119.8	6.0%	6749	119	491.5	8.1%
max	532	192	525	190	28.1	1.3%	525	190	57.6	1.3%	522	190	222.3	1.9%
mult	5681	120	5184	97	64.6	8.7%	5069	90	133.7	10.8%	4986	86	544.9	12.2%
sine	1347	62	1273	57	40.3	5.5%	1261	57	81.2	6.4%	1235	56	332.7	8.3%
sqrt	3286	1180	3246	1198	52.1	1.2%	3200	1188	103.8	2.6%	3127	1154	412.1	4.8%
square	3800	116	3380	77	94.1	11.1%	3346	77	184.8	11.9%	3281	74	730.3	13.7%
geomean						4.1%				5.2%				7.2%

In our experiment, the set of logic transformation techniques T consists of three elements: balance, rewrite, and refactor, with a uniform probability distribution $P = \{1/3, 1/3, 1/3\}$. We set $\gamma = 1$ in Algorithm 1. Throughout the experiment, we target mapping to 6-input LUTs. Of course, PIMap also supports other LUT architectures. For each design, we execute 40 trials, and each trial contains 100 iterations of mapping-guided logic optimization. For parallelization, we partition the original design to up to 16 sub-netlists, where each sub-netlist contains up to 100 LUTs. We run PIMap on up to eight machines, and each machine has a quad-core Xeon CPU operating at 2.66GHz.

We use two well-known benchmark suites to evaluate the effectiveness of PIMap: the 10 largest combinational benchmarks in the MCNC benchmark suite [15], as well as the entire EPFL arithmetic benchmark suite [1]. This collection of benchmarks contains a diverse set of designs ranging from common arithmetic units to realistic industrial designs. These designs also greatly differ in size.

5.1 Unconstrained Area Minimization

Table 1 shows the results of unconstrained area minimization for the 10 largest MCNC combinational benchmarks. For this set of benchmarks, we first apply ABC's compress2rs logic optimization script targeting area reduction. Based on our experiments with the available ABC synthesis scripts, compress2rs achieves the best area results for the majority of the designs. The optimized logic network is then mapped into 6-input LUTs using ABC's area-optimized mapper with command if -a -K 6. For PIMap, we record the size, depth, and runtime after 5, 10 and 40 trials. We also report the improvement of LUT counts in the PIMap-optimized designs over the baseline designs.

PIMap is able to reduce the LUT count by 4.8% on average after five trials, and 12.4% after 40 trials. For des and misex3, PIMap is able to reduce the size by more than 20%, showing the effectiveness of PIMap compared to ABC. The runtime of the 10 benchmarks are similar due to the similar sizes of the designs, averaging around 20 seconds for five trials, and 160 seconds for 40 trials. Although the runtime of PIMap is noticeably higher than existing mappers, which usually take less than a second for designs of similar sizes, we argue that PIMap is still valuable and viable in a high-effort FPGA implementation mode where technology mapping is unlikely the performance bottleneck.

Table 3. Area reduction under depth constraint using PIMap on the 10 largest MCNC combinational benchmarks —
We use the depth of the baseline designs as the depth constraint. `Base` = the baseline designs synthesized using ABC's `resyn2` script followed by a depth-oriented technology mapper (command `if -K 6`); `n Trials` = result after `n` number of trials using PIMap; `Size` = size of the design in terms of number of 6-input LUTs; `Dpt` = depth of the design defined as the highest LUT level; `Time` = runtime in seconds; `Improv` = improvement in size between PIMap and the baseline designs.

Designs	Base		5 Trials				10 Trials				40 Trials			
	Size	Dpt	Size	Dpt	Time	Improv	Size	Dpt	Time	Improv	Size	Dpt	Time	Improv
alu4	511	5	438	5	32.4	14.3%	438	5	68.0	14.3%	437	5	254.3	14.5%
apex2	674	6	511	6	31.3	24.2%	489	6	60.9	27.4%	469	6	250.2	30.4%
apex4	588	5	588	5	33.4	0.0%	588	5	63.9	0.0%	588	5	251.8	0.0%
des	818	5	651	5	50.3	20.4%	632	5	97.9	22.7%	584	5	395.4	28.6%
ex1010	655	5	654	5	30.5	0.2%	654	5	63.9	0.2%	652	5	258.2	0.5%
ex5p	351	5	351	5	25.4	0.0%	351	5	51.0	0.0%	351	5	202.7	0.0%
misex3	443	5	318	5	32.8	28.2%	314	5	65.0	29.1%	306	5	239.4	30.9%
pdc	1431	7	1430	7	55.0	0.1%	1430	7	107.4	0.1%	1427	7	441.0	0.3%
seq	693	5	590	5	33.3	14.9%	588	5	66.9	15.2%	588	5	282.9	15.2%
spla	1392	7	1387	7	61.9	0.4%	1361	7	128.0	2.2%	1361	7	479.7	2.2%
geomean						8.7%				9.4%				10.7%

We further apply PIMap to the EPFL arithmetic benchmark suite, and compare our results with the best known mapping records from the EPFL database that are publicly available [1]. Table 2 shows the comparison between PIMap and the existing best known results (used as baseline). PIMap is able to improve nine out of the 10 best known mapping results, with an average improvement of 7.2%. Notably, PIMap reduces the LUT count for `divisor`, `mult`, and `square` by more than 12%. In addition, PIMap improves the depth in eight out of the 10 designs even though it is not intended for depth optimization in this particular use case. We conjecture that existing area-oriented mappers that generate the best known min-area solutions have to make an unnecessary compromise in depth to gain additional area savings. We also note that even for the largest design `hyp` that has more than 44 thousand LUTs, the PIMap runtime remains reasonable, owing to the fact that we optimize multiple small sub-netlists in parallel instead of directly optimizing the entire design.

5.2 Depth-Constrained Area Minimization

Table 3 shows the result of depth-constrained area minimization on MCNC benchmarks. For the baseline designs, we first apply ABC's depth-minimizing `resyn2` script, then map the optimized logic network into 6-input LUTs using ABC's depth-oriented mapper with command `if -K 6`. We use the depth of the mapped baseline designs as the depth constraint for PIMap, and invoke PIMap to reduce the area of the baseline designs. PIMap is able to reduce the area for eight out of the 10 designs, with an average improvement of 10.7%, while preserving the depth from the baseline designs. It is noteworthy that PIMap achieves 30% area reduction for `apex2`, `des`, and `misex3`, showing that PIMap is still highly effective under a hard constraint on depth.

5.3 Scalability of Parallel Optimization

Figure 7 shows the scalability of PIMap. In our experiment, we partition an input netlist to up to 16 sub-netlists, each

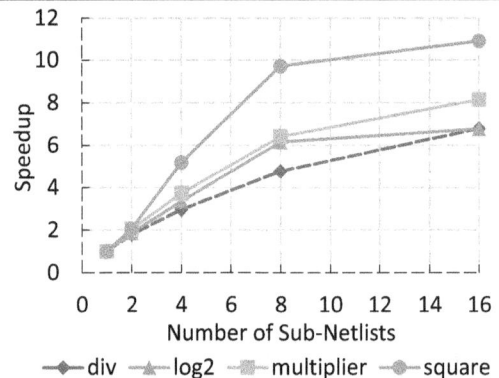

Figure 7. Scalability of the parallel optimization technique — We use PIMap for area reduction to test the scalability of parallelization. We measure the runtime to achieve a specific area target and plot the speedup in runtime versus number of sub-netlist partitions.

of which contains up to 100 LUTs. We select four large benchmarks in the EPFL benchmark suite, and study the runtime required to achieve a fixed area target. The area target of each benchmark is set to be the area of the PIMap-optimized design using one sub-netlist and 100 trials. In this experiment, we use four parallel threads to optimize one sub-netlist, which requires up to 64 threads in total for the 16 sub-netlists.

As shown Figure 7, PIMap scales reasonably well up to 16 sub-netlist partitions across multiple designs. In particular, PIMap scales near-linearly up to eight sub-netlists. With more sub-netlists, the overhead of netlist decomposition and reassembly becomes nontrivial and prevents PIMap from achieving the ideal speedup.

5.4 Runtime Breakdown of PIMap

Figure 8 shows the relative runtime of the four main steps in PIMap. Sub-netlist generation refers to the step of decomposing the original netlist into sub-netlists. The logic transformation step first proposes a transformation move, then applies the selected move to the network. The LUT mapping

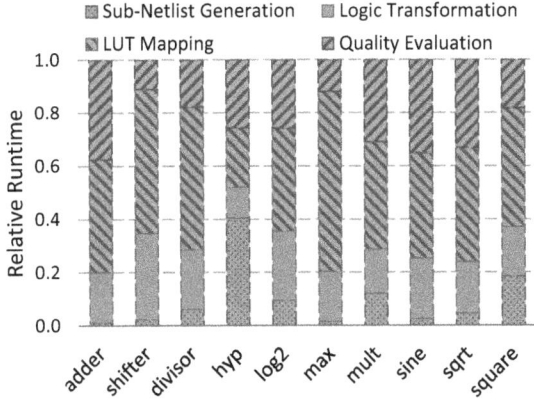

Figure 8. Runtime breakdown of PIMap.

step converts the logic networks into LUTs using ABC's built-in technology mapper named `if`. The quality evaluation step calculates the quality of the proposed transformation and decides whether to accept the proposed move.

Not surprisingly, the LUT mapping consumes the largest portion of the runtime, followed by quality evaluation and logic transformation. These three steps together dominate the runtime since they need to be iteratively invoked for many times in each trial (100 in our experiment). The runtime of the sub-netlist generation step is negligible for most of the benchmarks since the BFS-based extraction algorithm scales linearly as the size of the netlist. For `hyp`, the runtime of sub-netlist generation is noticeably higher than the other designs since it is significantly larger than other designs. Nevertheless, the runtime of sub-netlist generation for `hyp` is still on the same order of the other steps.

5.5 Impact of Sub-Netlist Size on PIMap Runtime

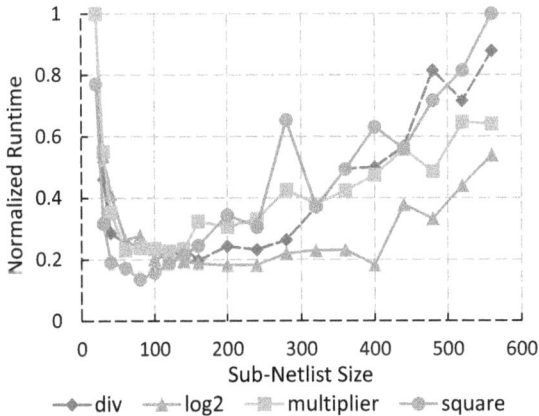

Figure 9. Impact of sub-netlist size on PIMap runtime.

Figure 9 shows the impact of the sub-netlist size on the PIMap runtime to achieve a fixed area target, defined as the area after 100 trials using a sub-netlist size of 20 LUTs. We partition the designs up to 16 sub-netlists. For smaller designs that do not admit 16 sub-netlists, we partition them into as many sub-netlists as feasible. The runtime in Figure 9

is normalized to the longest runtime of the corresponding design.

We observe that across the four benchmarks, the runtime inflection point is around the size of 100 LUTs. With smaller sub-netlists, each PIMap optimization thread runs faster, but overall progress may be slow since each sub-netlist only covers a small fraction of the entire design.

5.6 Area Reduction under a Tight Runtime Limit

Table 4. Area reduction using PIMap with 10 second runtime limit — `Base` = the best known results on EPFL benchmarks [1]; `PIMap` = solution of PIMap after 10 seconds. We highlight the designs that are improved by PIMap.

Designs	Base		PIMap	
	Size	Dpt	Size	Dpt
adder	201	73	**197**	69
shifter	512	4	512	4
divisor	3813	1542	**3787**	1536
hyp	44635	4194	44635	4194
log2	7344	142	**7305**	144
max	532	192	**526**	190
mult	5681	120	**5594**	118
sine	1347	62	**1309**	62
sqrt	3286	1180	**3279**	1181
square	3800	116	**3675**	102

Table 4 shows the performance of PIMap under a tight runtime limit, which is set to be 10 seconds. In this case, PIMap achieves less area savings but still manages to improve the best-known mapping results in eight out of the 10 EPFL benchmarks.

5.7 LUT Count vs. Gate Count Reduction

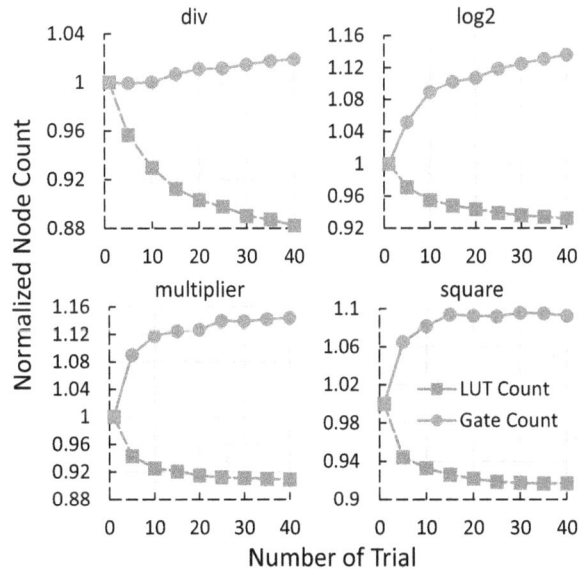

Figure 10. Relation between LUT count and AIG gate count at various design points of the same design.

Figure 10 shows the LUT count and the corresponding gate count in the AIG of the same design during the optimization process in PIMap, normalized to their initial values. For the four benchmarks, the LUT count decreases as the number of trials increases. However, we observe an opposite trend in gate count during the optimization, which agrees with our correlation study in Section 3.

6. Related Work

Mishchenko, et al. [11] describe a number of efficient rewriting techniques on AIGs, which serve as the basis for the logic transformations used in this work. The majority-inverter graph (MIG) proposed by Amarú, et al. [2] provides an alternative logic representation using three-input majority nodes and regular/complemented edges. MIG is shown to be beneficial for improving mapping quality in a number of cases. This is complementary to PIMap, since our iterative improvement framework is agnostic to logic representations.

Yang, et al. [16] propose a new way of logic synthesis by maintaining a precomputed library of optimal or near-optimal circuits for small practical functions. Their logic synthesis flow matches and replaces small circuit components in a new design to the elements in the precomputed library. However, this approach can only find optimal or near-optimal solution for small functions with no more than 12 inputs, and become sub-optimal for functions with more inputs. PIMap is orthogonal to [16] and it is not limited by the input size of the sub-netlist. It is also possible to incorporate Boolean matching techniques as new transformation moves in our iterative improvement framework.

STOKE [14] uses stochastic search to optimize x86 programs by randomly rewriting the x86 assembly instructions. Both STOKE and our approach randomly propose transformations using MCMC sampling to explore a large design space. Besides the different application domains, our work differs from STOKE in two major aspects: (1) STOKE focuses on using local moves that modify a single instruction at a time, while we make use of the logic rewriting techniques applied to multiple nodes in the network; (2) STOKE can only handle small programs with around one hundred instructions. In contrast, PIMap makes use of parallel optimization to effectively handle much larger circuits with tens of thousands LUTs.

7. Conclusions

We propose PIMap, a parallelized iterative improvement framework for area-oriented FPGA technology mapping. PIMap iteratively proposes logic transformation moves to optimize an input logic network for LUT mapping, and uses the actual mapping result to evaluate the quality of a proposed move. To improve the runtime, PIMap decomposes a large circuit netlist into multiple smaller sub-netlists, and optimizes them in parallel across different machines. Experimental results demonstrate significantly improvement in mapping quality for both unconstrained area optimization and depth-constrained area optimization compared to the state-of-the-art technology mappers. As a future direction,

we plan to investigate global restructuring techniques on the logic network to further improve the quality of PIMap.

8. Acknowledgements

This work was supported in part by NSF Awards #1337240, #1453378, #1512937, a DARPA Young Faculty Award D15AP00096, and a research gift from Xilinx, Inc.

References

[1] L. Amarú, P.-E. Gaillardon, and G. De Micheli. The EPFL Combinational Benchmark Suite. *International Workshop on Logic & Synthesis (IWLS)*, 2015.

[2] L. Amarú, P.-E. Gaillardon, and G. De Micheli. Majority-Inverter Graph: A New Paradigm for Logic Optimization. *IEEE Trans. on Computer-Aided Design of Integrated Circuits and Systems (TCAD)*, 35(5):806–819, 2016.

[3] Berkeley Logic Synthesis and Verification Group, ABC: A System for Sequential Synthesis and Verification, Release 60413. `http://www.eecs.berkeley.edu/~alanmi/abc/`.

[4] D. Chen, J. Cong, and P. Pan. FPGA Design Automation: A Survey. *Foundations and Trends in Electronic Design Automation*, 1(3):139–169, 2006.

[5] A. H. Farrahi and M. Sarrafzadeh. Complexity of the Lookup-Table Minimization Problem for FPGA Technology Mapping. *IEEE Trans. on Computer-Aided Design of Integrated Circuits and Systems (TCAD)*, 13(11), 1994.

[6] C. J. Geyer. Practical Markov Chain Monte Carlo. *Statistical Science*, pages 473–483, 1992.

[7] W. K. Hastings. Monte Carlo Sampling Methods using Markov Chains and Their Applications. *Biometrika*, 57(1):97–109, 1970.

[8] Y. Hu, V. Shih, R. Majumdar, and L. He. FPGA Area Reduction by Multi-Output Function Based Sequential Resynthesis. *Design Automation Conf. (DAC)*, 2008.

[9] S. Kirkpatrick, C. D. Gelatt, and M. P. Vecchi. Optimization by Simmulated Annealing. *Science*, 220:671–680, 1983.

[10] A. Mishchenko and R. Brayton. Scalable Logic Synthesis using a Simple Circuit Structure. *International Workshop on Logic & Synthesis (IWLS)*, pages 15–22, 2006.

[11] A. Mishchenko, S. Chatterjee, and R. Brayton. DAG-Aware AIG Rewriting a Fresh Look at Combinational Logic Synthesis. *Design Automation Conf. (DAC)*, 2006.

[12] A. Mishchenko, S. Chatterjee, and R. K. Brayton. Improvements to Technology Mapping for LUT-Based FPGAs. *IEEE Trans. on Computer-Aided Design of Integrated Circuits and Systems (TCAD)*, 26(2):240–253, 2007.

[13] P. Pan, A. K. Karandikar, and C. Liu. Optimal Clock Period Clustering for Sequential Circuits with Retiming. *IEEE Trans. on Computer-Aided Design of Integrated Circuits and Systems (TCAD)*, 17(6):489–498, 1998.

[14] E. Schkufza, R. Sharma, and A. Aiken. Stochastic Super-optimization. *Int'l Conf. on Architectural Support for Programming Languages and Operating Systems (ASPLOS)*, 2013.

[15] S. Yang. *Logic Synthesis and Optimization Benchmarks*. Microelectronics Center of North Carolina (MCNC), 1991.

[16] W. Yang, L. Wang, and A. Mishchenko. Lazy Man's Logic Synthesis. *Int'l Conf. on Computer-Aided Design (ICCAD)*, 2012.

A Parallel Bandit-Based Approach for Autotuning FPGA Compilation

Chang Xu[1,*], Gai Liu[2], Ritchie Zhao[2], Stephen Yang[3], Guojie Luo[1], Zhiru Zhang[2,†]

[1] Center for Energy-Efficient Computing and Applications, Peking University, Beijing, China
[2] School of Electrical and Computer Engineering, Cornell University, Ithaca, USA
[3] Xilinx, Inc., San Jose, USA

*changxu@pku.edu.cn, †zhiruz@cornell.edu

Abstract

Mainstream FPGA CAD tools provide an extensive collection of optimization options that have a significant impact on the quality of the final design. These options together create an enormous and complex design space that cannot effectively be explored by human effort alone. Instead, we propose to search this parameter space using autotuning, which is a popular approach in the compiler optimization domain. Specifically, we study the effectiveness of applying the multi-armed bandit (MAB) technique to automatically tune the options for a complete FPGA compilation flow from RTL to bitstream, including RTL/logic synthesis, technology mapping, placement, and routing. To mitigate the high runtime cost incurred by the complex FPGA implementation process, we devise an efficient parallelization scheme that enables multiple MAB-based autotuners to explore the design space simultaneously. In particular, we propose a dynamic solution space partitioning and resource allocation technique that intelligently allocates computing resources to promising search regions based on the runtime information of search quality from previous iterations. Experiments on academic and commercial FPGA CAD tools demonstrate promising improvements in quality and convergence rate across a variety of real-life designs.

1. Introduction

Over the last three decades, FPGAs have evolved from a small chip with a few thousand logic blocks to billion-transistor system-on-chips containing hardened DSP blocks, embedded memories, multicore processors, alongside millions of programmable logic elements. Concurrently, FPGA development tools have also grown into sophisticated design environments. Compiling an RTL design into bitstream typically involves heuristically solving a sequence of complex combinatorial optimization problems such as logic synthesis, technology mapping, placement, and routing [7].

To meet the stringent yet diverse design requirements from different domains and use cases, modern FPGA CAD tools commonly provide users with a large collection of optimization options (or parameters) that have a significant impact on the quality of the final design. For instance, the placement step alone in the Xilinx Vivado Design Suite offers up to 20 different parameters, translating to a search space of more than 10^6 design points [3]. In addition, multiple options may interact in subtle ways resulting in unpredictable effects on solution quality. Traditionally, navigating through such an enormous design space requires designers to rely on either prior design experience or vendor-supplied guidelines. Such ad hoc design practices incur costly manual effort to achieve the desired quality of results (QoR). Worse, each new design may require a drastically different set of options to achieve the best QoR [24].

One solution to improve design productivity is employing meta-heuristic search techniques to explore the parameter space automatically. Figure 1 shows the improvement of the worst negative slack (WNS) of three designs generated by Vivado, each tuned using three different search techniques: active learning, Bayes classification, and greedy mutation. From our experiments, it is evident that the most effective search technique (in terms of the number of Vivado runs needed to close timing) varies across different designs. Intuitively, distinct designs often present vastly different structures of the search space. Besides, different phases of the design space exploration benefit from different search techniques. For example, stochastic methods such as genetic algorithm may be more useful during the initial phase of the search, while first-order optimizations like gradient descent are very efficient in finding local minima when the promising search space is narrowed.

The above observations clearly motivate the use of an ensemble of search heuristics rather than one particular technique to effectively explore the design space of FPGA compilation. Similar insights were also gained in the OpenTuner project, which aimed to provide an extensible open-source framework for software program autotuning [4]. OpenTuner currently incorporates a collection of search techniques to

FPGA'17, February 22-24, 2017, Monterey, CA, USA
©2017 ACM. ISBN 978-1-4503-4354-1/17/02 ... $15.00
DOI: http://dx.doi.org/10.1145/3020078.3021747

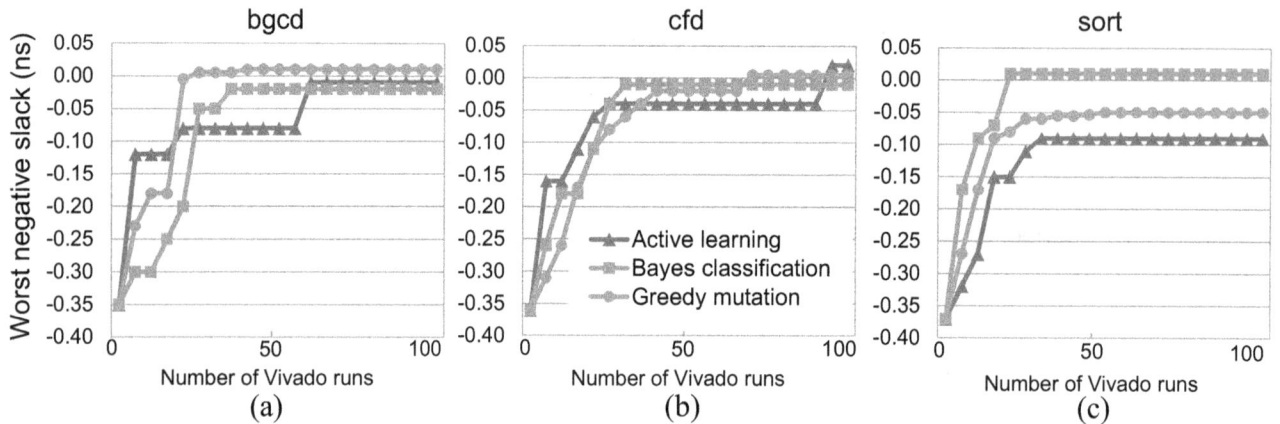

Figure 1: The search traces of three designs using three different search algorithms with the goal of improving worst negative slack — We use meta-heuristic algorithms to analyze results from Vivado, and guide the selection of Vivado configuration parameters. The x-axis denotes the number of Vivado runs. (a) `greedy mutation`, a simple genetic algorithm, is to first to close timing for binary GCD; (b) `active leaning`, a semi-supervised machine learning technique, is the first to close timing for computational fluid dynamics; (c) `Bayes classification`, the naïve Bayes classifiers, is the first to close timing for the bubble sort design.

provide robustness against different search spaces and uses the multi-armed bandit (MAB) algorithm [11] to determine the allocation of trials between the available techniques dynamically. In addition to applications in program autotuning [4], MAB has already been applied to many important optimization problems in various fields, such as artificial intelligence [19, 22] and operations research [9, 15].

Since FPGA CAD tools usually require long execution times (minutes to hours for real-world designs), it is crucial to significantly speed up the MAB-guided search without sacrificing the final QoR. An intuitive approach is launching multiple machines simultaneously, each conducting a MAB-guided search within the solution space independently. Alternatively, one can use a more efficient scheme that dynamically partitions the solution space into multiple partitions, and allocates additional computing resources to regions that are more likely to generate high-quality solutions.

In this paper, we propose *DATuner* — a parallel bandit-based framework for autotuning FPGA compilation. DATuner is built on OpenTuner but instead focuses on improving the productivity and quality of FPGA-targeted hardware designs. We also propose scalable and effective parallelization techniques based on dynamical solution space partitioning to speed up the convergence of DATuner. Our main contributions are as follows:

1. We adapt OpenTuner to tune the CAD tool parameters for FPGA compilation and demonstrate the effectiveness of the bandit-based approach in improving the design QoR.

2. We propose a scalable parallelization scheme which accomplishes the following: (1) efficiently partitions the global solution space into promising subspaces; (2) allocates compute resource among subspaces to balance the

exploration of unknown subspaces and the *exploitation* of subspaces with known high-quality solutions.

3. Experiments with DATuner on academic and commercial FPGA CAD tools demonstrate very encouraging improvements in design quality across a variety of real-life benchmarks. We believe that our framework is also applicable to many other EDA problems.

The rest of the paper is organized as follows: Section 2 introduces the preliminaries that serve as the basics of this work; Section 3 discusses our proposed techniques; Section 4 presents the experimental results; Section 5 summarizes the related work, followed by conclusions in Section 6.

2. Preliminaries

In this section, we provide an overview of the MAB problem formulation, its usage in OpenTuner, as well as the basics of the FPGA compilation process.

2.1 Multi-Armed Bandit Approach

The MAB problem and its solutions are extensively studied in statistics and machine learning [11]. The classic problem is formulated as a game, where the player has a fixed number of actions to choose from (i.e., *arms*), each of which having a reward given by an unknown probability distribution with an unknown expected value. The game progresses in rounds, and in each round, the player chooses one action (i.e., *pull an arm*) and obtain a reward sampled from the corresponding distribution. The reward loosely captures the effectiveness of an arm, and crucially, its probability distribution is learned during the process of the game. The objective is to maximize the total payoff after all the rounds. An effective MAB algorithm must find a right balance between *exploitation* (choosing the known best arm to obtain the highest ex-

158

pected reward), and *exploration* (selecting an infrequently used arm to gain more information about its reward distribution). Choosing an infrequently used arm sacrifices short-term gain for the possibility of discovering greater payoff in the long run. Existing methods are usually randomized algorithms, which pick an action in each round based on the history of chosen actions and observed rewards so far [5, 6]. The quality metric of an MAB algorithm is *regret*, which is the ratio between optimal payoff (obtained by pulling the optimal arm every round) and that generated from the MAB algorithm. Several known MAB algorithms can achieve a regret of $O(log N)$ for an N-round MAB, which has been shown to be asymptotically optimal [8].

Recently, an open-source autotuning framework called OpenTuner has adopted MAB to improve the runtime of software benchmarks [4]. Specifically, OpenTuner incorporates an ensemble of meta-heuristics for effectively searching the space of software compiler options. Examples of these heuristic methods include differential evolution, genetic algorithm, particle swarm optimization, and simulated annealing. The MAB algorithm used in OpenTuner treats each search method as an arm, and measures its reward using the area under curve mechanism — If an arm has yielded a new global best, an upward line is drawn, otherwise, a flat line is drawn. The area under this curve (scaled to a maximum value of 1) is the total payoff attributed to the corresponding arm. To balance exploitation and exploration, OpenTuner ranks each arm with a weighted sum of the area under curve metric and the frequency of its previous uses. Notably, OpenTuner reported up to 2.8x speedup at no programming cost by automatically tuning GCC flags.

2.2 FPGA Compilation Flow

The mainstream FPGA compilation flow takes an RTL design as input and generates a device-specific bitstream. This process involves several distinct and modular steps: logic synthesis, technology mapping, placement, and routing. Synthesis lowers the RTL design into a technology-independent logic or gate-level network. Technology mapping then maps this network into a netlist of look-up tables (LUTs). Placement determines the physical location of each LUT in the netlist, and routing connects all signal paths using the available programmable interconnects.

Many of these steps involve NP-hard problems. To tackle the difficulty of solving these problems, experts propose some approximated solutions with heuristic-based methods. FPGA CAD tools often provide designers with a set of configuration parameters that select between heuristics or influence the behavior of a heuristic. Examples of parameters include enabling remapping or retiming in logic synthesis, deciding how much to spread logic for congestion or how much to weight wire delay. Table 1 shows the tunable parameters available in the open-source Verilog-to-Routing (VTR) toolflow [16], covering logic synthesis, packing, placement and routing. With commercial FPGA CAD tools from Alter-

a/Intel and Xilinx, a much larger collection of switches are available (roughly 60 to 80 options are exposed to designers).

Table 1: List of tunable VTR configuration parameters.

Parameter	Value	Stage
resyn	{on,off}	logic synthesis
resyn2	{on,off}	logic synthesis
resyn3	{on,off}	logic synthesis
alpha_clustering	[0,1]	packing
beta_clustering	[0,1]	packing
allow_unrelated_cluster	{on,off}	packing
connection	{on,off}	packing
alpha_t	[0.5-0.9]	placement
seed	{1,2,3,4,5}	placement
inner_num	{1,10,100}	placement
timing_tradeoff	[0.3-0.7]	placement
inner_loop_recompute	{0,1,5}	placement
td_place_exp_first	{0,1,3}	placement
td_place_exp_last	{5,8,10}	placement
max_router_iterations	{20,50,80}	routing
initial_pres_fac	[0.3-100]	routing
pres_fac_mult	[1.2-2]	routing
acc_fac	[1-2]	routing
bb_factor	{1,3,5}	routing
astar_fac	[1-2]	routing
max_criticality	[0.8-1]	routing
criticality_exp	[0.8-1]	routing
base_cost_type	{'demand_only', 'delay_normalized'}	routing

2.3 Autotuning FPGA Compilation Parameters

Obviously, these tool options together create an enormous design space which cannot be effectively explored by human effort alone. Besides, there is no single set of compilation parameters that works for all designs [24]. Thus, we propose to automatically configure the FPGA tool options to achieve a faster design closure and better QoRs. The QoR metrics can be timing slack, resource usage, or power consumption. Due to the slow runtime of FPGA compilation, effective parallelization is paramount to ensure the viability of autotuning.

In this paper, we propose a parallel search methodology named DATuner. DATuner adopts OpenTuner as its core search engine to leverage the advantage of an ensemble over a single technique.

3. DATuner Techniques

In this section, we first propose a dynamic solution space partitioning method for parallelization. We also provide a MAB-based method for uneven computing resource allocation. Then we illustrate our paralellization framework.

3.1 Motivation

We formulate the EDA autotuning problem as a search problem in an N-dimensional solution space called S_0, where each dimension can be either continuous or discrete. Obviously, S_0 grows exponentially with the dimensionality of the solution space. When N is large, it is impractical to exhaustively traverse the search space to find the optimal solution. A simple approach is to partition S_0 into subspaces, launch multiple parallel searches, and assign each search instance to explore within one subspace. However, since some subspaces are more promising than others in terms of yielding good solutions, it is vital to properly partition the solution space in a way that the majority of search instances are assigned to the most promising subspaces. Of course, just as there is no single set of tool parameters that works well for all designs, no static partitioning of the solution space is optimal across designs.

Finding a suitable partitioning of the search space is key to improving the quality of the search. But doing so manually is usually hard, and requires adequate domain knowledge. In addition, just as there is no single set of parameters that works well for all designs, no static partitioning of the parameter space is optimal across designs. Thus, we propose a novel parallelization method, where we gradually identify promising subspaces via dynamic partitioning based on QoR samples obtained at runtime. We further propose an MAB-based compute resource allocation method for uneven sampling — more compute resources are assigned to promising subspaces to increase sampling quality.

3.2 Dynamic Solution Space Partition

We propose to partition the solution space dynamically, where the partitioning does not rely on any prior knowledge; instead it is decided by posterior knowledge learned during runtime. More specifically, our partitioning method iteratively constructs a *space partitioning tree* (SP tree), where the root node of the tree represents the initial solution space, and each intermediate node represents a subspace. The leaf nodes of the SP tree collectively form the active partitioning that is currently used by the parallel search instances. In each iteration, we select a subspace and divide it into multiple smaller partitions. As a result, a leaf in the SP tree will become an intermediate node that branches out to multiple new children, with which each "newborn" representing a newly created subspace.

Given an N dimensional solution space, we propose to dynamically partition the search space into subspaces and allocate more computing resources for searching within promising subspaces. This dynamic partitioning process is illustrated in Figure 2. S_0 represents the initial solution space and $S_1, S_2, ..., S_n$ are the subspaces iteratively created during space partitioning process. Figure 2(a) shows the known samples that are explored, where each grey dot indicates a sample with a good QoR and red crosses are those with poor QoRs. At each step of the partitioning process, a key decision is to select the most profitable dimension out of the N dimensions to partition, such that we can gain as much information about the solution space as possible. Here we propose to examine the entropy and information gain [20] when partitioning a specific dimension. Specifically, for each dimension i in the N-dimensional search space, we compute conditional entropy assuming we partition along dimension i and derive the corresponding information gain. We select the dimension with the highest information gain to partition.

Formally, for a subspace S_i, we define the set of known samples within S_i as D_i. We further label each sample as good or bad based on its associated QoR, and use Dg_i and Db_i to denote subset of good and bad samples within D_i, respectively (note that $Dg_i \cup Db_i = D_i$). Then we define the entropy of D_i as

$$H(D_i) = -(\frac{|Dg_i|}{|D_i|} \log(\frac{|Dg_i|}{|D_i|}) + \frac{|Db_i|}{|D_i|} \log(\frac{|Db_i|}{|D_i|}))$$

where $|D_i|$, $|Dg_i|$, $|Db_i|$ are the cardinalities of sets D_i, Dg_i, and Db_i, respectively. We next define the conditional entropy of D_i conditioned on a specific dimension of S_i. Suppose d represents the parameter chosen for the dth dimension of S_i, and we assume d has k possible discrete values. If we further define $H(D_i|d = j)$ as the entropy of D_i conditioned on d taking the value of j, we will have

$$H(D_i|d) = \sum_{j=1}^{k} \frac{|D_{i,d=j}|}{|D_i|} H(D_i|d = j)$$

Here $|D_{i,d=j}|$ is the cardinality of the set of samples in S_i with d set to j. With the above notations, we can formally define the information gain along dimension d as $G(D_i, d) = H(D_i) - H(D_i|d)$. Our dynamic space partitioning algorithm creates a new subspace by partitioning along the dimension with the highest information gain. If the chosen dimension has k possible parameter values (continuous value will be discretized), it will get partitioned and become an intermediate node in SP tree with $(k - 1)$ new children.

For the example in Figure 2(a), we have the following calculations when deciding whether to partition along x or y dimension. Here we assume have sampled 14 design points and eight of them have good QoRs. Therefore, the entropy of the initial solution space S_0 is $H(D_0) = -(\frac{8}{14}log(\frac{8}{14}) + \frac{6}{14}log(\frac{6}{14})) = 0.986$. We then compute the conditional entropy of D_0 conditioned on dimension x and y as $H(D_0|x) = \frac{8}{14} * 0.81 + \frac{6}{14} * 0.91 = 0.853$, and $H(D_0|y) = \frac{6}{14} * 1.00 + \frac{8}{14} * 0.96 = 0.977$. Finally, we compute the information gain for partitioning along x or y dimension as $G(D_0, x) = 0.133$ and $G(D_0, y) = 0.009$. Since the former information gain is higher, we decide to partition S_0 along the x dimension, which results in two new subspaces S_1 and S_2, as shown in Figure 2(b,c). In the next iteration of this process, we follow the same method and choose to further partition along the y dimension in S_2 as shown in Figure 2(d).

160

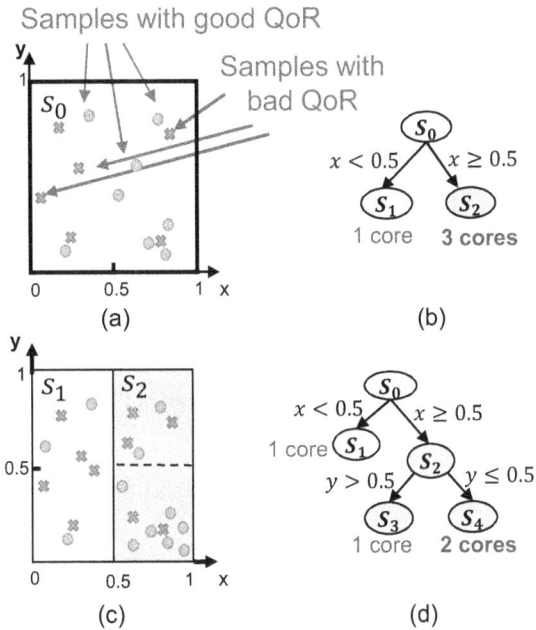

Figure 2: Conceptual illustration of the solution space partitioning method — The solution space is 2D with each dimension constrained to [0,1]. grey circles represent samples with good QoR and red crosses are poor samples. (a) and (c) show the partitions and the known samples at each iteration. (b) and (d) show the corresponding SP trees. Given four cores, we assign a different number of cores to each subspace based on the quality of solutions in that subspace. At each step, we choose the dimension with the highest information gain to partition.

3.3 MAB-directed Computing Resource Allocation

Once we obtain an SP tree, we need to properly allocate the available compute resources to the subspaces to maximize the overall sampling rewards. The key here is to balance exploitation (i.e., allocating more search instances to the most promising subspace) with exploration (i.e., sampling less promising subspaces to obtain a better estimate of enclosed solutions). Just as we can leverage MAB to choose the search technique when exploring within a subspace, we also propose to use it to solve the resource allocation problem. More concretely, we treat the subspaces as arms. To calculate the reward, we employ the UCBI algorithm [5], which defines the reward of a subspace S_i at round t as payoff$(S_i, t) = \overline{x_i} + \sqrt{\frac{2 \ln t}{n_i}}$. In this formulation, $\overline{x_i}$ is the average QoR of samples in S_i and n_i is the number of times (i.e., frequency) S_i has been chosen so far by the MAB. Essentially, the QoR and frequency terms are used to balance exploitation and exploration in the compute resource allocation.

3.4 Parallelization Framework

Figure 3 shows the overall flow of the proposed parallelization scheme, which follows a master-slave model. The master is responsible for distributing the parallel slave processes (search instances) to different subspaces. It starts with the original global space, and after collecting a sufficient number of samples, it performs dynamic space partitioning and allocates search instances to appropriate subspaces. A slave process invokes its search techniques to explore a specific subspace, and reports its result backs to the master. The master then further partition the search space and reallocates the slaves. This process iterates until attaining the target QoR or reaching timeout.

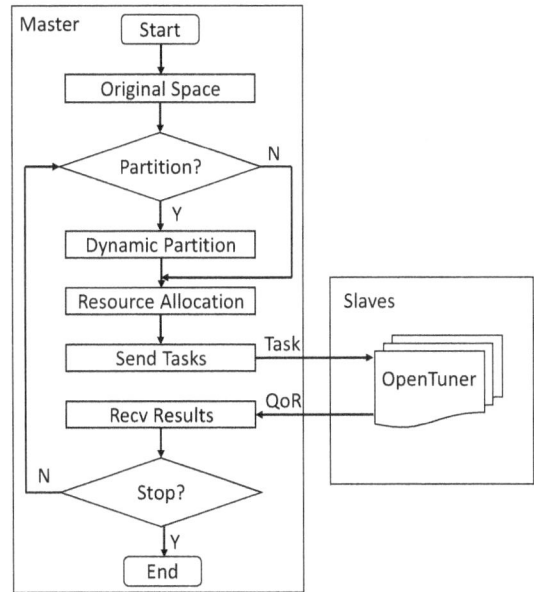

Figure 3: DATuner parallelization framework — We apply Master/Slave parallelization model and use MPI for communication. Master sends Tasks to slaves. Task specifies which subspace that slave instance should explore and may contain a historical best found QoR sample (if exists) in this subspace for slave instance to use as a search seed.

4. Experimental Results

In this section we evaluate the QoR improvement and convergence time of DATuner on two widely-used FPGA CAD tools: (1) the academic Verilog-to-Routing (VTR) framework [16] (version 7.0) and (2) Xilinx Vivado Design Suite [3] (version 2016.1). We run DATuner with eight machines (each machine with one search instance). Each machine has a quad-core Xeon processor running at 2.8GHz.

We make use of a set of real-life benchmarks from several different domains including image processing, general-purpose computing, communication, security, and computer vision. For the experiments targeting VTR, we choose 10 benchmarks covering different domains from the VTR-7.0

benchmark suite [16]. For the experiments using Vivado, we use five large industry designs. The characteristics of the VTR benchmarks and industry designs are summarized in Table 2 and Table 3, respectively.

Table 2: Profiles of the benchmarks used for VTR tuning.

Circuit	LUT	BRAM	Description
MkPktMerge	239	7344	Packet processing
Diffeq1	362	0	Scientific computing
Ch_intrinsics	425	256	Memory system
Raygentop	1884	5376	Ray tracing
MkSMAdapter4B	1960	4456	Packet processing
Sha	2001	0	Cryptography
Boundtop	3053	32768	Ray tracing
Or1200	3075	2048	RISC-V Processor
Blob_merge	8067	0	Image processing
Stereovision0	9567	0	Computer vision

Table 3: Profiles of the industry benchmarks used for Vivado tuning.

Circuit	FF	LUT	Constraint (ns)	Device
Design1	14545	14122	2.60	Virtex 7K160T
Design2	17847	29012	6.55	Virtex 7K70T
Design3	18204	28361	2.00	Virtex 7K160T
Design4	26098	17242	2.65	Virtex 7VX330T
Design5	27873	38261	4.30	Virtex 7VX330T

We select 23 tunable parameters from the VTR-7.0 manual [16] and 9 tunable parameters from Vivado flow covering logic synthesis, packing, placement and routing. The list of parameters for VTR and Vivado are shown in Table 1 and Table 4, respectively.

4.1 Tuning VTR

We first compare DATuner with a parallel baseline that performs a static partitioning scheme, denoted as *Static-Part* in Section 4.1.1. Then we compare DATuner with a serial baseline running OpenTuner on one machine, denoted as *Ser-MAB* in Section 4.1.2.

4.1.1 Comparison with Static Partitioning

For the case of static partitioning, we choose three parameters from the VTR parameter list as the pivots for partitioning and partition the solution space into eight subspaces. We empirically choose the partitioning pivots to be `alpha_t`, `allow_unrelated_clustering`, and `base_cost_type`, which usually have large impact on the timing quality.

In Figure 4, we compare DATuner with Static-Part, where both methods use eight machines for parallel searching. We conduct 100 iterations of searching for 10 VTR benchmarks and show the best-found frequency at different iterations. DATuner achieves better QoR as well as faster convergence

Table 4: List of tunable Vivado configuration parameters.

Parameter	Value	Stage
OptDirective	{Explore, ExploreSequentialArea, AddRemap, ExploreArea, Default}	logic synthesis
PlaceDirective	{Explore, ExtraNetDelay_high, ExtraNetDelay_medium, ExtraNetDelay_low, ExtraPostPlacementOpt, WLDrivenBlockPlacement, LateBlockPlacement, SSI_SpreadLogic_high, SSI_SpreadLogic_low, AltSpreadLogic_low, AltSpreadLogic_medium, AltSpreadLogic_high, ExtraTimingOpt, Default}	placement
Fanout_opt	{on,off}	post-placement
Placement_opt	{on,off}	post-placement
Critical_cell_opt	{on,off}	post-placement
Critical_pin_opt	{on,off}	post-placement
Retime	{on,off}	post-placement
Rewire	{on,off}	post-placement
RouteDirective	{Explore, HigherDelayCost, Default}	routing

rate than Static-Part for eight out of the ten designs. Besides, DATuner shows a significant improvement on average QoR than Static-Part, further demonstrating the benefits of dynamic partitioning. From our experiments, the SP trees learnt by DATuner at runtime through dynamic partitioning are indeed very different across different designs.

Table 5 provides a more detailed comparison between the best configurations found by DATuner and static partitioning in terms of the clock frequency, runtime, and area increase over the results from the default setting. It is not surprising to see frequency improvements from both dynamic and static partitioning, which indicates effectiveness of using MAB-guided search ensembles. In addition, DATuner with dynamic partitioning outperforms the static scheme in the majority of designs in terms of both frequency and LUT counts. The runtime overheads are also similar.

4.1.2 Comparison with Serial Search

We further compare DATuner with Ser-MAB in Figure 5. For fair comparison, we constrain DATuner and Ser-MAB with the same amount of compute efforts, where Ser-MAB runs on one machine for 800 iterations and DATuner runs eight search instances of 100 iterations each. While each MAB instance makes use of an ensemble of heuristic searches to avoid getting easily stuck in local optima, our

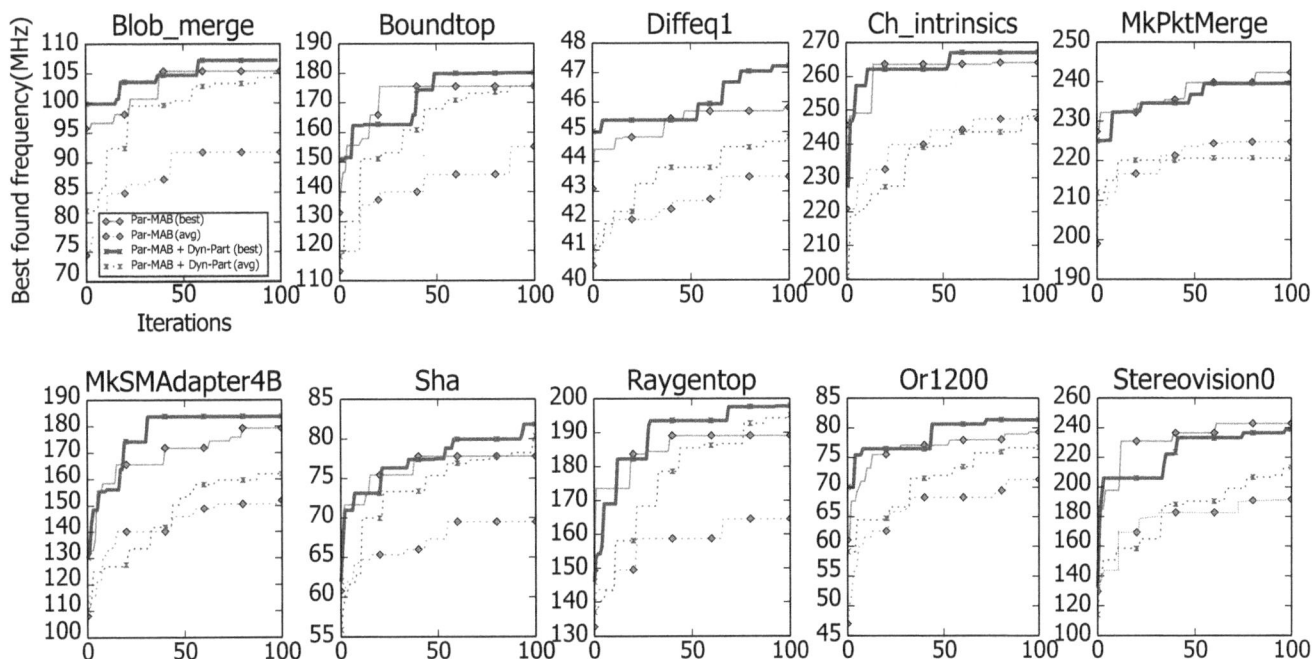

Figure 4: Comparison of dynamic and static partitioning schemes for VTR tuning — `Par-MAB` uses the Static-Part parallelization scheme and `Par-MAB+Dyn-Part` is the DATuner method. `best` is the best frequency found up to the current iteration and `avg` is the average frequency of all design points found up to the current iteration.

Table 5: Profiles of the best-found VTR configurations by DATuner and static partitioning — Freq., RT, and LUT are the ratios of the best configuration over default on clock frequency, runtime, and LUT count, respectively.

Circuit	DATuner			Static-Part		
	Freq. ratio	RT ratio	LUT ratio	Freq. ratio	RT ratio	LUT ratio
Blob_merge	1.11	5.22	1.01	1.09	2.54	1.01
Boundtop	1.17	3.85	1.08	1.14	3.21	1.06
Diffeq1	1.16	1.16	1.06	1.13	1.23	1.36
Ch_intrinsics	1.06	3.51	0.97	1.06	4.59	1.73
MkPktMerge	1.09	0.89	1.20	1.14	0.68	1.00
MkSMAdapter4B	1.04	1.86	0.99	1.01	0.69	1.00
Sha	1.12	2.28	1.00	1.06	1.69	1.00
Raygentop	1.12	3.62	0.99	1.07	2.09	1.42
Or1200	1.08	0.95	1.00	1.06	2.18	1.12
Stereovision0	1.18	1.74	1.29	1.21	2.04	1.24
Avg.	1.11	2.51	1.06	1.09	2.10	1.19

parallelization scheme further enables multiple MAB search instances to explore additional promising regions that cannot be quickly reached by a single search. In Figure 6, we attempt to visualize the search trajectory of one VTR design through dimensionality reduction. Here the black dash line captures the search trajectory of Ser-MAB, which is mostly trapped in one region. Other colored lines represent search trajectories of different search instances instantiated by DATuner, where they are simultaneously exploring different promising regions of the design space. We believe that this partly explains the results in Figure 5 where Ser-MAB results in a worse QoR than that from DATuner in six out of the ten VTR designs.

In Figure 7, we further compare DATuner with Ser-MAB in terms of the runtime to achieve a specific QoR target.

We set the QoR target to be 2% improvement in design frequency over the default design, and measure the speedup in runtime of DATuner (with eight search instances) over Ser-MAB. DATuner reaches the target QoR 11X faster than Ser-MAB.

4.2 Tuning Vivado

We have also applied DATuner to resolve the timing closure problem for five large industry designs, which are listed in Table 3. These designs are specified with very tight timing constraint, and are known as challenging benchmarks in terms of meeting timing.

In addition to showing the timing improvement over the default settings of Vivado, we also experiment with the Vivado exploration mode, a tool option that explores various

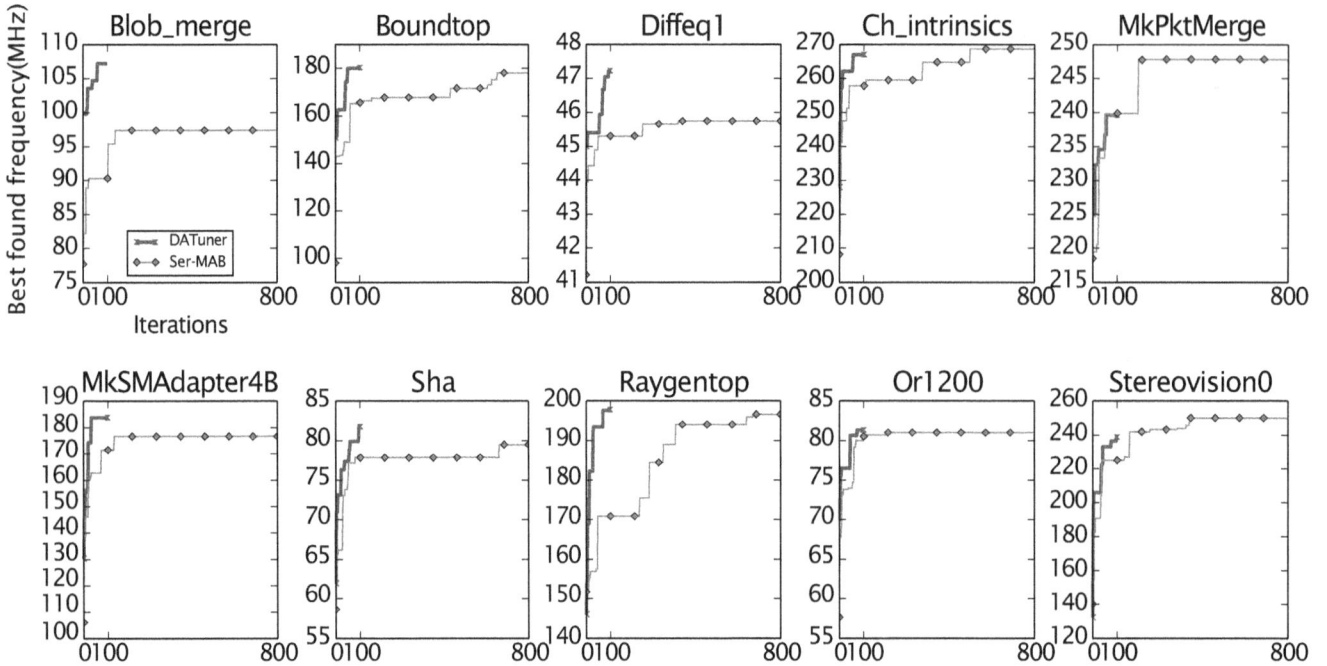

Figure 5: Comparison of DATuner and sequential search (Ser-MAB) for VTR tuning — We use the same total number of search iterations for DATuner and Ser-MAB.

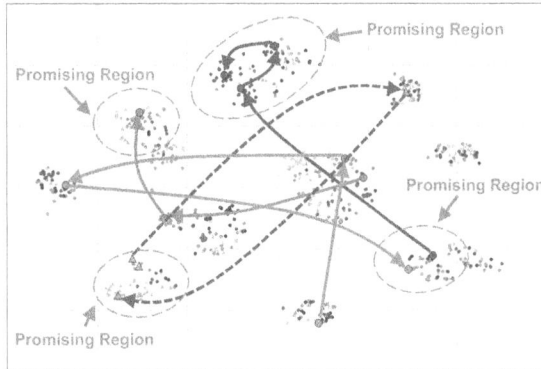

Figure 6: Search trajectory of VTR tuning for Diffeq1 — We use t-SNE package [23] to reduce dimensionality of the search space for VTR design Diffeq1 from 23 to 2 for the sake of visualization. Different colors represent samples of different search engines. Arrows indicate search time sequence. The black dash line represents trajectory of Ser-MAB. Other colored lines capture traces of DATuner. Ser-MAB is stuck in one promising region while DATuner leads to multiple promising regions.

optimizations in the placement and routing stages for improving timing. Figure 8 shows that this mode improves the WNS for four designs, but still fail to meet the timing constraint. In contrast, DATuner helps close timing for all designs.

We also study the profiles of the best-found configurations by DATuner. Figure 9 shows that average similarity

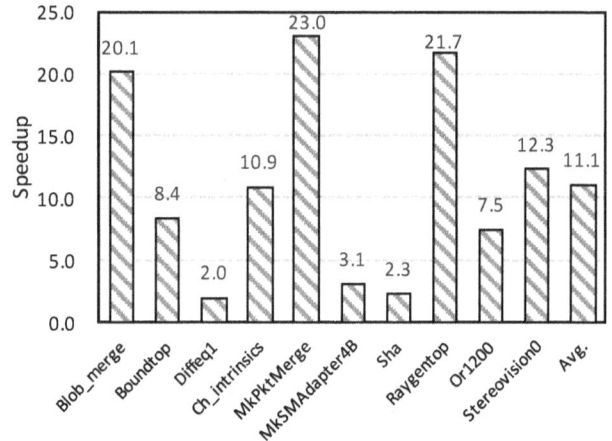

Figure 7: Runtime improvement using DATuner for VTR tuning — Compared with Ser-Search, DATuner reaches the same frequency target 11.1X faster on average using eight machines.

among the five designs is only 46%, indicating that the one-size-fits-all solution indeed does not exist. Table 6 further shows the ratios of worst negative slack (WNS), runtime, and area between the best-found configurations and default. On average, we reduce WNS by 11% and increase the runtime by a factor of 3.7X. The resource utilization is almost the same as the default configuration.

5. Related Work

Intelligent design space exploration and autotuning-based techniques have been proposed in the domain of high-

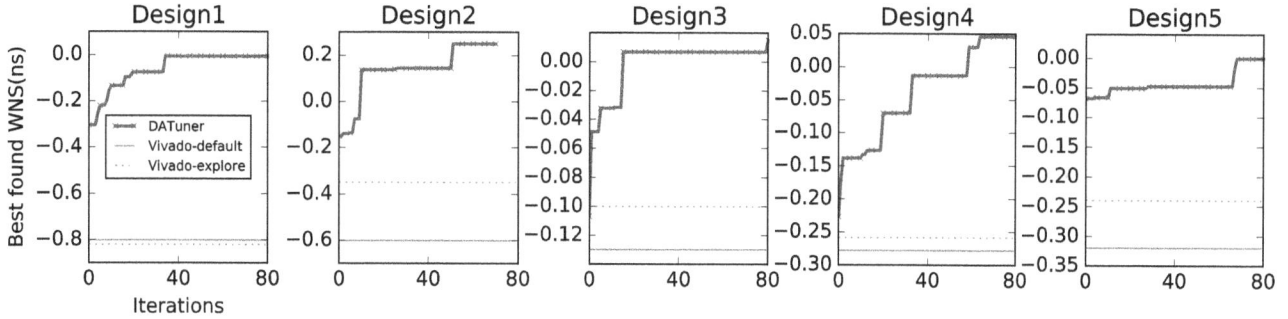

Figure 8: Vivado tuning by DATuner for large-scale industry designs — These designs fail to meet timing with both `Vivado-default` and `Vivado-explore` modes, whereas DATuner closes timing for all of them.

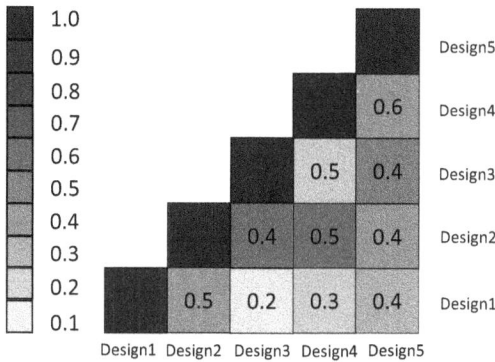

Figure 9: Similarity matrix of best-found configurations for Vivado designs — the average similarity is 46%.

Table 6: Profiles of the best-found Vivado configurations by DATuner — WNS, RT, LUT, and FF are the ratios of the best configuration over the default one in terms of worst negative slack, runtime, LUT count, and flip-flop count, respectively.

Circuit	WNS ratio	RT ratio	LUT ratio	FF ratio
Design1	0.77	2.38	0.83	1.00
Design2	0.93	6.80	1.00	1.00
Design3	0.94	3.26	1.00	1.00
Design4	0.88	4.30	1.03	1.00
Design5	0.90	1.62	1.00	1.00
Avg.	0.89	3.67	0.97	1.00

performance computing (e.g., stencil computation [10] and matrix computation [21]) and compiler optimization (e.g., a domain-specific compiler for image processing applications [18] and the compiler for Java Virtual Machine [12]).

Similar research efforts have recently emerged in the EDA field to configure CAD tool options to improve design quality automatically. Xilinx SmartXplorer [1] and Altera Design Space Explorer [2] use predefined or user-specified configuration bundles for design space exploration. They support parallel CAD runs with fixed sets of parameters and automatically report the best solution found. Unlike the fixed

heuristics used in these tools, DATuner dynamically determines the best search method for the current design.

InTime [13, 14] is a commercial autotuning tool for FPGA timing closure based on the naïve Bayesian classifier, and has recently been extended to include other machine learning techniques as well [24]. InTime builds a database of configurations from a series of preliminary runs and learns to predict the next set of CAD tool options to improve timing results, achieving 30% improvement in timing result compared to vendor-supplied design space exploration tools. The authors in [17] also propose machine learning techniques such as linear regression and random forest to autotune the performance and power consumption of FPGA designs. We note that the learning-based sampling and classification techniques used in InTime [14] and [17] are complementary to our proposal. It is possible to integrate these methods into DATuner as an additional arm in the MAB algorithm. Besides timing closure, our framework can also be applied to other EDA tools.

OpenTuner [4] leverages the MAB method to dynamically select the best searching technique from an ensemble of searching strategies to tune global compiler switches, which improves the performance of software compilers such as GCC by to 2.8x over the baseline using `gcc -o3`. Our work builds on OpenTuner, and targets hardware synthesis rather than software compiler optimizations, and investigates parallelization techniques to speed up the tuning process.

6. Conclusions

In this paper we propose DATuner, a parallel autotuning framework for FPGA compilation using the multi-arm bandit technique. To mitigate the high runtime cost incurred by the complex CAD optimization process, we devise an efficient parallelization scheme that enables many MAB-based autotuners to explore the design space simultaneously. Concretely, DATuner dynamically partitions solution space into promising subspaces based on information gains, and allocates compute resource among subspaces to balance the exploration of unknown subspaces and the exploitation of subspaces with known high-quality solutions. Applications of DATuner on VTR and Xilinx Vivado tools have demonstrated promising improvements in quality and convergence rate across a variety of academic and industry designs.

7. Acknowledgements

This research was supported in part by DARPA Young Faculty Award D15AP00096, Intel Corporation under the ISRA Program, a research gift from Xilinx, Inc., National Natural Science Foundation of China (NSFC) Grant 61520106004, Beijing Natural Science Foundation (BJNSF) Grant 4142022 and Chinese Scholarship Council.

References

[1] SmartXplorer for ISE Project Navigator Users Tutorial. *Xilinx Inc.*, 2010.

[2] Quartus II Handbook Volume 1: Design and Synthesis. *Altera Corporation*, 2014.

[3] Vivado Design Suite User Guide. *Xilinx Inc.*, 2015.

[4] J. Ansel, S. Kamil, K. Veeramachaneni, J. Ragan-Kelley, J. Bosboom, U.-M. O'Reilly, and S. Amarasinghe. OpenTuner: An Extensible Framework for Program Autotuning. *Int'l Conf. on Parallel Architectures and Compilation Techniques (PACT)*, 2014.

[5] P. Auer, N. Cesa-Bianchi, and P. Fischer. Finite-time Analysis of the Multiarmed Bandit Problem. *Machine Learning*, 2002.

[6] P. Auer, N. Cesa-Bianchi, Y. Freund, and R. E. Schapire. The Nonstochastic Multiarmed Bandit Problem. *SIAM Journal on Computing*, 2002.

[7] D. Chen, J. Cong, and P. Pan. FPGA Design Automation: A Survey. *Foundations and Trends in Electronic Design Automation*, 1(3):139–169, 2006.

[8] W. Chen, Y. Wang, and Y. Yuan. Combinatorial Multi-Armed Bandit: General Framework and Applications. *Intl Conf. on Machine Learning(ICML)*, 2013.

[9] V. F. Farias and R. Madan. The Irrevocable Multiarmed Bandit Problem. *Operations Research*, 59:383, 2011.

[10] J. D. Garvey and T. S. Abdelrahman. Automatic Performance Tuning of Stencil Computations on GPUs. *Int'l Conf. on Parallel Processing (ICPP)*, pages 300–309, Sept 2015.

[11] J. Gittins, K. Glazebrook, and R. Weber. Multi-Armed Bandit Allocation Indices. 2011.

[12] S. Jayasena, M. Fernando, T. Rusira, C. Perera, and C. Philips. Auto-Tuning the Java Virtual Machine. *Parallel and Distributed Processing Symposium Workshop (IPDPSW)*, pages 1261–1270, 2015.

[13] N. Kapre, B. Chandrashekaran, H. Ng, and K. Teo. Driving Timing Convergence of FPGA Designs through Machine Learning and Cloud Computing. *IEEE Symp. on Field Programmable Custom Computing Machines (FCCM)*, 2015.

[14] N. Kapre, H. Ng, K. Teo, and J. Naude. InTime: A Machine Learning Approach for Efficient Selection of FPGA CAD Tool Parameters. *Int'l Symp. on Field-Programmable Gate Arrays (FPGA)*, 2015.

[15] L. Lai, H. Jiang, and H. V. Poor. Medium Access in Cognitive Radio Networks: A Competitive Multi-Armed Bandit Framework. *Asilomar Conf. on Signals, Systems and Computers*, 2008.

[16] J. Luu, J. Goeders, M. Wainberg, A. Somerville, T. Yu, K. Nasartschuk, M. Nasr, S. Wang, T. Liu, N. Ahmed, K. B. Kent, J. Anderson, J. Rose, and V. Betz. VTR 7.0: Next Generation Architecture and CAD System for FPGAs. *ACM Transactions on Reconfigurable Technology and Systems (TRETS)*, June 2014.

[17] A. Mametjanov, P. Balaprakash, C. Choudary, P. D. Hovland, S. M. Wild, and G. Sabin. Autotuning FPGA Design Parameters for Performance and Power. *IEEE Symp. on Field Programmable Custom Computing Machines (FCCM)*, pages 84–91, 2015.

[18] R. T. Mullapudi, V. Vasista, and U. Bondhugula. PolyMage: Automatic Optimization for Image Processing Pipelines. *Int'l Conf. on Architectural Support for Programming Languages and Operating Systems (ASPLOS)*, pages 429–443, 2015.

[19] S. Ontanón. The Combinatorial Multi-Armed Bandit Problem and its Application to Real-Time Strategy Games. *Artificial Intelligence and Interactive Digital Entertainment Conference*, 2013.

[20] C. E. Shannon. A Mathematical Theory of Communication. *ACM SIGMOBILE Mobile Computing and Communications Review*, 2001.

[21] O. Spillinger, D. Eliahu, A. Fox, and J. Demmel. Matrix Multiplication Algorithm Selection with Support Vector Machines. 2015.

[22] L. Tran-Thanh, S. Stein, A. Rogers, and N. R. Jennings. Efficient Crowdsourcing of Unknown Experts using Bounded Multi-Armed Bandits. *Artificial Intelligence*, 214:89–111, 2014.

[23] L. Van der Maaten and G. Hinton. Visualizing Data Using t-SNE. *Journal of Machine Learning Research*, 2008.

[24] Q. Yanghua, N. Kapre, H. Ng, and K. Teo. Improving Classification Accuracy of a Machine Learning Approach for FPGA Timing Closure. *IEEE Symp. on Field Programmable Custom Computing Machines (FCCM)*, 2016.

FPGAs in the Cloud

George A. Constantinides (Moderator)
Imperial College London
g.constantinides@imperial.ac.uk

ABSTRACT

Ever greater amounts of computing and storage are happening remotely in the cloud, and it is estimated that spending on public cloud services will grow by over 19%/year to $140B in 2019[1]. Besides commodity processors, network and storage infrastructure, the end of clock frequency scaling in traditional processors has meant that application-specific accelerators are required in tandem with cloud-based processors to deliver continued improvements in computational performance and energy efficiency. Indeed, graphics processing units (GPUs), as well as custom ASICs, are now widely used within the cloud, particularly for compute-intensive high-value applications like machine learning. In this panel, we intend to consider the opportunities and challenges for broad deployment of FPGAs in the cloud.

In 2014, Microsoft announced the deployment of FPGAs in their datacenters for acceleration of Bing search. IBM's CAPI (coherent accelerator processor interface) facilitates connectivity and cache-coherent access between an FPGA-based accelerator and a POWER processor. More recently, in December 2016, Amazon announced the deployment of FPGAs in its EC2 F1 cloud instances. With these developments, FPGAs appear poised for widespread usage in cloud computing; however, obstacles undoubtedly remain.

Questions that will be explored by the panel include:

- Will cloud-based FPGA computing gain broad acceptance? Or will ASICs and GPUs ultimately win out for realization of cloud-based accelerators?

- What cloud-based applications or application domains are particularly suited to FPGAs?

- How would FPGAs be programmed in the cloud context? Is the current state of high-level synthesis sufficiently usable by software engineers?

- What fundamental differences exist in programming model and tool flow between FPGAs in the cloud and FPGAs for embedded systems?

- What infrastructure is needed for context switching between applications on an FPGA in the cloud? The Microsoft Catapult project has proposed the notion of a 'shell' of infrastructure surrounding an FPGA design. Is a single style of shell sufficient for all types of applications? Can a shell end up being an architectural bottleneck?

- Should the general public be able to write their own FPGA applications for cloud usage? Or should a library-based FPGA accelerator approach be taken? And what are the implications for design flows and IP?

- What are the security challenges for FPGA usage in the cloud and how might they be addressed?

- FPGAs (even those from the same vendor) are not bitstream compatible with one another. How might this be handled in the cloud where different compute nodes may be coupled with different FPGA hardware?

- How might FPGA cloud usage by best monetized?

CCS Concepts

•Networks → Cloud computing; •Hardware → Reconfigurable logic applications;

Keywords

FPGAs, reconfigurable computing, cloud computing

---

[1]"Roundup of Cloud Computing Forecasts and Market Estimates," Forbes, March 2016.

FPGA '17 February 22-24, 2017, Monterey, CA, USA

© 2017 Copyright held by the owner/author(s).

ACM ISBN 978-1-4503-4354-1/17/02.

DOI: http://dx.doi.org/10.1145/3020078.3030014

Hardware Synthesis of Weakly Consistent C Concurrency

Nadesh Ramanathan
Imperial College London
n.ramanathan14@imperial.ac.uk

Shane T. Fleming
Imperial College London
shane.fleming06@imperial.ac.uk

John Wickerson
Imperial College London
j.wickerson@imperial.ac.uk

George A. Constantinides
Imperial College London
g.constantinides@imperial.ac.uk

ABSTRACT

Lock-free algorithms, in which threads synchronise not via coarse-grained mutual exclusion but via fine-grained atomic operations ('atomics'), have been shown empirically to be the fastest class of multi-threaded algorithms in the realm of conventional processors. This paper explores how these algorithms can be compiled from C to reconfigurable hardware via *high-level synthesis* (HLS).

We focus on the scheduling problem, in which software instructions are assigned to hardware clock cycles. We first show that typical HLS scheduling constraints are insufficient to implement atomics, because they permit some instruction reorderings that, though sound in a single-threaded context, demonstrably cause erroneous results when synthesising multi-threaded programs. We then show that correct behaviour can be restored by imposing additional *intra-thread* constraints among the memory operations. We implement our approach in the open-source LegUp HLS framework, and provide both *sequentially consistent* (SC) and *weakly consistent* ('weak') atomics. Weak atomics necessitate fewer constraints than SC atomics, but suffice for many concurrent algorithms. We confirm, via automatic model-checking, that we correctly implement the semantics defined by the 2011 revision of the C standard. A case study on a circular buffer suggests that circuits synthesised from programs that use atomics can be 2.5x faster than those that use locks, and that weak atomics can yield a further 1.5x speedup.

Keywords

atomic operations, C/C++, FPGAs, high-level synthesis, lock-free algorithms, memory consistency models, scheduling.

1. INTRODUCTION

Gramoli [13] demonstrates in his comprehensive empirical study that, when writing multi-threaded programs for conventional multi-processors, the most efficient way to synchronise threads is to use fine-grained *atomic operations*

FPGA '17, February 22-24, 2017, Monterey, CA, USA

© 2017 ACM. ISBN 978-1-4503-4354-1/17/02. . . $15.00

DOI: http://dx.doi.org/10.1145/3020078.3021733

('atomics') – as opposed to, for instance, coarse-grained mutual exclusion based on locks. In this paper, we explore how lock-free programs can be compiled from C to reconfigurable hardware via *high-level synthesis* (HLS), and the performance benefits of doing so.

We focus on the *scheduling* stage of synthesis, in which software instructions are assigned to hardware clock cycles. Typical HLS schedulers seek to maximise instruction-level parallelism by allowing independent instructions to be executed out-of-order or simultaneously. In particular, non-aliasing memory accesses, or those that exhibit only read-after-read (RAR) dependencies (e.g. x=z; y=z), can be re-ordered. These reorderings are invisible in a single-threaded context, but in a multi-threaded context, they can introduce unexpected behaviours. For instance, if another thread is simultaneously writing to z, then reordering may introduce the behaviour where x is assigned the latest value but y gets an old one.

The implication of this is not that HLS tools are *wrong*, because these optimisations can only introduce new behaviours when the code already exhibits a race condition, and races are deemed a programming error in C [17, §5.1.2.4]. Rather the implication is that if these memory accesses are upgraded to become atomic (and hence allowed to race), then existing scheduling constraints are insufficient.

One approach for implementing atomics correctly is to enclose each in its own critical region, and ensure that the surrounding lock() and unlock() calls cannot be reordered. We show that this approach, which is the only approach available in LegUp [7], is expensive and scales poorly. Instead, we frame the implementation of atomics as a scheduling problem: we treat atomic accesses as regular memory accesses but impose additional intra-thread dependencies when devising a schedule for each thread.

By default, C atomics enforce *sequential consistency* (SC), which means that all threads have a completely consistent view of shared memory, and memory accesses always occur in the order specified by the programmer [20]. Although simple for programmers to understand, SC is an expensive illusion for language implementations to maintain in the presence of optimisations by compilers (such as constant propagation) and by architectures (such as store buffering) that confound SC.

In fact, many concurrent algorithms do not need all threads to share a completely consistent view of shared memory, and hence can tolerate *weakly consistent* atomics, which do not provide this guarantee in general. These 'weak atomics' include the *acquire/release* and *relaxed* atomics provided by the 2011 revision of the C standard ('C11') [17, §7.17.3], and later incorporated into OpenCL [19, §3.3.4]. The exact guarantees provided by these operations are specified by the language's *memory consistency model* (MCM); the rough idea is that while SC forbids *all* reorderings, acquire loads cannot be executed *later*, release stores cannot be executed *earlier*, and relaxed accesses can be moved freely. We show that C11's acquire/release and relaxed consistency can be implemented using fewer dependencies than SC, and hence offer the potential for more efficient scheduling.

Unfortunately, weak atomics are notoriously hard to implement correctly. A failure to anticipate their complex and counterintuitive behaviours has been the root cause of bugs in compilers [28], language specifications [4], and vendor-endorsed programming guides [2]. To build confidence that our work implements C11 atomics correctly, we use the Alloy model checker [18], first to debug our implementation during development, and then to verify automatically that any C11 program (with a bounded number of memory accesses) will be synthesised correctly.

We implement our approach in the LegUp HLS framework [6]. LegUp is an attractive starting point because it is open-source and already has some support for multi-threaded programs [7].

We evaluate our work via a case study: an application in which threads communicate via lock-free circular buffers. We show that using SC atomics yields a 2.5x speedup compared to locks, and that switching from SC atomics to weak atomics (where safe to do so) yields a further 1.5x speedup. Compared to an unsound implementation that omits locks and atomics altogether, our weak atomics incur only a 7% performance overhead and a 3% area overhead.

In summary,

- we show that LegUp cannot (in general) synthesise multi-threaded algorithms without relying on locks, because some instruction reorderings permitted by its scheduler can introduce erroneous behaviours (§2);

- we modify LegUp's scheduling algorithm to impose extra *intra-thread* dependencies on the atomics provided by the C11 standard, thus ensuring correct *inter-thread* communication (§4.2), and we show that a lock-free buffer implemented in this way is on average 2.5x faster than one that uses locks (§5);

- we further modify the scheduler to support *weak* atomics, also part of the C11 standard, which suffice for many algorithms despite requiring fewer dependencies (§4.3), and we show that using weak atomics instead of SC atomics in our lock-free buffer leads to a further 1.5x speedup (§5); and

- we confirm automatically, using the Alloy model checker, that our revised scheduler correctly implements SC and weak atomics as defined by the C11 standard (§4.4).

Experimental data, source code, and Alloy model files are available online [1].

2. MOTIVATING EXAMPLES

In this section, we provide two simple multi-threaded programs that can exhibit unexpected behaviours when compiled to hardware using LegUp, as a result of LegUp's relaxed scheduling constraints. In both cases, the unexpected behaviour only arises when particular instruction sequences

```
                int x=0;
┌─────────────────┬─────────────────┐
│ T1() {          │ T2() {          │
│ 1.1   r0=x;     │ 2.1   x=1;      │
│ 1.2   r1=x;     │       }         │
│       }         │                 │
└─────────────────┴─────────────────┘
        assert(r0 = 1 ⇒ r1 ≠ 0)
```

(a) A minimal violation of coherence.

```
              int x=0; int y=0;
┌─────────────────────┬─────────────────┐
│ T1(int a) {         │ T2() {          │
│ 1.1  r0=y+y+y+y+y+y; │ 2.1   x=1;      │
│ 1.2  r1=x;          │       }         │
│ 1.3  r2=x/a;        │                 │
│      }              │                 │
└─────────────────────┴─────────────────┘
        assert(r1 = 1 ⇒ r2 ≠ 0)
```

(b) A coherence violation witnessed in LegUp (where thread T1 is launched with a = 1).

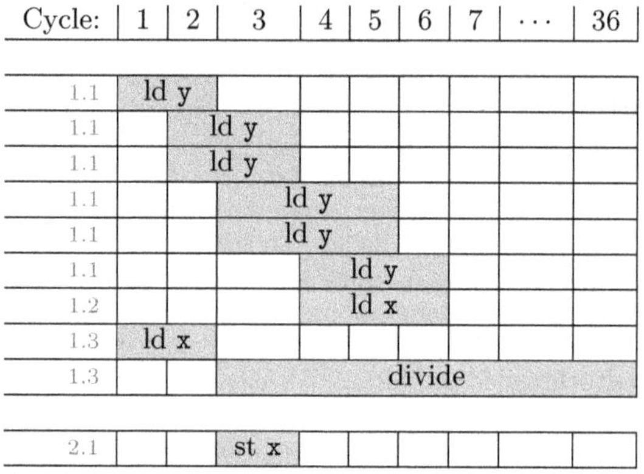

(c) Schedules for threads T1 (top) and T2 (bottom).

Figure 1: Violating *coherence* in LegUp.

are carefully contrived, but we argue that similar sequences could easily occur in 'realistic' programs too. We emphasise that the unexpected behaviours discussed in this section do not mean that LegUp's scheduler is *wrong*, because the programs are racy and are hence technically illegal. However, if these programs were rewritten to use *atomics* (which *are* allowed to race), and LegUp were to implement atomics simply as ordinary non-atomic accesses, then it *would* be wrong.

Coherence.

A multi-threaded program conforms to *sequential consistency* (SC) if all memory accesses occur instantaneously and in the same order as the corresponding instructions in each thread [20]. One of the simplest violations of SC is a *coherence* violation [24, §8], as illustrated in Fig. 1a. The variable x, initially zero, is shared between two threads, T1 and T2. A coherence violation occurs when the first load (line 1.1) observes x's new value but the second load (line 1.2) observes x's old value. This is detected by the failure of the final-state assertion.

We could not observe this particular coherence violation in LegUp-generated circuitry, but we *could* observe a coherence violation by first making some innocuous transformations to the source code, as shown in Fig. 1b. These involve dividing one of the loaded values by a variable that is set to 1 at run-time (so the compiler cannot optimise it away), and

```
        int x=0; int y=0;
  ┌──────────────┬──────────────┐
  │ T1() {       │ T2() {       │
  │ 1.1  x=1;    │ 2.1  if(y==1)│
  │ 1.2  y=1;    │ 2.2    r0=x; │
  │    }         │    }         │
  └──────────────┴──────────────┘
        assert(r0 ≠ 0)
```

(a) A minimal violation of message-passing.

```
        int x=0; int y=0;
  ┌──────────────┬──────────────┐
  │ T1(int a) {  │ T2() {       │
  │ 1.1  x=a/3;  │ 2.1  if(y==1)│
  │ 1.2  y=1;    │ 2.2    r0=x; │
  │    }         │    }         │
  └──────────────┴──────────────┘
        assert(r0 ≠ 0)
```

(b) A message-passing violation witnessed in LegUp (where thread T1 is launched with a = 3).

(c) Schedules for threads T1 (top) and T2 (bottom).

Figure 2: Violating *message-passing* in LegUp.

inserting extra loads of a second shared location, y. These transformations result in LegUp finding the schedule shown in Fig. 1c.[1] Because of the high latency of the division operation, LegUp seeks to schedule the second read of x as early as possible. It determines that line 1.3 depends neither on line 1.2 (there is only a read-after-read (RAR) dependency on x) nor on line 1.1, and hence can be executed first in its thread. The repeated reads of y cause a delay between the two reads of x, and it is during this gap that thread T2 updates x. In the main thread, threads T1 and T2 are forked successively, which offsets the starts of their respective executions by two cycles.

Message-passing.

Another example of an SC violation is illustrated by a failure of the *message-passing* paradigm [24, §3], which is illustrated in Fig. 2a. This example involves two shared locations, x and y, where x represents the message being passed from thread T1 to thread T2, and y is used as a 'ready' flag. A message-passing violation occurs if T2 observes that y has been set (line 2.1) but then goes on to observe that x is still zero (line 2.2).

As before, some innocuous code transformations are required to coax LegUp into revealing this behaviour, as shown in Fig. 2b. This time, we simply arrange that the value being stored to x is obtained by a division operation. As shown in the resultant schedule (Fig. 2c), this high-latency operation

---

[1] The schedule is constrained by dual-ported memory access.

delays the store to x. Because lines 1.1 and 1.2 are deemed independent, the schedule permits them to execute simultaneously, and the result is that y is written first. In the reading thread (T2), LegUp schedules both loads simultaneously, having used if-conversion [23] to replace the control flow with predicated statements (slt). By launching the reading thread two clock cycles after the writing thread, we can observe the new value of y but the old value of x – a violation of message passing.

3. BACKGROUND

We now summarise existing HLS support for concurrent programming (§3.1), and introduce the C11 MCM (§3.2).

3.1 High-level synthesis

Several HLS tools only accept sequential input, deriving parallelisation opportunities either automatically (e.g. ROCCC [27], LegUp [6]) or with the aid of synthesis directives (e.g. Vivado HLS [31]). Other tools accept multi-threaded input but only allow threads to synchronise via locks (e.g. Kiwi [14]) or via execution barriers (e.g. SDAccel [30]). Some HLS tools also support the OpenMP programming standard, which defines an atomic directive that enables lock-free programming. Leow et al. [21] transform OpenMP to Handel-C for hardware synthesis and Cilardo et al. [8] generate heterogeneous hardware/software systems with OpenMP. Neither of these works support the explicit multi-threading constructs defined by the Pthreads standard, so a direct comparison with the present work is difficult. Altera's SDK for OpenCL [3] supports lock-free programming via atomics [26], though the commercial nature of the tool makes it difficult to ascertain exactly how these operations are implemented. LEAP facilitates parallel memory access through its provision of memory hierarchies that potentially can be shared among Pthreads in a lock-free manner [32].

The most important point of comparison between the tools reviewed above and the present work is that we are the first to synthesise hardware from software that features *weak atomics* (as defined by C11 [17] and OpenCL 2.x [19]). Efficient implementations of weak atomics have been extensively studied in the conventional processor domain, and they have been shown to yield *average, whole-program* speedups of 1.13x on x86 (Core i7) CPUs [25, Fig. 5] over their SC counterparts. Our circular buffer case study suggests that on FPGAs, weak atomics can yield a 1.5x average speedup.

Finally, Huang et al. [16] and Cong et al. [9] have shown that compiler optimisations can affect the quality of HLS-generated hardware. Our work shows that in a multi-threaded context, some optimisations (as manifested through relaxed scheduling constraints) can even be unsound.

3.1.1 HLS Scheduling

An HLS front-end converts source code into a *control/data flow graph* (CDFG) [11]. A CDFG is a directed graph where each vertex is a basic block (BB) and each edge represents a control-flow path. Each BB is a data-flow graph (DFG) with operations as vertices (V_{op}) and dependencies as edges ($E_d \subseteq V_{op} \times V_{op}$). Scheduling determines the start and end cycles of each operation in a CDFG, taking into account the control-flow and data dependencies as well as additional constraints such as latency and resources. Scheduling is performed alongside the allocation of resources and the binding of operations and memory locations to these resources [11].

One of the most common scheduling techniques, used by Vivado HLS [31] and LegUp [6], expresses a CDFG schedule as a solution to a *system of difference constraints* (SDC) [10]. Various optimisations, such as as-soon-as-possible (ASAP) and as-late-as-possible (ALAP) scheduling, can be obtained by reformulating the objective function. We focus in this work on the constraint that captures data dependencies, which is formulated as:

$$\forall (v, v') \in E_d : end(v) - start(v') \leq 0.$$

That is, for every edge (v, v') where operation v' depends on v, the end of operation v must be scheduled before the start of operation v'.

3.1.2 *LegUp*

We utilise *LegUp*, an open-source HLS framework that enables applications to run on processors, as FPGA hardware accelerators, or both [6]. LegUp compiles an input C program to the LLVM Intermediate Representation (IR), which it analyses in order to generate a CDFG for SDC-based scheduling. To do this, LegUp firstly inserts control dependencies between BBs based on program order to ensure that only one BB is active at a time. These control dependencies eliminate any inter-BB instruction reordering or parallelism. Secondly, LegUp inserts data dependencies between instructions within a BB. LegUp insert two types of data dependencies (E_d): register (E_{reg}) and memory dependencies (E_{mem}), where

$$E_d = E_{reg} \cup E_{mem}.$$

LegUp analyses register dependencies (E_{reg}) by identifying producer-consumer relationships between instructions, where data produced by an instruction is consumed by other instructions.

Our focus is on memory dependencies (E_{mem}), which hold between memory operations, $V_{mem} \subseteq V_{op}$. LegUp preserves read-after-write (RAW), write-after-write (WAW) and write-after-read (WAR) dependencies to aliasing memory locations, as shown below:

$$E_{mem} = E_{LegUp} \tag{1}$$

where

$$E_{LegUp} = \{(v, v') \in V_{mem} \times V_{mem} \mid$$
$$(v \in V_{st} \lor v' \in V_{st}) \land sb(v, v') \land sloc(v, v')\}$$

and $V_{st} \subseteq V_{mem}$ is the set of store operations (and elsewhere, $V_{ld} \subseteq V_{mem}$ is the set of load operations), sb is the 'sequenced before' relation (as determined from the program order), and $sloc$ is the 'same location' relation (as determined by an alias analysis tool). That is, E_{LegUp} contains every pair of aliasing memory operations v and v', where at least one is a store and where v is sequenced before v'.

LegUp's existing memory dependencies do not enforce ordering between memory instructions that have only read-after-read (RAR) dependencies, or that are non-aliasing. The omission of these orderings allows the potential for intra-BB out-of-order or overlapping execution of memory accesses. Such optimisations are *legal* in a single-threaded context and can lead to more efficient schedules.

LegUp's Pthread support allows multi-threaded C programs to be synthesised for FPGAs [7]. LegUp maps each thread to a CDFG, each of which is scheduled independently. Because these threads can be executed in parallel, LegUp provides locks to allow each thread mutually exclusive access to shared memory.

Instead of resorting to using locks, we embrace fine-grained concurrency by extending LegUp's Pthread flow to support atomics. By default, LegUp's scheduler does not ensure sufficient memory consistency for atomics. We augment LegUp's scheduler to add additional intra-thread ordering edges to E_{mem}; this ensures globally-synchronised memory behaviour, without locks.

3.2 The C11 memory consistency model

The 2011 revision of the C and C++ languages, 'C11', defines a suite of instructions called 'atomics', for loading from and storing to shared memory without the need for locks [17, §5.1.2.4, §7.17]. Co-existing with these atomics are ordinary (non-atomic) memory loads and stores. Each atomic can be assigned a *consistency mode* (also known as a *memory order*). The available modes include: *relaxed* (for loads and stores) *acquire* (for loads) *release* (for stores), and *SC* (for loads and stores). Non-SC atomics can be more efficient than SC atomics, but do not guarantee that all threads have a consistent view of the memory they share. Each consistency mode can be *roughly* understood by assuming that all threads *do* share a consistent view of memory, but that some instructions can take effect out of order:

- an *atomic* load or store cannot be reordered with another atomic load or store that accesses the same location (this property is called *coherence*);

- a *relaxed atomic* load or store can be reordered anywhere within its thread (notwithstanding the other constraints);

- an *acquire atomic* load cannot be reordered with loads or stores that are sequenced after it in program order;

- a *release atomic* store cannot be reordered with loads or stores that are sequenced before it; and

- an *SC atomic* load or store cannot be reordered with any other load or store.

However, it is important to note that the explanations given above convey only a rough understanding. The official C11 standard defines the semantics of atomics not in terms of instruction reordering, but in terms of a detailed *memory consistency model* (MCM). The MCM specifies which complete executions of a program are allowed or forbidden. As a result of this discrepancy, some of the reorderings forbidden above are actually allowed under certain conditions.[2] This means that a program may actually exhibit more behaviours than a programmer following the rules above can anticipate.

The official semantics for C11 programs works by first mapping the program to a set of '*candidate*' traces [4]. This set of traces is obtained under the assumption that each load from a shared memory location can read a completely random value. In the second stage, candidate traces that exhibit inconsistent sequences of memory accesses among their events are rejected.

As an example of how this semantics works, consider the C11-style program in Figure 3a, and one of its candidate

---

[2] For instance, an acquire load *can* be reordered with a subsequent non-atomic load providing it is immediately preceded by another non-atomic load [12, §7.2].

```
int x=0; atomic_int y=0;
```

x=1;	r0=y.ld(ACQ);
y.st(1,REL);	if(r0==1)
	r1=x;

a: W_{na} x 1   c: R_{ACQ} y 1
$\downarrow sb$ rf $\downarrow sb, cd$
b: W_{REL} y 1   d: R_{na} x 0

(a) a program   (b) a candidate trace

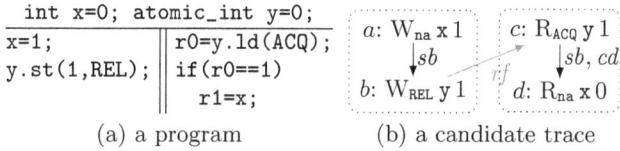

Figure 3: Example of C11 atomics.

traces (Figure 3b). We explain below why this particular candidate trace is deemed inconsistent. The trace contains four memory-related events (a, b, c, d), distributed between two threads as shown by the dotted rectangles. The store instructions give rise to write events (W) and the loads give rise to reads (R). Each event is tagged with the location it accesses (e.g., x or y), the value it reads or writes (e.g., 0 or 1), and whether it is non-atomic (na), atomic with consistency mode release (REL), or atomic with consistency mode acquire (ACQ). The *sequenced before* relation (sb) depicts the order of the instructions in the program, while the cd relation represents the control-flow dependency induced by the if-statement. The *reads-from* relation (rf) records that, in this particular trace, the read event c observes the 1 written by the write event b, and that the read event d (which has no incoming rf edge) observes the initial value, 0.

This trace is deemed inconsistent in C11 by the following reasoning. The rf arrow between the release and the acquire induces what is called 'release/acquire synchronisation' between the threads; we say that b *happens-before* c as a result. Taken together with the two sb arrows, we can further deduce that a happens-before d. C11 prescribes that reads must observe the most recent write in the happens-before relation, but d, which observes x's initial value, violates this rule. Hence, the trace is disallowed.

4. METHOD

This section describes how we extend LegUp's Pthread flow [7] to support sequentially consistent (§4.2) and weakly consistent (§4.3) atomics.

As we discussed in §3.1.2, LegUp's MCM requires mutual exclusion (locks) to ensure safe access to shared memory in a multi-threaded context. We propose strengthening LegUp's MCM so that multi-threaded programs can synchronise using atomics rather than locks. We build on the LegUp framework, as it offers Pthread support and is open source, but our method is generally applicable to HLS tools that use SDC-based scheduling because we simply inject extra ordering edges as SDC data dependency constraints.

We compile atomic operations from the C11 standard with Clang 3.5 into LLVM IR. From the LLVM IR we can extract the atomicity of each memory operation, and the consistency mode of each atomic operation, and use this information to decide which ordering edges to inject into the scheduler. We focus on atomic loads and atomic stores in this paper, but our full implementation also includes fences [1]. We do not consider atomic read-modify-write instructions (such as compare-and-swap).

We propose three different strengthenings of LegUp's existing MCM, E_{mem}, which was discussed in §3.1.2. A naive approach, which gives the strongest possible MCM, is to adhere to strict program order and forbid any parallel memory access (§4.1). We also define an MCM that only imposes or-

dering on *atomic* memory accesses (§4.2) and a third MCM that relaxes some ordering for weak atomics (§4.3).

To help visualise the scheduling implications of the various MCMs, we provide a running example: a single thread that loads from four different memory locations. The third load is atomic with the acquire (ACQ) consistency mode; the rest are non-atomic (na). Each schedule is obtained using ASAP scheduling assuming an unlimited number of memory ports.

Cycle:	1	2
r0=w;	ld_{na} w	
r1=x;	ld_{na} x	
r2=y.ld(ACQ);		ld_{ACQ} y
r3=z;		ld_{na} z

The schedule above shows our running example implemented with LegUp's current MCM. LegUp treats atomic operations as regular memory operations and since these memory accesses do not alias, all four memory operations are free to be scheduled simultaneously.

4.1 Preserving SC semantics

A naive solution for correct program behaviour is to serialise all memory operations, regardless of any alias analysis. This is achieved by redefining E_{mem} as follows:

$$E_{mem} = \{(v, v') \in V_{mem} \times V_{mem} \mid sb(v, v')\}. \quad (2)$$

E_{mem} now includes every pair of memory operations (v, v') where v is sequenced before v'. It overrides the memory dependencies generated by LegUp's existing MCM, E_{LegUp} (§3.1.2)

The schedule of our running example in this MCM is shown below.

Cycle:	1	2	3	4	5	6	7	8
r0=w;	ld_{na} w							
r1=x;			ld_{na} x					
r2=y.ld(ACQ);					ld_{ACQ} y			
r3=z;								ld_{na} z

Because of the serialisation, this schedule cannot utilise more than one memory port for shared memory access. This stifles any parallelism offered by a multi-ported memory controller.

4.2 Exploring atomics

We now define an MCM that specifies ordering dependencies only for the *atomic* operations within each thread, $V_{at} \subseteq V_{mem}$. We treat all atomic operations as SC, regardless of the consistency mode specified in the program. To do this, we augment LegUp's original scheduling constraints with those in $E_{at\uparrow}$ and $E_{at\downarrow}$:

$$E_{mem} = E_{LegUp} \cup E_{at\uparrow} \cup E_{at\downarrow} \quad (3)$$

where

$$E_{at\uparrow} = \{(v', v) \in V_{mem} \times V_{mem} \mid sb(v', v) \wedge v \in V_{at}\}$$
$$E_{at\downarrow} = \{(v, v') \in V_{mem} \times V_{mem} \mid v \in V_{at} \wedge sb(v, v')\}.$$

$E_{at\uparrow}$ specifies that for every atomic operation v and every memory operation v' sequenced before v, there must exist an ordering edge from v' to v. $E_{at\downarrow}$ specifies that for every atomic operation v and every memory operation v' sequenced after v, there must exist an ordering edge from v to v'. The combination of these two constraints and LegUp's existing MCM E_{LegUp} allows us to define an MCM that supports SC atomics.

The schedule of our running example when implemented in this MCM is shown below.

Cycle:	1	2	3	4	5	6
r0=w;	ld_{na} w					
r1=x;	ld_{na} x					
r2=y.ld(ACQ);			ld_{ACQ} y			
r0=z;					ld_{na} z	

The atomic load of y is constrained to happen after the loads of w and x (by $E_{\text{at}\dagger}$) but before the load of z (by $E_{\text{at}\ddagger}$). Even though the atomic load uses the acquire consistency mode, this MCM treats it as a SC atomic load. The MCM definition in (3) is generally less restrictive than the one in (2) because ordering is only enforced with respect to atomics, but in the worst case, it is equivalent to (2) when all memory accesses are atomic ($V_{\text{at}} = V_{\text{mem}}$).

4.3 Exploiting weak atomics

In §4.2, we defined an MCM that treats all atomic operations as SC atomics. This approach is suboptimal whenever any atomics have consistency modes that are weaker than SC. In this subsection, we take advantage of the relaxations allowed for these weak atomics by injecting fewer ordering edges compared to SC atomics.

Let V_{sc}, V_{acq}, V_{rel}, and V_{rlx} be the sets of sequentially consistent, acquire, release and relaxed atomics, such that $V_{\text{sc}} \cup V_{\text{acq}} \cup V_{\text{rel}} \cup V_{\text{rlx}} = V_{\text{at}}$. We define a MCM that can support weak atomics to be the union of LegUp's existing MCM, E_{LegUp}, and the five sets of constraints given below:

$$E_{\text{mem}} = E_{\text{LegUp}} \cup E_{\text{sc}\ddagger} \cup E_{\text{sc}\dagger} \cup E_{\text{acq}\ddagger} \cup E_{\text{rel}\dagger} \cup E_{\text{RAR}} \quad (4)$$

where

$$E_{\text{sc}\ddagger} = \{(v, v') \in V_{\text{mem}} \times V_{\text{mem}} \mid v \in V_{\text{sc}} \wedge sb(v, v')\}$$
$$E_{\text{sc}\dagger} = \{(v', v) \in V_{\text{mem}} \times V_{\text{mem}} \mid sb(v', v) \wedge v \in V_{\text{sc}}\}$$
$$E_{\text{acq}\ddagger} = \{(v, v') \in V_{\text{mem}} \times V_{\text{mem}} \mid v \in V_{\text{acq}} \wedge sb(v, v')\}$$
$$E_{\text{rel}\dagger} = \{(v', v) \in V_{\text{mem}} \times V_{\text{mem}} \mid sb(v', v) \wedge v \in V_{\text{rel}}\}$$
$$E_{\text{RAR}} = \{(v, v') \in V_{\text{mem}} \times V_{\text{mem}} \mid sb(v, v') \wedge$$
$$v \in V_{\text{at}} \cap V_{\text{ld}} \wedge v' \in V_{\text{at}} \cap V_{\text{ld}} \wedge sloc(v, v')\}.$$

We define five rules to implement an MCM that exploits the performance benefits of weak atomics. $E_{\text{sc}\dagger}$ and $E_{\text{sc}\ddagger}$ define the ordering dependencies for SC atomics, which are similar to $E_{\text{at}\dagger}$ and $E_{\text{at}\ddagger}$ from §4.2, except that they only apply to SC atomics rather than all atomics. $E_{\text{acq}\ddagger}$ represents the ordering edges for acquire atomics: for every memory operation v' sequenced after an acquire atomic v, there must exist an ordering edge from v to v'. $E_{\text{rel}\dagger}$ represents the ordering edges for release atomics: for every memory operation v' sequenced before a release atomic v, there must exist an ordering edge from v' to v. E_{RAR} enforces read-after-read dependencies for all atomics: we inject an ordering edge from v to v' whenever v is sequenced before v' and both load from the same memory location ($sloc$).

The schedule of our running example for this MCM is shown below.

Cycle:	1	2	3	4
r0=w;	ld_{na} w			
r1=x;	ld_{na} x			
r2=y.ld(ACQ);	ld_{ACQ} y			
r3=z;				ld_{na} z

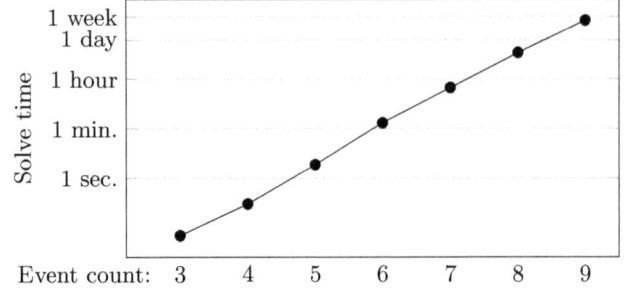

Figure 4: Solving time as the maximum number of events increases (y-axis is logarithmic).

Since the load of y is an acquire atomic, it must be completed before the load of z (by $E_{\text{acq}\ddagger}$), which is sequenced after it. However, the memory operations sequenced before the acquire load of y can be scheduled in parallel.

4.4 Ensuring correctness

Even though the scheduling constraints that we enforce are relatively straightforward, it is still challenging to justify that they are sufficient to rule out all executions deemed inconsistent by C11's MCM, because the specification of C11's MCM is so complex. Previous work has *proved* the correctness of implementations of C11's MCM both on CPUs [4] and on GPUs [28], but such proofs are laborious and fragile, and hence ill-suited to our prototype implementation.

Therefore, we turn to *lightweight* methods for verifying correctness. We employ the Alloy model checker [18] both to debug our implementation and to verify its correctness (up to a bound on the size of programs). Wickerson et al. [29] have previously used Alloy to check implementations of the C11 and OpenCL MCMs for several CPU and GPU architectures. Here, we port their work from the conventional processor domain to HLS.

Specifically, we use Alloy's constraint-solving abilities to search for a C11 trace T and a strict total order $\sqsubset_T$ over the events in T, such that

- T is *disallowed* by C11, but
- $v \sqsubset_T v'$ holds for all $(v, v') \in E_{\text{d}}$ – that is, $\sqsubset_T$ satisfies all of the scheduling constraints given in §4.3.

The $\sqsubset_T$ relation represents the order in which T's events occur at run-time. The existence of such a trace implies that the scheduling constraints need to be strengthened.

Figure 4 shows that Alloy's execution time increases exponentially with the upper bound on the number of events. The peformance figures were obtained on a machine with four 16-core 2.1 GHz AMD Opteron processors and 128 GB of RAM, and we used the Glucose SAT-solving backend. We were able to verify up to a maximum of 9 events. Although this bound appears small, many memory-related bugs can be revealed using even smaller programs [22]. We also confirmed that LegUp's original scheduling constraints are sufficient to avoid memory-related bugs in a single-threaded setting, again up to a 9-event bound.

5. EVALUATION

Thus far, our code examples have been relatively small, and designed to convey the problems of weak behaviour and

```
          atomic_int tail=0; head=0;
          int arr[SIZE]; res[MSGS];
1.1   while(prod<MSGS) {          while(cons<MSGS) {          2.1
1.2     chead = head.ld(ACQ);       ctail = tail.ld(ACQ);     2.2
1.3     ctail = tail.ld(RLX);       chead = head.ld(RLX);     2.3
1.4     ntail = (ctail+1)%SIZE;     nhead = (chead+1)%SIZE;   2.4
1.5     if(ntail != chead){         if(ctail != chead){       2.5
1.6       arr[ctail] = prod           res[cons] = arr[chead]; 2.6
1.7       tail.st(ntail,REL);         head.st(nhead,REL);     2.7
1.8       prod++;                     cons++;                 2.8
1.9     }                           }                         2.9
1.10  }                           }                           2.10
```

Figure 5: Acquire-Release semantics.

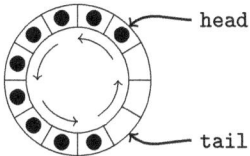

The head and tail pointers advance counterclockwise.

Figure 6: The circular buffer, diagrammatically.

demonstrate the potential of strengthening MCMs to implement atomics. In our evaluation, we investigate the performance of SC atomics and weak atomics on a real-world example: a lock-free single-producer-single-consumer (SPSC) circular buffer due to Hedström [15]. Data structures similar to this circular buffer are used in many real-time and memory-sensitive systems, and also appear in the Boost C++ library and the Linux kernel [5].

5.1 Case Study: SPSC Circular Buffer

Figure 5 shows the C-like code of a producer (on the left) and consumer (on the right) communicating via a circular buffer that is visualised in Figure 6. The buffer consists of atomic head and tail pointers, a buffer array (arr) and a result array (res). The producer only adds tasks and the consumer only removes tasks, as reflected by the store to arr (line 1.6) and the load from arr (line 2.6). The producer and consumer first check that the buffer is not full (line 1.5) and not empty (line 2.5), respectively. Finally, the producer and consumer update the tail (line 1.7) and head (line 2.7) pointers respectively with their next values. These next tail (line 1.4) and head (line 2.4) values are computed by a modular increment of SIZE to create a counterclockwise update, as depicted in Figure 6. We fix the buffer size (SIZE) at 64 and the number of messages transmitted (MSGS) to be 256. In addition, each atomic load (ld()) and atomic store (st()) is assigned a weak consistency mode: either ACQ for acquire, REL for release, or RLX for relaxed.

Ensuring correctness.

Hedström explains in detail why each memory access does not require full SC [15]. Roughly speaking, the non-atomic stores to arr (by the producer in line 1.6) do not race with the non-atomic loads of arr (by the consumer in line 2.6) because they are always separated by a release/acquire pair on the tail or the head pointer. These pairs ensure correct message-passing behaviour. The tail pair (lines 1.7 and 2.2) ensures that the consumer always reads from the latest write of the producer. Similarly, the head pair (lines 2.7 and 1.2) ensures that the consumer completes the read from arr before the producer writes to arr again.

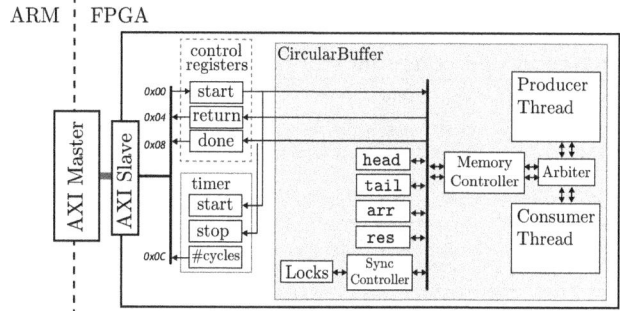

Figure 7: Architecture diagram.

Ensuring the correctness of any concurrent program in a weakly consistent setting is difficult because of the counter-intuitive behaviours allowed by a weak MCM, and testing is inconclusive because implementations of weakly consistent operations vary significantly between architectures. As such, to gain additional confidence in the correctness of this code, we turn to automatic verification. We use the Cpp-Mem tool [4] to confirm that the accesses of the shared non-atomic variable do not cause a race. Because CppMem does not support arrays, we replace arr with a scalar variable, and because CppMem's performance degrades rapidly with the number of events, we remove the while-loops. We give the actual code we verified online [1]. CppMem's result is of course weakened by the inclusion of these simplifications, but taken together with the informal argument for correctness given by Hedström, we obtain a reasonable degree of confidence in the program's correctness.

Implementation.

We map our buffer application to hardware via LegUp's pure hardware flow. We place-and-route our designs on a Xilinx Zynq 7000 (XC7Z020) with 53200 Look-up Tables (LUTs), 106400 registers, and 36 KB of block RAMs. Figure 7 shows the generated architecture. We synthesise each Pthread as a hardware accelerator, with global memory implemented on the FPGA either as registers or block RAMs. We accesses memory-mapped control registers from the ARM processor via an AXI slave connection, which we use to execute the accelerator system and extract both the verified results and the cycle counts from an on-board hardware timer. Shared memory access is protected by a memory controller. Although each thread has simultaneous dual-ported access to global memory, the memory controller can only perform two memory operations at a time. An arbiter ensures that only one thread is given access (to both ports) at a time. Also, LegUp's hardware locks are connected to the same memory controller via custom synchronisation logic.

5.2 Experiment Setup

We investigate the circular buffer on seven different design variations (as shown in Table 1): an unsound version, three lock-based versions, and three lock-free versions. Four of the seven are implemented with LegUp's pre-existing MCM and three are implemented with the MCMs discussed in §4.

The first version, Unsound, uses neither atomics nor locks. Although the results obtained from this implementation were verified to be correct experimentally, its correctness is coincidental and fragile. Small changes to the code, similar to those discussed in §2, could lead to incorrect results. We

Table 1: Design points. The last column gives the latency of one consume step and one produce step.

Short name	Description	MCM	Locks?	Lat.
Unsound	no atomics/locks (baseline)	orig	✗	10
OMP-criticals	OpenMP critical sections	orig	✓	14
Mutexes	Pthread mutexes	orig	✓	26
OMP-atomics	OpenMP atomics	orig	✓	41
SC	sequential consistency	§4.1	✗	17
SC atomics	sequentially consistent atomics	§4.2	✗	17
Weak atomics	weakly consistent atomics	§4.3	✗	12

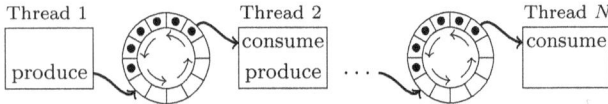

Figure 8: Chaining experiment (for N from 2 to 17).

treat this implementation as an upper bound for the circular buffer's performance.

OMP-criticals is implemented by wrapping the buffer's entire loop body with `#pragma omp critical`. LegUp implements these critical sections using a single global lock. Mutexes is similar, but in experiments that feature more than one circular buffer, each buffer is protected by its own mutex. This reduces the global contention to a single lock as can happen with OMP-criticals. OMP-atomics is implemented by wrapping each atomic instruction in a single-statement critical section. This is equivalent to OpenMP's `#pragma omp atomic`. Although this implementation is lock-free in source code, LegUp actually implements OpenMP atomics using a single global lock.

Of the lock-free designs, SC is the strictest because it serialises all memory operations regardless of their atomicity or consistency mode (see §4.1). SC atomics implements the MCM from §4.2 that takes into account the atomicity of memory operations but ignores the consistency mode of atomic operations. Weak atomics implements the MCM from §4.3 that considers the consistency mode of atomics.

We conduct two experiments on the circular buffer: chaining and bursting. Figure 8 shows the setup of the chaining experiment. The producer thread sends 256 messages across a chain of repeater threads to a consumer thread that verifies the results. Each repeater thread consumes from one buffer and immediately produces the same data to the next buffer in the chain. Table 1 provides the schedule latency of each repeater thread. In the chaining experiment, we observe the performance of our implementations as the number of repeater threads increases. In the bursting experiment, we increase the number of messages transmitted per transaction. We set up this experiment with three threads: one producer, one repeater, and one consumer. By increasing the number of messages per transaction, we increase the number of non-atomic memory accesses to the `arr` array. By doing so, we can investigate the relationship between the ratio of atomic accesses and the performance of our design points.

5.3 Results: Throughput

Figure 9 shows the throughput of the chaining and bursting experiments for all seven design points. For the chaining experiment, the overall throughput deteriorates with the increase in threads by an average of 20x across all design

points. This can be explained by the fact that the arbitration cost to access shared memory is increasing with increase in threads. In the burst experiment, the overall throughput improves with the increase in elements per transaction by an average of 5x. By transmitting more messages per transaction, we decrease the overall synchronisation cost required to transfer the same amount of data across threads.

In both experiments, the Unsound implementation has the best throughput, which can be attributed to this design point having the shortest schedule latency (as seen in Table 1). All three lock-based implementations have large throughput overheads compared to the upper-bound performance of Unsound. This can be explained by the longer schedule latencies (Table 1). For each mutually-exclusive access, LegUp performs a pair of function calls to lock and unlock a hardware lock. OMP-criticals has one pair, Mutexes has two pairs, and OMP-atomics has six pairs of these function calls per repeater thread. These calls introduce schedule delays and additional memory dependencies. These delays affect OMP-atomics, which has an average overhead of 28x (chaining) and 10x (bursting) compared to the Unsound implementation.

In the chaining experiment, Mutexes outperforms OMP-criticals for four threads or more. As we increase the number of threads, Mutexes tends to have less overhead than OMP-criticals because it distributes the contention between multiple hardware locks, whereas OMP-criticals relies on a single lock. On average, the best lock-based implementations have performance overheads of 4x (chaining) and 3.5x (bursting) compared to Unsound.

Of the three lock-free implementations, SC has the largest performance overhead for both experiments, with 1.7x on average (chaining and bursting) compared to Unsound. Although SC exploits neither the atomicity nor the consistency modes of memory operations, it still outperforms the best lock-based implementations by 2.5x (chaining) and 2x (bursting). This suggests that dealing with memory consistency as an intra-thread scheduling problem is better than incurring the overhead of locks.

SC atomics is, in the worst-case, as restrictive as SC, and we see this behaviour in the chaining experiment, since both of these implementations have the same schedule latency (Table 1). In the burst experiment, we see that SC atomics performs better than SC when there are more elements per transaction. This corresponds to more non-atomic memory operations. The fewer atomic memory operation there are, the better SC atomics performs compared to SC. SC atomics performs up to 1.5x faster than SC in the burst experiment.

Finally, Weak atomics only has a performance overhead of 1.04x (chaining) and 1.15x (bursting) compared to Unsound. We are able to recover most of the performance of the Unsound implementation, while guaranteeing correct behaviour. Compared to SC atomics, Weak atomics is on average 1.6x faster (chaining) or 1.2x faster (bursting). As we increase the number of elements per transaction, the SC atomics throughput approaches that of Weak atomics, because the increased potential for parallelising the non-atomic accesses dominates any difference in the treatment of atomic accesses between the two implementations.

5.4 Results: Resources

Figure 10 shows LUT utilisation for the chaining and bursting experiments. We see an increase in LUT utilisa-

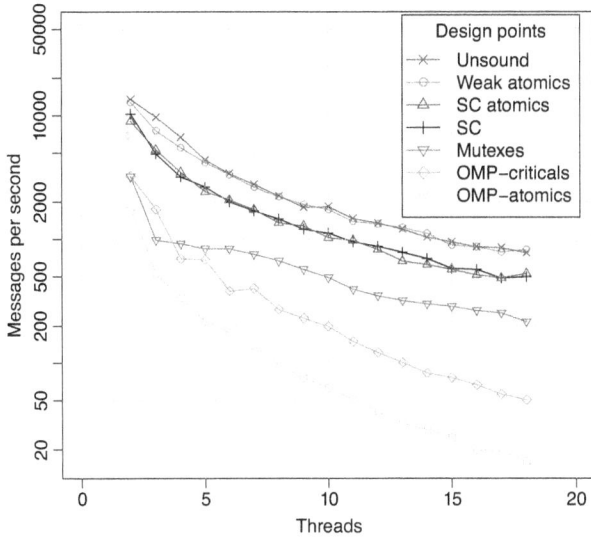

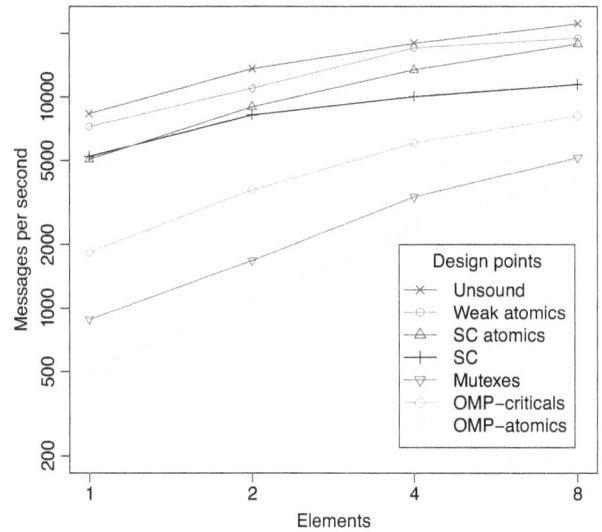

Figure 9: Throughput for the chaining experiment (left) and the bursting experiment (right).

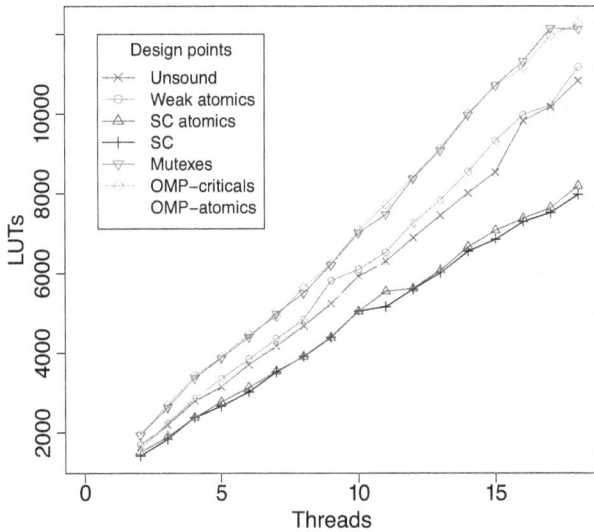

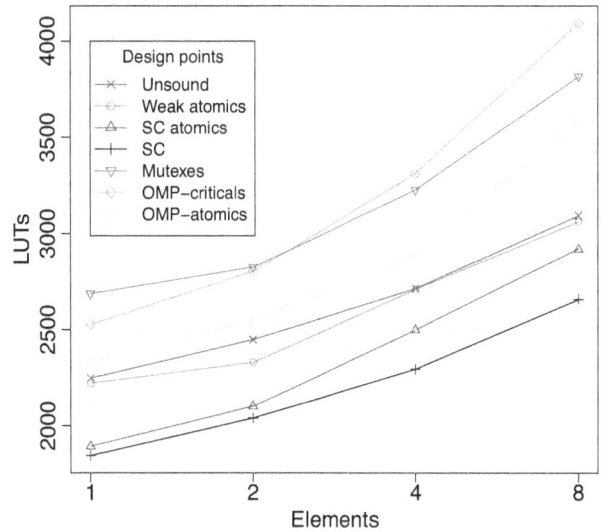

Figure 10: LUT utilisation for the chaining experiment (left) and the bursting experiment (right)

tion with the increase in threads and elements per transaction across all design points. At maximum LUT utilisation, we fill 22% of the FPGA fabric. OMP-criticals and Mutexes have the highest LUT utilisation. This can be attributed to both of these implementations requiring the synchronisation controller and hardware locks. SC and SC atomics have the smallest LUT utilisations, which can be attributed to them using only one memory port per thread due to serialisation (information we extract from LegUp's binding reports).

In the chaining experiment, we see that both the Unsound and the Weak atomics implementations use two memory ports per thread, resulting in their LUT utilisations being similar. For OMP-atomics, LUT utilisation lies between the SC and the Mutexes implementations. This may be because OMP-atomics requires the synchronisation controller and hardware locks (like Mutexes) but only uses one memory port per thread (like SC).

As we introduce more non-atomic memory accesses in the bursting experiment, some implementations can parallelise

their intra-thread memory accesses and hence exploit the second memory port provided by LegUp. This can explain the rise in LUT utilisation that is particularly noticeable for SC atomics and OMP-atomics.

6. CONCLUSION

This work has investigated how to implement lock-free algorithms on FPGAs using HLS. Our case study suggests that careful reasoning about memory consistency, as opposed to relying on locks, allows us to recover most of the performance of unsound implementations, while guaranteeing correctness. Even our worst-case lock-free implementation (SC in Table 1) is on average 2.5x faster than our best-case lock-based implementation (Mutexes). We have also shown that weakly consistent atomics have a smaller performance overhead than sequentially consistent atomics.

We hope our work will stimulate further support in HLS tools for fine-grained synchronisation in multi-threaded C programs, and raise awareness of the possibility of synthesising weakly consistent atomics on FPGAs. Previous work on implementing weak atomics has concentrated on mapping C to processor-specific assembly code [4], [28]; our work shows how HLS can compile weak atomics directly to hardware.

In the future, we hope to extend our approach beyond loads and stores to handle compound atomic operations (such as compare-and-swap), and thus enable a larger class of lock-free programs to be synthesised into hardware.

Acknowledgements

We thank David Thomas and Jason Anderson for helpful discussions. The support of the EPSRC Centre for Doctoral Training in High Performance Embedded and Distributed Systems (HiPEDS, grant reference EP/L016796/1), EPSRC grants EP/I020357/1, EP/K034448/1 and EP/K015168/1, the Royal Academy of Engineering, and Imagination Technologies is gratefully acknowledged.

REFERENCES

[1] Supplementary material is available on Zenodo, doi.org/10.5281/zenodo.200339, and GitHub, github.com/nadeshr/weak_atomics_FPGA17.

[2] J. Alglave, M. Batty, A. F. Donaldson, et al., "GPU concurrency: weak behaviours and programming assumptions," in Architectural Support for Programming Languages and Operating Systems (ASPLOS), 2015.

[3] Altera, Altera SDK for OpenCL (2016.05.02), 2016.

[4] M. Batty, S. Owens, S. Sarkar, et al., "Mathematizing C++ concurrency," in Principles of Programming Languages (POPL), 2011.

[5] T. Blechmann, "Lock-free single-producer/single-consumer ringbuffer," bit.ly/2dbqFq1, 2013.

[6] A. Canis, J. Choi, M. Aldham, et al., "LegUp: high-level synthesis for FPGA-based processor/accelerator systems," in Field-Programmable Gate Arrays (FPGA), 2011.

[7] J. Choi, S. Brown, and J. Anderson, "From software threads to parallel hardware in high-level synthesis for FPGAs," in Field-Programmable Technology (FPT), 2013.

[8] A. Cilardo, L. Gallo, A. Mazzeo, et al., "Efficient and scalable OpenMP-based system-level design," in Design, Automation & Test in Europe (DATE), 2013.

[9] J. Cong, B. Liu, R. Prabhakar, et al., "A study on the impact of compiler optimizations on high-level synthesis," in Languages and Compilers for Parallel Computing (LCPC), 2012.

[10] J. Cong and Z. Zhang, "An efficient and versatile scheduling algorithm based on SDC formulation," in Design Automation Conference (DAC), 2006.

[11] P. Coussy, D. D. Gajski, M. Meredith, et al., "An introduction to high-level synthesis," IEEE Design and Test of Computers, vol. 26, no. 4, 2009.

[12] M. Dodds, M. Batty, and A. Gotsman, "Compositional verification of relaxed-memory program transformations," Under review, 2016, bit.ly/2bmY7wI.

[13] V. Gramoli, "More than you ever wanted to know about synchronization," in Principles and Practice of Parallel Programming (PPoPP), 2015.

[14] D. Greaves and S. Singh, "Kiwi: synthesis of FPGA circuits from parallel programs," in Field-Programmable Custom Computing Machines (FCCM), 2008.

[15] K. Hedström, "Lock-free single-producer-single-consumer circular queue," bit.ly/2dbr8IK, 2014.

[16] Q. Huang, R. Lian, A. Canis, et al., "The effect of compiler optimizations on high-level synthesis for FPGAs," in Field-Programmable Custom Computing Machines (FCCM), 2013.

[17] ISO/IEC, Programming languages – C. International standard 9899:2011, 2011.

[18] D. Jackson, Software Abstractions – Logic, Language, and Analysis, Revised edition. MIT Press, 2012.

[19] Khronos Group, The OpenCL Specification. Version 2.0, 2013.

[20] L. Lamport, "How to make a multiprocessor computer that correctly executes multiprocess programs," IEEE Transactions on Computers, vol. C-28, no. 9, 1979.

[21] Y. Y. Leow, C. Y. Ng, and W. F. Wong, "Generating hardware from OpenMP programs," in Field-Programmable Technology (FPT), 2006.

[22] S. Mador-Haim, R. Alur, and M. M. K. Martin, "Litmus tests for comparing memory consistency models: how long do they need to be?" In Design Automation Conference (DAC), 2011.

[23] S. A. Mahlke, R. E. Hank, R. A. Bringmann, et al., "Characterizing the impact of predicated execution on branch prediction," in Microarchitecture (MICRO), 1994.

[24] L. Maranget, S. Sarkar, and P. Sewell, "A tutorial introduction to the ARM and POWER relaxed memory models," bit.ly/2dbpUNu, 2012.

[25] N. Minh Lê, A. Pop, A. Cohen, et al., "Correct and efficient work-stealing for weak memory models," in Principles and Practice of Parallel Programming (PPoPP), 2013.

[26] N. Ramanathan, J. Wickerson, F. Winterstein, et al., "A case for work stealing on FPGAs with OpenCL atomics," in Field-Programmable Gate Arrays (FPGA), 2016.

[27] J. Villarreal, A. Park, W. Najjar, et al., "Designing modular hardware accelerators in C with ROCCC 2.0," in Field-Programmable Custom Computing Machines (FCCM), 2010.

[28] J. Wickerson, M. Batty, B. M. Beckmann, et al., "Remote-scope promotion: clarified, rectified, and verified," in Object-Oriented Programming, Systems, Languages, and Applications (OOPSLA), 2015.

[29] J. Wickerson, M. Batty, T. Sorensen, et al., "Automatically comparing memory consistency models," in Principles of Programming Languages (POPL), 2017.

[30] Xilinx, SDAccel development environment - user guide (v2016.2), 2016.

[31] ——, Vivado design suite user guide: high-level synthesis (v2016.2), 2016.

[32] H.-J. Yang, K. Fleming, M. Adler, et al., "LEAP shared memories: automating the construction of FPGA coherent memories," in Field-Programmable Custom Computing Machines (FCCM), 2014.

A New Approach to Automatic Memory Banking using Trace-Based Address Mining

Yuan Zhou [*]   Khalid Al-Hawaj [*]   Zhiru Zhang

School of Electrical and Computer Engineering, Cornell University, Ithaca, NY

{yz882, ka429, zhiruz}@cornell.edu

ABSTRACT

Recent years have seen an increased deployment of FPGAs as programmable accelerators for improving the performance and energy efficiency of compute-intensive applications. A well-known "secret sauce" of achieving highly efficient FPGA acceleration is to create application-specific memory architecture that fully exploits the vast amounts of on-chip memory bandwidth provided by the reconfigurable fabric. In particular, memory banking is widely employed when multiple parallel memory accesses are needed to meet a demanding throughput constraint.

In this paper we propose TraceBanking, a novel and flexible trace-driven address mining algorithm that can automatically generate efficient memory banking schemes by analyzing a stream of memory address bits. Unlike mainstream memory partitioning techniques that are based on static compile-time analysis, TraceBanking only relies on simple source-level instrumentation to provide the memory trace of interest without enforcing any coding restrictions. More importantly, our technique can effectively handle memory traces that exhibit either affine or non-affine access patterns, and produce efficient banking solutions with a reasonable runtime. Furthermore, TraceBanking can be used to process a reduced memory trace with the aid of an SMT prover to verify if the resulting banking scheme is indeed conflict free. Our experiments on Xilinx FPGAs show that TraceBanking achieves competitive performance and resource usage compared to the state-of-the-art across a set of real-life benchmarks with affine memory accesses. We also perform a case study on a face detection algorithm to show that TraceBanking is capable of generating a highly area-efficient memory partitioning based on a sequence of addresses without any obvious access patterns.

1. INTRODUCTION

With the general-purpose CPU performance scaling significantly slowing in the past decade, heterogeneous computer architectures that integrate specialized accelerators are gaining popularity to achieve improved performance and energy efficiency. Along the line, field-programmable gate arrays (FPGAs) have evolved into an attractive option for fulfilling the role of application-specific hardware acceleration, owing to the many recent technological advances on FPGA hardware capabilities as well as the software tooling support for high-level design entries.

An FPGA-based hardware accelerator is typically highly parallelized and/or deeply pipelined in order to achieve a desirable throughput. As a result, multiple parallel accesses to a single on-chip memory are often required to provide the necessary data bandwidth to sustain the high throughput of the accelerator. However, the embedded memory blocks available on modern FPGA devices (e.g., BRAMs) only provide a very limited number of ports for concurrent reads/writes.[1] Simply replicating the memory blocks would not be feasible due to the steep area overhead and potential memory coherence overhead resulting from write operations.

A more viable solution is memory banking, which partitions a memory block into several smaller banks; thus, concurrent memory accesses are distributed to different banks, avoiding or minimizing banking conflicts. Since each memory bank only holds a subset of the original memory contents, memory banking usually yields a significantly lower storage overhead compared to memory duplication. Nevertheless, additional banking logic is still required to orchestrate the data movement between banked memories and compute units in the accelerator. For non-expert FPGA designers, devising a minimum-conflict banking scheme with low hardware overheads is certainly a challenging task. While commercial high-level synthesis (HLS) tools provide some basic support for array partitioning [8], the users remain responsible for manually specifying the banking scheme via vendor-specific pragmas or directives. For this reason, there is an active body of HLS research tackling the problem of automatic array partitioning (i.e., memory banking) given a throughput constraint that is usually specified in terms of pipeline initiation interval (II) [6, 12, 14, 16, 17].

In this paper, we also focus our study on automatic memory banking, and propose *TraceBanking*, a trace-based banking algorithm that is very different from the existing methods. Specifically, TraceBanking mines a stream of memory address bits to determine a banking scheme that minimizes the number of access conflicts and simplifies the banking logic. Unlike mainstream techniques that are mostly

---

[*] The first and second authors contributed equally to this work.

FPGA '17, February 22-24, 2017, Monterey, CA, USA

© 2017 ACM. ISBN 978-1-4503-4354-1/17/02. . . $15.00

DOI: http://dx.doi.org/10.1145/3020078.3021734

---

[1] Even for ASICs, it is not feasible to have a large number of memory ports due to the excessive area and power overhead [15].

based on static compiler analysis, TraceBanking only relies on simple source-level instrumentation to provide the memory trace of interest without enforcing any coding restrictions (such as static control parts often required by polyhedral analysis [3]). The major technical contributions of our work are threefold:

(1) We offer a fresh look at memory banking, by waiving the requirements of using static compile-time analysis. We show that from a trace of memory addresses, we can identify a set of "interesting" address bits that form the basis of the hardware-efficient memory banking function. In addition, our technique is able to form banking functions that do not belong to the solution space of the existing linear-transformation-based techniques.

(2) We propose a two-step heuristic to solve the trace-based memory banking problem. This heuristic is not only able to exploit regular memory access patterns, but can also generate efficient solutions for applications with irregular memory accesses.

(3) We propose an SMT-based checker that can formally verify if a memory banking solution is free of access conflicts under all possible execution traces. This allows the usage of a reduced (or incomplete) memory trace to significantly speed up TraceBanking, but without the risk of accepting an inferior banking solution. We believe that this formal verification technique is also useful for validating the soundness of existing memory banking algorithms, even though they are designed to be correct by construction.

The rest of this paper is organized as follows: Section 2 presents related work in memory banking; Section 3 formulates the trace-based memory banking problem; Section 4 provides motivational examples to illustrate the intuition behind our work; Section 5 describes our address mining algorithm in detail; Section 6 introduces the SMT-based banking solution checker; Section 7 reports the experimental results on commonly used benchmarks with affine memory accesses, which is followed by a case study on a face detection application with irregular memory accesses in Section 8; and Section 9 concludes this paper with discussion on future work.

2. RELATED WORK

There is a recent line of research that investigates the problem of automatic array partitioning in the context of HLS [20]. Initial efforts focus on one-dimensional arrays and attempt to find a proper cyclic partitioning with optimal scheduling to ensure conflict-free parallel data accesses [7, 11]. More recent proposals such as [16, 17] generalize these results to handle nested loops and multi-dimensional arrays.

Notably, linear transformation is extensively used among the existing array partitioning techniques. For example, the LTB approach [17] searches for a coefficient vector $\vec{\alpha}$ to construct a cyclic banking function $bank(\vec{x}) = (\vec{\alpha} \cdot \vec{x})\%N$, given the number of banks N and the affine memory access pattern. Meng et al. proposed a fast algorithm to generate the LTB coefficient vector $\vec{\alpha}$ according to the topology of the memory access pattern in multi-dimensional memory space [12]. The GMP approach is a generalization of LTB, which can generate block-cyclic banking function in the form of $bank(\vec{x}) = \lfloor (\vec{\alpha} \cdot \vec{x})/B \rfloor \%N$ [16]. More recently, Cilardo et al. proposed a lattice-based banking algorithm using polyhedron analysis [6].

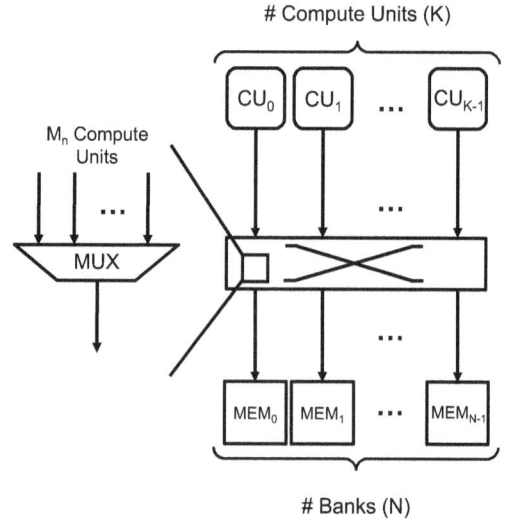

Figure 1: Hardware template for memory banking.

The aforementioned techniques all employ static compile-time analysis and are only effective with affine data access patterns. To our best knowledge, we are the first to introduce a comprehensive trace-based banking algorithm that is not limited to affine memory accesses. Along the lines of trace-based memory optimization, one relevant proposal is [4], which attempts to partition an array of data structures into distinct arrays by leveraging hints from software memory traces. However, this technique does not directly tackle memory banking for multi-dimensional arrays.

Besides memory partitioning, parallel data accesses can be further facilitated by creating data reuse buffer that exploits locality in memory access patterns. For many image processing and signal processing applications, data reuse is a more hardware-efficient solution due to the regular memory access patterns in stencil-like operations. Along these lines, a recent work by Su et al. introduced an efficient method of combining linear reuse analysis and cyclic memory partitioning to generate application-specific reuse-chains and memory-banking [14]. In this work, however, we focus on memory banking without data reuse; nevertheless, we believe that our trace-based approach can also be extended to generate data reuse buffers and will explore this topic in future work.

3. PROBLEM FORMULATION

In this section we provide the definitions and formulate the trace-based memory banking problem. An example of the hardware architecture under discussion, shown in Figure 1, contains a set of compute units and memory banks connected by a crossbar. The number of compute units is denoted as K, and the number of memory banks is denoted as N. For simplicity, we assume that each compute unit only has one memory load port, and each memory bank only has one read port. Our problem formulation as well as the proposed technique can be generalized to handle multi-bank and multi-port memories. In the following, we first define several important concepts before formulating the actual optimization problem.

Definition 1. **Memory Trace**: A memory trace T is a sequence of addresses that are grouped into L lists, where all addresses in the same list need to be accessed in parallel. Each of these lists is called a **step**. Each step contains K addresses which are issued by the compute units. In the following discussions, we refer to the l-th step in memory trace T as $T[l]$, and the memory operation requested by the k-th compute unit in step l as $T[l][k]$. If compute unit k does not issue any memory request in step l, $T[l][k]$ is marked as invalid.

Definition 2. **Memory Banking**: A memory banking solution of a trace T consists of a banking function $bank(A)$ and an offset function $offset(A)$. $bank(A)$ maps address A to a memory bank ID, while $offset(A)$ determines the intra-bank position. A memory banking solution can be fully represented by a set of binary variables $\{b_{A,n} \mid A \in T, 0 \leq n < N, n \in \mathbb{N}\}$, where $b_{A,n}$ evaluates to one if and only if address A is mapped to bank n, otherwise evaluates to zero.

Definition 3. **Banking Conflict**: A banking conflict occurs when two different addresses in the same step are mapped to the same memory bank.

Definition 4. **Mux Size**: The mux size of a memory bank n, M_n, refers to the number of compute units which access bank n in the memory trace. M_n can be represented by binary variables $\{b_{A,n}\}$ using the following equation:

$$M_n = \sum_{k=0}^{K-1} \bigvee_{l=0}^{L-1} b_{T[l][k],n}$$

With the above definitions, we can formulate the memory banking problem as an integer linear programming (ILP) problem:

Problem: Given a memory trace T, find a mapping function $bank(A)$ to optimize the following objective function, which minimizes memory access conflicts as the primary goal and reduces muxing overhead as the secondary goal.

$$Objective : \ \alpha \cdot Conflicts + \beta \cdot Muxing$$

$$= \alpha \cdot \sum_{l=0}^{L-1} \sum_{\forall A_i, A_j \in T[l]} s_{A_i, A_j} + \beta \cdot \sum_{n=0}^{N-1} M_n$$

subject to

$$i, j \in [0, K-1], i \neq j, \ s_{A_i, A_j} = \sum_{n=0}^{N-1} (b_{A_i,n} \cdot b_{A_j,n}).$$

Here the addresses A_i and A_j refer to the i-th and j-th address in step $T[l]$, respectively. The binary variable s_{A_i, A_j} equals to one if and only if addresses A_i and A_j are mapped to the same bank, otherwise equals to zero (we omit the linearization of non-linear terms due to page limit).

4. MOTIVATIONAL EXAMPLES

We use two examples to illustrate the intuition behind TraceBanking. We start with the very simple example in Figure 2, where Figure 2(a) shows a simple loop kernel containing two memory accesses per iteration, and Figure 2(b) shows the associated (truncated) memory trace. From Figure 2(b), it is not difficult to tell that the two addresses in each iteration always differ in the least significant bit (LSB). We refer to such bit as a **mask bit**. Informally, we define

Step	addr0	addr1
0	000000	000001
1	000001	000010
2	000010	000011
3	000011	000100
...	...	...

```
int A[SIZE+1];
for (int i=0; i<SIZE; i++)
    #pragma HLS pipeline II=1
    foo(A[i], A[i+1]);
```

(a) Loop Kernel   **(b)** Memory Trace

Figure 2: Simple loop example — **(a)** Pipelined loop kernel with two memory accesses in each cycle. **(b)** Memory trace of the loop kernel.

```
int A[Rows][Cols];
for (int i=1; i<Rows-1; i++)
    for (int j=1; j<Cols-1; j++)
        #pragma HLS pipeline II=1
        foo(A[i-1][j-1], A[i-1][j+1],
            A[i+1][j-1], A[i+1][j+1]);
```

(a) Loop Kernel   **(b)** Mem Pattern

Step	addr0	addr1	addr2	addr3
0	000|000	000|010	010|000	010|010
1	000|001	000|011	010|001	010|011
...	...	...	...	...
5	000|101	000|111	010|101	010|111
...	...	...	...	...
Cols-1	001|000	001|010	011|000	011|010
...	...	...	...	...

(c) Sample memory trace

(d) GMP solution   **(e)** An alternative solution

Figure 3: Bicubic interpolation — **(a)** Pipelined loop kernel with four memory accesses in each cycle. **(b)** Memory access pattern of the loop kernel in two-dimensional memory space. **(c)** Memory trace generated by concatenating array indexes: Addresses are formed by concatenating the two-dimensional array indexes i and j (for simplicity, i and j are both truncated to three bits). **(d)** GMP banking solution [16]. **(e)** An alternative solution generated by selecting mask bits.

the mask bits as a subset of address bits that can differentiate all memory addresses included in the same step. We argue that the mask bits provide important hints for finding a memory banking solution. In this particular case, if we partition array A based on the value of the LSB, we end up with a cyclic banking scheme that enables the loop to be fully pipelined.

Figure 3 shows another (and perhaps more interesting) example from bicubic interpolation [1]. In this case, the innermost loop has four memory accesses per iteration to a two-dimensional array. The memory access pattern is illustrated in Figure 3(b) and the corresponding address stream is shown in Figure 3(c). Existing techniques, such

181

as GMP [16], analyze the symbolic expression of memory accesses and search for appropriate coefficients to construct a banking function in the form of $bank(i, j) = \lfloor(\alpha_0 i + \alpha_1 j)/B\rfloor \% N$. Figure 3(d) shows the resulting 4-bank partitioning scheme, where $\alpha_0 = 1$, $\alpha_1 = 2$, and $B = 2$.

Figure 3(e) shows an alternative banking scheme, which is not in the solution space of the GMP approach.[2] By examining the memory trace in Figure 3(c), we can identify two mask bits: the second-to-last bit of i, plus the second-to-last bit of j. These two bits combined can differentiate the four memory accesses belonging to the same iteration. As a result, we can divide the original array into four memory banks according to the values of the two mask bits and arrive at the alternative scheme in Figure 3(e).

These two examples demonstrate the possibility of performing memory banking based on a stream of memory addresses. Although these examples both have affine memory access patterns, TraceBanking is also capable of generating memory partitioning for applications with irregular memory accesses. Regardless of the memory access pattern, it is important to identify the mask bits that form the basis of banking. The value of mask bits is referred to as **mask ID**. In the following sections, we will discuss how Trace-Banking identifies mask bits and derives efficient banking accordingly.

5. TRACEBANKING ALGORITHM

A straightforward method to optimize the objective function formulated in Section 3 is to use an ILP solver. However, ILP solvers are not scalable in general. Therefore, there is a need for heuristics which can find an optimal mapping between addresses and banks with a reasonable execution time.

In this section, we introduce TraceBanking algorithm, a flow of heuristics to solve the problem formulated in Section 3. Specifically, TraceBanking takes the number of available banks as a constraint and finds an optimized mapping by solving two sub-problems: (1) Finding a set of promising address bits to form mask bits, and (2) Finding a mapping between the generated mask IDs and available banks.

The flow of our algorithm is shown in Figure 4. The raw memory trace is first compressed, and a search is performed to find a feasible set of mask bits. Then, a graph will be generated based on the discovered mask bits. The generated graph will be colored such that each color represents a distinct memory bank. Since only the mask bits are used in the banking function, TraceBanking can potentially generate more area-efficient hardware to calculate bank IDs.

5.1 Finding Masks Bits

TraceBanking finds a set of bits from the address to form a mask in the first step. At the beginning, raw trace is pre-processed to remove redundant information, i.e. memory accesses with the same address in the same step; because having multiple accesses with the same address can be satisfied in the same cycle with no overhead. Then, the raw memory trace is compressed by initial-compression, which combines steps with identical accesses into a single step. A weight property is added to each step indicating its frequency in the raw trace. The resultant compressed trace is referred to as T_c. Figure 6(a) shows the compression process for our

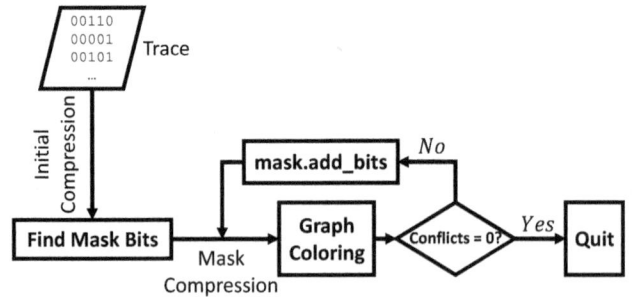

Figure 4: General structure of the proposed flow.

Algorithm 1 findMasksBits

Input : N – number of available banks;
          T_c – Compressed memory trace;
for $nbits \leftarrow \lceil log_2(N_A)\rceil$ **to** $address\_size$ **do**
  $mask \leftarrow$ all possible mask combinations with size $nbits$
  while $mask \neq null$ **do**
    $num_{conflicts} \leftarrow$ calculateConflicts(T_c, $mask$)
    if $num_{conflicts} \leqslant min_{conflicts}$ **then**
      /* Possible Solution   */
      $min_{conflicts} \leftarrow num_{conflicts}$
      /* Test graph colorability   */
      $G \leftarrow$ constructGraph(T_c, $mask$)
      if $\chi(G) \leqslant min_\chi$ **then**
        $min_\chi \leftarrow \chi(G)$
      end
      if $min_{conflicts} = 0$ and $min_\chi \leqslant N$ **then**
        break
      end
    end
    $mask \leftarrow next(mask)$
  end
end

Figure 5: The first heuristic in our flow to find mask bits.

bicubic example; no compression can be performed since no identical steps exist in the raw trace.

After cleaning up and compressing the trace, TraceBanking performs a multi-objective exhaustive search using the `findMasksBits` algorithm in Figure 5. This algorithm takes the available number of banks, N, as well as the compressed memory trace, T_c, as inputs. It evaluates any candidate mask using two objectives: *mask IDs' conflicts* and *conflict graph colorability*.

The search starts with masks that includes $\lceil log_2(N_A)\rceil$ bits, where N_A is the maximum number of memory accesses in all steps in the compressed memory trace. It tries all possible combinations of $\lceil log_2(N_A)\rceil$ bits; each combination constructs a unique mask which maps addresses to mask IDs. Going through the compressed memory trace, the algorithm evaluates mask IDs conflicts by counting the number of times when two addresses in the same step have the same mask ID.

After finding a mask that has the lowest number of mask IDs conflicts, the algorithm constructs a conflict graph — every node in the graph represents a mask ID; edges between nodes indicate mask IDs that appeared together in at least one step, and the edges' weights represent the frequency. Thus, the problem is transformed to a graph coloring problem. The algorithm calculates a lower bound for

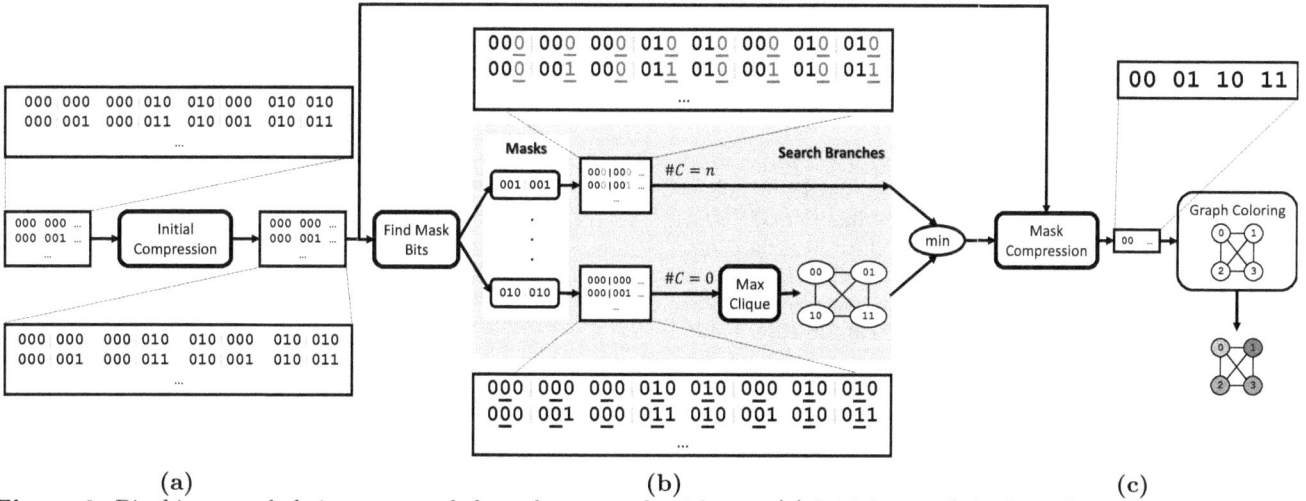

Figure 6: Bicubic example being processed throughout our algorithm — **(a)** Initial part of the flow where the raw memory trace is compressed and preprocessed; in this example, no compression nor preprocessing is possible. **(b)** The first heuristic of the flow conducting a search for mask bits; underlining shows the bits considered for masking and conflicts are highlighted with red colored mask bits. For masks with no conflicts, the heuristic checks colorability by max-clique. Then, the heuristic takes the mask with minimum conflicts and minimum max-clique ($\#C$ symbolizes number of conflicts for each search branch). For bicubic, the mask with no-conflicts and a max-clique of at most N, 4, is 010 010. **(c)** Finally, the second heuristic mask-compresses the trace and colors the generated graph. It is obvious that for bicubic the graph is rather simple to color as it is only a clique of size 4.

Algorithm 2 mapMaskIDsToBanks

Input : N – number of available banks;
$\quad\quad\quad\; T_c$ – Compressed memory trace;
$\quad\quad\quad\; mask$ – Initial Mask;
do
$\quad$ /* Perform mask-compression $\quad\quad\quad\quad$ */
$\quad T_{mc} \leftarrow \text{maskCompression}(T_c, mask)$
$\quad$ /* Construct a graph $\quad\quad\quad\quad\quad\quad\quad$ */
$\quad G \leftarrow \text{constructGraph}(T_{mc})$
$\quad$ /* Create a seed using greedy coloring */
$\quad S \leftarrow \text{greedyGraphColoring}(G, N)$
$\quad$ /* Color G using evolutionary algorithm */
$\quad num_{conflicts}, mapping \leftarrow \text{eaGraphColoring}(S, N)$
$\quad$ /* Ending conditions $\quad\quad\quad\quad\quad\quad\quad$ */
$\quad$ **if** $bits\_remaining(mask) = 0$ **then**
$\quad\quad |\;$ break
$\quad$ **else if** $num_{conflicts} \neq 0$ **then**
$\quad\quad |\; mask \leftarrow \text{performBestFirstSearch}(T_c, mask)$
$\quad$ **end**
while $num_{conflicts} \neq 0$;

Figure 7: The second heuristic in our flow to map mask IDs to banks.

the colorability of the conflict graph by finding the maximum clique; where graphs with maximum clique size greater than the number of banks, N, *cannot* be colored with N colors. Using bicubic as an example, Figure 6(b) shows the resulting graph; it is obvious that the graph has a maximum clique of 4; therefore, the first step concludes with the mask 010 010.

5.2 Mapping Mask IDs to Banks

The second step, with its algorithm shown in Figure 7, takes the mask found by `findMasksBits` and finds bank assignments for mask IDs such that the number of potential conflicts is minimized. To reduce complexity and re-

dundant work, the algorithm further compresses the trace by applying mask-compression, which is similar to initial-compression explained earlier except that the addresses are replaced with their corresponding mask IDs. After that, the algorithm will construct a conflict graph from the mask-compressed trace.

To find a coloring for the generated graph, the algorithm reduces the problem to maximum coloring.[3] The number of banks represents the number of colors available for coloring. The algorithm then generates a colored seed, S, using multiple order-based greedy heuristics [2, 10]. If the seed is not conflict-free, TraceBanking attempts to minimize the number of conflicts using an evolutionary algorithm [10]. In each evolutionary step, TraceBanking performs a set of heuristics that showed efficiency in coloring memory-accesses graphs [10]. Once a coloring for a conflict graph is found, the evolutionary algorithm concludes with banking function $bank(A)$ constructed from the coloring.

If the algorithm cannot find a conflict-free coloring in a bounded number of evolutionary steps, it is assumed that the graph is uncolorable. Then, TraceBanking proceeds to perform a best-first search. The search will modify the mask by adding one extra bit to it. It is reasonable to assume that address bits that are part of the final mask have an additive effect in reducing conflicts when considered; as a result, the best-first search tests the colorability of remaining bits by adding them to the mask in isolation. Then, the search includes the bit that yields a graph with the minimum number of conflicts permanently to the mask. Since this is a rough assumption, TraceBanking might use more bits than theoretically needed to find a feasible banking.

Taking the bicubic example from before, the algorithm will take the mask found by `findMasksBits` and its corresponding conflict graph. Then, it will attempt to color the four-node conflict graph shown in Figure 6(c). Because the

---

[3]In this paper we strictly target conflict-free solutions. However, TraceBanking is easily extended to adapt conflict-less solutions.

graph is actually a clique of four, it will be colored with four different colors, as shown in Figure 6(c). The resulting colored graph is conflict-free. Therefore, the algorithm finishes and produces the solution in Figure 3(e).

5.3 Offset Generation

After finding the mask bits and generating the banking function $bank(A)$, we need to find an offset function $offset(A)$ to transform an address A to a corresponding intra-bank offset. An intuitive method to generate the offset function is to simply scan every data element in the data domain and assign consecutive integers to data elements in each bank. Without any constraints on the offset function, this integer counting method is effective for both regular and irregular banking solutions. In addition, this method is optimal in terms of storage overhead since the data elements in each bank are guaranteed to have consecutive intra-bank offsets.

5.4 Uncovering Closed-Form Representations

The banking and offset functions obtained from Sections 5.2 and 5.3 are represented in the form of look-up tables by default. For applications with regular memory access patterns, it is possible to convert the look-up tables generated by TraceBanking into equivalent closed-form equations, which essentially uncovers and exploits the regularity in the original application.

Our key idea is to decompose the look-up table into multiple stages of smaller look-up tables, and use a simple search to map the sub-tables into equations. The composition of memory addresses is retrieved from source-level instrumentation. An example is shown in Figure 8. The original 5-bit mask shown in Figure 8(a) is divided into two disjoint sub-masks: i-Mask and j-Mask — according to the corresponding array indices. By grouping the entries with the same i-Mask ID, the original banking solution shown in Figure 8(a) is decomposed into two levels, where the first level is used to determine the look-up table for the second level. Figure 8(b) shows how to index the decomposed look-up tables, where the i-Mask ID is used to index the first-level table and j-Mask ID is needed to index the second-level table and retrieve the actual bank ID. As illustrated in Figure 8(b), each second-level look-up table can be represented by a modulus operation. By searching for coefficients to represent the relationship between i-Mask ID and the constants in the equations (highlighted in bold in Figure 8(b)), we can represent the original banking solution with one closed-form equation shown in Figure 8(b). Clearly, this approach can easily be generalized to arrays with higher dimensions. We also use a similar method to uncover the closed-form equation for an offset function, if such representation exists.

According to our experiments on a set of benchmarks with affine memory accesses, all of the results generated by TraceBanking can be represented by our equation template which is generalized from block-cyclic partitioning. Some of our solutions fall into the category of the cyclic partitioning scheme mentioned in the LTB approach [17]. Other solutions are not in the solution space of block-cyclic partitioning. Nonetheless, they can be efficiently represented with a few number of mask bits (e.g., bicubic solution in Figure 3(e)).

6. SMT-BASED VERIFICATION

The previous discussion in Section 5 assume that the input memory trace to TraceBanking is complete. In other

Address: i (6 bit) | j (6 bit)
Original Mask: 000111 | 000011
Partitioned Mask: i-Mask: 000111; j-mask: 000011

Mask ID	Bank ID	i-Mask ID	j-Mask ID
0	B0	0	0
1	B1	0	1
2	B2	0	2
3	B3	0	3
4	B1	1	0
5	B2	1	1
6	B3	1	2
7	B0	1	3
...	...	...	...

(a) Banking solution in a look-up table

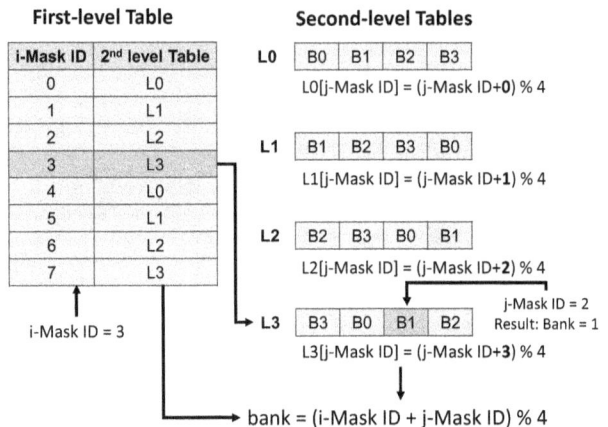

(b) Multi-level look-up table and closed-form solution

Figure 8: Example of mapping banking solution into closed-form equations — **(a)** Mask bits and the banking solution: An address bit noted as '1' is a mask bit, while an address bit noted as '0' is not. The mask bits are divided into two parts, i-Mask and j-Mask, according to the concatenation of array indices. **(b)** i-Mask is used to index the first-level table, and j-Mask is used to index the corresponding second-level table. Each second-level table can be represented with a closed-form equation. Constants in bold indicate the relationship between bank ID and i-Mask ID.

words, the input trace captures all memory accesses from the entire software execution. In this case, our solution is supposed to be sound in terms of guaranteeing no banking conflicts. When the given memory trace is incomplete or input-dependent, it is necessary to have a formal mechanism to verify if the resulting solution remains conflict-free under all possible scenarios.

To this end, we propose an SMT-based checker to validate the soundness of the solution with the aid of a simple compiler analysis. The checker takes the memory banking solution from TraceBanking, and the address expressions of the loop kernel from compiler analysis. With this information, we can formulate the SMT problem as shown in Figure 9(a). The integer variables for the SMT problem correspond to loop induction variables in the original application. We represent the banking solution as a function of array indices, and expressions of array indices as functions of loop induction variables. Then, we specify the iteration

Define loop induction variables as SMT variables:
int $\vec{i}$
Define banking function:
int $B(\overrightarrow{idx})$
/*definition of the banking function*/
Define expressions of array indices:
int[ ] $idx_0(\vec{i})$
/*represent array indices in the 1st load instruction*/
int[ ] $idx_1(\vec{i})$
/*represent array indices in the 2nd load instruction*/
...
/*define the total number of load instructions*/
const int instr_cnt = K
Construct iteration domain $\mathbb{D}$:
assert $((i[0] > 0)$ and $(i[1] > 0)$ and ...)
Constraint for having at least one conflict:
assert

$$\bigvee_{\forall \vec{i} \in \mathbb{D}} \bigvee_{\forall a,b \in [0, K-1], a \neq b} B(idx_a(\vec{i})) = B(idx_b(\vec{i}))$$

(a) General SMT formulation

Define loop induction variables as SMT variables:
int i, j
Define banking function:
int $B(i, j)$
/*select the mask bits from indices*/
return $(i$ & 0x2$) \| ((j$ & 0x2$) >> 1)$
Construct iteration domain $\mathbb{D}$:
assert $((i > 1)$ and $(j > 1)$ and
$(i < $ Rows-1$)$ and $(j < $ Cols-1$))$
Constraint for having at least one conflict:
assert ($(B(i-1, j-1) = B(i-1, j+1))$ or
$(B(i-1, j-1) = B(i+1, j-1))$ or
$(B(i-1, j-1) = B(i+1, j+1))$ or
$(B(i-1, j+1) = B(i+1, j-1))$ or
$(B(i-1, j+1) = B(i+1, j+1))$ or
$(B(i+1, j-1) = B(i+1, j+1)))$

(b) Example of Bicubic interpolation

Figure 9: SMT formulation of the banking solution checker — **(a)** General formulation. **(b)** Example of Bicubic interpolation.

domain as a constraint. Additionally, we add one constraint of having at least one banking conflict in the whole iteration domain. If the SMT problem is proven to be unsatisfiable, there is no memory access conflict in all iterations and the banking solution is valid.

The example shown in Figure 9(b) illustrates how the SMT-based checker validates the banking solution for bicubic interpolation shown in Figure 3(e): the loop induction variables i and j are used as SMT variables; and the banking function is represented symbolically. The constraints specify boundaries for the SMT variables, and compare every pair of addresses from the same iteration to check for conflicts.

As a formal verification technique, the SMT-based checker is also useful for validating the soundness of existing memory banking algorithms to detect any bugs in compiler analysis and code transformation, even though they are designed to be correct by construction.

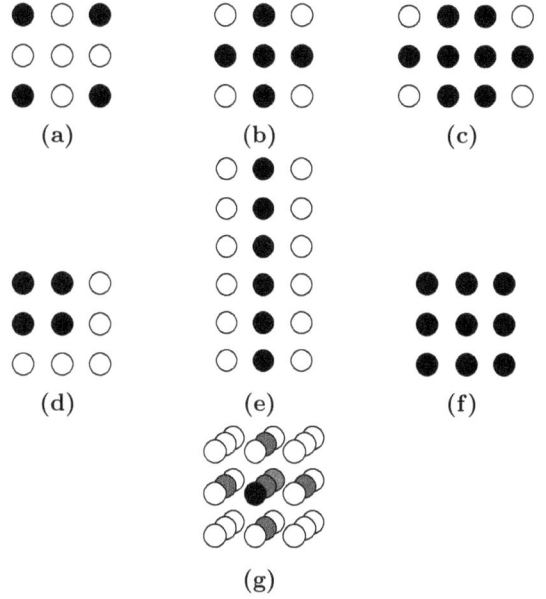

Figure 10: Memory access patterns of benchmarks — **(a)** BICUBIC, **(b)** DECONV, **(c)** DENOISE-UR, **(d)** MOTION_C, **(e)** MOTION_LV, **(f)** SOBEL, **(g)** STENCIL3D.

7. EXPERIMENTAL RESULTS

In our experiments, memory traces are generated by source-level instrumentation of the loop kernels. The addresses in the memory traces are constructed by concatenating multi-dimensional array indices. The core algorithm of Trace-Banking processes the memory trace and generates banking and offset functions. This algorithm is implemented in C. We use Vivado Design Suite 2016.2 from Xilinx [19] for high-level synthesis (HLS), logic synthesis and simulation. The target FPGA device is Xilinx Virtex-7. The memory banking flow takes in the memory trace and generates solutions in the form of look-up tables or close-form equations. We use Z3, an SMT theorem prover, to verify the generated solutions [9]. Each verified banking solution as well as the corresponding application are implemented as a synthesizable HLS code.

We adopt six different loop kernels from the GMP work [16]. In addition, we add Stencil3D benchmark from MachSuite [13], which accesses a three-dimensional array, to stress the robustness and scalability of our approach. The memory access patterns of these loop kernels are shown in Figure 10 — the solid dots represent the data elements being accessed in each iteration of the loop kernels. We substitute the processing phase of these loop kernels with a simple summation to better compare the overhead of different memory banking solutions. We also implemented the GMP method [16] as the baseline. All the designs are pipelined with II of one for maximum throughput. The input size of the designs is 64×48 ($5 \times 64 \times 48$ for Stencil3D), and the data size is 8-bit. We employ efficient algorithms from [18] and implement our own modulus functions to minimize area. These customized modulus functions are used in both the baseline and our approach.

7.1 Area Comparison

Table 1 shows comparison with the baseline, where the minimum number of banks is used. Both GMP and our ap-

Table 1: Timing and resource usage comparison with baseline using GMP [16], where the minimum number of memory banks is used — target clock period = 5ns; BRAM = # of BRAMs; Slice = # of slices; LUT = # of lookup-tables; FF = # of flip-flops; DSP = # of DSPs; CP = achieved clock period.

Benchmark	# Accesses	Method	# Banks	Mask Width	BRAM	Slice	LUT	FF	DSP	CP(ns)
BICUBIC	4	Baseline	4	-	4	74	217	163	0	3.89
		TraceBanking	4	2	4	74 (+0.0%)	212 (-2.3%)	184 (+13%)	0 (+0.0%)	3.66
DECONV	5	Baseline	5	-	5	185	531	383	10	3.52
		TraceBanking	5	12	5	182 (-1.6%)	541 (+1.9%)	383 (+0.0%)	10 (+0.0%)	3.37
DENOISE-UR	8	Baseline	8	-	8	180	616	391	0	4.15
		TraceBanking	8	4	8	188 (+4.4%)	623 (+1.1%)	427 (+9.2%)	0 (+0.0%)	3.62
MOTION_C	4	Baseline	4	-	4	76	186	153	0	3.58
		TraceBanking	4	2	4	68 (-11%)	193 (+3.8%)	190 (+24%)	0 (+0.0%)	3.65
MOTION_LV	6	Baseline	6	-	6	146	425	392	6	3.31
		TraceBanking	6	6	6	146 (+0.0%)	425 (+0.0%)	392 (+0.0%)	6 (+0.0%)	3.31
SOBEL	9	Baseline	9	-	9	405	1296	692	27	3.93
		TraceBanking	9	12	9	350 (-14%)	1059 (-18%)	719 (+3.9%)	27 (+0.0%)	3.96
STENCIL3D	7	Baseline	7	-	14	322	966	700	7	3.82
		TraceBanking	7	15	14	308 (-4.3%)	932 (-3.5%)	624 (-11%)	7 (+0.0%)	3.74
Average						-3.8%	-2.4%	+5.6%	+0.0%	

Table 2: Timing and resource usage comparison with baseline using GMP [16], where the number of memory banks is restricted to be a power-of-two — target clock period = 5ns; BRAM = # of BRAMs; Slice = # of slices; LUT = # of lookup-tables; FF = # of flip-flops; DSP = # of DSPs; CP = achieved clock period.

Benchmark	# Accesses	Method	# Banks	Mask Width	BRAM	Slice	LUT	FF	DSP	CP(ns)
DECONV	5	Baseline	8	-	8	129	418	278	0	3.63
		TraceBanking	8	4	8	125 (-3.1%)	411 (-1.7%)	302 (+8.6%)	0 (+0.0%)	3.11
MOTION_LV	6	Baseline	8	-	8	117	369	237	0	3.56
		TraceBanking	8	3	8	119 (+1.7%)	391 (+6.0%)	282 (+19%)	0 (+0.0%)	3.77
SOBEL	9	Baseline	16	-	16	328	1114	525	0	4.34
		TraceBanking	16	4	16	340 (+3.7%)	1129 (+1.3%)	472 (-10%)	0 (+0.0%)	3.89
STENCIL3D	7	Baseline	8	-	8	195	649	443	0	3.87
		TraceBanking	8	6	8	201 (+3.1%)	655 (+0.9%)	450 (+1.6%)	0 (+0.0%)	3.70
Average						+1.4%	+1.6%	+4.8%	+0.0%	

Table 3: Execution time of TraceBanking on Motion_LV with different array sizes.

Array Size	12×12	32×24	64×48	128×96	320×240	640×480
Runtime (s)	0.0096	2.19	4.88	6.94	12.87	33.38

proach can generate valid banking solutions with the minimum number of memory banks. Our approach is able to reduce the number of slices by 3.8% on average. One of the reasons is that our banking function does not always use all the bits in the address or array indices, which in turn reduces the complexity of the banking logic. For example, in Motion_C, we are able to save 11% of slices with a 2-bit mask. Another reason is that our approach is able to discover additional banking solutions that are not in the search space of the GMP method. For example, in Sobel, our design uses all the 12 index bits but still saves 14% of slices compared to the baseline; while the GMP solution has to perform mod 9 operations due to its block-cyclic nature, our solution alternates among three consecutive bank IDs in each row of the image, thus only requires mod 3 operations which is more area-efficient.

As pointed out by [16], an important design trade-off between logic complexity and storage overhead in memory partitioning is to enforce the number of memory banks to be a power-of-two instead of the minimum. Therefore, we conduct this experiment for the four benchmarks whose number of banks is not a power-of-two and compare our results with the baseline. Detailed experiment results are shown in Table 2. Comparing with the corresponding entries in Table 1, the designs in Table 2 generally have less area even though they use more memory banks and a more complex crossbar, because banking functions are significantly simplified when the number of banks is a power-of-two. For GMP designs, multiplication and division become simple shifting operations, while modulus operations are just selecting LSBs. For our designs, the resource saving comes from the reduction in mask width. Compared with baseline, our designs use a negligible 1.4% more slices. In general, the hardware generated by our trace-based memory banking approach is comparable with GMP in terms of area and timing.

7.2 Scalability

TraceBanking is able to generate competitive memory banking solutions from memory traces. However, using a complete memory trace may be expensive when the memory trace is large. Table 3 shows how the execution time of TraceBanking scales with an increasing array size. For applications with affine memory accesses, we can apply trace reduction to reduce the runtime. The general idea is to use

Table 4: Execution time of TraceBanking with reduced memory trace — Initial mask refers to the mask found by Section 5.1, while the Final mask refers to the mask found by Section 5.2.

Benchmark	Reduced Array Size	Mask Width Initial	Mask Width Final	Runtime (s)
BICUBIC	8×8	2	2	0.0093
DENOISE	10×10	4	8	3.45
DENOISE2	16×16	4	4	0.017
MOTION_C	8×8	2	2	0.0094
MOTION_LV	12×12	4	4	0.0096
SOBEL	18×18	6	10	5.94
STENCIL3D	$5 \times 14 \times 14$	6	11	4.37

a partial memory trace which covers an adequate number of steps. Because of memory access pattern redundancy in the trace, the generated banking scheme is likely to comply with banking schemes generated from a full trace. Since the banking scheme generated from a partial trace is not guaranteed to be valid, we use the SMT-based checker proposed in Section 6 to validate it. If the validation fails, we revert to using the complete memory trace.

We perform experiments with reduced memory traces for all the benchmarks listed in Table 1. For the size of the reduced trace, we use an empirical value of $2 \times \#Banks$ in each dimension of the array. For example, if the loop kernel conducts Sobel edge detection on an VGA image (640×480), rather than iterating through the whole image, we execute the loop kernel on an 18×18 sub-image and use this reduced trace as the input to TraceBanking. For all the benchmarks listed in Table 1, TraceBanking is able to generate solutions which are proven to be valid using the reduced traces as inputs. Moreover, these solutions are identical to the ones generated from complete traces. The execution time of the SMT-based checker is less than a second. As shown in Table 4, the execution time of TraceBanking is reduced significantly by using partial traces without sacrificing the quality of the solutions.

A critical observation from Table 4 is that, in most benchmarks, the final solution is either in the beginning or at the very end of the search space. TraceBanking exploits the aforementioned observation in pruning the search space by performing two simultaneous searches: forward search and backward search. Forward search starts from the mask with minimum number of bits upward to the mask with maximum number of bits, stopping with the first mask that yields no conflicts. On the other hand, backward search starts from the mask with the maximum number of bits downward to the mask with minimum number of bits, stopping when no bit can be removed without causing conflicts.

8. CASE STUDY: HAAR FACE DETECTION

In this section, we use Haar face detection [5] as a case study to show the efficacy of TraceBanking on applications with non-affine memory accesses. The Haar algorithm uses cascaded classifiers to detect human faces rapidly and robustly. Thousands of weak classifiers are integrated into a Haar system, and each of them has a distinct memory access pattern. A code snippet of the loop kernel in Haar algorithm is shown in Figure 11. The array `window` is a 25×25 im-

```
pixel window[25][25];
pixel coord[12];
int filter_no;

CLASSIFIER:
for (filter_no=0; filter_no<2913; filter_no++){
    #pragma HLS pipeline II=1
    // read array indexes from look-up tables
    int x0 = rectangles_array0[filter_no];
    int y0 = rectangles_array1[filter_no];
    int w0 = rectangles_array2[filter_no];
    ...
    // access 8 data elements from array
    coord[0] = window[y0][x0];
    coord[1] = window[y0][x0+w0];
    ...
    // if condition met, access 4 more elements
    if ( (w2!=0) && (h2!=0) ) {
        coord[8] = window[y2][x2];
        ...
    }
    else {
        coord[8] = 0;
        ...
    }
    // process data
    foo(coord);
}
```

Figure 11: Loop kernel of Haar face recognition.

age buffer and is steadily shifted in from the input image. Therefore, it is implemented with discrete registers. In each iteration, the loop kernel reads pixels into the array `coord` and process them in the function `foo()`. There are 2913 classifiers in total. The constant arrays `rectangles_array[]` store the constants needed to compute the array indices in each iteration. There is an `if` statement inside the loop kernel. When the condition is met, the loop kernel accesses 12 pixels from the `window` array in that iteration; otherwise, 8 pixels are accessed.

In order to maximize throughput, we need to fully pipeline the `CLASSIFIER` loop in Figure 11, where each classifier requires eight or 12 parallel accesses to the image buffer. Existing techniques cannot generate an efficient banking solution for this problem due to two reasons: (1) The 2913 classifiers have more than 2000 different memory access patterns in total, and (2) The array indices are non-affine without any linear relationship with the iteration variable `filter_no`. With TraceBanking, we are able to generate a conflict-free banking solution to partition the image buffer `window[25][25]` into 28 memory banks using the whole address as mask bits. The execution time is less than a second. Because the `window` array is a shifting window implemented using discrete registers, in this scenario, the memory banks are actually register banks.

Our baseline is a straightforward design that uses 12 instances of 625-to-1 multiplexer. We compare our design with the baseline and the result is shown in Table 5. The TraceBanking design in Table 5 refers to the memory banking design generated by our approach, and the Full Mux design refers to the baseline. For these two designs, we only extract the loop kernel part shown in Figure 11 to better compare the banking hardware overhead.

Table 5: Timing and resource usage comparison of the two designs — target clock period = 5ns; `BRAM` = # of BRAMs; `Slice` = # of slices; `LUT` = # of lookup-tables; `FF` = # of flip-flops; `DSP` = # of DSPs; `CP` = achieved clock period; `Latency` = latency of the loop kernel.

Implementation	BRAM	Slice	LUT	FF	DSP	CP(ns)	Latency
TraceBanking	34	4915	8266	12559	6	4.52	2923
Full Mux	22	21275	53553	23785	3	9.22	2919

Table 5 compares the Full Mux design with the TraceBanking design. Our TraceBanking design reduces Slice, LUT and Flip-Flop usage by 76.9%, 84.6% and 47.2%, respectively. Meanwhile, clock period is improved by 51.0%. BRAM usage increases because of the overhead in storing look-up tables for banking and offset functions. The reduction in logic resource usage results from the simplified muxing network in the TraceBanking design. In the TraceBanking design, two levels of multiplexers are used to connect the registers with the compute units, and each multiplexer has less than 30 inputs. In contrast, the Full Mux design uses 12 instances of 625-to-1 multiplexers, which consumes a lot more area. Even worse, the Full Mux design is extremely hard to route and unable to meet the 5ns timing target. Therefore, even though the Full Mux design has similar latency with the TraceBanking design, the total execution time of the loop kernel is much worse. Clearly, the banking scheme generated by TraceBanking helps improve both area and performance of the design, which contains very irregular memory accesses.

9. CONCLUSION AND FUTURE WORK

In this work, we propose TraceBanking, a memory banking approach using trace-based address mining. By analyzing the input memory trace of an application, we select the important address bits which can guide our banking decision, and apply a graph coloring algorithm to generate efficient banking solutions. We also propose an SMT-based checker to validate our solution. Experiments show that TraceBanking can generate comparable hardware with the state-of-the-art partitioning algorithm for applications with affine memory access patterns. In addition, a case study on Haar face detection demonstrates that TraceBanking can generate valid and efficient banking solutions for applications with non-affine memory accesses.

Our work opens a new path in automatically generating parallel hardware architecture using memory trace analysis, and we prove that this compute-intensive task can be accomplished within a reasonable amount of time. The execution time of our approach can be further reduced by launching parallel threads to exploit the heavy parallelism in the best-first search.

Furthermore, we believe our approach can be extended to generate other specialized parallel architectures, such as data reuse buffers commonly used for stencil-like applications. Additionally, trace analysis provides an opportunity for automatically generating a specialized on-chip caching system for applications with non-affine memory accesses, or even data-driven applications whose memory access pattern can not be statically determined.

Acknowledgements

This work was supported in part by Intel Corporation under the ISRA Program, NSF Awards #1337240 and #1453378, a DARPA Young Faculty Award, and a research gift from Xilinx, Inc. Khalid Al-Hawaj is supported by King Abdullah Scholarship Program (KASP) and King Fahd University of Petroleum and Minerals (KFUPM).

10. REFERENCES

[1] Bicubic Interpolation. http://www.mpi-hd.mpg.de/astrophysik/HEA/internal/Numerical_Recipes/f3-6.pdf.

[2] H. Al-Omari and K. E. Sabri. New Graph Coloring Algorithms. *American Journal of Mathematics and Statistics*, 2(4):739–741, 2006.

[3] C. Bastoul, A. Cohen, S. Girbal, S. Sharma, and O. Temam. Putting Polyhedral Loop Transformations to Work. In *Languages and Compilers for Parallel Computing*, pages 209–225. Springer, 2003.

[4] Y. Ben-Asher and N. Rotem. Automatic Memory Partitioning: Increasing Memory Parallelism via Data Structure Partitioning. *Proc. of the 8th Int. Conf. on Hardware/Software Codesign and System Synthesis (CODES+ISSS)*, pages 155–162, 2010.

[5] J. Cho, S. Mirzaei, J. Oberg, and R. Kastner. FPGA-Based Face Detection System using Haar Classifiers. *Int'l Symp. on Field-Programmable Gate Arrays (FPGA)*, 2009.

[6] A. Cilardo and L. Gallo. Improving Multibank Memory Access Parallelism with Lattice-Based Partitioning. *ACM Transactions on Architecture and Code Optimization (TACO)*, 11(4):45, 2015.

[7] J. Cong, W. Jiang, B. Liu, and Y. Zou. Automatic Memory Partitioning and Scheduling for Throughput and Power Optimization. *ACM Transactions on Design Automation of Electronic Systems (TODAES)*, 16(2):15, 2011.

[8] J. Cong, B. Liu, S. Neuendorffer, J. Noguera, K. Vissers, and Z. Zhang. High-level synthesis for fpgas: From prototyping to deployment. *IEEE Transactions on Computer-Aided Design of Integrated Circuits and Systems*, 30(4):473–491, 2011.

[9] L. De Moura and N. Björner. Z3: An Efficient SMT Solver. In *International conference on Tools and Algorithms for the Construction and Analysis of Systems*, pages 337–340. Springer, 2008.

[10] T. R. Jensen and B. Toft. *Graph Coloring Problems*, volume 39. John Wiley & Sons, 2011.

[11] P. Li, Y. Wang, P. Zhang, G. Luo, T. Wang, and J. Cong. Memory Partitioning and Scheduling Co-Optimization in Behavioral Synthesis. *Int'l Conf. on Computer-Aided Design (ICCAD)*, 2012.

[12] C. Meng, S. Yin, P. Ouyang, L. Liu, and S. Wei. Efficient Memory Partitioning for Parallel Data Access in Multidimensional Arrays. *Design Automation Conf. (DAC)*, 2015.

[13] B. Reagen, R. Adolf, Y. S. Shao, G.-Y. Wei, and D. Brooks. Machsuite: Benchmarks for Accelerator Design and Customized Architectures. In *Workload Characterization (IISWC), 2014 IEEE International Symposium on*, pages 110–119. IEEE, 2014.

[14] J. Su, F. Yang, X. Zeng, and D. Zhou. Efficient Memory Partitioning for Parallel Data Access via Data Reuse. *Int'l Symp. on Field-Programmable Gate Arrays (FPGA)*, pages 138–147, 2016.

[15] Y. Tatsumi and H. Mattausch. Fast Quadratic Increase of Multiport-Storage-Cell Area with Port Number. *Electronics Letters*, 35(25):2185–2187, 1999.

[16] Y. Wang, P. Li, and J. Cong. Theory and Algorithm for Generalized Memory Partitioning in High-Level Synthesis. *Int'l Symp. on Field-Programmable Gate Arrays (FPGA)*, 2014.

[17] Y. Wang, P. Li, P. Zhang, C. Zhang, and J. Cong. Memory Partitioning for Multidimensional Arrays in High-Level Synthesis. *Design Automation Conf. (DAC)*, 2013.

[18] H. S. Warren. *Hacker's Delight*. Pearson Education, 2013.

[19] Xilinx. Vivado Design Suite - HLx Editions, 2016.2. http://www.xilinx.com/products/design-tools/vivado.html.

[20] Z. Zhang, Y. Fan, W. Jiang, G. Han, C. Yang, and J. Cong. AutoPilot: A Platform-Based ESL Synthesis System. In *High-Level Synthesis: From Algorithm to Digital Circuit*, pages 99–112. Springer, 2008.

Dynamic Hazard Resolution for Pipelining Irregular Loops in High-Level Synthesis

Steve Dai[1], Ritchie Zhao[1], Gai Liu[1], Shreesha Srinath[1], Udit Gupta[*2],
Christopher Batten[1], Zhiru Zhang[1]

[1]School of Electrical and Computer Engineering, Cornell University, Ithaca, NY
[2]Computer Science, Harvard University, Cambridge, MA

{hd273, rz252, gl387, ss2783}@cornell.edu, ugupta@g.harvard.edu,
{cbatten, zhiruz}@cornell.edu

Abstract

Current pipelining approach in high-level synthesis (HLS) achieves high performance for applications with regular and statically analyzable memory access patterns. However, it cannot effectively handle infrequent data-dependent structural and data hazards because they are conservatively assumed to always occur in the synthesized pipeline. To enable high-throughput pipelining of irregular loops, we study the problem of augmenting HLS with application-specific dynamic hazard resolution, and examine its implications on scheduling and quality of results. We propose to generate an aggressive pipeline at compile-time while resolving hazards with memory port arbitration and squash-and-replay at run-time. Our experiments targeting a Xilinx FPGA demonstrate promising performance improvement across a suite of representative benchmarks.

1. Introduction

Over the past few years, high-level synthesis (HLS) has become an increasingly popular alternative to traditional register-transfer level (RTL) designs [4]. HLS automatically generates digital circuits from a behavioral specification, greatly improving productivity over the traditional tedious hardware design process. Pipelining is one of the most widely used optimizations in HLS because it allows successive loop iterations (or function invocations) to be overlapped during execution, effectively exploiting parallelism with fewer resources compared to outright hardware duplication.

Conventional HLS pipelining typically leverages modulo scheduling [12], a compile-time optimization which creates a static schedule for a single loop iteration that can be repeated at a fixed *initiation interval* (II). The modulo scheduling algorithm analyzes the program's control-data flow graph along with resource, data dependence, and other constraints to minimize the II while ensuring that the pipeline does not encounter hazards during execution. Specifically, the statically generated schedule must not allow multiple operations to access the same physical resource within a single cycle (*structural hazards*) and must ensure that dependences between memory loads and stores are not violated (*data hazards*). The need to avoid these two types of hazards on memory accesses often limit the throughput of the synthesized pipeline.

---

* Udit Gupta was affiliated with School of Electrical and Computer Engineering, Cornell University during the course of this work.

FPGA '17, February 22-24, 2017, Monterey, CA, USA
© 2017 ACM. ISBN 978-1-4503-4354-1/17/02...$15.00
DOI: http://dx.doi.org/10.1145/3020078.3021754

```
1  for (j=0...num_edges){
2    int s = e[j].src;          Cycle
3    int d = e[j].dst;            0    e[j].load    (line 2/3)
4                                 1    v[s].load    (line 5)
5    if (v[s]<0 && v[d]<0){       2    v[d].load    (line 5)
6      v[s] = d;                  3    v[s].store   (line 6)
7      v[d] = s;                  4    v[d].store   (line 7)
8  }}
```

(a) Source code.   (b) Schedule for one iteration.

Figure 1: **Maximal Matching example** — (a) Source code in C-like syntax. (b) Static schedule produced by conventional HLS pipelining with II=4. Only `load` and `store` operations are shown while others (e.g., comparisons) are omitted.

HLS pipelining makes extensive use of memory dependence and alias analysis to identify dependences and disambiguate memory accesses (for convenience, we use dependence and alias analysis interchangeably in subsequent discussions). Such techniques attempt to classify each pair of memory accesses as no-alias or must-alias if the analysis is conclusive, or may-alias if the analysis is inconclusive. Static alias analysis is able to return fairly accurate dependence information for programs with compile-time analyzable control flow and highly regular memory access patterns, allowing efficient pipeline schedules to be created. However, such static analysis techniques are ineffective against programs that contain conditional and/or data-dependent memory operations with memory addresses unknown at compile-time, making it difficult to prove the absence of aliases. As a result, the dependence information will be inexact and contains may-alias pairs that have to be treated as must-alias by the scheduler to ensure hazard-free execution under all circumstances.

While existing pipelining techniques are effective at generating high-throughput hardware for regular dataflow-centric applications with well-structured data access patterns, they cannot efficiently synthesize *irregular programs* (e.g. graph algorithms, data analytics, sparse matrix computations) because these programs exhibit data-dependent control flow, irregular memory dependence patterns, and dynamic workloads. In particular, irregular programs incur structural and/or data hazards caused by conditional and/or data-dependent memory operations whose occurrence pattern cannot be accurately predicted by static compiler analysis, even with advances in polyhedral model [10, 11]. To ensure functional correctness, the pipelining algorithm must conservatively assume that these hazards always occur, even if they rarely or never do in practice. Consequently, conservative static pipelining leads to pessimistic performance as the pipeline stalls needlessly to avoid hazards which may be *infrequent* during actual execution.

We illustrate this performance gap using Maximal Matching in Figure 1(a), a common graph algorithm that computes the set of independent edges without common vertices in a graph. The kernel examines the two endpoints of each edge of a graph and checks if

	Cycles																
	0	1	2	3	4	5	6	7	8	9	10	11	12	13	14	15	16
j=0	e.ld	v.ld	v.ld	v.st	v.st												
j=1					e.ld	v.ld	v.ld	~~v.st~~	~~v.st~~								
j=2									e.ld	v.ld	v.ld	~~v.st~~	~~v.st~~				
j=3													e.ld	v.ld	v.ld	~~v.st~~	~~v.st~~

(a) Execution following static schedule in (b) incurs 17 cycles. II=4 for all iterations.

	Cycles																
	0	1	2	3	4	5	6	7	8	9	10	11	12	13	14	15	16
j=0	e.ld	v.ld	v.ld	v.st	v.st												
j=1					e.ld	v.ld	v.ld	~~v.st~~	~~v.st~~								
j=2							e.ld	v.ld	v.ld	~~v.st~~	~~v.st~~						
j=3									e.ld	v.ld	v.ld	~~v.st~~	~~v.st~~				

(b) Ideal execution incurs only 13 cycles. II=2 after Cycle 4.

Figure 2: **Execution of Maximal Matching** — Assume a single-ported memory for each array. ~~v.st~~ indicates a `store` to array v that is not executed due to false conditional branch. (a) Execution following the static schedule in Figure 1(b). (b) Ideal latency-optimal execution.

they are marked. If not, the algorithm updates the vertices at the endpoints using two conditional stores. Note that there are conditional loop-carried dependences between the `load` operations on `line 5` and the `store` operations on `line 6/7`. However, these stores are executed infrequently for a dense graph because only a small subset of its edges are independent. Figure 1(b) shows the static schedule for one iteration of the loop. For this schedule, each array is mapped to a single-ported memory so only one memory access per array is allowed in each cycle. To avoid potential structural and data hazards, conventional techniques will pipeline this design to an II of 4 cycles, which results in a 17-cycle execution latency, as shown in Figure 2(a), for the first four iterations processing a fully-connected graph. Six cycles are unused because the condition on `line 5` in Figure 1(a) is evaluated false for all iterations except j=0, thus no stores need to be performed for those iterations.

To take advantage of the infrequent nature of conditional memory accesses and inter-iteration memory dependences in this case, a better solution would be to launch new iterations more frequently to increase the efficiency of the pipeline by saturating the available memory bandwidth. As shown in the ideal execution in Figure 2(b), aggressively launching a new iteration every two cycles from Cycle 4 onward reduces the execution latency to 13 cycles. However, aggressive pipelining causes structural hazards, when the `stores` from the current iteration collide with `loads` from the next iteration, as well as data hazards, when the loop-carried dependence is violated. For example, if the stores to array v in iteration j=1 were executed, they would collide with the loads from array v in iteration j=2. Moreover, a dependent load in iteration j=2 may read from an address in array v before a store in iteration j=1 writes to the same address, violating the inter-iteration read-after-write dependence between these memory accesses.

We propose to address the performance gap between conservative and aggressive pipelining by *speculatively* executing each iteration, launching each iteration before hazard-free execution can be guaranteed, and rely on a hardware dynamic hazard resolution mechanism to resolve any hazard that actually occurs. To achieve high throughput using this approach, two problems must be addressed: first, aggressive pipelining must be performed without pessimistically assuming that conditional or data-dependent hazards always occur; second, hazards that actually occur must be detected and resolved appropriately at runtime .

In this paper we propose a set of synergistic techniques which enable dynamic hazard resolution in pipeline synthesis. We address the scheduling problem by *virtualizing* the memory interface to make memory accesses appear independent. Virtualization hides structural hazards and dependences between memory operations, allowing any conventional HLS tools to perform aggressive scheduling without the need for programmer intervention. We next introduce hazard resolution logic which resolves structural hazards via port arbitration and data hazards via pipeline squashing. The hazard resolution hardware is automatically generated based on the number of virtual memory ports, the type (read or write) of each port, and the possible data dependences between memory accesses.

While our techniques are generally applicable to structural and data hazards for any expensive or limited hardware resources, this paper emphasizes memory-related hazards, because memory ports constitute a scarce resource and memory dependences are a common limiting factor of pipeline throughput in irregular programs. In particular, we focus on irregular loops with conditional memory accesses and inter-iteration memory dependences whose access patterns cannot be asserted at compile time. Our approach works for truly dynamic data dependences for which speculation, hazard detection, and replay are necessary for high-throughput pipelined execution. Our techniques provide the most performance benefit when the conditional accesses and data dependences are infrequent. Our approach is especially relevant as FPGA devices continue to attain higher memory bandwidths [6]. Specifically, our major technical contributions are threefold:

1. We identify a considerable performance gap in the HLS of irregular programs due to conservative nature of static pipelining in face of infrequent data-dependent dynamic hazards.

2. To our best knowledge, we are the first to propose and study structural hazard resolution and speculative execution as dynamic pipelining techniques to bridge this performance gap.

3. We compose our generated RTL with pipelines synthesized by a commercial HLS tool to achieve significant performance improvement on a suite of irregular benchmarks.

The remainder of the paper is organized as follows: Section 2 illustrates our dynamic hazard resolution techniques; Section 3 examines implementation details and discusses experimental results; Section 4 discusses related work; Section 5 concludes with the overall insight of this work.

2. Dynamic Hazard Resolution for HLS

We propose three synergistic techniques to augment the HLS-synthesized pipeline with dynamic hazard resolution to address the performance gap caused by static alias analysis and scheduling. Figure 3 illustrates the overall architectural template for the augmented pipeline with Maximal Matching from Figure 1(a), composed of an accelerator synthesized with a virtualized memory interface connected to a hazard resolution unit (HRU) customized for the Maximal Matching application. The HRU can be further divided into a data hazard resolution unit (D-HRU) and a structural hazard resolution unit (S-HRU). The HRU dynamically resolves structural and data hazards that occur in the Maximal Matching pipeline and communicates with memory. Our approach does not require any modification to current pipelining algorithms. HRU logic is automatically generated based on the schedule of the synthesized pipeline and a set of may-alias memory access pairs obtained from static analysis and/or user-specified directives. Our techniques also benefit from more accurate alias analysis to decrease the number of may-alias pairs and reduce the complexity of the customized HRU. We will use Maximal Matching to illustrate the customizable architecture.

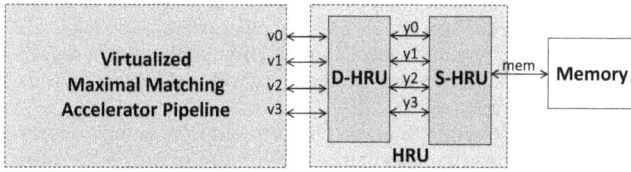

Figure 3: **Architectural template for the composed Maximal Matching accelerator** — HLS synthesized Maximal Matching pipeline with customized hazard resolution unit (HRU) consisting of a data hazard resolution unit (D-HRU) and a structural hazard resolution unit (S-HRU). A version with four virtual ports is shown.

```
1  for (j=0...num_edges){
2    int s = e[j].src;
3    int d = e[j].dst;
4
5    if (v0[s]<0 && v1[d]<0){
6      v2[s] = d;
7      v3[d] = s;
8  }}
```

Figure 4: **Maximal Matching example** — Virtualized source code in C-like syntax. Compared to Figure 1(a), accesses to array v have been replaced by accesses to v0, v1, v2, and v3, respectively.

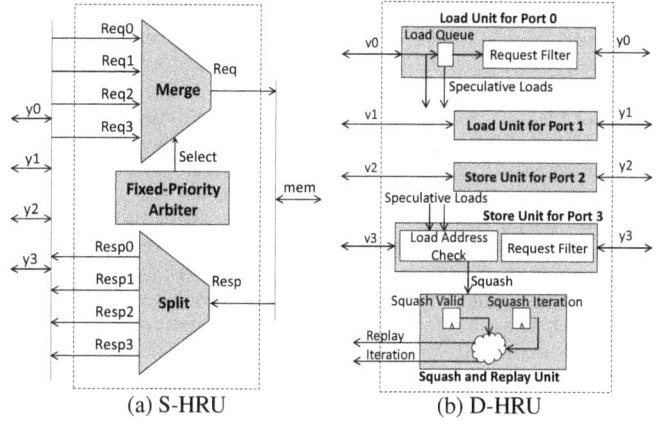

(a) S-HRU   (b) D-HRU

Figure 6: **Hazard resolution units (HRUs) for Maximal Matching** — (a) Structural hazard resolution unit (S-HRU). (b) Data hazard resolution unit employing speculative squash-and-replay (D-HRU).

2.1 Memory Interface Virtualization

Although we have identified a significant opportunity in improving the performance of synthesized pipelines by deferring the handling of infrequent hazards to runtime, we cannot take advantage of this opportunity unless we can easily reduce the pipeline II below what is deemed safe by the HLS tool. While it is possible to modify existing pipelining algorithms for this purpose, doing so would not be generally applicable to any HLS flows. It will also limit our ability to evaluate our techniques leveraging existing HLS tools.

We propose to relax infrequent resource and memory dependence constraints by *virtualizing* the memory interface to enable aggressive pipelining. Virtualization is a source-to-source transformation that alters each conditional or may-alias memory operations to access its own independent array. This technique decouples physical memory ports from the scheduling process to remove memory port constraints and inter-iteration memory dependences. In the perspective of the scheduler, the transformed memory operations do not share a common resource and thus do not alias. Hiding these infrequent hazards from the pipeline scheduler enables aggressive II reduction. Although the virtualized design contains more memory ports than the non-virtualized design, these ports interface with the HRU and will be arbitrated for actual physical memory ports, as shown in Figure 3.

To relax the constraints in Maximal Matching, we can virtualize its memory port interface by modifying the source code as shown in Figure 4 where the accesses to the same array v are transformed into accesses to four different arrays v0, v1, v2 and v3. With this transformation, the HLS tool no longer sees the dependence between those memory operations and no longer encounters memory port conflict because each memory operation accesses a different array. Assuming two physical memory ports and the same schedule as that in Figure 1(b), Figure 5 shows the execution trace of the first few iterations for virtualized Maximal Matching pipelined to II=2. There

exist two instances of potential dynamic data hazards between v.st in iteration j=0 and v.ld in j=1.

2.2 Structural Hazard Resolution

We first discuss the implications of aggressive scheduling on resources. Having bypassed unnecessarily conservative resource constraints during scheduling, it is necessary to complement the synthesized virtualized pipeline with an S-HRU to resolve structural hazards caused by infrequent conditional memory accesses that actually occur during runtime. While our proposed scheduling scheme with virtualization relaxes the constraints on memory ports, the number of physical memory ports is limited in reality. An S-HRU is required to appropriately arbitrate memory accesses that present at the virtual memory ports into a limited number of available physical memory ports. If there is only one physical memory port available for Maximal Matching, v.st from iteration j=0 cannot execute in parallel with v.ld from iteration j=1 as shown in Figure 7. In this case, the S-HRU prioritizes v.st in Cycle 3 and stalls v.ld until Cycle 4. Subsequent operations are similarly arbitrated and stalled. As shown in Figure 6(a), the S-HRU implements a fixed-priority arbitration policy that always services request(s) from the earliest iteration(s). This policy preserves consistency for some speculatively executed memory accesses to reduce the need for squash-and-replay. The policy is also important for preventing deadlock and allowing the pipeline to flush in case of stall.

While dynamic hazard resolution is able to arbitrate competing memory requests, it also allows an aggressively pipelined design to capture unused memory bandwidth when a conditional memory access is not executed due to a false conditional branch. As shown in Figure 7, dynamic memory port arbitration allows v.ld operations in iteration j=2 to capture the unused memory bandwidth from v.st operations that are not executed in iteration j=1 due to a false

	Cycles									
	2	3	4	5	6	7	8	9	10	11
j=0	v.ld	v.st		v.st						
j=1	e.ld		v.ld		v.ld	v̶.̶s̶t̶	v̶.̶s̶t̶			
j=2					e.ld	v.ld	v.ld	v̶.̶s̶t̶	v̶.̶s̶t̶	
j=3							e.ld	v.ld	v.ld	...

Figure 7: **Structural hazard resolution** — With a single-ported memory, memory access from an earlier iteration is prioritized while others are stalled. v.st from j=0 is prioritized over v.ld from j=1 even though they are in the same cycle on the HLS-generated schedule. v.ld operations from j=2 capture the unused bandwidth of v.st operations from j=1 that are not executed.

	Cycles									
	0	1	2	3	4	5	6	7	8	9
j=0	e.ld	v.ld	v.ld	v.st	v.st					
j=1			e.ld	v.ld	v.ld	v̶.̶s̶t̶	v̶.̶s̶t̶			
j=2					e.ld	v.ld	v.ld	v̶.̶s̶t̶	v̶.̶s̶t̶	
j=3							e.ld	v.ld	v.ld	...

Figure 5: **Execution of virtualized Maximal Matching** — With two physical memory ports and design pipelined to II=2. Note that there exist two instances of potential dynamic data hazard between v.st in j=0 and v.ld in j=1.

conditional branch. If the conditional accesses in Maximal Matching are infrequently executed, we can observe that the effective II will be very close to the target II of the aggressive pipeline.

The application-specific S-HRU architecture automatically generated for Maximal Matching is shown in Figure 6(a) targeting one physical memory port. Because there are four independent array accesses in the virtualized design in Figure 4, the customized S-HRU is composed of a merge unit with four input buses (Req0, Req1, Req2, and Req3) that arbitrates four incoming memory requests from the virtual request ports of the accelerator to the single physical memory request port (Req). Similarly, the S-HRU also includes a split unit that routes any memory response from the single physical memory response port (Resp) back to the appropriate virtual response port (Resp0, Resp1, Resp2, or Resp3) of the accelerator. A fixed-priority arbiter determines the priority of requests in the same cycle by always servicing request from the earliest iteration.

The proposed approach is able to elastically adapt to memory bandwidth that varies over time. This is especially applicable to emerging accelerator-rich architectures where many accelerators share the same memory ports [3]. For these architectures, statically assigning memory ports is either inefficient or impractical. In Section 3, we show that our hazard resolution techniques can effectively adapt to varying memory bandwidth.

2.3 Data Hazard Resolution

In addition to resource constraints, our aggressive scheduling scheme also relaxes inter-iteration dependence constraints by optimistically assuming that may-alias memory accesses would never alias. To ensure correct pipeline execution for the occasions when memory accesses do alias, however infrequent, we further complement the synthesized virtualized pipeline with a D-HRU to resolve runtime aliases not considered during static scheduling. In Figure 5, since the conditional accesses are actually executed in iteration j=0, v.ld in iteration j=1 is executed at Cycle 3 before v.st in j=0 is executed in Cycle 4. If the addresses of these may-alias memory accesses actually alias during runtime, the execution shown in Figure 5 would violate inter-iteration read-after-write dependence.

We propose to speculatively execute may-alias memory operations and perform squash and replay if the alias actually occurs during runtime. For Maximal Matching, we can speculatively execute the load operations from array v and squash and replay them only when memory aliasing is detected during the execution of a may-alias store. As shown in Figure 8, v.ld operations in iteration j=1 execute speculatively but are later squashed when v.st in j=0 executes in Cycle 4 and detects alias with the speculative v.ld from j=1 executed in Cycle 3. Due to the squash, iteration j=1 replays starting from Cycle 5, the cycle immediately after the alias is detected. On the other hand, v.ld operations executed speculatively in j=2 do not get squashed because v.st operations in iteration j=1 are not executed and cause no alias.

We propose a customized data hazard resolution unit with squash-and-replay capability (D-HRU) to enable a fully speculative pipeline. To prevent speculatively executed memory accesses from corrupting states, D-HRU is automatically generated to selectively include load queues and/or store queues to buffer speculatively executed requests until they are committed to memory. In addition, D-HRU selectively instantiates store-to-load forwarding unit to forward not yet committed store data. While the loads and stores reside in the queue, they are checked by other committing loads and stores to detect any mis-speculation. D-HRU implements a squash-and-replay mechanism that is able to cancel and replay any mis-speculated iterations.

While the idea of speculation is borrowed from complex superscalar processors, the customized architecture of an HLS synthesized pipeline provides a unique opportunity to greatly simplify the complexity of the speculation logic. As such, our hardware generation algorithm is designed to instantiate the minimum subset and minimum number of the aforementioned hardware modules to support the alias pattern of a particular application for a specific schedule. In Figure 6(b), the customized D-HRU instantiates a Load Unit for port 0 to buffer incoming load requests for array v0 (v[s].load), because these requests may alias with store requests on port 3 from array v3 (v[d].store). The size of the queue is determined by the difference between the worst-case schedule distance from the load to any potentially aliased stores (3 cycles in this case) and the II of the pipeline. Thus we need only one entry in the load queue to buffer incoming requests at port 0 for II=2.

In Figure 6(b), the Store Unit for port 3 instantiates a Load Address Check unit that reads the speculative load addresses from the Load Queue for port 0 and check whether the current store request in port 3 (v[d].store) aliases with any speculative load requests from port 0 (v[s].load). If so, it sends a squash signal to the Squash and Replay Unit which squashes and replays the appropriate iterations. Request Filter is instantiated as part of the Load Unit or Store Unit to drop squashed requests. No store buffers need to be instantiated because the store operations are not speculatively executed. Load Unit for port 1 and Store Unit for port 2 implement load buffer and load check similar to those of port 0 and 3, respectively.

3. Experiments

While we implement a source-to-source transformation to virtualize the memory interface of the design, we develop a highly-parameterized hardware generation algorithm to automatically generate the minimum amount of HRU logic necessary for the particular application and compose the HRU logic with the synthesized pipeline to achieve high performance. The hardware generation algorithm leverages profiling and dependence analysis passes to extract infrequent may-alias memory access pairs, along with metadata extracted from the schedule of the synthesized design to intelligently instantiate and connect HRU modules based on the architectural templates described in Section 2.

During hardware generation, the algorithm first extracts the necessary meta-data from the results of pipeline synthesis, including the II of the schedule, schedule distance between infrequent may-alias memory accesses, and the number of synthesized virtual memory ports. Then the algorithm generates the S-HRU based on the number of virtual and physical ports. Afterward, the algorithm instantiates a D-HRU if there exists dependence that must be resolved dynamically. The algorithm automatically customizes the composition of the D-HRU based on the number of virtual ports, a list of dependences, and the specification of each dependence. More specifically, a D-HRU is selectively composed of custom-size load/store queue, data forward unit, squash unit, replay unit, and filter units for resolving speculatively executed load and store operations.

We implement the hardware generation algorithm within a Python-based hardware modeling framework, which supports concurrent structural hardware modeling and provides a collection of tools for simulating and translating Python RTL models to Verilog [9]. To compose the synthesized pipeline with customized HRU, we instantiate a top-level model that integrates each HLS-generated accelerator design with appropriately-parameterized HRU models. Valid-ready interfaces are implemented to communicate between hardware units and stall the circuit when necessary.

| | Cycles | | | | | | | | | |
	3	4	5	6	7	8	9	10	11	12
j=0	v.st	v.st								
j=1	v̶.̶l̶d̶	v̶.̶l̶d̶	e.ld	v.ld	v.ld	v̶.̶s̶t̶	v̶.̶s̶t̶			
j=2		e.ld			e.ld	v.ld	v.ld	v̶.̶s̶t̶	v̶.̶s̶t̶	
j=3							e.ld	v.ld	v.ld	...

Figure 8: **Speculative squash-and-replay** — The execution of v.st in Cycle 4 detects alias with v.ld executed in Cycle 3. Executed v.ld operations in Cycle 3 and 4 from j=1 are squashed (indicated by v̶.̶l̶d̶). Iterations j=1 and onward are then replayed.

Table 1: QoR comparison between baseline (`base`), alternative with structural hazard resolution only (`s-hru`), and alternative with structural and data hazard resolution (`all`) using a single-ported memory. Target clock period is 5ns. Designs include Sorting (SORT), Connected Components Labeling (CC), Histogram (HIST), Maximal Matching (MM), Matrix Power (MATPOW), and N-Queens Algorithm (NQ).

Design	Latency (cycles)			Clock Period (ns)			#LUTs			#FFs			#DSPs		
	base	s-hru	all	base	s-hru	all	base	s-hru	all	base	s-hru	all	base	s-hru	all
SORT	3917	3153	3084	4.2	4.1	4.2	624	651	879	717	806	992	4	4	4
CC	2114	1513	1131	4.9	4.6	4.6	899	1047	1224	874	1308	1472	0	0	0
HIST	78014	78014	39382	3.9	4.1	4.2	508	592	652	529	602	753	2	2	2
MM	1973	1440	1150	3.9	4.3	4.6	487	586	960	479	516	852	0	0	0
MATPOW	16018	10529	6131	4.4	4.4	4.4	826	1789	1850	1228	2232	2413	13	12	12
NQ	2280	1344	1344	4.3	4.4	4.6	512	563	609	406	445	555	1	1	1

This composition can be simulated and synthesized with conventional tools. Both the C-level programs and composed RTL models are synthesized with Vivado 2015.1 targeting Xilinx Virtex-7 FPGA. Quality of results (QoR) is obtained post place-and-route, and performance is obtained from cycle-accurate RTL simulation.

3.1 Benchmarks

To understand the implications of our proposed approach, we experiment with designs that exhibit data-dependent structural and data hazards from a range of application domains. Our experiments emphasize irregularity typically not found in regular applications where current HLS tools excel. We discuss two applications in detail.

```
1  for (i=0; i<N; ++i){
2    int m = feature[i];
3    float wt = weight[i];
4    if (m>THRESHOLD){
5      float x = hist[m];
6      hist[m] = x + wt;
7  }}
```

```
1  for (k=1; k<=m; k++){
2    for (p=0; p<nz; p++){
3      x[k][row[p]] +=
4        a[p]*x[k-1][col[p]];
5    }
6  }
```

(a) `CountIf Histogram`   (b) `Matrix Power`

Figure 9: **Irregular loop kernels with conditional hazards** — (a) `CountIf Histogram` constructs a weighted histogram of an array of features above a specified threshold. Array `hist` incurs conditional hazards. (b) `Matrix Power` computes the set of vectors $A^i \vec{x}$ for $i = [0, m]$. Array `x` incurs conditional hazards.

In Figure 9(a), each iteration of the `CountIf Histogram` kernel increases the bin indexed by the current feature value by adding the current weight if the feature value is above a specified threshold. There is an inter-iteration read-after-write dependence between the `load` on `line 5` and the `store` on `line 6`, which may cause data hazards if a subsequent iteration reads from the same histogram bin before the current iteration writes to it. While such memory aliasing is usually rare during histogram computation, it is impossible to assert the absence of such alias without prior knowledge of the sequence of feature values. Thus the HLS tool must create a conservative schedule such that a subsequent iteration reads from the histogram after the current iteration finishes writing to the histogram. Moreover, static scheduling unconditionally allocates a memory port for each memory access in a cycle even if the access is conditional. This results in inefficient utilization of memory bandwidth when the conditional accesses are predicated false at runtime.

In Figure 9(b), the `Matrix Power` kernel computes the set of vectors $A^i \vec{x}$ for $i = [1, m]$. With A stored as a coordinate list of (`row`, `column`, `value`) tuples, this kernel performs m sparse matrix-vector multiplications. The indirect memory accesses `x[k][row[p]]` and `x[k-1][col[p]]` on `line 3` and `line 4` present a potential inter-iteration read-after-write dependence because the result of $A^i \vec{x}$ depends on that of $A^{i-1} \vec{x}$. To ensure functional correctness without complete knowledge of the run-time values of `row[p]` and `col[p]`, the HLS tool must conserva-

tively execute `load` from `x[k-1][col[p]]` only after `store` to `x[k][row[p]]` from a previous iteration has been completed.

3.2 Results

In Table 1, we first compare the achieved latency, clock period, and resource usage between the baseline designs, alternative designs with S-HRU only, and alternative designs with both D-HRU and S-HRU. The baseline designs consist of the highest-throughput pipelines generated by Vivado HLS, while our alternative designs are virtualized versions of the baseline designs synthesized with the same commercial tool but augmented with dynamic hazard resolution. With a single-ported memory, Table 1 shows that our alternative designs are able to achieve a significant latency reduction compared to the baseline designs with reasonable timing and area overhead. Note that the Histogram design excludes the condition in Figure 9(a) to present a case in which S-HRU provides no benefit.

The amount of speedup is dependent on the input data pattern, number of executed conditional memory accesses, and the available physical memory bandwidth. Table 1 breaks down how latency improves with only structural hazard resolution and both structural and data hazard resolution. For Histogram, including only S-HRU provides no performance benefit because the pipeline throughput is limited by a long inter-iteration dependence cycle. In this case, it is necessary to incur the overhead of the D-HRU. On the other hand, N-Queens reaps no benefit from speculation because structural hazard resolution has indirectly helped resolve any dynamic data dependence due to the limited number of memory ports. In this case, it is sufficient to include only the S-HRU.

By studying different design points, Table 1 demonstrates the inherent trade-off between performance gain and area. Our proposed techniques are important because loops that exhibit data-dependent hazards are often dominated by memory accesses. This is the reason that only a limited amount of compute resources are necessary. In addition, these loops usually contain only a couple of may-alias pairs, and thus require relatively lightweight hazard resolution logic that keeps timing and area well-contained.

We further study the effect of increasing memory bandwidth on performance and area by varying the number of physical memory ports. Figure 10 shows the speedup of each design for one to four memory ports normalized to the latency of the single-port case. For Sorting, Connected Components, Histogram, and N-Queens, performance saturates beyond two memory ports because these designs contain at most two unconditional memory accesses in each cycle most of the time. These two unconditional accesses need to be arbitrated only when there are less than two physical ports. Having more than two physical ports does not help because there aren't enough pipelined parallel accesses in these designs to utilize any ports beyond the two required. On the other hand, Maximal Matching and Matrix Power continue to reap the benefit of increasing memory bandwidth beyond two ports because both designs contain many memory accesses that can execute in parallel. Having a large number of memory accesses at each cycle allows the design to take full advantage of the available bandwidth.

Table 2 compares the achieved clock period and resource usage for different numbers of memory ports for Maximal Matching. Al-

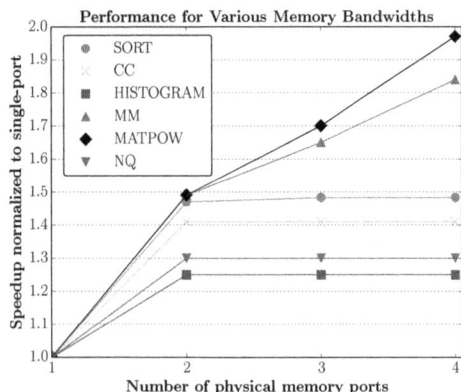

Figure 10: **Performance comparison for different memory bandwidths** — Speedup is normalized to the latency of single-ported memory case. The speedup saturates beyond two memory ports for designs with less pipelined parallelism or fewer memory accesses.

ternative designs with two to four ports incur `1.22x` to `1.70x` LUT counts and `1.02x` to `1.19x` FF counts with comparable timing. These overheads originate from the S-HRU shown in Figure 6(a) and apply equally to any benchmark. With an increasing number of physical memory ports, more complicated arbitration logic is needed to assign pending requests from the virtual ports to the available physical ports, which explains the increasing resource usage. According to Figure 10, Maximal Matching using four physical ports achieves over `1.8x` speedup compared to the single-ported case, which justifies the `1.70x` LUT and `1.19x` FF overhead.

Table 2: Timing and area overhead for increasing number of memory ports for Maximal Matching. No DSPs are used.

#Ports	Clock Period (ns)	#LUTs	#FFs
1	4.6	960	852
2	4.5	1171 (1.22x)	872 (1.02x)
3	4.5	1322 (1.38x)	941 (1.10x)
4	4.5	1629 (1.70x)	1010(1.19x)

4. Related Work

Many academic and commercial HLS tools, such as Vivado HLS [4] and LegUp [2], leverage static pipelining techniques to synthesize high-performance designs. Recent work in flushing-enabled pipelining [5] and multithreaded pipelining [13] extends these techniques to support dynamic memory behaviors. ElasticFlow enables the pipelining of irregular loop nests [14]. Zhao et al. synthesize irregular program by decoupling data structures from algorithms [15].

Alle et al. propose a runtime memory disambiguation technique where the address of a store is sent out before the store itself, allowing hardware to check whether an infrequently aliasing operation is expected to cause a hazard [1]. This information is leveraged to enable more aggressive pipeline II. We differentiate from this approach by considering structural in addition to data hazards for additional performance gain. We also study speculative execution to overcome the limitations pointed out by Alle et al.

Liu et al. extend polyhedral analysis to synthesizes pipelines that switches between aggressive (fast) execution, when hazards can be safely ignored, and conservative (slow) execution, when hazards are expected [7, 8]. Unlike this class of non-speculative stalling approach, our proposed approach does not require exact compile-time analysis to achieve high throughput. Our techniques tackle dynamic hazard resolution more broadly by emphasizing sophisticated runtime mechanisms complemented by relatively simple compile-time analysis. Nevertheless, our approach can benefit from the compile-time analysis proposed in this work.

5. Conclusions

Existing HLS tools rely on static pipelining techniques that extract parallelism only at compile-time, and are therefore not competitive for irregular programs with dynamic parallelism. As a result, we aim to create adaptive pipelining techniques that dynamically extract parallelism at run-time and efficiently handles statically unanalyzable program patterns. We address the problem of augmenting the HLS pipeline with application-specific dynamic hazard resolution to effectively resolve infrequent data-dependent structural and data hazards without sacrificing throughput. Our proposed approach achieve substantial performance improvement for a range of applications. For future work, it would be interesting to explore the trade-off between maximum effective pipeline throughput and complexity of the hazard resolution logic. It would also be useful to develop scheduling techniques to reduce the overhead of hazard resolution.

Acknowledgments

This work was supported in part by NSF Awards #1149464, #1337240, #1453378, #1512937, and DARPA YFA D15AP00096.

References

[1] M. Alle, A. Morvan, and S. Derrien. Runtime Dependency Analysis for Loop Pipelining in High-Level Synthesis. *Design Automation Conf. (DAC)*, Jun 2013.

[2] A. Canis, J. Choi, M. Aldham, V. Zhang, A. Kammoona, J. H. Anderson, S. Brown, and T. Czajkowski. LegUp: High-Level Synthesis for FPGA-Based Processor/Accelerator Systems. *Int'l Symp. on Field-Programmable Gate Arrays (FPGA)*, Feb 2011.

[3] J. Cong, M. A. Ghodrat, M. Gill, B. Grigorian, K. Gururaj, and G. Reinman. Accelerator-Rich Architectures: Opportunities and Progresses. *Design Automation Conf. (DAC)*, Jun 2014.

[4] J. Cong, B. Liu, S. Neuendorffer, J. Noguera, K. Vissers, and Z. Zhang. High-Level Synthesis for FPGAs: From Prototyping to Deployment. *IEEE Trans. on Computer-Aided Design of Integrated Circuits and Systems (TCAD)*, 30(4):473–491, Apr 2011.

[5] S. Dai, M. Tan, K. Hao, and Z. Zhang. Flushing-Enabled Loop Pipelining for High-Level Synthesis. *Design Automation Conf. (DAC)*, Jun 2014.

[6] M. Deo, J. Schulz, and L. Brown. Intel Stratix 10 MX Devices Solve the Memory Bandwidth Challenge. *Intel White Paper*, 2016.

[7] J. Liu, S. Bayliss, and G. Constantinides. Offline Synthesis of Online Dependence Testing: Parametric Loop Pipelining for HLS. *IEEE Symp. on Field Programmable Custom Computing Machines (FCCM)*, May 2013.

[8] J. Liu, J. Wickerson, and G. Constantinides. Loop Splitting for Efficient Pipelining in High-Level Synthesis. *IEEE Symp. on Field Programmable Custom Computing Machines (FCCM)*, May 2016.

[9] D. Lockhart, G. Zibrat, and C. Batten. PyMTL: A Unified Framework for Vertically Integrated Computer Architecture Research. *Int'l Symp. on Microarchitecture (MICRO)*, Dec 2014.

[10] A. Morvan, S. Derrien, and P. Quinton. Polyhedral Bubble Insertion: a Method to Improve Nested Loop Pipelining for High-Level Synthesis. *IEEE Trans. on Computer-Aided Design of Integrated Circuits and Systems (TCAD)*, 32(3):339–352, 2013.

[11] L.-N. Pouchet, P. Zhang, P. Sadayappan, and J. Cong. Polyhedral-Based Data Reuse Optimization for Configurable Computing. *Int'l Symp. on Field-Programmable Gate Arrays (FPGA)*, Feb 2013.

[12] B. R. Rau. Iterative Modulo Scheduling: an Algorithm for Software Pipelining Loops. *Int'l Symp. on Microarchitecture (MICRO)*, Nov 1994.

[13] M. Tan, B. Liu, S. Dai, and Z. Zhang. Multithreaded Pipeline Synthesis for Data-Parallel Kernels. *Int'l Conf. on Computer-Aided Design (ICCAD)*, pages 718–725, Nov 2014.

[14] M. Tan, G. Liu, R. Zhao, S. Dai, and Z. Zhang. ElasticFlow: A Complexity-Effective Approach for Pipelining Irregular Loop Nests. *Int'l Conf. on Computer-Aided Design (ICCAD)*, Nov 2015.

[15] R. Zhao, G. Liu, S. Srinath, C. Batten, and Z. Zhang. Improving High-Level Synthesis with Decoupled Data Structure Optimization. *Design Automation Conf. (DAC)*, Jun 2016.

Accelerating Face Detection on Programmable SoC Using C-Based Synthesis

Nitish Srivastava   Steve Dai   Rajit Manohar   Zhiru Zhang

School of Electrical and Computer Engineering, Cornell University, Ithaca, NY

{nks45, hd273, rm92, zhiruz}@cornell.edu

Abstract

High-level synthesis (HLS) enables designing at a higher level of abstraction to effectively cope with design complexity of emerging applications on modern programmable system-on-chip (SoC). While HLS continues to evolve with a growing set of algorithms, methodologies, and tools to efficiently map software designs onto optimized hardware architectures, there continues to lack realistic benchmark applications with sufficient complexity and enforceable constraints. In this paper we present a case study of accelerating face detection based on the Viola Jones algorithm on a programmable SoC using a C-based HLS flow. We also share our insights in porting a software-based design into a synthesizable implementation with HLS-specific data structures and optimizations. Our design is able to achieve a frame rate of 30 frames per second which is suitable for realtime applications. Our performance and quality of results are comparable to those of many traditional RTL implementations.

1. Introduction

As the complexity of applications and hardware platforms continues to escalate, high-level synthesis (HLS) emerges as a popular alternative to traditional register-transfer-level (RTL) methods for improving design productivity that is crucial in today's rapidly-evolving technology landscape. By automatically generating digital circuits from behavioral specifications, it is able to significantly reduce design effort while efficiently exploring a large multidimensional design space. Designers can leverage HLS to quickly convert software designs into customized hardware and obtain quality of results competitive to time-consuming manual RTL implementations.

While a growing interest in C-based design has led to the release of a range of commercial and academic HLS tools along with an ever-improving set of design techniques, there continues to be a lack of sufficiently complex software applications with realistic design constraints that can be used to benchmark these tools. Applications in current HLS benchmark suites often only contain small application kernels, which are too simple to effectively reflect the influence of specific optimizations and detail the strengths and limitations of different tools in achieving the desired design constraints. Furthermore, current benchmark applications rarely require hardware-software partitioning to leverage a co-design methodology that takes advantage of the capability of modern tightly-integrated programmable system-on-chips (SoCs).

To address the challenges of providing realistic benchmarks for HLS tools, we identify face detection based on the Viola Jones

FPGA '17, February 22-24, 2017, Monterey, CA, USA
© 2017 ACM. ISBN 978-1-4503-4354-1/17/02...$15.00
DOI: http://dx.doi.org/10.1145/3020078.3021753

algorithm [15] as a complex application whose achievable frame rate serves as a realistic performance constraint. Face detection is the task of finding faces within an image at different locations and irrespective of their size. It finds applications in a number of fields from photography to surveillance to robotics. The computationally intensive nature of the Haar feature classifiers in the Viola Jones algorithm makes face detection a suitable candidate for hardware acceleration.

In this paper we present a case study of accelerating a face detection system targeting a programmable SoC, emphasizing the insights from bringing a software design into a synthesizable implementation with specific data structures and optimizations. Our main contributions are twofold:

1. We identify Viola Jones face detection algorithm as a complex and realistic application for benchmarking HLS tools and provide a comprehensive case study to explore the flow from a pure software based implementation to an optimized C++ design suitable for HLS design flow.

2. We optimize our face detection system for performance, at the C/C++ level and synthesize it with a full-system compiler using SDSoC [9] from Xilinx. We show that our C-based design is suitable for real-time face detection applications achieving a frame rate of 30 fps. Our source code is publicly available on the authors' websites.

The rest of the paper is organized as follows: Section 2 examines the related work; Section 3 provides an overview of face detection based on the Viola Jones algorithm; Section 4 describes the baseline implementation; Section 5 discusses various optimizations performed; Section 6 presents performance and area results, followed by conclusions in Section 7.

2. Related Work

There have been many prior studies to evaluate state-of-the-art HLS tools [14, 16, 2]. Most of these works have used simple linear algebra and digital signal processing kernels such as matrix multiplication, FIR etc. CHStone represents a step towards benchmarking HLS with more realistic programs that make extensive use of high-level language features such as structs, pointers, and function calls [7]. However, most designs in CHStone remain small in size and are not necessarily good representatives of complex applications that can be handled by modern HLS tools. (e.g., those from the SoftFloat library [1]). MachSuite is a collection of 19 HLS benchmarks designed to span a variety of application domains that can potentially benefit from hardware acceleration [13]. These benchmarks are constructed to be kernels instead of complete applications. More recently, Liu et al. have made available an HLS implementation of an H.264 decoder design [11]. The authors have provided insights on porting a complex C reference design on FPGA by applying a set of code optimizations and HLS directives.

In this work we select Viola Jones face detection algorithm to benchmark FPGA-targeted HLS tool. FPGAs have become an attractive platform for real-time face detection systems. Several prior works have explored the RTL implementation of face detection algorithm on FPGAs. Lai et al. designed a parallel hardware architecture for FPGAs and were able to achieve 143 frames per second (fps) for the VGA image (640×480) [10]. However, the number of classifiers used was very small for real-world applications (52 as compared to 2,913 classifiers in our case), which led to a poor accuracy. Ngo et al. presented an efficient modular architecture for detection of multiple faces in video streams and were able to achieve a frame rate of 30 fps on QVGA (320×240) [12]. However, their results were based on simulations instead of real hardware implementation. Gao and Lu designed an RTL implementation and were able to achieve a frame rate of 98 fps for 16 classifiers in parallel [6], although they had to retrain the Haar classifiers such that each stage includes classifiers in the multiple of 16. He et al. proposed an SoC architecture for face detection using artificial neural networks and achieved a frame rate of 624 fps [4]. However, the number of sub-window sizes used were 11×11, 19×19, and 17×17, which would result in a poor detection accuracy for small faces. Jin et al. have shown the best performance among the reported FPGA-based face detection systems by attaining a frame rate as high as 307 fps for VGA images [8]. But it is worth noting that their algorithm was based on face uncertainty map using local binary pattern transform instead of Viola Jones. Cho et al. implemented the Viola Jones algorithm on a Virtex-5 FPGA and were able to achieve 26 fps for three classifiers processing the image in parallel and 15 fps for a single classifier [3]. This work is closest to our implementation in terms of the overall system architecture, but their implementation was in RTL as opposed to HLS. To our knowledge, we are the first to implement Viola Jones face detection algorithm on FPGA using C-based synthesis, and achieve a frame rate of 30 fps, suitable for many real-time applications.

3. Face Detection Algorithm

Viola Jones face detection algorithm is a widely-used method for real-time object detection. It uses Haar-like features, which are inner products between the image and Haar templates. A face candidate is a rectangular section of the original image. As images may have faces of different sizes, an image pyramid is constructed by downscaling the image by a constant factor. This multiscale representation of image is then searched for all possible 25×25 faces. The inner product of Haar features requires the sum of different rectangular sections of the downscaled image. Integral image is an efficient way to sum up the pixel values within a rectangular region. The value at any location (x,y) of the integral image is the sum of the image pixel value above and to the left of the location (x,y). The Haar features are mainly of two types – two-rectangle feature and three-rectangle feature. The value of two-rectangle feature is the difference between the weighted sum of pixels within two rectangular regions. A three-rectangle feature feature is the weighted sum within the two outside rectangles subtracted from the weighted sum in center rectangle. The weights and size of each feature is generated using AdaBoost machine learning algorithm. The area of any rectangle within the original image can be computed very easily using each corner of the rectangle in the integral image (as shown in Figure 1), where the area of the rectangular section D is computed by adding the diagonal elements e5, c3 and subtracting the off diagonal elements e3 and c5. To test every rectangle for a potential face, a 25×25 sliding window shifts around the whole image after downscaling, with a pixel offset of 1. Each time the window shifts, the image region within the window goes through the cascade classifier, which consists of multiple stages of classifiers (as shown in Figure 2(c)). If the input region fails to pass the threshold of a stage, the cascade classifier immediately rejects the region as a face. If a region pass all stages successfully, it is classified as

a candidate of face. The cascade filter can reduce the computation workload by rejecting a region at early stages. To compensate the effect of different lighting conditions, all the images are mean and variance normalized before sending them to the classifier.

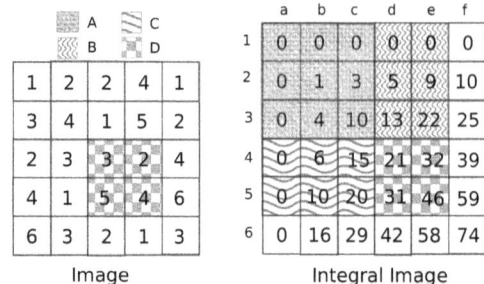

Figure 1: Image and its integral image — the value of the integral image at location c3 is the sum of the pixels in rectangle A. The value at location e3 is A+B, at location c5 is A+C, and at location e5 is A+B+C+D. The sum within the rectangle D can be computed as e5+c3-(e3+c5).

4. Baseline Implementation

In order to explore the flow from a software-based design to an optimized C/C++ based design suitable for HLS, we started with an open-source software implementation of Viola Jones face detection algorithm from [5]. The classifier used in this software implementation consisted of 25 stages, 2913 Haar classifiers, and Haar features trained by faces of size 25×25 pixels. We modified the source code to remove unsynthesizable constructs like system calls, heap accesses and recursive functions, to make it suitable for porting onto FPGA. This gave us a naïve hardware implementation of the face detection system with a frame rate < 3 fps.

Figure 2 provides an overview of the entire system used for our design. It consists of a CPU connected to FPGA where a host program is running on the CPU and a face detection accelerator is running on the FPGA. The CPU sends the image in pgm format, where each pixel value is an 8-bit number, to the hardware accelerator. The face detection system implemented on the FPGA processes the entire image to detect all possible faces and returns the coordinates of the rectangles that are detected as faces to the CPU. The CPU then marks the faces by printing rectangles on the image. The hardware implementation consists of three main modules which are detailed in the following sections.

4.1 Image Scaler

This module is responsible for downscaling the image to form an image pyramid. It takes the original image and a scaling factor as inputs and returns the downscaled image using a simple linear interpolation algorithm. The linear interpolation algorithm is implemented using two nested loops iterating over the image height and image width respectively. The inner loop body has shift, multiplication, and assignment operations to perform downscaling. The typical scaling factor used for our design is 1.2

4.2 Integral Image Generator

This module takes a downscaled image from the image scaler and constructs an integral image which is then stored in BRAMs. It consists of nested loops, with outer loop iterating over the height of the image and the inner loop iterating over the width of the image. The inner loop updates integral image pixel values by accumulating the pixels in the same row and to the left of a pixel location in the downscaled image and adding the pixel value at the same location but one row above in the integral image. This module also has

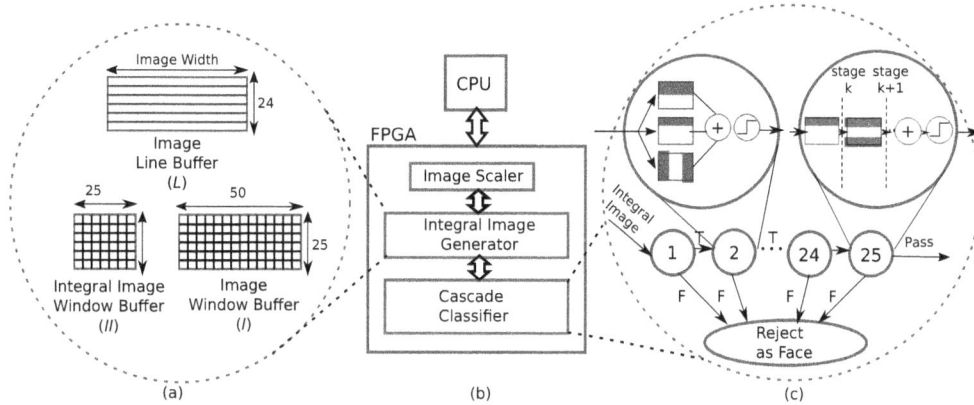

Figure 2: Face detection system — (a) Image line buffer, image window buffer and integral image window buffer for integral image generation, (b) Block diagram of the face detection system consisting of CPU and FPGA, and (c) Cascaded classifier with the classifiers in first 3 stages applied in parallel and in pipeline for rest of the stages

another nested loop which iterates over the rows and columns of the integral image and shifts the origin of the subwindow by one pixel location every iteration. The new subwindow location and the integral image is then sent to the cascaded classifier for further processing.

4.3 Cascade Classifier

This module receives an integral image and a subwindow location and passes the region inside the subwindow through the cascaded Haar classifiers as shown in Figure 2(c). For the pre-trained cascade classifier used for our implementation, there are 25 stages, each containing multiple Haar classifiers, ranging from 9 to 211. To implement cascading, this module contains a nested loop with the outer loop iterating over the number of stages and the inner loop iterating over the classifiers in each stage as shown in Figure 3. For each classifier in any stage, 12 values (x-y coordinates for the corner, plus width and height) corresponding to 3 rectangles in the Haar-classifier are read from the integral image subwindow, and the sum of each rectangle is obtained by adding the diagonal elements and subtracting the off diagonal elements of the rectangle. The sum of each rectangle is then multiplied by the corresponding weight and then added together and compared to a threshold value. Depending on whether the classifier sum exceeds the threshold value, one of the two classifier parameters α or β is accumulated into a running sum for that stage. For any stage, if the accumulated value exceeds the stage threshold, then it is considered to pass that stage and next iteration of the stage loop is processed, otherwise the function returns a negative value to the integral image generator, indicating that the given sub-window is not a face. In case the thresholds for all the stages are passed, then the subwindow is considered as a face and the cascade classifier notifies this by returning a positive value to the integral image generator, which then saves the upscaled version of those coordinates into a BRAM, so that they can be streamed out to the CPU when the processing of the entire image has finished. It also performs the normalization of the integral image by computing the mean and the standard deviation of the sub-window.

5. Optimizations

To improve the performance of our baseline implementation, we performed various optimizations as mentioned below:

5.1 Parallel and Pipelined Classifiers

We determined that the nested loop in the cascade classifier (Figure 3) is critical for the performance of the face detection system,

```
Cascade Classifier:
for (i=0;i < Nstages;i++) {
  for (j=0;j < Nclass[i];j++)
    stagesum += Classifier(II,classifierid,stddev);
  if (stagesum < sthresh[i]) break;
}

Classifier(II,k,stddev) {
  sum0 = (II[r0.y][r0.x]+II[r0.y+r0.h][r0.x+r0.w]
  -II[r0.y+r0.h][r0.x]-II[r0.y][r0.x+r0.w])*w0[k];
  sum1 = (II[r1.y][r1.x]+II[r1.y+r1.h][r1.x+r1.w]
  -II[r1.y+r1.h][r1.x]-II[r1.y][r1.x+r1.w])*w1[k];
  sum2 = (II[r2.y][r2.x]+II[r2.y+r2.h][r2.x+r2.w]
  -II[r2.y+r2.h][r2.x]-II[r2.y][r2.x+r2.w])*w2[k];
  finalsum = sum0+sum1+sum2;
  if (finalsum > cthresh[k]*stddev) return alpha[k];
  else return beta[k];
}
```

Figure 3: Unoptimized code for cascade classifier and a single classifier

as it is applied to all the subwindows in each downscaled image. The nested loop consists of a call to a Haar classifier and the best performance can be achieved when all the loops are completely unrolled and all the classifiers are processed in parallel. This requires a lot of hardware resources, making it infeasible to fit the design on the FPGA. Another approach is to pipeline the inner loop to exploit parallelism and to thus have a single pipelined classifier hardware whose classifier parameters change every cycle. This drastically reduces the amount of hardware resources required, but hurts the overall throughput. We wanted something in between these two approaches. We studied the number of sliding windows passing through each stage and the results obtained are shown in Figure 4. From the figure it can be seen that the number of subwindows passing through the first stage is two orders of magnitude more than the subwindows passing through the fourth and the fifth stages. Also, the subwindows passing through the second and third stages are an order of magnitude more than the ones passing from next two stages. This study clearly indicates that the first three stages are the throughput limiting factors. As the number of sliding windows passing through each stage is not the same due to cascading of the stages, the classifiers in the first three stages can be processed in parallel to increase the throughput at the cost of hardware resources. As the number of classifiers in the first three stages is small 9, 16, 27 respectively, this does not impose much area overhead and significantly improves the performance. For the next few stages, pipelining of the classifiers is more appropriate to save hard-

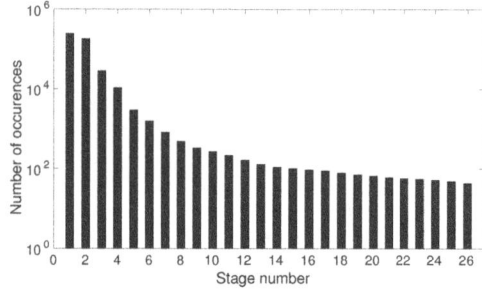

Figure 4: Number of occurrences of each stage on a 320×240 image

ware resources. Figure 2(c) shows an overview of the face detection system and optimized cascaded classifier with first 3 stages having classifiers in parallel and rest of them having pipelined classifiers.

To improve performance, we also stored the classifier values for the first three stages in registers, instead of BRAMs. The parallelization of the classifiers was done by making explicit function calls to each classifier, instead of doing it in a loop, as HLS tool we used schedules independent function calls outside the loop in parallel. Storing the classifier values in registers was done by hardcoding the constant values in the C code as shown in Figure 5. Hardcoding the classifier values reduces the need for BRAM accesses and gives the compiler more freedom to perform various optimizations. Some of these optimizations are shown in Figure 5, where multiplications by constants in the unoptimized code are replaced by shift and add operations in the optimized code produced by compiler. These kinds of optimizations, if lying on the critical path of the design as in our case, can help improve the performance of the design.

(a) Unoptimized Code

```
HardCodedClassifierk(II,variance){
    sum0=(II[6][5]+II[16][19]-II[16][5]-II[6][19])*-4096;
    sum1=(II[6][11]+II[15][13]-II[15][11]-II[6][13])*12288;
    sum2=0;
    if (sum0+sum1+sum2 > 58*variance) return 292;
    else return -89;
}
```

(b) Compiler Optimized Code

```
HardCodedClassifierk(II,variance){
    sum0=(-II[6][5]-II[16][19]+II[16][5]+II[6][19]);
    sum0=sum0 << 12;
    sum1=(II[6][11]+II[15][13]-II[15][11]-II[6][13]);
    sum1=(sum1 << 13) + (sum1 << 12);
    sum2=0;
    if (sum0+sum1+sum2 > 58*variance) return 292;
    else return -89;
}
```

Figure 5: Hardcoded classifier: (a) Unoptimized code with multiplication by constants (b) Compiler optimized code where multiplication is replaced by shift and add operations

5.2 Fast Integral Image Window Formation

As the coordinates of the classifiers are read from the integral image which is stored in BRAM, it requires 12 cycles to read the values of all the rectangle coordinates of a classifier. The classifiers are applied in the cascade classifier loop (Figure 3) which is critical for performance of the design. Reading classifier coordinates from BRAM imposes a resource constraint on the BRAM ports and prevents the tool pipeline the inner loop with the initiation interval of 1. To achieve an II of 1 in the inner loop, all the pixels of the

integral image need to be stored in registers instead of BRAM. To store the integral image for the entire 320×240 image in registers, it would require 1,920,000 1-bit registers, while the FPGA board that we are using has only 437,200 1-bit registers. Hence, if the integral image for the whole image is calculated all at once, it can only be stored in BRAMs. To address this issue, we used the integral image formation method mentioned in [3]. With this method, instead of producing the entire integral image at once, our design produces an integral image subwindow every clock cycle and stores it in an array of registers. As the integral image subwindow is stored in registers, it allows all the classifier coordinates to be read in parallel.

Here we describe the algorithm used for integral image generation. The integral image generator is provided with a 24×320 image line buffer, 25×50 image window buffer, 25×25 integral image window buffer, 25×50 square image window buffer and 2×2 square integral image window buffer as shown in Figure 2(a). For each incoming pixel with coordinate (x, y) representing the origin of the sliding window, the image line buffer performs a shift operation as in (1), where n is the row size of image line buffer, $p(x, y)$ is the incoming pixel value, and $L(x, y)$ represents a pixel in the image line buffer.

$$
\begin{aligned}
&L(x, (n-2) - k) := L(x, (n-2) - (k-1)), \\
&L(x, n-2) := p(x, y) \text{ where } 1 \leq k \leq n-2
\end{aligned}
\tag{1}
$$

If each row of the line buffer can be stored in different BRAMs, then it is possible to perform all these operations in parallel. The image window buffer I is a two dimensional array of registers which stores the pixel values from the image line buffer L and the current pixel value $p(x, y)$. The purpose of image window buffer is to store the necessary pixels for integral image window formation. For each incoming pixel $p(x, y)$, the image window buffer performs the following operations:

$$
\begin{aligned}
&I(i, j) := I(i+1, j), \text{where } 0 \leq i \leq m-2, 0 \leq j \leq n-1 \\
&I(m-1, j) := L(x, j), \text{where } 0 \leq j \leq n-2 \\
&I(m-1, n-1) := p(x, y) \\
&I(i, j) := I(i+1, j) + I(i+1, j-1), \text{where } i+j = m-1, \\
&\quad 0 \leq i \leq m-1, 1 \leq j \leq n-1, m = 2n,
\end{aligned}
\tag{2}
$$

The integral image window buffer II is used for classification of a face, and stores the integral pixel values moving from the image window buffer. For each incoming pixel $p(x, y)$, the integral image window performs the following operation:

$$
\begin{aligned}
&II(u, v) := II(u, v) + I(u+1, v) - I(0, v), \\
&\text{where } 0 \leq u \leq n-1, 0 \leq v \leq n-1
\end{aligned}
\tag{3}
$$

Similar operations are performed for the square integral image SII, except we store $square(p(x, y))$ instead of $p(x, y)$ in the square image window buffer. The square integral image is used to calculate the variance used to normalize the pixel values in the subwindow to handle lighting conditions.

The HLS tool we use provides synthesizable data structures for conveniently instantiating window and line buffers. However, the available methods do not allow add operations while performing left or right shift operations, as required in (2). Therefore, we implemented our own window buffers and line buffers using two dimensional arrays and partitioning them in dimension 0 and 1 respectively. When partitioned in dimension 0, HLS tool infer the arrays as array of registers and for dimension 1 as multiple BRAMs. The operations in (1), (2) and (3) if not coded properly, can end up with dependencies which may restrict the tool to schedule them in single cycle. As seen from the equations, to compute the current value of II, the value of I in the previous cycle is required; and to compute current value of I, the value L in the previous cycle is required. We adopted a methodology where the equations in (1), (2) and (3) are coded in reverse order as shown in Figure 6, to avoid any read-after-write dependency. Loops were unrolled to schedule all the operations in single cycle.

```
/* Integral Image Window Buffer */
for (u=0;u < WINDOW_SIZE;u++)
  #pragma HLS unroll
  for (v=0;v < WINDOW_SIZE;v++)
    #pragma HLS unroll
    II[u][v]=II[u][v]+(I[u][v+1]-I[u][0]);

/* Image Window Buffer */
for(j=0;j < 2*WINDOW_SIZE-1;j++)
  #pragma HLS unroll
  for(i=0;i < WINDOW_SIZE;i++)
    #pragma HLS unroll
    if( i+j != 2*WINDOW_SIZE-1 ) I[i][j] = I[i][j+1];
    else if (i > 0) I[i][j]=I[i][j+1]+I[i-1][j+1];

for(i=0;i < WINDOW_SIZE-1;i++)
  #pragma HLS unroll
  I[i][2*WINDOW_SIZE-1]=L[i][x];

I[WINDOW_SIZE-1][2*WINDOW_SIZE-1] = IMG[y][x];

/* Image Line Buffer */
for(k=0;k < WINDOW_SIZE-2;k++)
  #pragma HLS unroll
  L[k][x]=L[k+1][x];

L[WINDOW_SIZE-2][x] = IMG1[y][x];
```

Figure 6: Code for integral image formation avoiding RAW dependencies and unrolling the loops for single cycle updates

5.3 Integral Image Banking

To read 12 coordinates from the integral image window simultaneously, it requires twelve 625×1 18-bit MUXes. As this many MUXes require more than 170K LUTs, the HLS tool has a hard time generating and pipelining these MUXes. Even if the tool is able to generate them, they are not able to pipeline them efficiently, resulting in timing violations during the routing phase of the design. As the number of LUTs required is huge, this also adds a lot of area overhead and routing congestion. Using a 625×1 MUX means that for any rectangle coordinate in a classifier the value can be read from anywhere in the integral image. We profiled all the classifiers to see how many pixel locations does each of the 12 coordinates require and realized that a rectangle coordinate comes from a blob of pixels in the integral image and does not use all the 625 pixels. We leverage this information to bank the integral image into 28 banks, such that any of the 12 coordinates of a classifier do not lie in the same bank. Figure 7(a) shows an integral image window buffer with a giant 625×1 MUX to read a single coordinate from the integral image. Figure 7 (b) shows a two-level hierarchy of MUXes, where the first level of MUXes select the values from different banks, and the MUX in the second level selects a bank. As all the coordinates lie in different banks, different offsets are used as select signals for different MUXes in the first layer to read all the 12 coordinates from the integral image (the MUX selects are set to 0 for 16 banks that are not needed). The MUXes in the first level are shared between all the 12 coordinates; only the second layer is replicated. This integral image banking helped us reduce the LUT utilization from 179,712 to 16,722 and also allowed the tool to place and route the design quite easily.

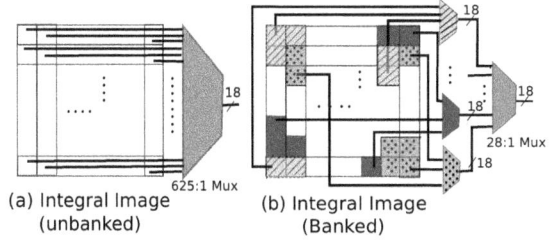

Figure 7: Integral image banking — (a) shows an unbanked integral image and a 625×1 MUX to read one coordinate from image. (b) shows an integral image banked into 28 banks, MUXes for 12 of these 28 banks read all the 12 coordinates and the MUX in the next layer is used to choose one of the banks for a coordinate

5.4 Square Root Approximation

As the first few stages constitute the throughput limiting factors, any logic before the cascaded classifier can bottleneck performance. To eliminate lighting effects, each subwindow has to be normalized. This requires the calculation of mean and standard deviation for every subwindow. As standard deviation is the square root of variance, we identified square root calculation as another throughput limiting factor because it takes 16 cycles on FPGA and is calculated for each subwindow. It is hard to parallelize due to inter-iteration dependencies in the loops. A better approach to achieve single cycle performance was to store the square root values in BRAMs and use direct look up for standard deviation calculations. As the number of bits required to represent the variance of a 25×25 window of 8 bit entries is 26, the square root look up requires a storage of $2^{26} \times 13$ bits. This translates to 47,331 BRAMs (each with 18Kb), which obviously would not fit on-chip. Hence we adopted a different approach where we treated variance as the sum of its most significant 10 bits left shifted by 16 and the lower 16 bits. The square root for the 16 bit numbers was stored in 32 BRAMs by declaring a statically initialized one dimensional array of 65536 elements. The square root calculation was performed by taking the square root of the upper and the lower halves of the number and left shifting the first result by 8 and adding them. We also made a separate case for the values which will be affected a lot by this approximation, and used upper 18 bits and lower 8 bits for them. We measured the percentage error for the approximated square root for all the 2^{26} bit numbers, and the error was less than 1% for 96% of the cases and less than 2% for 99.9% of the cases. For all our experiments, this 1-2% error did not effect the accuracy of face detection algorithm.

6. Experimental Results

The hardware-software setup used for our design consists of an ARM CPU and Zynq-7000 XC7Z045 FPGA available on a ZC706 board. We used Xilinx SDSoC 2016.1 to partition the application into software and hardware sections and automatically generate the data motion network between CPU and FPGA. SDSoC internally invokes Vivado HLS 2016.1 to synthesize the RTL from the design implementation in C. A high frame rate is very important for real time applications. Because the performance of our face detection system depends on the number of faces in the image, we measured the performance for different number of faces for both the software and hardware implementations. The software performance was measured on ARM Cortex-A9 present on ZC706 board.

Table 1 shows the performance of the implemented face detection system for 1, 2, 4 and 8 faces. It can be seen that the performance of the HLS-based face detection system is 8-9X higher than that of the software implementation in all four cases. The HLS design is able to achieve a frame rate of more than 30 fps for 1 to 4 faces, which is suitable for real-time application. Figure 8 shows the improvement in the frame rate for different optimizations. All the optimizations are performed along with fast integral image generation and integral image banking. From the figure it can be seen that baseline performance ranges from 1–3 fps, and all three optimizations (pipelined classifiers, parallel classifiers, and square root approximation) contribute almost equally to increasing the frame rate of the face detection system.

Table 1: Performance of our proposed face detection system with 320×240 resolution images for both hardware and software

# of faces	Software classifier	Hardware classifier
1	206 ms 4.8 fps	30 ms 33.4 fps
2	232 ms 4.3 fps	31 ms 32.1 fps
4	250 ms 4.0 fps	32 ms 31.3 fps
8	371 ms 2.7 fps	38 ms 26.3 fps

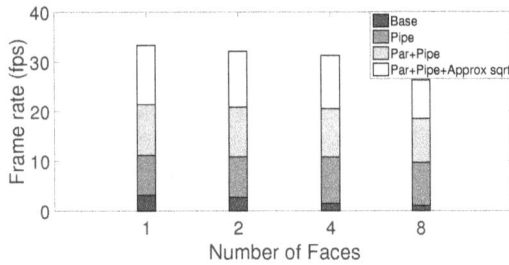

Figure 8: Frame rate improvement corresponding to various optimizations for 1, 2, 4 and 8 faces in 320×240 image

Table 2 shows the resource utilization of the face detection system. Most of the BRAM utilization comes from the storage of the original and the downscaled image in the on-chip BRAMs, each of which consumes 64 BRAMs. The rest of the BRAM utilization comes from the storage of different classifier parameters (weights, rectangle co-ordinates, thresholds, etc.). As we want single cycle access to all these parameters, any two classifier parameters that may be needed at the same time are stored in different BRAMs. The main factors of LUT consumption are the MUXes in integral image banking, logic for the integral image generation and arithmetic expressions, contributing 24%, 50% and 26% respectively toward the LUT utilization. Register utilization mainly comes from integral image generation (57%) and temporary storage (43%) in various modules and classifiers.

Table 2: Resource Utilization of our proposed face detection system with 320×240 resolution images

Logic	Total Used	Total Available	Utilization
LUT	62,522	218,600	28.6%
Registers	81,135	437,200	18.56%
DSP48E	111	900	12.33%
BRAM 18K	157	545	28.81%

7. Conclusions

In this paper, we provide insights for bringing a software design of Viola Jones face detection algorithm into a synthesizable C-based design. We describe various optimizations performed to achieve a frame rate suitable for real-time application. We acknowledge the strength of SDSoC and Vivado HLS in automatically generating the data motion network and pipelining complex loop structures. We also discuss the shortcomings of the tool in restricting the designer from having fine control over the design and synthesis process. We conclude that more advanced benchmarking is needed to create HLS tools with out-of-box quality-of-results competitive to traditional RTL implementations.

Acknowledgement

This research was supported in part by NSF Awards #1065307, #1337240, #1453378, and a research gift from Xilinx, Inc.

References

[1] SoftFloat, http://www.jhauser.us/arithmetic/SoftFloat.html.

[2] E. Casseau and B. L. Gal. High-Level Synthesis for the Design of FPGA-Based Signal Processing Systems. *Int'l Symp. on Systems, Architectures, Modeling, and Simulation (SAMOS)*, 2009.

[3] J. Cho, S. Mirzaei, J. Oberg, and R. Kastner. FPGA-Based Face Detection System Using Haar Classifiers. *Int'l Symp. on Field-Programmable Gate Arrays (FPGA)*, 2009.

[4] H. Chun, A. Papakonstantinou, and D. Chen. A Novel SoC Architecture on FPGA for Ultra-Fast Face Detection. *Int'l Conf. on Computer Design (ICCAD)*, 2009.

[5] F. Comaschi. https://sites.google.com/site/5kk73gpu2012/assignment/viola-jones-face-detection.

[6] C. Gao and S. L. Lu. Novel FPGA Based Haar Classifier Face Detection Algorithm Acceleration. *Int'l Conf. on Field Programmable Logic and Applications (FPL)*, 2008.

[7] Y. Hara, H. Tomiyama, S. Honda, H. Takada, and K. Ishii. Chstone: A Benchmark Program Suite for Practical C-Based High-Level Synthesis. *Int'l Symp. on Circuits and Systems (ISCAS)*, 2008.

[8] S. Jin, D. Kim, T. T. Nguyen, D. Kim, M. Kim, and J. W. Jeon. Design and Implementation of a Pipelined Datapath for High-Speed Face Detection Using FPGA. *IEEE Trans. on Industrial Informatics (IEEE T IND INFORM)*, 2015.

[9] V. Kathail, J. Hwang, W. Sun, Y. Chobe, T. Shui, and J. Carrillo. SDSoC: A Higher-Level Programming Environment for Zynq SoC and Ultrascale+ MPSoC. *Int'l Symp. on Field-Programmable Gate Arrays (FPGA)*, 2016.

[10] H. Lai, M. Savvides, and T. Chen. Proposed FPGA Hardware Architecture for High-Frame Rate (>>100 fps) Face Detection Using Feature Cascade Classifiers. *Int'l Conf. on Biometrics: Theory, Applications, and Systems (BTAS)*, 2007.

[11] X. Liu, Y. Chen, T. Nguyen, S. Gurumani, K. Rupnow, and D. Chen. High-Level Synthesis of Complex Applications: An H.264 Video Decoder. *Int'l Symp. on Field-Programmable Gate Arrays (FPGA)*, 2016.

[12] H. T. Ngo, R. C. Tompkins, J. Foytik, and V. K. Asari. An Area Efficient Modular Architecture for Real-Time Detection of Multiple Faces in Video Stream. *Int'l Conf. on Information, Communications and Signal Processing (ICICS)*, 2007.

[13] B. Reagen, R. Adolf, Y. Shao, G. Wei, and D. Brooks. Machsuite: Benchmarks for Accelerator Design and Customized Architectures. *Int'l Symp. on Workload Characterization (IISWC)*, 2014.

[14] S. Skalicky, C. Wood, M. ukowiak, and M. Ryan. High-Level Synthesis: Where Are We? A Case Study on Matrix Multiplication. *Int'l Conf. on Reconfigurable Computing and FPGAs (ReConFig)*, 2013.

[15] P. Viola and M. J. Jones. Robust real-time face detection. *Int'l Journal of Computer Vision (IJCV)*, 2004.

[16] F. Winterstein, S. Bayliss, and G. A. Constantinides. High-Level Synthesis of Dynamic Data Structures: A Case Study Using Vivado HLS. *Int'l Conf. on Field Programmable Technology (FPT)*, 2013.

Packet Matching on FPGAs Using HMC Memory: Towards One Million Rules

Daniel Rozhko, Geoffrey Elliott, Daniel Ly-Ma, Paul Chow, and Hans-Arno Jacobsen
Dept. of Electrical and Computer Engineering
University of Toronto, Toronto, ON, Canada
{daniel.rozhko, geoffrey.elliott, d.lyma}@mail.utoronto.ca
{pc, jacobsen}@eecg.toronto.edu

ABSTRACT

Packet processing systems increasingly need larger rulesets to satisfy the needs of deep-network intrusion prevention and cluster computing. FPGA-based implementations of packet processing systems have been proposed but their use of on-chip memory limits the number of rules these existing systems can maintain. Off-chip memories have traditionally been too slow to enable meaningful processing rates, but in this work we present a packet processing system that utilizes the much faster Hybrid Memory Cube (HMC) technology, enabling larger rulesets at usable line-rates. The proposed architecture streams rules from the HMC memory to a packet matching engine, using prefetching to hide the HMC access latency. The packet matching engine is replicated to process multiple packets in parallel. The final system, implemented on a Xilinx Kintex Ultrascale 060, processes 160 packets in parallel, achieving a 10 Gbps line-rate with approximately 1500 rules and a 16 Mbps line-rate with 1M rules. To the best of our knowledge, this is the first hardware solution capable of maintaining rulesets of this size. We present this work as an exploration of the application of HMCs to packet processing and as a first step in achieving a processing capability of a million rules at usable line-rates.

Keywords

FPGA; Reconfigurable; Accelerator; Networking; Packet Matching; Packet Classification; Hybrid Memory Cube; HMC

1. INTRODUCTION

FPGAs – with their reconfigurable nature and high bandwidth interfaces – represent a logical choice for networking infrastructure. However, their limited memory restricts the amount of information that can be stored within the chip, and off-chip memories are typically too slow to meet the demands of high-speed networks. As network managers attempt to match traffic against increasingly larger and more varied criteria, the small on-chip memories of the FPGA can quickly become a bottleneck.

Hybrid Memory Cube (HMC) based memories present one avenue to alleviate this bottleneck. At a high level, an HMC module consists of stacks of DRAM memory connected vertically by through silicon vias (TSVs) [1]. The memory controller of an HMC memory is integrated into the chip as one die in the stack, and is connected with TSVs to the layers of memory. Embedding the controller in the stack improves latency significantly since signals do not have to travel across the board to an off-chip controller, while also hiding complex DRAM communication protocols from the end user. Of particular importance for the work presented here is the increased bandwidth available from HMC memories. According to Micron, HMC memories have twelve times the bandwidth of traditional DDR3 and six times the bandwidth of newer DDR4 memories [1].

Through the use of HMC, we implemented an FPGA-based system that is capable of matching packets against a ruleset containing thousands to millions of rules. This high-rule processing capability is the primary novelty of our system. Such a system would be beneficial for firewalls, deep-network inspection, and intrusion detection, where large and diverse rulesets are often required [2]. We present this system as an early work in exploring the use of HMC for memory-based applications, in this case packet processing.

The remainder of the paper is organized as follows: Section 2 provides background information and a description of prior work. Section 3 details the architecture of our HMC-based packet matching system. The experimental setup used to test the system and the results obtained from these tests are presented in Sections 4 and 5, respectively. Finally, conclusions are presented in Section 6.

2. BACKGROUND AND RELATED WORK

Internet routers and switches operate by matching header fields of incoming packets against a set of rules and priorities. Based on a matching rule with the highest priority (in the case of multiple matches), a given action is performed on the packet, such as forwarding to a specific output interface, dropping the packet, or altering the headers or payload. The hardware and software tools that perform this process often support matching against different sets of packet header values; for example, the popular Berkeley Packet Filter [3] language used in many software tools supports matching against arbitrary ranges for source and destination port numbers [4], while the hardware-focused OpenFlow only supports exact matching for port numbers [5].

FPGA '17, February 22-24, 2017, Monterey, CA, USA

© 2017 ACM. ISBN 978-1-4503-4354-1/17/02...$15.00

DOI: http://dx.doi.org/10.1145/3020078.3021752

2.1 OpenFlow

OpenFlow [6] is a popular Software-Defined Networking (SDN) infrastructure platform. OpenFlow (and SDN as a whole) separates the data plane (transmission systems) of the network from the control plane (decision-making systems), resulting in a more adaptable network. Our system represents the routing component of the data plane and is capable of processing the fields present in the OpenFlow 1.1.0 standard [5]. The full list of fields, including the number of bits to represent each field, can be found in Table 1. The second term shown in the *Number of Bits* column represents the number of mask bits for that field, i.e., IP fields support an arbitrary bitmask while all other fields support exact match only. Note that in the full OpenFlow standard, MAC address matching supports an arbitrary bitmask, whereas our implementation is limited to exact matches (this is done in other state-of-the-art work as well [7][8]).

Table 1: OpenFlow 1.1.0 match fields

Field Name	Number of Bits
Ingress Port	32 + 1
Source MAC	48 + 1
Destination MAC	48 + 1
Ether Type	16 + 1
VLAN ID	12 + 1
VLAN Priority	3 + 1
MPLS Label	20 + 1
MPLS Traffic Class	3 + 1
Source IPv4	32 + 32
Destination IPv4	32 + 32
Protocol	8 + 1
Type of Service	6 + 1
Source Port	16 + 1
Destination Port	16 + 1
Priority	32

2.2 Related Work

Many FPGA-based approaches to packet classification exist, using bit-vector [8], TCAMs-on-FPGAs [6], or decision tree [7] approaches to rule storage. TCAM-based approaches attempt to mimic the performance of ASIC *Ternary Content Addressable Memories*, however, FPGAs are very power-inefficient for this task. Decision tree-based systems can be very memory-efficient by combining and merging similar rules, but do not allow for dynamic updates to the ruleset without rebuilding portions of the tree. Bit-vectors allow for fast parallel searches, but require more memory than TCAMs or decision trees [9]. Additionally, these systems exclusively use the on-chip memory of the FPGA to achieve high-speed line rates and to avoid the long wait times for DDR memories. As a result, such systems tend to be memory-limited and cannot store more than a few thousand rules at most.

Some approaches use a hybrid hardware-software approach, where only frequently-matched rules are stored in the hardware system [10]; for packets not matching the common

rules, the system must pass off the packet to a slower software-based system, which contains the remaining rules. These systems may also update the list of commonly accessed rules based on processed traffic to maintain minimum processing latency. While these systems can manage large rulesets, the packet processing latency is non-uniform and the average latency tends to be higher (depending on the ruleset and packets) because of the software processing. By storing all rules in fast HMC memory, our hardware-only system can compare all packets against all rules of a large ruleset at fast line-rates, while also maintaining the dynamic updatability found in software-based systems

3. PACKET MATCHING ARCHITECTURE

A high-level view of our system architecture is shown in Figure 1. The two central components (*Memory Prefetcher* and *Packet Matching Engine*) represent the proposed packet processing system, while the remaining peripheral components are simply part of the evaluation framework (described later in Section 4). The packet processing ruleset is stored in the HMC memory, with a memory prefetching component reading these rules in serially and forwarding them to a packet matching engine. Since rules can only be accessed serially from off-chip memory, the packet matching engine implements a simple search over the rules as they are streamed in. Throughput is increased by processing multiple packets in parallel. This section describes these architectural features in more detail.

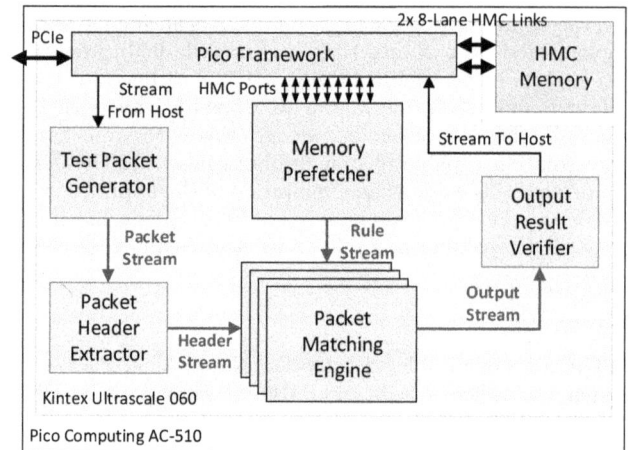

Figure 1: Complete system architecture.

3.1 HMC Memory Prefetcher

To maximize the utilization of the HMC link and provide rules to the matching circuits as quickly as possible, the system utilizes a memory prefetching circuit. Through the use of two instances of the Micron HMC IP Controller [11], the FPGA fabric has ten ports with which to access the HMC. The vendor-provided framework reserves one port for host access, leaving nine ports for use by the prefetcher. To simplify the request logic, the prefetcher distributes requests over eight of the nine ports.

As shown in Figure 2, each of the eight HMC ports is connected to an individual prefetching unit. Each unit issues 128-byte (2-rule) requests from the HMC in a sequential order to minimize the response time (typically, sequential

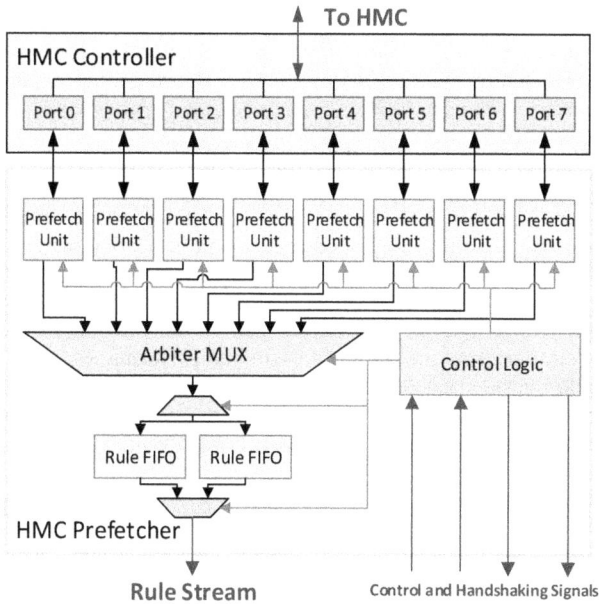

Figure 2: Memory prefetcher architecture.

memory accesses are faster than random ones). Each response is returned in eight 16-byte segments, which are collected and split into the two rules. Each unit feeds these rules into an arbiter multiplexer, which coalesces the eight streams into one. Once all the rules have been retrieved (based on the value of the global *RuleCount* register at the start of a cycle), the prefetcher then issues requests for up to 1/4 of the rules prior to the start of another match cycle. This minimizes the downtime of the HMC link, but does limit alterations to the ruleset – namely, that the ruleset cannot shrink by more than 75% on a given matching cycle. Since the responses can arrive out of request order, the circuit separates the original batch of rules from the prefetched ones by tagging the reads with a batch number (either 1 or 0). The tag is returned with the response, which is used to sort the rule into one of two FIFOs, which are pushed out to the matching circuits.

Since the rules are stored in the HMC, the rules can be updated dynamically by the host machine. The simple search method allows for rules to be rewritten without the need to recompute and update the entire set. For single rule changes, a blocking write can be issued to the 16-byte blocks containing the rule without affecting the prefetcher performance. For larger rule changes, the prefetcher supports multiple buffering. The 4GB of HMC is evenly divided into four partitions, each capable of holding 2 million rules. New rulesets should be written to an unused partition, and the system updated to point to the appropriate section of memory.

3.2 Matching Engine

The packet matching engine compares the headers of incoming packets against a ruleset and outputs the action of the highest priority matching rule. Rules and packet headers are streamed in from two FIFOs that are populated by the *Packet Header Extractor* and *Memory Prefetcher* circuits respectively as shown in Figure 1. The processing engine (PE) is at the heart of the matching engine. As shown in Figure 3, a PE compares all the fields in the packet with the

fields of each rule. The outputs of these comparisons are logically ANDed together to check if all fields of a particular rule have been matched. Exact match fields will output true if the mask bit is low. For IP source and destination fields, only the bits not set in the mask fields are used for comparison. Internal registers keep track of the highest priority rule and its corresponding action. Each new matching rule's priority is compared against the current highest priority and if the priority of the new rule is higher, these registers will take on the values of the new rule.

Since rules are read in sequentially, having more PEs will allow for more packets to be processed in parallel, thus increasing the throughput. Our first architecture, shown in Figure 3, was designed using Vivado HLS and uses a demultiplexer to load packets into an array of PEs and uses a multiplexer to sequentially send the outputs to the output FIFO. This architecture's simplicity makes it good for prototyping a proof of concept. However, we discovered that this architecture did not scale well with the number of PEs as it was difficult to meet timing for more than 100 PEs. This was due to the increasingly large fanout of the Rule Stream data signal and the deepening of the LUT levels required for the multiplexer and demultiplexer logic as the number of PEs increased.

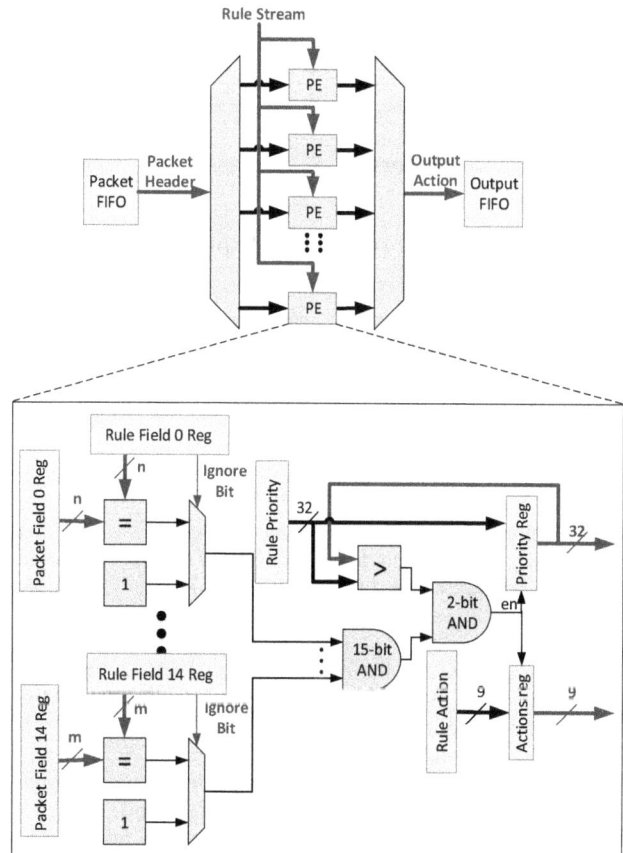

Figure 3: Simple matching engine and PE architecture.

Our second architecture, shown in Figure 4, tries to overcome these shortcomings. First, the PEs are placed in a systolic array architecture to reduce the fanout of the Rule

Stream data signal and remove the need for the large multiplexer and demultiplexer. Packet headers in the FIFO are sequentially shifted through the array until either the FIFO is empty or the array is full. The PEs load the header into their internal registers and rules are then sequentially shifted through the array for each PE to compare against its header. Once all the rules have been shifted through, the output of the PEs are loaded into a parallel shift register and then shifted into the output FIFO. To overcome the limitations of HLS, we designed this with SystemVerilog, which allowed us to optimize the PEs to use DSP slices for larger width comparisons, and to pipeline the comparisons aggressively. These optimizations allowed us to pack 60% more PEs (160 in total) into the matching engine.

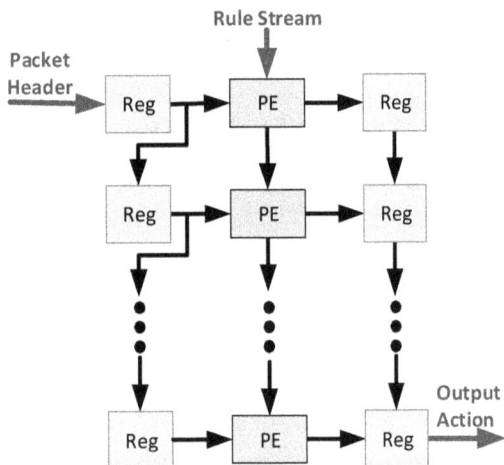

Figure 4: Systolic matching engine architecture.

4. EXPERIMENTAL SETUP

In this section, we describe the environment used to implement our designed system. This includes the design of both hardware and software components required to evaluate the performance of our system relative to other work.

4.1 HW and Development Framework

The system was designed to use a Micron AC-510 FPGA accelerator card, which features 4GB of HMC connected over two 8-lane SerDes links to a Xilinx Kintex Ultrascale 060 FPGA [12], and a maximum of 60GB/s of HMC memory bandwidth. The AC-510 is connected to a host CPU via a Micron EX-750 PCIe backplane, which can support up to four cards in parallel, though only one is used in the implementation of our system.

As part of the infrastructure to support the AC-510 and HMC, Micron provides the *Pico Framework* [13], a wrapper for the FPGA to include the PCIe and HMC links in hardware designs (as depicted in Figure 1), as well as software libraries and drivers for the host CPU. These libraries allow for simple software development and a simple protocol for communicating between the host and the FPGA/HMC.

Development of the system was done using a combination of Xilinx's Vivado and Vivado HLS toolkits, version 2015.4. Many of the system blocks were prototyped and finalized using Vivado HLS, with system integration done in Vivado. Due to the necessity of clock-related signaling, the

module for fetching rules from memory was written using SystemVerilog. To improve P&R results and allow for more matching circuits, the final version of the matching engine was also written in HDL.

4.2 Packet Generation and Verification

The Micron AC-510 Board was chosen for its HMC memory module, but it lacks the network interface that would allow our system to be tested in a real network deployment. Instead, our architecture was tested with a spoofed network interface: packets were generated and results verified on-chip. Note, this on-chip packet generation also decouples system performance from the PCIe bus performance, which would not be possible if the packet generation and result verification were done completely in software. The hardware components responsible for this spoofed evaluation framework are shown in Figure 1.

The *Test Packet Generator* creates and sends a continuous stream of packets at a line rate of up to 10 Gbps. Rather than generate random packets on-chip, this component holds a group of pre-generated packets in on-chip memory (up to 1024) and sends them in an infinite loop. The random packets themselves are generated in software and streamed to the test framework at initialization time through the *Pico Framework*. Note, since the random packets are generated in software, the expected match results can also be computed in software and sent to the system at initialization time.

The output of the generator is an octet-aligned stream of Ethernet packets, optionally with MPLS and Ethernet VLAN fields. The *Packet Header Extractor* parses the Ethernet stream and separates the packet header bits into their corresponding fields (see Table 1), to be processed by the Packet Matching Engine. This is done rather then sending pre-separated fields from the host directly so that the system can be tested with real packet data. Note, this component also tags each packet with an ingress timestamp (from a global counter), for the calculation of packet latency.

Finally, the *Output Result Verifier* receives the match results from the Matching Engine and verifies that the correct match was made. These correct matches are computed in software and streamed to the component at initialization time to be stored in on-chip memory. The verifier streams the number of errors and some statistics back to the host on a packet-batch basis (i.e. one iteration of the packet infinite loop). The statistics include the average packet latency for the batch (calculated using the global counter and packet timestamp), the total counter cycles taken for the batch (to calculate throughput), and the total number of rule fetch cycles taken for the batch (to calculate memory bandwidth).

4.3 Software Host Code

The software host code simulates a small network by first randomly generating a limited set of values for each possible field (e.g. 8 different MAC addresses), and then creating rules and packets based on that set. This ensures that each packet matches against at least some rules. Expected results are computed using a software implementation of the simple search algorithm. Packets, rules, and expected results are streamed to hardware using the *Pico Framework*.

5. RESULTS

In this section, we detail and summarize the results obtained from applying the above evaluation framework.

Table 2: Comparison of Packet Throughput & Processing Latency Against Prior Work

	# Rules	# Fields	Rule Storage	Max Throughput	Latency	FPGA
160 Systolic PEs	1504	15	770 Kb	10.2×10^9 bps	11.6×10^0 μs	Kintex Ultrascale
160 Systolic PEs	1048576	15	536 Mb	16.4×10^6 bps	52.7×10^3 μs	Kintex Ultrascale
Jiang [7]	9603	5	4896 Kb	80.23×10^9 bps	152×10^{-3} μs	Virtex-5
Jiang [7]	1000	12	552 Kb	40×10^9 bps	288×10^{-3} μs	Virtex-5
Qu [8]	1024	15	729 Kb	332.8×10^9 bps	700×10^{-3} μs	Virtex-6

5.1 Packet Processing Throughput

The main metric of merit for packet processing systems is the maximum packet throughput at a given number of rules, generally expressed as the Ethernet line rate required to transmit that number of minimum-sized packets. The results for three of our systems are presented in Figure 5. The best system achievable with our design, 160 systolic PEs, is represented by the top-most line. Note that the relation between rule count and line rate is linear on a log-log plot, which is expected given rules are streamed in serially. At 1500 rules, we note that our 160 PE system exceeds the 10 Gbps target line-rate, but at higher rule-counts this line rate is unachievable.

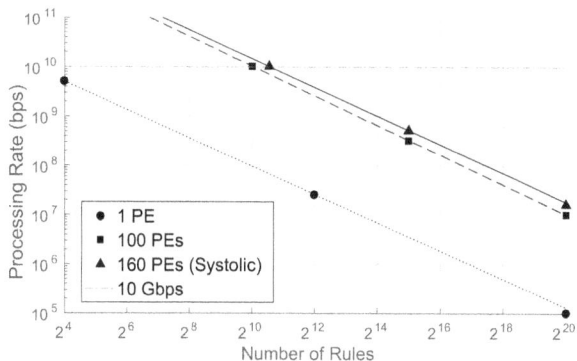

Figure 5: Maximum network throughput for varied rule set sizes.

Table 2 presents the packet throughput of our best system, 160 systolic PEs, along with other state-of-the-art hardware implementations of packet matching systems. Two entries in the table correspond to our work: the system tested with 1504 rules (max rule count at 10 Gbps) and $2^{20} = 1048576$ rules, as the first and second entries respectively. We note that previous systems outperform our implementation at lower rule counts; this is expected, since these systems utilize only on-chip memory. Our off-chip memory solution is the only hardware system (to the best of our knowledge) that can support much larger rule counts, achieving a processing rate of 16.4 Mbps at 1M rules.

5.2 Packet Processing Latency

Another key metric is the latency of processing a single packet. Since our system can only sequence through the rules at the rate at which we can receive them from off-chip memory (whereas existing systems might have access to all the rules in parallel), we expect a larger latency. In addition, existing systems are pipelined, allowing for new packets to

be pushed through every cycle; new packets in our system must be buffered while a previous match cycle completes, adding additional latency. The latency results for three of our systems are shown in Table 3. For comparison purposes, Table 2 presents the average latency of our best system, 160 systolic PEs, along with other state-of-the-art FPGA implementations. The results verify our expectations, as other state-of-the-art systems have better latency performance.

Table 3: Packet Latencies

# Rules	1 PE	100 PEs	160 Syst. PEs
1504	6.33×10^3 μs	55.0×10^0 μs	11.6×10^0 μs
1048576	6.06×10^6 μs	76.9×10^3 μs	52.7×10^3 μs

5.3 Sustained Memory Bandwidth

The standard versions of the Memory Prefetcher circuit provided the Match Engine with one rule per clock cycle. When implemented, this produced a sustained memory bandwidth of about 84.5 Gbps, or about 10.6 GB/s. These results are independent of the matching circuit architecture, since all versions consume up to one rule per cycle.

An alternative prefetcher was also tested, which instead provided two rules per cycle (by doubling the width of the FIFO), which increased the total memory bandwidth to about 161 Gbps or 20 GB/s. However, these double-match circuits were more difficult to place on-chip, resulting in fewer match circuits and, as a result, lower packet throughput. Because of this, only the one-rule per cycle architectures are discussed in the rest of this paper.

5.4 Resource Utilization

Table 4 details the resource usage for the systolic 160 PE system. The total available resources is presented in the first row, and the percentage of those resources used is shown in the subsequent rows, broken out based on the sub-module hierarchy. Note, *Test Framework* includes those blocks described in section 4.2, and *Pico Framework* is broken up into the HMC Controller, and everything else. The system caps out at between half and four-fifths of the chip resources, suggesting that more elements could be placed. However, beyond these points, the router is unable to find sufficient paths to meet the aggressive timing requirements (4ns or 6ns period, depending on the block). The *Test Framework* and the portions of the *Pico Framework* outside of the HMC Controller constitute five to eight percent of the total resource utilization; these components would not be required in a real deployment and thus these resources could be allocated towards more PEs.

Table 4: Resource Utilization – 160 Systolic PEs

	LUTs	FFs	BRAM	DSPs
Available Resources	331680	331680	1080	2760
Total Utilization	35.5%	81.4%	42.1%	40.6%
└ Packet Matcher	13.1%	52.7%	16.5%	40.6%
└ Prefetcher	0.6%	1.1%	11.9%	0.0%
└ Matching Engine	11.9%	51.0%	1.1%	40.6%
└ Test Framework	0.6%	0.7%	3.6%	0.0%
└ Pico Framework	22.4%	30.9%	25.6%	0.0%
└ HMC Controller	19.3%	26.3%	20.4%	0.0%
└ PCIe,Streams,etc.	3.1%	4.6%	5.2%	0.0%

6. CONCLUSION

In this paper we present a packet processing system capable of managing very large rulesets at usable line rates. Current systems are limited to 1000-10,000 rules; our HMC-based system can manage upwards of 2,000,000 rules. At the lower rule counts (~1000), our system meets a 10 Gbps line rate, a commonly used high speed Ethernet rate. The packet throughput decreases with increased rule count (to 16.4 Mbps at 1M rules), as expected given the serial nature of our architecture. The system uses 10 GB/s of memory bandwidth, though our extended results showed that just less than twice this amount of memory bandwidth is available (though in tradeoff with routeability). In addition, the FPGA on the AC-510 can only physically connect to two of the eight available links on the HMC module, so yet more bandwidth is available. We leave as future work the exploration of architectures able to effectively use the remainder of the memory bandwidth for increased throughput, perhaps employing multi-FPGA structures.

While our system is able to process the million-rule goal, the long processing time to cycle through the entire rule set introduces a significant amount of latency. Our system under performs with respect to latency compared to on-chip memory systems that can access many rules in parallel. Adapting the system to take advantage of algorithms with a lower memory footprint (such as a tree-based approach) should reduce the latency and improve throughput. Additionally, because of the high capacity of the HMC, the system can contain multiple sets of rules, which could allow for a rule tree to be updated without impacting performance. This is left as another avenue for potential future work.

As a final discussion, we believe our work demonstrates the potential of high-speed off-chip memory technologies, specifically in implementing fast hardware solutions for applications restricted by the available on-chip memory on FPGAs. Off-chip technologies need increased bandwidth to serve as effective on-chip memory replacements. The HMC technology helped accomplish this for our work, but further bandwidth increases are still needed (as evidenced by our system's poor latency performance). HBM memories may be one potential solution: Altera has announced that upcoming Stratix 10 MX devices will integrate up to four HBM2 tiles in-package with the FPGA, providing up to 1 TB/s of memory bandwidth [14]. Note however, that increased bandwidth can also strain the FPGA routing fabric, as it did in our tests with the HMC system. Using high bandwidth interfaces (all dedicated towards a single application)

on current routing resources is difficult and more care must be taken in designing hardware capable of distributing wide memory response signals across the FPGA. Providing some sort of infrastructure (possibly hardened) to augment the routing resources to distribute these high bandwidth signals would be a worthwhile FPGA architecture exploration, especially given how the available bandwidth already exceeds what is achieved in this work and is only increasing in the future. Multi-channel hardened memory controllers and perhaps hardened NoCs seem like worthwhile explorations.

7. ACKNOWLEDGMENTS

We would like to thank Micron and Pico Computing for the hardware donations provided for this work. Furthermore, we acknowledge Xilinx, NSERC, and the OFR CVST project for the funding and material provided for this project.

8. REFERENCES

[1] J. Thomas Pawlowski. Hybrid Memory Cube (HMC). In *HotChips 23*, Palo Alto, CA., August 2011.

[2] Richard E. Smith. *Elementary Information Security*. Jones & Bartlett Learning, 2015.

[3] Steven McCanne and Van Jacobson. The BSD Packet Filter: A New Architecture for User-level Packet Capture. In *USENIX winter*, volume 46, San Diego, CA., January 1993.

[4] *Berkeley Packet Filter (BPF) syntax*. http://biot.com/capstats/bpf.html.

[5] *OpenFlow Switch Specification version 1.1.0*, February 2011. http://archive.openflow.org/documents/openflow-spec-v1.1.0.pdf.

[6] Jad Naous, David Erickson, G. Adam Covington, Guido Appenzeller, and Nick McKeown. Implementing an OpenFlow Switch on the NetFPGA platform. In *ANCS '08*, San Jose, CA., November 2008.

[7] Weirong Jiang and Viktor K. Prasanna. Scalable Packet Classification on FPGA. *IEEE Transactions on VLSI Systems*, 20(9):1668–1680, Sept 2012.

[8] Yun R. Qu and Viktor K. Prasanna. High Performance and Dynamically Updatable Packet Classification Engine on FPGA. *IEEE Transactions on Parallel and Distributed Systems*, 27(1):197–209, January 2016.

[9] David E Taylor. Survey and taxonomy of packet classification techniques. *ACM Computing Surveys (CSUR)*, 37(3):238–275, September 2005.

[10] Naga Katta, Omid Alipourfard, Jennifer Rexford, and David Walker. Rule-Caching Algorithms for Software-Defined Networks. 2014.

[11] Micron. Hybrid Memory Cube (HMC) Controller IP. www.picocomputing.com/hybrid-memory-cube-hmc-controller-ip/.

[12] Micron. AC-510 UltraScale-based SuperProcessor with Hybrid Memory Cube. www.picocomputing.com/ac-510-superprocessor-module/.

[13] Micron. The Pico Computing Framework – the Ghost in the Machine. www.picocomputing.com/products/framework/.

[14] Manish Deo, Jeffrey Schulz, and Lance Brown. Stratix 10 MX Devices Solve the Memory Bandwidth Challenge. Technical Report WP-01264-1.0, Altera, May 2016.

Boosting the Performance of FPGA-based Graph Processor using Hybrid Memory Cube: A Case for Breadth First Search

Jialiang Zhang, Soroosh Khoram and Jing Li

Department of Electrical and Computer Engineering
University of Wisconsin-Madison

jialiang.zhang@ece.wisc.edu, khoram@wisc.edu, jli@ece.wisc.edu

Abstract

Large graph processing has gained great attention in recent years due to its broad applicability from machine learning to social science. Large real-world graphs, however, are inherently difficult to process efficiently, not only due to their large memory footprint, but also that most graph algorithms entail memory access patterns with poor locality and a low compute-to-memory access ratio. In this work, we leverage the exceptional random access performance of emerging Hybrid Memory Cube (HMC) technology that stacks multiple DRAM dies on top of a logic layer, combined with the flexibility and efficiency of FPGA to address these challenges.

To our best knowledge, this is the first work that implements a graph processing system on a FPGA-HMC platform based on software/hardware co-design and co-optimization. We first present the modifications of algorithm and a platform-aware graph processing architecture to perform level-synchronized breadth first search (BFS) on FPGA-HMC platform. To gain better insights into the potential bottlenecks of proposed implementation, we develop an analytical performance model to quantitatively evaluate the HMC access latency and corresponding BFS performance. Based on the analysis, we propose a two-level bitmap scheme to further reduce memory access and perform optimization on key design parameters (e.g. memory access granularity). Finally, we evaluate the performance of our BFS implementation using the AC-510 development kit from Micron. We achieved 166 million edges traversed per second (MTEPS) using GRAPH500 benchmark on a random graph with a scale of 25 and an edge factor of 16, which significantly outperforms CPU and other FPGA-based large graph processors.

1. INTRODUCTION

The explosion of data poses new challenges to emerging data-intensive workloads ranging from social network analysis to bioinformatics and neural networks. Large sparse graph, which usually contains millions of vertices and billions of edges, is one common data representation in these applications. Among all graph algorithms, breadth first search (BFS) is the most widely used one that serves as a basis of many other more complex algorithms. For instance, BFS is a key kernel in GRAPH500 [1], which is a widely used benchmark suite to measure the performance of super computers for data-intensive applications.

In traditional CPU-DRAM systems, efficient parallel large graph processing is challenging. Due to the *random* and *data-dependent* memory access pattern requirement of large graph workloads, it is difficult to exploit spatial or temporal locality in on-chip cache. As a result, the system performance is typically bounded by the throughput of external DRAM. However, traditional DDR DRAM suffers from poor random access performance due to the lack of memory level parallelism [2]. To make the situation worse, the high data transfer cost between DRAM and CPU makes it more challenging to parallelize large graph workloads efficiently on such systems, as the synchronization and locking between parallel kernels have become key performance bottlenecks [3].

To address the issues in traditional systems, in recent years, FPGA has been increasingly popular in accelerating graph workloads due to its flexibility, high performance and energy efficiency. Many existing works [4–6] have proposed different architectures to implement BFS on FPGA but are all based on one common scheme. By placing some key data – those used for synchronization between parallel kernels – on the on-chip block ram (BRAM) to alleviate the pressure on accessing external DRAM, the efficiency of processing sparse graph can be significantly improved. However, this scheme does not scale well with large graphs, as the on-chip storage capacity of FPGA is still very limited. As a consequence, these solutions unavoidably suffer from the DRAM bottleneck once the key data of a graph is too large to be fit in the FPGA's on-chip storage.

In this work, we propose a new scheme based on software/hardware co-design and co-optimization, to address the inefficiency of current BFS implementation on FPGA. It effectively combines the emerging hybrid memory cube (HMC) technology, which stacks multiple DRAM dies on top of a base logic layer, with FPGA to effectively accelerate large scale parallel graph workloads. HMC has much better random access performance than traditional DDR DRAM, due to its higher memory-level parallelism [2]. The parallelism mainly comes from two-folds: 1) bank level parallelism: It has a much smaller bank size compared to traditional DRAM, and therefore can fit more banks in a single chip. 2) vault level parallelism: The 3D stacking structure provides additional coarser-grained parallelism at the vault level, as will be explained in section 2.1. Furthermore, HMC supports near-memory operations, such as read-modify-write, locking, *etc.*, on the base logic layer. With all these properties, HMC provides a great opportunity for improving the efficiency of parallel BFS implementation despite of the limitation of FPGA's on-chip BRAM capacity. To leverage HMC's high memory level parallelism and near-memory operation, we propose an improved BFS implementation by taking full advantage of the HMC-FPGA platform, which includes modifications to the BFS algorithm and development of a platform-aware graph processing

FPGA '17, February 22-24, 2017, Monterey, CA, USA

© 2017 ACM. ISBN 978-1-4503-4354-1/17/02. . . $15.00

DOI: http://dx.doi.org/10.1145/3020078.3021737

architecture. More specifically, we need to change the original BFS execution flow and the data structure to enable the use of near memory operation, as will be explained in section 3.1. Also, by leveraging the parallel processing capability of FPGA-HMC platform, we introduce a Map-Reduce-like framework and present its FPGA implementation in section 3.2.

To achieve an optimal design, we further explore the design space of the FPGA-HMC based graph processing system through theoretical analysis and real hardware experiments. We use GRAPH500 [1] (i.e. BFS algorithm) as the benchmark to evaluate the performance and develop an analytical model to help us identify the potential performance bottlenecks as well as choosing the optimal design parameters. Based on the analysis results, we further propose to use a two-level bitmap to reduce the unnecessary HMC access. Finally, we perform both simulation and practical hardware implementation to validate our design choices.

The key contributions are summarized as follows:

- We develop a graph processing system based on software/hardware co-design and co-optimization, which comprises software modifications of level-synchronized BFS and a platform-aware graph processing architecture, to fully exploit the potential of FPGA and HMC.

- We propose an analytical performance model for our FPGA-HMC based BFS implementation. We then apply the model to perform an in-depth analysis on performance bottlenecks of the design.

- To address the bottlenecks, we propose a two-level bitmap scheme that effectively reduces the unnecessary HMC access to achieve high performance. We further apply our analytical model to perform efficient design space exploration for key design parameter optimization.

- We conduct experiments to verify the effectiveness of proposed techniques. Our implementation achieves $3\times$ performance improvement compared to CPU and outperforms other FPGA based graph processing system.

The rest of the paper is organized as follows. Section 2 presents the background of Hybrid Memory Cube (HMC) and Breadth First Search (BFS). In Section 3, we present the software design and the system architecture of our FPGA-HMC based graph processing system. In Section 4, we present an analytical performance model and apply it to analyze the performance bottlenecks. In Section 5, we present the design, performance analysis and the implementation of proposed two-level bitmap. Section 6 presents the experimental results and validates the proposed techniques. Section 6 concludes the paper.

2. BACKGROUND

In this section, we first provide an overview of the emerging Hybrid Memory Cube (HMC) technology. We analyze its structure and unique properties compared with the traditional DRAM. Then we present the background of breadth first search (BFS) and its parallel implementation.

2.1 Hybrid Memory Cube

HMC is an emerging memory module that stacks multiple DRAM dies on top of a CMOS layer to form a cube using through-silicon-via (TSV) technology. The word "hybrid" describes the fact that HMC combines both memory and logic dies into a single stack.

The architecture of HMC is optimized for parallel memory access. Each DRAM layer is divided into multiple partitions, and

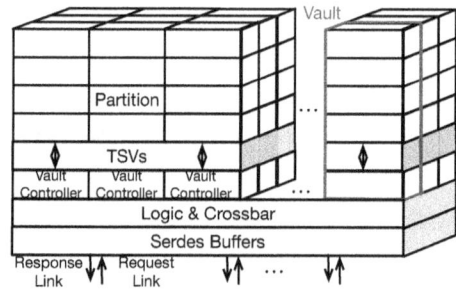

Figure 1: Architecture of Hybrid Memory Cube (HMC) [7]

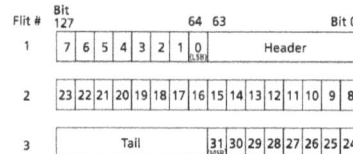

Figure 2: Example of FLIT with 32 Bytes payload

each partition comprises several memory banks. As shown in Figure 1, a vertically connected stack containing multiple partitions from different DRAM layers is called a *vault*. Moreover, each vault also contains a corresponding partition in the logic base layer, which serves as a vault controller. The vault controller manages the DRAM banks within the vault, and thus eliminates the need of off-chip memory controller in traditional DRAM module. Therefore, a HMC *vault* is analogous to the notion of a *channel* in traditional DRAM-based memory system, as it contains all components of a DRAM channel: a memory controller, several memory ranks (*partition*), and a bi-directional bus. We can therefore view HMC as a device that integrates the traditional multi-channel DRAMs into a single chip. In Table 1, we compare a 4 channel 8GB DDR DRAM memory system with a 8GB HMC. From the comparison, we show that HMC has highly fine-grained bank partitions which can be used to serve a large number of concurrent memory requests. Therefore, it offers much higher memory-level parallelism than traditional DRAM. More importantly, the page size of the HMC is only 16B, making it very suitable for random access and alleviates the over-fetch problem in traditional DRAM caused by large page size (several KB) [2]. Moreover, HMC provides an out-of-order memory access to fully exploit internal bank level and vault level parallelism. In general, HMC is expected to provide higher performance compared to traditional DRAM, especially for workloads with a large number of random accesses.

Table 1: Comparison of 8GB DDR4-2133 memory and HMC

	DDR4-2133	HMC
Total Capacity	8GB	8GB
No. of Vault (Rank)	2	32
No. Bank	256,128,64	512
Bank Capacity	32,64,128 MB	16 MB
Page size	1, 2 kB	16 B
Link Speed	19.2GB/s	up to 240GB/s

As shown in Figure 1, vault memory controllers are connected to a high-speed interface communicating with other HMCs or host devices (*e.g.* CPU, GPU, FPGA) via a crossbar switch. The high-speed interface consists of a serialized physical layer and a packetized transaction layer. The physical layer has several links, which can be used to connect to the different hosts. Each link consists of several lanes with a data rate typically higher than 10Gbps per lane. Different from the bi-directional bus of traditional DDR memory interface, the high-speed serial lane transmits data in both directions, which makes the HMC links *full-duplex*. HMC also incorporates a packetized transaction layer that differs from traditional

DDR interface but is similar to PCIe interface. Since the serial interface does not separate data bus from address bus, HMC includes the memory command, address and other information (*e.g.* tag) in the packet header, called "FLIT" (FLow unIT). As shown in Figure 2, FLIT is the smallest unit of data transmission on the high-speed interface. Each transaction may consist of several FLITs depending on the link granularity (ranging from 16 bytes to 128 bytes). *Choosing the size of data payload has significant impact on the performance of HMC.* In Section 4 , we will present the methodology for choosing an optimal data payload size.

32B:	33	3231	1312	109	54	43	0
	Ignored	DRAM[19:1]	Bank[2:0]	Vault[4:0]	DRAM[0]=Byte[4]	Byte[3:0]	

64B:	33	3231	1413	1110	65	43	0
	Ignored	DRAM[19:2]	Bank[2:0]	Vault[4:0]	DRAM[1:0]=Byte[5:4]	Byte[3:0]	

128B:	33	3231	1514	1211	76	43	0
	Ignored	DRAM[19:3]	Bank[2:0]	Vault[4:0]	DRAM[2:0]=Byte[6:4]	Byte[3:0]	

Figure 3: HMC address mapping scheme of 32B, 64B, 128B memory address granularity

Besides link granularity, HMC also has a configurable memory address granularity. As shown in Figure 3, the HMC uses an address field of 34 bits for internal memory addressing, which contains *vault* address, *bank* address, DRAM row and column address (within a bank) and byte address. For different memory access patterns, HMC provides four memory address modes with different granularities (16 bytes, 32 bytes, 64 bytes, 128 bytes). We can obtain different address mapping scheme by changing the size of byte address, which is the maximum payload size for a link packet, as each link packet can only access one vault. With the configurable memory address granularity, we can achieve different trade-offs between latency and throughput by distributing the memory access to different vaults or coalescing the memory access to one vault. In section 4, we will show how to obtain the optimal memory address granularity.

The base logic layer of HMC opens up opportunities for near-data computing. The HMC standard defines several locking and read-modify-write commands which are preferred to be executed by logic units near memory instead of host CPU. Although the idea of near data computing is not new, HMC is the first commercial device to practically implement the concept. In section 3, we will present software modifications to exploit near data operations to improve performance.

2.2 Breadth First Search

Breadth First Search (BFS) is a widely used graph traversal algorithm in broad applications ranging from data analysis in social networks [8] to routing optimization in Electronic Design Automation [9]. In this section, we formally define the BFS problem and its objective. These definitions will be referred to in later sections to analyze and optimize its implementation.

Assuming an unweighted graph G with vertex set V and edge set E, BFS finds a path from a source vertex $v_s \in V$ to all the other vertices in the graph G. In the output, for each vertex $v \in V$, BFS will produce a level value l, indicating its distance from v_s (v can be accessed from v_s by traveling through $l-1$ edges), and its father vertex id $f \in V$, indicating the vertex on the path to v which is the direct ancestor of v (naturally $(f, v) \in E$).

BFS traverses a graph by processing all vertices with the same distance from the source vertex iteratively. We define a *frontier* as the set of vertices which have the same distance from the source. We denote the latest known frontier as *current frontier*, and unknown frontier that will be generated based on current frontier as the next frontier in this iterative process.

A detailed description of level-synchronized BFS has been depicted in Algorithm 1. The *level* and *parent* are arrays that store the level and father information for all traversed vertices. Initially, all values in *level* and *father* arrays are set to 0 and -1 respectively. At the beginning of the algorithm (line 2-3), $level[v_s]$ and $father[v_s]$ are set to 1 and $NULL$ because v_s is added to the current frontier (line 4). Then, *current_level*, which holds the level number currently being processed, is set to 1 (line 5). During the iterative process (i.e. the while loop), at each level, for every vertex v in the *current frontier*, all unvisited neighbors of v (n) are added to next frontier (*next frontier* $\leftarrow$ n). Whether a neighbor has been visited or not is determined by checking if its level is non-zero (line 11). The *level* and *father* for these neighbor vertices are set to results calculated from *current_level* and the corresponding vertex in *current frontier*, v (line 12, 13). At the end of the iteration, the value of *current_level* is incremented, and *current frontier* and *next frontier* are swapped. The algorithm will not be terminated if the *current frontier* is not empty, which means there are still unvisited vertices in the graph. In a multi-thread context, threads that finish the traversal of their portions of the current frontier first should not further proceed until all threads finish the processing of the current frontier for synchronization purpose. Therefore, this algorithm is also called *level-synchronized BFS*.

Algorithm 1 Level-synchronized BFS

1: **procedure** BFS
2:      $level[v_s] = 1$
3:      $parent[v_s] = NULL$
4:      $current\ frontier \leftarrow v_s$
5:      $current\_level = 1$
6:      **while** $current\ frontier$ not empty **do**
7:          **for** $v \in current\ frontier$ **do**
8:              $current\ frontier = current\ frontier - v$
9:              $E_v = \{n \in V | (v, n) \in E\}$
10:              **for** $n \in E_v$ **do**
11:                  **if** $level[n]$ is 0 **then**
12:                     $level[n] = current\_level + 1$
13:                     $parent[n] = v$
14:                     $next\ frontier \leftarrow n$
15:          $current\_level = current\_level + 1$
16:          $Swap\ current\ frontier\ with\ next\ frontier$
---

3. BFS IMPLEMENTATION ON HMC-FPGA PLATFORM

In this section, we present our BFS implementation tailored to a system consisting of a FPGA and a HMC. We first describe the software design of the level-synchronized BFS that leverages the advantages of HMC. Then, we present the design details of our FPGA implementation using a Map-Reduce-like framework. Note that as there is no prior effort to implement BFS on FPGA-HMC platform, we will use this implementation as a baseline and compare it with an optimized design in Section 5.

3.1 Software Implementation

To best implement BFS on FPGA-HMC platform, it is important to carefully choose a design that best matches algorithmic behaviors with the available hardware resources to maximize performance and energy efficiency. Furthermore, the design needs to be scalable to accommodate real-world graphs at extremely large scales. Considering all these factors, we implement the following data structures and software execution flow, based on the unique characteristics of the BFS algorithm and hardware resources provided by our FPGA-HMC platform.

3.1.1 Data Structures

BFS requires different data structures for representing the graph, maintaining the intermediate meta data for frontiers, and storing the final results. Here, we describe these data structures, the reasons for choosing them, and how our BFS implementation uses them.

There are generally three types of data structures that are required for BFS algorithm: 1) an adjacency list, which is used to store the graph structure 2) two bitmaps that are used for bookkeeping the information of the current and the next frontiers 3) two arrays, which are required to store the level and parent information for all vertices. The adjacency list representation of a small graph has been depicted in Figure 4. In this data structure, a large adjacency array is allocated to store indices of neighboring vertices for each vertex in the graph back to back. In the vertex array, each slot stands for a vertex in the graph, and stores a pointer to the beginning of its neighbors in the adjacency array. Through this data structure, all neighbors of any random vertex can be easily accessed with one level of indirection. Overall, in case of a directed (or an undirected) graph with $|V|$ vertices and $|E|$ edges, adjacency list requires storage of $|V| + 1$ values in the pointers array and $|E|$ ($2|E|$ in case of an undirected graph) values in the adjacency array. This data structure provides a good balance between data compactness and random access speed.

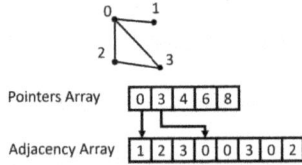

Figure 4: Adjacency list representation of a graph

Bitmaps are used to bookkeep the information for frontiers. A bitmap is an array containing $|V|$ bits, each of which indicates whether the corresponding vertex has been visited or not. To add a vertex to the frontier, we simply set its corresponding bit in the bitmap to 1. As shown in Algorithm 1, we only allocate two arrays to store the current frontier and the next frontier, respectively. At the end of each BFS iteration, we clear all bits in the bitmap of current frontier, and then use the bitmap of the next frontier as the new current frontier to start a new iteration (i.e. the role of the two bitmaps are swapped every time at the end of the iteration). We will theoretically analyze the performance of this process in Section 4.

3.1.2 BFS Execution Flow

The adjacency list, bitmaps, and two result arrays are all stored in the storage unit and are loaded into the processing unit for computation when needed. Based on the data structures defined, the data flow of Algorithm 1 can be implemented in hardware, as depicted in Figure 5. Within each iteration of the BFS algorithm (processing of one frontier), part of the bitmap for current frontier is loaded into the processing unit. For each marked vertex in the current frontier, its corresponding neighbors are marked in the bitmap for the next frontier.

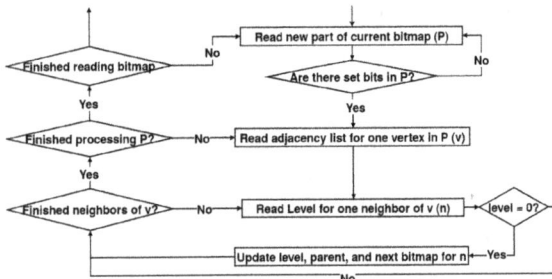

Figure 5: Flow of one iteration (level) of BFS

During the execution, BFS frequently accesses scattered locations in compact arrays stored in the HMC. This is an ideal case for us to fully exploit HMC's low random access latency and high parallelism. In addition to the significantly improved random access latency, HMC also provides native bit-level atomic updates, which is especially useful when updating the bitmap for the next frontier. Normally, updating the bitmap requires a reading of several bytes from main memory, an operation of bit updates in the processing element (set few bits to 1), and a writing back operation. Frequent bitmap modifications not only induce more traffic on the memory bus, but also are likely to result in frequent stalls when other processing elements are accessing the same address. With HMC, these unnecessary round-trip traffics can simply be avoided to save the memory bandwidth. Furthermore, by offloading the atomic operation to the HMC, the chance of stalls are considerably reduced.

3.2 FPGA-HMC based Graph Processor

In this subsection, we first introduce a Map-Reduce-like Framework to leverage the advantage of FPGA-HMC platform. Then, we present the implementation detail of proposed FPGA-HMC graph processor.

3.2.1 Map-Reduce-like Framework

Selecting a suitable execution framework is of great importance for an efficient hardware implementation. For BFS, this execution framework should be able to effectively manage irregular memory access patterns without much penalty. Additionally, as each part of the bitmap (frontier) can be processed independently in the level synchronized BFS, the framework should also be efficient in handling parallel tasks.

Based on the needs stated above, the Map-Reduce execution model is one ideal choice that well fits these descriptions. In this model, a task is divided into two phases – Mapping and Reduction. Mappers process a partition of the input data independently through a parallel streaming process. The output from mappers are then passed to reducers that produce the final results. This framework naturally offers a good degree of parallelism, making it possible to exploit random access capability of HMC by generating enough sporadic memory accesses.

Algorithm 2 depicts the Map-Reduce version of BFS. At the mapping stage, each mapper reads a partition of the bitmap, extracts the current frontier, and reads the adjacency list for these vertices. The reducers then read the level array for each neighbor, update parent and level arrays for previously unvisited vertices, and mark them by updating the bitmap for the next frontier. In the next subsection, we will convert these mappers and reducers into pipeline stages implemented on FPGA-HMC platform.

Algorithm 2 MapReduce BFS

1: **procedure** MAP(current_frontier[u:v])
2:     **for** $i = u : v$ **do**
3:         **if** $current\_frontier[i]$ **then**
4:             **for** $j = vertices[v] : vertices[v+1]$ **do**
5:                 $Emit\ (i, neighbors[j])$
6: **procedure** REDUCE$((i, [n_1, n_2, ...]))$
7:     **for** $j \in [n_1, n_2, ...]$ **do**
8:         **if** $level[j]$ *is* 0 **then**
9:             $level[j] = current\_level + 1$
10:             $parent[j] = i$
11:             $next\_frontier[j] = 1$

3.2.2 Platform-aware BFS Implementation

As discussed in Section 3.2.1, we propose a Map-Reduce-like Framework to leverage the capabilities of parallel execution and

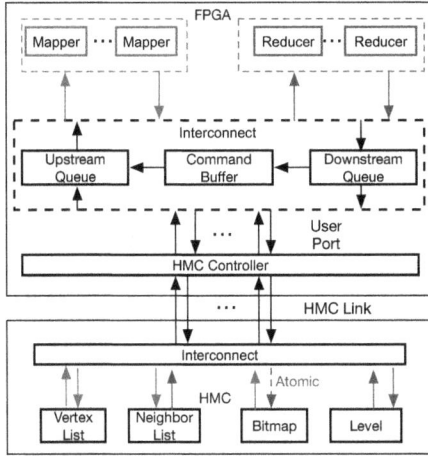

Figure 6: System diagram of FPGA-HMC based BFS implementation

the built-in atomic operation of HMC and the flexibility of FPGA. In this subsection, we will present the FPGA-HMC based BFS implementation that will be used as the basis of the analysis in Section 4. As shown in Figure 6, all mappers and reducers share the HMC Controller and HMC link via an interconnect which comprises a downstream queue, an upstream queue and a command buffer. The HMC controller is used to convert the high speed HMC link traffic into low speed user traffic. For example, a half-width HMC link (x8) will have 5 corresponding user ports, each of which could accept one downstream (to HMC) request packet and send one upstream (from HMC) response packet in one cycle. To fully utilize the bandwidth of HMC, we replicate the mapper and reducer by the same number of user ports to saturate the port resources. As there are more kernels than user ports inside the HMC controller, we add memory access queues between the BFS kernels and the HMC controller to buffer the requests that can not be served immediately. If the queue is full, the BFS kernels corresponding to the queue are stalled. In addition to memory queues, we further add a command buffer between the downstream queue and upstream buffer to log the destination of each HMC request, which decouples different kernel stages. For each HMC read request, the user needs to assign a tag to each request, which is used to keep track of the out-of-order HMC responses. The command buffer logs the tags and destination kernels of the memory accesses when sending HMC read requests, and forwards the HMC read responses to the corresponding kernels based on returned tags.

At the beginning of executing BFS, the bitmap will be reset except that the bit corresponding to the starting vertex will be set. At each cycle, the interconnect will first push the HMC access request from the mappers and reducers into the downstream queue and check 1) if HMC controller is ready to receive data, and 2) the availability of tag for HMC read request. When both conditions are satisfied, the TX interconnects will pass the memory requests to the HMC controller and store the destination in the command buffer using the tag as the effective address. Meanwhile, the interconnects will also check if there are incoming HMC responses generated at the HMC controller. If so, it will fetch the response using the tag and forward the returned data to the next destination. We will present more detailed design of mapper and reducer in section 5.3.

4. DEEPER INSIGHTS FOR PARALLEL BFS PERFORMANCE

Although we presented the data structures and execution flow of

BFS that can maximize the utilization of HMC in Section 3, there are still numerous design parameters and detailed design choices that cannot be easily determined by merely examining the general characteristics of the hardware. To that end, we propose an analytical performance model and will use this model to analyze the performance of our BFS design and identify optimization opportunities.

4.1 Analytical Performance Model

As BFS is a memory-heavy algorithm (as opposed to computation-heavy), the performance of the system is generally determined by memory performance. We thus first focus our attention on modeling the memory system. In the process of developing the model, our desire is to most accurately predict the performance of HMC by capturing its unique characteristics while avoiding too much complexity. Therefore, We derive the model based on a set of observations from the HMC architecture:

1. Packets are serialized through the IO. That means at each time stamp, the IO link between the HMC and the processing unit is occupied by only one packet. The duration for which the link is occupied is proportional to the size of the packet including the data being transferred, the header, and the tail.

2. The latency of processing a packet after it was received (the internal delay) by the HMC comprises a constant delay of processing the packet header in addition to internal data transfer delay which is proportional to data size.

3. The internal delay when multiple packets are serially received by the HMC, changes depending on whether these packets access different vaults or the same vault. Naturally, parallel access to different vaults result in less latency compared to accesses with vault conflicts.

Based on these guidelines, we propose the following model for processing a single access and then extend this model to encompass more complicated situations. Equation 1 shows the latency for a read and a write operation of g bytes. In this equation, g is the packet data size, H is the packet overhead including header and tail, b and B are internal and IO bandwidths in $Bytes/s$ respectively, and t_C is the constant header processing delay. In case of a read operation, we need to account for both a request packet as well as a response packet. The request consists of only a header and a tail which takes an additional delay of $\frac{H}{B}$ to travel through the link, resulting in a difference between read and write latencies.

$$t_r = \frac{g}{b} + \frac{g + 2H}{B} + t_C, \quad t_w = \frac{g}{b} + \frac{g + H}{B} + t_C \quad (1)$$

To model multiple accesses, we first consider two cases for n consecutive accesses with completely different access patterns. In the first case, all accesses are directed to the same vault. The resulting vault conflicts produce proportionally longer internal data transfer delay. On the other hand, the constant delay is hidden by overlapping processing requests. As a result, the read delay can be represented by:

$$t_r = n\frac{g}{b} + n\frac{g + 2H}{B} + t_C \quad (2)$$

On the other end of the spectrum, all n accesses are directed to different vaults. In this case, packets are processed in parallel inside the HMC. Therefore, the read latency would be:

$$t_r = \frac{g}{b} + n\frac{g + 2H}{B} + t_C \quad (3)$$

Based on these equations, we can now present the latency for a general case where vault conflict happens but, at the same time, some accesses can be processed in parallel as well. The read and write latencies with such access pattern would be:

$$t_r = \alpha \frac{g}{b} + n\frac{g+2H}{B} + t_C, \quad t_w = \alpha \frac{g}{b} + n\frac{g+H}{B} + t_C \quad (4)$$

where α ($1 \le \alpha \le n$) represents the maximum number of vault conflicts and is inversely proportional to the number of parallel accesses.

4.2 Performance Analysis

In this section, we analyze performance of BFS by estimating its execution latency using the HMC model we developed in the previous section. Note that although we only apply it to BFS in this work, the model is generically applicable to other algorithms.

Since BFS is memory bound, we can safely assume the total latency to be that of read and write operations of HMC. For this analysis, we only derive the results for bitmap operations (scanning current bitmap and updating next bitmap). A similar approach can be used to derive estimations for other portions of runtime, but results from bitmap operations accurately represent the scaling trends of the runtime and effectively help us identify performance bottlenecks and make design decisions.

Table 2 presents the terminology used in this analysis. As this table shows, these terms are closely related. More specifically, for a connected graph, the following equations hold.

$$\sum_{l=1}^{L} Q_l = V, \quad \sum_{i=1}^{V} q_{il} = Q_{l+1}, \quad \sum_{i=1}^{V} S_{il} = Q_l \quad (5)$$

Table 2: Analysis terminology

Term	Definition
V	Number of vertices
L	Maximum number of levels for which BFS operates
Q_l	Number of set bits in $currFront$ at the beginig of level l
q_{il}	Number of neighbors vertex i visits in level l
S_{il}	Whether vertex i was visited in level $l-1$. $S_{il} : \{0,1\}$

For convenience, we assume $Q_{V+1} = 0$, which means $\sum_{l=1}^{L} Q_{l+1} = V - 1$ (since $Q_1 = 1$). Also, for level 1 we have:

$$S_{v,1} = \begin{cases} 1, & v = v_s \\ 0, & Otherwise \end{cases} \quad (6)$$

We present our analysis in two parts. First, we analyze latency of reading bitmap for current level (current bitmap) and estimate the total amount of time spent on reading this array through the execution of BFS. Then, we do the same for updating the next frontier (the next bitmap). Although it is likely that this method results in overestimation of runtime by ignoring some overlappings of operations, it simplifies our analysis and provides a better picture of performance bottlenecks and improvement opportunities.

Reading Current Bitmap: Since the current bitmap is stored in the HMC and, for large graphs, is too large to read all at once, it has to be read in multiple partitions. We assume the number of partitions to be m and reading each partition is done by issuing several memory requests. Since we decide the order in which current bitmap is scanned, we can guarantee that requests issued to read a partition have maximum parallelism. We model this operation by k sets of n completely parallel read requests (in total we issue mkn read requests and read $D = mkng$ bytes of data). With this model, we can estimate the runtime for scanning current bitmap in level l to be:

$$\begin{aligned} T_{scan_l} &= m(k\frac{g}{b} + kn\frac{g+2H}{B} + t_C) \\ &= D\Big[\frac{1}{nb} + \frac{1}{B} + \frac{1}{g}\Big[\frac{2H}{B} + \frac{t_C}{kn}\Big]\Big] \end{aligned} \quad (7)$$

Here, D is determined by the graph size, n is determined by the number of vaults, and k is determined by the available on-chip

BRAM. For a large graph, D is going to be large while n and k are limited by available resources. Therefore, since the scan latency is proportional to D, reading the bitmap is going to be a bottleneck of the performance if the graph is large. We will later introduce the two level bitmap to address this issue in Section 5.

We can also see from this analysis that larger values of k and g (generating more read requests with larger granularity) can reduce latency. In the case of read granularity, this is due to the read overhead which is comparatively reduced for larger requests. Increasing k reduces the execution time as well by increasing the overlap between handling requests and hiding the constant request processing latency.

Writing to Next Bitmap: As shown in line 12 in Algorithm 1, when traversing edges from a visited vertex v, its newly visited neighboring vertex n has its corresponding bit in the next bitmap set. This operation is done for all neighbors using the native atomic operation of HMC. Similar to a write request, the atomic operation does not require a response. We can estimate the latency for updating bitmap for neighbors of v ($T_{wb_{vl}}$), time spent on writing to bitmap in level l (T_{wb_l}), and the total time spent on writing to bitmap as (T_{wb}).

$$T_{wb_{vl}} = \alpha S_{vl} \frac{g}{b} + q_{vl}\frac{g+H}{B} + S_{vl}t_C$$

$$\Rightarrow T_{wb_l} = \sum_{v=1}^{V} T_{wb_{vl}} = \alpha Q_l \frac{g}{b} + Q_{l+1}\frac{g+H}{B} + Q_l t_c \quad (8)$$

$$\Rightarrow T_{wb} = \sum_{l=1}^{L} T_{wb_l} = \alpha V \frac{g}{b} + (V-1)\frac{g+H}{B} + V t_c$$

This latency is dependent on g (the granularity of atomic writes), α (the average amount of access parallelism when writing to the bitmap), and V (the number of vertices). This result has a complexity of $O(V)$, which matches our expectation that this operation dominates the overall performance, as BFS in general has a complexity of $O(V+E)$ and the complexity becomes $O(V)$ for sparse graphs. In addition, since for atomic writes, g is fixed by the HMC architecture and V is a constant, the latency of this step is determined only by the amount of available write parallelism. Due to the random and data-dependent nature of memory accesses in BFS, the implementation can not adaptively change the amount of parallelism based on memory access patterns. However, it can be optimized using preprocessing with an intelligent strategy for storing the graph. We plan to investigate this optimization method in future works.

Insights from the Analyses: Using this analytical performance model, we identified the performance bottlenecks and improvement opportunities for bit-level operations of BFS. We also applied the same method to other operations performed in BFS and conducted similar analysis which generally confirms the findings from analyzing the bitmap portion of BFS. Therefore, we only discuss the results here without presenting more details.

The analysis shows how read and write granularity of accesses affects the runtime. Best read performance for reading bitmap, vertex, and adjacency analysis is achieved when larger read granularity is used. Conversely, write operations favor smaller granularity of accesses. That is because their low locality results in low access efficiency. The only exception happens when reading the level array to check whether a vertex was previously visited. Since this read also has low locality, it should be accessed with small granularity.

Another major bottleneck we identified is the scanning the bitmap during the time when the whole bitmap is read from the HMC. Usually in this data transfer process, as the graph is sparse, only a small part of it contains useful information. This problem can be addressed by using prior knowledge about the parts of the bitmap that will be used to look for the frontier information. In Section 5, we will present a scheme to implement this optimization.

5. OPTIMIZATION SCHEME

As discussed in Section 4, the bitmap scanning becomes the bottleneck of FPGA-HMC based BFS implementation. In this section, we propose a two-level bitmap design to eliminate unnecessary HMC accesses by leveraging the sparsity of the graph. We first present the idea of the two-level bitmap, and then find the optimal bitmap granularity using the analytical model. Finally, we will present the implementation of the two-level bitmap on the hardware.

5.1 Two-level Bitmap

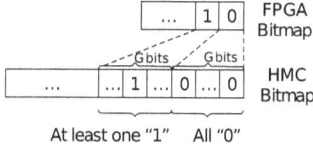

Figure 7: Illustration of two-level bitmap

In Section 4.2, it was shown that the scanning of the bitmap for current frontier creates a bottleneck for our BFS implementation. One important observation is that the bitmap is typically sparse (with regards to the placement of 1's in the whole array), resulting in a considerable amount of unnecessary data movement. Based on this observation, it is possible to take advantage of this sparsity with one level of indirection.

As shown in Figure 7, we propose a two-level bitmap scheme comprising a coarse-grained first level bitmap stored in the block ram (BRAM) on FPGA in conjunction with the fine-grained second level bitmap that we used in the baseline design. In this scheme, a block of G adjacent bits in the second level bitmap, called a range, are represented by one bit in the first level bitmap. A bit in the first level bitmap is set as long as one of the bits in the corresponding range of the second level bitmap is non-zero (each bit in the first level bitmap is the logic OR of its corresponding range in the second level bitmap). In this way, the first level bitmap can filter out reads to the second level bitmap when the bit in the first level bitmap is not set.

5.2 Bitmap Mapping Granularity

The performance of the two-level bitmap design depends on the granularity of the first level bitmap as well as the structure of the specific graph being analyzed. A more fine-grained first level bitmap provides more information about the second level bitmap, but with the trade-off of increased size. Therefore, it is important to find the lower bound for the size of on-chip bitmap that is necessary to deliver good performance. This lower bound depends on the actual structures of different graphs. A graph with fewer number of levels (higher average edges per vertex) will have less sparsity in its bitmap, resulting in a smaller lower bound. On the other hand, for a graph with a larger number of vertices and a larger off-chip bitmap, this bound should be larger. We will analytically determine this bound in a way that the performance of scanning bitmap in the two-level design is, on average, sufficiently higher than the single-level design.

To evaluate the performance improvement of the proposed two-level bitmap, we can apply the same analytical method we used in the previous section to this design. We assume the length of on-chip and off-chip bitmaps to be L_1 and L_2 bits respectively. This means that each bit in first level bitmap corresponds to $G = \frac{L_2}{L_1}$ adjacent bits in the second level bitmap. Each range, therefore,

requires $k' = \frac{L_2}{8g'L_1}$ read operations, where g' is the granularity of reads in the two-level bitmap scheme.

To estimate the time spent on reading all required bitmap ranges from the HMC in one iteration of BFS, we make two assumptions. First, we have enough on-chip BRAM to store a complete off-chip bitmap range. Second, in iteration l, there are M_l set bits in the first level bitmap. In other words, M_l bitmap ranges need to be read from the HMC. Based on these assumptions, T_{scan_l} can be estimated as follows.

$$T_{scan_l} = M_l(k'\frac{g'}{b} + k'\frac{g' + 2H}{B} + t_C) \qquad (9)$$

This result is similar to the latency we estimated previously for scanning the bitmap in the single-level scheme. The key difference is that the number of required steps to completely scan the off-chip bitmap is reduced from m to M_l and during each step, k' requests with g' granularity are generated. Note that, when calculating T_{scan_l}, we assume that all k' accesses are serially processed by the HMC (no vault-level parallelism). However, if G was large enough, we could break ranges corresponding to each bit in the on-chip bitmap and distribute them among multiple vaults. In this way, the k' accesses required to read one range could be parallelized to reduce T_{scan_l}.

Using this result, we can guarantee that performance is, on average, sufficiently high, with a judicious choice of L_1. Next, we present an optimization method of choosing L_1 so that scanning the bitmap in the two-level bitmap design would be on average β times faster than in the single-level bitmap design. This ratio β should not only be large enough to alleviate the bitmap update bottleneck, but also result in a reasonable size of on-chip bitmap that can fit within available on-chip resources. The following equations present a condition in which the two-level design is β times faster. Intuitively, we expect a large β to require a large first-level bitmap that represents the second level bitmap in a fine-grained granularity.

$$
\begin{aligned}
\beta T_{scan_l} &= \beta M_l(k'\frac{g'}{b} + k'\frac{g' + 2H}{B} + t_C) \\
&< \beta M_l k'(\frac{g'}{b} + \frac{g' + 2H}{B} + t_C) \\
&= \beta M_l k' T' < m(k\frac{g}{b} + kn\frac{g + 2H}{B} + t_C) = T \\
&\Rightarrow M_l k' < \frac{T}{\beta T'}
\end{aligned}
\qquad (10)
$$

Here, T and T' are known values that can be calculated based on architectural parameters of the HMC and available storage resources of the chip (k, n, b, B, etc.). As described before, we assume the number of set bits in the second level bitmap at the beginning of the l-th iteration to be Q_l. Therefore, we can find the expected number of set bits in the first level bitmap M_l based on Q_l, using statistical analysis. To find this value, equivalently, we can make an analogy to the problem where we have L_1 boxes and we randomly throw Q_l balls into these boxes with multiple occupancy allowed. To find the expected number of filled boxes at the end of this experiment, we can use the probability theory to calculate the value: $M_l = E(Q_l) = L_1(1 - (\frac{L_1-1}{L_1})^{Q_l})$ [10].

Assuming Q_l to be $\frac{V}{L}$ on average, we can use Equation 10 to find a bound for L_1.

$$M_l k' = E(\frac{V}{L})\frac{L_2}{8g'L_1} = (1 - (\frac{L_1 - 1}{L_1})^{\frac{V}{L}})\frac{L_2}{8g'} < \frac{T}{\beta T'} \quad (11)$$

Simplifying Equation 11 gives us a lower bound for L_1 as shown below.

$$\frac{1}{1 - (1 - \frac{8g'T}{L_2\beta T'})^{\frac{L}{V}}} < L_1 \qquad (12)$$

As shown in the equation above, in addition to β, the lower bound of L_1 depends on graph characteristics and a number of hardware dependent constants. We can not know the value of L in advance, but methods of estimating this value for large graphs have been proposed in previous works [11] and can be applied here. In Equation 13 both T and L_2 increase linearly with V. Thus, $\frac{8g'T}{L_2\beta T'}$ is typically independent of the graph size and is only proportional to $\frac{1}{\beta}$. Consequently, higher speedups require larger on-chip bitmaps. This relationship confirms our intuition. The lower bound also has a direct relationship with V and an inverse relationship with L which follows our initial expectations of the relationship between L_1 and the graph structure.

Finally, recalling that $G = \frac{L_2}{L_1}$, Equation 13 can be equivalently expressed as an upper bound for G.

$$G < L_2(1 - (1 - \frac{8g'T}{L_2\beta T'})^{\frac{L}{V}}) \qquad (13)$$

This equation indicates the trade-off between performance and storage space. A higher speedup, requires the bound to be smaller, resulting in a smaller G. This means that, to increase performance, the on-chip first level bitmap should represent the off-chip second level bitmap in a more fine-grained manner. Alternatively we can say, as long as G is smaller than this bound, choosing a larger value for G can achieve better space utilization without reducing performance.

5.3 Implementation of Two-level Bitmap

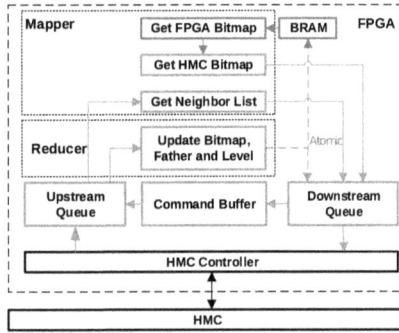

Figure 8: Detailed implementation of proposed HMC-FPGA based BFS processing system with two-level bitmap

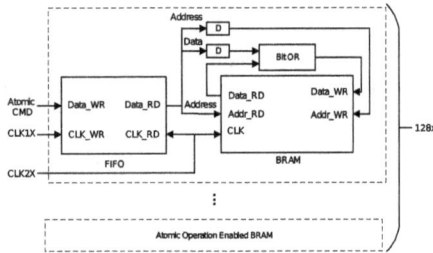

Figure 9: The implementation of atomic bitwise update operation using BRAM

To support the proposed two-level bitmap, we need to extend the FPGA implementation based on single level bitmap presented in section 3.2, which has a mapper design comprising two pipeline stages: getting the bitmap from HMC and getting the neighbor list from HMC. As shown in Figure 8, we add the following three components to the baseline design described in section 3.2.2: 1) BRAM for FPGA bitmap storage; 2) a third pipeline stage of mapper for scanning the FPGA bitmap; 3) supporting atomic updates for FPGA bitmap. In each BFS level, mappers first scan the FPGA

bitmap to find the asserted bit in the FPGA bitmap and read the corresponding HMC bitmap. Reducers need to update both FPGA bitmap and HMC bitmap atomically.

As shown in Figure 9, to support the atomic bitmap updates, we need to first read the memory content, conduct a bit-wise "OR" operation with the input, and then write it back to the BRAM. As the atomic read-modify-write procedure requires two cycles, and our kernel runs at a relatively low frequency, we use a double pump BRAM to reduce the latency of atomic operations to one kernel clock cycle. Since now the BRAMs and Map-Reduce BFS kernels are in different clock domains, we further add a FIFO between the kernel and the BRAM. The FIFO also buffers the atomic bitmap update commands when BRAM conflicts happen. To provide enough parallelism of the bitmap scan as well as to reduce the BRAM conflict of atomic bitmap update, we use 128 BRAM blocks to store the the on-chip bitmap. We use lower bits of the bitmap address as the byte address, and higher bits of the bitmap address as the BRAM address.

6. EVALUATION

In this section, we first introduce the experimental setup. Then, we present the simulation and experiment results to validate the effectiveness of design choices using proposed techniques. Finally, we show performance comparison between our results and prior works.

6.1 Experimental Setup

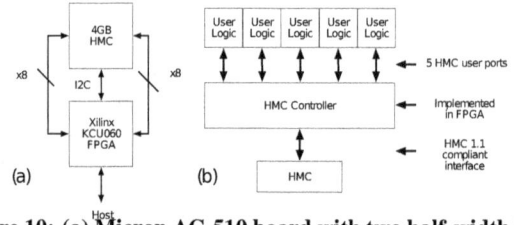

Figure 10: (a) Micron AC-510 board with two half-width HMC links [12] (b) HMC controller diagram [13]

We implement the proposed graph processor on an AC-510 FPGA module from Micron. As shown in Figure 10, AC-510 consists of a Xilinx KCU060 FPGA and a 4GB HMC chip. The AC510 board uses two half-width (8 lanes) 15G HMC links to connect HMC and FPGA, and provides an overall two-way bandwidth of 60GB/s. We implement our graph processing architecture under the PicoFramework, which provides communication between the host and the FPGA kernel. We use the HMC controller IP core from Micron as the interfaces between the FPGA kernel and the HMC. The host machine equips an Intel Xeon E5-1630V3 CPU and one DDR4 memory channel with 16GB capacity. We use Ubuntu 16.04.1 as the host operating system and compile our CPU implementation using gcc with flags "-Ofast" and "-march=native".

To accelerate the development process and facilitate evaluation of optimization methods, we develop an event-based HMC simulator. Using this simulator, we can gain better insights into the internal mechanisms of the HMC and avoid tedious trial-and-error cycles. Here, we discuss the details of our simulator and present simulation results for our experiments to show the improvements we can achieve using our optimization methods.

The HMC simulator is developed based on the analytical model presented in previous sections. Compared to those cycle-accurate simulators, this simulator sacrifices accuracy for better simulation speed and thus is more suitable for large workloads. Using this simulator, we can produce performance and event statistics for graphs with millions of nodes.

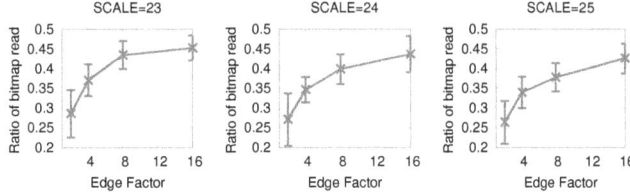

Figure 11: The ratio of HMC read request of bitmap scanning between two-level bitmap and single-level bitmap designs with different graph scale and edge factors

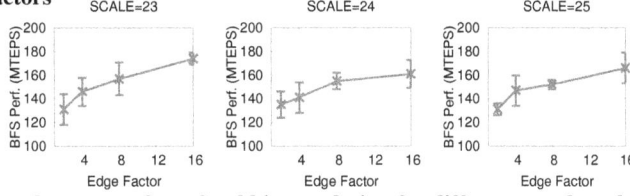

Figure 12: BFS performance of two-level bitmap design for different graph scales and edge factors

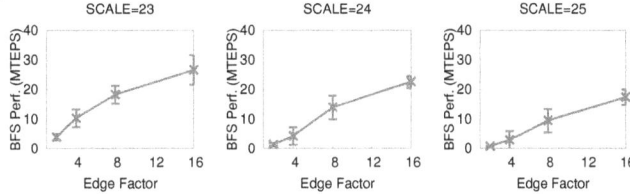

Figure 13: BFS performance of single-level bitmap design with different graph scales and edge factors

We use a similar method as stated in Graph 500 [1] to generate random graphs for testing our design. These graphs are generated with two tunable parameters, a scale (the number of vertices) and an edge factor (the ratio between total number of edges and total number of vertices). In other words, edge factor determines the average number of neighbors each vertex possesses. A larger edge factor results in a more connected graph. In the case of BFS, this means the algorithm would have to run for fewer numbers of iterations (L is smaller).

6.2 Results

We first use our event-driven simulator to verify the effectiveness of our two-level bitmap. A series of large sparse graphs with a scale of 23, 24, and 25 and different edge factors are generated. We plot the ratio of the number of bitmap reads between the two-level bitmap and the single-level bitmap scheme. As shown in Figure 11, the two-level bitmap scheme has consistently better performance (less reads). The sparser the graph is, the more effective this scheme can filter out unnecessary reads and the better the performance becomes. This trend also holds as the graph becomes larger. In Figure 13 and Figure 12, we further plot the BFS performance comparison between the single-level and the two-level bitmap schemes. It can be observed that the two-level bitmap leads to greater BFS performance gain on a sparser and larger graph. In contrast, due to the long off-chip latency and excessive reads generated in the single level bitmap scheme, the reference setup cannot saturate FPGA kernel resources by wasting a large portion of runtime waiting for the bitmap reads to be served.

We run a series of random access benchmarks from the Picoframework to evaluate the HMC access performance. As shown in Figure 14, we plot the traffic for four different cases: 100% READ, 100 % Write, Read-Modify-Write and Atomic Write with different payload sizes. If the size of the data payload is halved, the performance of random access does not double due to the overhead of packet head and tail. The results here confirmed our previous assumption that using larger payload size is suitable if the larger payload contains all useful data, which will be used by the kernels . Then, we plot memory access performance of our BFS implementation in Figure 15. We can see that our BFS implementation

Table 3: Performance comparison with existing works

System	Proposed	FPGP [4]	GRAPH Gen [3]	Torous-GRAPH [14]
Graph Type	Random	Twitter [15]	Twitter	Random
Max. Scale	26	25	26	22
Edge Factor	16	35	16	16
Runtime (s)	3.851	121.992	148,577	76.134
MTEPS	166.2	12.0	9.9	19.2

Table 4: Runtime comparison between single level bitmap, two-level bitmap and CPU (Scale=25, Edge Factor=16)

	Two-Level Bitmap	Single-level Bitmap	CPU
Runtime (s)	3.851	30.976	13.84
MTEPS	166.2	20.6	46.2

Table 5: Resource utilization

	FF	BRAM	DSP
Total	663360	2160	2760
Used	221894	580	64
Utilization	33%	27%	2%

could achieve the same memory access performance as the random access performance, which indicates that we have nearly saturated the HMC I/O.

In Figure 16, we further show that the BFS performance in the unit of million traversed edges per second (MTEPS) with different payload sizes. It can be seen that it has a similar trend as the ones shown in Figure 14, which indicates that the performance of our BFS implementation is largely determined by the random access speed. As long as the memory bandwidth can be further increased (i.e. a board with more high-bandwidth HMC links/lanes), we can achieve better BFS performance.

We compare the runtime of a CPU (Xeon E5-1630v3) and the proposed HMC-FPGA platform on a GRAPH500 graph with a scale of 26 and an edge factor of 16. Table 4 shows that our implementation achieves 3× performance compared with CPU. The two-level

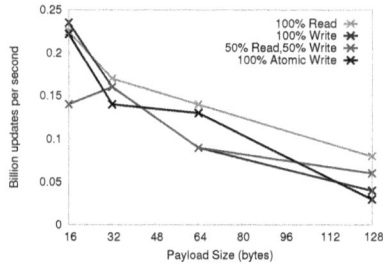

Figure 14: Benchmark of random access performance of HMC

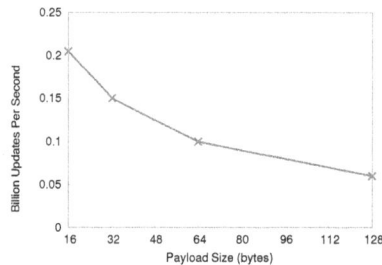

Figure 15: Memory access performance of BFS

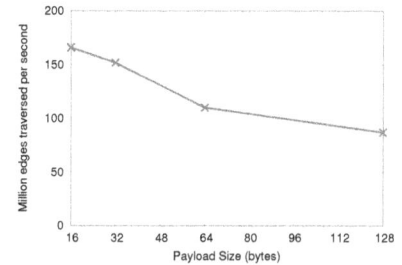

Figure 16: BFS performance with different payload size

bitmap scheme considerably boosts the performance of the proposed system by filtering out unnecessary reads and saving memory bandwidth.

In Table 3, we further compare the results with existing works. Due to the limited capacity of our HMC chip, we can only process a sparser graph but with the similar scale as the Twitter Graph [15] that is used in three prior works. Our implementation outperforms the prior works by nearly *one order of magnitude* and proves the effectiveness of proposed FPGA-HMC based graph processing system. Furthermore, as our previous analysis shows that our implementation tends to have better BFS performance with denser graphs, we expect to have much more performance gain (more than one order of magnitude) if using exactly the same Twitter Graph as the data input to the benchmark.

Finally, we show the resource utilization of our implementation in Table 5. As we store the full bitmap on HMC instead of on-chip BRAM, we only use 27% of the total 18Kb BRAM. This provides enough room for expansion if we have a faster and wider HMC link.

7. RELATED WORKS

There are several existing works on implementing graph accelerator using FPGA. GRAPHGEN [16] proposed an FPGA-based graph processing system using vertex centric model. However, it stores the whole graph in the on-board DDR DRAM, which severely limits the performance due to the bandwidth bottleneck of the memory. Also, the design does not provide any platform-aware software and/or hardware optimization for implementing BFS. TorusBFS [6] proposed a 2-D message passing structure to reduce the latency between parallel BFS kernels, but its performance is also limited by the poor random access performance of DRAM and the available on-chip resources. FPGP [4] employed interval-shared structure to maximize the the off-chip memory bandwidth and to fully exploit the parallelism of graph processing. However, its performance is in turn bounded by the capacity and bandwidth of FPGA's on-chip memory.

8. CONCLUSION

In this work, we present a graph processor design to fully exploit the capability of FPGA and HMC through collaborative software and hardware techniques. In particular, we first present the data structure and algorithm modifications, followed by Map-Reduce implementation of level synchronized BFS on FPGA-HMC platform. To gain deeper insights into the performance bottlenecks, we develop an analytical model for BFS runtime with respect to the HMC parameters and the graph properties. We found that the number of bitmap reads contributes a significant portion of the memory accesses and thus becomes the key performance limiting factor. To address the problem, we further introduce a two-level bitmap scheme, which leverages the sparsity of the bitmap and reduces the number of HMC accesses significantly. Finally, we use both simulation and experiment to verify the effectiveness of proposed techniques. Our implementation on Micron AC-510 development board achieves 166 MTEPS and outperforms CPU and other FPGA-based large graph processors.

ACKNOWLEDGEMENTS

We appreciate the insightful comments and feedback from the anonymous reviewers. We thank Micron for the donation of the development tool and hardware. We especially thank John Watson and Mark Hur for their support.

9. REFERENCES
[1] R. C. Murphy, K. B. Wheeler, B. W. Barrett, and J. A. Ang, "Introducing the graph 500," *Cray User's Group*, 2010.
[2] J. T. Pawlowski, "Hybrid memory cube (hmc)," in *IEEE Hot Chips*, 2011.
[3] A. Kyrola, G. Blelloch, and C. Guestrin, "Graphchi: large-scale graph computation on just a pc," in *USENIX OSDI*, 2012.
[4] G. Dai, Y. Chi, Y. Wang, and H. Yang, "Fpgp: Graph processing framework on fpga a case study of breadth-first search," in *ACM/SIGDA FPGA*, FPGA '16, 2016.
[5] Y. Umuroglu, D. Morrison, and M. Jahre, "Hybrid breadth-first search on a single-chip fpga-cpu heterogeneous platform," in *IEEE FPL*, 2015.
[6] G. LEI, R. LI, S. GUO, and F. XIA, "Torusbfs: A novel message-passing parallel breadth-first search architecture on fpgas," 10 2016.
[7] P. Rosenfeld, "Performance exploration of the hybrid memory cube," 2014.
[8] S. Kaur, S. Singh, and S. Kaushal, "Performance comparison of sampling techniques for web-based networks," in *International Conference on Recent Advances in Engineering Computational Sciences*, 2015.
[9] Y. S. Deng, B. D. Wang, and S. Mu, "Taming irregular eda applications on gpus," in *ACM ICCAD*, 2009.
[10] M. Mitzenmacher and E. Upfal, *Probability and computing: Randomized algorithms and probabilistic analysis*. Cambridge University Press, 2005.
[11] L. Gulyás, G. Horváth, T. Cséri, and G. Kampis, "An estimation of the shortest and largest average path length in graphs of given density," *arXiv preprint*, 2011.
[12] Picocomputing, "Ultrascale-based superprocessor with hybrid memory cube." http://picocomputing.com/ac-510-superprocessor-module.
[13] Picocomputing, "Hybrid memory cube (hmc) and controller ip." http://picocomputing.com/hybrid-memory-cube-hmc-controller-ip/.
[14] W.-S. Han, S. Lee, K. Park, J.-H. Lee, M.-S. Kim, J. Kim, and H. Yu, "Turbograph: a fast parallel graph engine handling billion-scale graphs in a single pc," in *ACM SIGKDD*, ACM, 2013.
[15] J. Yang and J. Leskovec, "Patterns of toral variation in online media," in *Proc. of the fourth ACM international conference on Web search and data mining*, 2011.
[16] E. Nurvitadhi, G. Weisz, Y. Wang, S. Hurkat, M. Nguyen, J. C. Hoe, J. F. Martínez, and C. Guestrin, "Graphgen: An fpga framework for vertex-centric graph computation," in *IEEE FCCM*, 2014.

ForeGraph: Exploring Large-scale Graph Processing on Multi-FPGA Architecture

Guohao Dai[1], Tianhao Huang[1], Yuze Chi[2], Ningyi Xu[3], Yu Wang[1], Huazhong Yang[1]
[1]Department of Electronic Engineering, TNLIST, Tsinghua University, Beijing, China
[2]Computer Science Department, University of California, Los Angeles, USA
[3]Hardware Computing Group, Microsoft Research Asia, Beijing, China
[1]dgh14@mails.tsinghua.edu.cn, [1]yu-wang@tsinghua.edu.cn, [3]xu.ningyi@microsoft.com

ABSTRACT

The performance of large-scale graph processing suffers from challenges including poor locality, lack of scalability, random access pattern, and heavy data conflicts. Some characteristics of FPGA make it a promising solution to accelerate various applications. For example, on-chip block RAMs can provide high throughput for random data access. However, large-scale processing on a single FPGA chip is constrained by limited on-chip memory resources and off-chip bandwidth. Using a multi-FPGA architecture may alleviate these problems to some extent, while the data partitioning and communication schemes should be considered to ensure the locality and reduce data conflicts.

In this paper, we propose ForeGraph, a large-scale graph processing framework based on the multi-FPGA architecture. In ForeGraph, each FPGA board only stores a partition of the entire graph in off-chip memory. Communication over partitions is reduced. Vertices and edges are sequentially loaded onto the FPGA chip and processed. Under our scheduling scheme, each FPGA chip performs graph processing in parallel without conflicts. We also analyze the impact of system parameters on the performance of Fore-Graph. Our experimental results on Xilinx Virtex Ultra-Scale XCVU190 chip show ForeGraph outperforms state-of-the-art FPGA-based large-scale graph processing systems by 4.54x when executing PageRank on the Twitter graph (1.4 billion edges). The average throughput is over 900 MTEPS in our design and 2.03x larger than previous work.

Keywords

large-scale graph processing; multi-FPGA architecture

1. INTRODUCTION

With demand for data analysis continuing to grow, the large-scale graph processing which discovers relationships among data is gaining increasing attention in many domains [1]. Previous work has provided large-scale graph processing systems, including CPU-based [2, 3, 4, 5, 6, 7, 8, 9, 10, 11, 12, 13], GPU-based [14, 15], FPGA-based [16, 17, 18, 19, 20, 21, 22, 23], and emerging systems [24].

As emphasized in this work, the key problem in large-scale graph processing is to provide a high bandwidth of data access [25, 26]. However, some characteristics of large-scale graphs bring challenges to fully utilizing bandwidth. These challenges include: (1) **Poor locality.** Graphs represent unstructured relationships between entities, and thus a small partition can have access to the whole graph. Poor locality leads to frequent global data access, while only local data access will have a large bandwidth in state-of-the-art computing platforms. (2) **Lack of scalability.** Communication over partitions causes heavy traffic in large-scale graph processing. Thus, it is difficult to design a system which scales to larger graphs. (3) **Random data access pattern.** The data access pattern of two neighboring vertices can be quite unlike. Such unstructured characteristic of graphs randomizes graph data access pattern. (4) **Heavy data conflicts.** Vertices from different partitions may read/write the same vertex simultaneously, leading to heavy conflicts. Moreover, unpredictable data access pattern brings great challenges to avoid conflicts. These four challenges need to be carefully considered so as to provide a high bandwidth and design a high-performance large-scale graph processing system.

To tackle these challenges, many solutions have been designed in previous work and most of them mainly focus on fully utilizing the bandwidth. GraphChi [4] divides a large graph into several *intervals* and *shards* as partitions of vertices and edges. Based on the partitioning scheme, the locality is ensured by accessing each partition in turns. Some previous work [10, 18, 4, 23] also sorts data to eliminate the randomness and conflicts of graph data access. However, the overhead of pre-processing on sorting data before execution needs to be reckoned especially when the graph may dynamically change during run-time. Compared with CPUs and GPUs, the random access feature of on-chip BRAMs is provided to implement random data access with high throughput on FPGA. However, the size of on-chip BRAMs of one FPGA chip is much smaller than the typical size of a large graph. Consequently, using the multi-FPGA architecture is a promising way to provide larger on-chip BRAM resources. However, most of FPGA-based systems are designed for one FPGA board [23] or require a global-accessible memory [18], with poor scalability for larger graphs.

To provide a high-performance large-scale graph processing system based on the multi-FPGA architecture, we design ForeGraph. We divide graphs into small partitions and as-

FPGA '17, February 22-24, 2017, Monterey, CA, USA
© 2017 ACM. ISBN 978-1-4503-4354-1/17/02. . . $15.00
DOI: http://dx.doi.org/10.1145/3020078.3021739

Table 1: Notations of a graph

Notation	Meaning
G	a graph $G = (V, E)$
V	vertices in G, $|V| = n$
E	edges in G, $|E| = m$
v_i	vertex i
$e_{i.j}$	edge from v_i to v_j
e_{src}	source vertex of edge e
e_{dst}	destination vertex of edge e
I_x	interval x
S_y	shard y
$B_{x \to y}$	block $x.y$ linked from I_i to I_j
$SI_{x,i}$	the i-th sub-interval of I_x
$SB_{x \to y,i,j}$	the (i, j) sub-block of $B_{x \to y}$
P	number of intervals
Q	number of sub-intervals in an interval
K	number of processing elements on a chip

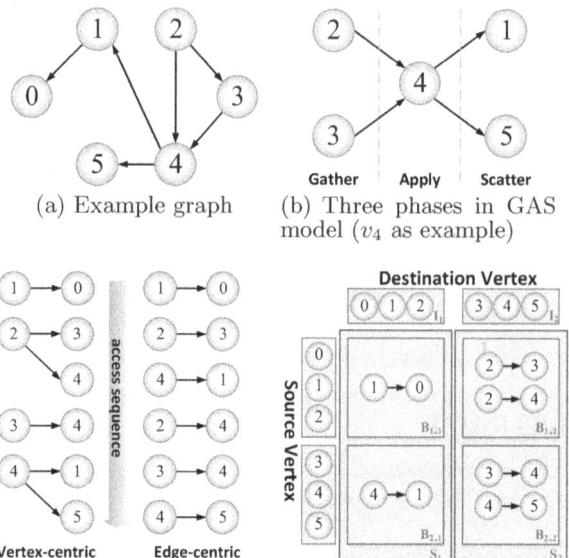

(a) Example graph

(b) Three phases in GAS model (v_4 as example)

(c) Access sequence of edges in VC and EC model

(d) Graph partitioning using intervals and shards

Figure 1: Example graph and corresponding models.

sign each partition to an FPGA board to ensure the locality of data access. Communication overhead among different FPGA boards is minimized to make ForeGraph scalable to large graphs. Vertices and edges are sequentially loaded onto FPGA chips to avoid random data access. Each partition is further divided into smaller ones and assigned to different processing elements (PEs) on FPGA chips, so conflicts are eliminated. Such multi-FPGA architecture can provide sufficient on-chip BRAM resources and off-chip bandwidth, which are essential to improve the performance of FPGA-based large-scale graph processing systems. Specifically, this paper makes the following contributions.

- **Scalable multi-FPGA graph processing.** The multi-FPGA architecture provides large on-chip BRAM resources with random access feature and sufficient off-chip bandwidth of graph data access. Data are allocated to each FPGA board rather than stored in a global-accessible memory (e.g. *Shared-Vertex Memory* in [18]) (Section 3.2 and Section 3.3). Moreover, communication overhead among boards is minimized (Section 3.4). These two technologies make our system scale to larger graphs.

- **Pre-processing with low overhead.** Vertices and edges are divided into partitions according to their indexes (Section 3.5). Data are not required to be sorted within each partition thus the overhead of pre-processing is reduced (from $O(m \log m)$ to $O(m)$, m denotes the number of edges). Locality is ensured, and conflicts are removed under our partitioning scheme.

- **Fully utilizing off-chip bandwidth.** We minimize data transmission on one board to fully utilize off-chip bandwidth. We adopt several optimization techniques in Section 4. For example, we compress the vertex index and use only 4 Bytes to represent an edge (2 Bytes for source and destination vertex respectively), even though there are millions of vertices in the graph.

- **Extensive experiments.** We have conducted comprehensive experiments to evaluate the performance in Section 6. Experimental results on five graphs show that ForeGraph can execute graph algorithms on graphs with billions of edges. ForeGraph outperforms state-of-the-art FPGA-based systems by 5.89x, and the average throughput is 2.03x larger than previous work.

The remaining of this paper is organized as follows. Section 2 introduces the background information of large-scale graph processing and correlative systems. The whole architecture of ForeGraph is shown in Section 3. Some optimization methods to fully utilize off-chip bandwidth are shown in Section 4. The performance of ForeGraph is analyzed and presented in Section 5 and Section 6 from both theoretical and experimental perspectives. We finally conclude this paper in Section 7.

2. BACKGROUND AND RELATED WORK

In this section, the background information of graph processing models is presented. Then, we will introduce previous FPGA-based large-scale graph processing systems. Notations used in this paper are shown in Table 1.

2.1 Graph Processing Models

Let V and E denote the vertex and edge sets in a graph G, the computation task over $G = (V, E)$ is to calculate the updated value of V and E. We assume each edge is directed, and an undirected graph can be realized by adding an opposing edge to each directed edge.

Gather-Apply-Scatter. When updating the value of V, updates are propagated from the source vertex to the destination vertex. Such model is known as the *Gather-Apply-Scatter* (GAS) model [2] which divides the update into three phases. In the *Gather* phase, a vertex receives value from source vertices of in-edges. Then, the updated value is calculated in the *Apply* phase. After that, the updated value is propagated to the destination vertices of out-edges. The GAS model can be executed in the form of iterations. In each iteration, each edge is accessed once to propagate updates from the source vertex to the destination vertex. Figure 1(b) illustrates the three phases of the GAS model.

Vertex-centric and edge-centric. As mentioned in the GAS model, updates are propagated from vertices to vertices through edges. Thus, the access sequence of edges differentiates different models, including *vertex-centric* (VC) model [6] and *edge-centric* (EC) model [12]. In VC model, a vertex scatters value to destination vertices of all out-edges (or

Algorithm 1 Pseudo-code of Breadth-First Search

Input: $G = (V, E)$, root vertex r
Output: depth of each $v \in V$, $d(v)$
1: $d(r) = 0$
2: **for** each $v \in V$ & $v \neq r$ **do**
3:    $d(v) = \infty$
4: **end for**
5: $finished = $ **false**
6: **while** ($finished = $ **false**) **do**
7:    $finished = $ **true**
8:    **for** each edge e **do**
9:       **if** $d(e_{src}) + 1 < d(e_{dst})$ **then**
10:         $finished = $ **false**
11:         $d(e_{dst}) = d(e_{src}) + 1$
12:       **end if**
13:    **end for**
14: **end while**
15: **return** $d(v)$, $v \in V$

gathers value from source vertices of all in-edges). In contrast, in EC model, all edges are sequentially accessed while the access sequence of source/destination vertices is disordered. Both VC and EC model have been implemented in previous systems and achieved excellent performance. Figure 1(c) shows an example of VC and EC model.

Interval-shard based partitioning. Graph partitioning is a widely used method which ensures the locality of graph data access. GraphChi [4] uses an interval-shard based partitioning model. Vertices and edges in a graph are divided into P *intervals* (vertex sets) and *shards* (edge sets). Later systems [10, 11] further divide edges into P^2 blocks according to the corresponding intervals of the source and destination vertices. For example, $B_{x \rightarrow y}$ contains all edges linked from I_x to I_y. Figure 1(d) shows an example of interval-shard based partitioning model.

Based on these models, the computation task is performed in the form of iterations. In each iteration, all blocks are accessed at most once. Updates are propagated from source vertices to destination vertices. Algorithm 1 shows the pseudo-code of Breadth-First Search (BFS) using these models. In the beginning, the depth of the root vertex is set to zero, and others are infinite. In each iteration, edges are sequentially accessed (Note that the accessing order of edges is not specified in Algorithm 1, we will explain the detailed order in ForeGraph in our implementation.). The depth of the corresponding destination vertex will be modified according to the depth of source vertex. Such algorithm can be easily transformed into other graph algorithms by modifying the code of propagation.

2.2 FPGA-based Graph Processing Systems

FPGA has been proved as a promising solution to many applications and previous work has provided large-scale graph processing systems based on FPGA [16, 27, 17, 18, 19, 20, 21, 22, 23]. Most of these systems are designed for a single FPGA chip. Some of these systems are only dedicated to specific algorithms, like Breadth-First Search (BFS) or PageRank (PR). There are also many general purposed systems which can apply to different graph algorithms, including GraphStep [20], GraphGen [21] and GraphOps [22]. GraphStep and GraphGen are two systems that applied VC model to FPGA. GraphOps provides a modular hardware library for constructing accelerators for graph analytics al-

gorithms. Shijie *et al.* [23] proposed a system to minimize row-conflicts using EC model. However, the size of graphs on all these systems is limited by memory resources on an FPGA board.

There are also some systems based on the multi-FPGA architecture. Betkaoui *et al.* [17] proposed a BFS solution on Convey HC-1 machine consisted of 4 FPGA boards. However, this system can hardly be applied to other graph algorithms. FPGP [18] provided a large-scale graph processing framework and it can be expanded to multi-FPGA architecture using a *Shared-Vertex Memory* (SVM). However, since all FPGA boards need to be connected to SVM, the system performance, as well as the scalability, is limited by the bandwidth of the SVM.

3. SYSTEM ARCHITECTURE

In this section, we will discuss the system architecture of ForeGraph. The data allocation and processing flow in ForeGraph will be explained in detail, followed by interconnection scheme and partitioning scheme.

3.1 Overall Architecture

The overall architecture of ForeGraph is shown on the left of Figure 2. ForeGraph consists of several FPGA boards. On each board, there is an FPGA chip to perform processing logic and off-chip memory to store graph data. All boards are connected by the interconnection. Such interconnection can be realized using the bus (e.g. PCI-e), directed optical fiber connections or other available structures. The detailed processing logic is shown on the right of Figure 2. The logic includes an interconnection controller, an off-chip memory controller, a data controller, a dispatcher and several processing elements (PEs).

- **Interconnection controller.** Data transmission among FPGA boards is controlled by interconnection controller.
- **Off-chip memory controller.** The off-chip memory controller arranges the data read/write of the off-chip memory. The controller can be realized by using existing IP core generators (e.g. Memory Interface Generator in Xilinx Vivado). When performing graph algorithms, data loaded to processing elements are all from the off-chip memory through this controller.
- **Data controller.** The data controller connects the off-chip memory controller and the interconnection controller. It packs and calculates the memory address and target board ID when transmitting data among boards.
- **Processing elements (PEs).** PEs are the kernel logic for executing graph algorithms on the FPGA board. As mentioned in Section 2.1, updates are propagated from the source vertex to the destination vertex using the corresponding edge. Thus, each PE contains a source buffer and a destination buffer storing source vertices and destination vertices respectively. Both source buffer and destination buffer are implemented using general purposed dual-port BRAMs. There is another edge buffer storing edges loaded from the off-chip memory. Edges are sequentially loaded from off-chip memory when updating. Both vertices and edges are sent to the processing logic, and the results will be calculated and written to the destination buffer. Different graph algorithms only differ in processing logic. When the updating for all vertices in the destination buffer finished, the results will be written to the off-chip memory, and new vertices and edges will

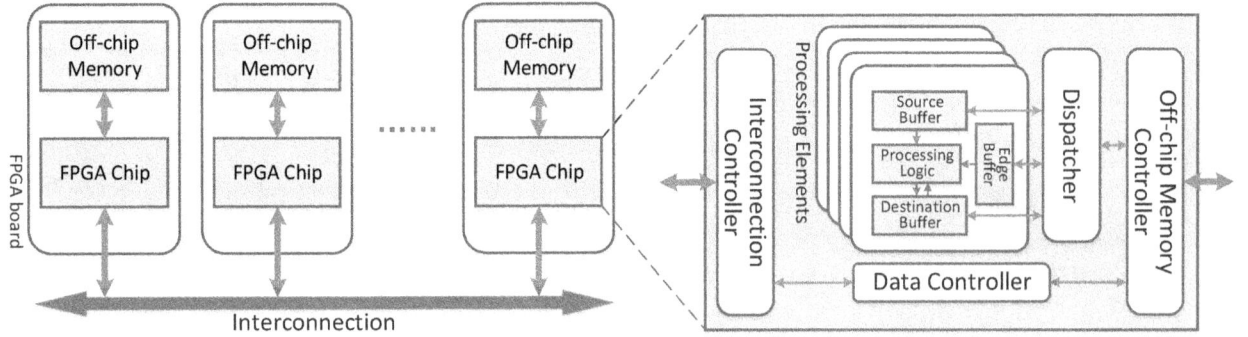

Figure 2: Overall architecture of ForeGraph (left) and on-chip processing logic (right).

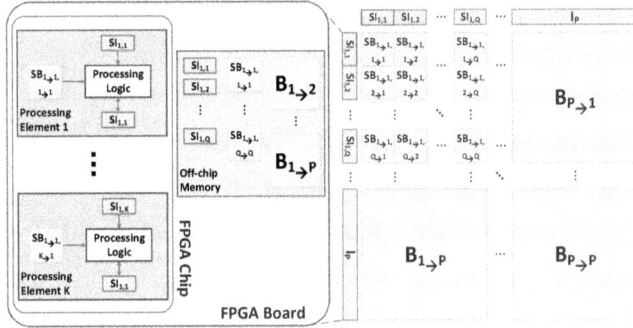

Figure 3: On-board data allocation (left) and two-level partitioning in ForeGraph (right).

be loaded to these buffers. Assuming the bandwidth of off-chip memory is around 10 GB/s per board, and the processing logic runs at the frequency around 200 MHz. We use 8 Bytes to represent an edge (4 Bytes for source vertex and destination vertex respectively). Based on the fact that the throughput of a single PE (200 MHz $\times$ 8 Bytes = 1.6 GB/s) is much smaller than the bandwidth of off-chip memory, using several PEs can fully utilize the off-chip memory bandwidth.

- **Dispatcher.** The dispatcher connects the off-chip memory controller and data buffers in PEs. When vertices and edges are loaded from the off-chip memory, the dispatcher sends data to corresponding PEs. The data allocation in different PEs is explained in detail in Section 3.2.

3.2 Data Allocation in Off-chip Memory

Graphs are divided into intervals (I) and shards (S) in ForeGraph. Each interval, as well as its corresponding shard, is assigned to the off-chip memory on an FPGA board. For example, in a ForeGraph system consisting of P FPGA boards, I_1 and S_1 are stored on the first FPGA board. S_1 consists of P blocks namely $B_{1\rightarrow 1} \sim B_{P\rightarrow 1}$. Each block is responsible for updating I_1 using different source intervals. These source intervals are stored in other FPGA boards and loaded to the first board in turn during run-time.

Considering there are several PEs in a chip and each PE contains two exclusive vertex buffers using BRAMs, the on-chip memory resources are not enough to store an interval as the graph size continues to grow. In ForeGraph, we adopt a two-level graph partitioning scheme shown on the right of Figure 3. Take the first interval I_1 as an example, in this two-level graph partitioning scheme, I_1 is further divided into Q sub-intervals, $SI_{1,1} \sim SI_{1,Q}$. Correspondingly, block $B_{1\rightarrow 1}$ is further divided into Q^2 sub-blocks, $SB_{1\rightarrow 1,1\rightarrow 1} \sim$

$SB_{1\rightarrow 1,Q\rightarrow Q}$. Each sub-block is responsible for updating a destination sub-interval using a source sub-interval.

When executing graph algorithms, different source sub-intervals are loaded to different PEs, while the destination sub-intervals are same in these PEs. These PEs update the destination sub-interval using corresponding sub-blocks. An example of data allocation when executing graph algorithms in ForeGraph is shown on the left of Figure 3. $SI_{1,1} \sim SI_{K,1}$ are loaded to PE 1 $\sim$ PE K and the destination sub-interval is $SI_{1,1}$ in all PEs. Edges in corresponding sub-blocks are loaded to edge buffers of each PE. When all PEs finished updating for $SI_{1,1}$, ForeGraph substitutes unused sub-intervals in the off-chip memory since those in PEs can continue to execute graph algorithms.

Intervals on other boards are loaded to local off-chip memory in turns. For example, the processing flow of the first board: updating I_1 using I_1 and $B_{1\rightarrow 1}$ $\rightarrow$ loading I_2 from the second board $\rightarrow$ updating I_1 using I_2 and $B_{2\rightarrow 1}$ $\rightarrow$ discarding I_2 on the first board, and so on.

3.3 On-chip Data Replacement Flow

When using an interval to update another interval, all Q^2 sub-blocks will be accessed. However, only K sub-intervals are processed at one time. Thus, ForeGraph schedules how to substitute sub-intervals in off-chip memory for those on the chip. An example of two different replacement strategies is shown in Figure 4. An interval is divided into four sub-intervals, and two PEs are implemented on the chip.

In the destination-first replacement (DFR) strategy, when two PEs finish updating the same destination sub-interval, ForeGraph writes it to the off-chip memory and replaces it with another sub-interval (Step 1 to Step 8 in Figure 4(a)). After all sub-intervals being updated using source sub-intervals in two PEs, ForeGraph replaces them with other new sub-intervals (Step 4 to Step 5 in Figure 4(a)). When all edges in $B_{1\rightarrow 1}$ have been accessed, other intervals will be loaded, and ForeGraph will repeat previous steps using these intervals as source intervals (Step 9 in Figure 4(b)).

In the source-first replacement (SFR) strategy, the source sub-intervals rather than the destination sub-intervals will be replaced (Step 1 to Step 2, Step 3 to Step 4, Step 5 to Step 6, Step 7 to Step 8 in Figure 4(b)). When a sub-interval has been updated by all sub-intervals, ForeGraph replaces it with a new sub-interval (Step 2 to Step 3, Step 4 to Step 5, Step 6 to Step 7 in Figure 4(b)). Similarly, other intervals will be loaded, and previous steps will be repeated after all edges in $B_{1\rightarrow 1}$ have been accessed (Step 9 in Figure 4(b)).

DFR and SFR differ in the data amount they read from/write

PE 1 / PE 2 — Destination-first replacement

	PE 1 src	PE 1 dst	PE 2 src	PE 2 dst	
Step 1	$SI_{1,1}$	$SI_{1,1}$	$SI_{1,2}$	$SI_{1,1}$	Update $SI_{1,1}$
Step 2	$SI_{1,1}$	$SI_{1,2}$	$SI_{1,2}$	$SI_{1,2}$	Update $SI_{1,2}$
Step 3	$SI_{1,1}$	$SI_{1,3}$	$SI_{1,2}$	$SI_{1,3}$	Update $SI_{1,3}$
Step 4	$SI_{1,1}$	$SI_{1,4}$	$SI_{1,2}$	$SI_{1,4}$	Update $SI_{1,4}$
Step 5	$SI_{1,3}$	$SI_{1,1}$	$SI_{1,4}$	$SI_{1,1}$	Update $SI_{1,1}$
Step 6	$SI_{1,3}$	$SI_{1,2}$	$SI_{1,4}$	$SI_{1,2}$	Update $SI_{1,2}$
Step 7	$SI_{1,3}$	$SI_{1,3}$	$SI_{1,4}$	$SI_{1,3}$	Update $SI_{1,3}$
Step 8	$SI_{1,3}$	$SI_{1,4}$	$SI_{1,4}$	$SI_{1,4}$	Update $SI_{1,4}$
Step 9	Load other source intervals from other board in turn. Repeat Step 1 to Step 8.				Update I_1 using other intervals

(Update I_1 using I_1)

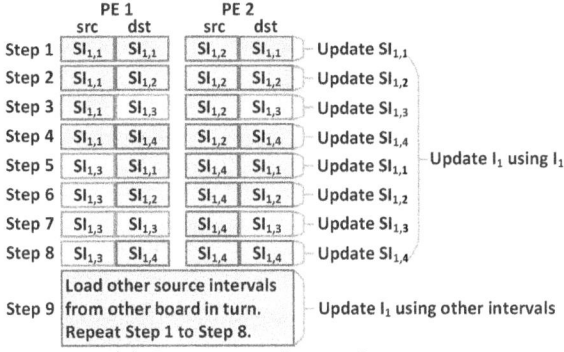

(a) Destination-first replacement.

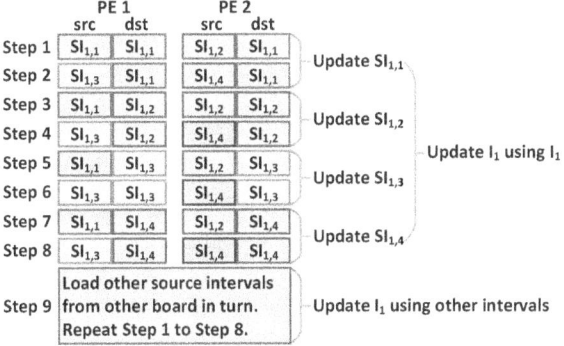

PE 1 / PE 2 — Source-first replacement

	PE 1 src	PE 1 dst	PE 2 src	PE 2 dst	
Step 1	$SI_{1,1}$	$SI_{1,1}$	$SI_{1,2}$	$SI_{1,1}$	Update $SI_{1,1}$
Step 2	$SI_{1,3}$	$SI_{1,1}$	$SI_{1,4}$	$SI_{1,1}$	
Step 3	$SI_{1,1}$	$SI_{1,2}$	$SI_{1,2}$	$SI_{1,2}$	Update $SI_{1,2}$
Step 4	$SI_{1,3}$	$SI_{1,2}$	$SI_{1,4}$	$SI_{1,2}$	
Step 5	$SI_{1,1}$	$SI_{1,3}$	$SI_{1,2}$	$SI_{1,3}$	Update $SI_{1,3}$
Step 6	$SI_{1,3}$	$SI_{1,3}$	$SI_{1,4}$	$SI_{1,3}$	
Step 7	$SI_{1,1}$	$SI_{1,4}$	$SI_{1,2}$	$SI_{1,4}$	Update $SI_{1,4}$
Step 8	$SI_{1,3}$	$SI_{1,4}$	$SI_{1,4}$	$SI_{1,4}$	
Step 9	Load other source intervals from other board in turn. Repeat Step 1 to Step 8.				Update I_1 using other intervals

(Update I_1 using I_1)

(b) Source-first replacement.

Figure 4: Two different replacement strategies.

to off-chip memory. In both DFR and SFR, all Q^2 sub-blocks (or sub-interval pairs) need to be processed. For there are K PEs on a chip, we need Q^2/K steps to finish the updating of a sub-block. For example, in Figure 4 with $K = 2$ PEs on a chip and $Q = 4$ sub-intervals in an interval, there are 8 ($= 4^2/2$) steps in total. In DFR, the destination sub-interval (same in all PEs) needs to be written to the off-chip memory, and a new sub-interval is loaded after each step. Thus, the read and write time for destination sub-intervals in DFR are both Q^2/K. Moreover, all Q source sub-intervals need to be loaded once. Consequently, the number of sub-intervals read/write are $(Q + Q^2/K)$ and Q^2/K respectively. In SFR, source sub-intervals in all K PEs need to be replaced after each step. Thus, the read time for source sub-intervals is $(Q^2 = Q^2/K \times K)$. Moreover, all destination sub-intervals need to be read/written once in SFR, which results in Q more read/write times of sub-intervals. According to the analysis, the number of sub-intervals read from/written to the off-chip memory is $(Q + Q^2)$ and Q respectively in SFR.

Table 2: Number of sub-intervals read from/written to the off-chip memory when processing a block

	read	write
destination-first replacement	$Q + Q^2/K$	Q^2/K
source-first replacement	$Q + Q^2$	Q

As we can see from Table 2, the advantage of DFR lies in the read time of sub-intervals while SFR costs less write time (we assume that $1 < K < Q$). Let T_r and T_w denote the average read/write time of a sub-interval, Formula (1) shows the situation where DFR outperforms SFR.

$$(Q + \frac{Q^2}{K}) \times T_r + \frac{Q^2}{K} \times T_w < (Q + Q^2) \times T_r + Q \times T_w \quad (1)$$

In ForeGraph, data are stored in DRAMs (same read/write bandwidth, different from other emerging devices like the non-volatile memory). Therefore, it is fair to assume that $T_r = T_w$. Formula (1) can be simplified into Formula (2).

$$(Q + 1)(K - 2) > -2 \quad (2)$$

Generally speaking, there are more than two PEs on a chip, which leads to $(Q + 1)(K - 2) \geq 0 > -2$. Thus, we adopt DFR in ForeGraph to minimize the data transmitted between the chip and the off-chip memory.

3.4 Interconnection

Much previous work proposed interconnection schemes among FPGAs like Catapult [28]. In Catapult, up to 48 FPGAs are connected using SerialLite III link in a torus network. It provides a peak theoretical bandwidth at 2×766 MB/s of each connection. The latency of each connection is around 400 ns. ForeGraph adopts the interconnection scheme in Catapult. We simulate the network consumption and compare it with other network structure (e.g. mesh, bus, and etc.) in Section 6.

Compared with distributed systems like Pregel [6] which transmits *messages* (update value from source vertices) to other computing nodes, we combine *messages* and update vertices locally in ForeGraph. Only updated the value of vertices are transmitted, and we minimize the data transmission amount so ForeGraph scales to larger graphs.

3.5 Index-based Partitioning

In ForeGraph, vertices are divided into P intervals and further into $P \cdot Q$ sub-intervals. Edges are also classified by their source and destination vertices. Different from previous systems like Graphchi [4] which needs to sort all edges in (sub-) blocks, ForeGraph only needs to assign vertices and edges to the corresponding (sub-) intervals and (sub-) blocks. Such implementation can significantly reduce the time consumption of pre-processing.

Before partitioning, we determine P and Q. Then all vertices are assigned to corresponding sub-intervals using *hash* function. For example, v_1, $v_{1 + \frac{n}{PQ}}$, $v_{1 + 2 \cdot \frac{n}{PQ}}$, and *etc.* are assigned to $SI_{1,1}$ (such partitioning method can balance the size of each block, shown in Table 8). Edges are also classified in this way without sorting. We reduce the overhead of pre-processing from $O(m \log m)$ to $O(m)$ by using index-based partitioning scheme (m denotes the number of edges).

Another advantage of this index-based partitioning is the fact that it can easily apply to dynamic graph algorithms. Previous systems need to sort all edges before updating, thus when the structure of the graph changes (e.g. inserting/deleting edges), the entire pre-processing needs to be redone. In ForeGraph, such overhead can be avoided because the order of edges in a (sub-) block is not required.

4. SYSTEM OPTIMIZATION

Based on the design for multi-FPGA in Section 3, we introduce three optimization methods to reduce data transmission amount and fully utilize PEs on one FPGA board.

4.1 Vertex Index Compression

Both vertices and edges are stored in off-chip memory thus compressing these data can significantly improve the performance of ForeGraph. In ForeGraph, we need to store the

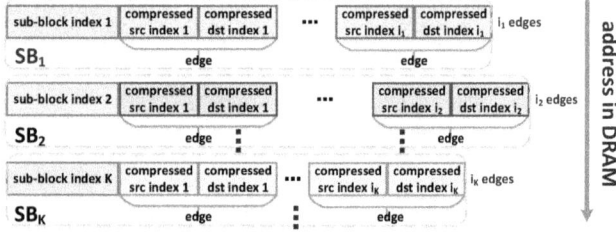

Figure 5: Vertex index compression using the sub-block index (SB_x contains i_x edges).

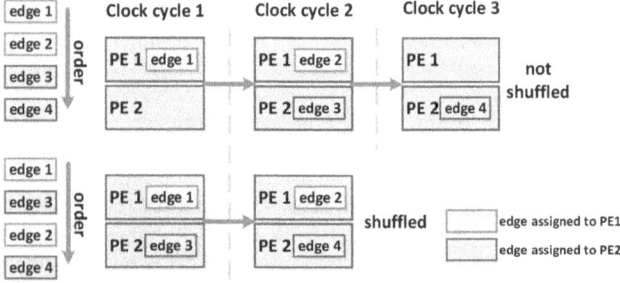

Figure 6: Shuffling edges to fully utilize PEs (FPGA chip can load two edges per clock cycle).

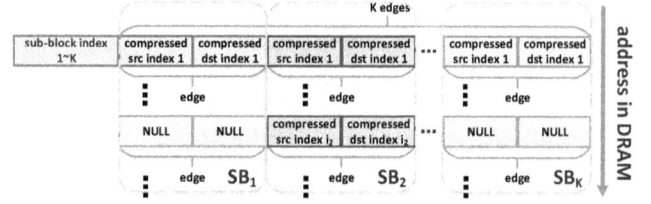

Figure 7: Shuffling edges in K sub-blocks (assuming SB_2 is larger than SB_1 and SB_K, $i_2 > i_1, i_2 > i_k$).

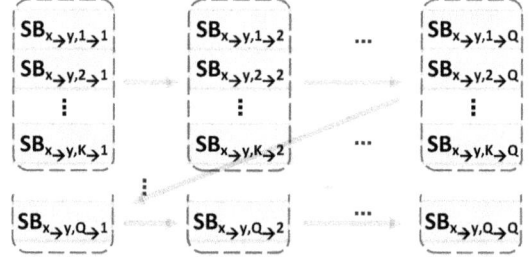

Figure 8: The order of accessing sub-blocks (sub-blocks in a dashed box are shuffled).

value of each vertex and the source/destination vertex indexes of each edge. The storage space for the value of each vertex is related to the dedicated algorithms (e.g. 8bits for the depth of each vertex in BFS). The compression of these data is not in the scope of this paper's discussion. The storage space for each edge is twice the size of the vertex index. For example, in the Twitter [29] graph which consists of 42 million vertices, we need $\log_2(42 \times 10^6) = 25$ bits to represent a vertex in this graph. The length of the vertex index can be even over 32 bits when the graph contains more than 4 billions ($= 2^{32}$) of vertices.

Source/Destination vertices of edges in a sub-block are all in the same sub-interval. We can use a sub-block index as a prefix to the vertex index. For instance, assuming there are 100 sub-intervals in the graph, we divide vertices with constant stride (100) into a sub-intervals. In this way, SI_1 includes $v_1, v_{101}, v_{201}...$ In this sub-interval, we use 1 as a prefix and all vertices in SI_1 can be indexed according to the position in sub-interval (e.g. v_{101} is the second vertices in SI_1). Thus, the indexes of vertices do not exceed $\frac{n}{100}$ (number of vertices in a sub-interval).

Figure 5 shows the data placement in DRAM using our vertex index compression method. Each sub-block begins with its sub-block index, followed by compressed edge index. In ForeGraph implementation, we use 2 Bytes (16 bits) to represent the vertex index. Thus, there are less than $2^{16} = 65536$ vertices in a sub-interval.

4.2 Shuffling Edges

As mentioned in Section 3.3, K PEs on a chip update one sub-interval using K consecutive sub-blocks. Utilization of PEs is inefficient in the way shown in Figure 5. Consecutive edges will be sent to only one PE because the source vertices are in the same sub-interval. However, a PE can only update one edge per clock cycle. Meanwhile, other PEs are idle in this situation. To settle such problem, we shuffle edges in these K sub-blocks.

Figure 6 shows an example of why shuffling edges can fully utilize all PEs. In Figure 6, there are two PEs and four edges are assigned to both of them. The bandwidth of the off-chip memory provides the throughput of loading two edges to the FPGA chip per cycle. If edges in a sub-block are in consecutive order, it takes three clock cycles to finish updating because only one edge is processed in the first and third clock cycle. However, if edges are shuffled, it only takes two clock cycles, and two edges are processed during each cycle.

Based on this shuffling method, we proposed the edge shuffling method which is shown in Figure 7. Edges in K consecutive sub-blocks are shuffled. K consecutive edges in DRAM are in different sub-blocks thus they are sent to different PEs. If the sizes of sub-blocks are different, Fore-Graph uses a NULL edge to fill in the blank position (gray blocks in Figure 7). We adopt DFR thus the destination sub-interval is replaced when all PEs finished updating. Figure 8 shows an example of the accessing order of sub-blocks in $B_{x \to y}$. K consecutive sub-intervals are loaded to the chip to update all sub-intervals. After loading sub-intervals, shuffled edges are loaded and dispatched to each PE.

4.3 Skipping Useless Blocks

In Algorithm 1, edges in all blocks are accessed in one iteration. However, previous work [30, 31] show that in algorithms like BFS, only some vertices are updated in one iteration. If a vertex is not updated, its neighbor vertices will not be updated in the next iteration. Thus, we do not have to access its outgoing edges.

Based on such observation, we can skip some edges if their source vertices are not updated in the prior iteration. Furthermore, if all vertices in one (sub-) interval have not been updated in one iteration, outgoing edges in (sub-) blocks with source vertices in the (sub-) interval do not need to be accessed in the next iteration. In this way, we can load fewer edges from the off-chip memory and skip (sub-) blocks which are unnecessary to be transmitted. In the implementation in ForeGraph, we use one bit in a bitmap [31] to represent if a sub-interval is updated in an iteration.

Table 3: Notations used in analysis

Notation	Meaning
BW_{mem}	bandwidth of the off-chip memory
BW_{int}	bandwidth of the interconnection
S_v	space used to store a vertex
S_e	space used to store an edge
M_{bram}	on-chip BRAM size
f	frequency of on-chip logic

5. THEORETICAL ANALYSIS

In ForeGraph, parameters like P and Q need to be set before implementation. In this section, we analyze how these parameters influence the performance of ForeGraph. Notations used in this section are listed in Table 3.

5.1 Modeling of ForeGraph

The processing time of an FPGA board mainly includes the following three parts:

- $T_{process}$, time of reading/writing sub-intervals from/to the off-chip memory before updating.
- T_{load}, time of loading edges from the off-chip memory when updating. We assume that on-chip throughput of all PEs is larger than off-chip bandwidth.
- $T_{transmit}$, time of loading intervals from other boards.

We assume that all n vertices and m edges are evenly divided into PQ and P^2Q^2 partitions (based on Table 8). Thus a sub-interval contains $n/(PQ)$ vertices and a sub-block contains $m/(P^2Q^2)$ edges. The first constraint is that on-chip BRAM size is sufficient to store all K source sub-intervals and destination sub-intervals.

$$M_{bram} \geq 2 \cdot K \cdot \frac{n}{PQ} \cdot S_v \rightarrow \frac{Q}{K} \geq \frac{2 \cdot n \cdot S_v}{P \cdot M_{bram}} \quad (3)$$

The second constraint relies on our vertex index compression method. We use no more than 16 bits to represent a vertex in a sub-interval. Thus a sub-interval contains less than $2^{16} = 65536$ vertices.

$$\frac{n}{PQ} \leq 65536 \quad (4)$$

The third constraint is that on-chip throughput is larger than off-chip bandwidth. We assume that the logic in PEs is designed in a pipelined architecture. Thus a PE can process one edge per clock cycle. The maximal on-chip throughput is $K \cdot S_e \cdot f$.

$$K \cdot S_e \cdot f \geq BW_{mem} \quad (5)$$

Formula (3)~(5) show the constraints in ForeGraph. Based on these constraints, we calculate the processing time of an FPGA board. Table 2 shows that in ForeGraph $(Q + 2Q^2/K)$ sub-intervals are read from/written to the off-chip memory when processing a block. A board needs to process P blocks in total thus we get $T_{process}$ in Formula (6).

$$T_{process} = \frac{(Q + \frac{2Q^2}{K})P\frac{n}{PQ}S_v}{BW_{mem}} = \frac{n \cdot S_v}{BW_{mem}} \cdot (1 + \frac{2Q}{K}) \quad (6)$$

Edges in P blocks are loaded to the FPGA chip. Thus, we get T_{load} in Formula (7).

$$T_{load} = \frac{\frac{m}{P} \cdot S_e}{BW_{mem}} \quad (7)$$

Intervals on other FPGA boards are transmitted to the board thus we get $T_{transmit}$ in Formula (8).

$$T_{transmit} = \frac{(P-1) \cdot \frac{n}{P} \cdot S_v}{BW_{int}} \approx \frac{n \cdot S_v}{BW_{int}} \quad (8)$$

Based on Formula (6)~(8), we can get the whole processing time of an FPGA board $T = T_{process} + T_{load} + T_{transmit}$.

5.2 Influence of Parameters on ForeGraph

Substitute Formula (3) into Formula (6), we get Formula (9).

$$T_{process} \geq \frac{n \cdot S_v}{BW_{mem}} \cdot (1 + \frac{4 \cdot n \cdot S_v}{P \cdot M_{bram}}) \quad (9)$$

We simplify $T_{process} \sim T_{transmit}$ and get T in Formula (10).

$$T = T_{process} + T_{load} + T_{transmit} \geq \alpha + \beta \cdot \frac{1}{P} \quad (10)$$

In Formula (10), α and β are two constants, show in Formula (11) and Formula (12).

$$\alpha = \frac{n \cdot S_v}{BW_{mem}} + \frac{n \cdot S_v}{BW_{int}} \quad (11)$$

$$\beta = \frac{4 \cdot n^2 \cdot S_v^2}{BW_{mem} \cdot M_{bram}} + \frac{m \cdot S_e}{BW_{mem}} \quad (12)$$

From Formula (10) we conclude that larger P (using more FPGA boards) leads to better performance in ForeGraph. However, in the real implementation, larger P leads to unbalance problem between partitions and decline of BW_{int}, thus simply increasing P cannot improve the performance when P reaches a threshold. Moreover, Q and K need to meet the condition for equality in Formula (3)~(5).

5.3 Comparison with Other Systems

We compare ForeGraph with two state-of-the-art FPGA-based large-scale graph processing systems, FPGP [18] and Shijie's work [23] (we call Shi in the following paper). We divide vertices into Q partitions. Both FPGP and Shi store vertices on the chip as many as possible. In FPGP, there is a *Shared-Vertex Memory* (SVM) connected to all FPGAs. Such implementation limits the scalability to multi-FPGA because the total bandwidth of SVM is limited. There are two source buffers on the chip thus it processes $K/2$ partitions equivalently. All edges are read once in FPGP. Shi uses the off-chip memory to store the temporary value of vertices, yet it cannot scale to the multi-FPGA architecture. All edges are read and written once respectively. On-chip BRAMs can store $2K$ partitions. Each partition needs to be read once when writing edge list and read/write once when reading the message list. Moreover, reading and writing of an edge in Shi are attached with a vertex value.

We compare the performance of the three systems on one FPGA board (FPGP does not scale well to multi-FPGA, and Shijie's work does not support multi-FPGA). The comparison result is shown in Table 4. Cells in the gray background show the system with the best performance from one perspective. ForeGraph outperforms the other two systems in terms of minimum data transmitting amount, maximal edges updated per cycle and scalability.

Table 4: Comparison between ForeGraph and other systems

	FPGP [18]	Shijie's work [23]	ForeGraph (ours)
read	$2Q/K \cdot nS_v + mS_e$	$2nS_v + mS_e + mS_v$	$(1 + Q/K)nS_v + mS_e$
write	nS_v	$nS_v + mS_v$	$Q/K \cdot nS_v$
read+write (assuming $m = 10n$ and $Q = 4K$)	$9nS_v + 10nS_e$	$23nS_v + 10nS_e$	$9nS_v + 10nS_e$
edges updated per cycle	two edges per cycle	at most K edges per cycle	K edges per cycle
multi-FPGA scalability	not scale well	no	scale well

6. EXPERIMENTAL RESULTS

Based on the system design and optimization methods, we conduct several experiments using different algorithms on different graphs. We also compare the performance of ForeGraph with state-of-the-art systems in this section.

6.1 Experimental Setup

We evaluate the performance of ForeGraph on the Xilinx Virtex UltraScale VCU110 evaluation platform with an xvcu190 FPGA chip. The target FPGA chip provides 16.61 MB on-chip BRAM resources. We verify the correctness of ForeGraph and get the clock rate as well as resource utilization using Xilinx Vivado 2016.2. All these results are from post-place-and-route simulations. The target off-chip memory is Micron MTA8ATF51264HZ-2G3 SDRAM (2GB, DDR4) and we use DRAMSim2 [32] to simulate the time consumption when accessing off-chip data. The memory runs at 1.2 GHz and provides a peak bandwidth of 19.2 GB/s. We simulate the time consumption of interconnection based on the Microsoft Catapult, it provides a stable latency around 400 ns and bandwidth around 12.25 Gb/s.

Table 5: Properties and acronyms of graphs

	# Vertices	# Edges
com-youtube (YT) [33]	1.16 million	2.99 million
wiki-talk (WK) [33]	2.39 million	5.02 million
live-journal (LJ) [33]	4.85 million	69.0 million
twitter-2010 (TW) [29]	41.7 million	1.47 billion
yahoo-web (YH) [34]	1.41 billion	6.64 billion

To evaluate the performance of ForeGraph, we implement it using three graph algorithms on five real-world graphs. Three graph algorithms include PageRank (PR), Breadth-First Search (BFS) and Weakly Connected Components (WCC). The properties of target graphs are shown in Table 5. The first three graphs can be implemented using one FPGA board while the latter two graphs need to be implemented on the multi-FPGA architecture. We use acronyms for these graphs and algorithms in our experimental results.

6.2 Resource Utilization

We use 8 bits to represent the depth of a vertex in BFS and 32 bits to represent the value of a vertex in PR and WCC. The average width of an edge is 32 bits (16 bits for the source vertex and 16 bits for the destination vertex) using our vertex index compression method. In this way, there are at most 65536 vertices in a sub-block. A sub-block uses 8 bits × 65536 = 64 KB BRAM resources in BFS and 32 bits × 65536 = 256 KB BRAM resources in PR/WCC. We implement 96 PEs when executing BFS and 24 PEs when executing PR/WCC. Detailed resource utilization, as well as clock rate, is shown in Table 6.

Table 6: Resource utilization and clock rate

	BFS	PR	WCC
# PEs	96	24	24
LUT	31.2%	33.4%	35.9%
Register	17.3%	20.6%	19.7%
BRAM	89.4%	81.0%	81.0%
Maximal clock rate	205 MHz	187 MHz	173 MHz
Simulation clock rate	200 MHz	150 MHz	150 MHz

6.3 Execution Time and Throughput

We implement three algorithms (BFS, PR, WCC) on four graphs (YT, WK, LJ, TW). Only one FPGA board is used when processing YT, WK, and LJ, while four FPGA boards are used when processing TW in our simulation.

Table 7: Execution time/throughput of ForeGraph

Algorithm	Graph	Execution time(s)	Throughput (MTEPS)
BFS	YT	0.010	897
	WK	0.027	929
	LJ	0.452	1069
	TW	15.12	1458 (364/board)
PR	YT	0.030	997
	WK	0.052	965
	LJ	0.578	1193
	TW	7.921	1856 (464/board)
WCC	YT	0.016	934
	WK	0.021	956
	LJ	0.307	1124
	TW	24.68	1727 (432/board)

Table 7 shows that the throughput of ForeGraph is around 1000 MTEPS when processing small graphs (e.g. YT, WK, and LJ). When processing larger graphs (e.g. TW) on the multi-FPGAs, the throughput decreases to 400 MTEPS because of the inter-FPGA communication and frequent substitution of on-chip data.

6.4 Benefits of Optimization Methods

6.4.1 Benefits of Vertex Index Compression

In ForeGraph, a vertex is indexed in its corresponding sub-interval using 16 bits. Table 5 shows the number of vertices in each graph with which we can calculate the required bit width to represent a vertex in each graph using the naive coding method. A vertex needs to be represented with $\log_2(1.1 \times 10^6) = 21$ bits in the YT graph and $\log_2(1.4 \times 10^9) = 31$ bits in the YW graph. Thus, ForeGraph reduces the edge data amount by 23.81%~48.39%.

6.4.2 Benefits of Edge Shuffling

ForeGraph processes K source sub-intervals simultaneously and edges in corresponding sub-blocks are loaded to PEs. We use the edge shuffling method to avoid the case that few PEs are overburdened, while others are idle waiting edges. We execute the PR (10 iterations) on four graphs using two different methods, the randomized (randomizing edges in each K sub-blocks) and shuffled order. [1] [2]

Table 8: Benefits of edge shuffling

		YT	WK	LJ	TW
# edges[1]	randomized	2.99m	5.02m	69.0m	1.47b
	shuffled[2]	393m	704m	12.5b	334b
	shuffled	3.77m	5.58m	92.6m	1.72b
edge data increased[2]		131x	140x	181x	234x
edge data increased		1.26x	1.11x	1.34x	1.17x
T_{exe}	randomized	0.041s	0.077s	0.952s	16.55s
	shuffled	0.030s	0.052s	0.578s	7.921s
speedup		1.37x	1.48x	1.65x	2.09x

Table 8 shows the comparison between two edge arrangement methods. In the edge shuffling method, we need to insert several *NULL* edges (Figure 7) thus it increases 1.22x edge data amount on average (If we divide consecutive vertices rather than vertices with a constant stride into an interval, the edge size is 172x on average due to the unbalanced size of each sub-block. The reason is the *power − law* characteristic of natural graphs, vertices with most in-edges are divided into one interval and sizes of its sub-blocks will be much large than other sub-blocks. Only one PE is working in this situation.). However, such increase of edges can lead to 1.66x performance improvement on average because we balance the workload of different PEs.

6.4.3 Benefits of Block Skipping

A source (sub-) interval, as well as corresponding out-edges, is skipped in an iteration when it is not updated in the prior iteration. Such optimization method leads to fewer data transmission between on-chip BRAMs and off-chip memories. We execute the BFS algorithm on four graphs and change the number of (sub-) intervals to show the ratio of transmitted (sub-) intervals/edges in Figure 9.

If we divide graphs into thousands of partitions, only 35%∼50% (sub-)intervals/edges are transmitted using our skipping method, shown in Figure 9. In this way, we reduce the transmitted data amount in ForeGraph.

6.5 Scalability

Section 5 shows that larger P leads to performance improvement. However, the interconnection scheme has the influence on the performance. We simulate four different interconnection schemes, including full interconnection (point-to-point connection), torus interconnection (implemented in

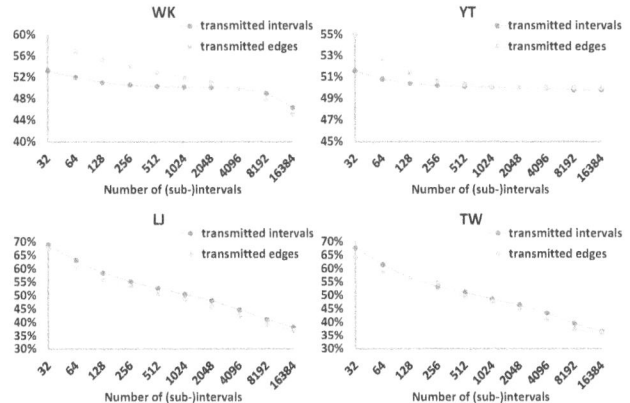

Figure 9: Transmitted (sub-)intervals/edges, executing BFS (varying number of (sub-)intervals).

Catapult), mesh (each FPGA board is connected to adjacent ones) and bus (all FPGA boards are connected using the bus). In these four schemes, the bandwidth and latency of a physical connection are all set to 12.25 Gb/s and 400 ns. We implement the PR algorithm on TW and YH.

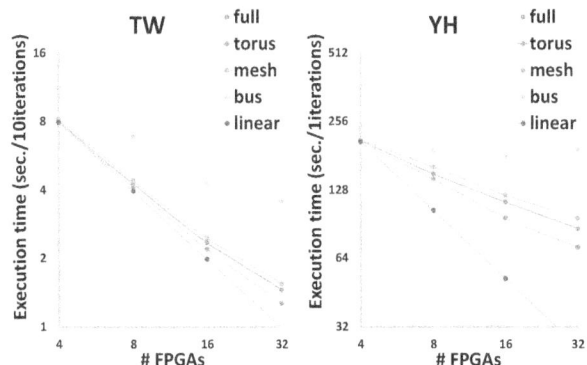

Figure 10: Scalability of ForeGraph.

We add a blue curve which provides a presumptive linear speedup (blue) in Figure 10. Both torus (orange) and mesh (gray) provide comparable performance to the full interconnection scheme (green). The comparison results of blue and green curves show that even the full interconnection cannot provide linear speedup because of the unbalanced workload of different FPGAs. Even so, ForeGraph scales well to the multi-FPGA platform.

6.6 Comparison with State-of-the-art Systems

We compare ForeGraph with state-of-the-art systems in Table 9. ForeGraph outperforms state-of-the-art systems on both execution time and throughput. Experimental results show that ForeGraph achieves 4.54x∼5.04x speedup to CPU-based systems and 8.07x speedup to the FPGA-based system. Moreover, the throughput of ForeGraph is 1.41x∼2.65x larger than previous FPGA-based systems.

7. CONCLUSION

In this paper, we propose a large-scale graph processing system, ForeGraph, based on the multi-FPGA architecture. ForeGraph provides larger on-chip BRAMs size and off-chip bandwidth which are essential to accelerate large-scale graph processing. Partitioning and communication scheme among FPGAs are also considered to ensure locality and reduce conflicts. ForeGraph achieves 5.89x speedup

---

[1] m stands for million and b stands for billion.

[2] We compare two partitioning methods. Results with this footnote divide consecutive vertices into an interval (e.g. $v_1, v_2, v_3...$). This partitioning scheme is widely used in many state-of-the-art systems like Gemini [7] and NXgraph [10]. Results without footnote are from our partitioning method which divides vertices with a constant stride into an interval (e.g. $v_1, v_{101}, v_{201}...$). Actually, the partitioning method is heavily dependent on the given vertex labeling, while natural graphs follow *power-law* and vertices with higher degrees seem to have smaller indexes.

Table 9: Comparison between ForeGraph and state-of-the-art systems

| Algorithm | Graph | Metric | ForeGraph | | Comparison system | | | Improve-ment |
			Platform	Performance	System	Platform	Performance	
BFS	TW	execution time(s)	4 FPGAs	15.12	TurboGraph [13]	CPU	76.134	5.04x
BFS	TW	execution time(s)	4 FPGAs	15.12	FPGP [18]	1 FPGA	121.99	8.07x
PR	TW	execution time(s)	4 FPGAs	7.921	PowerGraph [2]	512 CPUs	36	4.54x
BFS	WK	throughput(MTEPS)	1 FPGA	1069	Shijie's work [23]	1 FPGA	657	1.41x
BFS	–	throughput(MTEPS)	4 FPGAs	1458	CyGraph [16]	4 FPGAs	550	2.65x

compared with state-of-the-art designs, and 2.03x average throughput improvement compared with previous FPGA-based systems. Using on-chip BRAMs with random access feature is a promising way to accelerate large-scale graph processing, but it is still limited by the size of BRAMs. Both theoretical analysis and experimental results show that larger BRAM size leads to better performance. In future, it is reasonable to use FPGAs with more on-chip memory resources (e.g. UltraRAM in Xilinx UltraScale$^+$ [35], Altera Stratix 10 using 3D-stacking technology [36], and *etc.*) to achieve a superior performance.

8. ACKNOWLEDGMENT

This work was supported by National Natural Science Foundation of China (No. 61373026, 61622403, 61261160501) and Huawei Innovation Research Program (HIRP). We are also thankful to reviewers for their helpful suggestions.

9. REFERENCES

[1] Graph 500. http://www.graph500.org/.
[2] Je Gonzalez, Y Low, and H Gu. Powergraph: Distributed graph-parallel computation on natural graphs. In *OSDI*, pages 17–30, 2012.
[3] Joseph E Gonzalez, Reynold S Xin, Ankur Dave, Daniel Crankshaw, Michael J Franklin, and Ion Stoica. Graphx: Graph processing in a distributed dataflow framework. In *OSDI*, pages 599–613, 2014.
[4] Aapo Kyrola, Guy Blelloch, and Carlos Guestrin. GraphChi: Large-Scale Graph Computation on Just a PC Disk-based Graph Computation. In *OSDI*, pages 31–46, 2012.
[5] Yucheng Low, Danny Bickson, Joseph Gonzalez, Carlos Guestrin, Aapo Kyrola, and Joseph M Hellerstein. Distributed graphlab: a framework for machine learning and data mining in the cloud. *VLDB Endowment*, pages 716–727, 2012.
[6] Grzegorz Malewicz, Matthew H Austern, Aart JC Bik, James C Dehnert, Ilan Horn, Naty Leiser, and Grzegorz Czajkowski. Pregel: a system for large-scale graph processing. In *SIGMOD*, pages 135–146. ACM, 2010.
[7] Xiaowei Zhu, Wenguang Chen, Weimin Zheng, and Xiaosong Ma. Gemini: A computation-centric distributed graph processing system. In *OSDI*, pages 301–316, 2016.
[8] Nadathur Satish, Narayanan Sundaram, Md Mostofa Ali Patwary, Jiwon Seo, Jongsoo Park, M Amber Hassaan, Shubho Sengupta, Zhaoming Yin, and Pradeep Dubey. Navigating the maze of graph analytics frameworks using massive graph datasets. In *SIGMOD*, pages 979–990. ACM, 2014.
[9] Donald Nguyen, Andrew Lenharth, and Keshav Pingali. A lightweight infrastructure for graph analytics. In *SOSP*, pages 456–471. ACM, 2013.
[10] Yuze Chi, Guohao Dai, Yu Wang, Guangyu Sun, Guoliang Li, and Huazhong Yang. Nxgraph: An efficient graph processing system on a single machine. In *ICDE*, pages 409–420, 2016.
[11] Xiaowei Zhu, Wentao Han, and Wenguang Chen. GridGraph : Large-Scale Graph Processing on a Single Machine Using 2-Level Hierarchical Partitioning. In *ATC*, pages 375–386, 2015.
[12] Amitabha Roy, Ivo Mihailovic, and Willy Zwaenepoel. X-stream: edge-centric graph processing using streaming partitions. In *SOSP*, pages 472–488. ACM, 2013.
[13] Wook-Shin Han, Sangyeon Lee, Kyungyeol Park, Jeong-Hoon Lee, Min-Soo Kim, Jinha Kim, and Hwanjo Yu. Turbograph: a fast parallel graph engine handling billion-scale graphs in a single pc. In *SIGKDD*, pages 77–85. ACM, 2013.
[14] Farzad Khorasani. Scalable SIMD-Efficient Graph Processing on GPUs. In *PACT*, pages 39–50. ACM, 2015.
[15] Duane Merrill, Michael Garland, and Andrew Grimshaw. Scalable gpu graph traversal. In *ACM SIGPLAN Notices*, pages 117–128. ACM, 2012.
[16] Osama G Attia, Tyler Johnson, Kevin Townsend, Philip Jones, and Joseph Zambreno. Cygraph: A reconfigurable architecture for parallel breadth-first search. In *IPDPSW*, pages 228–235. IEEE, 2014.
[17] Brahim Betkaoui, Yu Wang, David B Thomas, and Wayne Luk. A reconfigurable computing approach for efficient and scalable parallel graph exploration. In *ASAP*, pages 8–15. IEEE, 2012.
[18] Guohao Dai, Yuze Chi, Yu Wang, and Huazhong Yang. Fpgp: Graph processing framework on fpga a case study of breadth-first search. In *FPGA*, pages 105–110. ACM, 2016.
[19] Nina Engelhardt and Hayden Kwok-Hay So. Gravf: A vertex-centric distributed graph processing framework on fpgas. In *FPL*, pages 403–406. IEEE, 2016.
[20] Nachiket Kapre, Nikil Mehta, Dominic Rizzo, Ian Eslick, Raphael Rubin, Tomas E Uribe, F Thomas Jr, Andre DeHon, et al. Graphstep: A system architecture for sparse-graph algorithms. In *FCCM*, pages 143–151. IEEE, 2006.
[21] Eriko Nurvitadhi, Gabriel Weisz, Yu Wang, Skand Hurkat, Marie Nguyen, James C Hoe, José F Martínez, and Carlos Guestrin. Graphgen: An fpga framework for vertex-centric graph computation. In *FCCM*, pages 25–28. IEEE, 2014.
[22] Tayo Oguntebi and Kunle Olukotun. Graphops: A dataflow library for graph analytics acceleration. In *FPGA*, pages 111–117. ACM, 2016.
[23] Shijie Zhou, Charalampos Chelmis, and Viktor K Prasanna. High-throughput and energy-efficient graph processing on fpga. In *FCCM*, pages 103–110. IEEE, 2016.
[24] Junwhan Ahn, Sungpack Hong, Sungjoo Yoo, Onur Mutlu, and Kiyoung Choi. A scalable processing-in-memory accelerator for parallel graph processing. In *ISCA*, pages 105–117. ACM, 2015.
[25] Andrew Lumsdaine, Douglas Gregor, Bruce Hendrickson, and Jonathan Berry. Challenges In Parallel Graph Processing. *Parallel Processing Letters*, pages 5–20, 2007.
[26] Andrew Lenharth, Donald Nguyen, and Keshav Pingali. Parallel graph analytics. *Communications of the ACM*, 59(5):78–87, 2016.
[27] Brahim Betkaoui, Yu Wang, David B Thomas, and Wayne Luk. Parallel fpga-based all pairs shortest paths for sparse networks: A human brain connectome case study. In *FPL*, pages 99–104. IEEE, 2012.
[28] Andrew Putnam, Adrian M Caulfield, Eric S Chung, Derek Chiou, Kypros Constantinides, John Demme, Hadi Esmaeilzadeh, Jeremy Fowers, Gopi Prashanth Gopal, Jan Gray, et al. A reconfigurable fabric for accelerating large-scale datacenter services. In *ISCA*, pages 13–24. IEEE, 2014.
[29] Haewoon Kwak, Changhyun Lee, Hosung Park, and Sue Moon. What is twitter, a social network or a news media? In *WWW*, pages 591–600. ACM, 2010.
[30] Virat Agarwal, Fabrizio Petrini, Davide Pasetto, and David A Bader. Scalable graph exploration on multicore processors. In *SC*, pages 1–11. IEEE, 2010.
[31] Sungpack Hong, Tayo Oguntebi, and Kunle Olukotun. Efficient parallel graph exploration on multi-core cpu and gpu. In *PACT*, pages 78–88. IEEE, 2011.
[32] Paul Rosenfeld, Elliott Cooper-Balis, and Bruce Jacob. Dramsim2: A cycle accurate memory system simulator. *IEEE Computer Architecture Letters*, 10(1):16–19, 2011.
[33] Stanford large network dataset collection. http://snap.stanford.edu/data/index.html#web.
[34] Yahoo! altavisata web page hyperlink connectivity graph, circa 2002. http://webscope.sandbox.yahoo.com/.
[35] https://www.xilinx.com/products/silicon-devices/fpga/virtex-ultrascale-plus.html.
[36] https://www.altera.com/solutions/technology/next-generation-technology/overview.html.

FPGA-Accelerated Transactional Execution
of Graph Workloads

Xiaoyu Ma, Dan Zhang and Derek Chiou
The University of Texas at Austin
{xma, dzhang, derek}@utexas.edu

ABSTRACT

Many applications that operate on large graphs can be intuitively parallelized by executing a large number of the graph operations concurrently and as transactions to deal with potential conflicts. However, large numbers of operations occurring concurrently might incur too many conflicts that would negate the potential benefits of the parallelization which has probably made highly multi-threaded transactional machines seem impractical. Given the large size and topology of many modern graphs, however, such machines can provide real performance, energy efficiency, and programability benefits. This paper describes an architecture that consists of many lightweight multi-threaded processing engines, a global transactional shared memory, and a work scheduler. We present challenges of realizing such an architecture, especially the requirement of scalable conflict detection, and propose solutions. We also argue that despite increased transaction conflicts due to the higher concurrency and single-thread latency, scalable speedup over serial execution can be achieved. We implement the proposed architecture as a synthesizable FPGA RTL design and demonstrate improved per-socket performance (2X) and energy efficiency (22X) by comparing to a baseline platform that contains two Intel Haswell processors, each with 12 cores.

Keywords

Graph Application; FPGA Accelerator; Transactional Memory; Throughput Compute; Multi-threaded Architecture

1. INTRODUCTION

Graph applications, widely used in many fields such as social network analysis, machine learning, data mining, electronic design automation and etc., have massive data parallelism because they iterate over a large number of vertices and/or edges using the same operators. Unlike regular data-parallel applications which can be well accelerated by SIMD (e.g. vector processing) or SIMT (e.g. GPUs) mechanisms,

however, graph workloads are dominated by pointer operations, leading to irregular memory accesses and control divergences which make those mechanisms inefficient. Therefore, parallelizing graph workloads requires more general, single-program-multiple-thread mechanisms, often achieved by thread-level parallelization techniques.

Transactions simplify parallel programming of graph applications by eliminating the need for fine-grained locks [1]. The scheduling of transactions is often combined with optimistic concurrent execution, which assumes transactions do not conflict, executes them in parallel and relies on transactional memory (TM) to detect conflicts and rollback conflicting transactions as needed. TM performs two main tasks: conflict detection and version management. Conflict detection signals an overlap between writes of one transaction and writes or reads of other concurrent transactions. Conflict detection is either eager (sometimes called pessimistic) if it detects offending accesses immediately or lazy (sometimes called optimistic) if it defers detection until later (e.g. when transactions commit). Version management defines where and how transactional writes are stored. The two main options for version management are lazy and eager. In a lazy approach, new values are stored in a temporary write buffer and are committed (or discarded) if the transaction succeeds (or fails). In an eager approach, new values are written into memory directly and old values are held in an undo-log. The undo-log is discarded (or flushed to memory) if the transaction succeeds (or fails).

The goal of this work is to accelerate transactional execution of graph applications. Towards this goal, we propose running many transactions in parallel to exploit the irregular data-parallelism available in graph workloads and an architecture to achieve this idea. The proposed architecture consists of lightweight multi-threaded processing engines that support the non-lockstep parallel execution of many transactions and high memory latency tolerance, a global shared memory with a hardware TM, and a work scheduler. While our idea is also applicable to CPUs and ASICs, we focus on using dedicated logic on FPGAs to exploit fine-grained parallelism and reduce general-purpose compute overheads like instruction fetch and decode. We implement the proposed architecture as a synthesizable FPGA RTL design and compare in performance and energy efficiency against a baseline platform using Intel 24-core Haswell processors.

2. MOTIVATIONAL EXAMPLE

As an example to motivate the techniques to be presented, the Vertex Exploration kernel (Figure 1) performs a BFS-

FPGA '17, February 22–24, 2017, Monterey, CA, USA.
© 2017 ACM. ISBN 978-1-4503-4354-1/17/02. . . $15.00
DOI: http://dx.doi.org/10.1145/3020078.3021743

```
Vertex-Exploration (graph);

  graph.init (); // init graph
  workQ.add (graph.root); // init workQ

  // main loop
  foreach (Vertex v in workQ) {
    // start of transaction
    if (v.visited == 0) {
      v.visit ();
      v.visited = 1;
      foreach (Vertex u : v.neighbors)
        workQ.add (u);
    }
    // end of transaction
  }
```

Figure 1: Vertex Exploration

like process that traverses all graph vertices reachable from the root and visits each vertex exactly once by updating a *visited* bit. During graph initialization, the *visited* bit is set to *0* for all vertices. The algorithm starts from the root node by putting it into a work queue. The work queue is a pool, with a scheduling policy e.g. FIFO, holding vertices to be processed in the future and supports dynamic work production and consumption, which is common for graph applications. The *foreach* loop body is transactional. Every iteration gets one vertex from the work queue and checks the *visited* bit of the vertex. If that vertex has been visited already, nothing happens and the iteration is done. Otherwise, the *visit()* function is called. Afterwards its *visited* bit is updated to *1* and its neighbor vertices are added into the work queue. If multiple vertices share a common adjacent vertex, each of them may generate a work item corresponding to that neighbor, leading to duplicated work. While duplicated work exists, transactional semantics ensure the vertex is visited only once since the *visited* bit is set by the first visitor to prevent others. If two transactions try to set the *visited* bit at the same time, a conflict is detected and handled so that only one can proceed and the other is aborted for re-execution.

The application exhibits massive loop-level data parallelism for large input datasets with e.g. millions of nodes. The available parallelism can be characterized by the number of work items available in the work queue as well as the likelihood of conflicts when they are executed in parallel. While initially the parallelism is limited to one vertex since only the root vertex is in the work queue, processing one vertex can cause all its neighbors to be inserted as new work into the work queue, leading to a quick increase of the available parallelism. Both the amount of parallelism and the likelihood of conflicts depend heavily on the size and topology of the input graph. In general, as the input graph gets bigger, the chance of conflicts decreases and the available parallelism increases accordingly until the algorithm runs out of work.

We propose running many transactions in parallel to exploit the exhibited parallelism. Transactions are viewed as software threads running on hardware substrate. Similar to GPUs, we emphasize high throughput rather than low single-thread latency. Unlike vector processors and GPUs that execute concurrent threads in a lockstep fashion, which

we call *synchronous execution*, we run transactions as independent threads not in lockstep, defined as *asynchronous execution*. We don't use *synchronous execution* models because they are inefficient due to the under-utilization issue of compute and memory resources [2–4] caused by control and data divergences of graph workloads. For the above example, assuming a real-world social network where some vertices are connected to thousands of edges while some are connected to only a few, the variation of transaction latency is significant, causing the synchronous model to not be a good fit because the overall latency of a group of concurrent threads is determined by the worst case in that group. In addition to high thread count and asynchronous execution, we employ hardware multi-threading for high latency tolerance to address the low spatial locality of point-based graph structures and support a large number of outstanding memory requests to explore memory-level parallelism, both ideas introduced by the Tera multi-threaded architecture [5].

3. KEY PROBLEMS

- While running transactions with increased concurrency exploits more parallelism, transaction conflicts increase accordingly because of more active transactions and higher single-thread latencies. Increased conflicts hurt scalability by undermining the performance gain brought by throughput compute, making the worthwhileness of running many transactions concurrently unclear.

- A scalable approach for conflict detection among a large number of asynchronous transactions is required to realize the proposed idea. While transactional memory (TM) designs have been proposed for GPU bulk synchronous execution with thousands of threads, they are not applicable to asynchronous systems. Other prior TMs do not target architectures with hundreds or thousands of threads.

- The slower a transaction, the higher the probability that it causes other transactions to fail because it does not release resources quickly enough. Transaction re-execution can also cause other transaction failure, leading to potential livelocks.

- The cache hierarchy is often affected by supporting transactions in existing TMs. A decoupled TM from the cache hierarchy would make the design cleaner and more flexible. In addition, it would enable replacing the silicon area that caches consume for additional computational capabilities, since caches are often area and energy inefficient for graph applications.

4. RELATED WORK

4.1 HW-Accelerated Graph Workloads

Hardware acceleration of graph workloads has gained a lot attention due to the explosion of digital data and the ever-growing need for fast data analysis. Several architectural requirements [6] were presented for hardware specialization of graph computations. Such requirements include an active work set, asynchronous execution with specialized synchronization mechanisms, memory latency tolerance, dynamic load balancing and customized memory subsystem. Many of these requirements have been realized in a variety of graph accelerator architectures. Betkaoui et al. proposed a reconfigurable architecture [7] which doesn't have a traditional cached memory hierarchy and tolerates off-chip memory latency by using a memory crossbar that connects many parallel identical processing elements to the shared off-chip memory. GraphStep [8] presented a concurrent system architecture for sparse graph algorithms that places graph nodes in small distributed memories paired with specialized graph processing nodes interconnected by a lightweight network. It also claimed the proposed architecture can be well mapped to FPGAs which have high-bandwidth and low-latency embedded memories. GraphGen [9] automatically compiles a vertex-centric graph specification onto an application-specific processor with a specialized memory subsystem and pipelined logic for user-defined instructions. Ozdal et al. [10] used System-C HLS flow to generate graph accelerators from programs based on the gather, apply and scatter model. The generated accelerator has a vertex-centric microarchitecture where tens of vertices and hundreds of edges are processed simultaneously and asynchronously for memory-level parallelism exploration. Tesseract [11] applied the concept of processing-in-memory (PIM) to graph processing by designing a programmable PIM accelerator with many in-order cores inside a memory chip, a new message passing mechanism to hide remote access latency and specialized graph prefetchers.

4.2 HW Transactional Memory (HTM)

HTM on CPUs. There are many HTM designs on CPUs [12–24], with focuses on version management, conflict detection, unbounded transaction support, scalability, flexibility and etc. Besides academic projects, HTMs are also available in industry implementations, such as Sun Rock [25], Intel Haswell and Broadwell [26,27], IBM BlueGene/Q [28], SystemZ [29] and POWER8 [30] processors. In general, these designs target a shared memory multiprocessor with a separate cache for each core and achieve HTM through modifying standard cache coherence protocols. Version management is performed by either buffering speculative state, typically in the cache or store buffer, or maintaining an undo-log. Metadata required by conflict detection is typically stored in Bloom filters or in bits added to each cache line.

HTM on GPUs. KILO TM [31] is an HTM design for GPUs to support thousands of concurrent transactions. It employs lazy version management and lazy conflict detection and leverages GPU's SIMT execution model. During the speculative execution, transactions within a thread block execute instructions like non-transactional code and buffer memory reads and writes in the local memory. After the thread block is done, a procedure is performed to detect conflicts among threads of the thread block and to commit/discard speculative results before the next thread block can be launched. Such a bulk synchronization assumed by KILO TM, however, doesn't exist in asynchronous execution which requires conflicts to be detected simultaneously with threads' speculative execution.

HTM on FPGAs. TMACC [32] offloaded conflict detection onto Bloom filter FPGA accelerators while having version management handled by software, and claimed by doing so the processor, caches, or coherence protocol do not need modifications in order to support accelerated transactional execution. Pusceddu et al. [33,34] presented a software layer to run TM on FPGA-based soft cores for small-scale embedded systems. Njoroge et al. [35] prototyped TCC [13] on an FPGA hosting two PowerPC soft cores. Kachris and Kulka-

rni [36] proposed an HTM design on four FPGA soft multiprocessors without private L1 caches. Grinberg and Weiss [37] took a similar approach in using FPGA-based HTM to simulate transactional systems. Labrecque and Steffan built NetTM [38] in an FPGA-based, multi-threaded, multicore architecture. They claimed that eager version management and eager conflict detection is a practical way of implementing FPGA-based HTM. NetTM supports eight threads running on two single-issue in-order cores, as well as large transactions through in-memory undo-logs.

Key Differences. Features that distinguish our work from prior HTM work are the capability of running hundreds to thousands of concurrent transactions in an asynchronous execution model and the worklist-based runtime control of transaction scheduling.

5. ACCELERATOR ARCHITECTURE

In this section we describe the accelerator architecture (Figure 2) that supports the execution of hundreds to thousands of transactions in the asynchronous execution environment.

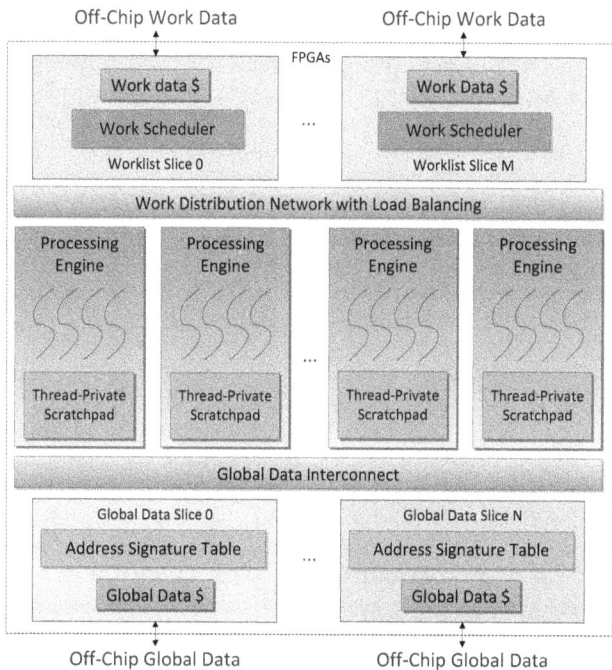

Figure 2: Architecture Overview

5.1 Memory Model

There are several memory spaces in the proposed architecture. **Global Shared Memory** presents a single view of the graph data structure. Global memory consistency is ensured by transactional semantics. Concurrent write/writes and read/writes to the same location from different threads are detected and handled by the transactional execution mechanism, eliminating the possibility of inconsistent states. **Work Memory** is a place for work data to be fetched by the worklist. Work memory requires off-chip storage since the work data can have an unbounded size. **Thread-Private Scratchpad Memory** holds each transaction's private data including intermediate results, speculatively created work, lock-log and versioning buffer (explained later). Since it's private to each thread, it cannot be used for communication among threads. Each thread starts with a clean scratchpad, eliminating the need of checkpointing before the transaction starts. Thread-private scratchpad uses on-chip buffer and may spill to off-chip for large transactions which cause hardware capacity overflow.

5.2 Processing Engines

Processing engines can be implemented using soft or hard processors or customized logic on FPGAs. They are fed with work data and process one work item at a time as a transaction. The work item definition and the operations that process the work item are application specific. For many applications the work item is a vertex or an edge, along with some attributes if needed. The processing of the work item typically touches that vertex or edge as well as a set of connected vertices and/or edges.

Processing engines access the global shared memory and the thread-private scratchpad memory as needed. One engine has multiple hardware threads, of which only one is active at any time. The engine switches among those threads in the event of off-chip memory accesses to hide memory latency. After a engine's currently active thread issues a memory operation, the engine switches to a different thread that is ready to proceed. When the result of the memory operation arrives, the thread that issued the operation earlier is rescheduled so that it becomes a candidate to be selected for continuation on a future context switch. Arithmetic operations of a thread can be executed either in-order or out-of-order to exploit parallelism within a thread. Global memory operations are issued in program order, eliminating single-thread memory write-after-write and write-after-read hazards and, therefore, simplifying the management of transactional states.

5.3 Worklist

The worklist feeds processing engines by fetching work data from work memory. The execution of a transaction may produce one or multiple new work items. Speculatively created new work is saved into the per-thread scratchpad memory. Later if that transaction commits, new work is sent to the worklist. Otherwise, new work is discarded and the work item processed by the failed transaction is sent back to the worklist to be scheduled for future re-execution.

The worklist has one or multiple instances, each called a worklist slice. Since producing/consuming work from the worklist usually has higher throughput than performing the computation, one worklist slice can feed many threads running on one or multiple processing engines. When there are multiple worklist slices, they are connected via an interconnect, e.g. a ring, and load balancing techniques can be employed to improve resource utilization. In each worklist slice, there is a scheduler that decides the order in which work items are sent to execution. For applications that require a specific execution order, bucket-based priority scheduling is widely used. A bucket-based priority scheduler [39] supports concurrent execution by allowing work items in the same bucket to execute in parallel. It also prioritizes buckets to achieve ordered execution, which is important to keep parallel execution efficient by reducing bad work, defined as updates of vertex/edge attributes to non-final values. While the bucket-based priority scheduler suppresses bad work, it doesn't scale well because bad work increases as the worklist

slice count increases. For some applications, the scheduling order has little performance impact and, therefore, simpler schedulers such as FIFO/LIFO are used for logic and power savings. In addition to scheduling, the worklist has done detection logic to terminate the execution when all worklist slices are empty and all processing engines are idle.

5.4 HW Transactional Memory

Threads are optimistically dispatched onto processing engines to execute by assuming the threads are isolated and do not conflict. Transactional memory detects and handles transactional semantics violations through version management, conflict detection and conflict resolution. Nested transactions are not supported. The proposed HTM does not rely on caches or coherence protocols.

5.4.1 Conflict Detection and Resolution

We adopt eager conflict detection because it identifies conflicts earlier and hence enables an earlier start of rollback to reduce wasted work. Conflict detection is performed for every global memory access. We provide scalable conflict detection by (1) using a shared directory to avoid broadcasting address signatures and (2) supporting concurrent conflict detection for memory accesses with different addresses. These ideas are achieved by **Address Signature Table** (AST), a shared directory for metadata that tracks memory footprints of all executing transactions. AST is like a cache whose set is chosen by a hash function. Given an address, the hash function maps it to a set that stores information needed to detect conflicts associated with that address. The stored information tells whether a live transaction has issued a memory request corresponding to the current AST set, indicated by a *valid* bit, and, if so, the *thread ID* of that transaction and whether it is a write or read using a *write* bit. Using the thread ID is space efficient because it has $\log_2 n$ (n is thread count) space complexity and leads to logarithmically increased AST size as the thread count increases. To allow multiple transactions to read the same address, an AST set can have multiple ways with each having these three fields, similar to a set associative cache. Although read-read overlaps should not cause conflict, a conflict must be assumed if there are not enough ways in that set. AST can be implemented using either on- or off- chip memory. On-chip AST supports faster conflict detection. Off-chip AST enables a larger signature table that reduces false sharing, a problem occurring when two different addresses are mapped onto the same AST set by the hash function. To support parallel conflict detection, the AST is partitioned into AST slices, each connected to processing engines through a network.

The conflict detection scheme is lock-based. Before a memory operation can be issued to memory, it arrives at its corresponding AST slice and set to reserve the entry by acquiring a lock on that set. During the AST entry reservation, the conflict detection algorithm (presented in the next paragraph) is performed to determine whether the memory operation conflicts with memory accesses of other concurrent threads. If a conflict does not occur, then the lock is acquired, the AST set is updated as needed, and the memory request will be sent to memory. Otherwise, the lock is not acquired by the requester thread. No further execution of that thread will be performed and that thread will abort. While detecting conflicts for every global data access is the default, it is not needed by an access to read-only data or an access with the same address as a preceding access that has been issued by the same thread and successfully acquired a lock. Such accesses can be marked as conflict free to bypass conflict detection.

The conflict detection protocol is as follows. (1) **Reads.** For a read, a valid way in the corresponding set of the read address with a matching thread ID indicates this thread already owns this location and, therefore, no conflict will be detected. Otherwise, if there is no write bit set for any valid ways and the set is not full, no conflict will be detected and one invalid way is allocated, setting the valid bit and the thread ID. In doing this, read-read overlaps are not detected as conflicts unless the associativity runs out. If there is a valid way with a different thread ID and a set write bit, which indicates another thread is writing to this location, then a conflict is detected. (2) **Writes.** Writes must be exclusive. If there exists a valid way in the corresponding set of the write address with a different thread ID, a conflict is detected because this implies another thread is writing to this location. Otherwise, no conflict is detected and one way of that set is allocated to the requester thread if needed, setting both the valid bit and the write bit.

One transaction can acquire locks on many addresses belonging to different AST slices and sets. Those locks need to be reclaimed during commit/abort so that they can be acquired later by other transactions. We use a per-thread **Lock-Log** residing in the thread-private scratchpad memory to keep track of each transaction's acquired locks by logging their addresses. The lock-log eliminates broadcasting the thread ID to all AST slices. Unlock requests are sent to AST slices associated with addresses recorded in the lock-log. Redundant entries of lock-log can be eliminated by logging an acquired lock only if a new AST entry has been allocated to the memory request. There is no required order in which lock-log entries are accessed during unlock. A simple solution is to organize the lock-log as an FIFO.

5.4.2 Version Management

Many prior HTM work leverages lazy version management by taking advantage of, and at the same time being constrained by, speculative execution that already exists in the microprocessor. Since we don't have that constraint, either eager or lazy can be used. The eager approach, which updates memory locations with speculative values and saves old values in a per-thread undo-log, allows faster commit by simply discarding the undo-log. It may hurt memory performance in two ways. First, each write introduces an extra read for the old value. The extra read can be eliminated if a preceding read has acquired the old value already, which is fortunately true for many graph applications. Second, memory bandwidth is wasted in performing and undoing the writes for aborted transactions. The lazy approach, which saves speculative values in a per-thread write-buffer and writes them to memory during commit, has faster abort by simply discarding the write-buffer. It also has the advantage of reducing memory traffic by coalesced writes but the disadvantage that the write-buffer must be searched for each read. In general, whether to use eager or lazy version management depends on how frequently rollback occurs. To achieve scalable performance, conflicts should be minimized and commit should be the common case. This makes the eager approach approach more attractive. In addition, the eager undo-log has a simpler structure than the lazy write-

buffer. The undo-log requires only sequential accesses. It can be achieved by an LIFO that saves old values of writes in program order and flushes to memory in reverse program order. In contrast, the lazy write-buffer requires an associative search on every read to load values from the latest write with the same address if single-thread read-after-write dependencies exist.

Version management is not needed when two conditions are satisfied. The first condition is limiting transactions to be cautious [1], that is, all reads occur before writes in program order and any write requires a preceding read to the same address. In fact, any non-cautious transaction is transformable to a cautious transaction by the programmer or compiler. The second condition is exclusive locking, meaning that a transaction holds an exclusive lock on data to prevent other transactions accessing the data (even if all accesses are read). Exclusive locking can be achieved by an one-way AST. When both conditions are met, the decision of transaction commit or rollback can be made before any write, eliminating the need of versioning buffer.

5.5 Livelock Avoidance

Livelocks are created by wasted work generating wasted work infinitely. For example, a thread that is aborting may not have had time to clear AST entries that another thread needs, causing the second thread unnecessarily to abort. If such abortings are circular and occur indefinitely, a livelock may occur. Making the abort process faster, e.g. through fast unlock and undo techniques, can reduce the chance of livelock, but cannot eliminate since it is impractical to make abort instantaneously fast. To tackle this problem, we introduce a concurrency control technique to dynamically turn on/off threads when needed. Each processing engine has logic that counts commits and aborts to compute the conflict rate. When the conflict rate during the past time interval is higher than the threshold, a certain number of threads are disabled. In case of livelock, no forward progress can be made so every transaction aborts. This would keep reducing the active thread count and eventually fall back to sequential execution which can always move forward since it has no conflicts. Likewise, threads that are disabled earlier can be re-activated if the conflict rate decreases. Besides avoiding livelocks, dynamic concurrency control can have positive performance impact by dynamically adjusting the execution width to the parallelism available to reduce conflicts.

5.6 Cache Hierarchy

Various caches can be introduced into the proposed architecture. A work data cache included in each worklist slice can be useful since work data has good spatial locality and fetching work data in a low-latency and high-throughput manner is important to keep processing engines busy. Per-engine L1 and/or global shared L2 caches for thread-private data such as intermediate results, lock-log and versioning buffer can help exploit short-term producer-consumer locality and speed up transaction commit/rollback. For graph data stored in the global shared memory, since it is required to send every graph data access to the global shared directory to detect possible conflicts, we eliminate per-engine L1 caches and, by doing so, eliminate the need for coherence. Instead, we support global shared L2 caches to service memory accesses that the AST determines are conflict free. To increase memory parallelism, conventional cache optimization techniques, such as banking, pipelining and non-blocking can be applied. Caches that have producer/consumer semantics and sequential memory footprint, e.g. work data cache for an FIFO worklist, can be further optimized to save unnecessary memory traffic. In addition, with the separation of HTM from cache hierarchy, each of these caches can be turned off to trade latency for logic and energy savings and the design would still work functionally.

6. EXPERIMENTAL EVALUATION

6.1 Experiment Methodology

6.1.1 Benchmarks

We study several benchmarks selected from the graph subcategory of graph exploration, shortest paths, connectivity analysis and graph coloring in the evaluation of our proposed approach. **Vertex Exploration** (VE) performs a BFS-like process to visit each vertex reachable from the root exactly once. **Bipartite Coloring** (BC) assigns one of two colors to each vertex of a bipartite graph such that no two adjacent vertices share the same color. **Transitive Closure** (TC) solves the reachability problem in graph theory. Given a graph in the form of adjacent matrix, it performs an iterative search to incrementally compute a two-dimensional reachability matrix, of which an element (i, j) represent whether there exists a path from vertex i to j in one or more hops. **Single Source Shortest Path** (SSSP) is a problem of finding shortest paths from a source vertex to all other vertices such that the sum of the weights of its constituent edges is minimized. The algorithm selected to solve this problem uses a demand-driven modification of the Bellman-Ford algorithm. **Breadth-First Search** (BFS) is a special case of SSSP with the distance being the number of hops required to reach from the source vertex. Its work scheduler requires very small bucket intervals and large per-bucket sizes, leading to significantly different dynamic behavior from SSSP. **Connected Components** (CC) performs a label propagation process to compute for each vertex the smallest component ID of all vertices reachable from that vertex.

S/L	ROAD		RAND		RMAT	
	Nodes	Edges	Nodes	Edges	Nodes	Edges
Small	1.9M	4.7M	1M	4M	256K	2M
Large	24M	58M	16M	64M	4M	32M

Table 1: Graph Categories and Sizes

Graphs are selected under three categories with different shapes characterized by graph diameter (the greatest distance between any pair of vertices in the graph) and vertex degree (the number of edges incident to the vertex). **Road** networks have large diameters and small vertex degrees. We use real-world road graphs such as the US road network. **Random** networks have constant degrees and medium diameters. They are synthetic graphs produced by a graph generator. **Scale-free** networks have small diameters and large vertex degrees following a power-law distribution. They are generated by a recursive matrix (RMAT) model [40]. For each of these categories, we run a small graph to obtain the scalability results shown in Section 6.2.1 and a large graph to get results listed in Section 6.2.2 (Table 1), except Transitive Closure that has a $O(V^3)$ worst case

complexity so it takes the first 1K and 4K nodes of small and large graphs respectively.

6.1.2 Baseline

The baseline platform uses 2.6GHz Intel Xeon E5-2690 v3 processors based on the Haswell-EP microarchitecture. The system has two processor sockets and each socket has 12 cores. Each core has private 32KB L1-Data, 32KB L1-Instruction and 256KB L2 caches. Cores on the same socket share a 30MB L3 cache. The system contains DDR4-2133 DRAM with a theoretical peak transfer rate of 17GB/s per channel. There are two connected DRAM channels on each of the two processor sockets, leading to an aggregated peak memory bandwidth of 68GB/s for the entire system. Total DRAM capacity of the system is 64GB. When needed, NUMA and huge pages are enabled for best performance.

Software is developed in C++ using Galois [1], a state-of-art high-performance graph computation framework. Code is compiled using gcc 4.9.3 version with -O3 flag enabled. A parameter sweep is done for each application and input pair to achieve the highest performance. The Intel vector extension instructions are not used because the SIMD execution model cannot efficiently support the asynchronous nature of graph applications. While HTM was originally available on the baseline processor, it is not used because a bug announced by Intel [41] caused the HTM to be disabled and the lack of runtime control on transaction scheduling leads to very poor performance. Baseline programs use the same algorithm as accelerator implementations. They are, however, not limited to transactional execution and use fine-grained locks and atomic instructions such as compare-and-swap to achieve higher performance. The execution time of baseline runs is measured by timers inserted into the source code. Power measurement leverages Intel Performance Counter Monitor (PCM) which collects the actual energy usage through the processor's on-chip sensors.

6.1.3 Accelerator Implementation

We implement the proposed design using tools provided by the FPGA Research Infrastructure Cloud [42]. The source is developed in Bluespec System Verilog and is passed to the Bluespec compiler to generate Verilog for synthesis and C++ for cycle-accurate simulation orders of magnitude faster than RTL simulation. The implemented processing engine is decoupled into engine infrastructure that is constant across applications and application-specific operators (not soft or hard processors) generated by a script from an FSM-based specification. Implemented worklists support bucket-based priority scheduling used by SSSP, BFS and CC and FIFO scheduling used by other applications. We use a ring network to connect worklist slices for load balancing. Conflict detection is through on-chip AST and implemented as a pipeline. We eliminate version management by making transactions cautious and using exclusive locking achieved by an one-way AST. A crossbar is used as the on-chip network connecting processing engines to AST. The implementation of cache hierarchy includes work data caches and per-engine caches for thread-private scratchpad memory. Graph data is not cached since graph memory access latency is hidden by hardware multi-threading. Implemented caches are direct-mapped, non-blocking, pipelined, and multi-banked.

We synthesize our design on Xilinx Virtex UltraScale 440 and tune our design to meet timing requirements of a 200

MHz clock speed. The whole design consists of one or more FPGAs depending on design parameters such as the number of engines and worklist slices, sizes of various on-chip buffers and etc. In a typical configuration, one FPGA has eight processing engines with each running 16 threads to keep the engine being fully utilized by hiding memory latency. The total 128 threads are fed by two worklist slices for applications using FIFO scheduling and four worklist slices for applications using bucket-based priority scheduling, a configuration that minimizes worklist stall cycles and keeps bad work at a low level. The total work data cache size per FPGA is 1MB. Since versioning buffer is eliminated, thread-private scratchpad memory only contains lock-log and intermediate results which are small enough to fit on LUT resources. AST is 640KB in size and is distributed in four slices. Such a single-FPGA configuration saturates the off-chip memory bandwidth we assume for each socket. The FPGA LUT utilization of such a configuration is around 45% for applications using FIFO scheduling and around 50% for applications using bucket-based priority scheduling, with little variation since application-specific logic is a small fraction of the entire design, and BRAM utilization is typically around 20%. When multiple FPGAs are used, we assume they all have the same image. This assumption is only for the purpose of evaluation simplicity. There are no reasons preventing proposed techniques being applied to a system consisting of different FPGA parts or images.

Cycle-by-cycle simulation is performed to produce performance results. In the simulation, we assume DDR SDRAM is used as the off-chip memory. The assumed memory I/O bus clock frequency is 800 MHz, which is supported by both Altera and Xilinx FPGAs when running user logic at 200 MHz. DRAM data are transferred at a burst length of eight, with each transfer being 64 bits and occurring at both positive and negative clock cycle edges, giving a theoretical peak transfer rate of 12.8GB/s per channel. It is also assumed that each FPGA socket has the same number of DRAM channels as one CPU socket of the baseline. The assumed DRAM device latency is 160ns for every DRAM access. Note that this latency is the wait time before the DRAM produces a response after it receives a request. It does not include the latency of sending DRAM requests and responses through AST (needed only for global data accesses), the on-chip network, various buffers and the memory controller. The actual round-trip DRAM read latency from the processing engine's perspective is around 300ns. For writes that need to reserve AST entries, the round-trip latency doesn't include the assumed DRAM access latency because write responses are sent back to engines without waiting for DRAM to complete the writes. For writes that are lock-free, no responses are expected by engines.

We use the power estimator incorporated in Xilinx Vivado Design Suite to measure power. The estimation is performed on fully placed-and-routed design and with the input of vector-based signal activity files generated by simulation.

6.2 Results and Analysis

6.2.1 Scalability

Due to the 13X lower FPGA clock speed and the focus on multi-threaded throughput, single-threaded execution of our approach is 8X to 32X slower than that of the software baseline (Figure 3). Therefore, executing many threads and

achieving scalable speedup is desired to achieve performance equal to or higher than the baseline. To study the scalability of our approach, we vary the thread count and report speedup over serial execution (Figure 4), the percentage rate of conflicts out of the total transaction count (Figure 5), the percentage increase of transaction commits compared to serial execution (Figure 6) and memory bandwidth utilization as a fraction of the theoretical peak (Figure 7).

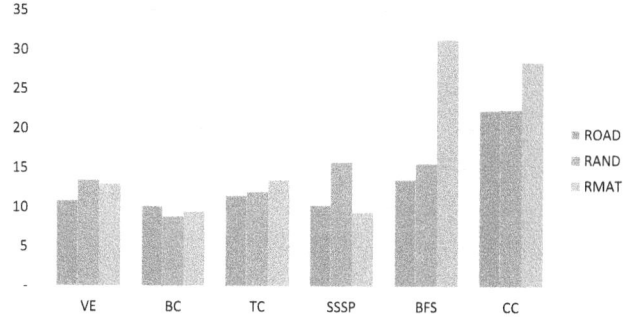

Figure 3: Single-Thread Execution Slowdown (Normalized)

One major limiting factor of scalability is wasted work which can be classified in two categories. The first category is transaction conflicts, which increase as concurrency increases. In some cases, moving from 128 threads to 256 or 512 threads decreases the conflict rate. This is because thread counts high than 128 use multiple FPGAs so the AST size is doubled or quadrupled to reduce conflicts due to false sharing. Another observation is that the conflict rate of road graphs is significantly higher than random and RMAT graphs because road graphs have smaller degrees and larger diameters, increasing the chance of conflicts. The second category of wasted work is bad work and is often associated with bucket-based priority scheduling. Take SSSP for example. Ideally we want all updates that lower the distance value of a node to its final value to minimize the work needed. With carefully chosen bucket intervals single-thread execution can achieve zero or very little bad work. Unfortunately, as concurrency increases it becomes harder to ensure the least distance update is applied in the first place, leaving to increased bad work. Besides SSSP, bad work also exists in BFS and CC, and as a consequence, increased commits are observed for them. Bad work becomes significant at 256 and 512 threads and hurts scalability.

Despite increased wasted work, scalable speedup over serial execution is achieved for most applications and inputs. Scalability persists even in some cases where the conflict rate is over 40%. This is because aborted transactions are usually lightweight, achieved by eager conflict detection and on-chip AST that enable detecting conflicts earlier and stopping further execution to avoid unnecessary work. Applications using worklists with bucket-based priority scheduling is in general not as scalable as applications with worklists with FIFO scheduling due to significant bad work at high thread counts. In addition, input graphs used in the scalability study are small graphs listed in Table 1. Our simulator runs high thread counts fast, but low thread count runs take a long time to complete because there are 10X/100X more cycles to simulate. For this reason we don't use larger graphs but we expect improved scalability as the graph gets bigger.

Memory bandwidth usage is proportional to the speedup. Single-FPGA memory bandwidth is saturated at 128 threads,

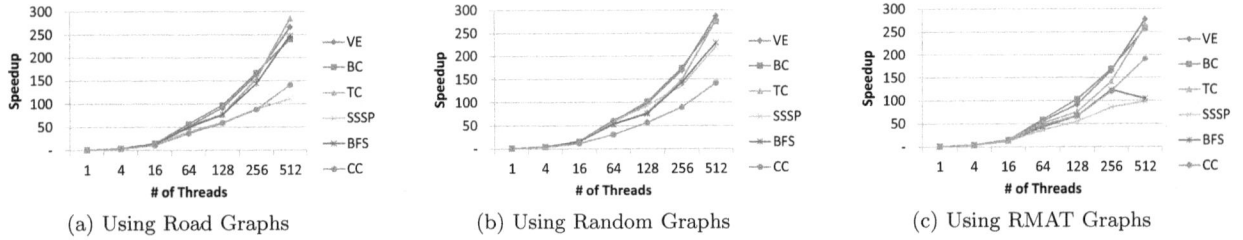

(a) Using Road Graphs (b) Using Random Graphs (c) Using RMAT Graphs

Figure 4: Speedup Over Serial Execution

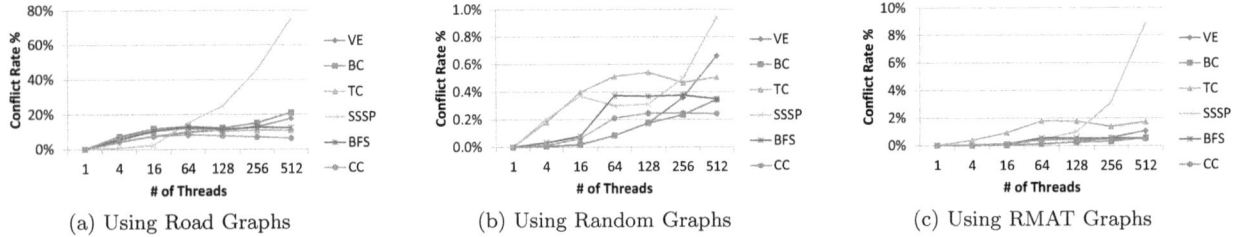

(a) Using Road Graphs (b) Using Random Graphs (c) Using RMAT Graphs

Figure 5: Conflict Rate

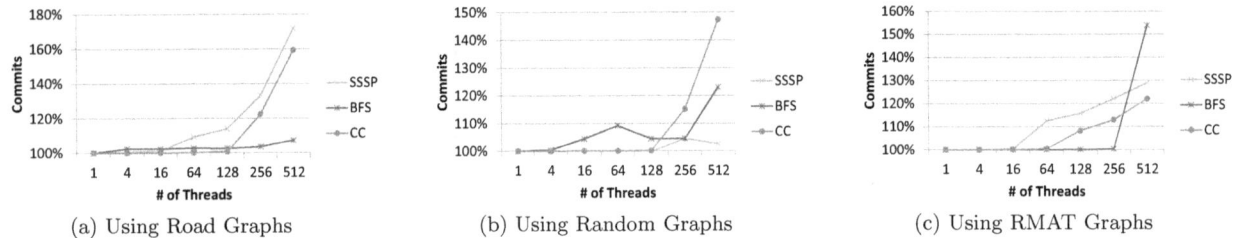

(a) Using Road Graphs (b) Using Random Graphs (c) Using RMAT Graphs

Figure 6: Commits

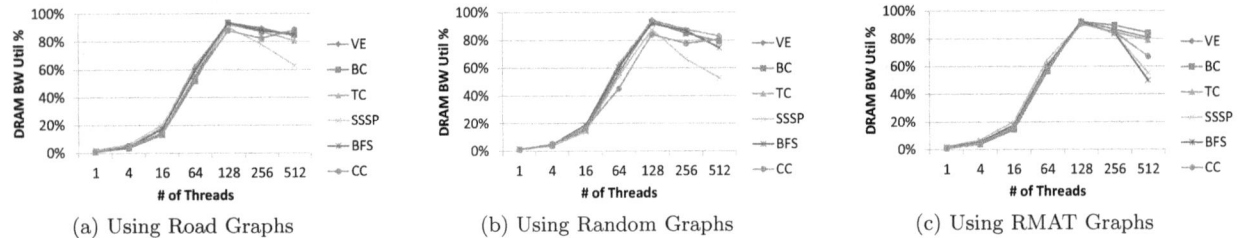

(a) Using Road Graphs (b) Using Random Graphs (c) Using RMAT Graphs

Figure 7: Memory Bandwidth Utilization

which explains why we run 128 threads per FPGA. Moving from 128 threads to 256 or 512 threads requires doubled or quadrupled FPGAs with the assumed available DRAM bandwidth increasing in a similar factor. So scaling continues and the actual memory use increases while its fraction out of the peak starts decreasing. At high thread counts, peak memory bandwidth utilization drops faster for applications and inputs that don't scale well.

6.2.2 Comparison Against CPUs

We compare performance achieved by our solution with a dual-FPGA-socket (256 threads) configuration against the dual-CPU-socket (24 threads) baseline (Figure 8a) by running on large graphs listed in Table 1. Note that time spent on loading graphs into memory and initializing data structure and worklist is excluded from the execution time. On average our approach performs 2.14X faster than the baseline. The only case of lower performance is BFS with RMAT graphs because serial execution on FPGA is over

30X slower than on CPUs and executing 256 threads is only 130X faster than serial execution (results from last section). The comparison of energy efficiency computed as performance per watt (Figure 8b) is based on single-socket. Moving from single-socket to multi-socket leads to linearly increased power but sub-linear speedup for both CPU and FPGA, so single-socket has the highest energy efficiency. For CPU, we use all threads on the first socket with NUMA disabled. We don't count the idle power consumption, which is around 20 watts, of the second CPU socket. In our measurement, a CPU socket with all cores being used consumes 80 to 120 watts while FPGA per-socket power is between 5 and 8 watts. Our comparison doesn't include the off-chip DRAM power, which is 5 to 7 watts, reported by Intel PCM, for a CPU socket, and unknown for FPGAs since it's not included in the power report. Due to the 10X power saving, our approach beats the baseline in all cases and is on average 21.93X more energy efficient. The performance and energy efficiency comparison results are summarized in Table 2.

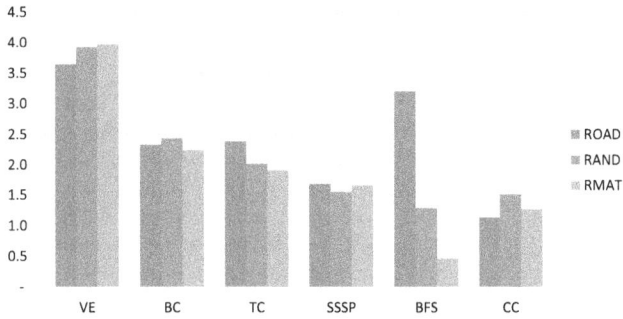

(a) Speedup (Normalized)

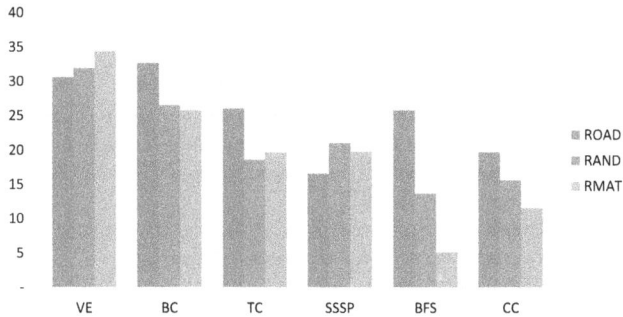

(b) Performance-Per-Watt (Normalized)

Figure 8: FPGAs VS. CPUs

	Clock	DRAM Bandwidth	Threads	Perf.	Perf. Per Watt
CPUs	2.6G	68.0GB/s	24	1X	1X
FPGAs	200M	51.2GB/s	256	2.14X	21.93X

Table 2: Comparison Summary

7. CONCLUSION

In this work we described a way to exploit the irregular loop parallelism of iterative graph workloads by executing loop iterations transactionally and asynchronously on many concurrent threads. We proposed microarchitectural techniques to realize such an idea on FPGAs and demonstrated their effectiveness in accelerating graph kernels. Our experimental results showed our approach beats the Intel 24-core Haswell CPU in per-socket performance while consuming 10X less power. Our future work includes an extensive study of various design choices in transactional state management, conflict detection, cache hierarchy and concurrency control and an evaluation of their impact on conflict rate, single-thread latency and overall performance.

8. REFERENCES

[1] K. Pingali, D. Nguyen, M. Kulkarni, M. Burtscher, M. A. Hassaan, R. Kaleem, T.-H. Lee, A. Lenharth, R. Manevich, M. MÃl'ndez-Lojo, D. Prountzos, and X. Sui, "The tao of parallelism in algorithms," in *Proceedings of the 32nd ACM SIGPLAN conference on Programming language design and implementation*, 2011.

[2] Q. Xu, H. Jeon, and M. Annavaram, "Graph processing on gpus: Where are the bottlenecks?," in *IEEE International Symposium on Workload Characterization*, 2014.

[3] M. Burtscher, R. Nasre, and K. Pingali, "A quantitative study of irregular programs on gpus," in *IEEE International Symposium on Workload Characterization*, 2012.

[4] N. Chatterjee, M. O'Connor, G. H. Loh, N. Jayasena, and R. Balasubramonian, "Managing dram latency divergence in irregular gpgpu applications," in *Proceedings of the International Conference for High Performance Computing, Networking, Storage and Analysis*, 2014.

[5] R. Alverson, D. Callahan, D. Cummings, B. Koblenz, A. Porterfield, and B. Smith, "The tera computer system," in *Proceedings of the 4th international conference on Supercomputing*, 1990.

[6] M. M. Ozdal, S. Yesil, T. Kim, A. Ayupov, S. Burns, and O. Ozturk, "Architectural requirements for energy efficient execution of graph analytics applications," in *Proceedings of International Conference on Computer-Aided Design*, 2015.

[7] B. Betkaoui, D. B. Thomas, W. Luk, and N. Przulj, "A framework for fpga acceleration of large graph problems: Graphlet counting case study," in *Proceedings of IEEE International Conference on Field-Programmable Technology*, 2011.

[8] M. deLorimier, N. Kapre, N. Mehta, D. Rizzo, I. Eslick, R. Rubin, T. E. Uribe, T. F. J. Knight, and A. DeHon, "Graphstep: A system architecture for sparse-graph algorithms," in *IEEE Symposium on Field Programmable Custom Computing Machines*, 2006.

[9] E. Nurvitadhi, G. Weisz, Y. Wang, S. Hurkat, M. Nguyen, J. C. Hoe, J. F. Martinez, and C. Guestrin, "Graphgen: An fpga framework for vertex-centric graph computation," in *IEEE Symposium on Field Programmable Custom Computing Machines*, 2014.

[10] M. Ozdal, S. Yesil, T. Kim, A. Ayupov, J. Greth, S. Burns, and O. Ozturk, "Energy efficient architecture for graph analytics accelerators," in *Proceedings of International Symposium on Computer Architecture*, 2016.

[11] J. Ahn, S. Hong, S. Yoo, O. Mutlu, and K. Choi, "A scalable processing-in-memory accelerator for parallel graph processing," in *Proceedings of International Symposium on Computer Architecture*, 2015.

[12] M. Herlihy and J. E. B. Moss, "Transactional memory: architectural support for lock free data structures," in *Proceedings of International Symposium on Computer Architecture*, 1993.

[13] L. Hammond, V. Wong, M. Chen, B. D. Carlstrom, J. D. Davis, B. Hertzberg, M. K. Prabhu, H. Wijaya, C. Kozyrakis, and K. Olukotun, "Transactional memory coherence and consistency," in *Proceedings of International Symposium on Computer Architecture*, 2004.

[14] C. S. Ananian, K. Asanovic, B. C. Kuszmaul, C. E. Leiserson, and S. Lie, "Unbounded transactional memory," in *Proceedings of International Symposium on High Performance Computer Architecture*, 2005.

[15] R. Rajwar, M. Herlihy, and K. Lai, "Virtualizing

transactional memory," in *Proceedings of International Symposium on Computer Architecture*, 2005.

[16] K. E. Moore, J. Bobba, M. J. Moravan, M. D. Hill, and D. A. Wood, "Logtm: Log-based transactional memory," in *Proceedings of International Symposium on High Performance Computer Architecture*, 2006.

[17] M. Lupon, G. Magklis, and A. Gonzalez, "Fastm: A log-based hardware transactional memory with fast abort recovery," in *Proceedings of International Symposium on Parallel Architecture and Compilation Techniques*, 2009.

[18] C. Blundell, J. Devietti, E. C. Lewis, and M. M. K. Martin, "Making the fast case common and the uncommon case simple in unbounded transactional memory," in *Proceedings of International Symposium on Computer Architecture*, 2007.

[19] J. Bobba, N. Goyal, M. Hill, M. Swift, and D. Wood, "Tokentm: Efficient execution of large transactions with hardware transactional memory," in *Proceedings of International Symposium on Computer Architecture*, 2008.

[20] L. Ceze, J. Tuck, C. Cascaval, and J. Torrellas, "Bulk disambiguation of speculative threads in multiprocessors," in *Proceedings of International Symposium on Computer Architecture*, 2006.

[21] L. Yen, J. Bobba, M. R. Marty, K. E. Moore, H. Volos, M. D. Hill, M. M. Swift, and D. A. Wood, "Logtm-se: Decoupling hardware transactional memory from caches," in *Proceedings of International Symposium on High Performance Computer Architecture*, 2007.

[22] A. Shriraman, S. Dwarkadas, and M. L. Scott, "Flexible decoupled transactional memory support," in *Proceedings of International Symposium on Computer Architecture*, 2008.

[23] H. Chafi, J. Casper, B. D. Carlstrom, A. McDonald, C. C. Minh, W. Baek, and C. K. andK. Olukotun, "A scalable, non-blocking approach to transactional memory," in *Proceedings of International Symposium on High Performance Computer Architecture*, 2007.

[24] C. C. Minh, M. Trautmann, J. Chung, A. McDonald, N. Bronson, J. Casper, C. Kozyrakis, and K. Olukotun, "An effective hybrid transactional memory system with strong isolation guarantees," in *Proceedings of International Symposium on Computer Architecture*, 2007.

[25] S. Chaudhry, R. Cypher, M. Ekman, M. Karlsson, A. Landin, S. Yip, H. Zeffer, and M. Tremblay, "Rock: A high-performance sparc cmt processor," in *Proceedings of International Symposium on Microarchitecture*, 2009.

[26] Intel, "Chapter 8. intel transactional synchronization extensions," in *Intel Architecture Instruction Set Extensions Programming Reference*, 2013.

[27] V.Leis, A. Kemper, and T. Neumann, "Exploiting hardware transactional memory in main-memory databases," in *Proceedings of International Conference on Data Engineering*, 2014.

[28] A. Wang, M. Gaudet, P. Wu, J. N. Amaral, M. Ohmacht, C. Barton, R. Silvera, and M. M. Michael, "Evaluation of blue gene/q hardware support for transactional memories," in *Proceedings of*

international conference on Parallel architectures and compilation techniques, 2012.

[29] C. Jacobi, T. J. Slegel, and D. F. Greiner, "Transactional memory architecture and implementation for ibm system z," in *Proceedings of International Symposium on Microarchitecture*, 2012.

[30] H. W. Cain, M. M. Michael, B. Frey, C. May, D. Williams, and H. Le, "Robust architectural support for transactional memory in the power architecture," in *Proceedings of International Symposium on Computer Architecture*, 2013.

[31] W. W. L. Fung, I. Singh, A. Brownsword, and T. M. Aamodt, "Hardware transactional memory for gpu architectures," in *Proceedings of International Symposium on Microarchitecture*, 2011.

[32] J. Casper, T. Oguntebi, S. Hong, N. G. Bronson, C. Kozyrakis, and K. Olukotun, "Hardware acceleration of transactional memory on commodity systems," in *Proceedings of international conference on Architectural support for programming languages and operating systems*, 2011.

[33] M. Pusceddu, S. Ceccolini, G. Palermo, D. Sciuto, and A. Tumeo, "A compact transactional memory multiprocessor system on fpga," in *Proceedings of International Conference on Field Programmable Logic and Applications*, 2010.

[34] M. Pusceddu, S. Ceccolini, A. Tumeo, G. Palermo, and D. Sciuto, "Emulating transactional memory on fpga multiprocessors," in *Proceedings of international conference on Architecture of computing systems*, 2011.

[35] N. Njoroge, S. Wee, J. Casper, J. Burdick, Y. Teslyar, C. Kozyrakis, and K. Olukotun, "Building and using the atlas transactional memory system," in *Proceedings of Workshop on Architecture Research using FPGA Platforms*, 2006.

[36] C. Kachris1 and C. Kulkarni, "Configurable transactional memory," in *IEEE Symposium on Field-Programmable Custom Computing Machines*, 2007.

[37] S. Grinberg and S. Weiss, "Investigation of transactional memory using fpgas," in *IEEE 24th Convention of Electrical and Electronics Engineers in Israel*, 2006.

[38] M. Labrecque and J. G. Steffan, "Nettm: Faster and easier synchronization for soft multicores via transactional memory," in *Proceedings of International Symposium on Field Programmable Gate Arrays*, 2011.

[39] A. Lenharth, D. Nguyen, and K. Pingali, "Priority queues are not good concurrent priority schedulers," tech. rep., The University of Texas at Austin, 2011.

[40] D. Chakrabarti, Y. Zhan, and C. Faloutsos, "R-mat: A recursive model for graph mining," in *Proceedings of the 2004 SIAM International Conference on Data Mining*, 2004.

[41] Desktop 4th Generation Intel Core Processor Family, Desktop Intel Pentium Processor Family, and Desktop Intel Celeron Processor Family: Specification Update (Revision 014).

[42] http://www.openfabric.org.

Enabling Flexible Network FPGA Clusters in a Heterogeneous Cloud Data Center

Naif Tarafdar, Thomas Lin, Eric Fukuda, Hadi Bannazadeh,
Alberto Leon-Garcia, Paul Chow
University of Toronto
{naif.tarafdar, t.lin}@mail.utoronto.ca, efukuda@ece.utoronto.ca,
{hadi.bannazadeh, alberto.leongarcia}@utoronto.ca, pc@eecg.toronto.edu

ABSTRACT

We present a framework for creating network FPGA clusters in a heterogeneous cloud data center. The FPGA clusters are created using a logical kernel description describing how a group of FPGA kernels are to be connected (independent of which FPGA these kernels are on), and an FPGA mapping file. The kernels within a cluster can be replicated with simple directives within this framework. The FPGAs can communicate to any other network device in the data center, including CPUs, GPUs, and IoT devices (such as sensors). This heterogeneous cloud manages these devices with the use of OpenStack. We observe that our infrastructure is limited due to the physical infrastructure such as the 1 Gb Ethernet connection. Our framework however can be ported to other physical infrastructures. We tested our infrastructure with a database acceleration application. This application was replicated six times across three FPGAs within our cluster and we observed a throughput increase of six times as this scaled linearly. Our framework generates the OpenStack calls needed to reserve the compute devices, creates the network connections (and retrieve MAC addresses), generate the bitstreams, programs the devices, and configure the devices with the appropriate MAC addresses, creating a ready-to-use network device that can interact with any other network device in the data center.

1. INTRODUCTION

Field-Programmable Gate Arrays (FPGAs) have recently proven to be a good computation alternative in data centers due to their compute capabilities and power efficiency. One example is the Microsoft Catapult project where FPGAs are deployed in the Bing search engine [1]. With a 10% power increase they are able to see a 95% performance increase. FPGAs allow users to create customized circuitry for their application. The performance and power-savings multiply at a data center scale. Provisioning FPGA resources from a shared cloud similar to the provisioning of CPUs can be very useful to allow users to create their own FPGA computing clusters. Related works have investigated the provisioning of a single FPGA tightly coupled with a CPU [2], or the creation of static FPGA clusters within the data center [3]. The provisioning of scalable and elastic FPGA clusters from a large general heterogeneous pool of devices has yet to be investigated, or at least disclosed if it is being done in any commercial systems.

In this work, our goal is to provide an easy way to orchestrate large FPGA clusters for large multi-FPGA and heterogeneous applications. We want the user to be able to make a heterogeneous cluster with the ratio of devices (e.g CPUs to FPGAs) and cluster size they require. We also wish to make the deployment and deallocation of these clusters from the cloud quickly, on the order of seconds. Dynamic cluster topologies will be created using the data center network. Our target is to provide the user an easy framework for building a large multi-FPGA application. An example can be a database query application where the query is divided into several sub-queries. Our goal is to provide the framework for the user to describe the query in terms of their query processing engines at a logical level, and then with our framework the user can place these query processing engines on multiple FPGAs and replicate the query many times.

We abstract away the FPGA connections and present the user with a large uniform platform that sits on top of a multi-FPGA backbone. These network FPGA clusters are seen as any other network device in the data center and with the appropriate network addressing information we can send and receive data from any other device in the data center (virtual CPU, other FPGA clusters etc.). Using our prototype system we do a detailed analysis of the whole virtualization stack: starting from mapping FPGA kernels to devices, using the cloud management software OpenStack to provision FPGAs and connect their network ports, map multi-FPGA topologies onto the network by configuring the FPGAs to use the appropriate network addresses, and ways to scale up by replicating nodes and inserting schedulers to communicate with the replicated nodes. Our system abstracts away the aforementioned stack and produces the cluster based on a description of the kernels and how they are connected, and which FPGAs these kernels will map to.

The rest of the paper is as follows: Section 2 will look into related work in FPGA virtualization and cloud cluster management tools, Section 3 will describe our data center resources, Section 4 will explain our design justifications, Section 5 describe the infrastructure we provide, Section 6 explores scalability of our infrastructure, Section 7 evalu-

FPGA'17, February 22–24, 2017, Monterey, California, USA.
Copyright © ACM. ISBN 978-1-4503-4354-1/17/02...$15.00
DOI: http://dx.doi.org/10.1145/3020078.3021742

ates our infrastructure and lastly we conclude the paper in Section 8.

2. RELATED WORK

In this section we describe previous work in virtualized FPGAs and other Cluster Management Tools in the cloud.

2.1 FPGA Virtualization and Clouds

There has been previous academic work providing FPGAs as virtualized resources within the cloud management tool OpenStack. The work presented by Byma et al. proposes FPGA resources sitting directly on the network to be allocated as OpenStack resources [4]. The hypervisor is programmed into hardware and communicates to the OpenStack controller via the network. Furthermore, the FPGA application region is split into four smaller regions allowing multiple users to share a single FPGA device. This requires modifying OpenStack to communicate to the hardware hypervisor in the FPGA.

The work proposed by Chen et al. also virtualizes FPGAs in OpenStack but does not consider FPGAs sitting directly on the network [5]. They implement the hypervisor in software by modifying KVM, which is a popular Linux hypervisor [6]. Instead, the FPGAs are coupled with a virtual machine. Similar to the previous work, this also requires modifying OpenStack to communicate to the software hypervisor.

Several industrial pursuits have started investigating provisioning FPGA resources from a cloud. One example is the Maxeler MPC-X project [7]. This project provides a virtualized FPGA resource to a user that can be implemented with a variable number of FPGAs. The user first allocates resources for the given cluster of FPGAs in the virtualized FPGA resource. Once the cluster has been made, the details are abstracted from the user during application run-time.

IBM's SuperVessel looks at providing an FPGA as a PCIe connected cloud resource with a CPU also provisioned with OpenStack [2]. In this model a single FPGA is provisioned to the user as an accelerator to which the user can upload FPGA code to be run and compiled onto the FPGA. This simplifies the process of provisioning an FPGA, but only with a single FPGA.

Microsoft has also continued their work with data center FPGAs with the second iteration of Catapult [3]. The FPGAs are connected directly to a host CPU via a PCIe link. The output of the host NIC connects to the FPGA and the FPGA connects to the network through a high-performance switch. Thus the FPGA has a direct network connection and the CPU accesses the network through the FPGA. FPGAs can communicate amongst each other through a low-overhead custom transport layer. The FPGAs in this environment are not provisioned as a part of a cloud service for external users, and are used internally within the Mircrosoft data center.

2.2 Cloud Cluster Management Tools

A key aspect of this project is to provide orchestration of clusters within our cloud environment. Heat [8] is a component in OpenStack that can orchestrate clusters using an orchestration template, which describes the virtual machines and networking within the desired cluster. This allows the creation of interesting network topologies within a cluster. Heat can be combined with user applications that can mod-

ify these clusters using other metrics such as performance, resource utilization, and CPU usage.

Other tools exist that combine orchestration and load balancing using the aforementioned metrics. The usual workflow for these tools are as follows. The tool first reserves a set of resources from a larger pool of compute nodes for a certain application. The allocated resources are then connected for the application and monitoring. The monitoring is used for user statistics as well as fault tolerance within the cluster.

These tools are helpful for getting reliable performance on a cluster as well as debugging a cluster. Debugging a cluster can be a daunting task as there are many variables within the cluster. These tools monitor events to gauge the status of different processes within an application and present the problem to the user in an easy to understand representation.

Most of these tools currently work for CPU clusters (e.g Apache Mesos [9]) and GPU clusters (e.g NVidia Management Library) [10]. Our challenge is to extend clustering capabilities to FPGAs by developing our own orchestration tool and then to investigate monitoring and updating our clusters using FPGA metrics, which will differ from the current set of CPU and GPU metrics current tools use.

3. BACKGROUND

This section describes the infrastructure underlying our platform, including the SAVI data center and SDAccel FPGA Programming Platform.

3.1 Smart Applications on Virtualized Infrastructure (SAVI) Testbed

The SAVI testbed is a Canada-wide multi-tier heterogeneous testbed [11]. Figure 1 shows the architecture of SAVI. This testbed contains various heterogeneous resources such as FPGAs, GPUs, Network Processors, IOT sensors and CPU-based servers. The virtualization of these resources is one focus of the research on SAVI, where our work focuses on the use of FPGAs. Resources other than CPUs such as GPUs and network processors, are provisioned to the user either by providing the entire server without virtualization or with the use of PCIe-passthrough.

The multi-tier property refers to the network architecture of SAVI. SAVI can be seen as multiple cloud networks. The Core consists of a large number of CPUs that provide the main compute resources of the data center. The Core is then connected to several Edges dispersed around Canada. Each of these Edges is a smaller cloud network that also contains the heterogeneous devices. Many of these heterogeneous devices are connected directly to the network through high performance 10 GbE switches. These devices are treated the same way any CPU would be treated as many of these devices are assigned network ports with valid MAC and IP addresses. These devices are addressable by any other node (CPU or other device) on the network, once they are registered to the network. This allows, for example, an IoT sensor in Toronto to send data to an FPGA cluster in Victoria and then have the data be accessible by a CPU cluster in Calgary. Furthermore the multi-tier architecture allows a lot of the processing to be done on the Edge network close to the heterogeneous devices before being sent to the Core where there are more compute resources.

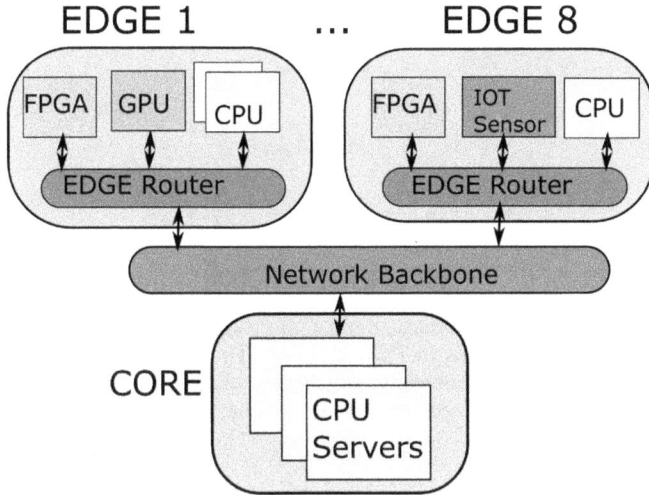

Figure 1: System diagram of the SAVI multi-tier architecture that has a CORE with many CPU Compute Servers and Edges physically dispersed around Canada. Each Edge is made up of compute CPUs and other heterogeneous devices (e.g FPGAs, GPUs, IOT Sensors).

3.1.1 OpenStack

OpenStack is the cloud management tool used by SAVI [8]. OpenStack is divided into several services. The two main services that we employ in our platform are Nova and Neutron, and these services are typically interfaced with a client machine. Nova is responsible for the deployment of compute infrastructure from the platform. This involves the generation of virtual machines on physical machines. The client machine specifies two fields when requesting a virtual machine: a software image, and the flavor. The software image refers to all the software that is to be installed on the virtual machine, including the operating system and any other applications that we want initialized on our virtual machine. These images are typically kept in a repository and can be updated by users of the testbed. The flavor refers to the physical specifications of the virtual machine, such as number the of CPU cores, RAM, and hard drive space.

Neutron is responsible for the provisioning of network resources. We can create network ports within our cluster, and these ports are assigned MAC addresses and IP addresses that will be valid within the cluster. When creating virtual machines, these ports are created implicitly, but we can explicitly create additional ports for non-virtual devices or non-CPU devices.

3.2 FPGA Hypervisor

In our design we use the Xilinx SDAccel [12] platform as an FPGA hypervisor, where the hypervisor is used to provide some basic services. The FPGA in this model is a PCIe-connected device and the platform first provides a driver to communicate to the FPGA. This is done through OpenCL, which provides the API to communicate to and manage devices.

OpenCL is both a programming language for heterogeneous devices and a programming API for a host application (conventionally run on a CPU) to manage and communicate to OpenCL compatible devices [13]. This envi-

ronment gathers all the OpenCL devices connected to the processor usually locally via PCIe. In the SDAccel Platform, as shown in Figure 2, the OpenCL API communicates to a driver provided by Xilinx called the Hardware Abstraction Layer (HAL) that provides driver calls to send/receive data from the FPGA and program the Application Region, in the FPGA. The Application Region is programmed using partial reconfiguration, and the region around the Application Region is the Hypervisor in our model. In this platform the kernels within the Application Region can be OpenCL kernels, Vivado HLS kernels, or even hand-coded Verilog/VHDL kernels.

The PCIe Module is a master to a DMA engine to read/write to off-chip DRAM. This is used to communicate data to the Application Region. The PCIe Module is also a master to an ICAP module (not shown) responsible for programming the Partial Reconfig region with a bitstream sent from the user in software. The HAL driver provides an API that abstracts away the addresses required to control the various slaves of the PCIe master.

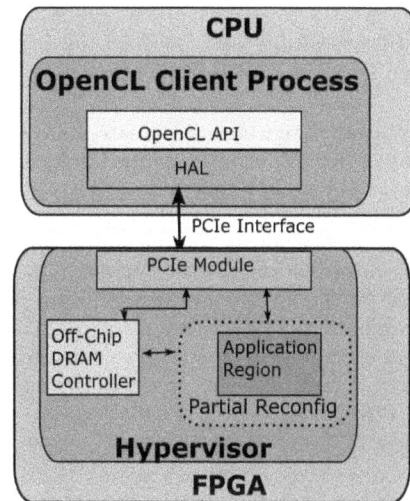

Figure 2: System diagram of the SDAccel platform.

For our cluster model we modified this base platform by adding a 1 GbE Ethernet core. For simplicity we do not use partial reconfiguration for the Application Region choosing instead to synthesize the application with the Hypervisor as a single design. This makes the programming flow simpler as there is only one bitstream to synthesize. The low-speed Ethernet core and the absence of a partially reconfigurable Application Region are limitations of our current modified version of the platform and will be addressed in the future.

4. DESIGN JUSTIFICATION

Our system looks at the creation of multi-FPGA clusters from a high-level kernel description. Our system can be broken down according to the infrastructure stack shown in Figure 3. We provide a high-level of abstraction where a user describes logical clusters independent of FPGA mappings, and our system provisions the cluster from a pool of resources accordingly. We take this approach as this is quite analogous to the modern FPGA system design approach that can be seen in Xilinx Vivado IP Integrator [14] or Altera Quartus QSys [15]. These tools are used to connect modules together to create larger systems. Our system provides a similar design space but the space is across multiple FPGAs. The interfaces between FPGAs are abstracted from the user, where the user's logical cluster description has no notion of which FPGA each user module will map to. We wish to provide a familiar environment to large system designers while providing abstractions to provide ways to scale to large multi-FPGA designs. Our system also provides ways to scale up nodes within a cluster by replicating those nodes, or entire clusters with the use of a directive.

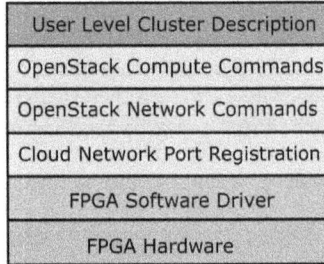

User Level Cluster Description
OpenStack Compute Commands
OpenStack Network Commands
Cloud Network Port Registration
FPGA Software Driver
FPGA Hardware

Figure 3: Infrastructure stack, most of this is abstracted from the user.

The multi-FPGA design cluster is created on the fly from a pool of resources in SAVI using OpenStack. Our system first builds single FPGA nodes, and then connects the network ports on the FPGAs in topologies that are determined from the logical cluster description the user provides. OpenStack is used to provision the single FPGA nodes, and to acquire network ports for the FPGAs in the SAVI data center. We use OpenStack because this is an open-source cloud management tool that is adopted in large data centers such as SAVI. Our placement in SAVI gives us access to the multi-tier infrastructure with the large pool of heterogeneous resources, which can be used to create large-scale heterogeneous applications.

5. INFRASTRUCTURE OVERVIEW

In this section we describe our infrastructure by examining each part of the infrastructure stack. First we will look at how a single FPGA is provisioned, then we will look at how clusters are provisioned and scaled.

5.1 Single FPGA Environment

The first step is to be able to provide an FPGA within a virtual machine. PCIe passthrough gives a virtual machine full access to a subset of the PCIe devices within a physical compute node. This can allow us to have multiple virtual machines on top of the physical machine able to access different PCIe devices. Figure 4 shows two virtual machines attached to PCIe devices using PCIe passthrough.

In our environment we use the Alpha Data ADM-PCIe-7V3 cards, which have a Virtex 7 FPGA. On these FPGAs, the Xilinx SDAccel static bitstream (the bitstream describing the Hypervisor) is programmed onto the flash memory. In our environment all the FPGAs are programmed with the same Hypervisor bitstream as OpenStack running on the server uses the PCIe Module connection to determine the type of PCIe-connected device. This PCIe Module might not be consistent across different FPGA Hypervisors and will not be recognized as the same device to OpenStack. This

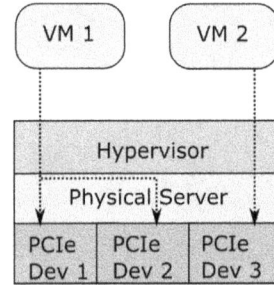

Figure 4: This figure shows PCIe passthrough. Two VMs have direct access to PCIe devices. The Hypervisor grants the first virtual machine full access to the first two PCIe devices and the second virtual machine has the third PCIe device.

static bitstream includes the PCIe Module that is detected by the physical compute node, and then registered with OpenStack Nova by including it in its PCIe passthrough White-List, which specifies the devices that can be attached to virtual machines.

The last step for the setup is the creation of a new Flavor, which defines a set of specifications for virtual machines. A Flavor can specify the type of PCIe device as well as the number of PCIe devices of that specific type (e.g there can be Flavors for for one FPGA, two FPGAs, one GPU, two GPUs etc.). In addition to PCIe devices, a Flavor also defines other machine specifications such as memory size and hard-disk space. Once these Flavors are created, they can be used to create multiple virtual machines described by the specifications of the Flavor.

We have been using this environment to provide an SDAccel service since Fall 2015, before IBM started to offer it in April 2016. We have Flavors that have simulated FPGAs and physical FPGAs.

5.2 Multi-FPGA Infrastructure

Our infrastructure provides a cluster of network-connected FPGAs to the user given a description of what a cluster of kernels will look like. The user provides a logical description of their desired FPGA cluster that describes how different FPGA kernels are to be connected together. The user also provides an FPGA mapping that specifies the number of FPGAs the user requires and places the kernels on the appropriate FPGAs. Kernel connections within a single FPGA are simple as they are directly connected, whereas kernel connections between FPGAs are implemented via the network. Furthermore kernels may also fan out to schedulers instead of directly connecting to other kernels.

5.2.1 Logical View of Kernels

The kernels in this system are streaming kernels and they use the AXI stream protocol for input and output. The AXI stream interface our system uses has the following fields: A 32-bit data field, 8-bit dest field, a 1-bit last field, a 1-bit ready field and a 1-bit valid field.

All kernel inputs to the system are addressed by a specific dest entry. Logically speaking, unless otherwise stated, any kernel output can connect to any input. This can be seen as all kernels being connected to a large logical switch. These kernels may be mapped to the same FPGA or to different

FPGAs. Furthermore these kernels can be replicated with directives in the input scripts and they can be scheduled in different ways with the use of schedulers.

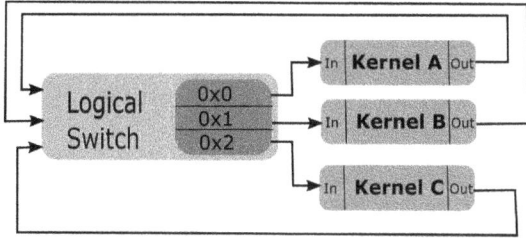

Figure 5: This highlights the simple logical view of a kernel cluster. In this situation all the kernels output to a switch and their inputs come from the switch.

Sub-Clusters

In Figure 5 we show three kernels connected via one logical switch. All kernels are connected to each other in a fully connected network. Edges can be removed if we directly connect kernels. Figure 6 shows four kernels with direct connections between some of the kernels. Such sub-clusters are then connected to the logical switch.

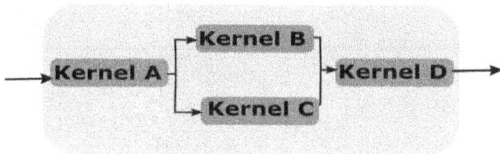

Figure 6: This is an example of a directly connected sub-cluster that would be connected to the logical switch.

We can also have our own schedulers where the output of a kernel might not be connected to all the other kernel inputs but to a subset of kernel inputs arbitrated by a scheduler. This type of sub-cluster is shown in Figure 7 and explained in more detail in Section 6.1.

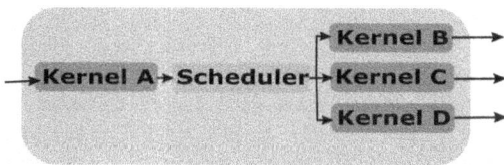

Figure 7: This is an example of a sub-cluster where a kernel is connected to a local scheduler that arbitrates between 3 kernels within the sub-cluster.

5.2.2 Physical Mapping of the Kernels

Each kernel in the logical topology is mapped to a physical FPGA. More than one kernel can be mapped to an FPGA. Direct kernel connections on the same FPGA are simply connected within the FPGA. Kernels with connections that cross an FPGA boundary are wrapped with logic to help with the crossing.

When connections on the large logical switch are divided across multiple FPGAs, the logical switch is implemented as physical switches on each of the FPGAs. Figure 5 shows three kernels fully connected with a logical switch. Now let's consider the following scenario: Kernels A and B are on FPGA 1 and Kernel C is on FPGA 2. The physical mapping is shown in Figure 8.

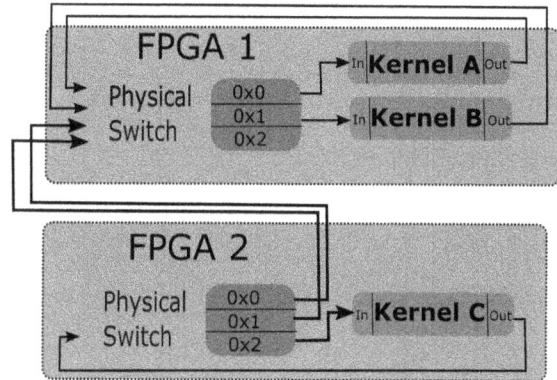

Figure 8: This figure translates the logical cluster shown in Figure 5 into a physical cluster with two FPGAs.

Figure 8 shows the logical switch split into two physical switches. The inputs to the respective kernels on the two FPGAs always come from the physical switch on the FPGA. The first FPGA sends all packets addressed to Kernel C to the switch in the second FPGA. Furthermore the second FPGA's switch sends all packets dedicated for Kernels A and B to the first FPGA. The output of each of the kernels feed into the physical switch on that FPGA. The physical switch can determine the destination FPGA of each packet.

For edges between kernels that are not connected to the large logical switch (sub-clusters), the direct connections must also be facilitated between FPGAs.

5.2.3 FPGA Application Region

The FPGA Application region includes helper modules for the User Kernel to interface directly with the network through the Ethernet interface. The helper modules are responsible for filtering packets, formatting packets and arbitrating for the network port. The Application Region is shown in Figure 9.

The configuration bus is used to configure the input and the output modules. These signals are driven by the PCIe Module on the FPGA, which receives signals from the PCIe-connected virtual CPU.

Input Module

All the packets that the FPGA receives via the Ethernet are forwarded to the input module. The packets that are received at the network port follow the Ethernet packet convention with a 14-byte header. On top of this we add our own protocol by appending two bytes (Kernel Address) to specify the destination kernel for the packet, as we may have multiple kernels on the FPGA that are requesting input packets.

Figure 10 shows the protocol details used by our FPGA infrastructure. Each FPGA in our infrastructure is assigned a MAC address within the SAVI infrastructure. The process

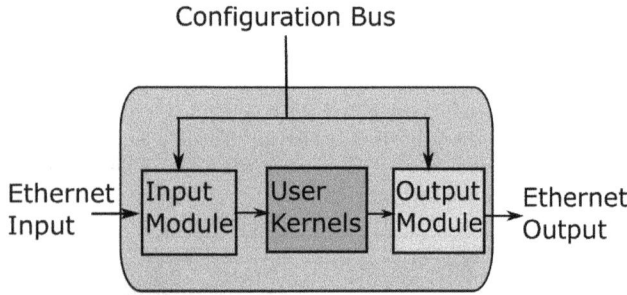

Figure 9: This figure shows the details of the Application Region. The input and output modules are both configured by the configuration bus.

Destination MAC (6 bytes)	Source MAC (6 bytes)	0x7400 (2 bytes)	Kernel Address (2 bytes)

Figure 10: The Ethernet protocol plus our custom protocol to differentiate the kernel.

by which we get the MAC address is discussed in Section 6.2. The destination MAC address should match the MAC address assigned to the particular FPGA. The source MAC address will be the source MAC address of the FPGA or of the virtual machine within SAVI that is sending the FPGA data. The next two bytes, according to the Ethernet frame protocol, are the ether-type that we hardcoded to 0x7400, and the last field is the address of the kernel within the FPGA.

The Input Module consists of an Input Bridge and an Input Demultiplexer. The Input Bridge is configured after the FPGA is programmed with the bitstream and before the application can run. The Input Bridge behaves as both a firewall and converts a packet from an Ethernet Packet into an AXI Stream packet. The Input Bridge's firewall is configured with the MAC address assigned to the FPGA. The Input Bridge also drops the Ethernet header and adds a dest field as part of the AXI stream. The dest field corresponds to the Kernel Address specified within the header. This Input Demultiplexer either outputs to kernels on this FPGA that are expecting Ethernet input, or it outputs to kernels on a different FPGA; in this case all packets matching the corresponding dest field will be sent straight to the output module. The input to the switch comes from both the Ethernet module and all other user kernels that can output to any other kernel on the FPGA. An example of an Input Module is shown in Figure 11. For details refer to Section 5.2.2.

Output Module

This module receives streams from the User Kernels and from the Input Demultiplexer. The Output Module consists of Packet Formatters (PF) and an Output Switch. Each stream (either from the User Kernels or from the Input Module) needs a Packet Formatter before it can be sent out to the network. Each stream is formatted with the appropriate MAC headers. The source MAC address is that of the FPGA. The destination MAC address is of the destination FPGA or virtual machine. The ether-type is 0x7400 as it was in the input stream and then we append the dest of the

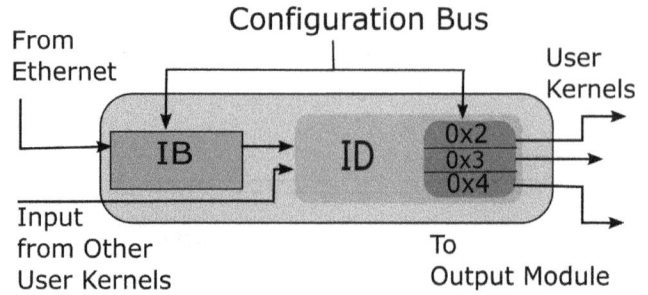

Figure 11: The input module consisting of the Input Bridge (labelled IB) and the Input Demultiplexer (labelled ID). In this example the dest fields 0x2, 0x3 feed into different User Kernels on this FPGA and 0x4 feeds into another FPGA by going through the Output Module.

stream into the header of the packet. All the Packet Formatters are fed into an output-switch that arbitrates using the last field of the AXI stream. The output switch uses a round-robin scheduling algorithm. The output module is shown in Figure 12. The input to the Packet Formatter is an AXI stream with a dest field. The formatter uses the dest field as the kernel address when it is outputting to the network.

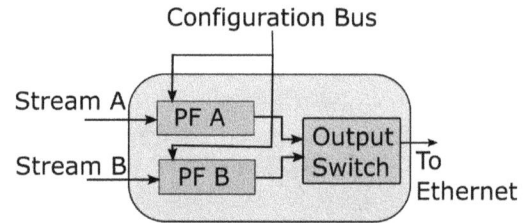

Figure 12: The output module for two streams consisting of Packet Formatters (labelled PF) for each stream that needs to be output.

6. SCALING UP FPGA CLUSTERS

A major feature of our infrastructure is the ability to scale the cluster. We can treat a whole cluster as a single processing unit and it can be replicated with a single directive within the script. For example, Figures 5 and 8 show a logical mapping transformed into a physical mapping without any replication. If this was to be replicated three times there would be a total of six FPGAs. The original FPGA mapping file listed only two FPGAs but six FPGA MAC addresses would be returned to the user.

6.1 FPGA Schedulers

Nodes within the cluster can be replicated as well without replicating the entire cluster. Replicating a node within the cluster will require all nodes that fan-in to that specific node to now include a Scheduler. The Schedulers currently support any-cast, which uses a round-robin scheduler, or broadcast. Figure 13 shows how a node is replicated within a cluster and where a Scheduler is inserted.

The Schedulers are also FPGA kernels. If the replicated kernels span across multiple FPGAs the scheduler will be placed on the FPGA with the most replications of that ker-

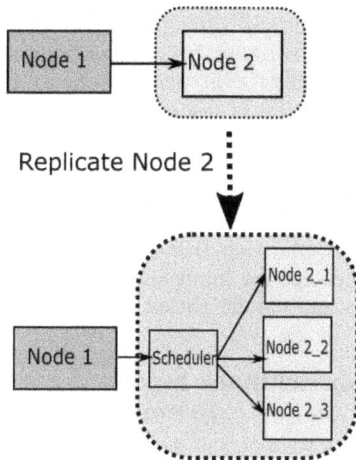

Figure 13: This shows the replication of Node 2. The replicated nodes are Node 2_1, Node 2_2 and Node 2_3. Node 1 has a Scheduler that fans out to the replicated nodes.

nel to reduce latency for the more common case. For example, in Figure 13, if two of three replications are on FPGA 1, and the other is on FPGA 2, then the script will place the Scheduler on FPGA 1. The script will then create connections from the Scheduler to the replicated nodes and one connection to the Output Module on FPGA 1. The remaining replicated kernel will be connected to the Input Module on FPGA 2. Figure 14 illustrates this scenario.

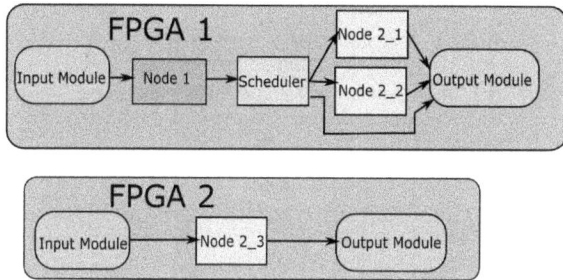

Figure 14: The physical configuration if Node 1, Node 2 _1 and Node 2_2 are on FPGA 1 and Node 2_3 is on FPGA 2.

6.2 FPGA Software Drivers and Network Connections

Each virtual machine with an FPGA is responsible for sending control signals to the FPGA. These control signals are to configure the Input Module and the Output Module with the appropriate MAC addresses. We choose to use the software to configure the Input and Output Modules because the alternative is to encode the MAC addresses in hardware, which will require resynthesizing FPGA bitstreams for different physical FPGAs when replicating the cluster. Our approach allows us the option to generate our cluster with one set of FPGAs and then replicate the clusters with the same bitstreams to more FPGAs.

The software drivers can configure the Input Bridge and the Packet Formatters in the hardware because the PCIe module in the hardware is a master (a driver of signals) to these modules. This means that writing to a certain address on the PCIe module can be used to send data to the Input

Bridge or the Packet Formatter. We can write to different addresses of the PCIe module with the HAL driver that was provided in the SDAccel tool kit. When a virtual machine with an FPGA is booted, the software driver is accepting bitstreams. Once a bitstream is received it will be programmed with the HAL and the Input Bridge and Packet Formatters will also be configured by the HAL. Our justification to provide the Packet Formatters as software configurable blocks is due to scalability. If we wish to scale up our cluster with more network FPGAs, the MAC address of each FPGA can be configured by software instead of synthesizing bitstreams on a per FPGA level.

Each FPGA obtains a network connection by first receiving a network port from the OpenStack service, Neutron. Each network port consists of a MAC address, and IP address. This port is then registered with the physical port on the network switch that has the FPGA connection. Our scripts can determine the physical switch port of a particular FPGA connection by observing which physical server hosts the virtual machine containing the PCIe server. In our setup we have one FPGA per physical server. If this were to change we would need a new mechanism to infer the physical network port of a particular FPGA. Once the port returned by Neutron is registered with the physical port, it is now accessible on the network from any other device in the SAVI data center, including other virtual CPUs, IoT devices and FPGA clusters.

6.3 Tool Flow

We summarize the use of our system by describing the tool flow. First the user submits a logical cluster description and FPGA mapping file to a global FPGA parser. Eventually, these could be generated by a higher-level framework or application. OpenStack calls are generated to create virtual machines, which are light-weight CPU virtual machines connected to an FPGA, and one virtual machine dedicated to synthesize bitstreams. Subsequent OpenStack calls are generated to create network ports, each with valid MAC and IP addresses. These ports are registered with the SAVI switch and now all packets sent to these addresses will be forwarded to the right switch port. After all the OpenStack calls are generated, the individual FPGAs are synthesized on the large virtual machine dedicated to synthesizing bitstreams. Once the bitstreams are synthesized they are forwarded to the individual FPGAs to be programmed onto the FPGA. Once programmed, the Packet Formatters are configured by the FPGA software driver running on the lightweight CPU attached to the FPGA via PCIe. After the user submits the initial cluster description files, the rest of the calls are automatically generated by our infrastructure.

7. EVALUATION

This section first examines the overhead of the infrastructure our design introduces and compares it to the SDAccel platform. This will quantify the overhead we introduce to support our multi-FPGA cluster. Then we test the latency and throughput of the input and output modules using a set of microbenchmarks. Finally, we test a full application using a database acceleration application. The designs are implemented on the Alpha Data 7V3 card, which has the following specifications: a Xilinx Virtex 7 XC7VX690TFFG-1157 FPGA (433200 LUTs, 866400 Flip Flops, 1470 BRAM Tiles), two 8GB ECC-SODIMM for memory speeds up to

1333MT/s and Dual SFP+ cages for high speed optical communication including 10 Gigabit Ethernet.

Our network infrastructure connects the 10 GbE SFP ports using 10 GbE to 1 GbE transceivers to a network switch. The switch can support 10 GbE links, but due to the 1 GbE FPGA core that is in our FPGA Hypervisor we have to use a 1 GbE cable. The goal of the evaluation is to demonstrate that our FPGA network modules add little overhead with respect to throughput and very little latency overhead. The absolute latency and throughput numbers are limited by the 1 GbE network connection but the infrastructure we have built can be used on 10 GbE, or better, systems where we would expect these numbers to be better. We also wish to highlight the scalability of our infrastructure with a case study, demonstrating that by simply changing a directive in the script, our clusters can replicate with the throughput scaling accordingly.

7.1 Resource Overhead

The resource overhead from our infrastructure is shown in Table 1. Absolute numbers are given with the percentage of the device total shown in brackets.

Table 1: Resource Overhead of our System

Hardware Setup	LUTS	Flip-Flops	BRAM
SDAccel Base	53346 (12.3 %)	64550 (7.45 %)	228 (15.5 %)
SDAccel Base with Ethernet Support	62344 (14.4 %)	76124 (8.79 %)	228 (15.5 %)
Input Module			
Input Bridge	87 (0.02 %)	170 (0.019 %)	2 (1.36 %)
Input Demultiplexer with 16 outputs	82 (0.019 %)	124 (0.014 %)	0 (0 %)
Output Module			
Ethernet FIFO Controller	26 (0.006 %)	12 (0.014 %)	2 (1.36 %)
Output Switch with 16 inputs	517 (0.119 %)	138 (0.016 %)	0 (0 %)
Packet Formatter (one per network output stream)	230 (0.053 %)	252 (0.029 %)	2 (1.36 %)
Total Available	433200	866400	1470

The SDAccel Base refers to the standard SDAccel environment that has no network connection for the FPGA. The SDAccel Base with Ethernet Support includes a 1 Gb Ethernet port. We can see that the addition of the Ethernet port requires only 2.1% of the resources of the whole device. The Input Module is divided into a Input Bridge and the Input Demultiplexer. The size of the Input Bridge is independent of the number of network input streams. The size of the Input Demultiplexer is dependent on the number of streams. Table 1 shows the overhead corresponding to a 16-port switch. The Output Module is divided into the Ethernet FIFO Controller, the Output Switch and the Packet Formatter. The Ethernet FIFO Controller overhead is independent of the number of output streams. The Output Switch size, analagous to the Input Demultiplexer size, is dependent on the number of output streams. The number of Packet Formatters we have on our FPGA is dependent

on the number of output streams. It can be seen that the resource usage of the Input Bridge, Input and Output Modules and Packet Formatter is small relative to the device and not significant in terms of resources.

7.2 Microbenchmarks

Our microbenchmarks consist of an application that is a direct connection between the Input Module and the Output Module of an Application Region. The goal of this is to show the overhead of our Input and Output Modules and to show that they can handle packets at line-rate as all of the modules are of single-cycle latency.

7.3 Microbenchmark Setup

For Microbenchmark 0 the CPU is directly connected to the FPGA. The CPU sends packets to the raw network interface and the FPGA echoes them back. The packets traverse through the Input Module, the Application Region FIFO and exit through the Output Module back into the CPU. The CPU for this data-point is not a virtual machine and the specifications of it are as follows: Intel Xeon 3.5 GHz CPU E5-2637, four cores with hyperthreading, 32 GB RAM.

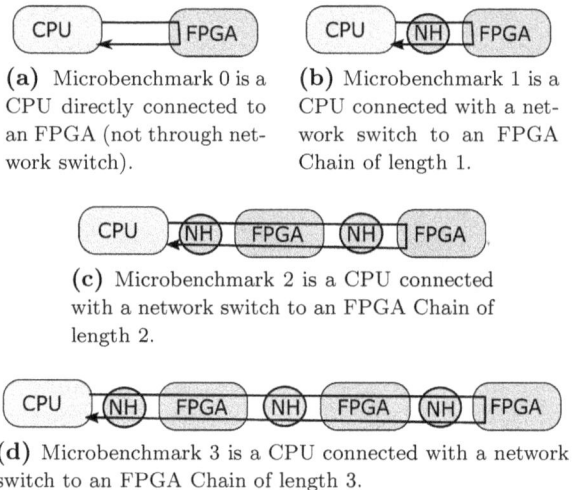

(a) Microbenchmark 0 is a CPU directly connected to an FPGA (not through network switch).

(b) Microbenchmark 1 is a CPU connected with a network switch to an FPGA Chain of length 1.

(c) Microbenchmark 2 is a CPU connected with a network switch to an FPGA Chain of length 2.

(d) Microbenchmark 3 is a CPU connected with a network switch to an FPGA Chain of length 3.

Figure 15: Microbenchmarks 1 to 3 have a network hop (NH). Each network hop travels to the network switch connected to all the FPGAs. Microbenchmark 0 does not use a virtualized CPU, where as the others use virtual CPUs provisioned in SAVI.

This is compared to three microbenchmarks using SAVI. These microbenchmarks consists of one virtual machine sending data to a chain of FPGAs. The chain of FPGAs is either a single FPGA, two FPGAs, or three FPGAs. The traversal through the FPGA chain requires packets to travel to the network switch to be routed. Figure 15 shows the setup of the four microbenchmarks. The specifications of the virtual machine sending data to the FPGA chain are as follows: QEMU Virtual CPU 2.0 GHz, two cores, 4 GB RAM.

7.3.1 Latency

The round-trip latencies are shown in Figure 16. There is no switch latency and no virtualization overhead for Microbenchmark 0. However after that point we notice a linear progression as we increase FPGAs. Each extra FPGA on the path requires two trips to the switch.

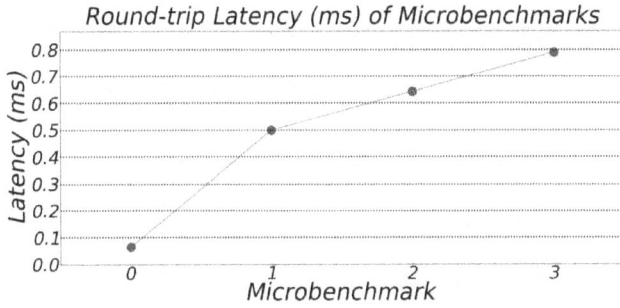

Figure 16: Round-trip Latency of the four microbenchmarks.

7.3.2 Throughput

Figure 17 shows the throughput for the different microbenchmarks. The red line is the bandwidth limit of the network cable. The throughputs of Microbenchmark 0 to 3 are measured with the iperf tool [16]. This is a network tool used to measure throughput of network connections. Microbenchmark 0 does much better because of the faster CPU as it approaches the theoretical maximum of 1 GB/s, which is the current speed of the Ethernet module in the SDAccel framework. When we look at Microbenchmarks 1 to 3, as expected the throughput remains consistent as more FPGAs are added to the chain. Figure 17 shows two additional data points. The first is the throughput between two virtual machines in the SAVI network (Microbenchmark 4). The second additional Microbenchmark is the calculated throughput within the FPGA (Microbenchmark 5). The internal FPGA bandwidth shows that the bottleneck observed is not within the FPGA but due to the virtual machine feeding the FPGA. The internal FPGA throughput is calculated by using the bus width, which is 4-bytes wide and multiplying that by the clock speed, which is 125 MHz. The network switch is designed to switch at 40G rates and therefore is not the bottleneck of our system.

Both the Input and Output Modules work with single-cycle latency. The Input Module needs a four-cycle warm-up period before it bursts the rest of the packet and the Output Module requires a five-cycle warm-up period. These warm-up periods are accommodated with additional FIFOs, which adds to the latency but does not affect the throughput.

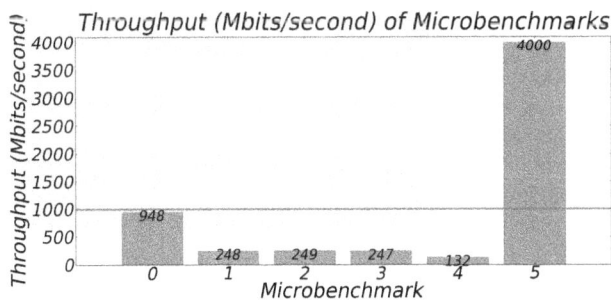

Figure 17: Throughput of the four microbenchmarks with two additional datapoints.

7.4 Application Case-study

Our application case study is a database query accelerator. Several works, such as [17] have shown FPGAs are a good target for such applications as they can perform low-latency, high-throughput applications. Furthermore, frameworks such as Apache Drill have shown that distributed clusters are a good way to accelerate database services [18]. The combination of those observations suggest that a distributed FPGA cluster is ideal for a database query accelerator.

The application we have built is a naive implementation of a query. The query is broken down into several sub-queries. Even though it is a naive implementation, the purpose of the infrastructure is to show that laying out the circuit is easy, and so is replication of that circuit (changing one number in the logical cluster file).

7.5 Query Implementation Details

The query is composed of five streaming components connected as a chain:

1. SQL Read: This component is responsible for reading SQL columns and outputting the data in a format that enables the rest of the components to process the data.

2. SQL Where: This operation is used to match column predicates and values with respect to a boolean operation (equal, greater than, less than, etc.)

3. SQL Like: This operation is used on a string column data and is used to match a string using a substring.

4. SQL Group: This operation aggregates different records using a grouping operation, such as counting.

5. SQL Write: This component is responsible for separating the stream coming out of SQL Group into columns.

Our infrastructure allows us to easily replicate the number of query processing engines, even across multiple FPGAs. When considering the number of processing engines, we first observe the resource usage of one replication of this processing engine, which is as follows: LUTs 11567 (2.7 %), Flip Flops 17176 (1.9 %), Block RAM 504 (34.3 %).

The Block RAM utilization limits our replication so we are limited to two query processing engines per FPGA (each query processing engine requires 35 % of the available BRAM). In our logical FPGA cluster file we would specify this as six replications and in our FPGA mapping we would divide the kernel nodes onto three FPGAs. We do the replication with a scheduler. The scheduler is located on one FPGA and forwards the data to either the replicated engines on the same FPGA or to another FPGA. This would send all the data to one destination and then the scheduler would be responsible for forwarding the data to the appropriate query processing engine. The first FPGA has a scheduler connected to two replicated query processing engines. The second and third FPGAs also have two replicated query processing engines connected directly to the Input Module as opposed to a Scheduler. The Scheduler on the first FPGA is responsible for scheduling work to all six replicated query processing engines across three FPGAs. This makes it simpler for the user since they do not have to change their interface to the cluster as they change the number of replications.

7.6 Case Study Evaluation

Our evaluation compares the throughput of one replication versus six replications across three FPGAs. As expected Figure 18 shows that the throughput increases as the replications increase and we expect it to continue to increase until it reaches the maximum of the FPGA chains observed earlier at about 240 MB/s. This example also highlights the scalability of our system. This would be at about 12 replications, which would require six FPGAs. The throughput limit of 240 MB/s is due to the speed of the CPU inputting table data into the FPGA chain. With a faster CPU we could theoretically saturate the network cable throughput limit of 1 GB/s, which can be increased with a faster network.

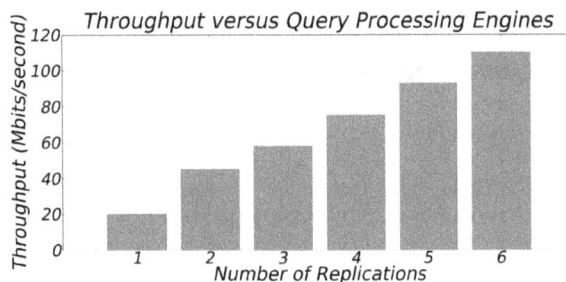

Figure 18: The throughput as we scale up the number of query processing engines.

8. CONCLUSION AND FUTURE WORK

The use of FPGA clusters can be useful as projects like the Microsoft Catapult project have shown. Our infrastructure provides a lightweight cluster provisioning tool. This tool, with a logical cluster description and FPGA mapping, can generate scalable clusters from a heterogeneous cloud. Moreover, these clusters are connected to the network as network devices ready to interact with other network devices. Our infrastructure makes it easy to scale up as with a simple directive we saw throughput scale almost linearly from one to six replicated processing units in our database case study.

The performance limitations in our experiments are due to the limits of our networking infrastructure. One area of future work is to address the slow 1 Gb Ethernet links by upgrading the Ethernet core. Our cluster example remains small but we also wish to upgrade our physical infrastructure to many more nodes so that we can demonstrate a large scale application. Our current case study application is limited due to the number of FPGAs available.

Another area of future work is to build true virtualization on top of this infrastructure. This can involve automatic placement of these kernels so the user will no longer provide an FPGA mapping, or the concept of making a large virtual FPGA out of an FPGA cluster. In both scenarios the cluster details are hidden from the user. Our infrastruture provides simple provisioning of FPGA clusters and can be the platform for using FPGA virtualization.

9. ACKNOWLEDGEMENTS

The authors would like to thank the SAVI testbed for providing the infrastructure, as well as NSERC, SAVI, Xilinx, and CMC/emSYSCAN for providing the equipment and funding for this project.

10. REFERENCES

[1] Andrew Putnum et al. A Reconfigurable Fabric for Accelerating Large-scale Datacenter Services. In *Computer Architecture (ISCA), 2014 ACM/IEEE 41st International Symposium on*, pages 13–24. IEEE, 2014.

[2] IBM Research. OpenPOWER Cloud: Accelerating Cloud Computing. https://www.research.ibm.com/labs/china/supervessel.html, 2016.

[3] Adrian Caulfield et al. A Cloud-Scale Acceleration Architecture. In *Proceedings of the 49th Annual IEEE/ACM International Symposium on Microarchitecture*, October 2016.

[4] Stuart Byma et al. FPGAs in the Cloud: Booting Virtualized Hardware Accelerators with OpenStack. In *Field-Programmable Custom Computing Machines (FCCM)*. IEEE, 2014.

[5] Fei Chen et al. Enabling FPGAS in the Cloud. In *Computing Frontiers*, 2014.

[6] KVM. Kernel Virtual Machine. http://www.linux-kvm.org, 2015.

[7] Maxeler Technologies. MPC-X Series. https://www.maxeler.com/products/mpc-xseries, 2015.

[8] Omar Sefraoui et al. OpenStack: toward an open-source solution for cloud computing. In *International Journal of Computer Applications*, 2012.

[9] Apache Software Foundation. Apache Mesos. https://mesos.apache.org, 2015.

[10] NVidia Inc. NVidia Cuda Zone, Cluster Management Library. https://developer.nvidia.com/cluster-management, 2015.

[11] Joon-Myung Kang et al. SAVI Testbed: Control and Management of Converged Virtual ICT Resources. In *IFIP/IEEE International Symposium on Integrated Network Management*, pages 664–667. IEEE, 2013.

[12] Xilinx Inc. SDAccel Development Environment. https://www.xilinx.com/products/design-tools/software-zone/sdaccel.html, 2016.

[13] The Khronos Group. OpenCL Standard. https://www.khronos.org/opencl/, 2015.

[14] Xilinx Inc. Accelerating Integration. http://www.xilinx.com/products/design-tools/vivado/integration.html, 2016.

[15] Altera Corporation. Qsys - Altera's System Integration Tool. https://www.altera.com/products/design-software/fpga-design/quartus-prime/features/qts-qsys.html, 2016.

[16] Iperf. Iperf – The TCP/UDP Bandwidth Measurement Tool. https://iperf.fr, 2014.

[17] Christopher Dennl et al. Acceleration of SQL Restrictions and Aggregations through FPGA-Based Dynamic Partial Reconfiguration. In *Field Programmable Custom Computing Machines (FCCM)*, pages 25–28, 2013.

[18] Apache Software Foundation. Apache Drill. https://drill.apache.org/, 2015.

Energy Efficient Scientific Computing on FPGAs using OpenCL

Dennis Weller[†], Fabian Oboril[†], Dimitar Lukarski[‡], Juergen Becker[†], & Mehdi Tahoori[†]
[†]Karlsruhe Institute of Technology (KIT), [‡]PARALUTION Labs
Contact Email: {dennis.weller,fabian.oboril,mehdi.tahoori}@kit.edu

ABSTRACT

An indispensable part of our modern life is scientific computing which is used in large-scale high-performance systems as well as in low-power smart cyber-physical systems. Hence, accelerators for scientific computing need to be fast and energy efficient. Therefore, partial differential equations (PDEs), as an integral component of many scientific computing tasks, require efficient implementation. In this regard, FPGAs are well suited for data-parallel computations as they occur in PDE solvers. However, including FPGAs in the programming flow is not trivial, as hardware description languages (HDLs) have to be exploited, which requires detailed knowledge of the underlying hardware. This issue is tackled by OpenCL, which allows to write standardized code in a C-like fashion, rendering experience with HDLs unnecessary. Yet, hiding the underlying hardware from the developer makes it challenging to implement solvers that exploit the full FPGA potential. Therefore, we propose in this work a comprehensive set of generic and specific optimization techniques for PDE solvers using OpenCL that improve the FPGA performance and energy efficiency by orders of magnitude. Based on these optimizations, our study shows that, despite the high abstraction level of OpenCL, very energy efficient PDE accelerators on the FPGA fabric can be designed, making the FPGA an ideal solution for power-constrained applications.

1. INTRODUCTION

Scientific computing is an integral part of our modern life enabling for instance artificial intelligence, improved health care or accurate weather forecasts. Yet, nowadays scientific computing is not only used on large-scale high-performance servers but also in low-power domains due to the growing interest in cyber-physical systems including autonomously operating smart devices [1]. Consequently, there is a strong demand for fast but low-power accelerators.

A key component in many scientific computing domains are *Partial Differential Equations (PDEs)*. Solving PDEs

efficiently is challenging and often requires numerical approaches based on the discretization of the problem space [2]. By this mean, the complex mathematical problem can be transformed into *systems of linear equations* (SLEs). These typically consist of millions of variables, and use special storage formats to avoid storing coefficients that are zero. As a result, solving these systems is computationally and storage-wise expensive [3], and a high memory bandwidth is key for high-performance solutions. However, due to irregular memory access patterns, efficient implementations w.r.t performance as well as energy demand are often challenging.

Traditionally, PDE solvers are implemented for many-core systems (CPUs), by dividing the problem space into several subdomains as well as by parallelizing the fundamental algebraic operations required by the iterative SLE solvers. In recent years also general purpose graphics processing units (GPGPUs) are gaining interest, and are now often used as accelerators, thanks to their superior performance and energy efficiency for massive data-parallel operations, such as the aforementioned algebraic operations [4].

Another group of accelerators are *Field Programmable Gate Arrays (FPGAs)*. Similar to CPUs and GPGPUs, FPGAs use the most recent manufacturing technologies, and with plenty configurable logic blocks they are well suited for data-parallel computations [5]. On top, even high-end FPGAs require less power than medium-class GPGPUs [6], and thus seem to be ideal candidates for power-constrained applications such as smart sensor systems[1]. Yet, FPGAs have been left out as accelerators for PDEs, so far. One reason is that writing efficient code for a heterogeneous platform using FPGAs has been very challenging, due to the lack of a universal programming framework. Consequently, separate codes had to be written for the host processor, for the accelerator and for the interfaces. This requires deep knowledge of the underlying FPGA architecture and use of hardware description languages, which is a major hurdle for software developers.

However, recently, both Altera and Xilinx, started to provide *OpenCL* support for their FPGAs [7, 8]. OpenCL is a framework for writing programs that execute across heterogeneous platforms [9]. By that means, OpenCL allows to write standardized C-like code for the host as well as for the accelerators, and thus relaxes the programming challenge for FPGAs. However, the increased level of abstraction makes it challenging to implement solvers at maximum performance or energy efficiency, as the developer has no direct influence on low-level characteristics such as resource

FPGA '17, February 22-24, 2017, Monterey, CA, USA
© 2017 ACM. ISBN 978-1-4503-4354-1/17/02. . . $15.00
DOI: http://dx.doi.org/10.1145/3020078.3021730

---

[1]E.g, a system steering an autonomous battery-powered vehicle based on sensor and camera input

usage, placement or timing constraints. Nevertheless, it was already demonstrated using OpenCL that FPGAs are very efficient platforms for DNA sequencing, FFT calculations, neural network implementations, image processing and option pricing [10–15]. While this is a great promise, the question of how well FPGAs are suited for solving PDEs efficiently using OpenCL remains unanswered.

Therefore, in this paper, *we propose a set of effective optimization strategies for fast and energy efficient OpenCL-based FPGA implementations of PDE solvers*. These include vendor-specific as well as vendor-independent techniques, data-set optimizations, algorithmic enhancements as well as data-flow and control-flow tuning to overcome the aforementioned implementation challenges for PDEs. The resulting implementations can be accessed at our project website [26]. In addition, we provide a *comprehensive study of the efficiency of FPGAs for solving PDEs using OpenCL* including a comparison with CPUs and GPGPUs. Our results of Xilinx and Altera FPGAs, show that our proposed optimization techniques improve performance and energy efficiency by orders of magnitude. As a result, very energy efficient solutions can be designed using OpenCL, despite the high abstraction level. For instance, our Altera FPGA is 2x more efficient than a quad-core processor, and 35% more efficient than a GPGPU with FPGA-like power consumption. Yet, conventional multi-core CPUs and high-performance GPGPUs still provide better performance. Nevertheless, thanks to the lower power consumption (≈ 30 Watt), FPGAs are the ideal candidates for power-constrained domains. Finally, the results also highlight fundamental differences among both manufacturers in terms of code implementation and optimization, as well as in terms of performance and efficiency.

The rest of this paper is organized as follows. The mathematical problem of our case study is introduced in Section 2, followed by a comprehensive discussion of the implementation for Xilinx and Altera in Section 3. Afterwards, the experimental results are presented and discussed in Section 4. Finally, Section 5 concludes the paper.

2. BACKGROUND AND RELATED WORK

2.1 Partial Differential Equations

Solving PDEs is a core component in many scientific computing domains. Consequently, there is a diversity of PDEs. Nevertheless, solving PDEs follows typically the same main steps, which are problem discretization, transforming the PDE into systems of linear equations and finally solving these systems. Hence, findings for one PDE and one solver apply to many other cases [3].

As a case study for PDEs we use the Poisson's equation in this work. The Poisson's equation occurs in various application domains, e.g. in electrostatics and mechanical engineering. One well known problem described by this PDE is the calculation of the electric potential for a given charge distribution. The equation in two dimensions is:

$$-\Delta u(x,y) = -\left(\frac{\partial^2}{\partial^2 x} + \frac{\partial^2}{\partial^2 y}\right) u(x,y) = f(x,y), \quad (1)$$

where $u(x,y)$ is the unknown potential, $f(x,y)$ is the known boundary condition and x and y are spatial coordinates. This PDE can be converted to an SLE by discretizing the continuous problem space with finite differences methods. The resulting SLE is:

$$A \vec{u} = \vec{b}, \quad (2)$$

where A is the Laplace matrix, $\vec{b}$ represents the boundary condition and $\vec{u}$ is the unknown vector, which represents, in the case of electrostatics, the electrical potential. It is worth mentioning, that the Laplace matrix is sparse, containing only up to 5 non-zero entries per row for the case of a 2D problem (see Figure 1).

2.1.1 Conjugated Gradient Method

To solve this sparse SLE, iterative schemes like the Conjugate Gradient (CG) method are advantageous [16]. The CG scheme is one of the most powerful iterative solvers suited for symmetric, positive-definite and sparse matrices [16], which all are properties of the Laplace matrix. The CG method is also a good choice for a case study, as it has many similarities to other iterative solvers, like the multigrid method [3], as it contains many fundamental algebraic operations like basic vector operations. Hence, the results of this work, have great importance for other iterative solvers implemented using FPGA-based OpenCL platforms.

The idea of the CG algorithm is to update the current approximation of the solution by a new vector with respect to the A-orthogonal projection of the residual $r = b - Au$ [3]. The corresponding algorithm is depicted in Algorithm 1, where A is the input matrix and b is the right hand side of the system, the initial guess is given by vector u_0 and the residual is denoted by r. Moreover, the discrete L_2-norm of a vector r is given by $\|r\| := \sqrt{r^T r}$. Each iteration of the CG method gives a new approximate solution u_k where the stopping criterion is evaluated by means of the corresponding residual $r_k = b - Au_k$, which is implicitly calculated in Step 6 $r = r - \alpha Ad$ (for more information see [3]).

2.2 OpenCL

Traditional methods to design FPGA-based accelerators involve register-transfer level descriptions, using hardware description languages like VHDL, Verilog or SystemC. Working with these languages is a time-consuming process, as they are akin to assembler languages and require detailed hardware programming knowledge as well as the understanding of underlying architecture for efficient use of hardware resources. To avoid such low-level programming languages, the biggest vendors of FPGAs, Altera and Xilinx, have recently released OpenCL frameworks with FPGA support [17]. Within these frameworks, it is possible to create high-level FPGA implementations without the requirement of deal-

---

Algorithm 1 CG algorithm

INPUT: A, b, u_0
1: $r_0 = b - Au_0$
2: $d_0 = r_0$
3: **repeat**
5: $\quad \alpha_k = \dfrac{r_k^T r_k}{d_k^T A d_k}$
6: $\quad r_{k+1} = r_k - \alpha_k A d_k$
7: $\quad u_{k+1} = u_k + \alpha_k d_k$
8: $\quad \beta_k = \dfrac{r_{k+1}^T r_{k+1}}{r_k^T r_k}$
9: $\quad d_{k+1} = r_{k+1} + \beta_k d_k$
10: $\quad k = k + 1$
11: **until** $\|r_{k+1}\| \leq \epsilon$
OUTPUT: u_{k+1}

$$b = A * \vec{u} = \begin{bmatrix} 4 & -1 & 0 & 0 & \cdots & -1 & 0 & 0 & \cdots & & 0 \\ -1 & 4 & -1 & 0 & 0 & \cdots & -1 & 0 & 0 & \cdots & 0 \\ 0 & -1 & 4 & -1 & 0 & 0 & \cdots & -1 & 0 & 0 & \cdots & 0 \\ & & & \ddots & & & & \ddots & & & \\ -1 & & & -1 & 4 & -1 & & & -1 & & \\ 0 & -1 & & & -1 & 4 & -1 & & & -1 & \\ 0 & 0 & -1 & & & -1 & 4 & -1 & & & -1 \\ & & & & & & & & & & \\ 0 & 0 & 0 & \ddots & & & \ddots & \ddots & \ddots & & \ddots \end{bmatrix} * \begin{bmatrix} u_{1,1} \\ u_{2,1} \\ \vdots \\ u_{x-1,y} \\ u_{x,y} \\ u_{x+1,y} \\ \vdots \\ u_{n-1,n} \\ u_{n,n} \end{bmatrix}$$

$$b_m = b_{x,y}$$
$$= 4u_{x,y} - u_{x,y+1} - u_{x,y-1} - u_{x+1,y} - u_{x-1,y}$$
$$= 4u_m - u_n - u_s - u_w - u_e$$

$$\triangle_h u(x,y) := -\frac{1}{h^2} * (4u(x,y) - u(x-1,y) - u(x+1,y) - u(x,y-1) - u(x,y+1))$$

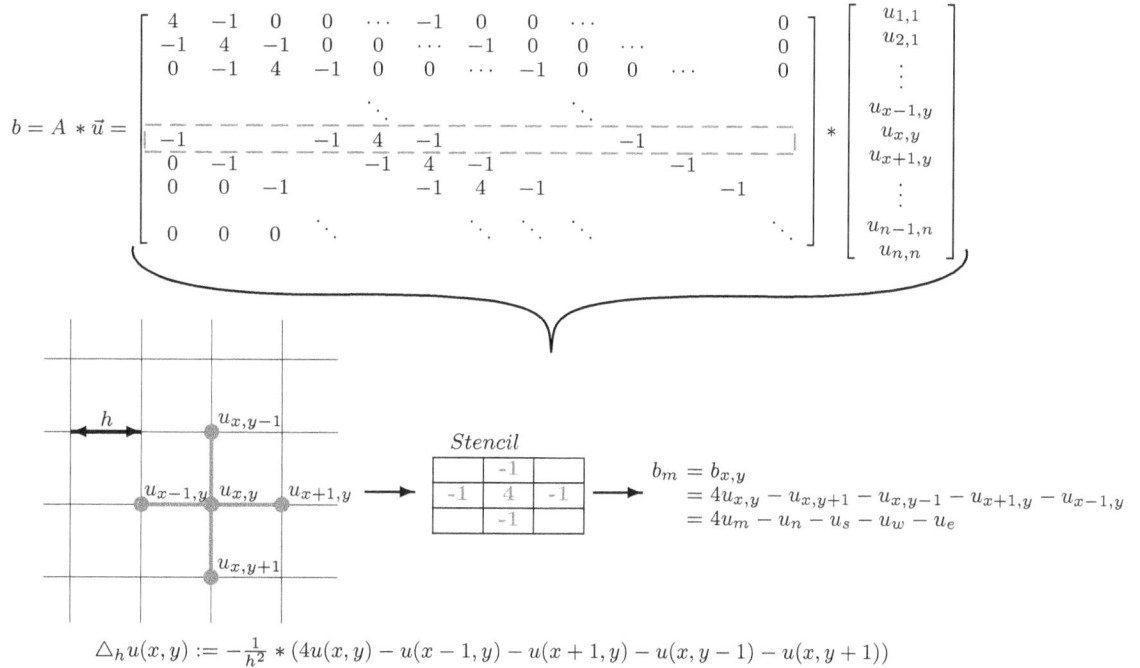

Figure 1: Laplace matrix (top) as the representation of the discretized solution for the Poisson's equation using a finite differences method. Each row is referred to the application of the discretized Laplacian operator on a grid point of the problem space (below), which takes the shape of a stencil with weights of -1 and 4.

ing with hardware description languages. Thus, investigations have been carried out, examining the potential of this new approach. As a result, in several application domains, FPGA implementations have been proposed as a mean to increase energy efficiency [10–15] (see Section 2.3 for details).

OpenCL specifies a C-like programming language, which enables the user to execute programs across heterogeneous platforms, through writing standardized code, without the need to refer to the underlying hardware. In order to implement designs, the OpenCL framework provides an application programming interface (API), which gives a host program running on a CPU platform, control over an accelerator. In the specific case of an FPGA accelerator, the host is able to load precompiled designs into the FPGA fabric, initiate data transfers and launch computations. In that regard it is important to note that software developers do not have to define the interfaces between host and accelerator, or between accelerator and memory. All interfaces as well as communication between host and accelerator are handled through the OpenCL framework. This is also a major advantage over other high-level synthesis approaches, as these focus only on the FPGA implementation. Because of that, in such high-level synthesis approaches, the software developers need to define all interfaces, and, more importantly, also need to implement all communication routines between host and accelerator manually.

Another major advantage of OpenCL is its task-based and data-based parallelism capability, potentially leading to designs with decent performance on a variety of platforms. Therefore, OpenCL partitions the original problem size into smaller junks (so called work-items), which represent single computation threads, dispatched to the accelerator and run in parallel. These work-items are grouped together into a work-group, whose size can be predefined. The size of a work-group is a design decision, and depends on the particular hardware structure (i.e. available resources) of the

accelerator. Moreover, we observed that the optimal work-group size depends also on the FPGA vendors. For Xilinx, the optimal work-group size was one, whereas Altera uses work-group sizes related to the problem size. Section 3.2 discusses this issue in depth.

Another main difference between the Altera and Xilinx OpenCL SDK is the use of optimization techniques. They are described in the next section along with implementation details of the CG algorithm. However, apart from these differences, both vendors provide the same platform model, consisting of multiple kernels and compute units (CUs). Each kernel can process data and deploys (multiple) CUs for parallel computing. The kernel design has to be determined before runtime using ahead-of-time-compilation. In contrast, OpenCL-based CPU and GPU platforms use just-in-time-compilation at runtime. This is because CPUs and GPUs have fixed architectures, whereas FPGAs are reconfigurable and their configuration is a time-consuming process (including high-level synthesis, timing analysis, place-&-route) that is not suitable for runtime compilation. In fact, the compilation of the CG solver requires several hours and an extensive amount of memory, which makes the process of optimizing the implementation very time consuming and costly.

2.3 Related Work

As OpenCL is a new alternative to include FPGAs as accelerators, there exist only few studies on the efficiency of OpenCL-based FPGA implementations. Yet, there is an increasing interest, as OpenCL promises to significantly shorten the software development time. Recently, [11] presented an OpenCL compilation framework which generated high-performance hardware for FPGAs, paving the way for further studies. Among these was [15], which presented an OpenCL-based approach to use FPGAs as energy efficient data center accelerators. In [13], it was demonstrated, how the OpenCL design of a genome sequencing algorithm, im-

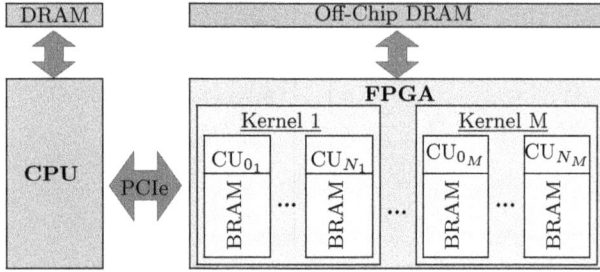

Figure 2: OpenCL platform with an FPGA accelerator: The CPU acts as host, provides the data for computation through the PCI-Express bus and controls the FPGA using the OpenCL-API. After the host has invoked the kernel execution the data is loaded from off-chip DRAM to local (BRAM) memory, and the FPGA starts processing the data.

plemented on a Xilinx FPGA, could surpass the performance and energy efficiency of CPU and GPU platforms. Further work has shown, how FPGA-based FFT accelerators can be realized [10]. The results supported the possibility of using FPGAs to achieve higher energy efficiency than GPUs under the means of OpenCL. Furthermore, [12] implemented Black-Scholes simulation for option pricing for Altera FPGAs, which were more energy efficient than comparable GPU platforms. Most recently, [14,18] demonstrated that OpenCL also allows the efficient implementation of neural networks and sparse matrix calculations on FPGAs.

However, up to now, there is no work related to solving complete PDEs or optimizing the solver efficiency on FPGAs using OpenCL. For that reason, here we propose a comprehensive set of optimization schemes to improve the performance and energy efficiency of FPGAs for solving PDEs using OpenCL. In addition, we analyze the performance and energy efficiency of this implementation compared to traditional approaches for CPUs or GPGPUs.

3. OPTIMIZATION SCHEMES FOR FPGA-BASED PDE SOLVERS USING OPENCL

For solving the discretized Poisson's equation, the CG method is implemented on the FPGA using OpenCL. Essentially, three kernel functions are required for the complete CG algorithm (Algorithm 1), which are representative for many PDE solvers [3]:

- Scaleadd() (line: 1,6,7,9): $\vec{z} = a \cdot \vec{x} + \vec{y}$
- Dotc() (line: 5,8): $a = \vec{x}^T \cdot \vec{y}$
- LaplaceApply() (line: 1,5,6): $\vec{y} = A \cdot \vec{x}$

In a first step, each of these kernels is designed standalone, and optimized with respect to performance. As the power consumption of FPGAs is dominated by leakage power [19], performance improvements directly result in a better energy efficiency. Moreover, the performance is limited by the memory bandwidth[2]. Hence, it is necessary to achieve a throughput as close as possible to the theoretical peak bandwidth, to realize good performance and energy efficiency.

To reach the maximum memory bandwidth is very challenging, in particular on FPGAs using OpenCL (see Section 4 for details). Therefore, we propose in the following

---

[2]Caused by the external DDR3-DRAM memory interface of the FPGA boards. Maximum on Xilinx FPGA and Altera FPGA is 10.6 GB/s or 21.2 GB/s, respectively.

a set of optimization techniques which include data-set optimizations, algorithmic enhancements, as well as data-flow and control-flow tuning. Some of these optimizations can be applied to the kernel designs as annotations in the code, represented as specific directives, while others require code and data restructuring. Hence, the use of these techniques is a challenging task, in particular, as not all optimization schemes always result in higher but decreased performance. For instance, excessive resource utilization can lead to reduced clock speeds resulting in degraded performance.

Another optimization challenge is the integration of the three kernels into one combined design, to load them onto the FPGA via one single bitstream. This step is required, as switching between different bitstreams is inefficient due to the switching overhead of more than 400ms (for our kernel design) compared to kernel execution times that are in the range of 10-60 ms. However, the integration of all kernels into one design is not trivial, as all resources have to be shared among the kernels. This can cause timing errors or excessive resource utilization, which in turn can lead to reduced clock frequencies. As a result, it is challenging to maintain the standalone kernel performance, even if multiple kernels are integrated in one single bitstream. Thus, optimizations and design complexity have to be carefully traded-off to achieve the best performance.

In the following, our proposed optimization strategies are described. Some of them are vendor-independent approaches, while there are also a couple of vendor-dependent schemes, that are required, as both companies follow different principles for their OpenCL SDK.

3.1 Vendor-Independent Optimizations

The proposed vendor-independent optimizations apply to the Xilinx and Altera OpenCL SDKs. However, the exact implementation way may differ. In addition, some of them are supported by OpenCL constructs and specific vendor commands, while others (in particular avoidance of branches and irregular memory access) need to be applied manually.

- **Loop Unrolling**: Loop Unrolling is a very effective tool to improve the performance of loops on FPGAs with no data dependency. If a loop is unrolled N times, N loop iterations are run in parallel leading to a speedup of N-times in best case. This leads to an improved performance, but more FPGA resources are utilized. To enable this feature, one can use either the directive _attribute_((opencl_unroll_hint(N))) or implement the unrolling manually.

- **Loop Pipelining**: Like Loop Unrolling, this technique implements another form of data parallelism, where all sequential operations in a loop are kept busy at all times. Instead of waiting until the complete loop has finished computation, new data is requested after the current operation block in the loop was processed, as shown Figure 3. The performance is increased at the cost of additional resources required for storing intermediate results after each block. For Xilinx FPGAs Loop Pipelining can be triggered with the pragma _attribute_((xcl_pipeline_loop)) and should be used whenever possible (see Figure 4), whereas the Altera compiler automatically employs this optimization.

- **Data Parallelism**: OpenCL enables the use of k-way single-instruction multiple-data (SIMD), which is supported by the FPGA vendors for a set of basic vector

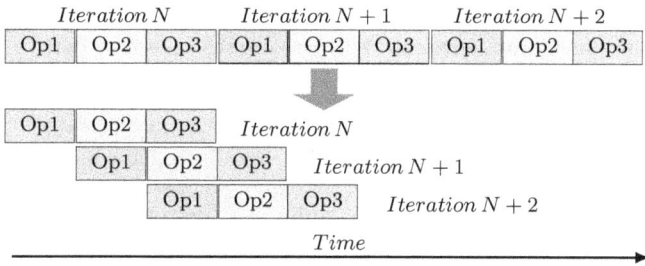

Figure 3: Loop Pipelining

operations like vector scaling. With vectorized processing, the throughput can be increased by a factor of k, which is typically 2,4,8 or 16. These k-way SIMD operations are induced by using vectorized data types. For instance, if 16-way SIMD is desired with floating point numbers, the data types have to be declared as float16. One float16 vector is the maximum data which can be transferred per clock cycle from the off-chip DDR3-DRAM memory to the on-chip local memory of the FPGA, as the related interface (for DDR3) is 512 bit wide (16 * 4 Byte (float) = 512 bit). Using vectorized processing widens the data path of the kernel as each operation is extended to process vectors instead of scalars, resulting in increased throughput but also resource utilization. Nevertheless, using float16 data types is key to achieve the best performance on FPGAs (see Figure 4 and Figure 5).

- **Replication of Compute Units**: The OpenCL framework supports the replication of compute units (CUs), which represent the implementation of a specific kernel function. Using this method, subsequent work-groups can be run in parallel instead of sequentially. As for the k-way SIMD technique, in the ideal case, the throughput can be increased by the number of replications. However, this only holds if the memory interface is not the performance bottleneck, otherwise the performance improvements are very limited. Moreover, using N CUs increases the resource utilization by more than N-times, due to additional control logic required to dispatch data to the different CUs. As a result, the number of CUs has to be carefully traded-off with resource demand. In case of PDE solvers, the *Dotc*-kernels highly benefit from using multiple CUs (see Figure 4 and Figure 5).

- **Dataflow-Driven Design**: The kernel implementations for FPGAs have to be designed under a dataflow-driven approach, using as few control structures as possible to maximize performance. These dataflow-driven designs are typically more efficient for FPGAs as control-driven approaches used for CPU implementations. The reason for this is that FPGAs do not have the sophisticated control-flow mechanisms of modern CPUs such as branch prediction or branch target buffers. As a result, the FPGA performance can be improved by 2x based on our observations, if branches/jumps are avoided. Thus, the use of control statements like "if-else" has to be restricted.

- **Regular Memory Accesses**: Due to the fact that the discretization matrix A is sparse, containing a huge number of rows and columns, sparse matrix formats like Compressed Sparse Row (CSR) are typically deployed for storage, as the traditional storage format

would require terabytes of storage. Using these sparse formats leads, however, to irregular, unaligned and complex memory access patterns during the matrix vector multiplications. Since FPGAs do not have big caches these access patterns cause massive performance drops, which is a major challenge for the design of efficient PDE solvers for FPGAs. In order to avoid this undesirable behavior, we propose to implement sparse matrix vector multiplications in form of stencils. This means that indexes of the required vector elements as well as the coefficients with which these vector elements are multiplied are hard coded in the OpenCL kernel. This avoids loading the matrix elements and facilitates the access for the vector elements (for instance it allows to use float16 data types). While this increases the performance on one hand, it also decreases the flexibility of the kernel, as then only one particular stencil is supported (in our case the 2D-Laplace stencil shown in Figure 1) instead of an arbitrary matrix.

3.2 Vendor-Specific Optimization Techniques

The aforementioned optimization techniques are key to improve the performance and energy efficiency of Altera and Xilinx FPGAs. Yet, both vendors follow different design philosophies, and thus require also very specific optimization schemes on top of the vendor-independent techniques.

A first important difference between Altera and Xilinx is the usage of the concept of work-items. For GPU devices, hundreds of work-items are used to represent the execution threads, which are dispatched to different cores and run in parallel. While this concept leads to high-performance designs for the Altera OpenCL SDK, it is not efficient for the Xilinx SDK. The best performance for the latter is achieved using only one work-item per compute unit, which takes full control of the data processing and data transfers.

Another Xilinx-specific optimization is that burst transfers have to be used to transfer data between the on-chip BRAMs and the off-chip memory. The reason is that each of these transfers, controlled by the memory controller integrated in the FPGA, consists of an initiation phase and the actual transferring phase. The effort for the former phase is always constant, regardless of the size of the transferred data, producing some type of overhead. While this turned out to be no issue for Altera FPGAs, it considerably limited the performance of our Xilinx FPGA, where the initiation phase takes about 50-70 clock cycles [20]. As a result, it is very inefficient, to transfer small amount of data, as the overhead dominates. We found out that fast transfer rates can only be achieved using large burst sizes of 16KB and more, in case of the Xilinx FPGA.

As a consequence of these differences between the Altera and Xilinx OpenCL SDKs, separate kernel code has to be written for Altera FPGAs and Xilinx FPGAs, which limits the portability between both vendors. In the following, we explain our proposed kernel designs comprising all aforementioned optimization techniques for both vendors in detail. All OpenCL kernels can also be found on our website [26].

3.2.1 OpenCL Kernels for Xilinx FPGAs

For all three Xilinx kernels (*Scaleadd*, *Dotc*, *LaplaceApply*) the optimization approaches are similar with regard to burst transfers, float16 data type and loop pipelining. Therefore, we will explain them using the *Dotc*-kernel as an example.

As it can be seen in Listing 1 for the *Dotc*-kernel for Xilinx FPGAs, all computations are carried out in a work group with a single work item, as the required work-group size is set to $1 \cdot 1 \cdot 1 = 1$ (Line 2). The required data for processing needs to be loaded and stored with burst transfers, implemented as pipelined loops (Line 11,16). We observed, that without burst transfers, the performance decreases by of 100x to 1000x. As a result of the pipelined loops, in each iteration one float16 vector is loaded into local BRAMs, processed and stored. This concept is advantageous, as the external memory interface is 512 bit wide [20], which corresponds to one float16 vector[3]. Thus, the maximum possible bandwidth can be achieved, in the case of perfect pipelined loops. Consequently, the design challenge is to reach an initial interval of 1, meaning that the loop can request new data every clock cycle. However, in practice, only an interval of 3 can be reached. To compensate this drawback, multiple compute units are deployed (here: 4 CUs), to perform calculations in parallel, and thus improve the throughput.

For the other two Xilinx kernels (*Scaleadd*, *LaplaceApply*) the optimization approaches are very similar. However, the *LaplaceApply*-kernel poses some special challenges. First, the implementation of 16-way SIMD operations is not trivial. This is due to the fact, that despite of using the 2D-Laplace stencil, still irregular memory accesses exist (only five non-continuous vector elements are accessed per operation as shown in Figure 1). To resolve this issue, the stencil (i.e., $4m - s - n - e - w$) is implemented with the help of scalar products on float16-data as follows:

$$
\begin{aligned}
out &= \vec{m} \cdot (0, \ldots, 0, -1, 4, -1, 0, \ldots, 0) \\
out &+= \vec{n} \cdot (0, \ldots, 0, 0, -1, 0, 0, \ldots, 0) \\
out &+= \vec{s} \cdot (0, \ldots, 0, 0, -1, 0, 0, \ldots, 0),
\end{aligned}
$$

where $\vec{m}$, $\vec{n}$ and $\vec{s}$ are float16 input vectors for the different rows required by the stencil routine (see Figure 1). Then, each vector $\vec{m}$, $\vec{n}$ and $\vec{s}$ is processed multiple times using different right-hand vectors, which differ in the stencil posi-

[3]float16 = 16 floats = 16 * 4 Byte = 16 * 32 Bit = 512 bit

tion, i.e. in the places with the non-zero-elements to compute all output elements. Furthermore, to minimize data traffic, multiple rows are loaded at once to maximize reuse of data in the local memory. The second challenge of the *LaplaceApply*-kernel is that the boundary elements of the grid require a special treatment, which leads to many if-else statements in the kernel code. To eliminate these branches, the input data is modified by adding an additional row of zeros below the bottom row to the grid as well as one row of zeros the top of the grid. By that means, the extra handling of the bottom and top row is avoided.

As a result, this implementation is very demanding in terms of resource utilization. In particular, the available BRAMs can limit the performance, as it determines the size of burst transfers as well as the amount of data that can be reused locally for the stencil computations.

3.2.2 OpenCL Kernels for Altera FPGAs

Using the Altera OpenCL SDK the concept of work-items is used differently, with multiple work-items per CU, resulting in completely different kernel designs as for Xilinx FPGAs. In general, the main idea behind our Altera kernels is that each work-item only processes one float16 element. To explain this further, the *Dotc*-kernel is used as example.

As it can be seen Listing 2, each work item (identified by gid in Line 6), processes only one float16 pair (Line 16), and stores the intermediate result in a local buffer. Thus, a reduction in a log-2-manner has to be carried out (Line 18-22), to obtain the final result. In comparison, the reduction is not required for the Xilinx kernel, which consists of only one work item which accumulates the intermediate results in each clock cycle (Line 20). Moreover, as it can be seen in the code, burst transfers are not required as explained before, while loop unrolling is performed (Line 14).

For the other kernels (*Scaleadd*, *LaplaceApply*) a similar implementation strategy is used. However, for the *LaplaceApply*-kernel, again some tricks are required to enable the usage of SIMD instructions, which, however, are different from

Listing 1: OpenCL *Dotc*-kernel for Xilinx [26]

```
1  #define BSIZE 2048 //to load 128KB in each burst
2  __kernel __attribute__((reqd_work_group_size(1,1,1)))
3  void kernel_dotc(__global const float16 *x, __global
       const float16 *y, float out, const int nloops) {
4      int gid = get_group_id(0); // use of 4 CUs
5      float temp = 0.0f;
6      __local float16 x_loc[BSIZE]; // local BRAMs
7      __local float16 y_loc[BSIZE];
8
9      for (int loop = 0; loop < nloops; loop++){
10         __attribute__((xcl_pipeline_loop))
11         for (int bid=0; bid<BSIZE; bid++) {
12             //load data to local memory
13             x_loc[bid] = x[bid+(loop+gid*nloops)*BSIZE];
14         }
15         __attribute__((xcl_pipeline_loop))
16         for (int bid=0; bid<BSIZE; bid++) {
17             //load data to local memory
18             y_loc[bid] = y[bid+(loop+gid*nloops)*BSIZE];
19             //Carry out dot-product and accumulate
20             temp += dot(x_loc[bid],y_loc[bid]);
21         }
22     }
23     out[gid] = temp;
24 }
```

Listing 2: OpenCL *Dotc*-kernel for Altera [26]

```
1  #define BLOCK_SIZE 64
2  __attribute__((num_compute_units(4))) // use 4 CUs
3  // work-group with 64 elements
4  __attribute__((reqd_work_group_size(64,1,1)))
5  __kernel void cdot(__global const float16 *x, __global
       const float16 *y, __global float *out, int size) {
6      int gid = get_global_id(0);
7      int lid = get_local_id(0);
8      int group = get_group_id(0);
9      int nl= get_local_size(0);
10     __local float intermed[BLOCK_SIZE];
11
12     // compute block-wise dot-products
13     intermed[lid] = 0;
14     #pragma unroll
15     for (int i = 0; i<16; i++)
16         intermed[lid] += x[gid][i]*y[gid][i];
17     // perform a binary-tree reduction
18     barrier(CLK_LOCAL_MEM_FENCE);
19     for (int i = (min(BLOCK_SIZE,nl))/2; i > 0; i /= 2) {
20         if (lid < i) intermed[lid] += intermed[lid + i];
21         barrier(CLK_LOCAL_MEM_FENCE);
22     }
23     //write result back
24     if (lid == 0) out[group] = intermed[lid];
25 }
```

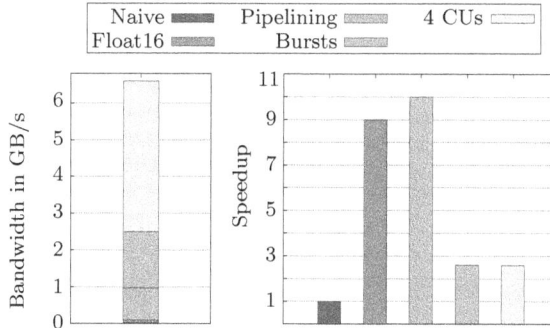

Figure 4: Performance optimization for the Xilinx *Dotc*-kernel. The optimization techniques are applied on top of each other in the given sequence.

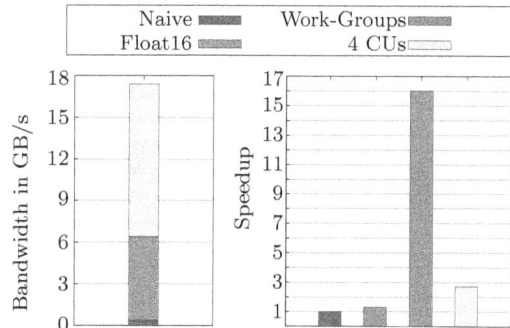

Figure 5: Performance optimization for the Altera *Dotc*-kernel. The optimization techniques are applied on top of each other in the given sequence.

those proposed for the Xilinx kernel. Instead of using scalar products, simpler vector-scaling routines are employed in combination with a clever data partitioning. First, to eliminate branches for the boundary elements, these are computed in separate kernels, which only compute the boundary elements. The runtime of these kernels is negligible in comparison to the main *LaplaceApply*-kernel, which computes the results for all points within the grid (see Figure 1). Hence, these kernels should be designed to consume as less resources as possible, to not induce restrictions for the other kernels. Second, all computations within the main kernel are performed using SIMD instructions. Therefore, the rows $\vec{n}$ and $\vec{s}$ are loaded as float16 vectors, while $\vec{m}$ contains now 18 float elements to include the left and right neighbors. Then, the output vector (again float16) is calculated as

$$\vec{out} = 4 \cdot \vec{m}[1:16] - \vec{s} - \vec{n} - \vec{m}[0:15] - \vec{m}[2:17].$$

Third, to minimize data transfer and maximize data reuse within the main *LaplaceApply*-kernel, each work-item calculates four float16 output vectors, namely two neighboring float16 packages for two adjacent rows. Processing more than four packages was not possible for our Altera FPGA due to resource limitations (available logic elements).

3.3 Impact of the Optimization Techniques

To highlight the potential of our proposed optimization schemes, we implemented the *Dotc*-kernels using different optimization strategies. As it can be seen from the corresponding results in Figure 4 for our Xilinx FPGA, a speedup of 620x can be achieved compared to the naive design using all techniques. Moreover, it is also noticeable that all schemes are necessary to obtain the best performance, as using SIMD instructions improves the baseline performance by 9x, loop pipelining adds another 10x, and using memory bursts as well as multiple compute units brings another 2.5x each. In this regard it is important to note that the sequence matters with which the optimization techniques are applied. In other words, using a different sequence of these optimization schemes will change the speedup values of each approach, however, the final combined value will remain the same. In addition it is worth to note that the results clearly show that the theoretical optimal speedup is

often not achievable (e.g. 16x for float16, or 4x with 4 CUs). This is due to dependencies in the control and data flow as well as due to timing adjustments during the compilation process, which lead to different clock frequencies for different designs containing different optimization levels.

The performance of the *Dotc*-kernel for the Altera FPGA also shows significant improvements using the proposed optimization schemes. Yet, the overall speedup is just 59x. The reason, why the Altera version benefits less than the Xilinx implementation is that the Altera OpenCL compiler already optimizes the naive implementation using for instance pipelining. Consequently, the naive kernel achieves a bandwidth of 300 MByte/s, 30x more than the Xilinx version. Again, a very effective measure is to use multiple CUs and float16. In addition, it is very important to use appropriate sizing for the work-group sizes, as only in this case float16 and multiple CUs can be as effective as illustrated. For instance, with a work-group size of 512 instead of 64 (see Listing 2) the performance drops from 17.7 GB/s to 14.6 GB/s.

4. RESULTS

4.1 Hardware Configuration

To evaluate the performance and efficiency of FPGAs, we use Xilinx (ADM-PCIE-7V3) and Altera (Terasic DE5-NET) PCIe-Boards and compare them against CPUs and GPGPUs. In this regard, we selected a low-power GPGPU using conventional DDR3-RAM (Intel HD Graphics) as well as a high-performance model equipped with very fast GDDR5-RAM (Nvidia GTX 980) to have a comprehensive analysis. The used platforms are listed in Table 1. For the CPU platform, OpenMP was deployed, which is an implementation of multithreading, capable of assigning computation threads to different processors to achieve parallelism and consequently increasing throughput. The Intel HD Graphics was accessed through the OpenCL framework, same as for the FPGAs (Xilinx SDAccel 2016.1 and Altera Quartus 15.1). In contrast, for the GTX 980, CUDA (v7.5) was used, which is, akin to OpenCL, a parallel computing platform. For the GPGPUs and the CPU, we used the Paralution library [21], which provides very efficient CG implementations. The implementations of the OpenCL kernels for the FPGA accel-

Table 1: Listing of platforms used for benchmarking of the CG method

	Platform	Specification	API	Theoretical Memory Bandwidth	Technology
CPU	Intel Core i5-4590	4 cores @ 3.3GHz	OpenMP	21.2 GB/s (dual-DDR3-1333)	22nm
GPU	Intel HD Graphics 4600	20 exec. units @ 1.15 GHz	OpenCL	21.2 GB/s (dual-DDR3-1333)	22nm
	Nvidia GeForce GTX 980	2048 CUDA Cores @ 1.1 GHz	CUDA	224 GB/s (256-bit GDDR5 @3.5 GHz)	28nm
FPGA	Xilinx Virtex 7	XC7VX690T @ 200 MHz	OpenCL	10.6 GB/s (DDR3-1333)	28nm
	Altera Stratix V GX	5SGXEA7 @ 300 MHz	OpenCL	21.2 GB/s (dual-DDR3-1333)	28nm

Table 2: Standalone kernel performance in GB/s.

	Naive		Optimized		Speedup	
	Xilinx	Altera	Xilinx	Altera	Xilinx	Altera
ScaleAdd	0.06	3.6	9.1	17.5	1492x	5x
Dotc	0.01	0.3	6.6	17.7	623x	59x
LaplaceApply	0.03	0.01	6.6	11.5	2000x	1150x

erators are published under [26]. All these devices are run on the same hardware platform, which uses an Intel Core i5-4590 as host CPU. More details about the specifications can be found in [22, 23]. All measurements were carried out with a vector size of 2^{26} (≈ 67 million), which is a reasonable problem size for discretized PDEs.

4.2 Performance Measurements

The performance of all kernels within the CG solver is limited by the available memory bandwidth, which itself is constraint by the maximum transfer rate of the employed memory devices. Thus, as a comparable measure, the ratio of achieved bandwidth to maximum bandwidth was used and expressed in percentage.

Using the aforementioned optimization methods, the performance of the Xilinx standalone kernels surpassed 6 GB/s, while more than 11 GB/s were achieved on the Altera board. In this regard, Table 2 lists the speedup between naive and optimized kernel designs. As it can be seen from the data, our proposed optimization strategies have a significant effect and boost the performance by orders of magnitude. However, neither for Altera nor for Xilinx, these standalone kernels could be combined into one single bitstream due to resource and timing constraints. Yet, having a single bitstream is essential to enable high performance, as switching between different bitstreams is inefficient (please see Section 3 for more details). Therefore, the designs of the *LaplaceApply*-Kernel had to be simplified. In case of Xilinx the compute units were reduced from 3 to 1, as otherwise not enough BRAMs were available for the other kernels. For Altera the kernel was modified to process only one float16 package instead of four (see Section 3.2.2), as otherwise the resource demand is that high (more than 80% of all logic elements), that the clock frequency drops from 300 MHz to less than 250 MHz which causes performance penalties for the other kernels and results in an overall worse performance.

Table 3 contains the throughput of each kernel (as part of a single bitstream in case of the FPGA platforms) in comparison between the platforms (see Table 1 for details). The Xilinx kernels are inferior to the Altera kernels, due to the fact that the available bandwidth is smaller (single-channel vs. dual-channel[4]), and some optimization strategies had to be discarded for the *LaplaceApply*-kernel, as just discussed. The Altera FPGA delivers a performance in the same range

---

[4]Please note that this restriction does not apply to all Xilinx PCIe boards. For instance, the ADM-PCIE-KU3 supports also dual-channel memory access under OpenCL which should result in 2x of the performance of the ADM-PCIE-7V3 used in this study

as the Intel Core and the Intel Graphics platforms. However, as expected, it could not beat the Nvidia GTX 980, which was superior in all kernel computations.

For all platforms, the *LaplaceApply*-kernel had the lowest throughput because of the irregular memory accesses. In contrast, the *Scaleadd*-kernel achieved the best performance due to its simplicity, except for the Nvidia and Altera platforms. A possible explanation, why these platforms achieve a better performance executing the *Dotc*-kernel is that this kernel requires only read operations, while the *Scaleadd*-kernel uses read and write memory accesses. In addition, it is obvious that the FPGAs have more problems with the *LaplaceApply*-kernels compared to the other platforms. This is due to the fact that these kernels require more control-flow operations as well as less regular memory accesses. CPUs and GPGPUs can handle these challenges much better due to their sophisticated microarchitectures and caches.

4.3 Power Measurements & Energy Efficiency

In addition to the performance measurements, also the power consumption was measured in order to determine the energy efficiency for each kernel and platform. Two methods were used for this purpose: a power meter pluggable in outlets, and Intel CPU registers for the CPU power consumption [24]. Using these tools, the total power consumption can be divided into the following components:

- System idle: Contains the power consumption of the host computer with its CPU, the DRAM and all other peripheries excluding the FPGA (GPU) board and without running any computations.
- FPGA (GPU) idle: Is related to the power consumption of the FPGA board (GPU) plugged into the host computer when no computations are running. This is essentially the difference of the idle system power with and without accelerator.
- CPU computation: Is the power consumption of the CPU cores which are exclusively used for the CG computation tasks. This value is obtained by reading out the corresponding power monitor registers inside the CPU and by subtracting the CPU power consumption during idle (included in System Idle).
- FPGA (GPU) computation: Is the power consumption which is required to carry out the CG computation in addition to the FPGA (GPU) idle power consumption. The data is obtained by measuring the total system power while computations are running, and then the idle and CPU consumption is subtracted.
- Host memory: This is the power consumed by the required host memory to execute the CG solver. Therefore, the total system power is measured with four memory modules and then with only one module to determine the consumption per module. This is then used to obtain the total memory power consumption.

With the help of this classification we are able to break down the power consumption and estimate only the power

Table 3: Throughput of the optimized kernels for each platform in GB/s and as percentage compared to the peak memory transfer rate. Moreover, the execution time for one iteration of the CG algorithm is given.

Vendor	Xilinx	Altera	Intel Core i5	Intel Graphics	Nvidia
Scaleadd	9.1 GB/s (85%)	17.5 GB/s (83%)	16.6 GB/s (78%)	17.9 GB/s (84%)	165 GB/s (67%)
Dotc	6.6 GB/s (62%)	17.7 GB/s (83%)	16.5 GB/s (77%)	16.5 GB/s (77%)	175 GB/s (73%)
LaplaceApply	2.8 GB/s (27%)	8.1 GB/s (38%)	11.2 GB/s (52%)	15.1 GB/s (71%)	143 GB/s (59%)
CG Runtime	. 710 ms	300ms	250ms	280ms	25ms

Table 4: Accelerator power consumption for the kernels of each platform in Watt. *A + B means: A is consumed by the accelerator incl. its memory, while the host CPU consumes B to manage the accelerator

Vendor	Xilinx	Altera	Intel Core i5	Intel Graphics	Nvidia
Scaleadd	35.3 + 18.7*	28.3 + 0.7	65 + 0	45.0 + 0.1	148.6 + 12.9
Dotc	35.8 + 18.7	27.5 + 0.7	66 + 0	45.4 + 0.1	153.6 + 12.9
LaplaceApply	37.8 + 18.7	27.8 + 0.7	71 + 0	45.6 + 0.1	230.1 + 12.9
CG	32.8 + 18.7	27.8 + 0.7	66 + 0	41.2 + 0.1	148.5 + 12.9

consumed by the CG computations as highlighted for the case of the *ScaleAdd*-kernel in Figure 6. The corresponding results for all kernels are presented in Table 4, which shows several interesting facts:

1. The FPGAs have the lowest power consumption (less than 30 Watt for the Altera board) making them ideal candidates for power-constrained applications. In comparison, the Intel Graphics performing similar to the Altera FPGA requires 45 Watt (including 15 Watt for its memory) and the quad-core processor has a 2x higher power consumption than the Altera FPGA. The most power-hungry platform is the Nvidia GTX 980, requires about 170 to 230 Watt for the kernels.

2. The consumption of the FPGA platforms is almost independent of the executed kernel, while there are significant differences for the CPU and Nvidia GTX 980. The reason for this behavior is that the power consumption of the FPGAs is dominated by leakage power, whereas dynamic power consumption is mostly responsible for the CPU and GPU power consumption.

3. Another interesting observation is that in case of the Xilinx platform the host CPU consumes a considerable amount of power (18.7 Watt), while this does not happen when the Altera board is used (0.7 Watt). This is because the host continuously polls the accelerator about the status of computation using the Xilinx SDK resulting in 100% load on two (out of four) CPU cores. In contrast, using the Altera FPGA for acceleration, almost no additional CPU power is required, as interrupts are used instead of polling, and this is more

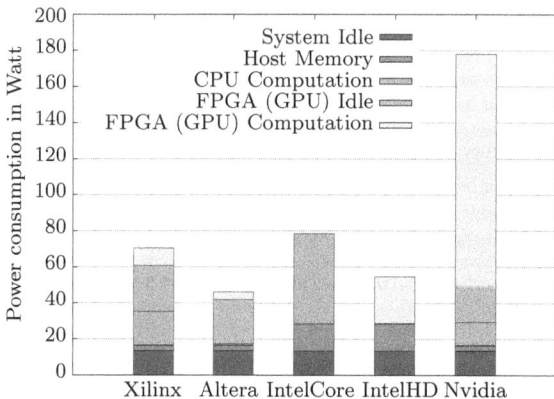

Figure 6: **Power consumption of *Scaleadd*-kernel (Note: PCIe accelerators require less host memory as they come with their own memory)**

efficient in the case of long kernel runtimes[5]. Also Nvidia's CUDA solution uses polling, yet the CPU load is less, resulting in less power demand for the host CPU compared to the Xilinx solution.

As a result, the Altera platform has in this scenario the best energy efficiency of all platforms using conventional DDR3 memory (see Table 5), achieving a throughput of up to 630 MB/Joule and requiring only 8.5 Joule per CG iteration. This is more than 2x less than the quad-core CPU and 35% less than the Intel Graphics. Hence, if power consumption is constrained, for instance because of cooling issues that limit heat dissipation as in many mobile and IoT platforms, an OpenCL-based FPGA solution is preferable over a low-performance GPGPU considering energy efficiency as well as raw power consumption.

The Xilinx platform has a worse energy efficiency, which however is mostly due to the fact that our Xilinx FPGA uses a single-channel memory interface resulting in only half the memory bandwidth compared to the Altera platform, and that polling is employed by the Xilinx SDK. Only the Nvidia platform has an even better energy efficiency than the Altera FPGA. Yet, it also has memory that offers a 10x higher bandwidth compared to the Altera platform. Consequently, the results of the Altera FPGA are very good.

In this regard it is worth noting that the energy efficiency and performance of the FPGA solutions can be massively improved if faster memory is used instead of conventional DDR-memory. By that means, FPGAs could even become a possible rival for high-performance GPGPUs. For instance Altera's new Stratix 10 generation supports "High Bandwidth Memory" (HBM) [25], which offers transfer rates upto 1 TB/s. Consequently, the energy efficiency can increase by 10x and more. In addition, the recent FPGAs also include integrated multi-core ARM-like processors, which can be exploited for computations like the reduction inside *Dotc*-kernel which do not perform that well on the FPGA. Nevertheless, compared to conventional CPUs, even the state-of-the-art FPGA solutions can offer a better energy efficiency (please note as before that the Xilinx solution has a poor energy efficiency due to the low performance caused by the single-channel memory interface, whereas all other solutions use multiple memory channels).

---

[5]Please note that for very short kernel execution times in the order of a few μs polling offers a performance advantage over interrupts. However, as our kernels require several ms for the computation, this advantage is negligible.

Table 5: Energy efficiency of each platform and kernel in MB/J and the resulting energy for one CG iteration.

Vendor	Xilinx	Altera	Intel Core i5	Intel Graphics	Nvidia
Scaleadd	169	604	256	438	1025
Dotc	105	628	252	400	1052
LaplaceApply	50	285	158	364	587
Joule/iteration	33.9	8.5	20.2	11.5	5.1

4.4 Utilization

One important parameter for the OpenCL designs on FPGAs is the resource utilization. A design is not configurable if resource constraints cannot be met. As shown in Table 6, the utilization of the Altera FPGA is about 50% for the logic elements. For the Xilinx FPGA, the utilization is in the same range, apart from the BRAMs, which are required for the burst transfers. Thus, efficient designs on the Xilinx FPGA have to consider this by distributing the number of BRAMs to the three kernel in an optimal way.

4.5 Portability of OpenCL Kernels

OpenCL enables the user to write code once and deploy it on different devices without modifying the code. In this work, this point has been examined by porting OpenCL programs between Xilinx SDK and Altera SDK. Our investigations clearly show that none of the used kernels can be ported efficiently without making significant modifications in the kernel code. This is due to the fact that each optimization technique applied, on the one hand increases performance, but on the other hand decreases the flexibility to reuse the code on other platforms. And second, a problem arises when porting kernels designed for CPU- or GPU-based platforms to FPGA-based platforms. This is because there exist different compilation policies. On CPU- and GPU-based platforms the kernel code is compiled at runtime and thus each kernel can use all resources, while FPGA-based platforms force the user to carry out offline compilations and share resources among all kernels. Therefore, utilization of resources must be determined before runtime which affects the way the kernel code is designed. Thus, portability of OpenCL code is only possible to a limited extent.

5. CONCLUSION

Scientific computing is of great importance for our modern life standard enabling high quality health care, ever improving artificial intelligence and smart cyber-physical systems. Consequently, fast and energy efficient approaches for scientific computing are required, in particular for power-constrained application domains including for instance smart sensor systems. This requires appropriate hardware accelerators, especially for solving partial differential equations (PDEs) which are an essential element of many scientific computing tasks. In this paper, we evaluated the advantages of using FPGA-based accelerators for solving PDEs using OpenCL. OpenCL allows to perform all necessary implementations in a C-like language rendering knowledge of the underlying hardware as well as hardware description languages unnecessary. This, however, makes it also very challenging to exploit the full FPGA potential and design fast yet energy efficient solvers. To tackle this challenge we proposed a comprehensive set of optimization techniques including data-set optimizations, algorithmic enhancements as well as data-flow and control-flow tuning schemes that improve performance by orders of magnitude, and thus enable designers to take full advantage from FPGAs. Yet, our comparison of Altera and Xilinx FPGA implementations show that efficient OpenCL code requires fundamentally different optimization approaches for Altera and Xilinx. As a byproduct, portability of OpenCL designs between Altera and Xilinx, is not given and does not conserve high efficiency. Nevertheless, the comparison with CPU- and GPGPU-platforms also shows that FPGAs are more energy efficient than conventional CPUs in solving PDEs and for power-constrained systems FPGAs deliver competitive performance to GPUs and offer even a better energy efficiency. Hence, FPGAs are the ideal solution for power-constrained PDE accelerators.

6. ACKNOWLEDGEMENT

The authors would like to thank Vinay Singh and Herve Ratinger from Xilinx, Nico Trost from PARALUTION Labs as well as Peter Figuli and Leonard Masing from KIT for their valuable inputs for this work.

7. REFERENCES

[1] D. P. Möller, *Guide to Computing Fundamentals in Cyber-Physical Systems: Concepts, Design Methods, and Applications.* Springer, 2016.
[2] W. Schiesser, *The Numerical Method of Lines: Integration of Partial Differential Equations.* Elsevier Science, 2012.
[3] Y. Saad, *Iterative methods for sparse linear systems.* Siam, 2003.
[4] J. Bolz et al., "Sparse matrix solvers on the gpu: conjugate gradients and multigrid," in *ACM TOG*, 2003.
[5] Altera, "A New FPGA Architecture and Leading-Edge FinFET Process Technology Promise to Meet Next-Generation System Requirements," 2015.
[6] Nvidia, "Tesla K8 GPU Active Accelerator ," 2014.
[7] "Altera OpenCL SDK," https://www.altera.com/products/design-software/embedded-software-developers/opencl/overview.html.
[8] "SDAccel - Xilinx OpenCL SDK," http://www.xilinx.com/products/design-tools/software-zone/sdaccel.html.
[9] J. E. Stone et al., "Opencl: A parallel programming standard for heterogeneous computing systems," *Computing in science & engineering*, pp. 66–73, 2010.
[10] J. Andrade et al., "From OpenCL to Gates: The FFT," in *Global Conference on Signal and Information Processing*, Dec 2013, pp. 1238–1241.
[11] T. S. Czajkowski et al., "From opencl to high-performance hardware on FPGAS," in *Proceedings of FPL*, 2012.
[12] D. P. Singh et al., "Harnessing the Power of FPGAs Using Altera's OpenCL Compiler," in *Proceedings of FPGA*, 2013.
[13] A. Sirasao et al., "FPGA Based OpenCL Acceleration of Genome Sequencing Software," *System*, p. 11.
[14] N. Suda et al., "Throughput-optimized opencl-based fpga accelerator for large-scale convolutional neural networks," in *Proceedings of FPGA*, 2016.
[15] J. Cong et al., "Software Infrastructure for Enabling FPGA-Based Accelerations in Data Centers: Invited Paper," in *Proceedings of ISLPED*, 2016, pp. 154–155.
[16] J. R. Shewchuk, "An introduction to the conjugate gradient method without the agonizing pain," p. 1, 1994.
[17] F. Richter-Gottfried et al., "Opencl 2.0 for fpgas using oclacc," *arXiv preprint arXiv:1508.07977*, 2015.
[18] H. Giefers et al., "Analyzing the energy-efficiency of sparse matrix multiplication on heterogeneous systems: A comparative study of GPU, Xeon Phi and FPGA," in *Proceedings of ISPASS*, April 2016, pp. 46–56.
[19] F. Li et al., "Architecture Evaluation for Power-efficient FPGAs," in *Proceedings of FPGA*, 2003, pp. 175–184.
[20] Xilinx, "SDAccel Development Environment Methodology Guide: Performance Optimization," 2016.
[21] D. Lukarski, "Paralution-library for iterative sparse methods," 2015.
[22] "7 Series FPGAs Overview ," www.xilinx.com/support/documentation/data_sheets/ds180_7Series_Overview.pdfXC.
[23] Altera, "Altera Stratix-V family overview table," 2015.
[24] F. Oboril et al., "High-resolution online power monitoring for modern microprocessors," in *Proceedings of DATE*, 2015.
[25] Altera, "Enabling Next-Generation Platforms Using Altera's 3D System-in-Package Technology," 2015.
[26] http://cdnc.itec.kit.edu/OpenCLFPGA.php.

Table 6: Utilization of FPGA resources for CG

Vendor	LUT	Registers	BRAMs	DSPs
Altera	50%	25%	26%	31%
Xilinx	35%	15%	65%	18%

Secure Function Evaluation
Using an FPGA Overlay Architecture

Xin Fang
Dept of Electrical and
Computer Engineering
Northeastern University
Boston, MA, USA
fang.xi@husky.neu.edu

Stratis Ioannidis
Dept of Electrical and
Computer Engineering
Northeastern University
Boston, MA, USA
ioannidis@ece.neu.edu

Miriam Leeser
Dept of Electrical and
Computer Engineering
Northeastern University
Boston, MA, USA
mel@coe.neu.edu

ABSTRACT

Secure Function Evaluation (SFE) has received considerable attention recently due to the massive collection and mining of personal data over the Internet, but large computational costs still render it impractical. In this paper, we leverage hardware acceleration to tackle the scalability and efficiency challenges inherent in SFE. To that end, we propose a generic, reconfigurable implementation of SFE as a coarse-grained FPGA overlay architecture. Contrary to tailored approaches that are tied to the execution of a specific SFE structure, and require full reprogramming of an FPGA with each new execution, our design allows repurposing an FPGA to evaluate different SFE tasks without the need for reprogramming. Our implementation shows orders of magnitude improvement over a software package for evaluating garbled circuits, and demonstrates that the circuit being evaluated can change with almost no overhead.

Keywords

FPGA; Secure Function Evaluation; Garbled Circuits

1. INTRODUCTION

Mining behavioral data is a ubiquitous practice among Internet companies, and is presently happening at an unprecedented scale. Google, Netflix, Amazon, and Facebook routinely monitor and mine a broad array of behavioral signals collected from their users, including ad clicks, pages visited, and products purchased. Such information is monetized through targeted advertising or personalized product recommendations. Behavioral data collection is therefore of considerable business value to online companies [ ]; moreover, there are often benefits to society at large: mining such data can aid in the detection of medical emergencies or the spread of diseases [ ], in polling to assess political opinions [ ] or news adoption [ ], in the assessment of terrorist threats [ ], etc. On the other hand, this massive data collection and mining has given rise to significant privacy concerns, extensively documented by researchers [, , , , , , ,] as well as the popular press [,]. Such concerns are only likely to further increase with the emergence of the "Internet of things", as wearable devices and home automation sensors connected to the Internet proliferate.

This state of affairs gives rise to the following challenge: given the benefits of mining behavioral data to both online companies and the society at large, is it possible to *enable data mining practices without jeopardizing user privacy*? A series of recent research efforts [, , , –] have attempted to address this issue through cryptographic means and, in particular, through secure function evaluation (SFE). SFE allows an interested party to evaluate any desirable polynomial-time function over private data, while revealing only the answer and nothing else about the data. This offers a strong privacy guarantee: an entity executing a secure data-mining algorithm over user data learns only the final outcome of the computation, while the data is never revealed to the entity. SFE can thus enable, e.g., a data analyst, a medical professional, or a statistician, to conduct a study of sensitive data, without jeopardizing the privacy of the participants (online users, patients, etc.).

Any algorithm to be executed over amounts of data at the scale encountered in the above settings needs to be highly efficient and scalable. SFE over private data therefore poses a significant challenge, as it comes at a considerable additional computational cost compared to execution in the clear. Prior work has made positive steps in this direction, showing that a variety of important data mining algorithms [–] can be computed using Yao's Garbled Circuits (GCs) [,] in a parallel fashion. The function to be evaluated is converted to a binary circuit which is "garbled" in such a way that an evaluator of the circuit learns only the values of its output gates. Execution of this circuit is subsequently parallelized, e.g., over threads [ ] or across a cluster of machines [ ].

Nevertheless, this approach to parallelization leaves much to be desired: for example, in [ ], even under parallelization over 128 cores, executing a typical data-mining algorithm like Matrix Factorization through SFE is of the order of 10^5 slower compared to (parallel) execution in the clear. In practice, this means that applying MF to a dataset of 1M entries requires roughly 11 days under SFE, a time largely prohibitive for practical purposes.

In this paper, we advocate leveraging hardware acceler-

FPGA '17 February 22-24, 2017, Monterey, CA, USA

© 2017 Copyright held by the owner/author(s).

ACM ISBN 978-1-4503-4354-1/17/02.

DOI: http://dx.doi.org/10.1145/3020078.3021746

ation to tackle the scalability and efficiency challenges inherent in SFE. FPGAs are by design an excellent hardware platform for the implementation of SFE primitives and, in particular, garbled circuits. This is precisely because FPGAs are tailored to executing nearly identical operations in parallel. The types of operations encountered in garbled circuits (namely, garbling and un-garbling gates) fit this pattern precisely: they involve, e.g., a series of symmetric key encryptions, XORs, and other well-defined primitive operations (see also Section 3). In that sense, an FPGA implementation of SFE benefits from both high speed evaluation and hardware-level parallelization.

On the other hand, the amount of computation required to evaluate a garbled circuit for an application at the usual data-mining scale cannot fit in a single FPGA. For this reason, evaluating a function securely entails partitioning computations into sub-tasks to be programmed and evaluated over a single FPGA. A practical implementation therefore needs to allow repurposing an FPGA to quickly compute different SFEs or different sub-tasks of a larger SFE. For this reason, tailored approaches that are tied to the execution of a specific SFE structure, and require full reprogramming of an FPGA with each new execution, cannot be applied efficiently to the types of SFE problems we wish to address.

To address these challenges, we propose a *generic, reconfigurable implementation of SFE as a coarse-grained FPGA overlay architecture*. As FPGAs have become more dense and capable of holding a large number of gate equivalents, there has been an increased interest in FPGA overlay architectures [, , , – ,]. An FPGA overlay consists of two parts: (1) a circuit design implemented on the FPGA fabric using the usual design flow, and (2) a user circuit mapped onto that overlay circuit. Garbled circuits are excellent candidates for an FPGA overlay design. Precisely because components of a circuit follow a generic structure, an overlay approach that does not reprogram FPGAs from scratch, but simply *reroutes* connections between elementary components (in our case, garbled AND and XOR gates) leads to important efficiency improvements.

This paper makes the following contributions:

- We design and implement a generic FPGA overlay architecture for the execution of arbitrary garbled circuit topologies. In our design, FPGAs are programmed once to contain implementations of garbled components (AND, XOR gates). Wiring and instantiation is determined at execution time through writing to registers and memory. Thus, the overhead for repurposing the FPGA for different circuit computations is kept very low.

- We integrate our implementation with ObliVM [ ], a framework mapping code written in a high-level language to a garbled circuit, allowing arbitrary programs written in ObliVM to be mapped to our FPGA overlay architectures.

- We evaluate the performance of our GC overlay architecture on several examples and demonstrate orders of magnitude speedup over ObliVM. We demonstrate the effects of using the overlay architecture, which results in change time for different circuit computations that have little effect on overall performance.

The remainder of the paper is organized as follows. We present related work in Section 2 and background on garbled circuits in Section 3. Our implemented system and overlay architecture are presented in Section 4 and experimental results in Section 5. Finally, we present our conclusions and future work in Section 6.

2. RELATED WORK

Garbled Circuits. Although garbled circuits were proposed by Andrew Yao nearly three decades ago [,], it is only in the last few years that the research community has made progress at improving their efficiency, bringing their application closer to practicality. Several improvements over the original protocol have been proposed, including the point-and-permute [ ], row reduction [ ], and the Free-XOR [ ] optimizations; we use all of these in our implementation.

Building on these optimizations, there has been a surge of recent programming frameworks, such as TASTY [ ], FastGC [ ], Fairplay [ ], and ObliVM [ ], that provide software implementations of GCs. These frameworks, particularly ObliVM, allow developers without any cryptography expertise to convert algorithms expressed in a high-level language to GCs. None of these frameworks focus on hardware acceleration. We provide an interface to ObliVM in our work; this allows us to describe algorithms in a high level language, map them to circuits through ObliVM, and then use our software to execute these circuits over our FPGA overlay architecture.

FPGA overlays. Recently, as FPGAs have become more dense and capable of holding a large number of gate equivalents, there has been an increased interest in FPGA overlay architectures. An FPGA overlay consists of two parts: (1) a circuit design implemented on the FPGA fabric using the usual design flow, and (2) a user circuit mapped onto that overlay circuit. Overlays are in general used for two purposes. The first is to create FPGA designs that are independent of the specific structures on a particular FPGA and therefore to make designs portable, or, in other words, able to be mapped to FPGAs from different vendors and to different devices from the same vendor. This class of FPGA overlay designs [,] creates basic FPGA structures, such as Look-Up Tables (LUTs) and routing, built on top of those provided in silicon on the target FPGA chip. We are using an FPGA overlay for the second purpose; namely, to reduce the amount of time to translate a design to an FPGA implementation. FPGAs offer a great deal of reconfigurability and flexibility; however, this comes at the cost of programming. Generating designs that run efficiently on FPGAs can be challenging for the end user. In addition, the *compilation* process for a high end FPGA design can take several hours. Here *compilation* refers to the complete set of steps from specification (in a hardware description language (HDL) or high level language) to generating a bit stream to download to the FPGA. These steps include synthesis, place-and-route and bit stream generation for the target FPGA. Examples of this style of FPGA overlay architecture include Network on a Chip (NoC) overlays [,] and instruction set extension overlays [ ]. In these cases, structures are built on the FPGA and the overlay architecture provides flexible routing among them.

Hardware Implementations of Garbled Circuits. Recent studies have used FPGAs as well as GPUs [,] for hardware implementations of garbled circuits. TinyGarble [ ] uses techniques from hardware design to implement GCs as sequential circuits and then optimize these designs, reporting on results using high level synthesis tools and simulation, but do not report any actual hardware implementations. TinyGarble produces more efficient solutions for a single GC instance, but does not handle multiple pieces of a GC or different garbled circuits the way our overlays do. Järvinen et al. [ ] target embedded system and describe the first FPGA implementation of GC. This implementation is at a completely different design point than ours: while generic and able to support a wide range of hardware implementations, the proposed FPGA design implements only one encryption core. In contrast, our overlay architecture implements hundreds of encryption cores on a single FPGA and executes them in parallel.

A recent FPGA implementation of garbled circuits by Songhori et al. [ ] take a different approach. Rather than implement garbled circuits directly, they implement a *garbled* MIPS core. Problems to be evaluated securely are written in code, that is compiled to MIPS assembler and then run securely on their garbled MIPS processor. The goal of [ ] is to fabricate this MIPS core; FPGAs are used for prototyping the design. Using MIPS assembly code to represent the problem being evaluated alleviates the problem of lengthy FPGA place and route cycles. However, the FPGA is not used as efficiently as in our implementation: Songhori et al. use considerably fewer encryption cores, and running code on a MIPs processor creates an extra level of overhead.

Our architecture uses much more parallelism than other FPGA implementations of garbling. For starters, we implement four SHA-1 cores in hardware for each AND gate, while others use one encryption core serially [ ]. In addition, we implement as many garbled AND gates as we can keep busy at the same time, and implement garbled circuits directly on top of an efficient overlay.

3. TECHNICAL BACKGROUND

Yao's protocol (a.k.a. *garbled circuits*) [ ] is a generic cryptographic protocol for secure function evaluation. In short, it allows the secure evaluation of an arbitrary function over private data, provided this function can be represented as a circuit. We give a brief overview of the protocol below (see, e.g., [ ], for a detailed treatment).

3.1 Garbled Circuits Overview

In the variant we study here (adapted from [,]), Yao's protocol runs between (a) a set of private input owners (e.g., Google's users), (b) an Evaluator, (e.g., a data analyst working for Google), that wishes to evaluate a function over the private inputs, and (c) a third party called the Garbler, that facilities and enables the secure computation. Formally, let n be the number of input owners, and let $x_i \in \{0,1\}^*$ denote the private input of individual i, $1 \leq i \leq n$, represented as a binary string. Finally, let $f : (\{0,1\}^*)^n \to \{0,1\}^*$ be the function that the Evaluator wishes to compute over the private data. The protocol satisfies the following property: at the conclusion of the protocol, the Evaluator learns *only* the value $f(x_1, x_2, \ldots, x_n)$ and nothing else about $x_1, \ldots, x_n$, while the Garbler learns nothing.

A critical assumption behind Yao's protocol is that the function f can be expressed as a *Boolean circuit*, and, more specifically, as a directed acyclic graph (DAG) of AND and

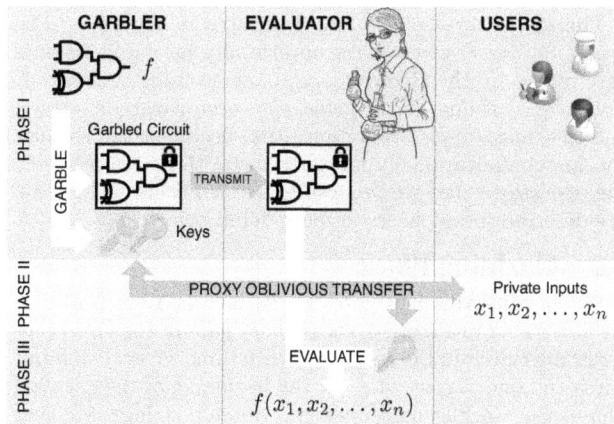

Figure 1: Yao's protocol. The Evaluator wishes to evaluate a function f, represented as a binary circuit of AND and XOR gates, over private user inputs $x_1, x_2, \ldots, x_n$. In Phase I, the Garbler "garbles" each gate of the circuit, outputting (a) a "garbled circuit", namely, the garbled representation of every gate in the circuit representing f, and (b) a set of keys, each corresponding to a possible value of the inputs $x_1, \ldots, x_n$. In Phase II, through proxy oblivious transfer, the Evaluator learns the keys corresponding to the true user input values, while the Garbler learns nothing. In the final phase, the Evaluator uses the keys as input to the garbled circuit to evaluate the circuit, ungarbling the gates in breadth-first order. At the conclusion of Phase III, the Evaluator learns $f(x_1, \ldots, x_n)$.

XOR gates.[1] The structure of the circuit – and, thus, the function to be computed – is known to all participants: e.g. the circuit could be computing the sum or the maximum among all inputs x_i.

Overall, Yao's protocol consists of three phases:

1. **Garbling Phase.** During the garbling phase, the Garbler prepares (a) a set of encrypted (i.e., "garbled") truth tables for each binary gate in the circuit, as well as (b) a set of random strings, termed *keys*, one for each possible binary value in the strings representing the inputs. At the conclusion of this phase, the Garbler sends to the Evaluator the garbled truth tables; each such table is referred to as a "garbled gate", and all gates together constitute the "garbled circuit".

2. **Oblivious Transfer Phase.** Subsequently, the Evaluator, Garbler, and the input owners engage in a proxy oblivious transfer [, ,]. Through this, the Evaluator retrieves the input keys from the Garbler that correspond to true input binary values held by the owners. Oblivious transfer ensures that, although the Evaluator learns the correct keys, the cleartext input values are never revealed to either the Garbler or the Evaluator.

3. **Evaluation Phase.** Finally, the Evaluator uses these input keys to "evaluate" the gates of the circuit, effectively decrypting the garbled gates. Each such decryption reveals a new key that allows the Evaluator to ungarble/decrypt subsequent gates connected to it. Ungarbling the output gates reveals the value $f(x_1, \ldots, x_n)$.

---

[1]Recall that any Boolean circuit can be represented using only ANDs and XORs.

The above three phases are illustrated in Figure 1. The execution flow (as well as the opportunity for parallelism) is determined by the Boolean circuit representing function f. Both the "garbling" of the gates, that occurs at the Garbler, and the "ungarbling/evaluation", that occurs at the Evaluator, are computationally intensive tasks; these are precisely the operations that we propose to accelerate using FPGAs. We describe these phases in more detail below.

3.2 Garbling Phase

We now describe how gates are garbled in Yao's protocol. As illustrated in Figure 2, each binary gate in the DAG representing the circuit is associated with three wires: two input wires and one output wire. At the beginning of the garbling phase, the Garbler associates two random strings, $k_{w_i}^0$ and $k_{w_i}^1$, with each wire w_i in the circuit. Intuitively, each $k_{w_i}^b$ is an encoding of the bit-value $b \in \{0, 1\}$ that the wire w_i can take. For each gate g, with input wires (w_i, w_j) and output wire w_k, let $g(b_i, b_j) \in \{0, 1\}$ be the binary output of the gate given inputs $b_i, b_j \in \{0, 1\}$ at wires w_i and w_j, respectively. For each gate g, the Garbler computes the following four ciphertexts, one for each pair of values $b_i, b_j \in \{0, 1\}$:

$$\text{Enc}_{(k_{w_i}^{b_i}, k_{w_j}^{b_j}, g)}(k_{w_k}^{g(b_i, b_j)}) = \text{SHA1}(k_{w_i}^{b_i} \| k_{w_j}^{b_j} \| g) \oplus k_{w_k}^{g(b_i, b_j)}, \quad (1)$$

where SHA1 is the SHA1 hash function, $\|$ indicates concatenation, g is an identifier for the gate, and $\oplus$ is the XOR operation.

The "garbled" gate is then represented by a *random permutation* of these four ciphertexts. An example of a garbled AND gate is illustrated on Fig. 2. Observe that, given the pair of keys $(k_{w_i}^0, k_{w_j}^1)$ it is possible to successfully recover the key $k_{w_k}^1$ by decrypting $c = \text{Enc}_{(k_{w_i}^0, k_{w_j}^1, g)}(k_{w_k}^1)$ through[2]:

$$\text{Dec}_{(k_{w_i}^0, k_{w_j}^1, g)}(c) = \text{SHA1}(k_{w_i}^{b_i} \| k_{w_j}^{b_j} \| g) \oplus c. \quad (2)$$

On the other hand, the other output wire key, namely $k_{w_k}^0$, cannot be recovered having access only to $(k_{w_i}^0, k_{w_j}^1)$. More generally, it is worth noting that the knowledge of (a) the ciphertexts, and (b) keys $(k_{w_i}^{b_i}, k_{w_j}^{b_j})$ for some inputs b_i and b_j yields *only* the value of key $k_{w_k}^{g(b_i, b_j)}$; no other input or output keys of gate g can be recovered.

At the conclusion of the garbling phase, the Garbler sends the garbled gates (each comprising a random permutation of four ciphertexts) to the Evaluator. It also provides the correspondence between the garbled value and the real bit-value for the circuit-output wires (the outcome of the computation): if w_k is a circuit-output wire, the pairs $(k_{w_k}^0, 0)$ and $(k_{w_k}^1, 1)$ are given to the Evaluator. Finally, the Garbler keeps the random wire keys $(k_{w_i}^0, k_{w_i}^1)$ that correspond to circuit-input wires w_i, i.e., wires at the very first layer of the circuit, encoding user inputs; all other wire keys are discarded.

3.3 Oblivious Transfer Phase

To transfer the correct keys of the circuit-input wires to the Evaluator, the Garbler engages in a proxy oblivious transfer (OT) with the Evaluator and the users. Through proxy OT, the Evaluator obliviously obtains the circuit-input value keys $k_{w_i}^b$ corresponding to the actual bit b of

---

[2]Note that the above encryption scheme is *symmetric*, as Enc, Dec are the same function.

b_i	b_j	$g(b_i, b_j)$	Garbled value
0	0	0	$\text{Enc}_{(k_{w_i}^0, k_{w_j}^0, g)}(k_{w_k}^0)$
0	1	1	$\text{Enc}_{(k_{w_i}^0, k_{w_j}^1, g)}(k_{w_k}^1)$
1	0	1	$\text{Enc}_{(k_{w_i}^1, k_{w_j}^0, g)}(k_{w_k}^1)$
1	1	1	$\text{Enc}_{(k_{w_i}^1, k_{w_j}^1, g)}(k_{w_k}^1)$

Figure 2: A garbled AND gate. Each of the three wires w_i, w_j, w_k is associated with two random keys k^0, k^1, representing the value 0 and 1, respectively. The garbled AND gate consists of the four ciphertexts appearing on the rightmost column of the table above: each possible output value key is encrypted using the corresponding input pair of keys, along with a string g representing the gate id. A random permutation of these four ciphertexts is revealed by the Garbler to the Evaluator.

circuit-input wire w_i. Proxy OT ensures that (a) the Garbler does not learn the user inputs, (b) the Evaluator can compute the function on these inputs alone, and (c) the Garbler learns nothing. Note that this OT only pertains to circuit-inputs (the first layer of the circuit); as such, its communication cost is typically several orders of magnitude smaller than the Garbler to Evaluator transfer occurring at the end of the previous phase. As proxy OT is not as intensive in computation or communication as the other two phases, and does involve hardware acceleration, we do not describe it in detail. We refer the interested reader to [, ,] for a formal description and implementation.

3.4 Evaluation Phase

Having the keys corresponding to true user inputs, the Evaluator can "evaluate" each gate, by decrypting each ciphertext of a gate in the first layer of the circuit through Eq. (2): only one of these decryptions will succeed[3], revealing the key corresponding to the output of this gate. Each output key revealed can subsequently be used to ungarble/evaluate any gate that uses it as an input. The evaluator can thus proceed ungarbling gates in breadth first order over the DAG blueprint of the Boolean circuit, until finally obtaining the keys of gates at the last layer of the circuit. Using the table mapping these keys to bits, the Evaluator learns the final output.

3.5 Optimizations

Several improvements over the original Yao protocol have been proposed recently, that lead to both computational and communication cost reductions. These include the point-and-permute [ ], row reduction [ ], and Free-XOR [ ] optimizations, all of which we implement in our design. Point-and-permute reduces the four decryptions at the evaluator to one. Row-reduction reduces the number of ciphertexts that need to be transmitted by the Garbler to the Evaluator from four to three. Free-XOR significantly reduces the computational cost of garbled XOR gates. XOR gates do not need to be encrypted and decrypted, as the XOR output wire key is

---

[3]This can be detected, e.g., by appending a prefix of zeros to each key $k_{w_k}^b$, and checking if this prefix is present upon decryption. In practice, the point-and-permute optimization of [ ] eliminates the need for attempting to decrypt all four ciphertexts.

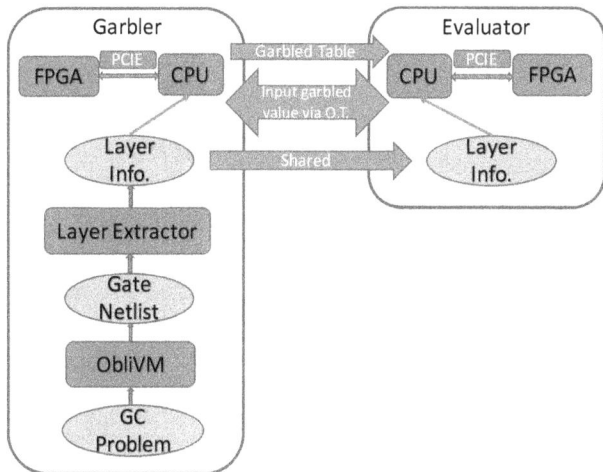

Figure 3: System Overview. An algorithm written in high-level language is translated to a Boolean circuit using ObliVM. The resulting circuit is passed through a layer extractor, identifying layers through BFS. The Boolean circuit DAG, annotated with layer information for each gate, is passed to the Garbler and Evaluator CPUs, that use it as a "blueprint" for execution. The CPUs subsequently use this blue print to garble gates and evaluate them at the FPGAs of the Garbler and Evaluator, respectively.

computed through an XOR of the corresponding input keys. In addition, the free-XOR optimization fully eliminates communication between the Garbler and the Evaluator for XORs: no ciphertexts need to be communicated between them for these gates. Our implementation takes advantage of all of these optimizations. We note that, as a result, the circuit for computing an AND gate, illustrated in Fig. 5, differs slightly from the AND gate garbling algorithm outlined above.

4. FPGA OVERLAY ARCHITECTURE FOR GARBLED CIRCUITS

4.1 System Overview

Our FPGA acceleration of GC works as follows. We start with a function f we wish to evaluate securely and a set of user inputs and generate an output of the function without revealing the data. This is done by (a) translating the function to a Boolean circuit and providing commands to the FPGA to garble/evaluate the function, and (b) accelerating the garbling or evaluation making use of an FPGA overlay architecture. We first describe how the system is partitioned between CPU and FPGA processing, and then describe the FPGA implementation.

Our system consists of two host PCs (instantiating the Garbler and Evaluator, respectively) equipped with FPGA cards for acceleration, as shown in Figure 3. On the Garbler side, the function f is first translated to a Boolean circuit before it can be garbled. Toward this end, we make use of ObliVM [22], a software framework that allows developers without any cryptography expertise to convert algorithms expressed in a high-level language to GCs. A user writes their problem in Java, and ObliVM translates it to a Boolean

circuit and handles the garbling and evaluation. On the garbler, we take the Boolean circuit representation output from ObliVM, disabling garbling and evaluation through the framework. The Boolean circuit is sent to our layer extractor: this program extracts the Boolean circuit's *layers* using breadth first search. The resulting layered Boolean circuit (i.e., the "blueprint" for the garbling and execution) is sent to the Evaluator. This "blueprint" is subsequently used by the two hosts CPUs to dictate the garbling and evaluation to be performed by each FPGA.

In more detail, on each CPU, the Boolean circuit is represented as a DAG whose nodes are AND and XOR gates. Layers are defined recursively: gates whose input wires are global inputs are at layer 0, while a gate is at layer k if one of its input wires connects to a gate at layer $k-1$ and the other connects to a gate at layer $\leq k-1$. Note that gates in the same layer can be executed (i.e., garbled or evaluated) in parallel. Layer information is used to guide the CPU on the order with which gates are to be loaded to the FPGA, to be gabled or evaluated.

The FPGA implements a sea of garbled AND gates and XOR gates as described in Section 4.2. Each wire of the Boolean circuit has a unique wire ID associated with it. These wire IDs are also used as the memory addresses on the FPGA: these memory locations store the keys corresponding to these wires, used to garble or evaluate a gate. The CPU is responsible for mapping Boolean circuit gates to the FPGA hardware AND and XOR gates that realize them. For XOR gates this is trivial, since we implement one XOR gate in hardware (see below). AND gates are a different matter, as our FPGA architecture implements as many AND gates in parallel as can be kept busy. Suppose the FPGA realizes A AND gates in hardware. If there are more than A AND gates in a layer, our FPGA architecture is designed in such a way that the first hardware AND gate will complete processing before the information for the $A+1$st garbled gate is received by the FPGA. Thus, the CPU can transmit all the AND gates in a layer, and assign them to gates modulo A. More details of the FPGA architecture are given in Section 4.2.

When a layer is completed, the CPU then transmits the next layer of the circuit, until the circuit has been fully garbled. The CPU determines the order to send AND and XOR gates to the FPGA. Currently we send all the AND gates followed by all the XOR gates in a layer. Since the latency of an AND gate is much longer (82 cycles) than the latency of an XOR (one cycle), this results in a relatively efficient ordering.

For each layer, the Garbler sends to the FPGA (a) the number of gates in the layer, (b) the input and output wire IDs for the layer, (c) labels indicating whether a gate is AND or XOR, and (c) for the AND gates, which hardware gate the AND is mapped to (among the A available gates). Layer 0 requires key values for the inputs, which are 80 bit random values generated for each possible input value, i.e., $k_{w_i}^0$ and $k_{w_i}^1$. These strings are generated using a random number generator on the host for each of the input wires w_i and communicated to the FPGA. The output of the FPGA garbling includes the ciphertext values (i.e., the garbled gates), as well as keys for output wires. These are sent by the FPGA to the host CPU; the Garbler CPU sends garbled gates directly to the Evaluator CPU. The Garbler CPU also provides input keys to the Evaluator CPU via proxy oblivious transfer

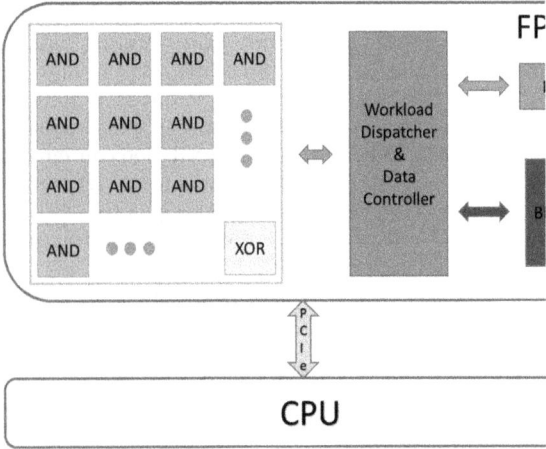

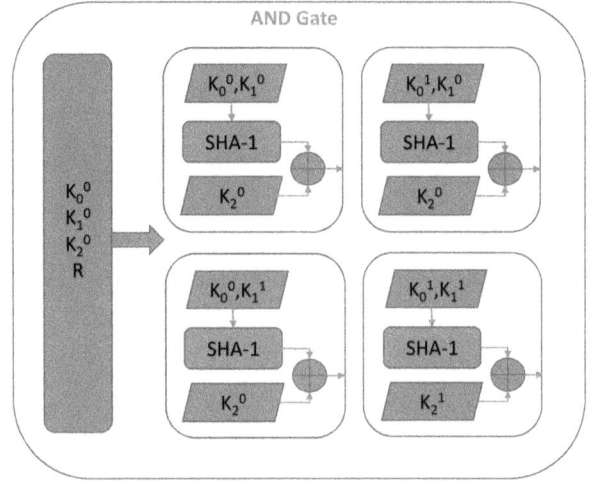

Figure 4: Overlay Architecture for Garbled Circuits overlay consists of as many AND gates as can be kep in parallel, a single XOR gate, BRAM for storing g wire values, and a FIFO for communicating values from the FPGA to the CPU. The workload dispatcher coordinates all operations.

Figure 5: A Garbled AND Gate. The garbling of an AND gate consists of four SHA-1 cores operating in parallel.

between the Garbler, Evaluator, and the users/input owners, as described in Section 3.1.

4.2 FPGA Overlay Architecture

Our FPGA overlay architecture differs from other overlays in that it is designed to only support garbled circuits, whose implementation consists entirely of AND and XOR gates. Note that the overlay for the garbler and the evaluator are different. We support communication between gates by storing all inputs and outputs in on-chip block RAM. This is a coarse grained overlay, as both AND gates and XOR gates are quite complex, as described below.

A big advantage of implementing the garbler (and evaluator) as an overlay architecture is that it eliminates the lengthy place and route times incurred when using an FPGA. Different pieces of the same problem, as well as different problems, can easily be mapped to the overlay without incurring this expense. As the garbler is more complex than the evaluator, the rest of the paper describes the garbler and its implementation in detail.

The complete design of the overlay architecture for garbling, shown in Figure 4 includes XOR and AND gates, BRAM, a FIFO for communicating the garble table and outputs with the CPU, and a workload dispatcher. We describe these components and their design in this section.

BRAM. We use Block Random Access Memory (BRAM) to store the garbled values for each wire (i.e., every input and output for every gate). We treat all of the on-chip memory as one monolithic sequential memory device. The memory is 81 bits wide (80 bits of data plus a valid bit), and implemented with one read port and one write port. The unique wire IDs in the circuit, generated on the host CPU, correspond to memory locations. The maximum number of wire IDs that BRAM can hold is 2^{21}, assuming all memory locations are used for garbled values. This monolithic memory simplifies our design since no decision making is required in determining where to find inputs or where to store outputs.

It also means that the BRAM is the current bottleneck in our design.

AND and XOR gates. We stress that the AND gates and XOR gates required for garbling are much more complicated than single bit gates. Inputs to all gates are represented as 80 bits in our implementation. Thus, a so called "free" XOR gate consists of eighty single bit XORs.

A garbling AND gate implements the functionality described in Section 3.1 and shown in Fig. 2. Each line is implemented according to Equation 1. This implementation requires four SHA-1 cores, using 512 bits of input derived from the garbled inputs and additional information. The implementation is based on an open source SHA-1 core [39]. Our garbled AND gate requires 82 clock cycles on the FPGA and uses 3070 ALMs and 3750 one bit registers on a Stratix V FPGA. Note that, while SHA-1 in and of itself is no longer considered secure, it is adequate for preserving privacy in the context of garbled circuits, where cryptography is applied at many levels. In addition, new garbled values and keys are generated whenever new input values are applied to a circuit, making any attack unlikely to succeed. Figure 5 shows the implementation of four SHA cores in parallel in our design.

We implement in hardware the maximum number of AND gates that can be kept busy, taking the latency of the AND operations and the availability of the BRAM for reading into account. In our current design, this results in $A = 43$ AND gates. We implement a single XOR gate, as the computation has one cycle latency and additional XORs cannot be provided with inputs. Fig. 6 shows the timeline for garbling a circuit consisting of only AND gates. Our overlay architecture implements 43 AND gates. If more ANDs are in a layer the 44th gate runs on the first gate when it is completed. In our implementation, the XOR gates in a layer will be computed after all the AND gates have started. An XOR gate has four cycles of latency total, two for reading inputs, one for computing XOR and one for writing the output. There may be contention for writing BRAM if XOR and AND gates complete at the same time. This contention is handled by the workload dispatcher.

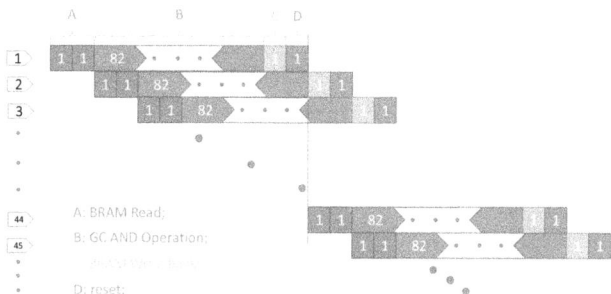

Figure 6: Garbled Circuit AND Gate Operation Sequence. Reads and writes from BRAM are the bottleneck, since BRAM has one read and one write port. An AND gate can begin operation after its two (80 bit) inputs are read from BRAM. Each AND gate has 82 clock cycle latency. This diagram assumes there are no XOR gates. Latency for processing XOR gates is much shorter.

FIFO. The FIFO enables communication from the FPGA to the CPU; data is sent over the PCIe bus. The values transmitted include the ciphertexts for each AND gate and the keys of each gate's (AND and XOR) output wires. The garble table values are written to the FIFO when each AND garbling completes. The FIFO is wide enough for this to take one clock cycle. This is done during the "reset" cycle shown in Fig. 6. At the completion of garbling the output wire values are also written to the FIFO.

Workload Dispatcher. The workload dispatcher is a state machine that receives input from the host, reads and writes the correct values from BRAM, and properly dispatches outputs and the garble table values. Specifically, the workload dispatcher implements the following steps:

1. Determine if next gate to be processed is an AND or XOR gate.

2. Read the inputs, and forward to the assigned gate (recall that AND gates are assigned by the host).

3. When a gate is finished computing, write the output of the garbled gate to the correct location in BRAM.

4. When an AND gate is finished computing, push the gate ID and garble table values to the FIFO for transmission to the host PC over the PCIe interface.

5. At the end of garbling, read the garbled output value(s) from the wire ID(s) provided by the CPU and push them to the FIFO for transmission to the CPU.

5. EXPERIMENTAL RESULTS

We use the ProcV board from Gidel as our target platform. It is a Stratix V FPGA-based platform with 16+GB external memory. It provides high-speed communication between host and FPGA via a PCIe*8 generation 3 bus which makes the system suitable for high-performance computing and low latency networking projects. The ProcV system is supported by Gidel's ProcWizard software and IPs. The Altera Stratix V FPGA on board provides high capacity and high speed for many designs and contains 234K ALMs and 52M memory bits.

Table 1: Resource Utilization

Module	ALMs	M20Ks	1 bit Register
One AND	3,070	0	3,750
One XOR	40	0	81
BRAM	0	1,060	0
FIFO	510	280	404
Whole Design	176,893/234,720 75.4%	1,340/2,560 52.3%	215,308

PCIe generation 3 is a serial computer bus standard which has been available since 2010. It doubles the data rate compared with generation 2 with 8 Giga transfers per second(GT/s) per lane. The ProcV board, with 8 lanes, will provide about 7.88 Gb/s throughput. This high throughput benefits the data transfer between the host CPU and the Stratix FPGA on board. For garbled circuits the amount of data to transfer is not high, but having high speed interconnect ensures that communication between FPGA and host is not the bottleneck.

Table 1 shows the resource utilization for our system. For this system, the total logic utilization (in ALMs) is about 75% of those available. The BRAM can hold 2^{21} words, where a word is a garbled value. Any garbled circuit problem with fewer than 2^{21} wire IDs can fit in our system.

We use ObliVM [ ] to generate the Boolean circuit representation fed into the FPGA. We also use it to run our experiments to completion. We compare our results with ObliVM to validate our designs and also compare run times to show speed up. Our design is not fully working in hardware so the experimental results we provide are estimates based on the design tools and placed and routed circuits. The maximum frequency achievable for this overlay architecture is just over 200 MHz.

We compare the number of clock cycles for both ObliVM garbling a circuit and our approach. ObliVM is written in Java; we insert some C code which can precisely monitor the clock cycle count. We sum the clock cycle times for the XORs and ANDs to provide the computing time on both the FPGA and host CPU. Note that these operations are performed serially on the CPU, but in parallel on the FPGA. We do not include some of the setup time in ObliVM. A complete end-to-end test should show an even greater advantage for GC on FPGAs.

The problems that we garble are: Millionaire's problem, addition, Hamming Distance (HD), multiplication and sorting. The size of these problems is shown in Table 2. For different problems we use different numbers of input bits. The millionaire's problem uses 2 bits for each person, the adder is 6 bits wide. Sorting orders a sequence of inputs; in this example the inputs are ten four bit integers. In addition to explore scalability, we implement several different sizes of HD and multiplication. For HD, we show results for two 10, 20 and 30-bit inputs. For multiplication, we show results for 8, 16, 32 and 64 bit multipliers. Table 2 shows the number of AND and XOR gates for each of these problems, as well as the number of layers and maximum number of AND gates per layer.

Table 3 compares clock cycles for our FPGA design and ObliVM software. The FPGA implementation requires about 10^4 times fewer clock cycles than ObliVM, and demonstrates the advantage of implementing garbling using FPGAs. The

Table 2: Size of the Examples

Problem	# of AND Gate	# of XOR gate	# of layers	Max # of AND gate in One Layer
Millionaire (2)	2	11	7	1
Addition (6)	6	24	18	1
Hamming Distance (10)	20	90	22	5
Hamming Distance (30)	60	270	28	15
Hamming Distance (50)	100	450	33	25
A * B (8)	120	352	57	64
A * B (16)	496	1472	122	256
A * B (32)	2016	6016	250	1024
A * B (64)	8128	24320	505	4096
Sorting (10*4)	848	4683	278	32

Table 3: Clock Cycle Comparison

Problem (Input Size in bit)	Our Approach (Clock Cycle)	ObliVM (Clock Cycle)
Millionaire (2)	$1.9 * 10^2$	$1.1 * 10^6$
Addition (6)	$5.6 * 10^2$	$1.7 * 10^6$
Hamming Distance (10)	$1.2 * 10^3$	$4 * 10^6$
Hamming Distance (30)	$2.2 * 10^3$	$1.1 * 10^7$
Hamming Distance (50)	$2.8 * 10^3$	$1.7 * 10^7$
A * B (8)	$4.4 * 10^3$	$3 * 10^7$
A * B (32)	$3.6 * 10^4$	$1.1 * 10^8$
A * B (64)	$1.1 * 10^5$	$3.2 * 10^8$
Sorting (10*4)	$1.1 * 10^4$	$1.4 * 10^8$

Table 4: Real Time Speedup

Problem	Speedup
Millionaire (2 bits)	422
Addition (6 bits)	222
Hamming Distance (10 bits)	243
Hamming Distance (30 bits)	357
Hamming Distance (50 bits)	434
A * B (8 bits)	498
A * B (32 bits)	218
A * B (64 bits)	208
Sorting (10*4 bits)	929

software platform runs on a computer with Intel Core i7-2640 CPU at 2.80 GHz; the FPGA design runs at 200 MHz. Taking this into consideration, Table 4 presents the expected speedup of our approach compared with ObliVM. Our approach is two to three orders of magnitude faster. In addition, we expect the FPGA implementation to consume much less power. Runtime results for HD show that the speed up increases with the size of the inputs. For multiplication, we see the opposite trend with speedup decreasing as the problem gets larger. This is partly due to the fact that the large multiplication examples have more layers, and some of these layers have very few AND gates. In our design, much of our parallelism, and therefore speedup, comes from processing multiple garbling AND gates in parallel. In future work, we will examine partitioning schemes other than "layer by layer" which should allow us to take better advantage of the available parallelism.

This project has two goals. The first is to accelerate garbled circuits on an FPGA. The second is to be able to rapidly garble different problems without incurring long recompile and programming costs. Compiling a garbled circuit design from scratch could take hours or even days. Our overlay architecture is compiled and downloaded once. This initial time is about an hour for the current design. The time to change between problems on the FPGA is very small. The FPGA design needs to be reset to clear all sequential elements, and then new values can be transmitted. For the small problems evaluated here, the longest step for garbling a compete function is the time to translate a problem to a Boolean circuit. This time can be minimized by keeping a library of garbled circuit implementations available, essentially caching the output of the ObliVM circuit generator for future use.

6. CONCLUSIONS AND FUTURE WORK

We have presented an implementation of Garbled Circuits on an FPGA using a coarse-grained overlay architecture. Our implementation is the first FPGA overlay architecture designed for this purpose, makes use of the parallelism available on the FPGA to accelerate garbling, and can achieve more than two orders of magnitude speedup over existing software implementations. This advantage is due to the fact that the operations encountered in GCs, (well defined primitive operations involving key encryptions, hashing and XOR computation) are a good match for an FPGA architecture implemented as an overlay. The design is demonstrated on small problems, but is designed to scale up to much larger ones. Larger problems can be divided into partitions and each part can be sequentially implemented on the FPGA overlay. The overhead for switching between parts of the same problem or between different problems consists of a few words of information communicated over a high speed PCIe interface.

In the future, we plan to examine much larger GCs, and expect the advantage of the FPGA implementation to grow as the problem size increases. We will implement the host code to partition and schedule garbled circuits onto the FPGA fabric and consider problems that map to multiple FPGAs on multiple nodes in a data center setting. Our architecture is the initial step to making privacy preserving computation on a large scale feasible by accelerating it with FPGAs.

Acknowledgments

This research was supported by Google through a Faculty Research Award.

7. REFERENCES

[1] L. A. Adamic and N. Glance. The political blogosphere and the 2004 US election: divided they blog. In *Proceedings of the 3rd international workshop on Link discovery*, pages 36–43. ACM, 2005.

[2] J. Angwin. The web's new gold mine: Your secrets: a journal investigation finds that one of the fastest-growing businesses on the internet is the business of spying on consumers; first in a series. *Wall Street Journal*, 2010.

[3] D. Beaver, S. Micali, and P. Rogaway. The round complexity of secure protocols. In *Proceedings of the twenty-second annual ACM symposium on Theory of computing*, pages 503–513. ACM, 1990.

[4] M. Beye, Z. Erkin, and R. L. Lagendijk. Efficient privacy preserving k-means clustering in a three-party setting. In *IEEE International Workshop on Information Forensics and Security*. IEEE Press, 2011.

[5] A. Brant and G. G. Lemieux. ZUMA: An open FPGA overlay architecture. In *IEEE Symposium on Field-Programmable Custom Computing Machines*, pages 93–96. IEEE, 2012.

[6] W. Du, Y. S. Han, and S. Chen. Privacy-preserving multivariate statistical analysis: Linear regression and classification. In *4th SIAM International Conference on Data Mining*. SIAM, 2004.

[7] S. Even, O. Goldreich, and A. Lempel. A randomized protocol for signing contracts. *Communications of the ACM*, 28(6), 1985.

[8] O. Goldreich. *Foundations of Cryptography: Volume 2, Basic Applications*. Cambridge university press, 2009.

[9] W. Henecka, S. Kögl, A.-R. Sadeghi, T. Schneider, and I. Wehrenberg. TASTY: tool for automating secure two-party computations. In *ACM Conference on Computer and Communications Security*, 2010.

[10] Y. Huang, D. Evans, J. Katz, and L. Malka. Faster secure two-party computation using garbled circuits. In *USENIX Security*, 2011.

[11] Y. Huang, L. Malka, D. Evans, and J. Katz. Efficient privacy-preserving biometric identification. In *Network and Distributed System Security Symposium*, 2011.

[12] N. Husted, S. Myers, A. Shelat, and P. Grubbs. GPU and CPU parallelization of honest-but-curious secure two-party computation. In *Asia-Pacific Computer Science and Application Conference*, 2013.

[13] A. K. Jain, S. A. Fahmy, and D. L. Maskell. Efficient overlay architecture based on DSP blocks. In *IEEE Symposium on Field-Programmable Custom Computing Machines*, pages 25–28. IEEE, 2015.

[14] A. K. Jain, D. L. Maskell, and S. A. Fahmy. Are coarse-grained overlays ready for general purpose application acceleration on FPGAs? In *Proceedings of IEEE International Conference on Pervasive Intelligence and Computing*. IEEE, 2016.

[15] K. Järvinen, V. Kolesnikov, A.-R. Sadeghi, and T. Schneider. Garbled circuits for leakage-resilience: Hardware implementation and evaluation of one-time programs. In *Cryptographic Hardware and Embedded Systems*, pages 383–397. Springer, 2010.

[16] N. Kapre and J. Gray. Hoplite: Building austere overlay NoCs for FPGAs. In *International Conference on Field Programmable Logic and Applications*, pages 1–8. IEEE, 2015.

[17] N. Kapre, N. Mehta, M. Delorimier, R. Rubin, H. Barnor, M. J. Wilson, M. Wrighton, and A. Dehon. Packet switched vs. time multiplexed FPGA overlay networks. In *IEEE Symposium on Field-Programmable Custom Computing Machines*, pages 205–216. IEEE, 2006.

[18] D. Koch, C. Beckhoff, and G. G. Lemieux. An efficient FPGA overlay for portable custom instruction set extensions. In *International Conference on Field Programmable Logic and Applications*, pages 1–8. IEEE, 2013.

[19] V. Kolesnikov and T. Schneider. Improved Garbled Circuit: Free XOR Gates and Applications. In *International Colloquium on Automata, Languages and Programming*, 2008.

[20] M. Kosinski, D. Stillwell, and T. Graepel. Private traits and attributes are predictable from digital records of human behavior. *Proceedings of the National Academy of Sciences*, 110(15):5802–5805, 2013.

[21] J. Leskovec, L. Backstrom, and J. Kleinberg. Meme-tracking and the dynamics of the news cycle. In *Proceedings of the 15th ACM SIGKDD international conference on Knowledge discovery and data mining*, pages 497–506. ACM, 2009.

[22] C. Liu, X. S. Wang, K. Nayak, Y. Huang, and E. Shi. Oblivm: A generic, customizable, and reusable secure computation architecture. In *IEEE Symposium on Security and Privacy*, 2015.

[23] D. Malkhi, N. Nisan, B. Pinkas, and Y. Sella. Fairplay-secure two-party computation system. In *USENIX Security*, volume 4, 2004.

[24] A. Mislove, B. Viswanath, K. P. Gummadi, and P. Druschel. You are who you know: Inferring user profiles in Online Social Networks. In *International Conference on Web Search and Data Mining*, 2010.

[25] M. Naor, B. Pinkas, and R. Sumner. Privacy preserving auctions and mechanism design. In *1st ACM Conference on Electronic Commerce*, 1999.

[26] A. Narayanan and V. Shmatikov. Robust de-anonymization of large sparse datasets. In *IEEE Symposium on Security and Privacy*, 2008.

[27] K. Nayak, X. S. Wang, S. Ioannidis, U. Weinsberg, N. Taft, and E. Shi. GraphSC: Parallel secure computation made easy. In *IEEE Symposium on Security and Privacy*, 2015.

[28] V. Nikolaenko, S. Ioannidis, U. Weinsberg, M. Joye, N. Taft, and D. Boneh. Privacy-preserving matrix factorization. In *ACM Conference on Computer and Communications Security*, 2013.

[29] V. Nikolaenko, U. Weinsberg, S. Ioannidis, M. Joye, D. Boneh, and N. Taft. Privacy-preserving ridge regression on hundreds of millions of records. In *IEEE Symposium on Security and Privacy*, 2013.

[30] J. Otterbacher. Inferring gender of movie reviewers: exploiting writing style, content and metadata. In *Conference on Information and Knowledge Management*, 2010.

[31] S. Pu, P. Duan, and J.-C. Liu. Fastplay-a parallelization model and implementation of SMC on CUDA based GPU cluster architecture. *IACR Cryptology ePrint Archive*, 2011:97, 2011.

[32] M. O. Rabin. How to exchange secrets by oblivious transfer. Technical Report TR-81, Aiken Computation Laboratory, Harvard University, 1981.

[33] M. Ramos-Casals, P. Brito-Zerón, B. Kostov, A. Sisó-Almirall, X. Bosch, D. Buss, A. Trilla, J. H. Stone, M. A. Khamashta, and Y. Shoenfeld. Google-driven search for big data in autoimmune geoepidemiology: Analysis of 394,827 patients with systemic autoimmune diseases. *Autoimmunity reviews*, 2015.

[34] D. Rao, D. Yarowsky, A. Shreevats, and M. Gupta. Classifying latent user attributes in twitter. In *2nd International workshop on Search and mining user-generated contents*, 2010.

[35] S. Ressler. Social network analysis as an approach to combat terrorism: past, present, and future research. *Homeland Security Affairs*, 2(2):1–10, 2006.

[36] S. Salamatian, A. Zhang, F. du Pin Calmon, S. Bhamidipati, N. Fawaz, B. Kveton, P. Oliveira, and N. Taft. How to hide the elephant-or the donkey-in the room: Practical privacy against statistical inference for large data. In *2016 IEEE Global Conference on Signal and Information Processing*, 2013.

[37] E. M. Songhori, S. U. Hussain, A.-R. Sadeghi, T. Schneider, and F. Koushanfar. TinyGarble: Highly compressed and scalable sequential garbled circuits. In *IEEE Symposium on Security and Privacy*, 2015.

[38] E. M. Songhori, S. Zeitouni, G. Dessouky, T. Schneider, A.-R. Sadeghi, and F. Koushanfar. GarbledCPU: a MIPS processor for secure computation in hardware. In *Proceedings of the 53rd Annual Design Automation Conference*, page 73. ACM, 2016.

[39] J. Strömbergson. SHA1 core. https://github.com/secworks/sha1.

[40] U. Weinsberg, S. Bhagat, S. Ioannidis, and N. Taft. Blurme: Inferring and obfuscating user gender based on ratings. In *ACM conference on Recommender systems*, 2012.

[41] T. Wiersema, A. Bockhorn, and M. Platzner. Embedding FPGA overlays into configurable systems-on-chip: ReconOS meets ZUMA. In *2014 International Conference on ReConFigurable Computing and FPGAs*, pages 1–6. IEEE, 2014.

[42] J. Wortham. Facebook and privacy clash again. *The New York Times May*, 6, 2010.

[43] A. Yao. How to generate and exchange secrets. In *Foundations of Computer Science*, 1986.

[44] A. C.-C. Yao. Protocols for secure computations. In *IEEE Symposium on Foundations of Computer Science*, volume 82, pages 160–164, 1982.

FPGA Acceleration for Computational Glass-Free Displays

Zhuolun He* and Guojie Luo*†‡
Center for Energy-efficient Computing and Applications, School of EECS, Peking University, China*
Collaborative Innovation Center of High Performance Computing, NUDT, China†
PKU-UCLA Joint Research Institute in Science and Engineering‡
{juicehe, gluo}@pku.edu.cn

ABSTRACT

The increasing computational power enables various new applications that are runtime prohibitive before. FPGA is one of such computational power with both reconfigurability and energy efficiency. In this paper, we demonstrate the feasibility of eyeglasses-free displays through FPGA acceleration. Specifically, we propose several techniques to accelerate the sparse matrix-vector multiplication and the L-BFGS iterative optimization algorithm with the consideration of the characteristics of FPGAs. The experimental results show that we reach a 12.78X overall speedup of the glass-free display application.

1. INTRODUCTION

FPGAs have been increasingly popular as accelerators for large scale compute-intensive applications because of their inherent parallelism. With massive on-chip logics and flexible on-chip memories, FPGAs can be expediently customized as high throughput, low latency computing systems. Nevertheless, the degree of computational parallelism is limited by either on-chip memory bandwidth or IO rate of external memory.

Light field, defined as a part of space studied from the standpoint of transmission of radiant energy within that space by Gershun [1], can now be recorded, manipulated and displayed with the advent of computers, color displays and inexpensive digital sensors [2]. While an image is a 2D slice of the 4D light field, computational light field display applications aim to construct a 4D light field from a set of 2D images of different angle's original view, where a significant amount of raw data is required. On the one hand, the compute-intensive nature of light field display applications makes them a particularly good fit for FPGA-based processing. On the other hand, relevant issues concerning the vast amount of data should be overcome to enhance the performance of the FPGA-based application.

We explore light field display application on FPGA. In particular, we make the following contributions:

FPGA '17, February 22-24, 2017, Monterey, CA, USA

© 2017 ACM. ISBN 978-1-4503-4354-1/17/02. . . $15.00

DOI: http://dx.doi.org/10.1145/3020078.3021728

1. We apply ideas of matrix compression and table lookup to minimize the data volume to transfer.

2. We search for the optimal partitioning factor of array to increase the concurrency of on-chip BRAM access.

3. We put forward an FPGA-friendly algorithm that effectively reduces both computational load and data transmission of the L-BFGS optimization method.

The remainder of this paper is organized as follows: Section 2 gives a brief introduction of our application and FPGA acceleration. Section 3 shows the overall structure of the system. Section 4 and 5 demonstrate our key techniques in SpMV and L-BFGS in detail. Section 6 shows our experimental results. Section 7 and 8 are related work and conclusions sections.

2. BACKGROUND

There are estimates that about 2.5 billion people (one-third of the world's population) could be affected by myopia by the end of this decade [3], and thus, they need eyeglasses or contact lenses to read or see clearly. Huang and Wetzstein [4] have introduced a computational display technology that predistorts the presented content for the observer so that the desired image is perceived without the need for eyewear. However, the long runtime of solving linear systems in the eyeglass-free display algorithm acts as a significant obstacle to process images at required rate. Therefore, we focus on the interesting and useful subject of accelerating the algorithm.

While section 2.1 gives a brief introduction of the algorithm, section 2.2 shows the time profiling. Section 2.3 discusses the basic idea of FPGA acceleration.

2.1 Light Field Reconstruction Problem

The goal of Huang and Wetzstein's algorithm is to present a 4D light field to the observer, such that a desired 2D retinal projection is perceived. Figure 1 demonstrates the application. Formally speaking, given the desired 2D image $u \in \mathbf{R}^M$ and the 2D-to-4D transformation matrix $P \in \mathbf{R}^{M \times N}$ encoding the projection of the screen-side light onto the retina, the light field reconstruction problem is to find a proper light field $x \in \mathbf{R}^N$ emitted by the display as follows:

$$\begin{aligned} \text{minimize} \quad & f(x) = \|u - Px\|_2 \\ \text{subject to} \quad & \mathbf{0} \le x \le \mathbf{1} \end{aligned} \tag{1}$$

Here, M is the discretized locations on the retina ($M = 128 \times 128$ in our program), and N is the number of emitted

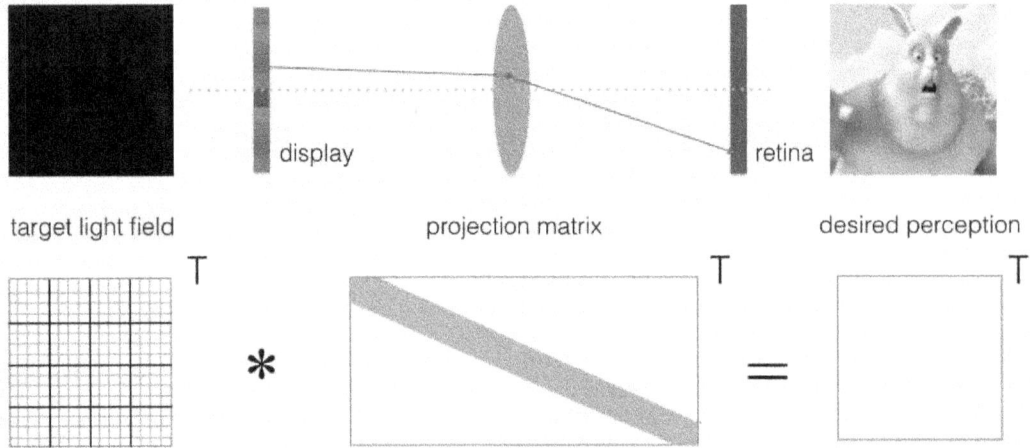

Figure 1: Glass-free Display Application

light rays ($N = 700 \times 700$ is applied for iPod Touch 4 according to Huang and Wetzstein).

The matrix P is constant under the rule of light field transformation [5], when viewing distance, pupil size, and other parameters are fixed. Therefore, the process of building the projection matrix P needs to be done merely once, and can be considered as pretreatment and input of the algorithm. In other words, for each input image, the only work of the algorithm is to calculate the light field by Equation 1.

Equation 1 can be solved using standard convex optimization algorithms, and we employ the L-BFGS algorithm [6] here. However, this is still of high calculation strength due to the high dimensionality of P and u.

2.2 The Algorithm and its Runtime Profiling

As mentioned above, since P can be treated as the input of the algorithm, we want to focus on the runtime of solving Equation 1 and other processes that need to be done respectively for each input image.

In a C++ prototype of the reconstruction algorithm[1], processing a 128×128 image needs approximately 124.5s, where L-BFGS accounts for 122.5s, namely 98.4% of runtime. The high percentage pushes us to concentrate on the acceleration of the L-BFGS algorithm.

Listing 1 is a rough outline of the L-BFGS algorithm. We timed respectively for the four primary procedures in L-BFGS algorithm in line 2-5, and the result is as Figure 2.

Besides, we also timed for the basic matrix-vector operations. The result is shown in Figure 3, from which we can see multiplication and inner product operations take up over 70% of runtime.

These profiling results indicate that the matrix-vector multiplication, the inner product, and the vector addition are the most time-consuming matrix-vector operations in the L-BFGS algorithm. They are the focus of acceleration.

---

[1]We test it using the same configuration as the baseline described in Section 6.1.

Listing 1 L-BFGS Algorithm Outline [7]

Input: starting point x_0, integer history size $m > 0$, $k = 0$;
Output: the position x with a minimal objective function
1: **while** not converge **do**
2:     Calculate gradient $\nabla f(x_k)$ at position x_k;
3:     Compute direction p_k using two-loop recursion as Listing 2;
4:     Search for step length α_k which satisfies Wolfe conditions;
5:     Update $x_{k+1} = x_k + \alpha_k p_k$, $k = k + 1$ and other information;
6: **end while**
7: **return** final x

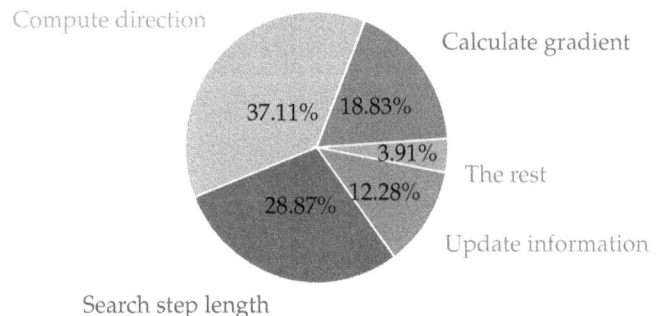

Figure 2: Time of Procedures (Totally 123.72s)

268

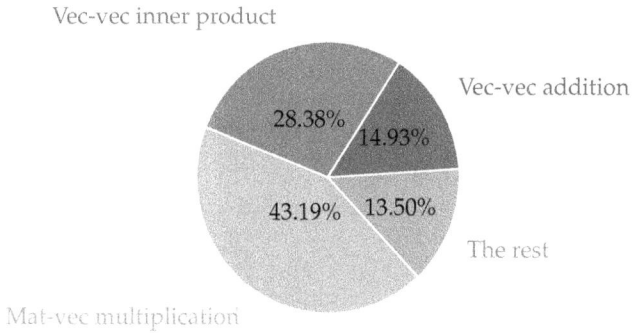

Figure 3: Time of Operations (Totally 122.48s)

2.3 FPGA Acceleration and Challenges

FPGA acceleration is a promising technique to implement energy-efficient and low-latency computational tasks. Let's take the computation of inner product as an instance here.

Ideally, the speed of inner product calculation is limited by the computational resources, assuming that on-chip memory is large enough to hold the two operand vectors. Suppose F_m floating-point multiplications and F_a floating-point additions are performed per second. For an inner product operation between two vectors in $\mathbf{R}^N$, totally N times multiplications and $N - 1$ times additions are needed. Therefore, the sequential computation time $T_{comp} = N/F_m + (N-1)/F_a$. Thanks to the inherent parallelism structure of FPGA, we can directly implement a parallel design for inner product calculation. If the design consists of K multipliers and a reduction tree for summation, the computation time is reduced to $T_{comp} = N/(K \cdot F_m) + \log_2(N-1)/F_a$.

However, the limited on-chip block RAM (BRAM) imposes a barrier for exposing the peak computational performance of FPGAs. If memory bandwidth is denoted by B elements per second, the memory I/O time $T_{I/O} = 2N/B$. Then the total time for inner product takes $T \geq \max(T_{comp}, T_{I/O})$. Typically, $T_{I/O}$ is the bottleneck.

In this paper, we apply the idea of data compression and data reuse to reduce the requirement of data transfer and improve the performance.

3. OVERALL ACCELERATOR DESIGN

Figure 4 shows the overall structure of our system. The Flow Controller assembles the modules to form the application. The Memory Manager sees to BRAMs management and off chip data transfer management. Mul-Add, SpMV, and InnerProduct are the processing modules. Whenever the control flow reaches the three operations, the Memory Manger is invoked to read required data from external memory and store them in on-chip BRAMs, after which the corresponding processing module starts computation. Results are written back to external memory if necessary.

4. SPARSE MATRIX-VECTOR MULTIPLICATION

In this sparse matrix-vector multiplication section, we primarily focus on the memory issues within the problem, which significantly affect the performance. Specifically, we reduced the data transfer time by compressing the sparse matrix size

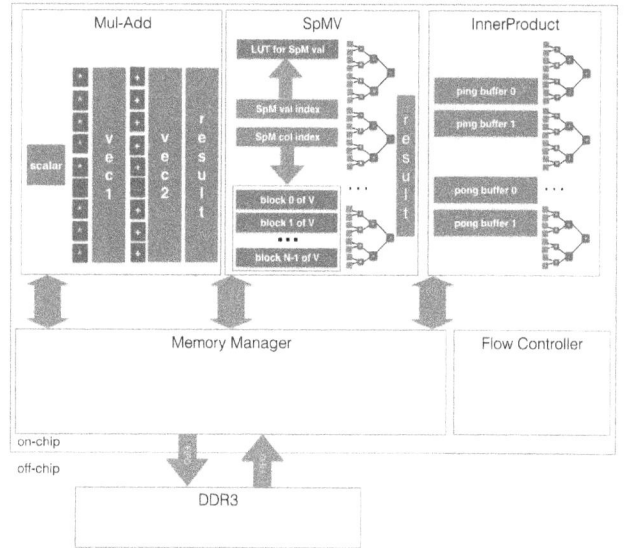

Figure 4: Overall Structure of Accelerator

(elaborated in section 4.1) and reduced the data access time by partitioning the vector (elaborated in section 4.2).

We have to emphasize here that our problem is not very similar to the traditional deconvolution problem, since the projection matrix (namely the sparse matrix here) is an analog result generated by the simulation of the projection process. That is to say, building the matrix involves analog phases, such as sampling and rounding, which makes the matrix anomalous and so that access pattern of the vector is not affine-access for the matrix.

4.1 Storage of the Sparse Matrix

4.1.1 Bitwidth Reduction for COO and CRS

Note that the projection matrix P is a large matrix with billions of elements, but only no more than a million of them are non-zero. Spontaneously, the matrix should be represented in a sparse format. And the simplest one, the coordinate list (COO), is to use a triplet $\langle (r,c), v \rangle$ to denote each non-zero element, where r and c are the row index and column index of an element and v is its corresponding value. Here, r and c are integers range from 0 to $M - 1$ and 0 to $N - 1$, and can be stored in a $\lceil \log_2 M \rceil$-bit integer and a $\lceil \log_2 N \rceil$-bit integer, respectively. v is a floating-point number range from 0-1, and takes up 32-bit width space as a single-precision floating-point number in IEEE 754. Suppose there are totally n_z non-zero elements in the matrix, the matrix can be stored in $(\lceil \log_2 M \rceil + \lceil \log_2 N \rceil + 32)n_z$ bits, namely $(\frac{1}{8}(\lceil \log_2 M \rceil + \lceil \log_2 N \rceil) + 4)n_z$ bytes space.

If all the non-zero elements in triplet are sorted in a row-major order and are placed together, we get a n_z-row table with three columns: row-index column, column-index column, and value column. Notice that the elements are sorted in row-major order, which means the elements from the same row are placed successively, and the duplicate row indices are redundant. Therefore, we can compress the row-index column. In this Compress Row Storage (CRS), the row-index column contains only M elements. The ith element stores the row index in the table of the first non-zero element in the ith row. There are n_z non-zero elements so the row index of an entry is no more than $n_z - 1$, and thus can be store in $\lceil \log_2 n_z \rceil$ bits. With the column-index column and value column remained the same, the matrix can be stored in $M\lceil \log_2 n_z \rceil + \lceil \log_2 N \rceil + 32n_z$ bits, namely $\frac{M}{8}\lceil \log_2 n_z \rceil + (\frac{1}{8}\lceil \log_2 N \rceil + 4)n_z$ bytes.

4.1.2 Compression using Look-up Table of Values

We have different strategies to store and transfer the value column. As mentioned above, we need n_z 32-bit floating-point numbers to store the values directly, and that counts for $4n_z$ bytes storage space.

However, in the algorithm, the value is something like light intensity and is calculated as the number of samples falling on a discrete screen light field coordinate divided by total number of samples generated. Given that, since the total number is fixed, we can only store the number of samples for each coordinate, and calculates the actual value when necessary. According to the result of building projection matrix, the max number of samples is less than 600, and can be represented as a 10-bit integer, so we need only $1.25n_z$ bytes storage space, at the cost of an extra division for each value.

Moreover, we notice that there are only 350 different values, so the idea of the index table is under consideration here. We can use a 9-bit number to represent an unsigned integer less than 512, which means we reduce the storage space to $1.125n_z$ bytes for the values, but have to keep an index table in memory with a size of about 0.5 Kbytes (350×10 bits), and have to look up the index table and calculate for each value. The compressed row-index column and col-index column remain the same as that in section 4.1.1.

4.1.3 Overall Matrix Size Reduction

The effects of different storage methods are summarized in Table 1. Our CRS+LUT representation achieves a $1.81\times$ reduction in the matrix storage compared to the conventional CRS, and thus greatly relieve the bandwidth bottleneck of the sparse matrix-vector multiplication.

Format	Space complexity (bytes)	Storage (MB)
flat	$4MN$	32112.64
COO	$\frac{1}{8}\lceil \log_2 M \rceil n_z + (\frac{1}{8}\lceil \log_2 N \rceil + 4)n_z$	6.63
CRS	$\frac{M}{8}\lceil \log_2 n_z \rceil + (\frac{1}{8}\lceil \log_2 N \rceil + 4)n_z$	5.24
CRS+LUT	$\frac{M}{8}\lceil \log_2 n_z \rceil + (\frac{1}{8}\lceil \log_2 N \rceil + 1.125)n_z$	2.90

Table 1: Storage of the single-precision sparse matrix with $M = 16384$ rows, $N = 490000$ columns, and $n_z = 816272$ non-zero entries in our application. The CRS+LUT format has an overhead of 437.5 bytes for the look-up table (LUT).

4.2 Partitioning of the Vector

Typically, a block RAM in FPGA provides up to $16Kb$ storage size (if not using parity bits). In our problem, the vector consists of 490000 32-bit floating-point numbers, which takes 980 BRAMs to hold the whole vector. Due to the limited number of read ports of the BRAMs, the mapping from

an array (e.g., a vector in SpMV) to the BRAMs is important to fetch enough data in every clock cycle during pipelining.

As we mentioned, the access pattern of the vector is irregular on the matrix rows, because the matrix simulates some analog processes. Therefore, conventional methods for stencil computation to partition the vector is no longer feasible. The good thing is that since the matrix is constant during computation and thus, the access pattern is statistically analyzable, it is possible to search for an optimal partitioning factor to reach a maximum access rate of the vector elements. With the sparse matrix donated as P and the vector donated as x, we divide the vector into N blocks to minimize the memory access latency. Formally, we search for such an N that:

$$\underset{N}{\text{argmin}} \sum_{r=1}^{P.rows} \max_{b=1}^{N} acc_{r,b} \qquad (2)$$

Here, $acc_{r,b} = k$ indicates that when we calculate the inner-product between the rth row of P and x, there will be k read transactions for block b. Since different BRAMs can be read or written in parallel, the number of cycles for each row-vector multiplication is decided by the block with the most read transactions, and the equation 2 is rather straightforward.

We enumerate the factors of $|x|$ as potential partitioning factors, which is intuitive and avoids small storage fragmentation. We also try both block partition and cyclic partition. Considering both the search time and the BRAM resource limitation, we set an upper bound of 1500 for N during the enumeration. Table 2 shows part of the results. In this case, 980 is a perfect partitioning factor, which not only cause no conflict in memory access, but also brings about no storage fragmentation.

Factor N	Method	Min cyc/r	Max cyc/r	Total cyc
980	cyclic	1	1	16384
1225	cyclic	1	1	16384
1250	cyclic	1	2	19840
...	...	...	...	...
1400	block	4	18	188564
1250	block	5	18	193276
...	...	...	...	...
1	N/A	37	54	816272

Table 2: Partition Results of Various N

5. DECOMPOSED L-BFGS ALGORITHM

5.1 Vector-free L-BFGS

The major component of the overall algorithm is the iterative L-BFGS algorithm, where the computation of inner products consumes most of the time. The computational kernel of the L-BFGS algorithm is a two-loop recursion, as shown in Listing 2. The direction p_k depends on the the current gradient direction $\nabla f(x_k)$ and the last m updates $s_i = x_{i+1} - x_i$ and $y_i = \nabla f(x_{i+1}) - \nabla f(x_i)$ for $i = k - m, ..., k - 1$.

We adopt the vector-free L-BFGS algorithm [7] which can reduce both the efforts in computation and data transfer. The key idea is to represent the vector p_k as a linear combination of the precomputed inner products, as shown in figure 5. Specifically, let $b_j^k = s_{k-m-1+j}$, $b_{m+j}^k = y_{k-m-1+j}$ for

Listing 2 The original L-BFGS two-loop recursion [7]

Input: $\nabla f(x_k)$, s_i, y_i for $i = k - m, ..., k - 1$
Output: new direction p_k
1: $p_k = -\nabla f(x_k)$
2: **for** $i = k - 1$ **to** $k - m$ **do**
3:     $\alpha_i = \frac{s_i \cdot p_k}{s_i \cdot y_i}$
4:     $p_k = p_k - \alpha_i y_i$
5: **end for**
6: $p_k = \frac{s_{k-1} \cdot y_{k-1}}{y_{k-1} \cdot y_{k-1}} p_k$
7: **for** $i = k - m$ **to** $k - 1$ **do**
8:     $\beta = \frac{y_i \cdot p_k}{s_i \cdot y_i}$
9:     $p_k = p_k + (\alpha_i - \beta)s_i$
10: **end for**

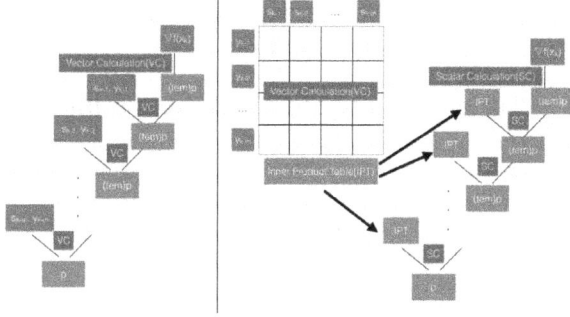

Figure 5: Two-loop recursion in the original L-BFGS (the left) and the vector-free L-BFGS (the right)

Listing 3 The vector-free L-BFGS two-loop recursion [7]

Input: inner product table $T^k[\,][\,]$ of size $(2m + 1)^2$
Output: coefficients δ_i^k for $i = 1, 2, ..., 2m + 1$
1: **for** $i = 1$ **to** $2m + 1$ **do**
2:     $\delta_i^k = (i < 2m) \, ? \, 0 : -1$
3: **end for**
4: **for** $i = k - 1$ **to** $k - m$ **do**
5:     $j = i - (k - m) + 1$
6:     $\alpha_i = \frac{\sum_{l=1}^{2m+1} \delta_l^k T^k[l][j]}{T^k[j][m+j]}$
7:     $\delta_{m+j}^k = \delta_{m+j}^k - \alpha_i$
8: **end for**
9: **for** $i = 1$ **to** $2m + 1$ **do**
10:    $\delta_i^k = \frac{T^k[m][2m]}{T^k[2m][2m]} \delta_i^k$
11: **end for**
12: **for** $i = k - m$ **to** $k - 1$ **do**
13:    $j = i - (k - m) + 1$
14:    $\beta = \frac{\sum_{l=1}^{2m+1} \delta_l^k T^k[m+j][l]}{T^k[j][m+j]}$
15:    $\delta_j^k = \delta_j^k + (\alpha_i - \beta)$
16: **end for**

$j = 1, 2, ..., m$, and $b_{2m+1}^k = \nabla f(x_k)$, we can write the direction p_k as $\sum_{i=1}^{2m+1} \delta_i^k b_i^k$. In this way, we can replace the vector computations in Listing 2 by the scalar computations in Listing 3.

Each time when executing Listing 3, we need a look-up table for the inner products among $\nabla f(x_k)$, s_i and y_i for $i = k - m, ..., k - 1$. There are $2m + 1$ vectors in total, so the table

size is $(2m + 1)^2$. The entry $T^k[i][j]$ stores the value of the inner product $b_i^k \cdot b_j^k$.

When iterating from k to $k + 1$, we only need to update the look-up table by discarding the outdated vectors and inserting new entries. The new entries include the inner products between $\nabla f(x_{k+1})$, s_k, y_k and the remaining vectors. Noticing that $s_k = x_{k+1} - x_k$ and $y_k = \nabla f(x_{k+1}) - \nabla f(x_k)$, there are many computations that can be shared when computing the new inner products relating to s_k or y_k.

5.2 TESC for VL-BFGS

Here we put forward an efficient algorithm to update the look-up table in VL-BFGS called "Transfer Equation and Shared Computation" (TESC). Our algorithm is shown in Listing 4, and it has the minimum inner product computations so that it highly improves the performance of VL-BFGS.

TESC is based on the following two observations:

1. When entering an iteration, most of the vector entries are overlapped with the previous ones.

2. When finishing an iteration, $\nabla f(x_k)$ is the only vector that cannot be linearly represented by previous vectors.

From the first observation, we obtain the following transfer equation:

$$\begin{cases} b_i^k = b_{i+1}^{k-1}, & \text{for } i = 1, ..., m - 1 \\ b_{m+i}^k = b_{m+i+1}^{k-1}, & \text{for } i = 1, ..., m - 1 \end{cases} \quad (3)$$

From the second observation, we can conclude that the inner products involving the newly produced vector $\nabla f(x_k)$ are inevitable. In fact, with equation 3, the rest of the look-up table entries can be calculated from the previous look-up table and other scalars. For example:

$$\begin{aligned} b_m^k \cdot b_m^k &= (\alpha_{k-1} \sum_{i=1}^{2m+1} \delta_i^k b_i^{k-1}) \cdot b_m^k \\ &= \alpha_{k-1} \sum_{i=1}^{2m+1} (\delta_i^k b_i^{k-1} \cdot (\alpha_{k-1} \sum_{j=1}^{2m+1} (\delta_j^k b_j^{k-1}))) \\ &= \alpha_{k-1}^2 \sum_{i=1}^{2m+1} \sum_{j=1}^{2m+1} (\delta_i^k \delta_j^k b_i^{k-1} \cdot b_j^{k-1}) \\ &= \alpha_{k-1}^2 \sum_{i=1}^{2m+1} \sum_{j=1}^{2m+1} (\delta_i^k \delta_j^k T^{k-1}[i][j]) \end{aligned} \quad (4)$$

The expression to calculate $b_m^k \cdot b_m^k$ above consists of only scalar operations, so no direct inner product is needed here. Most of the derivations are evident, so we just omit them here. Some operations involve the two discarded vectors after the last iteration, so we just postpone discarding until finishing updating the look-up table.

Listing 4 shows the outline of TESC.

5.3 Complexity Analysis and Comparison

In TESC, with the history size m and the vector dimension d, the computational complexity of updating the inner product table for each iteration is $(2m + 4)d$, compared to the origin $6md$ in VL-BFGS. Even better, the $2m + 4$ inner product computations involve the same vector, which means we can

Listing 4 TESC for VL-BFGS

Input: previous look-up table $T^{k-1}[\,][\,]$, $\nabla f(x_k)$, and the relevant scalars and vectors
Output: new look-up table $T^k[\,][\,]$
1: **for** $i = k - m$ **to** $k - 1$ **do**
2:     compute $\nabla f(x_k) \cdot s_i$ and $\nabla f(x_k) \cdot y_i$
3: **end for**
4: compute $\nabla f(x_k) \cdot \nabla f(x_k)$ and $\nabla f(x_k) \cdot \nabla f(x_{k-1})$
5: compute $\nabla f(x_k) \cdot (s_{k-m-1})$ and $\nabla f(x_k) \cdot (y_{k-m-1})$
6: **for** $r = 1$ **to** $2m + 1$ **do**
7:     **for** $c = 1$ **to** r **do**
8:         Update $T^k[r][c]$ using $T^{k-1}[\,][\,]$, the inner product results above and the relevant scalars
9:     **end for**
10: **end for**

keep that vector in the BRAM on FPGA during the computations, and thus reduce the data transfer. We will discuss the details in the following paragraphs.

Originally, L-BFGS needs $2 \cdot (2m)$ inner product computations in its two-loop recursion, and another $(2m + 2)d$ multiplications to calculate the new direction p_k. Therefore, the total complexity of the origin algorithm is $(6m + 2)d$ multiplication for each iteration. Intuitively, $(6m + 2)d$ multiplications bring about $(12m + 4)d$ data transfer. However, since some data can be shared between the multiplications due to the certain calculation pattern here, data transfer can be lowered to $(8m + 4)d$ per iteration.

For VL-BFGS, with the consideration of the commutative law of multiplication since $s_i \cdot y_j \equiv y_j \cdot s_i$, each new iteration only need to calculate $6m$ new dot products which involve new s_k, y_k and g_k. The other and the final step is to calculate the new direction p based on δ^k and the base vectors, i.e. $b_1^k, \ldots, b_{2m+1}^k$. The complexity is another $2md$ multiplications, which means the overall complexity of the algorithm is $8md$ multiplications. Similarly, the idea of data reuse can be applied here. For example, when we are calculating inner products related to new s_k, we simply have s_k stored in the block RAM of FPGA and fetch the other party of the product from on-board memory one by one. Therefore, data transfer can also be reduced to $8md$ per iteration.

Things get much more amazing when it comes to VL-BFGS with TESC. As mentioned above, the computational complexity of updating the inner product table is $2m + 4$ inner products involving the same vector, so data transfer complexity is $2m + 4$ here. With the addition of the calculation for the new direction p, the overall complexity is $(4m + 4)d$ multiplications with $(4m + 4)d$ data transfer.

Table 3 shows and compares the analysis results.

	Multiplication	Data transfer
L-BFGS	$(6m + 2)d$	$(8m + 4)d$
VL-BFGS	$8md$	$8md$
VL-BFGS with TESC	$(4m + 4)d$	$(4m + 4)d$

Table 3: Complexity Analysis and Comparison

6. EXPERIMENTAL EVALUATIONS

6.1 Experimental Setup

We tested our optimizations on VC707 evaluation board featuring the Virtex-7 XC7VX485T-2FFG1761C FPGA. Designs are implemented as IP cores with Vivado High-Level Synthesis v2015.2 and synthesized and place-and-route by Vivado v2015.2.

The Huang and Wetzstein's original algorithm was implemented in MATLAB. And we convert the original implementation into C++ as the baseline for the following comparisons. The baseline uses Eigen (a C++ template library for linear algebra) and CppNumericalSolvers (an L-BFGS implementation in C++11 based on Eigen) for the matrix-vector manipulation and optimization. We tested on a server with a 20-core Intel Xeon CPU E5-2630 v3 @ 2.30GHz and $64GB$ main memory, hereinafter inclusive.

6.2 Analysis of the SpMV Optimization

In section 4.1, we introduced the idea of matrix compression using bitwidth reduction and look-up table, which achieves a $2.28X$ reduction in storage compared with the conventional CRS representation. Naturally, it saves 56.1% data transfer time of the sparse matrix, and that is 43.0% of IO for each SpMV execution.

In section 4.2, we partitioned the vector with the optimal factor to achieve the maximum on-chip memory bandwidth. Besides, we also notice that there are approximately fifty to sixty non-zero elements in a sparse matrix row, and none of them holds more than 64 non-zeros. To simplify our design, we propagate a constant of 64 elements down the processing unit chain and the reduction tree each trip, and the accesses of corresponding vector elements cause no conflict because of the array partition.

To take full advantage of previous ideas, we first rewrite the original MATLAB-style SpMV operation (which looks like a dense matrix-matrix multiplication) as an FPGA-friendly one (which uses CRS and LUT as mentioned) in C++. The change greatly reduces the runtime of the CPU version application from over two minutes to 65.49 seconds.

We employ ping-pong buffer in our FPGA design, and the performance is entirely limited by the external memory bandwidth in this situation. Runtime comparison and source utilization are listed in section 6.4.

6.3 Analysis of the L-BFGS Enhancement

By adopting vector-free L-BFGS, as shown in Listing 3, inter-data dependencies between iterations are removed in the two-loop recursions of L-BFGS. Not only can we divide the operand vectors into blocks for parallel computing, but we may parallelize different inner-product operations. The greater granularity of parallelism is also applicable to FPGA clusters or distributed systems.

Listing 4 shows our TESC algorithm that updates the look-up table in VL-FBGS efficiently using transfer equation and shared computation. With TESC, the runtime of the CPU version decreases to around 47.47 seconds.

Before we load certain computations onto FPGA, we tested different history size m (see Listing 1), and we take $m = 3$ as the history size hyperparameter, which guarantees convergence and lowers calculation cost. In this case, the runtime is reduced to 25.26 seconds.

6.4 FPGA Speedup of each Component

With the consideration of the nature of the algorithm and the optimizations, we conclude three most basic operations in VL-BFGS with TESC:

1. Sparse matrix-vector multiplication (SpMV)
   ($vector_{res} = SpM * vector$)

2. Inner product of vectors (InnProd)
   ($scalar_{res} = vector_1 \cdot vector_2$)

3. Scalar multiplication and vector addition (Mul-Add)
   ($vector_{res} = scalar \cdot vector_1 + vector_2$)

It is reasonable to compare the runtime between FPGA implementation and multi-threading implementation of each operation. We use OpenMP to implement the multi-threading version from the C++ code, where Eigen is adopted as the linear algebra library, as mentioned above.

According to the analysis of VL-BFGS with TESC in section 5.3, there are $2m + 4$ consecutive inner products in the updating phase and $2m$ multiple-additions in the phase of calculating new direction p. Therefore, we test the two operations in loops that repeat them for corresponding times and add OpenMP directives to the loops. The SpMV operation will not be tested with repetitive computation, and we add the OpenMP directives to the for loops inside the operation.

Table 4 shows the runtime comparison of each component, while figure 6 illustrates the speedup comparison. Table 5 shows the resource utilizations of each component and the summation on FPGA.

	SpMV	InnProd	Mul-Add
FPGA	0.0085s*	0.0237s	0.0635s
1-thread	0.0312s	0.1247s	0.1920s
2-threads	0.0204s	0.1120s	0.1437s
4-threads	0.0121s	0.0741s	0.1091s

   * estimated

Table 4: Runtime Comparison of each Component

	LUT	FF	BRAM	DSP
SpMV	8290	6038	1058	10
InnProd	21722	26372	39	0
Mul-Add	27834	40959	169	0
Total	57846	73369	1266	10
Available	303600	607200	2060	2800
Utilization(%)	19	12	61	~0

Table 5: Resource Utilizations of each Component

6.5 The Overall Speedup and Discussions

Finally, we can obtain the overall speedup. The FPGA version takes totally 9.74 seconds to accomplish, which reaches a $12.78\times$ speedup compared with the baseline. $3.64\times$ speedup is closely FPGA-related, including L-BFGS enhancement and FPGA acceleration of some operations. L-BFGS enhancement contributes $1.38\times$ to the speedup directly and more importantly, it enables the employment of FPGA. Yet our system didn't fully utilize the external memory bandwidth. Currently, the peak memory bandwidth in our experiment is less than $800MB/s$. Therefore, there is still considerable room for performance improvement.

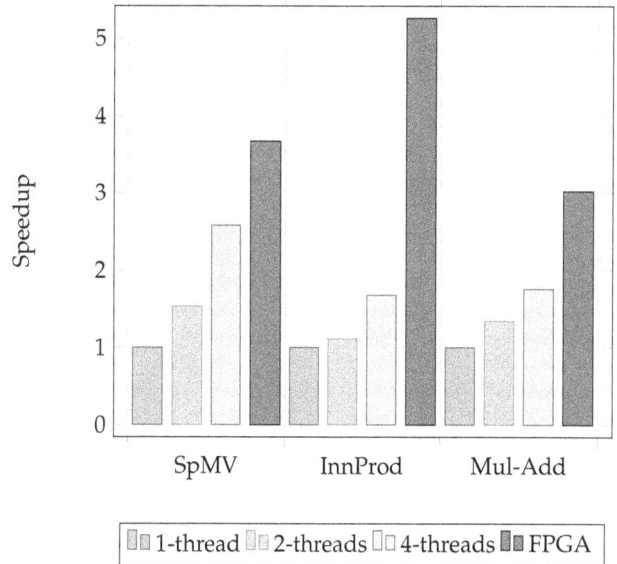

Figure 6: Speedup Comparison

7. RELATED WORK

Though our FPGA acceleration of the light field reconstruction problem is quite different from the previous problems, some challenges are solved by our novel techniques, which are partly inspired by the following works.

SpMV on FPGA The sparse matrix-vector multiplication is one of the most important kernels in scientific computing. P. Grigoras and et al. [8] have used the Bounded CSRVI Format to compress the sparse matrix values on CPU and decompress in runtime. Y. Umuroglu and M. Jahre [9] [10] have described a scalable backend architecture that exploits column-major traversal and interleaving to achieve high bandwidth utilization. They have also proposed a hardware-software caching scheme that exploits preprocessing to enable performant and area-effective SpMV acceleration. S. Guo and et al. [11] have presented a deeply-pipelined SpMV accelerator by exploiting a hardware-friendly storage scheme.

Memory Partition Memory partitioning can efficiently map data elements in the same logical array onto multiple physical banks so that the accesses to the array are parallelized. Y. Wang and et al. [12] have proposed a generalized memory-partitioning framework using a polyhedral model. J. Cong and et al. [13] have presented an automatic memory partitioning technique which can efficiently improve throughput and reduce the energy consumption of pipelined loop kernels for given throughput constraints and platform requirements.

System Optimization It is always important to balance the resource usage of different processing modules to reach better performance. P. Li and et al. [14] have developed an algorithm to determine the optimal resource usage and initiation intervals for each loop in the applications to achieve maximum throughput within a given area budget.

8. CONCLUSIONS AND FUTURE WORK

In our experiment, we achieve a $12.78X$ speedup for the light field reconstruction application using FPGA. On-chip memory bandwidth and IO rate turn out to be the greatest limitation for FPGA performance, so we compress the matrix and partition the vector in SpMV operations to get better properties. Besides, we come up with a novel and efficient algorithm to update the look-up table in the vector-free L-BFGS.

In the future, we would like to explore real-time light field reconstruction technique with a more customized system. Besides, the system should apply to various viewing distance with eyeball tracking feature, which bound to be attractive and practical.

9. ACKNOWLEDGMENT

This work is partly supported by National Natural Science Foundation of China (NSFC) Grant 61520106004, Beijing Natural Science Foundation (BJNSF) Grant 4142022, and the Peking University Principal Undergraduate Research Foundation
(URTP2015PKU004).

10. REFERENCES

[1] A. Gershun, "The light field," *Journal of Mathematics and Physics*, vol. 18, no. 1-4, pp. 51–151, 1939.

[2] M. Levoy, "Light fields and computational imaging," *Computer*, vol. 39, no. 8, pp. 46–55, 2006.

[3] E. Dolgin, "The myopia boom," *Nature*, vol. 519, pp. 276–278, mar 2015.

[4] F. Huang and G. Wetzstein, "Eyeglasses-free display: towards correcting visual aberrations with computational light field displays," *ACM Transactions on Graphics (SIGGRAPH)*, pp. 1–12, 2014.

[5] F.-c. Huang, G. Wetzstein, and B. A. Barsky, "Supplementary Material : Eyeglasses-free Display : Towards Correcting Visual Aberrations with Computational Light Field Displays Derivation of the Light Field Transport,"

[6] B. J. Nocedal, "Updating Quasi-Newton Matrices With Limited Storage," vol. 35, pp. 773–782, 1980.

[7] W. Chen, Z. Wang, and J. Zhou, "Large-scale L-BFGS using MapReduce," in *Proceedings of Neural Information Processing Systems (NIPS 2014)*, 2014.

[8] P. Grigoras, P. Burovskiy, E. Hung, and W. Luk, "Accelerating spmv on fpgas by compressing nonzero values," in *IEEE International Symposium on Field-Programmable Custom Computing Machines*, pp. 64–67, 2015.

[9] Y. Umuroglu and M. Jahre, "An energy efficient column-major backend for fpga spmv accelerators," in *IEEE International Conference on Computer Design*, pp. 432–439, 2014.

[10] Y. Umuroglu and M. Jahre, *A Vector Caching Scheme for Streaming FPGA SpMV Accelerators*. 2015.

[11] S. Guo, Y. Dou, Y. Lei, and G. Wu, "A deeply-pipelined fpga-based spmv accelerator with a hardware-friendly storage scheme," *Ieice Electronics Express*, vol. 12, no. 11, pp. 20150161–20150161, 2015.

[12] Y. Wang, P. Li, and J. Cong, "Theory and algorithm for generalized memory partitioning in high-level synthesis," in *Acm/sigda International Symposium on Field-Programmable Gate Arrays*, pp. 199–208, 2014.

[13] J. Cong, W. Jiang, B. Liu, and Y. Zou, "Automatic memory partitioning and scheduling for throughput and power optimization.," in *IEEE/ACM International Conference on Computer-aided Design*, pp. 697–704, 2011.

[14] P. Li, P. Zhang, and J. Cong, "Resource-Aware Throughput Optimization for High-Level Synthesis,"

Hardware Acceleration of the Pair-HMM Algorithm for DNA Variant Calling

Sitao Huang[†], Gowthami Jayashri Manikandan[†], Anand Ramachandran[†],
Kyle Rupnow[‡], Wen-mei W. Hwu[†], Deming Chen[†]

[†]University of Illinois at Urbana-Champaign, USA
{shuang91, mankndn2, aramach4, w-hwu, dchen}@illinois.edu

[‡]Advanced Digital Sciences Center, Singapore
k.rupnow@adsc.com.sg

ABSTRACT

With the advent of several accurate and sophisticated statistical algorithms and pipelines for DNA sequence analysis, it is becoming increasingly possible to translate raw sequencing data into biologically meaningful information for further clinical analysis and processing. However, given the large volume of the data involved, even modestly complex algorithms would require a prohibitively long time to complete. Hence it is the need of the hour to explore non-conventional implementation platforms to accelerate genomics research. In this work, we present an FPGA-accelerated implementation of the Pair HMM forward algorithm, the performance bottleneck in the HaplotypeCaller, a critical function in the popular GATK variant calling tool. We introduce the PE ring structure which, thanks to the fine-grained parallelism allowed by the FPGA, can be built into various configurations striking a trade-off between instruction-level parallelism (ILP) and data parallelism. We investigate the resource utilization and performance of different configurations. Our solution can achieve a speed-up of up to $487\times$ compared to the C++ baseline implementation on CPU and $1.56\times$ compared to the best published hardware implementation.

Keywords

Hardware Acceleration; FPGA; forward algorithm; Pair-HMM; Computational Genomics; PE ring

1. INTRODUCTION

Bioinformatics is a fast-growing field, with increasing demand for high computational capabilities for several applications. Next Generation Sequencing (NGS) technologies and the increasing availability of genome data through public databases, have enabled us to develop comprehensive pipelines to sequence and process complex genomes.

FPGA '17, February 22-24, 2017, Monterey, CA, USA

© 2017 ACM. ISBN 978-1-4503-4354-1/17/02. . . $15.00

DOI: http://dx.doi.org/10.1145/3020078.3021749

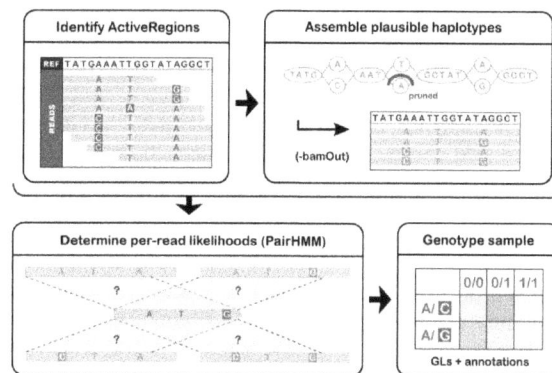

Figure 1: The major steps in HaplotypeCaller [13].

Translation and interpretation of the raw sequencing data to biologically meaningful information for further clinical analysis like disease prediction, drug performance evaluation etc., are of utmost importance now. Several algorithms have been developed to address problems like DNA sequence alignment [1, 2, 3, 4], error correction [5, 6, 7] and variant calling [8]. Many bioinformatics workflows suffer from very high computational times brought forth by the explosion in data available from low-cost, high-throughput sequencing. In response to this, several bioinformatics algorithms have been implemented on alternative computing platforms like FPGAs and GPUs to reduce their execution times. Such recent developments point to workflows being executed on heterogeneous computing platforms where instructions for the critical and computation intensive parts of an algorithm will be off-loaded for execution on an FPGA or a GPU to achieve significant speed-ups compared to a CPU-only implementation. Parallelization and acceleration of complex bioinformatics algorithms has become an area that is being widely explored [9, 10, 11, 12].

Our work deals with a specific bioinformatic analysis called variant calling. Variant calling identifies differences between a given subject's DNA and a standard reference DNA. The input data to the analysis are the standard reference DNA and the sequencing data of the individual in the form of alignment files. Alignment files are a specific type of representation of the sequencing data showing the sequenced reads and the most likely areas they are sequenced from with respect to the reference sequence. These associations are determined by minimizing the edit-distance between a read sequence and regions in the reference sequence.[1, 2] Edit-distance minimizations may be considered valid because the error rates involved in the sequencing technologies of interest are small and localized, and we are primarily interested in small variations from the reference.

GATK's HaplotypeCaller [14, 13] is one of the most popular variant calling tools available today. The tool does the analysis in two steps. In the first step, it identifies locations in the genome where the chances are high that a variation is present based on simple computations. These locations, called active sites, are processed further to confirm the initial assessment.

To determine if an active site in the sample is a variant or not, the tool assembles what it thinks are the probable haplotypes in the region surrounding the active site. The probable haplotypes in a location are the tool's initial guess regarding the different sequences of DNA present in that particular location. More than one sequence may be found at a given location in the genome because, for instance, the human genomic material is made up of pairs of chromosomes, and two chromosomes in a pair can be different locally, while being very similar globally. Once the probable haplotypes are constructed, the tool assesses which of the candidate haplotypes are most likely present in the individual's genome by calculating the likelihood of alignment of each haplotype to the read sequences in that region in the input alignment file. If the established haplotypes are different from the reference sequence, the tool determines that there is a variation at that location. The general flow of the HaplotypeCaller is summarized in Figure 1.

GATK's HaplotypeCaller assumes that haplotypes and read sequences follow a pair hidden Markov model (Pair-HMM). Pair-HMM [15] is a popular statistical model to study pairwise alignment probabilities of two sequences. We can infer several aspects of the alignment using various inference algorithms of the Pair-HMM model such as, optimal sequence alignment (Viterbi algorithm) and the overall alignment probability (forward algorithm). The forward algorithm of the Pair-HMM gives the statistical measure of the similarity between two sequences. It computes the overall alignment probability by summing the likelihood of all possible alignments between the two sequences. The forward algorithm for the Pair-HMM model are used in several applications like gene prediction, functional similarity analysis between two protein sequences and variant calling [16, 17, 18]. Specifically, it is used by GATK's HaplotypeCaller to measure similarity between reads and probable haplotypes.

Table 1 shows the runtime results of each stage of the HaplotypeCaller for Chromosome 20 from sample NA12878 (Whole Genome Sequence data) as published by Mauricio et al. of Broad Institute [19]. This shows that the major bottle-neck is the forward algorithm computations of the Pair-HMM. In the Pair-HMM stage, every candidate haplotype is compared to each input read to compute the likelihood score using the forward algorithm. The number of computations involved is of the order $N \times M \times R \times H$, where N is the number of input reads, M is the number of candidate haplotypes, R is the length of the input reads and H refers to the length of the candidate haplotype.

In this work, our objective is to achieve a speed-up of the Pair-HMM's forward algorithm on an FPGA-based comput-

Table 1: Profiling results for HaplotypeCaller run on Chromosome 20 of NA12878 Whole Genome Sequence (WGS) sample [19].

Stage	Time	Runtime
Assembly	2,598s	13%
Pair-HMM (forward algorithm)	14,225s	70%
Traversal + Genotyping	3,379s	17%

ing platform to minimize the bottleneck of computing flows similar to GATK's HaplotypeCaller that utilize such a Pair-HMM model to compute the overall alignment probability.

Pair-HMM is a type of more complicated dynamic programming algorithm, compared to many other programming algorithm. The propagation operator in Pair-HMM is complicated combination of floating-point additions and multiplications, rather than simple `min` or `max` operators as in many other dynamic programming algorithms. And, there are three matrices that each has data dependencies on the other two. Besides, Pair-HMM requires all the values to be at least single-precision floating-point numbers. Normalizing to fix point domain will lead to either overflow or underflow problem. Performing floating-point operations efficiently usually a hard problem for FPGAs.

Traditionally, in FPGA-accelerated solutions to the Pair-HMM, systolic arrays have been commonly used. However, the systolic array structure lacks the flexibility of handling variable input lengths and hence lacks design scalability and configurability. In this work, we propose a Processing Element (PE) ring structure to compute the forward algorithm. To the best of our knowledge, this is the first PE ring structure based implementation of the Pair-HMM forward algorithm. The PE ring structure can be configured for inputs of varied lengths without any changes to the hardware. In the following sections, we will demonstrate how our PE ring structure exhibits significant advantage in terms of performance and flexibility.

The contributions in this work may be summarized as follows:

- We propose a ring-based hardware implementation of the Pair-HMM's forward algorithm, which can support flexible lengths for input read sequences. Our implementation can achieve significant speed-ups of up to 487× compared to the C++ baseline implementation on CPU, and 1.56× compared to the published best hardware implementation.

- Several optimization techniques for improving PE ring's performance are proposed and discussed, the PE ring structure and the optimization may be readily extended to accelerate other applications that are based on similar dynamic programming algorithms.

- Based on both the above implementation and optimization techniques, we present experimental results to illustrate the trade-offs and other design considerations in using the PE ring structure to accelerate dynamic programming algorithms.

- Our work provides an example of how to effectively accelerate complicated floating-point dynamic programming calculation with FPGA.

The rest of the paper is organized as follows: Section 2 provides an overview of the prior implementations of bioinformatics algorithms that are similar to the Pair-HMM; Section 3 introduces the fundamentals of the forward algorithm of the Pair-HMM; Section 4 presents the details of our ring-based implementation of the forward algorithm; Section 5 illustrates the experimental results and presents a comparison of the performance of the ring-based implementation to other implementations of the Pair-HMM algorithm; Section 6 concludes the paper.

2. RELATED WORK

There are many illustrative examples of the speed optimizations offered by FPGA accelerators for bioinformatics algorithms. FPGA acceleration of Error Correction in NGS reads has been achieved in [12]. The work gets a significant $35\times$ speed-up compared to the software implementation of its base error correction algorithm presented in [5].

Dynamic Programming algorithms have been explored and implemented on varies types of hardware platforms, such as GPU, FPGA and ASICs; For the FPGA platform, most of the work use systolic arrays structures, e.g. the work in [20]. An FPGA accelerated version of the Smith-Waterman algorithm that identifies the best local alignment between two DNA sequences is presented by Isaac TS Li et al. [11]. The work achieved a $160\times$ acceleration compared to the baseline software version. In [21], ring-based structure is proposed to accelerate the dynamic time warping algorithm, which is a type of dynamic programming algorithm whose propagation operator is `min` operator. In that problem, the data could be processed in the fixed point number domain. Ring-based structure is also adopted to accelerate dynamic programming algorithm in this work. However, the dynamic programming algorithm this work accelerate, Pair-HMM, is more complicated. Pair-HMM's propagation operator is a complicated combination of floating-point additions and multiplications, and there are three matrices involved at the same time. This is the reason why Pair-HMM is hard to accelerate using FPGA. There are some other work accelerates dynamic programming algorithm with novel circuit design. In [22], the accumulated score/penalty in dynamic programming problem is represented by the latency of a path in combinational circuit, which corresponding to the dynamic programming search path. This novel design achieve significant speedup compared to the computation based methods. However, this latency based design could only be applied to the those dynamic programming problems whose propagation operator is `max` or `min` operator.

An FPGA implementation of the Pair-HMM stage of HaplotypeCaller on Convey computers is reported in [19]. It achieves $13\times$ speedup compared to the Java implementation of the Pair-HMM algorithm on CPU. The Convey machine contains four high-end FPGAs. In our work, we target a single FPGA chip. However, we leverage most of the optimization techniques feasible through the ring-based RTL-design modifications and achieve higher performance and flexibility of the Pair-HMM's forward algorithm. We achieve a faster and efficient implementation of the Pair-HMM's forward algorithm that can be used in similar flows that utilize it for other applications.

A recent work from Altera [23] accelerates the Pair-HMM algorithm with Altera OpenCL SDK and FPGAs. Their work achieves significant speedup compared to software. The hardware structure in this work is the systolic array. Processing elements are placed in a grid structure. Grid structures are very common in FPGA acceleration designs. However, using the grid structure to process dynamic programming matrices introduces additional overhead of having to store intermediate results back to memory in every step of computation. Our PE ring implementation eliminates this overhead. In the PE ring, the output of one PE is delivered to the neighbor PE and consumed immediately. The whole PE ring produces at most one intermediate result that needs to be stored every cycle. Besides, the PE ring is very amenable to trade offs through restructuring which can reduce the number of idle PEs when boundary conditions (starting or ending of processing a single sequence pair) happen. This can be thought of as a trade-off between Instruction Level Parallelism (ILP) and data-parallelism. In the case of using a single PE ring, the execution goes over one set of dynamic-programming matrices with identical dimensions, while when using multiple smaller rings, we concentrate in parallel on many, possibly differently sized, sets of dynamic programming matrices which may not be amenable to simultaneous processing by a single PE ring. We will discuss more about such techniques later.4.3.

3. FORWARD ALGORITHM

When used as a generative model, the Pair-HMM maybe thought of as emitting a pair of aligned sequences X and Y. To model an alignment based on edit-distance, as opposed to Hamming distance, the model has match, insert and delete states. The Pair-HMM allows us to draw inferences about the alignment quality of a pair of sequences under the assumption that the sequence pair was emitted by itself [Figure 2]. In the HaplotypeCaller, the overall alignment quality between a candidate haplotype and an input read is computed using the Pair-HMM.

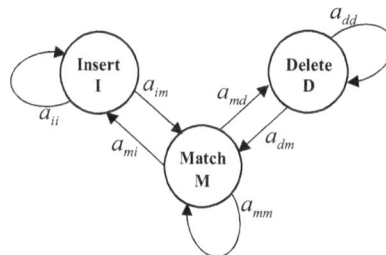

Figure 2: Insert, delete, and match states of Pair-HMM.

Table 2: An example of hidden-state sequence generation using Pair-HMM.[16]

Seq X:	A	G	G	T	A	-
Seq Y:	-	-	G	T	A	A
Hidden state Sequence:	I	I	M	M	M	D

Figure 2 shows the state transitions in a Pair-HMM model. The hidden states are represented as M, D and I. When in state M, the pair-HMM emits symbols from both sequences, implying that the symbols may align to each other. When in state I, it emits one symbol from sequence X, and a blank symbol - meaning no symbol from sequence Y, indicating an insertion in sequence X. Similarly D state represents a deletion in sequence X (or an insertion in sequence Y). The edge-weights between the states represent transition probabilities. Table 2 illustrates how a particular alignment between two sequences may be represented using a Pair-HMM state sequence. The probability of the particular alignment is the product of the corresponding state transition probabilities. To find the overall alignment probability, we need to find the sum of the probabilities of all such alignments between the two sequences. However, if we follow a brute-force approach to evaluate each possible sequence alignment, it can be computationally expensive as there can be a large number of possible alignments between two sequences. Instead, the forward algorithm is used to efficiently compute the overall alignment probability.

The forward algorithm is essentially a dynamic programming approach, which uses three matrices: f^M, f^I and f^D. i and j correspond to the position indices in the sequences X and Y. $f^k(i,j)$ is the *forward variable* that represents the combined probability of all alignments up to positions (i, j) that end in state k. The forward algorithm may be summarized as:

Initialization:

$$
\begin{cases}
f^M(0,0) = 1 \\
f^X(0,0) = f^D(0,0) = 0 \\
f^M(i,0) = f^I(i,0) = 0 \\
f^M(0,j) = f^D(0,j) = 0
\end{cases}
\tag{1}
$$

Recursion:

$$
\begin{cases}
f^M(i,j) = Prior \cdot (a_{mm}f^M(i-1,j-1) \\
\quad + a_{im}f^I(i-1,j-1) + a_{dm}f^D(i-1,j-1)) \\
f^I(i,j) = a_{mi}f^M(i-1,j) + a_{ii}f^I(i-1,j) \\
f^D(i,j) = a_{md}f^M(i,j-1) + a_{dd}f^D(i,j-1)
\end{cases}
\tag{2}
$$

Termination:

$$
Result = f^M(N_h, N_r) + f^I(N_h, N_r) + f^D(N_h, N_r) \tag{3}
$$

where N_h and N_r are the lengths of the haplotype (seq. X) and input read (seq. Y) respectively.

Many quantities in the forward algorithm recursion need elaboration. These quantities are evaluated from additional information available in the input dataset pertaining to the quality of a read sequence and various characteristics related to its alignment at each position in the sequence. Specifically, four different quality score values are used in GATK's formulation of the Pair-HMM, which we base our implementation on. Three of them assign penalties to gaps in the alignment, namely the insertion gap open penalty (or base insertion quality Q_i), the deletion gap open penalty (or base deletion quality Q_d) and the gap continuation penalty (Q_g). In addition, there is also data that indicates the level of confidence in the correctness of each symbol in each read sequence, which we represent as Q_{base}. In the forward algorithm recursion presented here, a_{ij} represents a transition probability from state i to state j. For example a_{mm} represents a transition from the match state to the match state. The *Prior* value represents the probability of emitting an aligned pair of symbols. The emission and transition probabilities are computed in the Pair-HMM implementation for the HaplotypeCaller as follows [24]:

$$
Prior = \begin{cases}
1 - Q_{base}; & \text{if the bases match} \\
Q_{base}; & \text{if the bases don't match}
\end{cases}
\tag{4}
$$

$$
\begin{aligned}
a_{mm} &= 1 - (Q_i + Q_d) & &- \text{match continuation} \\
a_{im} &= 1 - Q_g & &- \text{insertion to match} \\
a_{dm} &= 1 - Q_g & &- \text{deletion to match} \\
a_{mi} &= Q_i & &- \text{match to insertion} \\
a_{ii} &= Q_g & &- \text{insertion continuation} \\
a_{md} &= Q_d & &- \text{match to deletion} \\
a_{dd} &= Q_g & &- \text{deletion continuation}
\end{aligned}
\tag{5}
$$

This set of prior probabilities and transition probabilities need to be computed for each input read, as they differ for each position in the read.

4. DESIGN AND IMPLEMENTATION

The flow for Pair-HMM computations in GATK's HaplotypeCaller is as follows: The Pair-HMM input datasets are parsed to get the read and haplotype bases, read base qualities and other gap penalty scores. The prior and transition probability matrices for each read-haplotype pair are computed using these quality scores. The input matrices are fed to the ring-based forward algorithm computation block on the FPGA to get the overall alignment likelihood. To parse and pre-process the read-sequences and the haplotypes, and obtain the various quality scores in the right form, we use the reference software implementation of the Pair-HMM stage of the HaplotypeCaller[19]. The original order of computations of the forward algorithm's Dynamic Programming(DP) matrix is row-wise (or column-wise). These computations cannot be parallelized as they are due to the data dependencies between the successive computations according to equation 2. Modifying the array access patterns will help us leverage the parallel nature of the computations and design a Processing Element (PE) ring structure to maximize performance. Figure 3 shows the data dependencies within the forward algorithm matrix and the computing order in our implementation. PEs are placed along the diagonal and all diagonal values are computed in parallel and stored in internal registers. These register values are used to calculate the values of the next diagonal of the matrix. The forward algorithm involves computations for 3 such DP matrices f^M, f^D and f^I.

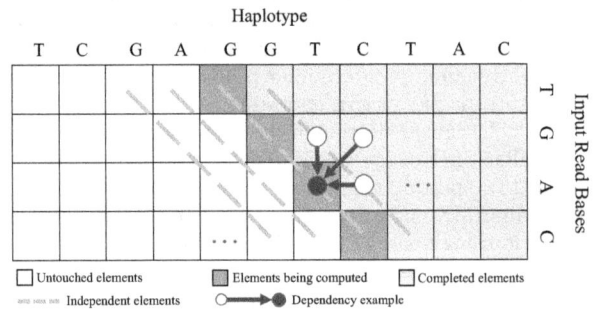

Figure 3: Diagonal matrix access pattern: computations along the diagonal can be parallelized as there are no dependencies among them

The forward algorithm essentially requires a series of arithmetic operations on probability values. Software implementations can comfortably work with floating-point numbers

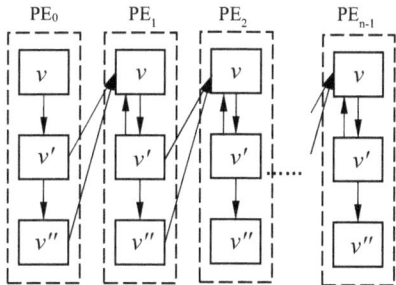

Figure 4: The internal shift registers and their data dependencies among PEs

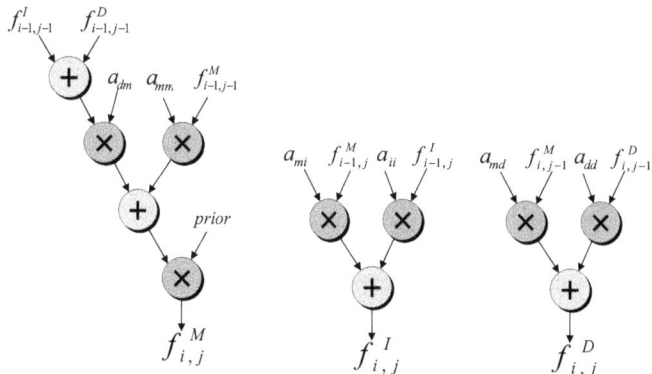

Figure 5: Arithmetic operations inside PEs

to represent data and execute computations. For FPGA-based acceleration, it is common practice to normalize all the floating-point numbers to be within a range of fixed point numbers, and use the FPGA to process those fixed point numbers. However, based on our experiments, the values that turn up in the forward algorithm's computations cover a large range of values, tens of orders of magnitude larger than what fixed point numbers can represent. Working with the fixed point domain will lead to overflow or underflow issues for this algorithm, or a very large loss of precision. Thus, our design needs to use floating-point numbers and computations to obtain the requisite accuracy and correctness of computation.

Generally, the hardware design for a dynamic programming algorithm consists of a series of PEs, similar to what was described in Figure 3. In our design, a fixed number of processing elements are arranged in a ring-based structure. Ring-based organization has been proposed and used to accelerate other dynamic programming algorithms[21]. However, given that the forward algorithm requires two different types of critical operations (both addition and multiplication) and given the fact that we need to use floating point operations for accurate execution of the algorithm, the forward algorithm poses a new set of challenges to tackle. According to equations 2, there are 7 multiply operations and 4 add operations for Pair-HMM calculation in each PE. The critical path consists of 2 adders and 2 multipliers. All the operations are implemented using Altera's floating-point IPs, and are fully pipelined. However this adds many cycles of latency; floating-point multiplication requires 5 cycles while floating-point addition requires 7 cycles (at an operating frequency of 200MHz). Thus, the overall latency of the critical path is 24 cycles (on Stratix V). Without careful optimizations, the initiation interval of each PE will be too large to provide useful acceleration. We will discuss the techniques we use to improve the performance of these arithmetic operations in section 4.3.

4.1 PE Array

Figure 6 shows a simplified organization of the PE array, the core component of the PE ring structure. The figure also illustrates how various PEs in the design process the DP matrix elements. Our design consists of n basic PEs, where n is the optimal number of read bases to be processed. As shown in Figure 6, during any step of processing, the processing elements (PEs) are "placed" (processing) along a diagonal of the matrix. One may notice that there are no dependencies along such a diagonal (Figure 3), and all the PEs can

compute at the same time, given the results of computation of the previous diagonal. After each computation, the ring moves along the horizontal direction of the matrix to place itself on the next diagonal parallel to the current one. Though there are no dependencies among the PEs within a diagonal, there are dependencies among the neighboring PEs across consecutive diagonals. There are several data buses between the neighboring PEs to share intermediate results to satisfy these dependencies.

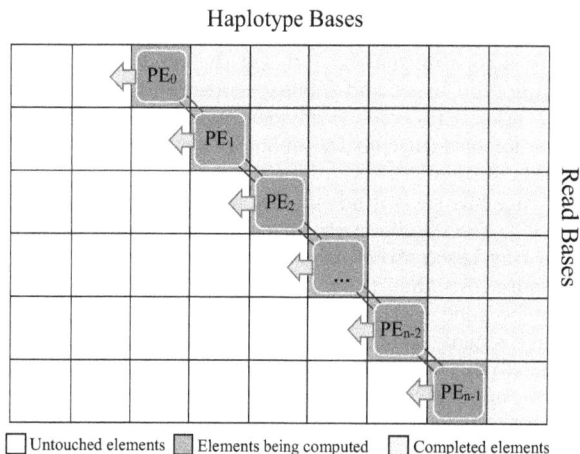

Figure 6: PE array processing the corresponding matrix elements

Let $v(PE_i)$ be the temporary calculation result produced by the i-th PE in the current clock cycle, and $v'(PE_i)$ be the result produced by the i-th PE at the last clock cycle, and $v''(PE_i)$ be the result produced by the i-th PE at the clock cycle before the last clock cycle. Then, based on the data dependency relationships among the matrix elements of the forward algorithm, we get the following formula.

$$v(PE_i) = f(v'(PE_i), v'(PE_{i-1}), v''(PE_{i-1})) \qquad (6)$$

where f is a function that summarizes the forward algorithm recursion (equation (2)). In our design, $v(PE_i)$, $v'(PE_i)$, and $v''(PE_i)$ are stored in three sets of registers. The value of $v'(PE_i)$ and $v''(PE_i)$ can be stored for computations through shift registers. Figure 4 shows the internal registers in the PEs and the data dependencies among those PEs.

Moreover, equation (6) is a general equation that can be used to describe many dependency patterns. Thus, a similar hardware structure can be used to accelerate other dynamic programming algorithms with dependencies that look like equation 6.

4.2 PE Ring

The PE array structure can be extended to a PE ring-based organization by connecting the first PE and the last PE with an internal buffer. The ring-based structure provides extra flexibility and scalability for the design. Figure 7 demonstrates how we use the PE ring structure to calculate the values of the forward algorithm matrix.

With the PE ring structure, the first n rows of the forward-algorithm matrix are calculated first, where n is the number of instantiated PEs (different from the input read length and the haplotype length). After the first PE reaches the last element in the first row, it can continue to process the $(n+1)^{th}$ row in the matrix. In the PE ring structure, the first PE, PE_0, and the last PE, PE_{n-1}, are connected to an internal data buffer. This internal buffer is used to store the temporary results produced by the last PE, PE_{n-1}, so that the first PE can use this data when it processes the new row in the matrix. This way, the design can handle computations for different sizes of the dynamic programming matrix irrespective of the number of PEs instantiated in the design.

In our PE ring implementation, only one of the PEs, the PE that computes the first element of the first row of the forward algorithm matrix, (labeled the "first PE") takes in the haplotype bases and quality scores, and the inputs to all the other PEs come from their neighboring PEs. This saves a lot of data transfer among a large number of PEs, and data storage.

PE ring has several advantages over the other organizations, e.g. the systolic array and the PE array. First of all, with a ring-based structure, we are able to process matrices with more rows than the number of instantiated PEs. This cannot be done with a PE array. The second advantage of PE ring is that there are at most two intermediate results produced per PE which are consumed within two cycles by itself or by neighboring PEs (equation 6). This reduces a lot of data transfer and data storage overhead in some other organizations, e.g. systolic arrays. In the case that a $m \times n$ 2-dimensional systolic array is used to compute the dynamic programming algorithm, after each step of calculation, n or m of intermediate data items are produced and need to be stored in the local on-chip buffer or external off-chip memory until the entire matrix computation is complete.

4.3 Optimizations

We adopt several techniques to further improve the hardware described in Sections 4.1 and 4.2.

4.3.1 Shorten critical paths in arithmetic operations

Figure 5 shows the arithmetic operations inside each PE. The naive implementation of Figure 5 has 24 cycles of latency (based on Altera's Stratix V floating-point IPs), which is a big drawback from the point of view of overall latency. If we analyze the critical path in Figure 5 carefully, we will find that the operands of the first adder and first 2 multipliers in the critical path ($f_{i-1,j-1}^I$, $f_{i-1,j-1}^D$, and $f_{i-1,j-1}^M$) have been ready 2 rounds earlier than the current round.

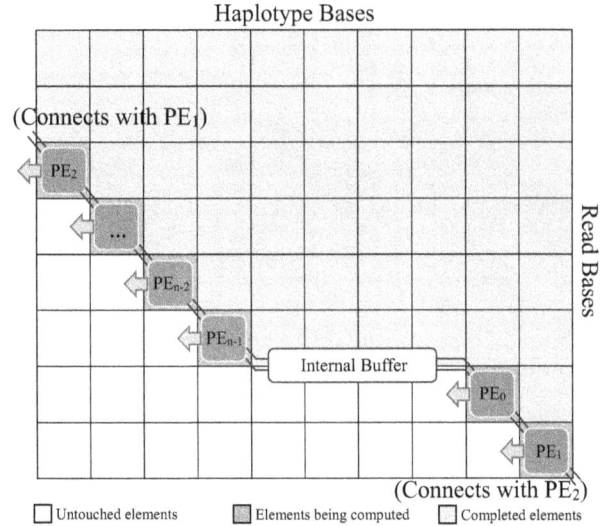

Figure 7: PE ring processing the corresponding matrix elements.

This means that we would be able to start the computation of the critical path earlier and re-distribute the operations among PEs. Based on this idea, we move the first adder and the first two multipliers to the previous PE, and start computation as soon as the operands are ready. After adopting this scheme, the arithmetic operations within each PE are shown in Figure 8. Intermediate computation results $t_{i,j}^a$ and $t_{i,j}^b$ are sent to the next PE in the PE ring. Note that, compared to Figure 5, the operands' indices of first adder and first two multipliers (f^M, f^I, and f^D) have changed, because they are used to compute t^a and t^b in advance.

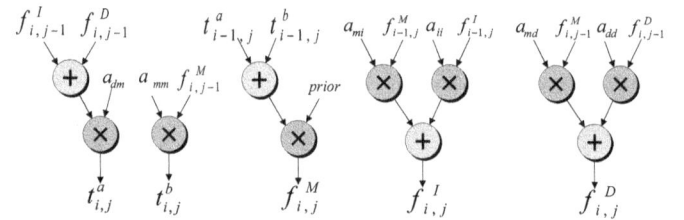

Figure 8: Optimized arithmetic operations inside PEs

With this optimization, the critical path of arithmetic operations is shortened to have only one adder and one multiplier with 12 cycles of latency (on Stratix V), while the overall number of adders and multipliers remains the same.

4.3.2 Pipelining and resource sharing

Note that all the adders and multipliers in the PEs are fully pipelined and the critical path has the latency of 12 cycles (on Stratix V). During this 12-cycle period, we could initiate the computation of other matrices corresponding to another read-haplotype pair. Since the computations of DP matrices are independent from each other, the PEs could compute 12 matrices at the same time.

Figure 9 shows an example of computing multiple matrices at the same time with full pipelining. In the different

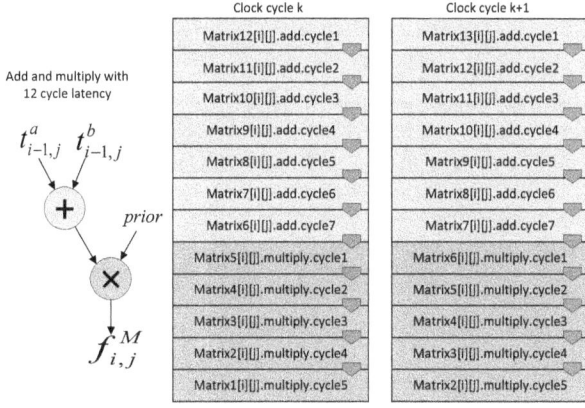

Figure 9: Example of pipelining inside i^{th} PE

pipeline stages of the arithmetic operators, operands from different matrices are used to do the computation.

4.3.3 Tuning PE ring size and number of PE rings

Another property that can be used to tune the design is the size of the PE rings, i.e., the number of PEs in a single PE ring. If the number of PEs in the PE ring is small, we can place a larger number of PE rings inside the FPGA chip.

Having smaller, but many PE rings could have some potential benefits. First of all, with multiple PE rings, multiple matrices can be processed at the same time. It is to be noted that this parallelism is different from that described in section 4.3.2. The parallelism utilized with multiple PE rings is more coarse-grained. Second, a smaller PE ring will potentially have lesser number of idle PEs during the first and the last few cycles of processing a matrix.

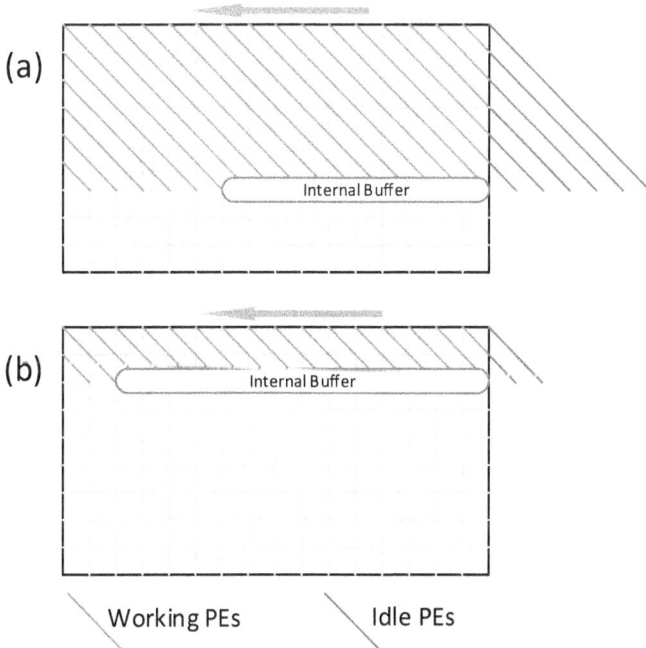

Figure 10: Idle PEs at the beginning of processing and depth of internal buffer when using (a) long PE ring; (b) shorter PE ring

Note that there are idle PEs for a small number of cycles at the beginning of matrix computations or at the last few rounds (when the number of remaining rows is smaller than the number of PEs in the ring). This also means that there are no idle PEs when processing the middle rows of the DP matrix since the PEs that finish the computation of a row will move to uncomputed rows below.

Figure 10 illustrates the idle PEs when the PE ring is processing the DP matrix during the first few cycles. The parallel diagonal lines represent the positions of PE ring at consecutive cycles. The PE ring starts from the top right corner, and moves to the left. Comparing (a) and (b) in Figure 10, we can see that if the PE ring is shorter, there will be less idle PEs during processing. Considering the fact that while using shorter PE rings, we can place more PE rings on the FPGA; we can also compare the idle $\#PE \times \#cycle$ product for the whole FPGA design. Figure 11 shows one intuitive way to do the comparison. In the figure, the area of triangles represents the idle $\#PE \times \#cycle$ product. Assuming that the maximum total number of PEs that can be placed into an FPGA chip is a constant, i.e. if $\#PE \times \#ring$ is a constant, then we can see that the idle $\#PE \times \#cycle$ product of a single longer PE ring is a single big triangle, while the sum of idle $\#PE \times \#cycle$ product of the shorter PE rings are several smaller triangles. Comparing the areas of two set of triangles, we could see that the configuration of shorter PE rings has less idle PEs in general.

We could also count the number of idle PEs directly. Let M be the total number of PEs that can be placed in the FPGA, i.e. the length of a PE ring when we try to deploy a single large PE ring on the FPGA. Let $M = kN$, where N is the length of smaller PE rings, and there are k PE rings. Then, for the single PE ring case, the number of idle PEs are

$$\sum_{i=1}^{M-1} i = \frac{1}{2}M(M-1). \quad (7)$$

For the smaller PE ring case, the number of idle PEs are

$$k\sum_{i=1}^{N-1} i = \frac{k}{2}N(N-1) = \frac{1}{2}M(N-1). \quad (8)$$

Thus a design with multiple smaller PE rings only has $\frac{N-1}{M-1}$ of the idle PEs of the design with a single long PE ring.

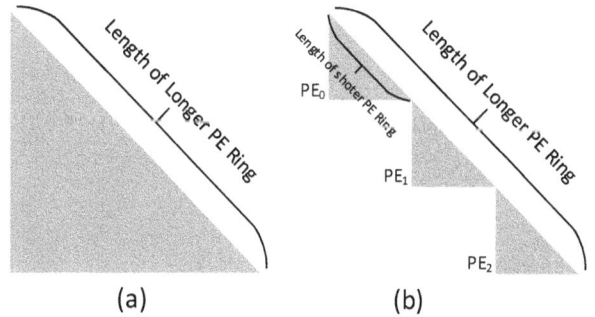

Figure 11: Comparing $\#idle\_PEs \times \#idle\_cycles$ when using (a) one single longer PE ring; (b) multiple shorter PE rings

Then, consider idle PEs while processing the last few rows of the DP matrix. Figure 12 illustrates this case. This case of idle PEs happens when the number of matrix's rows could not be divided exactly by the number of PEs. This is common because the number of matrix's rows, which is the read sequence's length could be an arbitrary positive integer. If we assume the distribution of read sequence's length is uniform, then any number of idle PEs could happen with the same probability, giving a mean value of half of the PE ring length. This means the number of idle PEs is proportional to the length of PE rings. If the total number of PEs is a constant, then the total numbers of idle PEs for different configurations are similar. Based on this analysis, using shorter PE rings would not reduce the number of idle PEs during the computation of the final rows of the DP matrix. Figure 12(b) shows only the processing steps of one of the n short PE rings.

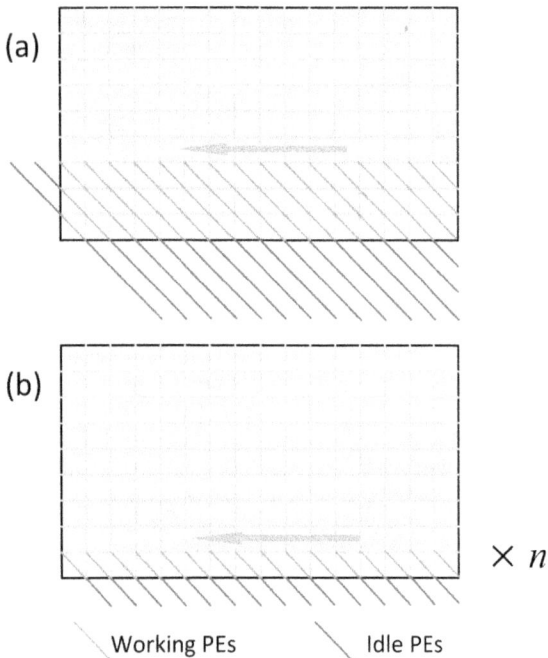

Figure 12: Idle PEs at the last stage of processing when using (a) one single long PE ring; (b) n short PE rings (showing only one of n PE rings in the figure)

Even though using shorter PE rings could reduce the number of idle PEs at the beginning of processing, using shorter PE rings could also have some disadvantages. While using a shorter PE ring, the internal buffer needs to be larger. This is because there will be more intermediate results produced before the next iteration on columns starts. That will significantly increases memory block utilization. This point is also illustrated in Figure 10. Besides, too many small PE rings will lead to potential memory port contention, because each PE ring will need to fetch data in every clock cycle.

4.3.4 Floating-point operator implementation

All the floating-point addition and multiplication operators are built with Altera's floating-point IPs. Those arithmetic IPs could be instantiated and mapped to either DSP blocks or logic elements in FPGA. Both two mappings give operators with the exact same functionality. However, the amount of available logic resource and DSP resource could be different on a target FPGA, thus the ratio of IPs mapped to logic elements and that mapped to the DSPs should be carefully tuned to achieve maximum resource utilization in the FPGA chip. In our implementation, we calculate the maximum number of operators that can be implemented using logic elements and with DSPs. Based on this calculation, we figure out the best ratio of number of IPs mapped to logic and of those mapped to DSP. In our final design for Stratix V FPGA, we utilize 83% of the logic elements and 75% of DSP blocks. Generally, when considering the mapping of IPs, given a fixed target frequency, the latency in terms of cycles could be less important than resource utilization. This is because when all the operators are fully pipelined, we may be able to almost completely hide the effects of latency by feeding in new data to occupy the different pipeline stages of the operators, as shown in Figure 9.

This type of tuning of the IP implementation becomes even more important if there are multiple mapping choices, multiple latency options and multiple frequency choices. In our case, there aren't many options, thus manual tuning works good enough. If the number of options grows, this could become an interesting design space exploration problem.

5. EXPERIMENTAL RESULTS

5.1 Test Data and Target FPGAs

The test data comes from a Whole Genome Sequence (WGS) dataset available at [24] that represents Pair-HMM inputs generated by HaplotypeCaller from GATK version 2.7. The benchmark consists of individual datasets each having different haplotype sizes and input read lengths. Each dataset contains testcases consisting of read and haplotype pairs of lengths varying from 10 to 302 bases.

To fully analyze the performance and resource utilization of our implementation, we synthesize our design targeting two FPGAs, Altera's Stratix V FPGA (5SGXEA7N2F45C2), which is the FPGA on Terasic's DE5-Net experiment board, and the new Arria 10 FPGA (10AX115H1F34E1SG). Altera's Stratix V is built with 28nm process technology, and it is one of Altera's high-end FPGAs. Altera's new Arria 10 FPGA uses 20nm process technology, and it has more logic and DSP resources. Besides, the Arria 10 FPGA has hard floating-point elements, which makes floating-point computations more efficient. We collect the performance data of our design by running simulations of our design.

5.2 Performance

5.2.1 Compared with Other Implementations

We compare our performance data with that of other representative implementations [19], including CPU, GPU, multi-cores, and FPGAs. The comparison shows that our implementation is faster than other reported implementations.

Table 3 compares the performance of our implementation versus a few others. The performance data for CPU and GPU platforms are reported in [19]. The dataset used is the "10s" dataset available along with the original Java implementation in GATK. We present our results with this

Table 3: Performance comparison across various implementations

Platform	Runtime(ms)	Speedup
Java on CPU	10800	1×
C++ Baseline	1267	9×
Intel Xeon AVX Single Core	138	78×
NVidia K40 GPU	70	154×
Intel Xeon 24 Cores	15	720×
Altera OpenCL (Stratix V)	8.3	1301×
PE Ring (Stratix V)	**5.3**	**2038×**
Altera OpenCL (Arria 10)	2.8	3857×
PE Ring (Arria 10)	**2.6**	**4154×**

dataset because this allows us to compare to other implementations. We also run the experiments using larger datasets, and significant speedup is also achieved for larger datasets. The execution time on other datasets is listed in Figure 13.

Our performance data in the table is based on 8 PEs/ring × 8 rings configuration on the Stratix V FPGA, and 8 PEs/ring × 16 rings configuration on the Arria 10 FPGA. Our performance numbers are based on the overall FPGA frequency of 200MHz. Our FPGA synthesis targets have the same number of logic elements and DSP blocks as that of Altera's OpenCL implementation [23].

Prior to our work, the state-of-the-art implementation has been Altera's OpenCL implementation of the Pair-HMM on FPGA. These performance results come from Altera's whitepaper [23]. As shown in the table, on Stratix V, our PE ring design could achieve 1.56× further speedup compared with Altera's implementation. On Arria 10, our design is 7.7% faster than Altera's implementation. The speedup from our Arria 10 implementation is smaller because our implementation contains 128 PEs while Altera's implementation has 208 PEs. In comparison to other platforms, our proposed PE ring design for Arria 10 could achieve 5.77× speedup over Intel Xeon 24 core AVX implementation, 26.92× speedup over K40 GPU implementation, and more than 4000× speedup over the original Java implementation.

5.2.2 Impact of PE Ring size

Based on our synthesis results, Altera Stratix V FPGA can accommodate a single PE ring consisting of 64 PEs or multiple rings of shorter lengths. For example, 8 PE rings each consisting of 8 PEs can be put into the Stratix V FPGA. We synthesize designs with various lengths and numbers of PE rings, and run simulations to get performance data.

Figure 13 shows the normalized execution time on three datasets when the PE ring sizes are varied keeping the total number of PEs constant. The figure legend "$m \times n$" stands for the configuration of m PEs/ring × n rings. As discussed in section 4.3.3, using multiple smaller PE rings could reduce the total number of idle PEs during the processing. Figure 13 supports this observation.

Note that we do not further reduce the size of the PE rings below 8 PEs/ring. There are two reasons. First of all, too many small PE rings will lead to potential memory port contention, because each PE ring needs to read input data every clock cycle. Second, multiple smaller PE rings require more and larger internal buffers, which significantly increases memory block utilization.

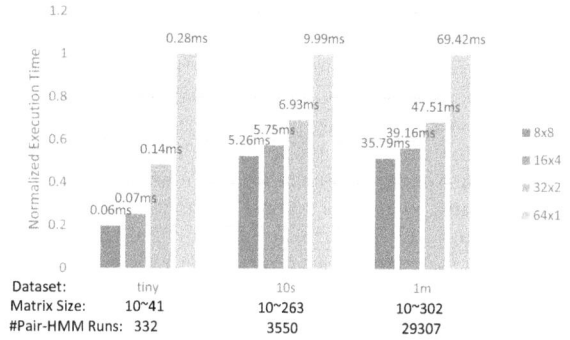

Figure 13: Normalized execution time on three datasets when using different sizes of PE rings (Stratix V). "$m \times n$" stands for the configuration of m PEs/ring × n rings.

5.2.3 Implementation on Stratix V and Arria 10

To explore performance trends with more PEs and hard floating-point IP blocks, we synthesize our design targeting Altera's Arria 10 FPGA as well. Arria 10 FPGA has hard floating-point elements that shorten the latency of floating operations. On Arria 10, the latencies of single precision floating-point addition and multiplication are both only 3 cycles when using hard floating-point elements. Besides, the amount of logic resources available on the Arria 10 FPGA is more than what is available on Stratix V. The Arria 10 synthesis target has 427,200 Adaptive Logic Modules (ALM), while the Stratix V target has 234,720 ALMs. Also, Arria 10 has 1,518 DSP blocks, while Stratix V has 256 DSP blocks. Arria 10 FPGA is able to accommodate 128 PEs, and the total latency of arithmetic operations in each PE is only 6 cycles, while the Stratix V FPGA can accommodate 64 PEs, and the total latency of arithmetic operations in each PE is 12 cycles.

Table 4: Synthesis Results for both target FPGAs

FPGA	#PEs	Fmax	Logic	DSP
Stratix V	64	200.16 MHz	83%	75%
Arria 10	128	230.73 MHz	4%	93%

Table 4 shows the maximum number of PEs, maximum frequency, and resource utilization for the two implementations. We observed that our design on Arria 10 is able to achieve a higher frequency. However, the implementation on Arria 10 utilizes almost all the DSP resources while utilizing a very small percentage of logic elements. This is because the synthesis tool (Altera Quartus Prime) maps all the floating-point IPs for Arria 10 to DSP blocks. If those floating-point operators could be mapped to the logic elements, the Arria 10 FPGA will be able to fit in much more PEs, and thus gain further speedup. In the Stratix V case, the resource utilization is more balanced, as a fraction of the operations are also mapped to the logic elements.

6. CONCLUSION

Pair-HMM forward algorithm computation is a major bottleneck in several DNA sequence analysis flows. Essentially, the Pair-HMM's forward algorithm is a complicated floating-point number based dynamic programming algorithm with a high computational complexity. The forward algorithm involves the computation of three matrices while respecting data dependencies among the matrix elements, and it involves a series of floating-point add and multiply operations. In this work, we propose an efficient and flexible ring-based hardware implementation of the Pair-HMM forward algorithm, as well as several optimization techniques to further boost the performance of the PE ring structure. Our ring-based design achieves a significant speed-up of up to 487× compared to the C++ baseline implementation on CPU, and up to 1.56× further speedup compared to the published best hardware implementation. In our design, the ring structure exhibits its unique advantages of flexibility allowing trade-offs between coarse and fine-grained parallelism, and reduced data transfers between the hardware kernel and memory components. We also analyze at depth, the details of how dynamic programming calculations implemented on hardware could benefit from varying PE ring size. The proposed design could be configured as multiple shorter PE rings, which has less idle PEs during computation. This configuration could be adjusted accordingly based on the resources available on the specific FPGA.

Acknowledgment

This work is partially supported by IBM Faculty Award and C-FAR, one of the six centers of STARnet, a Semiconductor Research Corporation program sponsored by MARCO and DARPA.

7. REFERENCES

[1] Temple F Smith and Michael S Waterman. Identification of common molecular subsequences. *Journal of molecular biology*, 147(1):195–197, 1981.

[2] Saul B Needleman and Christian D Wunsch. A general method applicable to the search for similarities in the amino acid sequence of two proteins. *Journal of molecular biology*, 48(3):443–453, 1970.

[3] Stephen F Altschul, Warren Gish, Webb Miller, Eugene W Myers, and David J Lipman. Basic local alignment search tool. *Journal of molecular biology*, 215(3):403–410, 1990.

[4] Heng Li, Jue Ruan, and Richard Durbin. Mapping short dna sequencing reads and calling variants using mapping quality scores. *Genome research*, 18(11):1851–1858, 2008.

[5] Yun Heo, Xiao-Long Wu, Deming Chen, Jian Ma, and Wen-Mei Hwu. Bless: bloom filter-based error correction solution for high-throughput sequencing reads. *Bioinformatics*, page btu030, 2014.

[6] Wei-Chun Kao, Andrew H Chan, and Yun S Song. Echo: a reference-free short-read error correction algorithm. *Genome research*, 21(7):1181–1192, 2011.

[7] Lucian Ilie, Farideh Fazayeli, and Silvana Ilie. Hitec: accurate error correction in high-throughput sequencing data. *Bioinformatics*, 27(3):295–302, 2011.

[8] Qingguo Wang, Peilin Jia, Fei Li, Haiquan Chen, Hongbin Ji, Donald Hucks, Kimberly Brown Dahlman, William Pao, and Zhongming Zhao. Detecting somatic point mutations in cancer genome sequencing data: a comparison of mutation callers. *Genome medicine*, 5(10):1, 2013.

[9] Michael C Schatz, Cole Trapnell, Arthur L Delcher, and Amitabh Varshney. High-throughput sequence alignment using graphics processing units. *BMC bioinformatics*, 8(1):474, 2007.

[10] Chi-Man Liu, Thomas Wong, Edward Wu, Ruibang Luo, Siu-Ming Yiu, Yingrui Li, Bingqiang Wang, Chang Yu, Xiaowen Chu, Kaiyong Zhao, et al. Soap3: ultra-fast gpu-based parallel alignment tool for short reads. *Bioinformatics*, 28(6):878–879, 2012.

[11] Isaac TS Li, Warren Shum, and Kevin Truong. 160-fold acceleration of the smith-waterman algorithm using a field programmable gate array (fpga). *BMC bioinformatics*, 8(1):1, 2007.

[12] Anand Ramachandran, Yun Heo, Wen-mei Hwu, Jian Ma, and Deming Chen. Fpga accelerated dna error correction. In *Proceedings of the 2015 Design, Automation & Test in Europe Conference & Exhibition*, pages 1371–1376. EDA Consortium, 2015.

[13] Broad Institute. Haplotypecaller overview. https://www.broadinstitute.org/gatk/guide/article?id=4148.

[14] Aaron McKenna, Matthew Hanna, Eric Banks, Andrey Sivachenko, Kristian Cibulskis, Andrew Kernytsky, Kiran Garimella, David Altshuler, Stacey Gabriel, Mark Daly, et al. The genome analysis toolkit: a mapreduce framework for analyzing next-generation dna sequencing data. *Genome research*, 20(9):1297–1303, 2010.

[15] Richard Durbin, Sean R Eddy, Anders Krogh, and Graeme Mitchison. *Biological sequence analysis: probabilistic models of proteins and nucleic acids*. Cambridge university press, 1998.

[16] Byung-Jun Yoon. Hidden markov models and their applications in biological sequence analysis. *Current genomics*, 10(6):402–415, 2009.

[17] Chuong B Do, Mahathi SP Mahabhashyam, Michael Brudno, and Serafim Batzoglou. Probcons: Probabilistic consistency-based multiple sequence alignment. *Genome research*, 15(2):330–340, 2005.

[18] William H Majoros, Mihaela Pertea, and Steven L Salzberg. Efficient implementation of a generalized pair hidden markov model for comparative gene finding. *Bioinformatics*, 21(9):1782–1788, 2005.

[19] Broad Institute. Accelerating variant calling, 2013.

[20] Sean O Settle. High-performance dynamic programming on fpgas with opencl. In *Proc. IEEE High Perform. Extreme Comput. Conf.(HPEC)*, pages 1–6, 2013.

[21] Zilong Wang, Sitao Huang, Lanjun Wang, Hao Li, Yu Wang, and Huazhong Yang. Accelerating subsequence similarity search based on dynamic time warping distance with fpga. In *Proceedings of the ACM/SIGDA international symposium on Field programmable gate arrays*, pages 53–62. ACM, 2013.

[22] Advait Madhavan, Timothy Sherwood, and Dmitri Strukov. Race logic: A hardware acceleration for dynamic programming algorithms. In *ACM/IEEE 41st International Symposium on Computer Architecture (ISCA)*, pages 517–528. IEEE, 2014.

[23] Altera. Accelerating genomics research with opencl and fpgas, 2016.

[24] Pair-hmm test data. https://github.com/MauricioCarneiro/PairHMM/tree/master/test_data.

Poster Session 1

Measuring the Power-Constrained Performance and Energy Gap between FPGAs and Processors

Andy Gean Ye, *Ryerson University*
Karthik Ganesan, *University of Toronto*
Contact: aye@ee.ryerson.ca

This work measures the performance and power consumption gap between the current generation of low power FPGAs and low power microprocessors (microcontrollers) through an implementation of the Canny edge detection algorithm. In particular, the algorithm is implemented on Altera MAX 10 FPGAs and its performance and power consumption are then compared to the same algorithm implemented on the STMicroelectronics' implementation of the ARM M-series microcontrollers. We found an extremely high, four- to five-orders of magnitude, performance advantage of the FPGAs over the microcontrollers, which is much greater than any previously reported values in FPGAs vs. processors studies. Furthermore, this speedup only comes at a cost of 1.2x to 15x higher power consumption, which gives FPGAs a significant advantage in energy efficiency. We also observe, however, the current generation of low power FPGAs have significantly higher static power consumption than the microcontrollers. In particular, the low power FPGAs consume more static power than the total power consumption of the lowest power consuming microcontrollers, rendering the FPGAs inoperable under the power budgets of these processors. Furthermore, this high static power consumption exists despite the fact that the FPGAs are implemented on a low leakage 55nm process with dual supply voltages while the microcontrollers are implemented on a conventional, single supply voltage, 90nm process. Consequently, our results indicate that it is particular important for future research to address the static power consumption of low power FPGAs while maintaining logic capacity so the performance and energy efficiency advantages of the FPGAs can be fully utilized in the extremely low power application domain that are driven by batteries with very small form factors and emerging small scale energy harvesting technologies.

Keywords: Field Programmable Gate Arrays (FPGAs); Low-Power FPGAs; FPGA vs. Microcontroller; Performance; Energy Efficiency

DOI: http://dx.doi.org/10.1145/3020078.3021756

A Mixed-Signal Data-Centric Reconfigurable Architecture enabled by RRAM Technology

Yue Zha, *University of Wisconsin-Madison*
Jialiang Zhang, *University of Wisconsin-Madison*
Zhiqiang Wei, *Panasonic*
Jing Li, *University of Wisconsin-Madison*
Contact: jli@ece.wisc.edu

This poster presents a data-centric reconfigurable architecture, which is enabled by emerging non-volatile memory, i.e., RRAM. Compared to the *heterogeneous* architecture of commercial FPGAs, it is inherently a *homogeneous* architecture comprising of a two-dimensional (2D) array of mixed-signal processing "tiles". Each tile can be configured into one or a combination of the four modes: logic, memory, TCAM, and interconnect. Computation within a tile is performed in analog domain for energy efficiency, whereas communication between tiles is performed in digital domain for resilience. Such flexibility allows users to partition resources based on applications' needs, in contrast to fixed hardware design using dedicated hard IP blocks in FPGAs. In addition to better resource usage, its "memory friendly" architecture effectively addressed the limitations of commercial FPGAs i.e., scarce on-chip memory resources, making it an effective complement to FPGAs. Moreover, its coarse-grained configuration results in shallower logic depth, less inter-tile routing overhead, and thus smaller area and better performance, compared with its FPGA counter-part. Our preliminary study shows great promise of this architecture for improving performance, energy efficiency and security.

Keywords: Reconfigurable architecture; Non-volatile memory; Ternary content addressable memory; mixed-signal processing; coarse-grained configuration

DOI: http://dx.doi.org/10.1145/3020078.3021759

A Framework for Iterative Stencil Algorithm Synthesis on FPGAs from OpenCL Programming Model

Shuo Wang, Peking University
Yun Liang, Peking University
Contact: ericlyun@pku.edu.cn

Iterative stencil algorithms find applications in a wide range of domains. FPGAs have long been adopted for computation acceleration due to its advantages of dedicated hardware design. Hence, FPGAs are a compelling alternative for executing iterative stencil algorithms. However, efficient implementation of iterative stencil algorithms on FPGAs is very challenging due to the data dependencies between iterations and elements in the stencil algorithms, programming hurdle of FPGAs, and large design space. In this paper, we present a comprehensive framework that synthesizes iterative stencil algorithms on FPGAs efficiently. We leverage the OpenCL-to-FPGA tool chain to generate accelerator automatically and perform design space exploration at high level. We propose to bridge the neighboring tiles through pipe and enable data sharing among them to improve computation efficiency. We first propose a homogeneous design with equal tile size. Then, we extend to a heterogeneous design with different tile size to balance the computation among different tiles. Our designs exhibit a large design space in terms of tile structure. We also develop analytical performance models to explore the complex design space. Experiments using a wide range of stencil applications demonstrate that on average our homogeneous and heterogeneous implementations achieve 1.49X and 1.65X performance speedup respectively but with less hardware resource compared to the state-of-the-art.

Keywords: Stencil; FPGA; OpenCL

DOI: http://dx.doi.org/10.1145/3020078.3021761

Scala Based FPGA Design Flow

Yanqiang Liu, *Shanghai Jiao Tong University*
Yao Li, *Shanghai Jiao Tong University*
Weilun Xiong, *Shanghai Jiao Tong University*
Meng Lai, *Shanghai Jiao Tong University*
Cheng Chen, *Morgan Stanley*
Zhengwei Qi, *Shanghai Jiao Tong University*
Haibing Guan, *Shanghai Jiao Tong University*
Contact: qizhwei@sjtu.edu.cn

With the rapid growth of data scale, data analysis applications start to meet the performance bottleneck, and thus requiring the aid of hardware acceleration. At the same time, Field Programmable Gate Arrays (FPGAs), known for their high customizability and parallel nature, have gained momentum in the past decade. However, the efficiency of development for acceleration system based on FPGAs is severely constrained by the traditional languages and tools, due to their deficiency in expressibility, extendibility, limited libraries and semantic gap between software and hardware design. This paper proposes a new open-source DSL based hardware design framework called VeriScala that supports highly abstracted object-oriented hardware defining, program-matical testing, and interactive on-chip debugging. By adopting DSL embedded in Scala, we introduce modern software developing concepts into hardware designing including object-oriented programming, parameterized types, type safety, test automation, etc. VeriScala enables designers to describe their hardware designs in Scala, generate Verilog code automatically and interactively debug and test hardware design in real FPGA environment. Through the evaluation on real world applications and usability test, we show that VeriScala provides a practical approach for rapid prototyping of hardware acceleration systems. (This work is supported by the National Key Research & Development Program of China 2016YFB1000500)

Keywords: FPGA; DSL; VeriScala

DOI: http://dx.doi.org/10.1145/3020078.3021762

Thermal Flattening in 3D FPGAs Using Embedded Cooling

Girish Deshpande, *University of Texas at Dallas*
Dinesh Bhatia, *University of Texas at Dallas*
Contact : girish.deshpande@utdallas.edu

Thermal management is one of the key concerns in modern high power density chips. A variety of thermal cooling techniques that have been in use in industrial applications are now also being applied to integrated circuits. In this work, we explore the integration of thermal aware CAD techniques with embedded cooling solutions to achieve smoother thermal profiles in 3D FPGAs. We also present some results on coolant temperatures and flow rates and their effect on thermal gradients on the chip.

Keywords: FPGA; Microchannels; Embedded cooling

DOI: http://dx.doi.org/10.1145/3020078.3021764

A Machine Learning Framework for FPGA Placement

Gary Grewal, *University of Guelph*
Shawki Areibi, *University of Guelph*
Matthew Westrik, *University of Guelph*
Ziad Abuowaimer, *University of Guelph*
Betty Zhao, *University of Guelph*
Contact: ggrewal@uoguelph.ca

Many of the key stages in the traditional FPGA CAD flow require substantial amounts of computational effort. Moreover, due to limited overlap among individual stages, poor decisions made in earlier stages will often adversely affect the quality of result in later stages. To help address these issues, we propose a machine-learning framework that uses training data to learn the underlying relationship between circuits and the CAD algorithms used to map them onto a particular FPGA device. The framework does not solve the problem at an arbitrary stage in the flow. Rather, it seeks to assist the designer or the tool to solve the problem. The potential capabilities of the framework are demonstrated by applying it to the *placement* stage, where it is used to recommend the best placement flow for circuits with different features, and to predict placement and routing results without actually performing placement and routing. Results show that when trained using 372 challenging benchmarks for a Xilinx UltraScale device, the classification models employed in the framework achieve average accuracies in the range 92% to 95%, while the regression models have an average error rate in the range of 0.5% to 3.6%.

Keywords: Machine Learning; Optimization; FPGA Placement; Heterogeneous UltraScale devices

DOI: http://dx.doi.org/10.1145/3020078.3021765

Precise Coincidence Detection on FPGAs: Three Case Studies

Ralf Salomon, *University of Rostock*
Ralf Joost, *University of Rostock*
Contact: ralf.joost@uni-rostock.de

In high-performance applications, such as quantum physics and positron emission tomography, precise coincidence detection is of central importance: The quality of the reconstructed images depends on the accuracy with which the underlying system detects the coincidence of two events. This paper explores the utility of three different hardware modules for this very task. In contrast to most of the state-of-the-art systems, these modules are edge triggered rather than being voltage-level based. This change in the modus operandi increases the accuracy of the resulting coincidence window by about one order of magnitude. In addition, this paper considers the entire detector arrays, which host a large number of selected detectors. Due to additional signal propagation delays, these arrays yield a coincidence window width as short as 70 ps within an effective range of up to 10 ns.

Keywords: Coincidence Detector; Edge-Triggered; Detector Array; High Precision; FPGAs

DOI: http://dx.doi.org/10.1145/3020078.3021766

Towards Efficient Design Space Exploration of FPGA-based Accelerators for Streaming HPC Applications

Mostafa Koraei, *University of Tehran*
Magnus Jahre, *NTNU Trondheim*
S.Omid Fatemi, *University of Tehran*
Contact: m.koraei@ut.ac.ir

Streaming HPC applications are data intensive and have widespread use in various fields (e.g., Computational Fluid Dynamics and Bioinformatics). These applications consist of different processing kernels where each kernel performs a specific computation on its input data. The objective of the optimization process is to maximize performance. FPGAs show great promise for accelerating streaming applications because of their low power consumption combined with high theoretical compute capabilities. However, mapping an HPC application to a reconfigurable fabric is a challenging task. The challenge is exacerbated by need to temporally partition computational kernels when application requirements exceed resource availability. In this poster, we present work towards a novel design methodology for exploring design space of streaming HPC applications on FPGAs. We assume that the designer can represent the target application with a Synchronous Data Flow Graph (SDFG). In the SDFG, the nodes are compute kernels and the edges signify data flow between kernels. The designer should also determine the problem size of the application and the volume of raw

data on each memory source of the SDFG. The output of our method is a set of FPGA configurations that each contains one or more SDFG nodes. The methodology consists of three main steps. In Step 1, we enumerate the valid partitions and the base configurations. In Step 2, we find the feasible base configurations given the hardware resources available and a library of processing kernel implementations. Finally, we use a performance model to calculate the execution time of each partition in Step 3. Our current assumption is that it is advantageous to represent SDFG at a coarse granularity since this enables exhaustive exploration of the design space for practical applications. This approach has yielded promising preliminary results. In one case, the temporal configuration selected by our methodology outperformed the direct mapping by 3X.

Keywords: Reconfigurable Computing, FPGA, HPC, SDFG, Acceleration, Application mapping

DOI: http://dx.doi.org/10.1145/3020078.3021767

Accurate and Efficient Hyperbolic Tangent Activation Function on FPGA using the DCT Interpolation Filter

Ahmed M. Abdelsalam, *Polytechnique Montreal*
J. M. Pierre Langlois, *Polytechnique Montreal*
Farida Cheriet, *Polytechnique Montreal*
Contact: ahmed.abdelsalam@polymtl.ca

Implementing an accurate and fast activation function with low cost is a crucial aspect to the implementation of Deep Neural Networks (DNNs) on FPGAs. We propose a high accuracy approximation approach for the hyperbolic tangent activation function of artificial neurons in DNNs. It is based on the Discrete Cosine Transform Interpolation Filter (DCTIF). The proposed interpolation architecture combines simple arithmetic operations on the stored samples of the hyperbolic tangent function and on input data. The proposed implementation outperforms the existing implementations in terms of accuracy while using the same or fewer computational and memory resources. The proposed architecture can approximate the hyperbolic tangent activation function with 2×10^{-4} maximum error while requiring only 1.12 Kbits memory and 21 LUTs of a Virtex-7 FPGA.

Keywords: Deep Neural Network (DNN); Embedded FPGA; Deep learning; Activation function; Hyperbolic tangent.

DOI: http://dx.doi.org/10.1145/3020078.3021768

An FPGA Overlay Architecture for Cost Effective Regular Expression Search

Thomas Luinaud, *Polytechnique Montréal*
Yvon Savaria, *Polytechnique Montréal*
J.M. Pierre Langlois, *Polytechnique Montréal*
Contact: thomas.luinaud@polymtl.ca

Snort and Bro are Deep Packet Inspection systems which express complex rules with regular expressions. Before performing a regular expression search, these applications apply a filter to select which regular expressions must be searched. One way to search a regular expression is through a Nondeterministic Finite Automaton (NFA). Traversing an NFA is very time consuming on a sequential machine like a CPU. One solution so is to implement the NFA into hardware. Since FPGAs are reconfigurable and are massively parallel they are a good solution. Moreover, with the advent of platforms combining FPGAs and CPUs, implementing accelerators into FPGA becomes very interesting. Even though FPGAs are reconfigurable, the reconfiguration time can be too long in some cases. This paper thus proposes an overlay architecture that can efficiently find matches for regular expressions. The architecture contains multiple contexts that allow fast reconfiguration. Based on the results of a string filter, a context is selected and regular expression search is performed. The proposed design can support all rules from a set such as Snort while significantly reducing compute resources and allowing fast context updates. An example architecture was implemented on a Xilinx® xc7a200 Artix-7. It achieves a throughput of 100 million characters per second, requires 20 ns for a context switch, and occupies 9% of the slices and 85% of the BRAM resources of the FPGA.

Keywords: overlay; FPGA; NFA; regular expression; SoC

DOI: http://dx.doi.org/10.1145/3020078.3021770

FPGA'17, February 22–24, 2017, Monterey, CA, USA.
ACM ISBN 978-1-4503-4354-1/17/02.

Poster Session 2

Using Vivado-HLS for Structural Design: A NoC Case Study

Zhipeng Zhao, *Carnegie Mellon University*
James C. Hoe, *Carnegie Mellon University*
Contact: zzhao1@andrew.cmu.edu

There have been ample successful examples of applying Xilinx Vivado's "function-to-module" high-level synthesis (HLS) where the subject is algorithmic in nature. In this work, we carried out a design study to assess the effectiveness of applying Vivado-HLS in structural design. We employed Vivado-HLS to synthesize C functions corresponding to standalone network-on-chip (NoC) routers as well as complete multi-endpoint NoCs. Interestingly, we find that describing a complete NoC comprising router submodules faces fundamental difficulties not present in describing the routers as standalone modules. Ultimately, we succeeded in using Vivado-HLS to produce router and NoC modules that are exact cycle- and bit-accurate replacements of our reference RTL-based router and NoC modules. Furthermore, the routers and NoCs resulting from HLS and RTL are comparable in resource utilization and critical path delay. Our experience subjectively suggests that HLS is able to simplify the design effort even though much of the structural details had to be provided in the HLS description through a combination of coding discipline and explicit pragmas. The C++ source code and a more extensive description of this work can be found at http://www.ece.cmu.edu/calcm/connect_hls.

Keywords: C; High-Level Synthesis; Structural Design; Network-on-Chip

DOI: http://dx.doi.org/10.1145/3020078.3021772

Automatic Generation of Hardware Sandboxes for Trojan Mitigation in Systems on Chip

Christophe Bobda, *University of Arkansas*
Taylor Whitaker, University of Arkansas
Charles Kamhoua, Air Force Research Lab
Kevin Kwiat, Air Force Research Lab
Laurent Njilla, Air Force Research Lab
Contact: cbobda@acm.org

Component based design is one of the preferred methods to tackle system complexity, and reduce costs and time-to-market. Major parts of the system design and IC production are outsourced to facilities distributed across the globe, thus opening the door for malicious Trojan insertion. Hardware Sandboxing was introduce as a means to overcome the shortcomings of traditional static Trojan mitigation methods, which use intense simulation, verification, and physical tests to detect the evidence of malicious components before system deployment. The number of test patterns needed to activate with certainty potential hidden Trojans is very large for complex IPs and SoCs with dozens of inputs, outputs, states, and memory blocks, thus limiting the effectiveness of static testing methods. The rationale is to spend less effort testing pre-deployment. Instead, guards should be built around non-trusted components to catch malicious activities and prevent potential damage. While feasibility of hardware sandboxes has been proven with case studies and real-world applications, manual design was used and no systematic method was devised to automate the design process of system-on-chips that incorporate hardware sandboxes to provide high-level of security in embedded systems. In this work, we propose a method for automatic generation of hardware sandboxes in system-on-chips. Using the interface formalism of De Alfaro and Hetzinger to capture the interactions among components, along with the properties specification language to define non-authorized actions, sandboxes are generated and made ready for inclusion in a system-on-chip design. We leverage the concepts of composition, compatibility, and refinement to optimize resources across the boundary of single component and provide minimal resource consumption. With results on benchmarks implemented in FPGA, we prove that our approach can provide high-level of security, with less resource and no increase in delay.

Keywords: Hardware Sandboxes, Hardware Trojan, SoC Security, FPGA, Automatic Generation

DOI: http://dx.doi.org/10.1145/3020078.3021774

Accelerating Financial Market Server through Hybrid List Design

Haohuan Fu, *Tsinghua University*
Conghui He, *Tsinghua University*
Huabin Ruan, *Tsinghua University*
Itay Greenspon, *Maxeler Technologies*
Wayne Luk, *Imperial College London*
Yongkang Zheng, *China Financial Futures Exchange*
Junfeng Liao, *Tsinghua University*
Qing Zhang, *China Financial Futures Exchange*
Guangwen Yang, *Tsinghua University*
Contact: haohuan@tsinghua.edu.cn

The financial market server in exchanges aims to maintain the order books and provide real time market data feeds to traders. Low-latency processing is in a great demand in financial trading. Although software solutions provide the flexibility to express algorithms in high-level programming models and to recompile quickly, it is becoming increasingly uncompetitive due to the long and unpredictable response time. Nowadays, Field Programmable Gate Arrays (FPGAs) have been proved to be an established technology for achieving a low and constant latency for processing streaming packets in a hardware accelerated way. However, maintaining order books on FPGAs involves organizing packets into GBs of structural data information as well as complicated routines (sort, insertion, deletion, etc.), which is extremely challenging to FPGA designs in both design methodology and memory volume.

Thus existing FPGA designs often leave the post-processing part to the CPUs. However, it largely cancels the latency gain of the network packet processing part. This paper proposes a CPU-FPGA hybrid list design to accelerate financial market servers that achieve microsecond-level latencies. This paper mainly includes four contributions. First, we design a CPU-FPGA hybrid list with two levels, a small cache list on the FPGA and a large master list at the CPU host. Both lists are sorted with different sorting schemes, where the bitonic sort is applied to the cache list while a balanced tree is used to maintain the master list. Second, in order to effectively update the hybrid sorted list, we derive a complete set of low-latency routines, including insertion, deletion, selection, sorting, etc., providing a low latency at the scale of a few cycles. Third, we propose a non-blocking on-demand synchronization strategy for the cache list and the master list to communicate with each other. Lastly, we integrate the hybrid list as well as other components, such as packets splitting, parsing, processing, etc. to form an industry-level financial market server. Our design is applied in the environment of the China Financial Futures Exchange (CFFEX), demonstrating its functionality and stability by running 600+ hours with hundreds of millions packets per day. Compared with the existing CPU-based solution in CFFEX, our system is able to support identical functionalities while significantly reducing the latency from 100+ microseconds to 2 microseconds, gaining a speedup of 50x.

Keywords: FPGA; low latency; database; market server; finance

DOI: http://dx.doi.org/10.1145/3020078.3021775

Joint Modulo Scheduling and Memory Partitioning with Multi-Bank Memory for High-Level Synthesis

Tianyi Lu, *Tsinghua University*
Shouyi Yin, *Tsinghua University*
Xianqing Yao, *Tsinghua University*
Zhicong Xie, *Tsinghua University*
Leibo Liu, *Tsinghua University*
Shaojun Wei, *Tsinghua University*
Contact: luty15@mails.tsinghua.edu.cn

High-Level Synthesis (HLS) has been widely recognized and accepted as an efficient compilation process targeting FPGAs for algorithm evaluation and product prototyping. However, the massively parallel memory access demands and the extremely expensive cost of single-bank memory with multi-port have impeded loop pipelining performance. Thus, based on an alternative multi-bank memory architecture, a joint approach that employs memory-aware force directed scheduling and multi-cycle memory partitioning is formally proposed to achieve legitimate pipelining kernel and valid bank mapping with less resource consumption and optimal pipelining performance. The experimental results over a variety of benchmarks show that our approach can achieve the optimal pipelining performance and meanwhile reduce the number

of multiple independent memory banks by 55.1% on average, compared with the state-of-the-art approaches.

Keywords: Modulo Scheduling; Memory Partitioning; Multi-bank; HLS

DOI: http://dx.doi.org/10.1145/3020078.3021778

A Batch Normalization Free Binarized Convolutional Deep Neural Network on an FPGA

Hiroki Nakahara, *Tokyo Institute of Technology*
Haruyoshi Yonekawa, *Tokyo Institute of Technolgy*
Hisashi Iwamoto, *Poco a poco networks*
Masato Motomura, *Hokkaido University*
Contact: nakahara.h.ad@m.titech.ac.jp

A pre-trained convolutional deep neural network (CNN) is a feed-forward computation perspective, which is widely used for the embedded systems, requires high power-and-area efficiency. This paper realizes a binarized CNN which treats only binary 2-values (+1/-1) for the inputs and the weights. In this case, the multiplier is replaced into an XNOR circuit instead of a dedicated DSP block. For hardware implementation, using binarized inputs and weights is more suitable. However, the binarized CNN requires the batch normalization techniques to retain the classification accuracy. In that case, the additional multiplication and addition require extra hardware, also, the memory access for its parameters reduces system performance. In this paper, we propose the batch normalization free CNN which is mathematically equivalent to the CNN using batch normalization. The proposed CNN treats the binarized inputs and weights with the integer bias. We implemented the VGG-16 benchmark CNN on the NetFPGA-SUME FPGA board, which has the Xilinx Inc. Virtex7 FPGA and three off-chip QDR II+ Synchronous SRAMs. Compared with the conventional FPGA realizations, although the classification error rate is 6.5% decayed, the performance is 2.82 times faster, the power efficiency is 1.76 times lower, and the area efficiency is 11.03 times smaller. Thus, our method is suitable for the embedded computer system.

Keywords: Binarized Deep Neural Network; FPGA

DOI: http://dx.doi.org/10.1145/3020078.3021782

A 7.663-TOPS 8.2-W Energy-efficient FPGA Accelerator for Binary Convolutional Neural Networks

Yixing Li, *Arizona State University*
Zichuan Liu, *Nanyang Technological University*
Kai Xu, *Arizona State University*
Hao Yu, *Nanyang Technological University*
Fengbo Ren, *Arizona State University*
Contact: yixingli@asu.edu

FPGA-based hardware accelerator for convolutional neural networks (CNNs) has obtained great attentions due to its higher energy efficiency than GPUs. However, it has been a challenge for FPGA-based solutions to achieve a higher throughput than GPU counterparts. In this paper, we demonstrate that FPGA acceleration can be a superior solution in terms of both throughput and energy efficiency when a CNN is trained with binary constraints on weights and activations. Specifically, we propose an optimized accelerator architecture tailored for bitwise convolution and normalization that features massive spatial parallelism with deep pipeline (temporal parallelism) stages. Experiment results show that the proposed architecture running at 90 MHz on a Xilinx Virtex-7 FPGA achieves a computing throughput of 7.663 TOPS with a power consumption of 8.2 W regardless of the batch size of input data. This is 8.3x faster and 75x more energy-efficient than a Titan X GPU for processing online individual requests (in small batch size). For processing static data (in large batch size), the proposed solution is on a par with a Titan X GPU in terms of throughput while delivering 9.5x higher energy efficiency.

Keywords: FPGA; Hardware Acceleration; Deep Learning; Convolutional Neural Network; Binary Neural Network; High-throughput; Energy Efficiency

DOI: http://dx.doi.org/10.1145/3020078.3021786

CPU-FPGA Co-Optimization for Big Data Applications: A Case Study of In-Memory Samtool Sorting

Jason Cong, *University of California, Los Angeles*
Zhenman Fang, *University of California, Los Angeles*
Muhuan Huang, *University of California, Los Angeles*
Libo Wang, *University of California, Los Angeles*
Di Wu, *University of California, Los Angeles*
Contact: mhhuang@cs.ucla.edu

To efficiently process a tremendous amount of data, today's big data applications tend to distribute the datasets into multiple partitions, such that each partition can be fit into memory and be processed by a separate core/server in parallel. Meanwhile, due to the limited scaling of general-purpose CPUs, FPGAs have emerged as an attractive alternative to accelerate big data applications due to their low power, high performance and energy efficiency. In this paper we aim to answer one key question: *How should the multicore CPU and FPGA coordinate together to optimize the performance of big data applications?*

To address the above question, we conduct a step-by-step case study to perform CPU and FPGA co-optimization for in-memory Samtool sorting in genomic data processing, which is one of the most important big data applications for personalized healthcare. First, to accelerate the time-consuming compression algorithm and its associated cyclic redundancy check (CRC) in Samtool sorting, we implement a portable and maintainable FPGA accelerator using high-level synthesis (HLS). Although FPGAs are traditionally well-known to be suitable for compression and CRC, we find that a straightforward integration of this FPGA accelerator into the multi-threaded Samtool sorting only achieves marginal system throughput improvement over the software baseline running on a 12-core CPU. To improve system performance, we propose a dataflow execution model to effectively orchestrate the computation between the multi-threaded CPU and FPGA. Experimental results show that our co-

optimized CPU-FPGA system achieves a 2.6x speedup for in-memory Samtool sorting.

Keywords: Compression and CRC; Genome data sorting; Dataflow execution

DOI: http://dx.doi.org/10.1145/3020078.3021787

Stochastic-Based Multi-stage Streaming Realization of a Deep Convolutional Neural Network

Mohammed Alawad, *University of Central Florida*
Mingjie Lin, *University of Central Florida*
Contact: mingjie@eecs.ucf.edu

Large-scale convolutional neural network (CNN), conceptually mimicking the operational principle of visual perception in human brain, has been widely applied to tackle many challenging computer vision and artificial intelligence applications. Unfortunately, despite of its simple architecture, a typically sized CNN is well known to be computationally intensive. This work presents a novel stochastic-based and scalable hardware architecture and circuit design that computes a large-scale CNN with FPGA. The key idea is to implement all key components of a deep learning CNN, including multi-dimensional convolution, activation, and pooling layers, completely in the probabilistic computing domain in order to achieve high computing robustness, high performance, and low hardware usage. Most importantly, through both theoretical analysis and FPGA hardware implementation, we demonstrate that stochastic-based deep CNN can achieve superior hardware scalability when compared with its conventional deterministic-based FPGA implementation by allowing a stream computing mode and adopting efficient random sample manipulations. Overall, being highly scalable and energy efficient, our stochastic-based convolutional neural network architecture is well-suited for a modular vision engine with the goal of performing real-time detection, recognition and segmentation of mega-pixel images, especially those perception-based computing tasks that are inherently fault-tolerant, while still requiring high energy efficiency.

Keywords: Stochastic computing; FPGA; convolutional neural network

DOI: http://dx.doi.org/10.1145/3020078.3021788

fpgaConvNet: Automated Mapping of Convolutional Neural Networks on FPGAs

Stylianos I. Venieris, *Imperial College London*
Christos-Savvas Bouganis, *Imperial College London*
Contact: stylianos.venieris10@imperial.ac.uk

In recent years, Convolutional Neural Networks (ConvNets) have become the state-of-the-art in several Artificial Intelligence tasks. Across the range of applications, the performance needs vary significantly, from high-throughput image recognition to the very low-latency requirements of autonomous cars. In this context, FPGAs can provide a potential platform that can be optimally configured based on the different performance needs. However, the complexity of ConvNet models keeps increasing leading to a large design space. This work presents fpgaConvNet, an end-to-end framework for mapping ConvNets on FPGAs. The proposed framework employs an automated design methodology based on the Synchronous Dataflow (SDF) paradigm and defines a set of transformations on the SDF graph in order to efficiently explore the architectural design space. By treating high-throughput and latency-critical systems separately, the presented tool is able to efficiently explore the architectural design space and to generate hardware designs from high-level ConvNet specifications, explicitly optimised for the performance metric of interest. Overall our framework yields designs that improve the performance density and the performance efficiency by up to 6× and 4.49× respectively over existing highly-optimised FPGA, DSP and embedded GPU work.

Keywords: FPGA; Synchronous Dataflow; Convolutional Neural Networks; Design Space Exploration

DOI: http://dx.doi.org/10.1145/3020078.3021791

FPGA'17, February 22–24, 2017, Monterey, CA, USA.
ACM ISBN 978-1-4503-4354-1/17/02.

Poster Session 3

FPGA-based Hardware Accelerator for Image Reconstruction in Magnetic Resonance Imaging

Emanuele Pezzotti, *University of Illinois at Chicago*
Alex Iacobucci, *University of Illinois at Chicago*
Gregory Nash, *University of Illinois at Chicago*
Umer Cheema, *University of Illinois at Chicago*
Paolo Vinella, *University of Illinois at Chicago*
Rashid Ansari, *University of Illinois at Chicago*
Contact: epezzo2@uic.edu

Magnetic Resonance Imaging (MRI) is widely used in medical diagnostics. Sampling of MRI data on Cartesian grids allows efficient computation of the Inverse Discrete Fourier Transform for image reconstruction using the Inverse Fast Fourier Transform (IFFT) algorithm. Though the use of Cartesian trajectories simplifies the IFFT computation, non-Cartesian trajectories have been shown to provide better image resolution with lower scan times. To improve the processing time of MRI image reconstruction for these optimized non-Cartesian trajectories using a Non-uniform Fast Fourier Transform (NuFFT) algorithm, dedicated accelerators are required. We present an FPGA-based MRI solution to implement NuFFT for image reconstruction. The solution is based on the design of an efficient custom accelerator on FPGA using OpenCL, and covers all the phases necessary to reconstruct an image with high accuracy, starting from raw scan data. The architecture can be easily extendable to tackle 3D imaging, and k-space properties have been analyzed to reduce the number of samples processed, achieving satisfactory reconstruction accuracy while positively impacting processing time. Our solution achieves a marked improvement over previously published FPGA- and CPU-based implementations and, due to its scalability, it is suitable for the image sizes common in MRI acquisitions.

Keywords: FPGA; Hardware Acceleration; Image Processing; MRI; OpenCL

DOI: http://dx.doi.org/10.1145/3020078.3021793

Storage-Efficient Batching for Minimizing Bandwidth of Fully-Connected Neural Network Layers

Yongming Shen, *Stony Brook University*
Michael Ferdman, *Stony Brook University*
Peter Milder, *Stony Brook University*
Contact: yoshen@cs.stonybrook.edu

Convolutional neural networks (CNNs) are used to solve many challenging machine learning problems. These networks typically use convolutional layers for feature extraction and fully-connected layers to perform classification using those features. Significant interest in improving the performance of CNNs has led to the design of CNN accelerators to improve their evaluation throughput and efficiency. However, work on CNN accelerators has mostly concentrated on accelerating the computationally-intensive convolutional layers, while a major bottleneck of the existing designs arises due to the data-intensive fully-connected layers. Unfortunately, the leading approaches to reducing bandwidth of the fully-connected layers are limited by the storage capacity of the on-chip buffers.

We observe that, in addition to the possibility of reducing CNN weight transfer bandwidth by adding more on-chip buffers, it is also possible to reduce the size of the on-chip buffers at the cost of CNN input transfer. Paradoxically, shrinking the size of the on-chip buffers costs significantly less input bandwidth than the weight bandwidth saved by adding more buffers. Leveraging these observations, we develop a design methodology for fully-connected layer accelerators that require substantially less off-chip bandwidth by balancing between the input and weight transfers. Using 160KB of BRAM enables the prior work to reduce off-chip bandwidth by 5x on the most bandwidth-intensive fully-connected layers of the popular AlexNet and VGGNet-E networks. With our newly proposed methodology, using the same 160KB of BRAM produces a design with 71x bandwidth reduction on the same networks.

Keywords: FPGA accelerators; Convolutional neural networks; Bandwidth optimization

DOI: http://dx.doi.org/10.1145/3020078.3021795

ASAP: Accelerated Short Read Alignment on Programmable Hardware

Subho S Banerjee, *University of Illinois at Urbana-Champaign*
Mohamed el-Hadedy, *University of Illinois at Urbana-Champaign*
Jong B. Lim, *University of Illinois at Urbana-Champaign*
Daniel Chen, *University of Illinois at Urbana-Champaign*
Zbigniew T. Kalbarczyk, *University of Illinois at Urbana-Champaign*
Deming Chen, *University of Illinois at Urbana-Champaign*
Ravishankar K. Iyer, *University of Illinois at Urbana-Champaign*
Contact: ssbaner2@illinois.edu

The proliferation of high-throughput sequencing machines allows for the rapid generation of billions of short nucleotide fragments in a short period. This massive amount of sequence data can quickly overwhelm today's storage and compute infrastructure. This poster explores the use of hardware acceleration to significantly improve the runtime of short-read alignment (SRA), a crucial step in pre-processing sequenced genomes. It presents the design and implementation of ASAP, an accelerator for computing Levenshtein distance (LD) in the context of the SRA problem. LD computation is a prominent underlying mathematical kernel that is common to a large number of SRA tools (e.g., BLAST, BWA, SNAP) and is responsible for 50–70% of their runtime. These algorithms mentioned above calculate the exact value of LD between nucleotide strings but only use them to build a total ordering (an ordered list) of the most likely point of origin in the genome. ASAP computes an approximation of LD by encoding computation in propagation delay of circuit elements. This approximation is calculated in an accelerated fashion in hardware and preserves the original total ordering of LDs produced by the traditional algorithms. This computation is performed by constructing circuits that comprise the recursive definition of the LD computation and measuring propagation delay of a signal entering and leaving the circuit. Additionally, ASAP can explore large portions of the search space (substrings of the strings being compared) within one clock cycle, and ignore parts of the search space that does not contribute to an answer. Our design is implemented on an Altera Stratix V FPGA in an IBM POWER8 system using the CAPI interface for cache coherence across the CPU and FPGA. Our design is 200x faster (median measurement) than the equivalent C implementation of the kernel running on the host processor and 2.2x faster for an end-to-end alignment tool for 120-150bp short-read sequences.

Keywords: FPGA; Bioinformatics; Genomics

DOI: http://dx.doi.org/10.1145/3020078.3021796

RxRE: Throughput Optimization for High-Level Synthesis using Resource-Aware Regularity Extraction

Atieh Lotfi, *UC San Diego*
Rajesh K. Gupta, *UC San Diego*
Contact: alotfi@cs.ucsd.edu

Despite the considerable improvements in the quality of HLS tools, they still require the designer's manual optimizations and tweaks to generate efficient results, which negates the HLS design productivity gains. Majority of designer interventions lead to optimizations that are often global in nature, for instance, finding patterns in functions that better fit a custom designed solution. We introduce a high-level resource-aware regularity extraction workflow, called RxRE that detects a class of patterns in an input program, and enhances resource sharing to balance resource usage against increased throughput. RxRE automatically detects structural patterns, or repeated sequence of floating-point operations, from sequential loops, selects suitable resources for them, and shares resources for all instances of the selected patterns. RxRE reduces required hardware area for synthesizing an instance of the program. Hence, more number of program replicas can be fitted in the fixed area budget of an FPGA. RxRE contributes to a pre-synthesis workflow that exploits the inherent regularity of applications to

achieve higher computational throughput using off-the-shelf HLS tools without any changes to the HLS flow. It uses a string-based pattern detection approach to find linear patterns across loops within the same function. It deploys a simple but effective model to estimate resource utilization and latency of each candidate design, to avoid synthesizing every possible design alternative. We have implemented and evaluated RxRE using a set of C benchmarks. The synthesis results on a Xilinx Virtex FPGA show that the reduced area of the transformed programs improves the number of mapped kernels by a factor of 1.54X on average (maximum 2.8X) which yields on average 1.59X (maximum 2.4X) higher throughput over Xilinx Vivado HLS tool solution. Current implementation has several limitations and only extracts a special case of regularity that is subject of current optimization and study.

Keywords: High-level Synthesis; Regularity Extraction; Resource Sharing; Throughput Optimization

DOI: http://dx.doi.org/10.1145/3020078.3021797

GRT 2.0: An FPGA-based SDR Platform for Cognitive Radio Networks

Haoyang Wu, *Peking University*
Tao Wang, *Peking University*
Zhiwei Li, *Peking University*
Boyan Ding, *Peking University*
Xiaoguang Li, *Peking University*
Tianfu Jiang, *Peking University*
Jun Liu, *Peking University*
Songwu Lu, *University of California, Los Angeles*
Contact: wuhaoyang@pku.edu.cn

Although there is explosive growth of theoretical research on cognitive radio, the real-time platform for cognitive radio is progressing at a low pace. Researchers expect fast prototyping their designs with appropriate wireless platforms to precisely evaluate and validate their new designs. Platforms for cognitive radio should provide both high-performance and programmability. We observed that for the parallel and reconfigurable nature, FPGA is suitable for developing real-time software-defined radio (SDR) platforms. However, without a carefully designed "middleware architecture layer", Real-time programmable wireless system is still difficult to build.

In this paper, we present GRT 2.0, a novel high-performance and programmable SDR platform for cognitive radio. This paper focuses on the architecture design of media access control (MAC) layer and radio frequency (RF) front-end interface. We allocate different MAC functions into different computing units, including a dedicated, light-weight embedded processor and several peripherals, to ensure both programmability and microsecond-level timing requirements. A serial-to-parallel converter is adopted to solve the issues of frame type matching and precise timing between PHY and RF. To support mobile host computers, we use the more portable USB 3.0 interface instead of PCIe. Finally, with the design of an efficient "gain lock" state machine, automatic gain control (AGC) processing time has been reduced to less than 1us. The evaluation result shows that with 802.11a/g protocol, GRT 2.0 achieves maximum throughput of 23Mbps in MAC, which is compatible to commodity fixed-logic wireless network adaptors. The latency of RF front-end is less than 2us, over 10X performance improvement to the Ethernet cable interface. Moreover, by carefully designed

FPGA'17, February 22–24, 2017, Monterey, CA, USA.
ACM ISBN 978-1-4503-4354-1/17/02.

"middleware architecture layer" in FPGA, we provide good programmability both in MAC and PHY.

Keywords: Software Defined Radio; Cognitive Radio; FPGA; Wireless

DOI: http://dx.doi.org/10.1145/3020078.3021798

FPGA Implementation of Non-Uniform DFT for Accelerating Wireless Channel Simulations

Srinivas Siripurapu, *Indian Institute of Technology Madras*
Aman Gayasen, *Xilinx Inc.*
Padmini Gopalakrishnan, *Xilinx Inc.*
Nitin Chandrachoodan, *Indian Institute of Technology Madras*
Contact: ee13d009@ee.iitm.ac.in

FPGAs have been used as accelerators in a wide variety of domains such as learning, search, genomics, signal processing, compression, analytics and so on. In recent years, the availability of tools and flows such as high-level synthesis has made it even easier to accelerate a variety of high-performance computing applications onto FPGAs. In this paper we propose a systematic methodology for optimizing the performance of an accelerated block using the notion of compute intensity to guide optimizations in high-level synthesis. We demonstrate the effectiveness of our methodology on an FPGA implementation of a non-uniform discrete Fourier transform (NUDFT), used to convert a wireless channel model from the time-domain to the frequency domain. The acceleration of this particular computation can be used to improve the performance and capacity of wireless channel simulation, which has wide applications in the system level design and performance evaluation of wireless networks. Our results show that our FPGA implementation outperforms the same code offloaded onto GPUs and CPUs by 1.6x and 10x respectively, in performance as measured by the throughput of the accelerated block. The gains in performance per watt versus GPUs and CPUs are 15.6x and 41.5x respectively.

Keywords: High performance computation; NUDFT; Wireless channel simulation; FPGAs; acceleration; high-level synthesis

DOI: http://dx.doi.org/10.1145/3020078.3021800

FPGA'17, February 22–24, 2017, Monterey, CA, USA.
ACM ISBN 978-1-4503-4354-1/17/02.

Learning Convolutional Neural Networks for Data-Flow Graph Mapping on Spatial Programmable Architectures

Shouyi Yin, *Tsinghua University*
Dajiang Liu, *Tsinghua University*
Lifeng Sun, *Tsinghua University*
Xinhan Lin, *Tsinghua University*
Leibo Liu, *Tsinghua University*
Shaojun Wei, *Tsinghua University*
Contact: liudj@tsinghua.edu.cn

Data flow graph (DFG) mapping is critical for the compiling of spatial programmable architecture, where compilation time is a key factor for both time-to-market requirement and mapping successful rate. Inspired from the great progress made in tree search game using deep neural network, we proposed a framework for learning convolutional neural networks for mapping DFGs onto spatial programmable architectures. Considering that mapping is a process from source to target, we present a dual-input neural network capturing features from both DFGs in applications and Process Element Array (PEA) in spatial programmable architectures. In order to train the neural network, algorithms are designed to automatically generate a data set from PEA intermediate states of preprocessed DFG. Finally, we demonstrate that the trained neural network can get high identifying accuracy of mapping quality and our proposed mapping approach are competitive with state-of-the-art DFG mapping algorithms in performance while the compilation time is greatly reduced.

Keywords: DFG; reconfigurable architecture; mapping; convolutional neural network;

DOI: http://dx.doi.org/10.1145/3020078.3021801

Cache Timing Attacks from The SoCFPGA Coherency Port

Sumanta Chaudhuri, Université Paris-Saclay
Contact: sumanta.chaudhuri@telecom-paristech.fr

In this presentation we show that side-channels arising from micro-architecture of SoCFPGAs could be a security risk. We present a FPGA trojan based on OpenCL which performs cache-timing attacks through the accelerator coherency port (ACP) of a SoCFPGA. Its primary goal is to derive physical addresses used by the Linux kernel on ARM Hard Processor System. With this information the trojan can then surgically change memory locations to gain privileges as in a rootkit.

We present the customisation to the Altera OpenCL platform, and the OpenCL code to implement the trojan. We show that it is possible to accurately predict physical addresses and the page table entries corresponding to an arbitrary location in the heap after sufficient (~300) iterations, and by using a differential ranking.

The attack can be refined by the known page table structure of the Linux kernel, to accurately determine the target physical address, and its corresponding page table entry. Malicious code can then be injected from FPGA, by redirecting page table entries. Since Linux kernel version 4.0-rc5 physical addresses are obfuscated from the normal user to prevent Rowhammer attacks. With information from ACP side-channel the above measure can be bypassed.

Keywords: SoCFPGA; OpenCL; Cache Timing Attack; Cache Coherency; Embedded Systems Security; Rowhammer

DOI: http://dx.doi.org/10.1145/3020078.3021802

Dynamic Partitioning for Library based Placement on Heterogeneous FPGAs

Fubing Mao, *Nanyang Technological University*
Wei Zhang, *Hong Kong University of Science and Technology*
Bingsheng He, *National University of Singapore*
Siew-Kei Lam, *Nanyang Technological University*
Contact: fmao001@ntu.edu.sg

Library based design and IP reuses have been previously proposed to speed up the synthesis of large-scale FPGA designs. However, existing methods result in large area wastage due to the module size difference and the waste area inside each module. In this paper, we propose an efficient and dynamic module partitioning approach for the library based design flow that minimizes the area wastage. Our proposed approach efficiently utilizes the pre-placement module information such as relative positions of blocks including CLBs, DSPs and RAMs, and the module sizes (width, height) for placing these blocks. We introduce a B*-tree representation to enable a fast modular placement. Simulated annealing algorithm is adopted to direct each round of the placement and to search for the optimization. We develop a set of efficient rules to guide the module selection and partition during placement, to eliminate the waste area inside and between modules and achieve a more compact final placement. In addition, the proposed approach can adapt to different architectures and address the fixed-outline constraint. Experiment results show that our approach can reduce the FPGA area utilization by up to 19% compared with the state-of-the-art approach while with acceptable runtime. More detailed description of this poster can be found in our technical report. "Dynamic Partitioning for Library based Placement on Heterogeneous FPGAs" https://github.com/Frankfbmao/BMPR/blob/master/dypartition.pdf

Keywords: FPGA; B*-tree; Placement; Dynamic Partitioning

DOI: http://dx.doi.org/10.1145/3020078.3021803

An Energy-Efficient Design-Time Scheduler for FPGAs Leveraging Dynamic Frequency Scaling Emulation

Wei Ting Loke, *National University of Singapore*
Chin Yang Koay, *Xilinx*
Contact: elelwt@nus.edu.sg

We present a design-time tool, EASTA, that combines the feature of reconfigurability in FPGAs and Dynamic Frequency Scaling to realize an efficient multiprocessing scheduler on a single-FPGA system. Multiple deadlines, reconvergent nodes, flow dependency and processor constraints of the multiprocessor problem on general task graphs are rigorously taken into consideration. EASTA is able to determine the minimum number of processing elements required to create a feasible schedule and dynamically adjust the clock speed of each processing element to reclaim slack. The schedule is represented by an efficient tree-based lookup table. We evaluate the EASTA tool using randomly generated task graphs and demonstrate that our framework is able to produce energy savings of 39.41% and 33% for task graphs of size 9.

Keywords: Field Programmable Gate Array; Low Power; Dynamic Frequency Scaling; Design-Time Scheduling

DOI: http://dx.doi.org/10.1145/3020078.3021805

Author Index

www.ingramcontent.com/pod-product-compliance
Lightning Source LLC
Chambersburg PA
CBHW080934220326
41598CB00034B/5778